Experiencing Jazz

Experiencing Jazz

Richard J. Lawn

*Dean of the College of Performing Arts at
The University of the Arts*

McGraw Hill

Boston   Burr Ridge, IL   Dubuque, IA   Madison, WI   New York   San Francisco   St. Louis
Bangkok   Bogotá   Caracas   Kuala Lumpur   Lisbon   London   Madrid   Mexico City
Milan   Montreal   New Delhi   Santiago   Seoul   Singapore   Sydney   Taipei   Toronto

The McGraw·Hill Companies

Mc Graw Hill **Higher Education**

EXPERIENCING JAZZ
Published by McGraw-Hill, a business unit of The McGraw-Hill Companies, Inc., 1221 Avenue of the Americas, New York, NY, 10020.
Copyright © 2007 by The McGraw-Hill Companies, Inc. All rights reserved. No part of this publication may be reproduced or
distributed in any form or by any means, or stored in a database or retrieval system, without the prior written consent of The McGraw-
Hill Companies, Inc., including, but not limited to, in any network or other electronic storage or transmission, or broadcast for
distance learning.
Some ancillaries, including electronic and print components, may not be available to customers outside the United States.

This book is printed on acid-free paper.

Printed in China

3 4 5 6 7 8 9 0 CTPS/CTPS 0 9 8

ISBN-13: 978-0-07-245179-5

ISBN-10: 0-07-245179-3

Vice President and Editor-in-Chief: *Emily Barrosse*
Publisher and Sponsoring Editor: *Christopher Freitag*
Signing Representative: *Janet Taborn*
Associate Development Editor: *Beth S. Ebenstein*
Editorial Assistant: *Marley Magaziner*
Managing Editor: *Jean Dal Porto*
Lead Project Manager: *Susan Trentacosti*
Manuscript Editor: *Pat Steele*
Art Director: *Jeanne Schreiber*
Lead Designer and Cover Designer: *Gino Cieslik*
Text Designer: *Maureen McCutcheon Design*
Art Editor: *Katherine McNab*
Photo Research Coordinators: *Nora Agbayani and Sonia Brown*
Photo Researcher: *David A. Tietz*
Production Supervisor: *Janean A. Utley*
Lead Media Project Manager: *Marc Mattson*
Media Producer: *Jocelyn Spielberger*
Composition: *10/12 Times Roman, by Carlisle Publishing Services*
Printing: *45# Pub Matte Plus, Courier Kendallville*
Cover: Red Jazz. *Didier Lourenco/Winn Devon Art Group LTD*
Credits: The credits section for this book begins on page C–1 and is considered an extension of the copyright page.

Library of Congress Cataloging-in-Publication Data

Lawn, Richard.
 Experiencing jazz/Richard J. Lawn.
  p. cm.
 Includes bibliographical references, discography, and index.
 ISBN-13: 978-0-07-245179-5 (softcover : alk. paper)
 ISBN-10: 0-07-245179-3 (softcover : alk. paper) 1. Jazz—History and criticism. 2. Jazz—Analysis,
 appreciation. I. Title.
 ML3506.L39 2007
 781.65—dc22
                                              2006014898

The Internet addresses listed in the text were accurate at the time of publication. The inclusion of a Web site does not indicate an
endorsement by the authors or McGraw-Hill, and McGraw-Hill does not guarantee the accuracy of the information presented at these
sites.

www.mhhe.com

I am deeply indebted to Susan Lawn for "putting her life on hold" while helping immeasurably to make this book become a reality. In addition, I thank the many students who served as its inspiration.

RICHARD (RICK) LAWN is Dean of the College of Performing Arts at The University of the Arts. Formerly, Rick was affiliated with the University of Texas (UT) at Austin where he served as Director of Jazz Studies, Chair of the Department of Music, and Associate Dean for Academic Affairs. He also served as Director of the Center for Advanced Studies in the Arts at UT. Before joining the Texas faculty he was Director of Jazz Studies at the University of Northern Iowa and began his teaching career in the Oneonta, New York, public school system and Hartwick College. Rick holds undergraduate and graduate degrees from the Eastman School of Music, where he specialized in woodwind performance and jazz studies. His primary teachers have been Rayburn Wright, Bill Dobbins, Manny Albam, Chuck Mangione, and William Osseck.

Rick has received several notable composition grants from the National Endowment of the Arts and, as a member of the Nova Saxophone Quartet, has recorded on the Musical Heritage Society, Crystal, and Equilibrium labels. The Sea Breeze record label issued *Unknown Soldiers,* a CD recorded by the Third Coast Jazz Orchestra featuring his compositions and arrangements. It has received favorable reviews in *Cadence Magazine* and *The Austin American Statesman.* Kendor Music, CL Barnhouse, Walrus Music, Concept Music, Alfred Music, Dorn, and UNC Press, among others, publish his music. His arrangement of "Donna Lee" was recorded by Bobby Sanabria's New York Latin big band on his 2001 Grammy-nominated CD. Rick's books entitled *The Jazz Ensemble Directors Manual* and *Jazz Theory and Practice* (which includes interactive software) have become staples among jazz educators and students.

Ensembles under his direction have won acclaim at national conferences and festivals throughout the United States and Europe. Performing experiences include extended engagements with Lionel Hampton, Chuck Mangione, the Rochester Philharmonic, and the Austin Symphony. He has performed in backup orchestras for Dizzy Gillespie, Joe Williams, Natalie Cole, Marian McPartland, The Temptations, The Four Tops, Dianne Schuur, Rosemary Clooney, and a host of others. The Selmer Company has sponsored Rick's performances and clinics, and in 2004 he was elected to serve as Treasurer of the International Association for Jazz Education.

CONTENTS

4 The Roots of Jazz   48

PART 2 Classic Jazz, 1917–1945

5 Jazz Takes Root   76

The Jazz Age: From Chicago to New York   106

The Swing Era: Jazz at Its Peak   134

Midwest Swing and a Few More Among Many   170

PART 3   Modern Jazz

The Bebop Revolution   200

10 Be Cool: Fifties and Early Sixties Cool, Intellectual, and Abstract Jazz   240

PART 4   Postmodern Jazz

11

Tradition Meets the Avant-Garde: Moderns and Early Postmoderns Coexist   272

12

Miles and Miles of Miles: Miles Davis and His Sidemen Redefine Postmodern Jazz   302

13 The Electric 1970s and 1980s 342

14 The Unplugged, Eclectic 1970s and 1980s 370

Jazz at the Close of the Century   400

The Afro-Latin and Caribbean Connection   430

Jazz is about America. It is as American as apple pie and baseball, but surprisingly few people understand it or appreciate its wonder and appeal. Jazz represents the spirit and cultural fabric of the country and has served as the basis of most popular music styles. Perhaps this is why our lives are invaded daily with jazz music—on television, in commercials selling everything from cars to banks and clothing, in films, in elevators and doctors' offices, in restaurants and shopping malls, and in countless other public places. It is music that evokes basic human emotions and can be soothing, chilling, sensual, raucous, uplifting, spiritual, meditative, annoying, or jarring. Sometimes it strikes controversy among listeners. Anyone is capable of enjoying these fundamental feelings, but the experience is enhanced beyond expectation when one knows more about how the music is produced and its roots, developments, and place in American history.

Music is the most elusive, abstract, and in some ways the most intangible of all art forms. It cannot be touched, felt, or seen. It does, however, evoke any number of emotional responses, which is why it has become such an important part of the human experience. The only way to truly understand music, like any art form, is to experience it. No art form can be genuinely appreciated without an intimate experience with it. By working with clay, one gains a new perspective on what the sculptor faces when creating a work of art. By closely examining jazz performance practice, one gains a new view and appreciation of the music-making process.

Jazz is a performance art—a spontaneous art designed for the moment. While it can be described in words, analyzed, and placed in an historic continuum, it cannot be fully understood and appreciated without experiencing the music firsthand and hearing the musicians describe it. Words alone cannot do justice to the listening experience and it is important to understand that it is the music that defines the words we use to describe it. Jazz is a work in progress, an ongoing experiment and music in constant evolution. To quote jazz guitarist Larry Coryell, "jazz is a workshop."

Like any of the other art forms, music can be divided into numerous subcategories that, over time, have been described in great detail and consequently named. It is the naming of these styles that often tends to confuse the less-informed listener since there are often only subtle differences between them. The naming of various styles is the result of historians and critics who attempt to better explain and describe the music. To some extent, these stylistic names are also the result of commercial marketing strategies. The term "jazz," used to describe this uniquely American music, is no less confusing than the terms "classical" or "pop" music. Each of these general headings can imply numerous substyles. What is unique about jazz compared to classical music, among other things, is the rate at which jazz styles have evolved. In a mere 100 years, this American music has been transformed to include countless innovations in performance practice. These stylistic changes are so significant that the jazz of today bears only subtle similarities to the earliest forms from 100 years ago, yet buried beneath the surface are common threads binding all of the uniquely different styles together to form a rich tapestry. The fun lies in finding these common characteristics. The essence of jazz is its ability to absorb, transform, and change. Like any art form, it is periodically renewed by various influences. Throughout its development, jazz has been viewed variously as folk music, entertainment, and art music. All three views often existed simultaneously, a fact still true today. It is a music that crosses all social, economic, racial, and geographic boundaries. Centuries from now, only the unique American innovations will be recognized and remembered. These will be sports like baseball, inventions like the personal computer, and no doubt jazz.

COVERAGE

Experiencing Jazz provides clear explanations of each jazz style and how it functions in contrast to other styles. Each style is presented in association with its primary innovators. The material is presented in a logical chronological sequence, but art is never that clean and easy to categorize or sort out. The reader will find the occasional paradox within a single chapter created by the juxtaposition of one style against a polar opposite. This approach was chosen rather than compartmentalizing styles and artists and confining their discussions to nice, cleanly sectionalized chapters. The multiplicity of styles is precisely what was often encountered at the time, particularly from about 1945 on, leaving audiences, critics, and the musicians to make sense of it all. *Experiencing Jazz* goes beyond most textbooks by placing the music in a historical, cultural, and social context, helping readers to relate the music to their own interest areas, and to understand why, to some extent, the music may have developed as it did.

Experiencing Jazz and the companion media provide the reader with an understanding of how jazz works, how and why it evolved, who its primary innovators were, how to listen to it, and how in some cases jazz has been informed by certain aspects of American society. The book and accompanying CD-ROM will familiarize the student with basic building blocks of music as they relate to a discussion of jazz. Without an elementary understanding of music construction and jazz performance practices, it is impossible to fully appreciate jazz performance. It is for this reason that such topics are discussed in Chapters 2 and 3 rather than at the end of the book as appendixes. *Experiencing Jazz* is designed to create educated listeners, not just to present facts, dates, figures, lists of tunes, and performers.

Each style chapter includes a retrospective glimpse at the reception of jazz in America by providing the reader with some insight into how the music was perceived by critics, historians, and fans.

Since this book embraces and recognizes the needs of nonmusicians and musicians alike, a great deal of emphasis is placed on materials that will enhance their understanding and appreciation of jazz by providing a more informed listening experience. It is not enough to merely read about jazz; it must be keenly listened to. A collection of audio recordings, combined with numerous video and audio tutorials located on the CD-ROM, reinforces the principles and performance practices associated with jazz. Emphasis is placed on artists who made significant contributions to jazz rather than inundating the reader with lists of performers who are indeed noteworthy when considering the evolution of jazz but, in retrospect, are not considered to be major trendsetters or innovators. A few musical examples have been included on the CD-ROM and in the text to challenge readers who may be musicians. In most cases these examples are supported by audio interpretations on the CD-ROM and graphic representations that can easily be interpreted by the nonmusician.

RECORDINGS

Experiencing Jazz has a listening program featuring landmark recordings by leading performers that provides examples of the various jazz styles discussed throughout the text. A two-CD set is packaged with each new copy of the text, and an additional third audio CD is available for separate purchase. A listing of tracks for the CDs appears on the inside covers.

Not every significant recording or artist can be represented on a three-disk collection. The selection of recordings to include confronted me with difficult choices. In some cases, recording companies were unwilling to license some landmark recordings. Additional analysis and discussions of other significant recordings are provided on the CD-ROM and a Web site supporting this publication.

SUPPORT FOR STUDENTS

Experiencing Jazz Multimedia Companion CD-ROM

Experiencing Jazz is packaged with an interactive CD-ROM. A wealth of support material is included on this disk that closely follows readings in the text. It should not, therefore, be considered as supplementary to this book, but rather a closely integrated companion to it. While it would be useful to have ready access to the CD-ROM as each chapter is studied, it is not imperative or mandatory. Readers are encouraged, however, to make use of the CD-ROM designed to enhance their comprehension of each chapter in the text. All CD-ROM activities are highlighted with icons inside the text so students know which concepts are covered.

This CD-ROM provides a wide range of support for the student:

- Interactive materials that clearly explain fundamentals of melody, rhythm, harmony, form, blues, and performance practice in jazz.

- Instructional videos to provide a keen awareness of form, the instruments associated with jazz and their roles in an ensemble, solo jazz piano styles, and jazz drum-set performance techniques.

- An audio introduction to each instrument associated with jazz that also acquaints the user with special effects, performance techniques, and brass mutes associated with the jazz style. An instrument identification quiz is provided as well.

- Listening guides and easily understood discussions of each recording included in the companion CD audio anthology.

- Photos and documents that relate to each stylistic era.

- Numerous audio excerpts from interviews with noted musicians including Miles Davis, Gil Evans, Chick Corea, Charles Mingus, Herbie Hancock, Pat Metheny, Charlie Parker, Dexter Gordon, Stan Kenton, Stan Getz, John Coltrane, Billie Holiday, Louis Armstrong, Gerry Mulligan, Dizzy Gillespie, and others bring authenticity to the text.

Online Learning Center

The Online Learning Center (OLC) that accompanies this text can be found at www.mhhe.com/lawn. It provides students with an abundance of additional resources such as multiple-choice, true/false, and for further study questions; projects; and links to useful Web sites. All material on the OLC is available in a cartridge for WebCT and Blackboard for use in online courses or course Web sites. A supplementary chapter discussing the relationships between jazz and classical music is offered as well as a condensed history of disk recording and a discussion of the relationship of this medium to jazz.

SUPPORT FOR INSTRUCTORS

Instructor's Edition/Online Learning Center

The Online Learning Center at www.mhhe.com/lawn includes a separate, password-protected Instructor Site with a wide range of resources for instructors. The Online Learning Center contains

- An Instructor's Manual, by David Aaberg of Central Missouri State University, with comprehensive teaching suggestions for each chapter as well as suggestions for how to integrate the CD-ROM in the classroom.

- A Test Bank, by Robert Hughes of Saint Louis University, with 30–40 questions for each chapter.

- McGraw-Hill's EZ Test, a flexible and easy-to-use electronic testing program that allows instructors to create tests from book-specific items. It accommodates a wide range of question types, and instructors may add their own questions. Multiple versions of the test can be created and any test can be exported for use with course management systems such as WebCT, Blackboard, or PageOut. EZ Test Online is a new service and gives you a place to easily administer your EZ Test–created exams and quizzes online. The program is available for Windows and Macintosh environments.

- Student Projects associated with each chapter, prepared by Christopher Kocher of The University of South Dakota.

- Multiple-choice, true/false, and for further study questions associated with each chapter, prepared by Mathew Buchman of University of Wisconsin–Stevens Point.

- Chapter-by-chapter links to appropriate Web resources, prepared by Janice Jarrett of University of Arizona.

ACKNOWLEDGMENTS

I acknowledge with gratitude the many reviewers who took the time to read and critique the manuscript: David Aaberg, *Central Missouri State University*; Matthew Buchman, *University of Wisconsin–Stevens Point*; David Champouillon, *East Tennessee State University*; Brian Coyle, *Hope College*; Lawrence Dwyer, *University of Notre Dame*; Paul Fehrenbach, *Penn State University-DuBois Campus*; Jeffrey Haskell, *University of Arizona*; Clarence Bernard Henry, *University of Kansas*; Janice Jarrett, *University of Arizona*; Eugene Jones, *East Tennessee State University*; Richard Lowenthal, *New Jersey City University*; Peter Madsen, *University of Nebraska at Omaha*; David B. Niethamer, *Longwood University*; Patricia P. Norwood, *University of Mary Washington–Mary Washington College*; Michael Pagán, *University of Colorado at Boulder*; and J. B. Scott, *University of North Florida*.

I offer my sincere thanks and appreciation to the following individuals for their significant contributions and assistance during various stages in the development of this text and CD-ROM. Special thanks go to: Dan Morgenstern, Tad Hershorn, and the staff of the Rutgers Institute of Jazz Studies; UT–Austin College of Fine Arts Information Technology staff Jim Kerkhoff, Frank Simon, Andy Murphy, and Tyson Breaux; Paul Young, Glenda Smith, Todd Hastings, and Paul White who, as students at The University of Texas, helped in the development of the CD-ROM prototype; David Aaberg for his editorial suggestions and concise chapter summaries; Ben Irom and Mark "Kaz" Kazanoff who helped create listening guides; David Fudell and the staff of the Center for Instructional Technologies at The University of Texas; The Harry Ransom Humanities Research Center at UT–Austin; Jack Cooper for his composition *Video Blues*; Austin, Texas, musicians Greg Wilson, Randy Zimmerman, Pat Murray, Mike Koenning, Craig Biondi, Paul Haar, John Fremgen, Steve Snyder, Chris Maresh, Eric Middleton, Russell Scanlon, and John Kreger for their recorded contributions; Charlie Richard, Steve Hawk and the Hawk–Richard Jazz Orchestra whose Sea Breeze Jazz CD (SB-2093) *The Hawk Is Out* provided a source for brief audio examples; Paul DeCastro, Jeff Benedict, and members of Rhumbumba for their self-titled Sea Breeze Jazz CD (SB-3067) that provided Afro-Cuban examples; members of the Third Coast Jazz Orchestra whose Sea Breeze Jazz CD (SB-2116) *Unknown Soldiers* provided a source for additional audio clips; Marc Dicciani and Marlon Simon from The University of the Arts School of Music for their Afro-Cuban demonstrations; Dave Laczko who helped to unearth a few interview clips; Sara MacDonald from the UArts Library; Carl Woideck at the University of Oregon; Lewis Porter at Rutgers University; Brady Ajay for efforts in the production of the CD-ROM; Wesley Hall for his dogged pursuit of permissions for the CD-ROM; David Tietz for his perseverant photo research; and Chris Freitag, Jocelyn Arsht, Melody Marcus, Beth Ebenstein, and the production staff at McGraw-Hill for believing in the value of this project.

Jazz has become a universal music, recognized worldwide and identified with the United States. It is a unique nationalist style representing the most significant cultural contribution that America has made to the global arts landscape. Jazz has become synonymous with modern American thought and is a metaphor for democracy and freedom of expression. It should be studied, experienced and treasured!

Richard J. Lawn

Experiencing **Jazz**

The Nature of Jazz

"Jazz isn't a noun. It's a verb. It's a process, a way of being, a way of thinking."[1]

PAT METHENY

THAT FOUR LETTER WORD

"Jazz up your wardrobe." "Put some jazz in your savings account." "Don't give me all that jazz." "Own the jazziest car on the road." "Quit jazzin' me!" This word "jazz" that we hear daily first appeared in American vocabulary in the early 1900s. Existing as a slang term before it was used to describe music, its origins have puzzled historians for many years.

Theories about the origins of the word jazz are largely unsubstantiated. The only sure fact is that none of the theories can be proven true. Some have associated the word with the red light district of New Orleans and sexual intercourse. Garvin Bushell, a circus band musician from New Orleans, offers the following observation:

> They said that the French had brought the perfume industry with them to New Orleans, and the oil of jasmine was a popular ingredient locally. To add it to perfume was called "jassing it up." The strong scent was popular in the red light district, where a working girl might approach a perspective customer and say, "Is jazz on your mind tonight, young fellow?"[2]

As late as 1947 Berry's *American Dictionary of Slang* cited the word under *copulate.* The term jazz was supposedly related to the act of intercourse itself—"he's jazzin' her."[3] *The New York*

3

New Orleans, early 1900s

Times used the term in their February 2, 1917 issue, in an advertisement taken by Reisenweber's club to promote "The First Eastern Appearance of the Famous Original Dixieland Jazz Band."[4] According to Nick LaRocca, the group's cornetist, "jass" was changed to "jazz" to discourage people from defacing signs by erasing the letter j. The associations of the word jazz to vulgarity, sex, and the bordello is probably why some jazz musicians rarely if ever use the word in discussing their own music.[5]

Others attribute the word's origins to linguistic variations. One writer points out the word's relationship to the French word "jaser," which means "to chat," "to chatter," "to prattle" or "to talk a lot and say nothing." Prior to the Louisiana Purchase in 1803, the French owned the Mississippi Delta area, often referred to as the birthplace of jazz. **Creoles,** a racial mix resulting from a union between French, African-American, and sometimes Spanish, spoke a hybrid form of French. Some theorists suggest that the word "jazz" in Creole meant to speed things up. Another theory to consider is the claim that the term jazz is derived from West African languages, a natural conclusion because the Gold (West) Coast of Africa served as the point of origin for many slaves. Early jazz artist names like James and Charles morphed from their formal spellings (Charles and James) to nicknames like Chaz and Jas or Jazz.[6] A 1919 article in the *Music Trade Review* refers to the wild, barbaric music played by trumpeter Jasbo Brown after having a few drinks. Patrons who enjoyed his musically gregarious behavior shouted "More Jasbo," which eventually distorted to just "more jazz."[7] Jazz historian Robert Goffin attributed the word to a black musician named Jess who played in a "jerky, halting style." As early as 1904, James Reese Europe, a black bandleader, believed the word was a distortion of the name of a New Orleans band known as Razz's Band. Other historians speculate that the term "jazz" stemmed from a vaudeville expression meaning to excite, stir things up, or make things go faster.[8]

Songsheet publication cover (1918) for music performed by the Original Dixieland Jazz Band, the first group to make a commercial jazz recording.

As jazz developed into a more sophisticated, acceptable art form, efforts were even made to rename the music and discard "jazz" due to its undesirable connotations. In 1949, *Down Beat* magazine sponsored a contest to find a new name for jazz. The publisher announced prizes and a distinguished panel of judges (including well-known contemporary big band leader Stan Kenton and author S. I. Hayakawa). After months of deliberation, the winner was announced—CREWCUT. The winner collected her $1,000 first prize from the magazine and defended her entry as "simply the exact opposite of the slang name for classical music—'Longhair.'" Other winning selections were Amerimusic, Jarb, Syncope, Improphony, and Ragtibop. The results were announced in the magazine but this surprising statement was added: "The judges were unanimous in the opinion, shared by the editors of *Down Beat,* that none of the hundreds of words submitted is adequate as a substitute for Jazz."[9]

Whatever the true story is about the derivation of this uniquely American word, the music and the word quickly gained recognition worldwide. One can fully experience jazz only by exploring how it is unique, how it can be described and identified, and how to evaluate and appreciate its forms and variety.

> **Before reading the following definition of jazz, use the CD-ROM to listen to the collage recording that traces approximately 80 years of recorded jazz. This recording is found in the corresponding chapter on the CD-ROM. Make note of how different each excerpt is from one another.**

DEFINING JAZZ

Jazz is a direct result of West African influences on European derived music styles and popular American music. Since its beginnings at the turn of the century, it has shown an ability to absorb aspects of other music styles and transform them into something entirely new and different. Emerging in the first decades of the 1900s as an unpolished folk music, jazz reflected diverse influences. Among them are the blues, marching bands, polkas, field hollers and work songs, religious music, ragtime, and of course, West African music with its emphasis on individualistic expression, spontaneity, and rhythmic complexity. Even from these beginnings, jazz was a chameleon, absorbing and reflecting all of these musical influences present in America at the turn of the century.

While jazz is a distinctive style recognizable worldwide, it has been difficult to define and has confounded many critics and historians. Defining jazz is exacerbated because it remains in a constant state of metamorphosis, influenced by popular culture, by advancements in technology, and by the musicians' own desire for change and self-improvement. Therefore, like the music itself, there is no absolute set of criteria for defining it. Nonetheless, different combinations of certain traits always characterize jazz music.

Jazz is a rhythmically vibrant and complex music that often includes a rhythm section (piano, bass, and drums). The rhythms of jazz are richly complex, creating an element of tension. Rhythm is not the sole source of this tension, for it is also found in the sometimes dissonant harmonies and complex improvisations associated with jazz.

In true West African tradition, jazz is shaped by the performers' individual musical gestures and spontaneous variations. It is a music in which the performers assume the most prominent role and bear the greatest responsibility. It features

Jazz soloist Bobby McFerrin

certain instruments and special effects that are synonymous with the style. Many of its instrumental affectations may have been an effort to emulate the flexibility and expressiveness of the human voice. These instrumental effects alter and color the sound in unusual ways, and exerted an impact on twentieth-century "classical" music (see CD-ROM). While jazz is closely associated with certain instruments, any instrument can be used to imply the style. A wide range of instrumentalists and/or singers can present jazz, from solo performers to large orchestras. Self-proclaimed inventor of jazz, Jelly Roll Morton, advocated that almost any kind of music could sound like jazz since jazz is a way of playing and interpreting music.

Some definitions of jazz assert that swing, a certain rhythmic phenomenon, and improvisation, are two absolute criteria for authentic jazz. While these can be important features, they are not entirely unique to jazz, nor are they required for the music to be considered jazz. Much contemporary jazz post-1970 does not swing by the classic definition of the term. Music in a jazz style may not contain much improvisation, but can still be identified as jazz. On the other hand, some non-jazz may contain jazz characteristics. For example, does jazz saxophonist Phil Woods' improvised solo on Billy Joel's pop hit "Just the Way You Are" make it jazz?

Jazz has become a truly eclectic music, embracing musical styles from around the world and transforming them into a uniquely American form of artistic expression that frequently requires the performer to improvise. The blues, in itself an individualistic and spontaneous form of expression, remains an important component of jazz and a significant contribution by black Americans. Black performers have been the primary developers of jazz and blues though some white performers and composers contributed significantly to advancing the music and to developing it as a viable commercial product. At the dawn of the twenty-first century, jazz can easily be considered one of the most significant musical accomplishments of the previous century and one that shows promise for continued advancement.

The jazz sounds of the World Saxophone Quartet

The subsection Characterizing Jazz, found in the corresponding chapter of the accompanying CD-ROM, provides an excellent supplement to this section and includes excerpts of interviews with many performers.

Note: All terms in bold are also found in the glossary included on the CD-ROM and in the Glossary section of this book.

CHAPTER SUMMARY

Jazz is a music that developed in America at the dawn of the twentieth century. Many styles of music and music making that influenced the beginnings of jazz reflect the melting pot that is America. This mix includes elements from both European and African music. A product of these diverse influences, jazz is a music containing a great variety of substyles, from early ragtime- and blues-influenced jazz to free jazz and rock-influenced fusion (see Example 1.1).

Succinctly defining the word "jazz," considering its many substyles and the fact that jazz is constantly changing, is challenging. Origins of the word itself are also murky, with no single explanation substantiated. Change in approach to improvisation is one of the most important factors in the development of the various styles of jazz, yet examples of jazz containing little or no improvisation exist.

EXAMPLE 1.1 Jazz styles timeline.

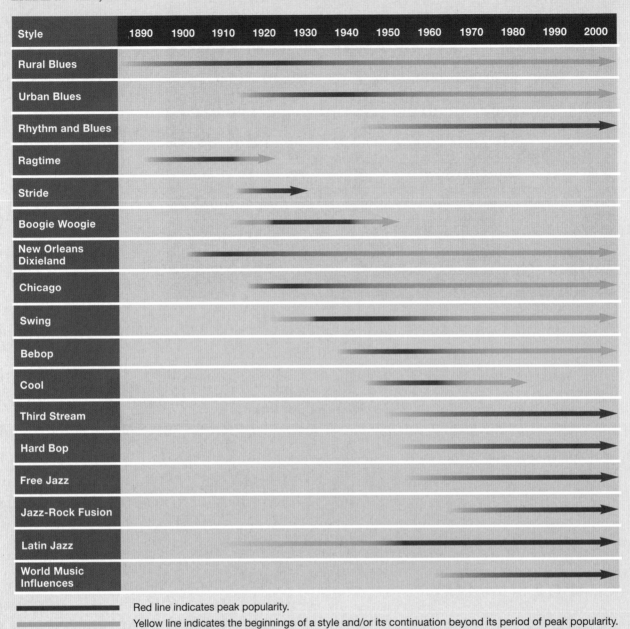

Style	1890	1900	1910	1920	1930	1940	1950	1960	1970	1980	1990	2000
Rural Blues												
Urban Blues												
Rhythm and Blues												
Ragtime												
Stride												
Boogie Woogie												
New Orleans Dixieland												
Chicago												
Swing												
Bebop												
Cool												
Third Stream												
Hard Bop												
Free Jazz												
Jazz-Rock Fusion												
Latin Jazz												
World Music Influences												

Red line indicates peak popularity.
Yellow line indicates the beginnings of a style and/or its continuation beyond its period of peak popularity.

At one time, jazz was played exclusively in a swing feel. Approaches to playing swing evolved with each new style of jazz, and, because jazz continues to evolve and adapt, embracing music styles from around the world, jazz is no longer played exclusively in a swing feel. Certain instruments and performance techniques have become associated with jazz, which can be played or sung by any number of performers. Individuality, spontaneity, and the importance of the performer instead of the composer have always been at the core of jazz. What can be unequivocally stated about jazz is that it was pioneered primarily by black Americans, is often improvised, rhythmically driven, and combines European, African, American, and sometimes Afro-Latin elements. Further, jazz continually evolves as it is influenced by technology, current events, different cultures, and music from throughout the world.

KEY TERMS

Your instructor should clarify which terms and aspects of this chapter are of primary importance. You should be familiar to some extent with the following term:

Creole

REVIEW QUESTIONS

1. What are some of the theories regarding the origins and derivation of the word jazz?
2. Name some of the identifying or salient characteristics of jazz, regardless of substyle.
3. Jazz was the result of what primary non-European or American influence?
4. What styles of music, European or American, were factors in the formation of early jazz styles?
5. Is the composer or performer more important to the jazz style?
6. Music from what four countries or regions played into the formation of jazz?
7. Can any piece of music be played in a jazz style? Explain your answer.
8. An aspect of rhythmic interpretation that is unique to jazz is called _____ .
9. Define the term Creole.
10. What style, born in America, is undoubtedly the most important African-American contribution to jazz?

MAPLE
LEAF
RAG.

By King of Ragtime writers
Scott Joplin.

Composer of...
The Cascades
Sunflower Slow Drag
Elite Syncopations

The Elements of **Jazz**

"Jazz did not exist until the twentieth century. It has elements that were not present either in Europe or in Africa before this century. And at any of its stages it represents . . . a relationship among rhythm, harmony, and melody that did not exist before."[1]

MARTIN WILLIAMS

While brief discussions of musical terms important to your understanding of jazz are provided throughout this chapter, you should use the CD-ROM in order to more fully understand these concepts. The section entitled the Elements of Jazz provides audio demonstrations and more in-depth explanations of these terms and concepts.

Jazz, since its simple, uncomplicated beginnings as a folk music, has become a complex music that reflects a constantly changing American society. Despite the many influences and changes that jazz has experienced over a century of development, and its uniqueness when compared to other music styles, jazz shares ingredients common to all forms of music.

Jazz can be examined and discussed in the same ways that apply to any style of music. All music is discussed in terms of *rhythm, melody, harmony, texture,* and *form.*

11

RHYTHM

Rhythm is accomplished through varying lengths of notes, combined with space, all in relationship to a steady pulse. Some notes in a melody last longer than others and some move more quickly. So, duration is an expression of rhythm. Without rhythm, music has no sense of motion and melodies would be monotonous and boring. It is the rhythm of music that propels it forward and ensures that it is not static. Without using complex musical notation, consider the graphic symbols in Example 2.1 that illustrate the familiar tune "Happy Birthday." Some notes are lower or higher in pitch (vertical scale), some are louder than others (indicated by darker images), and some are shorter or longer in duration (horizontal scale) indicating rhythm. Silence, or rests seem to separate some of these notes. Sing the familiar tune to yourself as you move through the graphic from left to right.

EXAMPLE 2.1

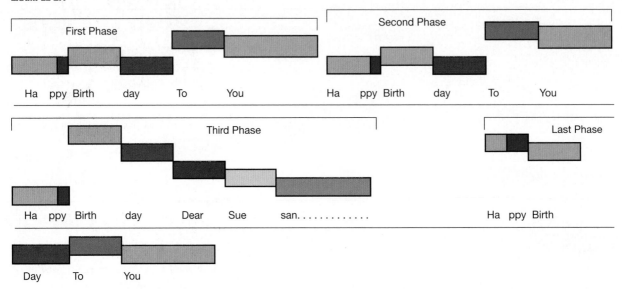

Meter and Tempo

Meter defines the number of primary beats, or pulses, in each measure of music, and is an expression of the organization of rhythms. **Measure** (or **bar**) is a unit that serves as a container, holding a specific number of beats as defined by the meter. A waltz emphasizes a triple meter (1-2-3) where each measure has three beats, and a march features a duple meter (1-2) with two beats per measure.

Poetry has rhythm and meter. Sonnets, rhymes, and limericks all project rhythm and meter. Think of measures as inch marks on a ruler. In 4/4 meter, each beat would be represented by 1/4-inch marks since there are four quarters to each inch. The 1/4-inch subdivision can be further divided into smaller increments, as is the case with music note values. To continue this analogy, how quickly or slowly we move across a tape measure or yardstick, progressing from one inch to the next, is a measure of the tempo. **Tempo,** another concept important to the understanding of how music works, is an expression of the pace or speed at which the music moves. It could also be compared to the pace of someone walking or running. Some songs seem to have no regular tempo, moving slowly and described as **rubato.**

It is safe to say that jazz performers and composers were content for decades to deal largely with music in duple meter—primarily 2/4, and 4/4 meters (see Example 2.2). For example, most ragtime piano music was written in 2/4 meter, while nearly all the instrumental jazz literature that followed well into the 1940s was in common time, or 4/4 meter. Jazz musicians were most concerned during the first three decades of the formative years with honing skills as improvisers. Attention was placed on developing performance technique necessary to face the challenges presented to the soloist by simple forms like the 12-bar (measure) blues with reasonably complex harmonies. It was not until the 1950s that jazz artists began to venture outside the safe confines of duple meters. Jazz waltzes were not popular until the 1950s and 1960s. Jazz composers, who rarely have enjoyed the same high profile as the "classical" composer or jazz performer, began to stretch their imaginations during this time.

EXAMPLE 2.2

Two measures shown with 2/4 meter signature and a tempo of 60 to the quarter note (one beat per second)

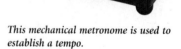

This mechanical metronome is used to establish a tempo.

Listen to all or a portion of the following tracks from the CD anthology that serve as excellent examples of different meters. "Take Five" for example is in 5/4 meter, while much of "Suite for the Americas" is in 7/4. Compare these tunes to "Every Tub," "Summertime," or "Daahoud" written in the more common 4/4 meter.

Symphony orchestras and bands have conductors to control the pace of the music—jazz ensembles have rhythm sections. There is flexibility in terms of the tempo associated with a "classical" music ensemble performance. In larger ensembles such as symphony orchestras, the conductor controls the tempo. In smaller ensembles, the performers control the tempo and must work carefully together to adjust the tempo or risk a poor, disorganized performance. The rate of the steady pulse, or tempo, in a jazz or pop/rock group is consistent and generally maintained throughout the piece by the **rhythm section,** which is comprised of piano, bass, drums, and often guitar. Within this group of instruments, there is likely to exist a hierarchy of time-keeping responsibilities that may be somewhat dependent on the particular style of jazz. The other musicians in the ensemble must then strive to rhythmically coexist within this tempo. At times, performers in a jazz band may seem to rush or drag behind the rhythm section's steady pulse, but it is frequently by choice, not by error. The dragging sensation is often described as **laying back** and is often associated with the sound of a particular band and defines its style.

The subject of rhythm as it relates to jazz is a thorny one that has puzzled many and provoked debate for many years. Attempts to define the special rhythmic

French jazz muscians Stéphan Oliva at the piano, Bruno Chevillon on bass, and American drummer Paul Motian.

qualities of jazz have sometimes ended in poetic metaphors and metaphysical phrases in attempts to make feelings and individual interpretations tangible. The very existence of a group of instruments described as the "rhythm section" points to the importance of this basic musical element to the jazz style. What other music ensemble, other than related popular music styles that share similar roots with jazz (rock, R & B, pop) includes a group of instruments known as the "rhythm section"? The emphasis on steady rhythm is a distinguishing feature of this music and, aside from the spontaneously improvised aspect of jazz, its unique rhythmic features are among the most important characteristics establishing jazz as a truly original style.

Listen to all or a portion of the following tracks from the CD anthology that serve as excellent examples of different tempos. Chick Corea's "Excerpt From the First Movement of Heavy Metal" features two tempos—the introductory slow, rubato without strict tempo (0:00–0:23) followed by a set tempo established by the piano beginning at 0:24. Compare this track to the slow, but steady tempo of "Moon Dreams."

Rhythmic Devices Important to Jazz

Much has been said about the relationship of African music to jazz. Some scholars find the relationship to be exaggerated, while others testify to certain unique qualities that define jazz as being related directly to the African experience in America. Since there has been no evidence left behind in terms of recordings from the period of slavery in the United States, we are left to sort out this mystery based largely on written artifacts from this early period of American history. These artifacts make it plausible to conclude that the unique and complex rhythmic aspects of jazz stem directly from the influences of the West African tradition on American and European music. It is important to this discussion to understand certain characteristics of jazz rhythm that find their heritage in West African concepts. (See Chapter 4 for additional information about African music and its relationship to jazz.)

The rhythmic terms "syncopation" and "swing" are synonymous with jazz. **Syncopation** is a rhythmic phenomenon that occurs when one regularly occurring rhythm or major beat emphasis (when your foot pats down) interacts with a rhythm that occurs on a weak, normally unemphasized, portion of a beat (when your foot moves up). The rhythm that is normally unemphasized becomes accented and creates a syncopation or tension. In one sense, this is the result of a **polyrhythm,** or a combination of two or more rhythms occurring simultaneously. Often times the various rhythms in a polyrhythmic texture imply more than one meter (3/4 and 6/8) simultaneously. They then could be referred to as **polymetric,** implying many meters. See Examples 2.3 and 2.4.

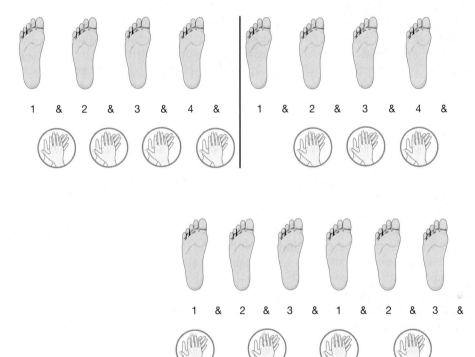

EXAMPLE 2.3

This example illustrates a simple syncopation in measure one that results from handclaps on off beats that create a tension between major beats represented by the left foot tapping a steady pulse. By the second beat of the second measure, the hand claps are lined up precisely with the foot tapping on beats 2, 3, and 4, hence no syncopation and no tension.

EXAMPLE 2.4

Using similar graphics, this example illustrates a simple polyrhythm. In this case, the meter implied by the foot taps is 3/4. The handclapping introduces a cross rhythm in opposition to the foot tapping. If the foot tapping suddenly stops, the handclaps give the illusion of 2/4 meter. The combined result when both are executed simultaneously is a polyrhythm that also implies a polymeter.

While there are numerous styles of African music found throughout the continent, several important aspects of West African music key to the formation of jazz styles are illustrated by the first track on the accompanying CD anthology. Traditional West African music is not known for its complex harmonies and melodies. It is, however, highly developed rhythmically, sporting numerous examples of polyrhythms, syncopations, and polymeters. It was the rhythmic and spontaneous aspect of West African music that exerted significant influence on the formation of early jazz. In some ways **swing,** a rhythmic phenomenon associated with jazz, is evidence of the syncopated, polyrhythmic nature of jazz. (More information about African music is presented in Chapter 4)

Listen to the following track from the CD anthology that offers excellent examples of syncopations and polyrhythms. The opening section of Keith Jarrett's "The Windup" (0:00–0:39) juxtaposes a regular rhythm played by one hand with improvised syncopated rhythms that work against the regular rhythm and are played by the other hand.

Audio clips illustrating all of these abstract terms used to describe various aspects of rhythm can be found in the corresponding chapter of the CD-ROM. Here you can explore the subsection about rhythm.

Swing as an Aspect of Jazz Rhythm

Have you ever tried to explain how a food tastes to someone? It is almost impossible to truly appreciate the flavor of a particular food without actually tasting it. That same analogy is true for describing "swing." It is certainly one of the most difficult characteristics to define when discussing jazz rhythm. Musicians and analysts alike have struggled to respond to the frequently posed question—what is swing? Big band leader Count Basie when asked to define swing said things like "pat your foot" or "tap your toe."[2] Jazz pioneer Louis Armstrong is reputed to have said, "If you have to ask, you'll never know."[3] Big band swing era trumpeter Jonah Jones may have come closest when he implied that it was a feeling.[4] Duke Ellington defined swing as "the un-mechanical but hard driving and fluid rhythm over which soloists improvise."[5] None of these responses, however, provides a real explanation of the rhythmic phenomenon that began to be described in the 1920s as "swing."

André Hodeir, author of the important 1956 publication *Jazz: Its Evolution and Essence*, said that "jazz consists essentially of an inseparable but extremely variable mixture of relaxation and tension,"[6] and that the "feeling of tension and relaxation coexist at the same moment."[7] In other words, some performers are playing things on the beat while others are simultaneously playing syncopated accents on other portions of the beat. The combined result is a forward momentum we describe as swing, and there can be many subtle variations of swing—as many variations as there are players. Swing can be compared to skipping. When we skip, we divide our even pace unevenly, which is a characteristic of swinging in jazz. We make an otherwise even paced walk uneven; we make it skip, even though we may get from point A to point B in the same amount of time as it would have taken had we walked with an even pace (tempo).

A sound byte is worth 1,000 words in helping to define swing. Listen to The Count Basie Band on your CD anthology play "Every Tub." This great band set the standard for swing and the Basie rhythm section illustrates this concept at 0:32–0:55. You may be intrigued enough to listen to the entire track.

MELODY

Melody is the result of an organization of notes that move by varying distances—by step and leap—either ascending or descending, to form a musical statement. Melody is thought of as moving in a linear, horizontal fashion. A complete musical idea or statement is often termed a **phrase.** The term phrase can refer to a melodic, harmonic, or rhythmic statement. Short melodic phrases are strung together to create entire tunes.

Melody is by far the easiest ingredient to understand. Melodies can stand alone, be coupled with other melodies, or be sung and/or played with accompaniment. Melody is the aspect of most musical styles usually remembered more easily than harmony or even rhythm. A melody is often easy to recognize and remember because it may consist of only a few notes. Does anyone remember the three-note NBC television sound logo, the more contemporary four-note ABC identifier, or the four-note (two pitches) motive Beethoven used in his *Symphony Number 5?* Most listeners identify a lyric with a melody and hear them as one ingredient. Lyrics even help to clarify the overall form or architecture of a piece. Instrumental jazz is perhaps less easily grasped because it lacks a lyric to help listeners keep track of the various twists and turns of the melody. Remove the lyrics of a tune and many listeners lose their way. The memorable melody of a show or pop tune that serves as the basis for an instrumental jazz treatment can become altered beyond easy recognition since instrumentalists are not bound by lyrics. These show and pop tunes from the 30s and 40s were used in jazz improvisations. As jazz matured, performers discarded popular dance and show tunes from their repertoire, and the new, original jazz melodies became less easily recognized and more difficult to follow and remember.

The **key** of a piece of music is defined by a central note, scale, or chord that provides a musical center of gravity. Most melodies are governed by a **key signature** (sharps or flats) and most pieces are written in a particular key with the exception of some contemporary music. A piano keyboard is grouped into repeating sets of 12 different notes, defined as an octave. There are 12 different key signatures used to define 12 keys used in music, and they correspond to the 12 different black and white notes on the piano keyboard. A melody can begin on any of these 12 different notes. The first note in a melody sometimes helps to define the key of the piece. Certain keys are more widely used than others, and some musicians feel that certain keys are more somber, while others are more lighthearted and optimistic, though this is entirely subjective. Singers often practice a song in different keys until they find the one that they feel most suits the mood of the tune and best accommodates their own voice range. When a song changes key it is said to **modulate.** Keys fall into one of two categories and define a tonality—major or minor. **Tonality** helps to describe the aural character of a piece of music, a melody or a single harmony. Harmony and melody work together to establish a tonality. If a piece of music lacks a key center it is termed **atonal** (lacking of any specific tonality). Only some very contemporary avant-garde music lacks tonality. A song may have more than one tonality depending on its complexity. Tonality could be compared to a painting where many colors may be used but one seems dominant. Example 2.5 illustrates how key signatures are used to dictate key and tonality.

EXAMPLE 2.5

Key signatures for E flat major or C minor, A flat major or F minor, and G major or E minor.

 Most of the music presented on the companion CD anthology is considered tonal. The Ornette Coleman track "Mind and Time," however, is a good example of atonal improvisation since Coleman pays no real regard to key, harmony, or prescribed melody. Begin your listening either at the beginning to listen first to the composed tune or at the start of his solo at 0:23.

 For a more detailed explanation of melody and keys along with musical examples, use the CD-ROM and explore the section on melody found in the corresponding chapter Elements of Jazz.

Blues

A distinguishing aspect of many jazz melodies is the blues. Blues melodies are based on alterations of a traditional scale. Some believe that the altered thirds, fifths and sevenths of the blues scale can be attributed to certain African singing practices. A **scale** is a logical progression of ascending and descending notes arranged in half and whole step intervals. The piano keyboard shown in the following graphic makes it easy to see these two basic intervals that serve as building blocks for all scales. Note names are labeled. The distance from C to D is a whole step interval while the black key in between represents a half step interval. Scales are comprised of eight consecutive notes, following a particular key signature, and named in accordance with the starting note. On this keyboard, the C scale would be played as C-D-E-F-G-A-B-C (Example 2.6). The third, fifth, and seventh notes of this traditional scale are altered to form the "blues scale," (see Glossary **blue notes**) as shown in Example 2.6. The blue shaded notes indicate the lowered third (E♭), lowered fifth (G♭), and lowered seventh (B♭). There are gradations of blue notes, since singers and instrumentalists are less capable of being precise than a pianist when lowering these pitches. The **chromatic** scale (Example 2.7) includes all 12 different pitches each separated by half steps, therefore including all white and black keyboard notes.

EXAMPLE 2.6

"Blue notes" indicated by color.

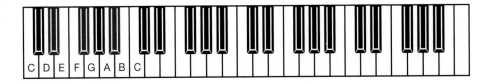

EXAMPLE 2.7

Chromatic scale.

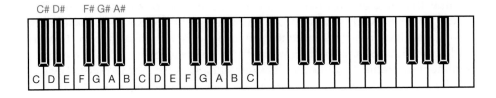

The blues scale is almost an amalgamation of pitches from the major and minor tonalities. Leroy Ostransky, author of *Understanding Jazz*, felt that "early jazz players probably saw little distinction between major and minor modes [scales] and used major and minor thirds interchangeably."[8] Whatever the origins, these slightly flatted pitches (third, fifth, and seventh scale degrees) became known as **blue notes** and are responsible for much of the special melodic and harmonic character that distinguishes jazz from other forms of music. Blue notes often help to communicate a melancholy feeling. Blues songs are often associated with a depressed, downtrodden, or melancholy mood. The use of blue notes does not always, however, achieve this feeling, nor are these alterations always used to create this "blue" mood. They are merely one way to make a melodic line more personalized and expressive. The blues will be discussed further in Chapters 3 and 4 and in the sections on form and harmony that follow.

Use the CD-ROM to gain more insight into melodies and how they work. The section about Melody found in the corresponding chapter includes many examples that can be played from your computer and help you to understand simple concepts.

HARMONY

Harmony is a collection of two or more notes played together and, in contrast to melody, is viewed as a vertical event since notes are stacked one on top of another and sounded simultaneously. **Chords** are similarly defined. Harmony is typically used to accompany a melody.

The harmonic aspects of jazz were, for many years, the least inventive and original. Jazz began as a folk style and folk styles rarely feature any kind of harmonic conflict, dissonance, or complexity aside from rhythmic. Many folk songs feature only a few chords that are repeated many times in support of the melody. A succession of chords is called a **chord progression,** or just **progression.** The **harmonic rhythm** defines the pace at which chords move from one to another in a progression. The harmonic rhythm in prejazz folk and blues styles and early jazz was very predictable and usually slow moving, often following a vocal lyric. The harmonic language of jazz is largely borrowed from light classical, popular dance, religious, and various forms of entertainment music. The earliest forms of jazz were based on marches, cakewalks, quadrilles, and polkas—all dance forms popular in the nineteenth century. Since the primary interest for the earliest jazz performers was improvisation, there was less concern for intricate harmonies and chord progressions or fast moving harmonic rhythms. The naiveté of the simple harmonies provided the freedom needed to be adventuresome in the creative improvisation of new melodies. It was the simple harmonies and structures borrowed from these non-jazz forms that gradually became influenced by the blues.

Perhaps the only truly unique aspect of jazz harmony for many years was introduced through the application of blue notes. Those altered tones that we identify with a blues melody were incorporated into the harmonies to form more colorful and dissonant chords beyond the simple three-note **triad** (shown in Example 2.8) or unaltered, four-note **seventh chord.**

EXAMPLE 2.8

Top line melody accompanied by three- or four-note chord harmony.

 Use the CD-ROM to gain more insight into how harmony is constructed and functions. The section about Harmony is found in the corresponding chapter and includes many examples that can be played from your computer, helping you to understand these concepts.

Eventually, jazz harmony adopted a more sophisticated vocabulary that included tones above the seventh (known as **extension tones**—ninth, eleventh, thirteenth) and chromatically altered tones that were not uncommon in twentieth-century "classical" music by composers such as Stravinsky, Debussy, and Bartók. Chords become richer and denser as more tones are added. Chromaticism adds tension to a chord. See Example 2.9.

EXAMPLE 2.9

Four-note seventh, five-note ninth, and six-note eleventh chords illustrating extension tones beyond the three-note triad. The eleventh chord also indicates two chromatically altered notes outside the key signature of three flats.

On the audio anthology listen to the lush, slow moving but changing harmonies used to support the melody of "Moon Dreams" from Miles Davis's *Birth of the Cool* recording. Listen to the entire track or just the opening section from 0:00 to 0:25.

Most jazz tunes feature a progression of chords, indicated through notation or by Roman numerals, that create tension by first moving away from a **key center** (central pitch, tonic or I chord) before eventually progressing back to this key center as shown in Example 2.10.

EXAMPLE 2.10
Chord symbols are used to represent a Ima^7 vi^7 ii^7 V^7 Ima^7 in the specific key of B♭ major.

Tonic is the home key, which in this example is B♭ major. This practice, known as **functional harmony,** is based on the notion that there are certain tendencies that lead one chord logically to another. This practice serves as the basis for a high percentage of jazz tunes and American popular music. The sense of key, or center of tonal gravity, helps jazz players to create logical improvisations—melodies that relate back to this center of gravity. Jazz tunes often feature only one or two key centers, depending on how many uniquely different sections there are to the tune. It is essential that jazz improvisers are thoroughly conversant in functional harmony since it is these principles that guide the soloist to create new melodies. The best soloists can identify the chords in a progression by hearing them and without the aid of printed music.

TEXTURE

Music can be perceived as a mosaic or fabric where melodies and harmonies interact and intertwine, serving as the tiles or fibers in the completed work. The ways in which each tile or fiber interacts with one another—melody with harmony or several melodies with one another—contributes to what is described as the music's **texture.** Texture can be dense or sparse, busy or static—transparent or dark and rich. Melodies are described by textural descriptors such as monophonic, homophonic, or polyphonic. **Monophonic** describes a single line unaccompanied melodic texture. Music is **homophonic** when only one melody line is predominant, supported by chord accompaniment. Chords, discussed in more detail in the section on harmony and on the CD-ROM, are the result of three or more notes sounded simultaneously. Homophonic textures are therefore denser than monophonic ones. **Polyphonic** music features two or more equally dominant and intertwined melodic lines creating yet another different texture. The different melodic lines are said to be moving in **counterpoint** (literally note against note) to one another. Textures with a greater number of elements become increasingly challenging for the listener.

Excellent examples of these textural concepts can be heard on tracks included on the companion CD anthology. For example, "Line For Lyons" offers an excellent example of polyphony or counterpoint from 0:00 to 0:45. Keith Jarrett's unaccompanied solo in the "Windup" beginning at 1:55–2:30 serves to further describe a monophonic texture, and "Take Five" beginning at 0:22 provides a good illustration of a homophony.

Using Example 2.1, "Happy Birthday," you can see and hear illustrations of many concepts discussed to this point. For example, the first three *phrases* continue to ascend, but the melody begins to descend in the third phrase. The melody, which constantly changes direction, is constructed of close steps and more distant leaps. Where is the climax reached, at least in terms of the highest note? How many phrases comprise this familiar tune? If you sang it by yourself, unaccompanied, the texture would be described as monophonic. If you were accompanied, the texture would be described as homophonic. If after singing it once, you began again on a different starting pitch, you would be changing key, or modulating.

FORM

Form in music describes its overall architecture—how many melodies are there? Do they repeat and how many times? Are sections repeated exactly or with variation? Form gives music structure similar to the organization we find in other art forms, in nature, everyday life, and in architecture (suspension bridge, building, etc.). It is an important musical ingredient to comprehend in order to understand what you hear. While on the surface form may seem to be the easiest element to understand, without the benefit of lyrics and a singer it may be difficult for the untrained listener to discern.

Most jazz compositions have more than one clearly defined section. A letter—A, B, C, and so on—defines each large section in the overall form. Each of these sections usually features a distinctly different melody and accompanying chord progression. For example, ragtime pieces are often based on the following formal scheme: AABBACCDD. This form is derived from the **rondo,** a European "classical" model also evident in the march and the polka. The rondo describes a form where one section (A) reoccurs and is juxtaposed with contrasting sections (B, C, and D). The consecutive letters in such a scheme indicate that there is a repeat of that particular theme before moving on to a new one. Often a piece that follows this model changes key at the C section.

Listen to the recording of Scott Joplin's "Maple Leaf Rag" included on the companion CD anthology as it provides an excellent example of the more complex rondo form with multiple themes and changing keys.

Many American popular songs that served as springboards for jazz improvisations followed the **song form** model usually represented by ABA or AABA. The return to A to end the form gives one a sense of symmetry and finality. Each section (A and B) is typically eight measures in length. Jazz musicians often refer to the B section as the **bridge** or "channel." The blues is the simplest of all forms since it is usually only 12 measures long, lacking a B or C theme.

IN THE NICK OF TIME

RICK LAWN

Copyright © 2002

Typical lead sheet that represents the tune dissected in Chapter 3 on the CD-ROM in the section on Performance Practice.

Once again, "Take Five" on the audio anthology offers a good example of the classic song form—ABA. Each section of the form is divided up into two, four-measure phrases. Following a brief introduction by the rhythm section, the A section begins at 0:22 with the second phrase occurring at 0:30 through repeat of the first. The first phrase of the B section begins at 0:38 with the second phrase following at 0:45. The A section returns at 0:52 and the second phrase occurs at 1:00. The improvised solo begins at 1:08.

The Billie Holiday rendition of "Body and Soul" and Stan Getz's recording of "Só Danço Samba," also included on the CD collection, provide additional examples of AABA song form structure that is easy to follow because of the lyric content.

"Jimmy and Wes," included on the CD anthology, is a good illustration of a simple 12-bar instrumental blues based on a repetitive melody.

The section about Form found in the corresponding chapter on the CD-ROM provides a thorough explanation of form in music with examples drawn from the jazz repertoire.

IMPROVISATION

Extemporaneous playing; spontaneous composition; creating music on the spur of the moment. These are simple phrases to describe the act of improvising. People now think of jazz at the mere mention of the term improvisation, though there are often improvised solos in pop tunes and improvisation is often a component of Indian music. Descriptions of jazz from almost any era agree that improvisation is a salient feature. Jazz historian Ostransky stated that in jazz "reading music is considered a lesser accomplishment than improvising it."[9] Discussing the importance of improvisation to jazz, noted jazz scholar James Lincoln Collier wrote that "it is always the soloist that is written about, always the solo that is analyzed."[10] Earlier writings about jazz portrayed improvisation as a mysterious or divine process, adding to the music's mystique. Recently, more thoughtful discussions have helped us to understand the true process behind this unique form of creativity. Since improvisation is an important feature of jazz, the intelligent listener needs to learn about its nature in order to develop skills for identifying and appreciating it.

Something Borrowed—The European Tradition

An early tradition of improvised music is found in medieval chants and in music from the Renaissance (cir. 1450–1600) and Baroque (cir. 1600–1750) periods. Composers were expected to deviate from the original melodies as did Baroque composer Georg Phillipp Telemann when he composed the *Methodical Sonatas*. He provided the basic melody on one line and on another line suggestions for improvisation like that used by modern jazz soloist Charlie Parker.[11] In 1765 violinist and composer Karel von Dittersdorf wrote that: "A new custom developed . . . To show their improvisational creativity they [the soloists] start fantasias in which they play a simple subject which they then very artfully vary several times according to the best rules of composition."[12] Baroque composers J. S. Bach and G. F. Handel also included passages where improvisation was invited and this practice continued until the beginning of the Romantic period (cir. 1820–1900). Although a fine improviser, Ludwig van Beethoven, an extraordinary composer from this period, began a new trend away from this improvisation. The increasing complexity of the music, the growth of music publishing businesses, and the increasing number of amateur musicians caused "classical" composers like Beethoven to seek more control over their compositions. Franz Liszt, another composer and improviser, summed up this new trend by saying "the most absolute respect for the masterpieces of the great masters has replaced the need for novelty and individuality."[13] More attention was paid to interpretation of the musical composition as written, and by the late 1800s, the role of improvisation was diminishing in European music. However, at the same time, in the United States new styles of music were emerging that once again placed a high value on spontaneity and individuality.

Something New, Something Blue—The Jazz Tradition

The roots of American jazz can be compared to any folk tradition—impromptu, spontaneous, and simplistic. These characteristics as well as rhythm, lyric, and melody were of utmost importance in early vocal styles. Perhaps the closest thing to true improvisation in the late 1800s and early 1900s in America could be found in African-American vocal styles such as work songs and field hollers improvised by slaves and chain gang workers, and especially in the blues. This vocal style featured blue notes, slightly altered tones where a special inflection was given to the third and seventh scale tones by lowering the pitch slightly. Instrumentalists later imitated this blues vocal style.

An excellent example of this vocal blues style, including embellishments and "blue notes" associated with the blues can be found on the CD Anthology. Listen to tracks 5, 6, and 9 to see if you can identify these blue tones and vocal embellishments in track 6.

As a whole, the earliest jazz instrumentalists were not known for their ability to improvise new solos each time they performed. Typically, these early musicians performed a piece the same way each time once their approach to a particular song had been refined. Their playing was largely a theme and variation style in which a melody was merely embellished and ornamented in new ways. Thematic variation is the simplest form of improvisation and is probably what Alphonse Picou (1878–1961), a New Orleans clarinetist, referred to when he described this early form of jazz as a "style of playing without notes."[14]

The study of the development of early instrumental jazz is difficult because during this era the music could be preserved only in a written format. No audible artifact remained for study. As each jazz performance is an interpretation of a composition, the printed page could not totally capture the live performance and its unwritten subtleties. However, after the turn of the twentieth century, jazz became perhaps the first music to be greatly influenced by the advent of sound recording, for it directly paralleled the growth of jazz (see the brief History of Recording included on the Online Learning Center.) Recordings provided a lasting aural artifact that faithfully reproduced the live performance other musicians could now be influenced by and imitate. Recordings were also responsible for the very rapid changes in jazz compared to the slower pace in previous musical history where one style was popular for decades before a significant change occurred. Recordings, though, became both an asset and a disadvantage. On one hand, they quickly spread the music and were models for younger musicians trying to learn through imitation. On the other hand, musicians with a popular record now found that the public often wanted to hear live performances exactly as they remembered the recording. The pressures of popularity, customer satisfaction, and marketing could then discourage improvisation.

As jazz matured, largely through the work of Louis Armstrong in the mid-1920s, the concept and importance of improvisation solidified. There are many levels of improvisation at work within the hierarchy of a jazz ensemble. For example, drummers and bassists probably improvise the greatest percentage of the time, though often what they play is not new to them. They rely on familiar patterns that they have played many times. There is no precise duplication, however, and what they improvise often depends on the style of the tune, the tempo, and, of course, with whom they are playing. The amount of improvisational content in a particular performance is dependent to a great extent on the size of the ensemble and the intent of the music. Larger ensembles usually mean a lesser amount of improvisation, while small, chamber-size ensembles like trios and quartets rely a great deal more on improvisation. Jazz aimed at a dance audience usually features less improvisation because the music assumes a more subservient role.

The performance environment can also have a significant influence on how musicians play. Their solos are in part a reflection of their emotions at the time and

Duke Ellington orchestra members at a BBC broadcast.

can be motivated by mood, audience (receptive or antagonistic), and performance environment (cramped stage, smoky bar, concert hall stage). If the players in a band are not compatible on a musical level or a personal level, the music is sure to suffer.

There is a musical dialogue that occurs between the ensemble or soloist and rhythm section, each complementing the other while suggesting new ideas for elaboration by the other. Many performers have described the jazz solo as a story with a beginning, middle, and end. To tell a good story there are characters; in musical situations memorable melodic phrases serve the role of characters and are often repeated with some variation to provide continuity to an improvisation. A musician's relationship to the audience is fragile and requires a proper balance between variety and repetition. The performer's duty is to establish for the listeners what is important and then take them on a journey to these important points. Two Yale University researchers determined that the listener who is led to make certain subconscious predictions by the performer must come out right about 50 percent of the time in order to enjoy a performance. If the predictions are too successful, boredom results and the music is judged too trite, derivative, or banal. If the prediction rate drops too far below 50 percent, the listener loses interest and considers the music chaotic and disorganized.[15] This observation bears out by the frequent use of forms such as rondo and song form (AABA) where composers rely heavily on repetition.

With each style, a new improvisational language is developed. A new vocabulary is created initially by the innovators, and then further developed by the followers. Each style borrows from the vocabulary of a previous style(s), though it is inappropriate to use solely the improvisational vocabulary from one era on tunes from an entirely different style period. In other words, the improvised bebop style, which came about in the mid-1940s developed by Charlie Parker and

Dizzy Gillespie, is inappropriate to use on a Dixieland style tune from the 1920s because bebop is too dissonant, featuring chromatically altered chord tones not found in Dixieland. The language of jazz improvisation is in continual evolution, always borrowing devices from previous generations.

Jazz players tend to copy and borrow from exceptional innovators. The great jazz soloists such as Louis Armstrong, Charlie Parker, Dizzy Gillespie, and John Coltrane, each created a new vocabulary and are still copied years after their deaths. Nevertheless, there is a downside to learning from models, for originality can be sacrificed. The great Swing Era tenor saxophonist Lester Young spoke out in *Down Beat* magazine about the problem of "copy cats" in his 1949 interview with Pat Harris entitled "Pres Talks About Himself, Copycats." Young told Harris "The trouble with most musicians today is that they are copycats. Of course you have to start out playing like someone else. You have a model or a teacher, and you learn all that he can show you. But then you start playing for yourself. Show them that you're an individual. And I can count those who are doing that today on the fingers of one hand."[16] The problem of authenticity, originality, and recreation through imitation has been hotly debated and each jazz improviser must evaluate how important it is to reflect the tradition when playing jazz and how much is too much. Pianist McCoy Tyner in a clinic for college students suggested that "you should become proficient at taking chances"[17] (rather than spending too much time copying other players since that often only ends in losing your personal identity).

> After reading this section, you should read and play the examples included in the sections on Melody and Harmony found in the corresponding chapter on the CD-ROM. A tutorial about Improvisation can also be found in Chapter 3—Listening to Jazz and by further exploring the subsection Performance Practice.

It will be important, as you listen to examples of the various styles of jazz presented throughout the remainder of this book, to relate what you hear and read to the musical concepts presented in this chapter. You will find that the instrumental roles and performance practices change, and the application of musical concepts may also vary from style to style helping to identify, define, and clarify each stylistic change, while making them uniquely different by comparison.

CHAPTER SUMMARY

Jazz, like all music, can be broken down to the basic elements of rhythm, melody, harmony, texture, and form. Of these elements, rhythm is significant in setting jazz apart from other styles of music. Included under the heading of rhythm are syncopation, meter, and swing. Swing refers both to a specific jazz style period and to a way of performing music. Jazz groups most often perform at steady tempos set by a rhythm section rather than by a conductor. The way in which the rhythm section plays and interacts has changed with each specific style of jazz.

Improvisation is simultaneous composition and performance. While in no way exclusive to jazz, improvisation is a key ingredient to jazz. Many feel that some level of improvised content needs to be present for music to be considered jazz. Similar to the evolution of rhythm section styles, approaches to improvisation have changed throughout the history of jazz. Early jazz performers often did little more than ornament the previously stated melody in their improvisations, while performers of other jazz styles may create an entirely new idea based on the same chord structure as the melody. In some styles of jazz, it may be difficult to differentiate a melody statement from an improvised solo.

Technology has had a profound effect on the development of jazz. Since much of the evolution of jazz has centered on changes in approach to improvisation, the technology to record performances provided models from which new ideas in improvisation could spring. The same was not true for composed music, since it could be recreated by performing it from the printed page. Other technological developments including the electric guitar, electric bass, synthesizer, and digital sampler have opened new possibilities in available sounds for jazz and altered the roles instruments play within a jazz group.

KEY TERMS

Your instructor should clarify which terms and aspects of this chapter are of primary importance. You should be familiar to some extent with the following terms:

rhythm	key signature	extension tones
meter	modulate	key center
measure (bar)	tonality	tonic
tempo	atonal	functional harmony
rubato	scale	texture
rhythm section	chromatic	monophonic
lay back	blue notes	homophonic
syncopation	harmony	polyphonic
polyrhythm	chord	counterpoint
polymeter	chord progression	form
swing	(progression)	rondo
melody	harmonic rhythm	song form
phrase	triad	bridge
key	seventh chord	

REVIEW QUESTIONS

1. Briefly discuss the relationship of African music to jazz from the rhythmic standpoint.
2. What is meant by swing?
3. What is the difference between a melody and a phrase, or is there any difference?
4. Discuss the various aspects of the blues and its significance to jazz.
5. What three terms can be used in discussing the texture of a piece of music?
6. In general, what is meant by functional harmony?
7. What are the most common forms used in jazz?
8. Is improvisation unique to jazz? Explain your answer.
9. Discuss the improvisational tradition in jazz.
10. In the standard song form, what term is used to describe the middle section?

> **Make sure that you also review material on the corresponding chapter of the CD-ROM.**

Listening to **Jazz**

"To appreciate music the listener must be actively involved. Passive listening to music does not bring about intelligent musical enjoyment, but active listening, which includes understanding and active participation with emotional responses, can foster musical enjoyment."[1]

PAUL TANNER, DAVID MEGILL, AND MAURICE GEROW, *JAZZ*

PERFORMANCE PRACTICE

People often listen passively to music because they are bombarded daily by all kinds of it in so many different environments (doctor's office, elevator, supermarket, coffee shop, mall). Consequently, they become nearly oblivious to it. This book and the accompanying CD-ROM are designed to enhance the ability to be a more active listener by increasing your level of appreciation and understanding of jazz without detracting from the enjoyment of casually listening to music.

Everyone is entitled to their own opinion about music, but in order to have a valid opinion, it is wise to have criteria to consider while listening to and evaluating a performance. Learn to be an observant member of the audience, know what to listen to and look for, and the experience will be substantially enhanced.

Since jazz is considered an art form where so much is left to the personal interpretation of the performer and arranger, an overview of the techniques employed to personalize their performance is significant to our study of jazz.

The Instruments of Jazz

Different styles of music are often associated closely with certain instruments. We frequently can make an educated guess about the style of music that a band plays by merely looking at the band. We see a violin, we think of classical music, and a saxophone reminds us of jazz. Any instrument is capable of being played in a jazz style; however, the established tradition has drawn associations to certain instruments such as the saxophone and the drum set. Neither of these instruments is typically found in symphony orchestras. On the other hand, violins, cellos, violas, bassoons, oboes, and harps are rarely heard playing in a jazz style. When we see a group that consists of a three- or four-piece rhythm section, a saxophone, and a trumpet, it is very safe to assume that the music they play is associated in some way with jazz.

Some instruments have fallen out of favor in terms of their use in jazz. For example, the tuba, a holdover from brass bands, was commonplace in jazz ensembles well into the early 1930s, but is rarely used by more contemporary jazz groups. The clarinet, which was a very well-established instrument during the early jazz periods and through the mid-1940s, is now less frequently heard in this setting. The guitar gradually replaced the banjo, often found in early Dixieland style bands. The soprano sax, first made popular by Sidney Bechet in the 1920s, fell out of favor until it was reintroduced by John Coltrane in the early 1960s. So while some instruments have remained mainstays of the jazz band since the beginning, others have come and gone. Some instruments such as the drum set went through radical changes stimulated by both technological advancements and the musicians themselves. The guitar, which eventually became amplified, is another example of how technology has had a direct impact on the music and performance practices.

The instruments associated with jazz are members of the brass, woodwind, percussion, and string instrument families. Members of the brass family include the cornet, trumpet, flugelhorn, trombone, tuba, and French horn. Only the cornet, trumpet, flugelhorn, and trombone are common to jazz. Brass players often use mutes in the jazz setting. Many different kinds of mutes were actually first made popular by jazz players and later adopted by modern "classical" composers. The woodwind family consists of the flute, clarinet, oboe, saxophone, and bassoon. Those woodwinds most common to jazz are the saxophone, clarinet, and flute. The bass is a member of the string family and, of course, the drum set and various Latin instruments are considered members of the percussion family. The piano was actually once considered a member of the percussion family along with the pitched, keyboard percussion instruments like the vibraphone and marimba. With the advent of electronic organs and modern synthesizers, the piano and its relatives might now best be associated with the keyboard family.

The Drum Set and Swing

Drummers, who serve to motivate the swing feel, have incorporated the polyrhythmic and polymetric aspects of the African drum ensemble. These ensembles are comprised of many drummers, all playing different rhythms on different percussive instruments. The single jazz drummer on his drum set (also known as "**kit**") is able to incorporate the rhythms played by many African drummers into one cohesive style. The fundamental or ground rhythm is maintained by the hi-hat cymbals (also known as sock cymbal) played on beats two and four and sometimes by the bass drum that often defines each beat of the measure (1-2-3-4). The hands are kept free to embellish this fundamental pulse and are expected to apply shifting accents on the other drums and cymbals as the steady time flow is maintained by the hi-hat, ride cymbal, and bass drum. A modern drum set is pictured in Example 3.1. Done properly, the jazz drummer's one-man drum ensemble produces a swinging pulse of subtle, ever-changing tensions and relaxations created by the interactions of irregular patterns played by the hands and regular patterns played by the feet. Bear in mind, too, that the bass generally maintains the steady, predictable pulse of a tempo by playing notes on each beat

EXAMPLE 3.1
The jazz drum set.

Crash cymbal

Ride cymbal

Shell tom

Hi hat or
sock cymbal

Floor tom

Snare
drum

Bass drum

of the measure (1-2-3-4). As Count Basie's long-time guitarist Freddie Green said in an interview with Stanley Dance "the rhythm section is the foundation of it [swing]. If the rhythm section isn't swinging, then you can forget about it. If it isn't clicking, moving together. . . ."[2]

The swing **ride cymbal** rhythm, which gradually evolved as an additional means of providing a regular pulse, is as impossible to precisely notate as are many African rhythms. Many West African characteristics are evident in the shifting ride cymbal rhythm that resembles the skipping analogy presented in Chapter 2. The ride cymbal is used to create a smooth, connected flow of skipping attacks that help to propel the music forward. Only recently has computer hardware and software enabled scientific studies to determine the true mathematical subdivision of each beat in various swing jazz styles. Here, suffice it to say that in a swing phrase, notes played on downbeats are lengthened and upbeats shortened and accented slightly since they occur as anticipations of upcoming major beats or downbeats. Tap your foot in an even tempo and sing the syllable "ga" with a slight emphasis as your foot comes up on every other tap. This exercise will give you the sensation of swinging by emphasizing the second half of each beat. You can also try using the following syllables to verbally imitate the feeling of swing. Example 3.2 represents two measures that can be repeated multiple times.

| Ding | Ding-**ga** | Ding | Ding-**ga** | Ding | Ding-**ga** | Ding | Ding-**ga** | **EXAMPLE 3.2** |
| 1 | 2 | 3 | 4 | 1 | 2 | 3 | 4 | |

Tap a steady tempo with your foot and imagine the irregular punches and jabs of a boxer intermingled with this steady pulse. This exercise helps to portray the approach of the more modern drummer. Listen and watch the drummer on *Video Blues* found on the CD-ROM to hear and see a good example of this style particularly during trumpet and saxophone solos.

No special musical notation is used to express swing and it cannot be accurately notated. If the piece is identified as jazz, then it is played in the appropriate style. Much has been said about the oral and aural traditions that are important to the very existence of various folk music styles, and these same traditions have had a significant impact on the formation of jazz styles. It is not possible to swing if one has never heard it and learned first to duplicate it through imitation. In this way, jazz is very different than traditional Western European classical music. It is also important to realize that as time passed and jazz changed, swing rhythms became both more subtle and more complex.

Swing is a phenomenon indigenous to jazz and resulted from the gradual evolution of this music during the acculturation process of the black race in America. One of the primary reasons why "swing" has been so difficult to define is that jazz performance practices have changed significantly about every 10 years since the beginning of instrumental jazz in the early twentieth century. The music has continued to swing as styles changed, but the actual interpretation of swing has changed. Swing means different things to different people, but the rhythmic spirit of jazz is identifiable in all of its numerous styles

Once again, you should use the CD-ROM and examine the section on swing in the Elements of Jazz section found under Rhythm and Meter. It will also be helpful to explore the drum set that is found in the corresponding Chapter 3, Listening to Jazz, on the CD-ROM. You can listen to some of the drum styles and look at the pieces of a drum set.

A Jazz Veteran Discusses the Rhythm Section

The primary importance of a rhythm section to jazz is most evident when one traces the stylistic evolution of this music from the earliest New Orleans styles (polka, ragtme, brass band) to the more recent explorations by Miles Davis and his disciples who melded state-of-the-art electronics with a rhythmically driving blues/riff tradition. The rhythm section and the evolution of its modified playing techniques consistently appear to be at the heart of each major stylistic innovation from the early part of the twentieth century to the present day. It has functioned as the necessary catalyst to catapult jazz from its birth near the turn of the century through a rapid maturation process leading logically to current stylistic trends. There is no better way to learn about the rhythm section and the essence of jazz than through the eyes and ears of a veteran such as jazz bassist Gene Ramey. He learned on the bandstand and in the recording studio with many of jazz's dignitaries such as Jay McShann, Charlie Parker, Tadd Dameron, Fats Navarro, Teddy Wilson, Lester Young, Stan Getz, and Thelonious Monk. The rhythm section provides the heartbeat of jazz, or as Gene Ramey so aptly put it, "the rhythm section is the motor." Bassist Gene Ramey devoted a lifetime to supplying the heartbeat of many outstanding jazz organizations. Ramey, who served alongside many of the masters of their art, offered the following comments about the heartbeat of jazz.

> The rhythm section has to work as a team that concentrates on the band and on the soloist. You have to know who you're going to cooperate with. It's better for the rhythm section not to have written notes unless it's for special little phrases. Most of the black bands believe in turning the rhythm section loose and giving them a chart [written music] only for chords and let them improvise from that. That doesn't mean for the bass player and drummer to go wild. The drummer and everyone else in the rhythm section is supposed to stay at home [provide a basic foundation] and remember that you're working as a team and not individually. If I'm playing behind you I'm supposed to know

every note you're playing. What you're supposed to play on a hot chorus is according to what the soloist is playing. If you listen to him and if you've got your smoke signals working, you're going to follow what he's doing and you'll fit nicely together. The rhythm section is the motor and the drummer is the painter; he's the decorator. The drummer can prepare the soloist to go into the middle part of a chorus. He can prepare the soloist to come out of the middle part and go into the last part of the chorus, and he can prepare them for the next chorus. If he does it right, he's going to inspire that soloist. Now what we would do is let Bird [Charlie Parker] take it easy for the first chorus. We just played around behind him and then all of a sudden we'd set fire to his tail and the audience and the rest of the band.[3]

The CD-ROM offers a close look at the modern jazz drum set. The drum set is discussed in great detail along with video clips that are found by exploring the Performance Practice section in the corresponding chapter.

The best way to become associated with the instrumental sounds of jazz is to explore the Instrumentation and Performance Practice sections in the corresponding chapter on the CD-ROM. Pictures and sound files of the instruments and mutes commonly found in jazz ensembles can be found in this section. You can also test yourself on your ability to recognize the sound of various instruments.

Orchestration and Instrumentation

Orchestration refers to which instruments are used to play the music. Orchestration, or **instrumentation,** can, and usually does vary throughout a piece of music. Orchestration can provide originality to a composition. A single composition can be rendered with many different orchestrations, though it is most often associated with the one originally conceived by the composer and/or arranger.

Compare the orchestration of two tracks included on your audio anthology— "Summertime," arranged by Gil Evans and "Piece 1" by Anthony Braxton.

The Arrangement While performers tend to occupy the most prominent position in jazz, the arrangers (who oftentimes are also the performers) also serve an all-important function. The **arrangement** refers to the way a group of musicians presents a particular piece of music when compared to the original model. The arrangement is considered an adaptation of the original. Since much of the jazz repertoire during the first 50 years was based on popular songs of the day, adaptations were required to suit the needs of the jazz performer. These adaptations were and continue to be important in providing a unique identity for the performer or band. The "arrangement" is unique to jazz and American popular music. While there are examples of arrangements in classical literature, they are of much less significance to the history and development of the music.

Since there is no standard instrumentation for jazz bands and they can range in size from duos to large ensembles consisting of 16 or more musicians, it is

EXAMPLE 3.3

spontaneous and consider what to play next, soloists rely on "licks," or prelearned patterns and phrases. These phrases, used throughout an improvised solo, often refer to the tradition, as they may be quotes of melodies played by another soloist years earlier. Even the great improviser Charlie Parker in a bebop improvisation quoted a Louis Armstrong solo recorded many years earlier. These quotes and memorized phrases can be strung together in many different ways to create new material. Phrases borrowed from the tradition could be compared to the many ways that we can express an idea in words. For example, take a phrase like "The new fallen snow is beautiful." This simple idea could be expressed and embellished in many different ways. One could have said "The new snow that fell last night is beautiful," or "New snow like we got last night is really beautiful." This multiple means of expression is exactly what jazz players do when they use a prelearned phrase and put it to use in an improvised solo. In using a prelearned phrase, the soloist creates the illusion to the listener of pure spontaneity. While the sequence or prelearned ideas are assembled and reassembled in new ways from performance to performance, many of the memorized ideas are repeated. Ostransky wrote about this phenomenon in his book *The Anatomy of Jazz*. He said, "They [jazz improvisers] do not compose on the spur of the moment; their significant improvisations are the result of long practice and experience."[4] Through years of listening, borrowing, assimilating, analyzing, and imitating, soloists amass a collection of jazz phrases that suit their individual style and can be recalled at any time in the course of a solo. In other words, soloists play what they enjoy playing. It is obvious that not everything played during a jazz solo is spontaneously created. These solos, more frequently than not, are based on a series of recreations—bits and pieces of prelearned material coupled with newly created ideas to form a fresh, new improvisation. In the fall of 1958, Duke Ellington traveled to England for a tour with his orchestra. He expressed his thoughts and feelings about jazz improvisation in an article entitled "The Future of Jazz" included in the souvenir program. In this article he said:

> There are still a few die-hards who believe there is such a thing as unadulterated improvisation without preparation or anticipation. It is my belief that there has never been anybody who has blown even two bars worth listening to who doesn't have some idea about what he was going to play, before he started. If you just ramble through the scales or play around the chords, that's nothing more than musical exercise. Improvisation really consists of picking out a device here, and connecting it with a device there; changing the rhythm here, and pausing there; there has to be some thought preceding each phrase, otherwise it is meaningless.[5]

Other forms of quotes used by jazz soloists include humorous ones, like "Here Comes the Bride" (from the opera *Lohengrin* by Richard Wagner), which almost everyone knows, and melodies from other standard tunes that fit the particular chord progression. Quotes of this nature sometimes serve as an homage to earlier players and a display of machismo, demonstrating to fellow musicians and informed listeners how much is known about the tradition. The player's ultimate objective is to have an effective dialogue with the other musicians while creating exciting new ideas and incorporating significant and appropriate aspects of the tradition. To quote contemporary trumpeter Tom Harrell, "He improves on his heritage, but he also tries to invent music that has never been heard before."[6] Only the greatest soloists, the true virtuosos on their instruments, are capable of spontaneously creating a high percentage of completely new material each time they improvise. The most innovative improvisers in the history of jazz were those who dared to break from tradition and forge new pathways that relied less on what had come before.

What most jazz players strive for is to find the "Zone," which they describe as a mental state in which complete relaxation and intense concentration coexist. The late great jazz pianist Bill Evans described his creative process to author, historian Dan Morganstern in a 1964 *Down Beat* magazine interview by saying that "Everybody has to learn certain things, but when you play, the intellectual process no longer has anything to do with it . . . I am relying on intuition then. I have no idea of what is coming next."[7] Evans is describing the "Zone" that so many jazz players have referred to and strive each night to attain.

A section about Improvisation can be found on the CD-ROM in the corresponding chapter. Further explore the subsection about Performance Practice on this tutorial. Listening to the examples will enhance your understanding of this most important aspect of jazz performance practice.

UNDERSTANDING THE PERFORMANCE

There are common features in all jazz performances and it can be helpful to review some aspects of the typical jazz performance, and the sequence in which they occur. Keep the following outline handy while listening to the music included on the companion CD anthology. Many jazz performances adhere to the following scheme:

- Introduction—often 4, 8, or 16 bars long (sometimes there is no introduction).
- Tune—blues (12 bars), extended blues (16 or 24 bars), or song form (AABA, ABA, AAB).
- Improvised solo(s)—usually adhering to the form of the piece though sometimes abbreviated.
- Interlude—interludes are sometimes used to link solos and are composed sections. Often there is no interlude, only additional solos.
- Shout chorus—newly composed material featuring the entire ensemble. This section is common in big band arrangements but often not found in small group jazz.
- A return to the tune.
- Ending—sometimes referred to as **coda** (musical term for ending) or **tag**.

"Take Five" or "Daahoud," included on your CD anthology, provides a fine example of this classic small group presentation formula.

There can be many exceptions to this scheme; however, a high percentage of performances follow this general model. Exceptions sometimes occur when the constructing an effective solo. Do you sense good communication during the performance?

2. Is there obvious communication between the soloists and the rhythm section?

3. Do the soloists project self-confidence?

4. Does the audience applaud? Unlike soloists in a classical piece, audiences typically applaud a good jazz soloist before the end of a piece. This practice probably stemmed from the informal places in which jazz was presented for many years before entering the concert hall.

5. Is the performance spirited and does it seem sincere? Are the players involved in the performance and do they hold your attention?

6. Did the singer improvise in a scat vocal style?

 The CD-ROM includes examples to help you identify whether a performance is out of tune, rushes, drags, or is generally sloppy. These examples will help to further clarify these concepts and aid you in assessing the quality of a performance. They can be found in the corresponding chapter on the CD-ROM.

Originality and spontaneity are very important to a good jazz performance, though sometimes difficult to recognize and evaluate. The improvised nature of jazz is one area that makes it radically different from classical music. Classical musicians are expected to be flawless and consistent in their presentation of a piece from performance to performance. Jazz musicians, on the other hand, are evaluated on their ability to be consistently spontaneous, uniquely different, and original. The ability to play entirely new improvisations from one performance to the next is risky but makes a jazz musician stand out from the crowd. To do something unique, unusual, or unpredictable is often the mark of an exceptional jazz performer. To determine if a performance or recording meets this criteria, ask yourself the following questions. It may, however, take a more seasoned listener to find answers to some of these questions.

- Is the performance pedestrian and predictable, or are there some unusual aspects that catch you off guard and hold your attention? For example, are any pieces played in a style different from the expected—a tune usually played in the swing style played instead as a Bossa Nova?

- Is there some variation in the overall presentation or do all the pieces sound the same and have the same tempo and style?

- Is the overall ensemble performance well rehearsed and balanced?

- Do the performers execute the music precisely in a cohesive manner?

- Do the improvised solos project a sense of daring and originality?

Author and jazz pianist Ted Gioia in his book *The Imperfect Art* points out that jazz, if measured against classical music performance standards, is often flawed. In jazz, the emphasis is placed on individual creativity and spontaneity and as a result it is not uncommon to detect slight imperfections in a live performance. If the performers are really "going for it" and striving for an emotion-packed performance, mistakes can occur. The most polished performers, however, are skilled at masking mistakes in their improvisations even turning them into creative ideas.[8]

THE JAM SESSION

Since the beginning, jazz musicians have gathered in jam sessions for their own amusement and stimulation. The jam session provides a social gathering and networking opportunities. New musicians in town attend the local jam session to make contacts for future employment. Musicians often stop by jam sessions after their regular gig, often a more commercial job providing little opportunity for improvisation. The musicians at a jam are unencumbered by the dictates of public taste and so more apt to experiment taking chances. As Scott DeVeaux put it in his book *The Birth of Bebop,* the jam session was [is] "the pursuit of virtuosity for its own sake; the shift of focus away from the mass audience to the personal struggle of musicians to master the art of improvisation."[9] Therefore, jam sessions provide a unique opportunity for audiences to see musicians at work, learning, exploring, experimenting, and, of course, sometimes failing in the difficult art of improvisation.

Once they became public, jam sessions attracted the public's attention despite the musicians' general disregard for the audience's likes and dislikes. In fact, jam sessions can often bypass the casual listener altogether unless they are well informed about jam session protocol, generally standardized worldwide. Even before the swing era, jam sessions were popular with black and white musicians. In New York, black musicians frequented the Harlem Rhythm Club, while white musicians attended sessions at the Onyx. In the 1920s, musicians sponsored "rent parties" and charged admission to what was, in essence, a jam session. The income helped pay a fellow musician's rent. Even today jam sessions can be found in many U.S. cities, sponsored by the local union hall, university, or jazz club.[10]

At a jam session, there is usually a house band, or a house rhythm section, employed to ensure accompaniment for the horn players who drop by. Aside from the house band, musicians are not paid for their participation. Sometimes these jam sessions can turn into competitive "cutting sessions" in which the rivalry between two or more musicians (usually horn players) can become very intense. There are cutting session tales involving some of the most famous performers in jazz history. There is generally a tacit understanding among the musicians as to the pecking order of those in attendance. Status is based on a well-established reputation and a reigning local kingpin can be challenged in a cutting session by a newcomer. In the 1930s, some clubs featured exclusive jam sessions called "suppers" showcasing only exceptional players performing by invitation only. A reputation could be made or destroyed at a jam session.

Despite this competitiveness, musicians are generally supportive and encouraging to one another. Jam sessions keep seasoned musicians on their toes and offer younger musicians the opportunity to learn from the masters. These sessions also provide a safe haven in which to try new ideas and to practice. Author Ralph Ellison described the jam session as "the jazz man's true academy."[11] The jam session holds an important place in the history and advancement of jazz improvisation.

What Happens in a Jam Session?

The jam session follows a traditional pattern. The house band or house rhythm section forms the nucleus. As different horn players, guitarists, and rhythm section players who wish to "sit in" take their place on stage, the group must first decide on a tune to play. There is a generally accepted jazz canon or repertoire of popular and show tunes (usually from the 1930s and 40s) as well as jazz standards known by many musicians and varying by region. Experienced musicians are familiar with this canon of tunes, while for the younger, less experienced musicians

Jam session at Jimbo's Bop City in San Francisco (1952) featuring (left to right): Dexter Gordon, Jimmy Heath on tenor saxophones; Roy Porter, drums; Percy Health, bass; Hampton Hawes, piano; Sonny Criss, alto saxophone.

there may be a "fake book" on hand as a crutch and containing hundreds of these tunes with melody and chord symbols.

Once everyone agrees on the tune they must also decide on a key, tempo, and style. Most of this repertoire is usually played in one or two standard keys. (Remember that any tune can be played in any of the 12 keys.) Singers perform a song in a particular key because of their individual voice range. Tunes can be performed in a broad range of tempi and styles. More experienced musicians might choose a particular tune, key, or fast tempo in order to discourage less-experienced musicians from participating. Any one of these difficulty factors can cause the novice to sit out rather than risk embarrassment. Before starting the tune, an introduction may be contrived and agreed upon. In some cases, the rhythm section creates an introduction by playing the last four or eight measures of the tune.

The musicians might also discuss an order of soloists or they may just let this happen spontaneously. If there is more than one horn player, they might decide to share the responsibility of playing the tune, allowing for more variety and flexibility in the rhythmic interpretation of the melody. For example, the trumpet player might play the "A" section while the saxophonist takes over at the "bridge" or "B" section. Sometimes it takes a while for the musicians to agree on all of these performance aspects.

To begin, someone sets the tempo by counting in time, often snapping their fingers on alternate beats, that is, 1-2-1234. After the introduction is stated and the original tune, the group launches into individual improvised solos. Horn players not soloing might improvise **riffs** (simple repeated phrase) as backgrounds. Remember that the rhythm section accompanying a horn soloist or singer is improvising the accompaniments on the given chord progression. When everyone has soloed, there might be a chorus (one complete cycle through the chord progression) or more during which the soloists trade four- or eight-measure phrases, sometimes alternating with the drummer during this trading sequence. The practice of **trading fours** stems from the African musical tradition in which the **call and response,** or question answer format, was common practice. Eventually, once all solos have concluded, the band returns to restate the tune. A singer might return to the "bridge" or "B" section of the form following the solos on a slow ballad to avoid making tunes too long and redundant. There is often a tag or coda (musical ending section) to conclude the tune. This tag could be a restatement of the introduction. There is also an understanding among musicians that the final four measures of a tune can be repeated several times as an ending. Contrarily some tunes end very abruptly, usually dictated by the nature of the melody. It takes a great deal more time to explain the jam session performance protocol than it actually does to happen. Try to attend a jam session to experience firsthand this interesting phenomenon that originated with jazz.

VIDEO BLUES

Look at the short movie entitled *Video Blues* found in the corresponding chapter on the CD-ROM. The following outline will help guide you through this video and enable you after one or two viewings to answer the list of questions that follows. Don't try to concentrate on identifying too many details on the first viewing. This video will help to clarify a number of standard jazz performance practices discussed in this chapter.

Video Blues was composed and arranged by Jack Cooper. While *Video Blues* is not a jam session played entirely by professionals, but represents a staged, instructional performance, it does provide insight into many aspects of a jazz blues performance. This piece is a 12-bar blues arranged for three horns and a rhythm section. As you listen and watch try to keep track of the 12-measure form that repeats throughout this video. To assist you in following the 12-bar blues form conduct a simple 4/4 pattern (found on the CD-ROM) or count silently as you or tap your foot: 1234 2234 3234 4234 5234, and so on.

- The first chorus serves as an introduction and acquaints us with the members of the rhythm section. This introduction lasts approximately 22 seconds.

- The horn section makes the first statement of the main theme: 22 seconds to approximately 44 seconds. Can you explain what occurs during this first chorus?

- The second statement of the tune features the trombone in call and response style with the other horns. This section lasts from approximately 44 seconds to 1:05.

- The third chorus begins at 1:05 and features an ensemble "break" followed by a trumpet solo. This chorus ends at approximately 1:27.

- The fourth chorus, which begins at 1:27, features an improvised bass solo. The chorus ends at approximately 1:49.

- The alto sax is featured from approximately 1:49 to 2:11.

- A drum solo begins the next chorus at approximately 2:12. The drummer exchanges solos in a dialogue with the piano. The chorus ends at approximately 2:33.

- The final chorus features the entire ensemble and begins at approximately 2:34. A final short ending, sometimes referred to as a "tag," is added following this last chorus. This tag begins at approximately 2:51.

After viewing this video you should be able to answer the following questions about the music.

- Did the bass player use an electric or acoustic instrument?
- What instruments accompanied the bass solo?
- What did the other horns do during the alto sax solo?
- Did the saxophonist play alto, tenor, or both?
- Did the sax soloist begin his solo at the exact beginning of a chorus, or did his entrance overlap with the end of the bass solo?
- When did the drummer switch from sticks to brushes and why?
- How many measures long was the ensemble "break?"
- What kind of mute did the trumpet soloist use?
- How many measures did the trumpet soloist play during the third chorus?
- Did the bass player use a bow?
- Did the piece ever return to the two-beat style featured during the introductory chorus?
- Was the guitar ever used as a single line instrument as opposed to playing only chords?
- How many choruses of the blues were played and specifically what happened during each chorus?

You should be familiar with the following terms and their use throughout this performance:

call and response	syncopation
measure	trading fours
unison	phrase
break	bar
fill	shout chorus
comping	kicks
pizzacato	fermata
background figure	

Once you have completed this chapter you should have a much clearer understanding of how the various elements of music work together in a jazz context, and how musicians communicate in a performance, interpret the music, and construct jazz music. This newly acquired knowledge will serve you well as you progress through this book, listen to jazz recordings, and attend live performances.

CHAPTER SUMMARY

In listening to jazz, it is very important to hone one's active listening skills. We have become a society of passive listeners, whether it is the way in which background music influences our shopping and eating habits or even the need some feel to have music in the background while doing other tasks (like studying). Active listening involves noticing different details of a recording (the bass, the ride cymbal, the piano, etc.) during numerous listenings of the performance, as opposed to attempting to absorb all of the details of the performance simply by listening to the composite sound (everything at once).

Although it is possible for any instrument to be used in a jazz setting, some instruments (like saxophone, flugelhorn, and drum set) are often associated with jazz, while others (such as violin, bassoon, and French horn) are more commonly associated with a symphony orchestra. In jazz, the way an instrument is played is much more important than the specific instrument being played. It is common for jazz artists to use techniques often foreign to the classical tradition. This may include such devices as growls, smears, and falls.

Improvisation is an important element of jazz. The improviser creates new melodies using only chord symbols as a basic guide to the harmony of a tune. Although one might get the impression that the performer is creating entirely new music on the spot, typically jazz musicians often create solos by interspersing countless memorized short figures/phrases that they have played before with new, improvised material. In listening to alternate takes of recordings done by some of the great jazz masters, one often finds not only similarities in the solos, but sometimes identical figures occurring at the same place in the form of the tune as other recordings of the artist playing that same tune. Specific figures/phrases are often closely associated with an artist acting as a musical signature. In most styles of jazz, improvised solos follow the same form and harmony as the melody statement. Listeners can hum the melody to themselves during an improvised solo in order to keep track of the form.

Jam sessions, while sometimes entertaining, take place more for the benefit of the participating musicians than for the audience. This is a time when jazz musicians can experiment and take risks, as well as make contact with other players. As such, a jam session is often a learning situation for the participants. These sessions can take place after hours, sometimes lasting until the morning and have been part of the jazz tradition since the beginning.

KEY TERMS

Your instructor should clarify which terms and aspects of this chapter are of primary importance. You should be familiar to some extent with the following terms:

kit	phrasing	scat
ride cymbal	accents	shout chorus
orchestration	coda	soli
instrumentation	tag	riffs
arrangement	rubato	trading fours
articulation	chorus	call and response

REVIEW QUESTIONS

1. Name the instruments usually found in the jazz rhythm section.
2. What wind instrument commonly associated with jazz is rarely heard in a classical music context?
3. What woodwind instrument popular in early jazz bands has fallen somewhat out of favor in more modern times?
4. Name the woodwind instruments commonly associated with jazz.
5. Name the brass instruments.
6. Explain the significance of the "arrangement" to jazz.
7. Name some of the special effects associated with jazz playing, especially wind instrument performance practice, and discuss why these affectations are important to jazz as a style.
8. Discuss the typical architecture that defines many jazz performances. Use letters and short musical terms to express the form and shape.
9. Describe those factors that would contribute to an excellent jazz performance or recording.
10. What is the significance of the jam session to jazz?
11. What are the important things that musicians must consider at a jam session in order to enjoy a successful performance?
12. When a singer scats, what are they doing?
13. What is meant by swing?
14. Discuss the roles of the rhythm section instruments.

Make sure that you also review material on the corresponding chapter of the CD-ROM.

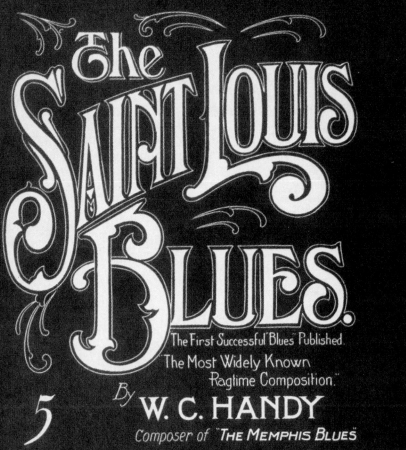

The Saint Louis Blues.

The First Successful "Blues" Published.

The Most Widely Known Ragtime Composition."

By **W. C. HANDY**

Composer of "The Memphis Blues"

5

Publishe...

PACE & HANDY

MEMPHIS

The New York Times.

"All the News That's Fit to Print."

THE WEATHER.

NEW YORK, TUESDAY, APRIL 16, 1912—TWENTY-FOUR PAGES.

ONE CENT

TITANIC SINKS FOUR HOURS AFTER HITTING ICEBERG; 866 RESCUED BY CARPATHIA, PROBABLY 1250 PERISH; ISMAY SAFE, MRS. ASTOR MAYBE, NOTED NAMES MISSING

Col. Astor and Bride, Isidor Straus and Wife, and Maj. Butt Aboard.

"RULE OF SEA" FOLLOWED

Women and Children Put Over in Lifeboats and Are Supposed to be Safe on Carpathia.

PICKED UP AFTER 8 HOURS

Vincent Astor Calls at White Star Office for News of His Father and Leaves Weeping.

FRANKLIN HOPEFUL ALL DAY

Manager of the Line Insisted Titanic Was Unsinkable Even After She Had Gone Down.

HEAD OF THE LINE ABOARD

J. Bruce Ismay Making First Trip on Gigantic Ship That Was to Eclipse All Others.

Biggest Liner Plunges to the Bottom at 2:20 A. M.

RESCUERS THERE TOO LATE

Except to Pick Up the Few Hundreds Who Took to the Lifeboats.

WOMEN AND CHILDREN FIRST

Cunarder Carpathia Rushing to New York with the Survivors.

SEA SEARCH FOR OTHERS

The California Stands By on Chance of Picking Up Other Boats or Rafts.

OLYMPIC SENDS THE NEWS

Only Ship to Flash Wireless Messages to Shore After the Disaster.

The Lost Titanic Being Towed Out of Belfast Harbor.

CAPT. E. J. SMITH,
Commander of the Titanic.

PARTIAL LIST OF THE SAVED.

Includes Bruce Ismay, Mrs. Widener, Mrs. H. B. Harris, and an Incomplete, suggesting Mrs. Astor's.

The Roots of **Jazz**

"If you play a recording of American Jazz for an African friend . . . he may say, as he sits fidgeting in his chair, `What are we supposed to do with this?' He is expressing the most fundamental aesthetic of African music: without participation there is no meaning. . . . The music of Africa invites us to participate in the making of a community."[1]

JOHN MILLER CHERNOFF

America is undoubtedly the most ethnically and culturally diverse country in the world. African slaves, brought to the United States largely from the western shores of the Continent, provided an indentured work force for Southern plantations. This African influence provided the most essential catalyst for creating a new American music. Also immigrating to the United States, well before the twentieth century, were immigrants from throughout Europe, including Scots, Irish, English, French, Spaniards, Germans, Eastern Europeans, as well as Cubans, Puerto Ricans, and Asians. Seeking their fortunes, new opportunities, and freedom, each of these populations contributed to the cultural stew. It is no surprise that a new, native music would develop reflecting all this diversity.

It was important for transplanted African slaves to preserve some aspects of their cultural heritage since in many cases entire families were broken up at the auction block. Husbands, wives, and children were often separated. Without the comfort and security of the family and village, the preservation of social, religious, and musical customs became even more important. By maintaining these traditions, the link to a homeland they would likely never again see would not be broken. The need to preserve these cultural and aesthetic ideals stimulated the development of a new music style. Jazz has become the most universally recognized original American art form as a byproduct of this cultural milieu.

OUT OF AFRICA: THE SIGNIFICANCE OF AFRICAN MUSIC TO JAZZ

Jazz would not exist without the influences exerted by African-Americans on the music styles already existing in America. These musical influences can be seen and heard in nearly every aspect of jazz including the rhythms, melodies, harmonies, and forms. Since no recordings exist to document the process that led to the creation of early instrumental jazz, certain aspects of this process are at best sketchy. Conclusions about this process, however, can be drawn based on what is known about African culture and early American music of the times.

Musical Aesthetic

The African concept of art and music is vastly different from that of the Western world. There is no special word for art in many African languages. Rather the making of art, be it visual or performance in nature, is part of the everyday life experience. It is functional and participatory. Music exists in African society to fulfill a specific function. For example, music played an important role in the African funeral service, a custom that migrated to New Orleans. Brass bands played somber music as mourners made their way to the cemetery to commit the deceased to the hereafter and following the burial, picked up the tempo in celebration of the individual's life on earth and freedom in death.

Contrary to Western musical practices, in Africa everyone is a participant. While there are skilled professional musicians who supply music for special occasions in African life, there is always a sense of community participation. As a result of this attitude, the African is less apt to be inhibited or concerned about the ability to contribute to a performance. Music making in Africa is a form of socialization and therefore goes far beyond the Western concept of performance, where strong boundaries are established between audience and performers. This same aesthetic is found in the work of the earliest jazz musicians who broke from Western tradition and performance practices that dictated how music should be played. Not encumbered by Western practices, jazz musicians appear to be uninhibited performers more concerned with engaging their audience. This is not to say that African music lacks tradition or organization, for in many ways the music that accompanies certain rituals and ceremonies is somewhat standardized and passed down from generation to generation through the practice of oral and aural tradition. It is an ensemble art much like early New Orleans style jazz where each instrument had a specific, well-defined role. But within the context of this role, whether in African music or jazz, there is often room for, and an expectation of, some personal interpretation.

Rhythm in African Music

Music in Africa is closely linked to dance and commonly associated with numerous ceremonies and rituals both secular and sacred in nature. Jazz existed during its first several decades as an accompaniment to dance. Rhythm and dance are in fact inseparable. Of the three primary ingredients in all music, rhythm is clearly most predominant and important to the music of Western Africa, the source of much U.S. slave trade. Rhythmic grouping and natural accents define certain meters, although meter and bar lines are of no great relevance to African music. Complex polyrhythms and polymeters are implied through various combinations of simultaneously occurring rhythm patterns. All three rhythms can be played simultaneously to the same fundamental pulse or beat. (See Example 4.1.)

EXAMPLE 4.1

You don't have to read music to understand these rhythmic examples. The graphic representation of these music rhythms are expressed below. Each line corresponds to the music notation above.

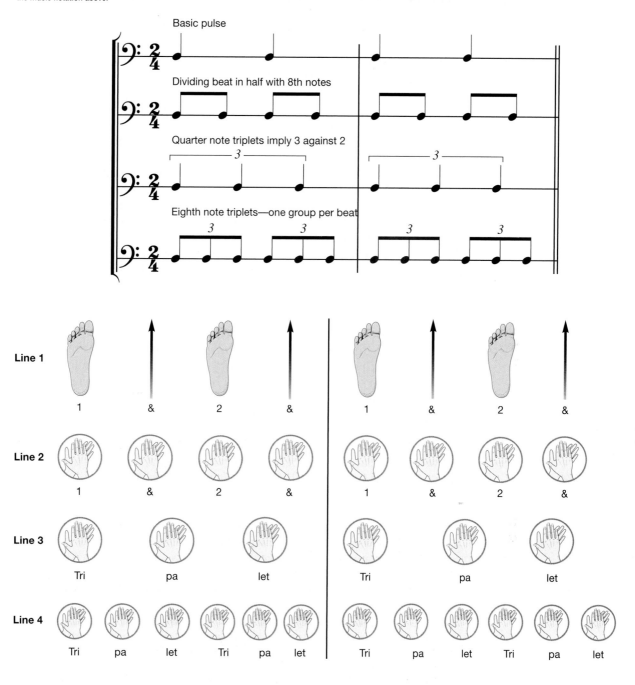

You can find an audio version of this polyrhythm on the CD-ROM in the corresponding chapter.

Listen to Track 1 on the companion CD anthology to hear a good example of polyrhythmic African drumming and the preponderance of rhythm in this music. The interaction of these opposing rhythms frequently leads to intricate forms of rhythmic tension. One of these rhythmic layers usually outlines a ground or regular rhythm pattern that serves as the basic foundation upon which other, more intricate and sometimes improvised rhythms are layered. Can you distinguish the different rhythmic layers?

A common **ground pattern** (fundamental, reoccurring rhythm pattern) in much African music is shown in Example 4.2, labeled Habanera. This same rhythm serves as the basis for many ragtime and early jazz instrumental pieces (see Chapter 16). The **habanera** is also the basis for Caribbean rhythms and numerous Latin dance styles including the **meringue** and **conga**. The habanera is thought to be the forefather of the popular 1920s dance known as the Charleston. Review the illustrations shown in Example 4.2 to compare these forms. The "Reindeer Rag" is attributed to composer Joseph Lamb and closely resembles a Latin meringue rhythm, as does the excerpt from James Scott's "Hilarity Rag." An excerpt from "King Porter Stomp," a 1929 composition in a ragtime influenced style by early jazz composer/pianist Jelly Roll Morton, has been re-notated from the original 4/4 meter to 2/4 to make the rhythmic comparison to the meringue more obvious. Notice that all of these brief examples show the natural accent and anticipation created by the tied notes ♪♪ that appear in the same position in each excerpt. You don't need to read music to see the resemblance between each of these examples.

Each of the rhythms in Example 4.2 offers a feeling of forward motion created by the anticipation of beat 2 created by the tied note (the handclap in the middle of the bar). Anticipations of a major beat create a natural accent that helps to propel the music forward. Try tapping your foot in a regular tempo while you clap your hands just before your foot comes down. If you clap consecutively in this manner, then syncopation occurs. The constant feeling of forward motion created by rhythmic anticipations and syncopations played by one group, which collide with notes placed on the beat by other ensemble players, creates tension. It is this tension that provides the buoyant, swinging, bouncy feeling associated with jazz usually referred to as "swing" and caused by syncopation.

Unlike much of the European derived music found in early Americana (like the march, cakewalk, and polka), which have well-defined strong beats (1 and 3) and weak beats (2 and 4), African music tends to be more variable with less predictable accents. Listen again to the African excerpt included as track 1 on the accompanying CD anthology. When accents are somehow shifted away from those pulses typically and predictably stressed, **syncopation** is said to occur. A simple form of syncopation could occur by merely moving the typical accent on beats one and three of a march to beats 2 and 4. Much has been said about the predominance of syncopation in jazz, its importance in contributing to the unique nature of jazz rhythms, and the relationship to African music. To quote Gunther Schuller from his book *Early Jazz*:

> By transforming his natural gift for against-the-beat accentuation into syncopation, the Negro was able to accomplish three things: he reconfirmed the supremacy of rhythm in the hierarchy of musical elements; he found a way of retaining the "democratization" of rhythmic impulses [meaning that any portion of a beat could have equal emphasis]; and by combining these two features with his need to conceive all rhythms as rhythmicized melodies, he maintained a basic, internally self-propelling momentum in his music.[2]

EXAMPLE 4.2

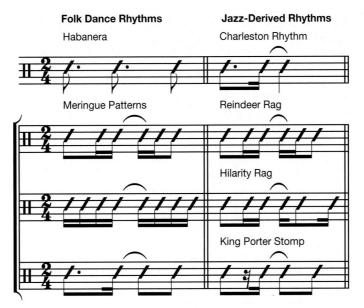

Folk Dance Rhythms   **Jazz-Derived Rhythms**

Habanera   Charleston Rhythm

Meringue Patterns   Reindeer Rag

Hilarity Rag

King Porter Stomp

The habanera rhythm is simplified below. Try to coordinate your hands and feet in a steady tempo. The hand clap emphasizes the habanera rhythm while the feet establish a basic tempo, beating out each eighth note in the measure.

Habanera

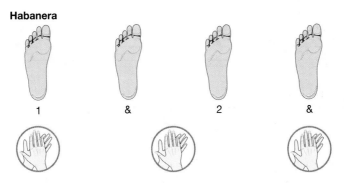

The example that follows is a simplified version of the "Charleston" rhythm derived from the habanera.

Charleston

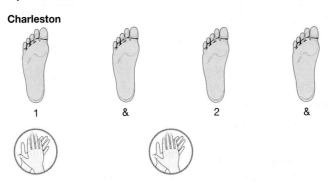

Schuller is also defining to some degree what **swing** is. It is this form of propulsion or forward momentum that we feel when something "swings." (See Chapter 2.)

Syncopation was no doubt what James Reese Europe, an early Black military and society bandleader, was referring to in 1919 when he talked about his band members "accenting notes which originally would be without accent."[3] It was the results of these early attempts at rhythmic interpretation that led to the beginnings of jazz, swing, and those subtle ingredients that cannot be notated accurately using the Western system of notation. Just like African music, jazz rhythms cannot be precisely notated. This fact no doubt frustrated the French musicians who tried without success to duplicate the sound of Europe's 1919 military band by merely reading the music he gave them. Hence we can conclude that neither jazz nor African music can be played authentically by reading notes on the page. Traditional music notation must be translated by musicians familiar with the jazz style in order for the music to sound like jazz.

Louis Armstrong, among other early jazz innovators, commonly employed similar polyrhythms and syncopations by using rhythmic figures that implied 3/4 meter against 4/4 as shown in the following excerpt from Louis Armstrong's solo on "Hotter Than That" (included in the *Smithsonian Collection of Classic Jazz*, SCCJ). Rhythmic groups of three are shown bracketed in Example 4.3.

EXAMPLE 4.3

For those readers that do not read music, the graphic representation will help to clarify the rhythms expressed in the music example. The graphic example represents only the first two measures of this Armstrong excerpt.

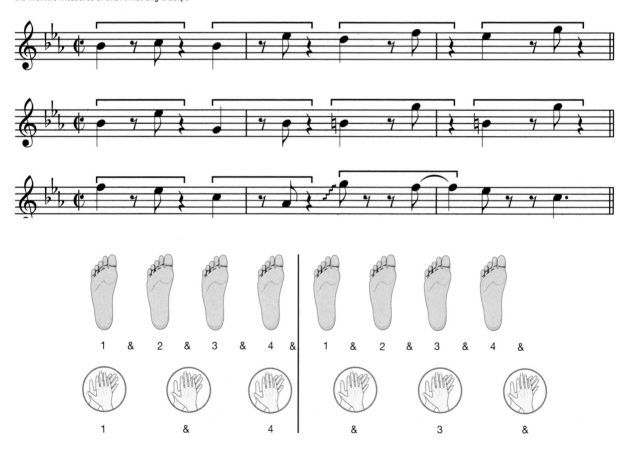

If necessary, review the concepts presented on the CD-ROM in the Elements of Music section that discusses rhythm and meter. Example 4.3 can be heard on the CD-ROM in the corresponding section.

Melody in African Music

Melody occupies a more secondary role in the music of Western Africa. African melodies are quite simple in comparison to jazz or most styles of Western music and in fact often consist of only a few pitches. This collection of pitches can be called a **motive.** Motives are often repeated many times throughout the course of an African song. These melodies are further described as **monophonic,** meaning a single melodic line without accompanying harmony.

Traditional African music does not always utilize the Western 12-tone system or key signatures but is often based on a simple five-note pentatonic scale that communicates a sense of key center through regular repetition. Some historians believe that when African singing practices collided with Western hymns and other forms of music found in the United States, these **pentatonic scales** served to inspire the blues scale and blues tonality that is so much a part of the jazz tradition. One could say that the blues scale may have evolved as a result of the Africans' attempt to reconcile the pentatonic scale with the Western eight-note scale and harmony they found in the United States.

The similarity between blues and pentatonic scales is illustrated by an audio example found on the CD-ROM in the corresponding chapter.

African Music as a Means of Communication

Some African groups have been known to use music as a means of communication. They use drums, voices, and instruments to actually express words and ideas through music. A parallel can be seen in jazz from the standpoint that instrumentalists attempt to develop a very personalized style on their instruments that is often vocally inspired. In the eyes of many jazz performers, the best-improvised solos tell a story and communicate this story to the listener. This jazz performance practice stems from the African tradition of communicating through music.

Improvisation in African Music

There is actually not that much improvisation in African music as the performers do not deviate radically from the primary prescribed melodic or rhythmic material. The early jazz performers actually improvised very little and was bound fairly closely by their ensemble role; but as the music matured, more emphasis was placed on creativity, spontaneity, and real improvisation that departed radically from the basic theme or preconceived musical ideas.

There is much repetition, both melodically and rhythmically, in African music. This repetition can also be found in many jazz styles that feature recurring melodic fragments, bass patterns, chord progressions, and other musical devices. Variation, sometimes achieved through the process of improvisation, is common to African music performance practice even though these variations may be subtle. By comparison, early jazz instrumentalists also varied their statement of a melody slightly from performance to performance, but the essence of the original tune was kept intact.

Form in African Music

A significant feature of much African music that influenced jazz is the **call-response** form. This scheme involves a solo voice or small group of singers and an opposing choir of voices and/or instrumentalists. The soloist or small group makes a musical statement that evokes a musical response by the larger group. The same question-answer or call-response pattern can be found in many compositions throughout the history of jazz. Numerous arrangements were crafted for the big bands of the swing era based on this simple scheme. The classic vocal blues style also resembles this same African model as will be illustrated later in this chapter. The idea of soloists exchanging or trading improvised phrases, a concept also discussed in Chapter 3, stems from the call-response format.

This first track on the companion audio anthology does much to support the descriptions you have read about African music performance practice. Listen to it and describe the various layers added to form the complex polyrhythmic texture. Listen to the call–response format and other characteristics that might be found later in jazz.

EARLY AMERICAN VOCAL MUSIC

Some forms of African music promulgated in the United States by slaves had a subtle impact on the formation of early jazz. For example, the performance of **work songs** and field hollers by slaves had little audience outside the plantations. Aside from the white overseers supervising the slave work force, white listeners were well insulated from this kind of African-based music unless they had an occasion to visit **Congo Square** in New Orleans. The Square was a parklike place where blacks were permitted to congregate and participate in various ceremonies and rituals, both secular and sacred. Such gatherings often featured music and dance, improvisational in nature. While it is true that the improvisatory nature of some of the work songs, designed to rhythmically mimic a work task and take one's mind off the drudgery of indentured slavery, may have eventually exerted some influence on American music, the influences on early jazz and blues are less than obvious and not well documented through recordings.

Slaves had the most contact with whites and European-derived music through their participation in religious worship services often sponsored, or at least encouraged, by their owners. Africans, who typically worshipped many gods, were comfortable with religious ceremony and ritual, so they adapted easily to the Christian beliefs taught to them by their white masters. It was in this context that African musical influences were gradually exerted on traditional Christian hymns. These transformed, African influenced religious songs eventually became know as **spirituals, gospels,** and **jubilees.** Spirituals were derived from white folk hymns and camp-meeting songs. They were often based on Bible scripture or sacred themes that illiterate slaves and whites attending the worship services could not read. To involve the congregation, the preacher intoned, or lined out, one phrase of text at a time. The parishioners responded by singing the line back using some familiar folk or religious hymn tune of the day as a basis. Once again, the call-response format already familiar to Africans was put to use in the lining-out of religious text using song. Since the tunes were slow, the congregation often embellished the melodies, singing them as they had remembered them or been taught by their elders, and in their own personal styles often resulting in harmony. The

African Americans laboring in the cotton fields. Photograph ca. 1890.

themes were based on ridding themselves of the devil and returning to the Promised Land. Spirituals typically feature long, sustained melodies and communicate sadness. "Nobody Knows the Trouble I've Seen" and "Swing Low Sweet Chariot" are well-known examples of the spiritual, which is often associated with and influenced by the blues. The gospel and jubilee, on the other hand, tend to be quicker in tempo, more rhythmic, and generally more high-spirited, featuring hand clapping and other forms of rhythmic accompaniment. The gospel, which developed some years later as an offshoot of the spiritual, was intended to be sung in harmony and accompanied by instruments. Blacks and whites practiced spiritual and gospel styles; therefore both styles were influenced by African and European musical traditions. In both cases, the bending of pitches and other similar blues inflections were evident. Gospels might feature lyrics that are more secular in nature, or project a message that could be interpreted with religious or secular overtones. The jubilee was a high-spirited song of praise and celebration. Most of us have heard "When the Saints Go Marching In," which is a fine example of what began as a jubilee before being transformed into a widely performed New Orleans style Dixieland instrumental piece. The Fisk Jubilee Singers, a product of Fisk University in the late 1800s, traveled widely performing in these various vocal styles. Mark Twain wrote to a friend in 1897 after hearing a performance by this group saying: "I think that in the Jubilees and their songs, America has produced the perfect flower of the ages; and I wish it were a foreign product so she would worship it and lavish money on it and go properly crazy over it."[4] At this point, Americans still looked to Europe for inspiration, guidance, and approval when it came to the arts and Twain seems to lament the fact that Americans could not yet appreciate the beauty and originality in their own, original product.

The Fisk Jubilee Singers. Photographed in 1880.

GETTING THE BLUES

Considering all the early black vocal styles, it is safe to say that the **blues** has had the most far-reaching impact. No one seems to know precisely how the characteristics of the blues came about, but it seems logical to assume that the blues was born as a consequence of the Africanization of Western music. The blues tonality may be the result of the African-Americans' efforts to reconcile their own pentatonic melodies with Western harmonic and melodic practices.

To learn more about the blues and hear why the pentatonic scale theory has some credence, use the CD-ROM and find the sections discussing melody and harmony found in Chapter 2—The Elements of Jazz.

The blues is perhaps as misunderstood a term as "jazz" or "swing." It can imply a mood or emotional state, a chord progression, or a tonality achieved by embellishing a melodic line. To make matters worse, blues became so popular in the early years of the twentieth century that the word was frequently used in song titles even though the song bore absolutely no classic blues characteristics. The poetry of a blues lyric, in the case of a vocal blues, often tells the story of lost love, persecution, or any of life's other tribulations. The blues originated as a folk music with solo singers/song writers who often improvised the melody and lyrics, accompanying themselves on a guitar or piano. Because these early blues songs were improvised by solo performers, there was a high degree of spontaneity and there was no consistency in terms of length, chord progression, or meter. The rhythm, accent, and meter of the lyrics dictated how many beats to a measure and how many measures long the chorus would be. Through the use of vocal inflections such as bends, shakes, scoops, shouts, and varying vibrato speed, these early blues singers delivered emotionally charged performances. So it was the high level of raw emotion projected rather than the sophistication of the music that was of most significance. The accompaniment, rather than consisting of a series of chords, might be little more than a single drone note on the guitar or a simple reoccurring blues melody, perhaps derived from a pentatonic or blues scale.

There are many styles of blues—classic, country, urban, and so on. There is not universal agreement on the character of each of these blues styles and the lines that differentiate one from the other can be quite blurred. By the early 1920s, blues singers like Mamie Smith, Ma Rainey ("Mother of the Blues"), Bessie Smith, and Robert Johnson began to exert an influence on early jazz instrumentalists. This collaboration between singers and instrumentalists led to the gradual standardization of the blues form that continues to be recognized today.

For additional information on the blues and harmony, refer to these discussions on the CD-ROM in Chapter 2—The Elements of Jazz. If you haven't already done so, look at the *Video Blues* movie also on the CD-ROM and found in Chapter 3—Listening to Jazz.

The classic blues form consists of 12 measures and essentially three primary chords—the I, IV, and V chords. As jazz matured, this simple three-chord progression became only the skeletal outline for increasingly complex blues progressions through the addition of many more chords. Blues can be in a minor or major key, and the general tonality or lyric does not have to communicate melancholy. In fact, many blues pieces from the swing and bebop periods of jazz are actually quite uplifting. Some blues progressions have been extended to 16 measures while others have been shortened to only 8. A bridge or middle section, usually 8 measures in length, can be added to extend the more typical 12-bar blues even further. In this case, the entire form would resemble the A-B-A song form format for a total of 32 measures (each A is 12 measures in length plus an 8-bar bridge).

The classic 12-bar blues is usually presented as three four-measure phrases. The first line of text is usually repeated, followed by a third that acts as a contrast and summary to the first line. Each verse follows this same antecedent–consequent pattern. Since the lyric typically occupies only about two measures, or half the length of each four-measure phrase, an instrumentalist usually improvises during the second half of each phrase. The two-measure improvisation serves as a "response" to the lyric, which represents the "call" in this African derived format. Example 4.4 shows a template for this classic 12-bar blues form.

EXAMPLE 4.4
Classic 12-Bar Blues Form

Each block represents one measure.

Lyric (Call) Improvisation (Response)

Lyric (Call) Improvisation (Response)

Lyric (Call) Improvisation (Response)

U.S. postage stamp featuring Robert Johnson.

Robert Johnson (1911–1938) is one of the foremost examples of this rich tradition, though his recordings were issued years after the blues emerged around the turn of the century. Only 11, 78-rpm "race" records were released during his lifetime, but his work has become recognized worldwide, influential in the commercialization of rock and roll and R & B styles years later. He lived in relative obscurity most of his life, but was canonized as an innovator in 1994 when the U.S. Postal service issued a commemorative stamp with his portrait.

Johnson, known in some circles as "King of the Delta Blues," was as much a blues poet as he was a solo singer/songwriter. He wrote and sang about his own experiences as a musician wandering the Mississippi Delta region in hopes of establishing a reputation that would help him to escape a life of sharecropping and migrant itinerate fieldwork. In the early stages of his career, he performed largely at jook joints and roadhouses that catered to loggers, migrant workers, and crews building roads for the WPA (Works Progress Administration federal relief program) project. He became attracted to alcohol, gambling, and women, and it was his obsession with finding the right woman that lead to his untimely death, supposedly at the hand of a jealous man who laced his whiskey with poison.

While Johnson became well known in the Delta region, especially Mississippi and Arkansas, it wasn't until the release of his first recordings that his reputation spread, enabling him to tour outside the region with performances in Chicago, New York, Detroit, St. Louis, and Canada. His first hit record for the Vocalion Records, "Terraplane Blues," served to advance his career and no doubt lead to John Hammond's quest to book him as an opening act for his 1938 "From Spirituals to Swing" extravaganza at Carnegie Hall. Hammond, a jazz impresario and champion of Black performers, was unaware of Johnson's untimely death.

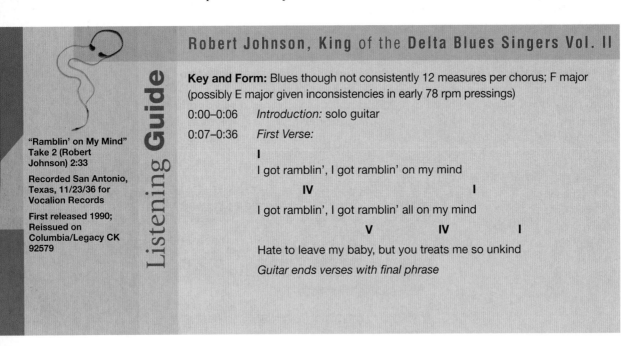

Robert Johnson, King of the Delta Blues Singers Vol. II

Listening Guide

"Ramblin' on My Mind" Take 2 (Robert Johnson) 2:33

Recorded San Antonio, Texas, 11/23/36 for Vocalion Records

First released 1990; Reissued on Columbia/Legacy CK 92579

Key and Form: Blues though not consistently 12 measures per chorus; F major (possibly E major given inconsistencies in early 78 rpm pressings)

0:00–0:06   *Introduction:* solo guitar

0:07–0:36   *First Verse:*

I

I got ramblin', I got ramblin' on my mind

IV   I

I got ramblin', I got ramblin' all on my mind

V   IV   I

Hate to leave my baby, but you treats me so unkind

Guitar ends verses with final phrase

0:37–1:103   *Second Verse:*

I

And now babe, I will never forgive you anymore

          IV   **I**

Little girl, little girl, I will never forgive you anymore

                V   **IV**   **I**

You know you did not want me, baby, why did you tell me so?

Guitar ends verses with final phrase

1:04–1:28   *Third Verse:*

I

And I'm runnin' down to the station, catch that first mail train I see
(spoken softly: I hear her comin' now)

          IV   **I**

An' I'm runnin' down to the station, catch that old first mail train I see

               V   **IV**

I've got the blues 'bout Miss So-and-So, and the child got the blues

        I

about me

Guitar ends verses with final phrase

1:29–1:55   *Fourth Verse:*

I

An' they's de'ilment*, she got devilment* all on her mind

          IV   **I**

She's got devilment, little girl, you got devilment all on your mind

           V   **IV**   **I**

Now I got to leave this mornin', with my arm' fold' up and cryin'

Guitar ends verses with final phrase

1:56 to end   *Fifth Verse:*

I

I believe, I believe my time ain't long

IV   **I**

I believe, I believe that my time ain't long

      V   **IV**   **I**

But I'm leavin' this mornin', I believe I will go back home

Guitar ends with final phrase

*Devilment means devilish, cruel, or wicked behavior.

Ramblin' On My Mind, Words and Music by Robert Johnson. Copyright ©(1978) 1990, 1991 Lehsem II, LLC/Claud L. Johnson. Administered by Music & Media International, Inc. International Copyright Secured. All Rights Reserved.

Bessie Smith (1894–1937), American early jazz singer known as the "Empress of the Blues."

The recording included in the companion audio anthology demonstrates this great rustic blues tradition. Johnson's original style marries his vocal poetry with a free-style guitar accompaniment that ranges from rhythmic chords in a boogie-woogie shuffle-like feel, to single-line, soloistic gestures that respond to his lyrics. By modern standards, his performance might be considered crude or rough around the edges; but there is an austere beauty, rhythmic savvy, and overall complexity to his emotionally charged performance that is unmistakable. Notice how he does not strictly adhere to balanced phrases, each with four measures of four beats. What comes naturally seems to be of greater importance, though one suddenly gets the sense that a beat was skipped here or there, or a measure added to the expected fixed, modern 12-bar blues form. Johnson does adhere to the typical three-chord sequence (I-V-IV) and each chord has been noted above the lyric. Each line is completed by solo guitar.

Known as the "Empress of the Blues," Bessie Smith is another classic blues singer from the period. In contrast to Johnson, she frequently shared the stage and recordings with jazz players who accompanied her. Listen to Bessie Smith's performance of "Lost Your Head Blues" included on the SCCJ while following the lyrics provided below. Roman numerals and chord symbols have also been provided to help you follow the chord progression. Bessie begins singing after a brief four-measure introduction improvised by cornetist Joe Smith. This performance follows the classic blues format outlined above and in this case, Joe Smith assumes the role of brilliantly improvising in a call and response format following each lyric.

Listening Guide

Bessie Smith

"Lost Your Head Blues"

Recorded 5/4/26.

Bessie Smith: *vocal*

Joe Smith: *cornet*

Fletcher Henderson: *piano*

(Roman numeral chord symbols are indicated above the lyrics of each verse.)

Four Measure Instrumental Introduction

I Chord 4 bars

Verse 1: I was with you baby when you did not have a dime—*J. Smith improvises 2 bars*

IV Chord 2 bars   **I Chord 2 bars**

I was with you baby when you did not have a dime—*J. Smith improvises*

V7 Chord 2 bars

Now since you got plenty money you have throw'd your good gal down—*Joe Smith improvises on I chord for 1 bar and V7 chord for 1 bar to end form*

I Chord 4 bars

Verse 2: One things for always you ain't worth my while—*J. Smith improvises 2 bars*

IV Chord 2 bars   **I Chord 2 bars**

One things for always you ain't worth my while—*J. Smith improvises*

V7 Chord 2 bars	I Chord 1 bar V7 / Chord 1 bar

When you get a good gal you'd better treat her nice—*J. Smith improvises*

I Chord 4 bars

Verse 3: When you were lonesome I've tried to treat you kind—*Smith improvises 2 bars*

IV Chord 2 bars	I Chord 2 bars

When you were lonesome I've tried to treat you kind—*J. Smith improvises*

V7 Chord 2 bars	I Chord 1 bar V7 / Chord 1 bar

But since you've got money it done change your mind—*J. Smith improvises*

I Chord 4 bars

Verse 4: I'm gonna leave baby ain't gonna say goodbye—*J. Smith improvises 2 bars*

IV Chord 2 bars	I Chord 2 bars

I'm gonna leave baby ain't gonna say goodbye—*J. Smith improvises*

V7 Chord 2 bars	I Chord 1 bar V7 / Chord 1 bar

But I'll write you and tell you the reason why—*J. Smith improvises*

I Chord 4 bars

Verse 5: Days are lonesome nights are so long long—*J. Smith improvises 2 bars*

IV Chord 2 bars	I Chord 2 bars

Days are lonesome nights are so long long—*J. Smith improvises*

V7 Chord 2 bars	I Chord 1 bar V7 / Chord 1 bar

I'm a good ole gal but I just been treated wrong—*J. Smith improvises*

W. C. HANDY—"FATHER OF THE BLUES"

William Christopher Handy (1873–1958), a bandsman, composer, and cornet player, is remembered as the "father of the blues" following the publication of his autobiography by the same name published in 1941. While there is some debate about this prestigious title, since others claim to publishing or performing in this style before Handy's "Memphis Blues" in 1912, history does show that it was W. C. Handy that brought the blues to widespread popularity. Handy was the son of a Methodist minister who had been freed from slavery. He readily admitted that he patterned his versions of the blues after black folk songs with their roots in the South, though he also heard blues being sung on the streets of St. Louis well before his first publications. He heard these songs performed during his travels as a minstrel musician. **Minstrel shows** were early touring variety shows popular during the mid-1800s. Traveling with small bands, actors, comedians, jugglers, and other entertainers, the

Composer W. C. Handy (1873–1958).

shows offered humor, musical numbers, dancing, and often a parody play based on an "Uncle Tom's Cabin"–like theme. Minstrel shows are significant to a discussion of jazz for they provided a means of employment for many early jazz musicians. Handy's travels with such shows took him all over the United States and as far away as Havana, Cuba, where he initially heard the Afro-Latin rhythms that would later have a major impact on his compositions.

Handy's first published composition was "Memphis Blues," originally written as a campaign song for a Memphis politician and titled "A Southern Rag." He and a partner formed a publishing company, one of the first black companies to enter this business. While "Memphis Blues" enjoyed steady sales and has been recorded by numerous artists, it was Handy's "St. Louis Blues," published in 1914, that earned him the title "Father of the Blues." It was first recorded in 1915 and subsequently became the most widely recorded song in America. To quote David A. Jasen and Gene Jones who authored *Spreadin' Rhythm Around: Black Popular Songwriters, 1880–1930*, "By 1930 ["St. Louis Blues"] was the most famous blues in the world. By 1930 it was the best-selling song in any medium—sheet music, recordings, and piano rolls."[5] Not only were its lyrics innovative, but "its harmonies literally put new notes into the pop music scale, and its structure showed writers a new way to build popular songs."[6] Handy actually used the blues scale in the body of this composition, which had never been done before in a published work. The success of this Handy original helped to pave the way for a blues sensation that swept the country in the early 1920s. Many new labels, or subsidiary labels of larger companies, were formed for the specific purpose of recording blues singers such as Mamie Smith, Ma Rainey (known as the "Mother of the Blues"), Alberta Hunter, Blind Lemon Jefferson, Ethel Waters, Robert Johnson, and, of course, Bessie Smith. The Black Swan label, founded by Handy's publishing partner, was just such a label and targeted its marketing to the growing black population congregating around major cities such as New York, Chicago, and Detroit. Of great surprise to these record companies was the fact that much of their sales were attributed to white buyers. The label reported a $100,000 profit in its first year. These so-called "race records," intended for the African-American market, were immensely successful especially for blues artists such as Mamie Smith who sold millions for the Okeh label. White owned record labels took advantage of this successful trend in the '20s and started secondary labels reserved for black artists. They dropped the term "race records" in the 1930s in favor of referring to them as the "sepia series."

In 1929 Handy's "St. Louis Blues" became the subject of a short film starring Bessie Smith, her only appearance on film. It was very likely her poignant recording of Handy's popular blues, also featuring Louis Armstrong, that led to her being selected for this role. This film is barely 15 minutes long but features an all black cast including a large choir and stride pianist/composer James P. Johnson. Racial attitudes at this time prohibited mixing of blacks and whites on film though it became increasingly common in the late 1920s to hear mixed companies of actors and/or musicians on radio, a faceless medium.

Every aspect of Handy's hit song "St. Louis Blues" was innovative from the lyrics, which tell a frank tale of love lost, to the harmony, melody, and formal aspects of his composition. The formal structure is perhaps the most clearly innovative aspect of Handy's presentation of the blues. Most blues of the day were only 12 measures in length with a formal scheme of simply "A" that was repeated numerous times. The formal scheme found in "St. Louis Blues," however, follows an AABA song form pattern, where each A represents a typical 12-bar blues chord progression. The lyrics in these blues sections follow the same predictable pattern found in many blues tunes including "Lost Your Head Blues," previously discussed. The first two measures of each four-bar phrase in the A section are dedicated to lyrics, followed by impressive two-measure improvisations by Louis Armstrong. This A section architecture is typical in that it represents the classic question–answer or call and response format, in this case contrasting vocalist and improvising cornet soloist. The B section in this case is 16 measures in length, deviating from the blues norm. The chord progression in the final A section following B returns to the blues form, however, it is slightly different than the chord progression found in the initial "A" sections that begin the chorus. The "B" section departs from this standard blues sequence and features a tango influenced rhythm, though barely discernable in this version. The form is sometimes changed, however, and performers have moved sections around putting the B section before the A. For example, Handy's 1922 recording with his own band shows the tango B section first. Handy's earlier travels to Cuba and the 1914 tango dance craze in the United States were no doubt responsible for this obvious influence. The formal outline, harmonic scheme, and lyrics that follow will help guide you through the performance of this historic recording included as track 2 on disc 1 of the accompanying CD anthology.

W. C. Handy

Listening Guide

Key and Form: D Major; AA¹ (12 bars blues repeated); BB¹ (8 bars repeated in parallel minor key of D min.); A¹¹ (12-bar blues back in original key of D major)

0:00–0:04   Introduction

0:04—First "A" Section—12-Bar Blues

D(I)   G7(IV7)   A7(V7) D(I)   D7(I7)

I hate ta see the eve'nin sun go down—*Armstrong improvises second 2 measures*

G7(IV7)   B♭7(♭VI7) A7(V7) D(I)   D7(I7)

I hate ta see the eve'nin sun go down—*Armstrong improvises second 2 measures*

A7(V7)   Emi(ii)   A7(V7) D7   F#° G7 B♭7 D/A G7 B♭7 A7

It make me think I'm on my last go'round—*Armstrong improvises second 2 measures*

0:49—Second "A"—12-Bar Blues

D(I)   G7(IV7) A7(V7)   D(I)   D7(I7)

Feelin' tomorrow like I feel today—*Armstrong improvises second 2 bars*

G7(IV7)   B♭7(♭VI7) A7(V7) D(I)   D7(I7)

Feelin' tomorrow like I feel today—*Armstrong improvises second 2 bars*

"St. Louis Blues" by W. C. Handy 3:09

Bessie Smith: *vocal*

Louis Armstrong: *cornet*

Fred Longshaw: *harmonium*

Recorded in New York, January 14, 1925

Columbia 14064-D

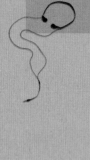
W. C. Handy *concluded*

A7   Emi(ii)   A7(V7)   D7 F#° G7 B♭7 D/A G7 B♭7 A7

I'll pack my grips [bags], n' make my get-a-way—*Armstrong improvises second 2 bars*

1:33—"B" Section (16)—(Often played as a tango but not in this version)

Dmi(I)   A7(V7)

St. Louis woman, with her diamond rings—*Armstrong improvises second 2 bars*

A7(V7)   Dmi(I)

Pulls dat man around by her apron strings—*Armstrong improvises second 2 bars*

Dmi(I)   A7(V7)

Wasn't for powder an' the store-bought hair—*Armstrong improvises second 2 bars*

A7(V7)   Dmi(I)   E7(II7) A7(V7)

The man I love wouldn't go nowhere, no __ where ____

I got dem (Smith begins last verse as an anticipation of the next full chorus, Armstrong begins accompaniment)

2:29—Return to "A" section—12-Bar Blues

D(I) A7   D   A7   D   A7 D A7 D   D7(I7)

St. Louis Blues and as blue as I can be (Armstrong accompanies in harmony)—*Armstrong improvises second 2-bars*

G7(IV7)   A7(V7)D7(I7)

He's got a heart like a rock cast in the sea—*Armstrong improvises second 2 bars*

G7(V7)   B♭7(♭VI7) A7(V7)   D   D7/F#bass G7   A♭dim D

Or else he wouldn't have gone so far from me.

RAGTIME

The blues and **ragtime** styles actually emerged concurrently in the United States, though the blues continues to exert significant influence on jazz while ragtime does not. Most historians agree that ragtime enjoyed the limelight as a very influential style from about 1895–1915, though it is not considered jazz. It is considered to be the first style of American music to enjoy widespread popularity and demonstrate that a native form of American music, highly influenced by black performers and composers, could actually be the basis of commercial success. This music not only impressed many Americans who bought sheet music versions, piano rolls and pianos, but it also showed significant influence on classical composers of the day (covered in Chapter 17 on the Online Learning Center). In fact, one could say that this early pre-jazz style found its greatest champions in those classical musicians of the day who were enamored with its fresh and unique rhythmic qualities.

Both black and white musicians championed this piano style. Black pianist/composer Tom Turpin gained the first copyright for a rag in 1883 while white pianist/composer William Krell was the first to publish a ragtime composition in 1897 entitled the "Mississippi Rag." It was Scott Joplin, James Scott, and Joseph Lamb, however, who were most responsible for advancing the style.

Once again, the term "rag" was frequently misused and often interchanged with the terms "blues," "two-step," and "cakewalk." The term "rag" supposedly stemmed from a black folk dance style of the day referred to as clog dancing. The word ragtime is thought to be a composite of two words—rag, meaning syncopated, and time, meaning rhythm. Therefore ragtime implies a style of playing where rhythms are syncopated. The **cakewalk** was an upbeat, syncopated dance style popular prior to the beginning of the twentieth century. Cakewalks continued to provide rousing finales to minstrel shows and often involved the entire cast dancing to rag-like music. Ragging was also considered a way of playing or interpreting music through the use of spontaneous syncopation.

What clearly differentiates a rag from a blues is the formal structure. Ragtime compositions have little resemblance to African styles as the formal scheme and harmonic style for rags are clearly derived from European models. The AABBACCDD **rondo form** found in most rags is closely related to the same form found in marches, reels, coon songs, polkas, and cakewalks of the day. Each section is usually eight measures in length and there is typically a modulation (key change) away from the primary key at the "C" theme much like the key change found in marches at the trio. The "March King" and great American bandmaster John Phillip Sousa admired this style and often featured a "rag" or a "march and two-step" in his concert band performances.

Song sheet cover of Scott Joplin's "The Entertainer," 1902.

Racism in the United States was born out of slavery, Jim Crow laws, minstralsy, and other forms of bigotry and stereotyping. Coon songs were folk songs with lyrics that were generally degrading of blacks and serve to exemplify racist attitudes of the time. In a sense, they were racist musical jokes, which bore titles such as "Every Race Has a Flag But the Coon" and "You're Just a Little Nigger, But You're Mine All Mine." White male and or female singers in black face often sang these songs, perhaps as minstrel show entertainers. The same syncopated rhythms found in these early folk songs were the basis for similar syncopations and rhythmic vitality found in rags. Authors Jasen and Jones described the impact of this late 1800s coon song on ragtime as follows:

> Their constant use of syncopation attuned the public ear for the ragtime that would appear around the turn of the century. And their slangy, "low-class" lyrics took a big step away from politer European operatic song models. Their commercial success introduced "black" subject matter—and the work of many black songwriters—into middleclass white parlors on sheet music and cylinder records. In this time of families entertaining themselves at home around the piano, part of the fun was the naughtiness of playing at being black. Other ethnic groups took their lumps in songs but blacks got the worst of it.[7]

Rags also bore a remarkable similarity to tunes like "Turkey in the Straw" (subtitled "Ragtime Fantasie") and "Camptown Races" composed by popular American folk song writer Stephen Foster.

The classic rag was a strictly composed solo piano style that incorporated little or no improvisation or blues influences, at least by its early primary practitioners.

Rags were composed in either 2/4 or 4/4 meter and featured a very regular, oom-pah-like left hand that supplied the fundamental rhythm while outlining the harmonies. The right hand added syncopated melodies to these regular, left-hand striding rhythms that served to emphasize strong beats (1 and 3). It was a percussive, mechanical style of syncopation though and did not swing, as would be the case some years later. For example, listen to Jelly Roll Morton's recording of "Maple Leaf Rag" included on the SCCJ. Not only has it been rhythmically transformed to swing, but Morton also altered the form and significantly embellished the melody (no doubt through improvisation) compared to the original Joplin recording included in the anthology that accompanies this text. Some classic syncopated rhythms found in rags are shown in Example 4.5.

EXAMPLE 4.5
Rag Rhythms

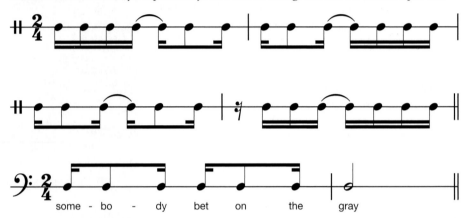

Final rhythm from Stephen Foster's "Camptown Races"

Scott Joplin (1868–1917), American composer; oil over a photograph.

While the popularity of rags quickly spread from coast to coast, the geographic region that is generally considered as the epicenter of ragtime was the Midwest—specifically the cities of St. Louis and Sedalia. It was here that the major ragtime publishers began mass-producing sheet music in this style for distribution nationwide. Many of the next generation's band leader/composers and jazz pianists like Duke Ellington, Fletcher Henderson, Fats Waller, and James P. Johnson were first introduced to the piano through rags. It is believed that Duke Ellington first learned to play the piano by mimicking the key motion on a player piano spinning piano rolls of this kind of music.

Those composers deeply committed to the ragtime style were convinced that this was the new classical music of America, and that they were destined to achieve fame and fortune as its progenitors. Joplin and later James P. Johnson composed large-scale concert works including operettas, symphonies, choral works, and ballets in the ragtime style, though none of these efforts were successful, may never have been published, and in some cases were never performed publicly. Joplin's opera **"Treemonisha"** saw only one self-produced public performance that was not well received. It was finally reproduced in 1976, winning the Pulitzer Prize. Joplin never recovered from the earlier failure, however, and despite their best efforts to transform this style into a serious American national style, these composers began to witness the decline of public interest in ragtime around

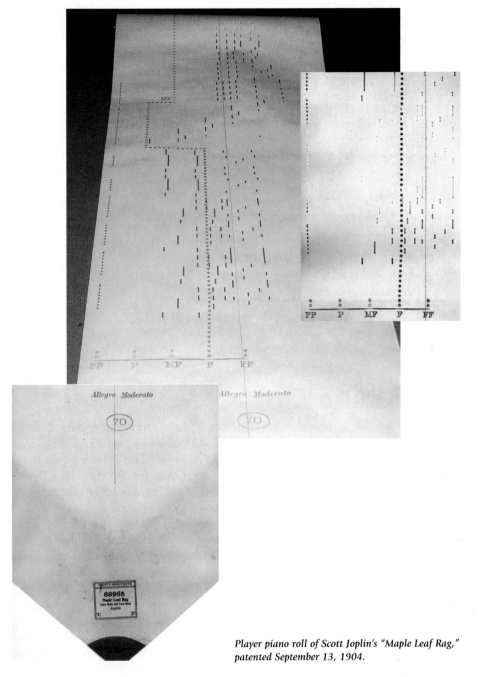

Player piano roll of Scott Joplin's "Maple Leaf Rag,"
patented September 13, 1904.

1914. While the influences of the ragtime piano style can be seen in the instrumental jazz of the era and served as the direct predecessor of the **stride** solo piano style, ragtime had outlived its time and was eclipsed by the onslaught of instrumental jazz featuring the daring, exciting, and virtuosic improvising soloist as the centerpiece.

Track 3 on disc 1 of the companion CD anthology features a modern recording of Scott Joplin's performance of "Maple Leaf Rag." The original piano roll was made by the composer in 1916 and rerecorded using a player piano and modern recording equipment in 1986. This recording, therefore, is not completely accurate in representing Joplin's performance skill. Nonetheless, it does give us a glimpse of his artistry as a composer and pianist. This popular rag follows the classic model containing four uniquely different themes. The formal scheme is represented as AABBACCDD. A key change occurs at the C theme. The time chart that follows should help you follow these themes as they unfold.

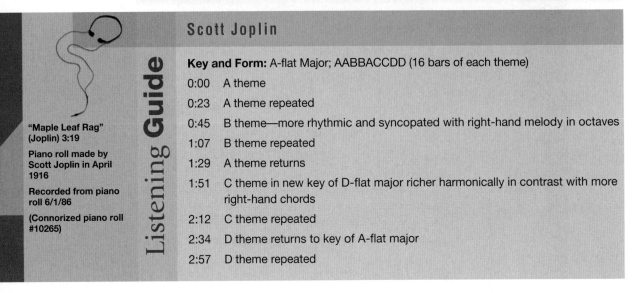

Listening Guide

"Maple Leaf Rag" (Joplin) 3:19

Piano roll made by Scott Joplin in April 1916

Recorded from piano roll 6/1/86

(Connorized piano roll #10265)

Scott Joplin

Key and Form: A-flat Major; AABBACCDD (16 bars of each theme)

0:00	A theme
0:23	A theme repeated
0:45	B theme—more rhythmic and syncopated with right-hand melody in octaves
1:07	B theme repeated
1:29	A theme returns
1:51	C theme in new key of D-flat major richer harmonically in contrast with more right-hand chords
2:12	C theme repeated
2:34	D theme returns to key of A-flat major
2:57	D theme repeated

BRASS BANDS

Brass bands were an American tradition borrowed from Europe and popular in many towns around the United States well before World War I and the beginnings of jazz. Some of the early jazz musicians began their careers as members of such bands, many situated in and around New Orleans. Early jazz instrumentalists Jimmy Noone, Sidney Bechet, Buddy Bolden, Bunk Johnson, and Joe "King" Oliver were all initially members of these brass bands. Brass band repertoire ranged from instrumental arrangements of piano rags, blues, marches, polkas, czardaszes (Slovakian folk dance), schottisches (Bohemian or Czech folk dance), cakewalks, and coon songs. Bands like the Olympia and Excelsior Bands included cornets, clarinets, trombones, drums, tubas, and sometimes stringed instruments like the banjo, guitar, and violin. It is believed that the banjo was actually derived from a similarly constructed African instrument.

These bands performed indoors and outdoors for various functions including weddings, funerals, street parades advertising a touring show, a product or a business, and special occasions sponsored by various fraternal organizations. While James Reese Europe and Will Marion Cook's society bands and orchestras in New York were recorded prior to the first jazz recording in 1917, no authentic recordings exist to document the sounds of these early New Orleans brass bands. There was no recording industry at the time as the new technology for the preservation of sound had not yet been perfected. These bands served as a springboard for much smaller, more mobile ensembles that eventually became an essential ingredient of the New Orleans nightlife.

The influences of African music were widespread by 1915 and, coupled with the blues, ragtime, brass bands, and early vocal styles, set the stage for a profound musical revolution in America serving as an emblem of democracy while affecting music worldwide. All that was necessary now was a mechanism to disseminate the music on a large scale to listeners and future generations of musicians throughout the United States and abroad.

The Eagle Band. This 1916 version shows leader Frankie Dusen, trombone, Louis Nelson, clarinet, and cornetist Buddy Petit.

Jazz in Perspective

The timeline that follows will put the developments of jazz discussed in this chapter into a larger historical context, providing you with a better sense of how landmark musical events may relate to others that match your personal areas of interest.

1905

- The years leading up to the beginnings of instrumental jazz saw a tremendous influx of immigrants from Europe.

- Oklahoma becomes 46th state in 1907.

- Women not welcome to work force though many employed by telephone company.

- Lightbulb still being perfected by General Electric.

1908

- Long-distance radio broadcast still only dreamed about.

- A rebellious group of painters known as "The Eight" focused on works depicting the coming of a new age—the industrialization and urbanization of America. Their touring show also focused on growing population of immigrants.

- President Theodore Roosevelt forms commission to save natural resources.

- Competition begins between early auto manufacturers—Ford, Buick/GM.

- Jack Johnson becomes first black boxer to win world heavyweight championship.

- Gustav Mahler (composer) and Toscanini (conductor) make U.S. debuts.

1909
- Admiral Peary reaches North Pole.
- Psychologists Freud and Jung become well know for their theories and writings.
- W. C. Handy's (Father of the Blues) "Memphis Blues" was composed for Edward "Boss" Crump's election campaign song. This is believed to be the first black authored blues tune to become published.
- Architect Frank Lloyd Wright establishes reputation.
- First opera broadcast live on radio from the MET by Lee de Forest, inventor of the radio vacuum tube.

1910
- NAACP founded.
- George Eastman develops first easy-to-use portable camera.
- Urban league formed to help blacks migrating to northern cities from the south.

1911
- Composer Irving Berlin's "Alexander's Ragtime Band" is huge hit.
- Workers begin to unionize and strike for better wages.

1912
- Minimum wage law established.
- Wilson elected U.S. president on "New Freedom" slogan and human rights ticket.
- Jazz pianist/composer Jelly Roll Morton publishes "The Jelly Roll Blues."

- HMS *Titanic* sinks killing 1,500 passengers.

1913
- Congress passes income tax amendment.
- Buffalo nickel makes its debut.
- Ford opened assembly line to build Model T automobile.
- Woman makes first air flight as a passenger.
- Cecil B. DeMille produces first full-scale Hollywood film at cost of $47,000 for six reels.
- Scott Joplin makes piano roll of "Maple Leaf Rag."

1914–1916
- W. C. Handy published (1914) "St. Louis Blues" that was first recorded in 1915.
- Tango craze hits United States.
- War spreads throughout Europe threatening to involve the United States.
- Industry booms in the United States.
- AT&T sends first wireless message across Atlantic Ocean in 1916.
- First birth control clinic signals new morals and erosion of puritan Victorian ideals.

CHAPTER SUMMARY

The diverse influences of West African music, early American vocal music, blues, brass bands, and ragtime all contributed to the beginnings of jazz. From West Africa the use of polyrhythms was very important in the development of syncopated ragtime melodies and later to the swing feel of early jazz. Work songs, field hollers, spirituals, gospels, and other aspects of American vocal music contributed many of the inflections/effects that identify jazz.

Ragtime is a composed music that flourished in the late 1890s and in the first decade and a half of the twentieth century. It is a very syncopated music written primarily for the piano. Its beginnings can be traced to the Midwest cities of St. Louis and Sedalia, Missouri. While not actually jazz, ragtime bears a resemblance to the later, more improvised stride jazz piano style that featured similar left- and right-hand roles. Many jazz pianists and bandleaders had roots in ragtime including Duke Ellington, Fletcher Henderson, Fats Waller, and James P. Johnson. In comparison to early jazz, ragtime was typically played in a more strict and rigid manner than jazz. The best known of the ragtime composers is Scott Joplin. Other notable composers of the style include James Scott and Joseph Lamb.

Blues is a style especially dependent on vocalists, who developed it about the same time that jazz emerged. The 12-bar blues form has been used not only by blues musicians but also by the jazz community throughout the history of jazz. While numerous early blues examples include a self-accompanied singer (Robert Johnson) performing often in variable/flexible tempos (rubato), other examples feature larger groups using musicians primarily associated with jazz (Bessie Smith). Portions of some of these early blues recordings are virtually indistinguishable from early jazz.

KEY TERMS

Important terms, people, bands, and places.

TERMS
ground pattern
habanera
meringue
conga
syncopation
swing
motive
monophonic
pentatonic scales
call-response
work song
spiritual
gospel

jubilee
blues
minstrel show
ragtime
cakewalk
rondo form
"Treemonisha"
stride

PEOPLE
James Reese Europe
Louis Armstrong
Ma Rainey
Bessie Smith

W. C. Handy
James P. Johnson
Scott Joplin
Buddy Bolden
Will Marion Cook

ENSEMBLES
Olympia Band
Excelsior Band

PLACES
Congo Square

REVIEW QUESTIONS

1. Describe the form of a classic blues lyric.
2. Who is remembered as the "father of the stride style"?
3. The stride style generally refers to what instrument?
4. Who is known as the "father of the blues" and why?
5. Who is considered the "empress of the blues"?
6. Describe the essence of the ragtime style, discussing why it was influential to early jazz.
7. When was ragtime popular?

8. Describe the similarities between early jazz and African music.

9. Explain the difference between spiritual, gospel, and jubilee.

10. What was the significance of minstrelsy to early jazz?

11. Describe the typical blues form.

12. Who composed "St. Louis Blues"?

13. What non-American or European influence can be heard in "St. Louis Blues"?

14. What is the significance of early black vocal styles to instrumental jazz?

15. Aside from Scott Joplin, name two ragtime composers noted for their early work.

16. Clarify the meaning of call and response and discuss the heritage of this term and practice.

SUGGESTED SUPPLEMENTARY LISTENING

The abbreviation (iT) indicates that a particular recording cited in the text, or particularly demonstrative of the artist, is available from the Apple iTunes Web site. Other Web-based music distributors may also prove to be valuable resources. SCCJ indicates *Smithsonian Collection of Classic Jazz.*

James Reese Europe's 369th U.S. Infantry "Hell Fighters Band, **Memphis Archives, MA7020**
W.C. Handy Memphis Blues Band, **Memphis Archives, MA7006**
Fisk Jubilee Singers **"Ezekiel Saw De Wheel" Sony (iT)**
Robert Johnson King of the Delta Blues **Sony/Muze (iT)**

Bessie Smith

Bessie Smith: The Complete Recordings Vols.1–4 **Sony (iT)**
The Bessie Smith Collection **Sony (iT)**
The Essential Bessie Smith **Sony (iT)**
"Lost Your Head Blues" SCCJ

5

Jazz Takes Root

> "[Jazz] expresses our American nature—and as long as our nature is expressed by anything so simple and straightforward we will have no cause to worry."[1]
>
> FRANK PATERSON IN *MUSICAL COURIER*, 1922

While musical seeds were sown by 1917 for a new American music style to take root, germination required a special set of circumstances to fertilize its growth. Perceived as little more than a controversial folk music, "jass," or jazz as it was eventually called, was not taken seriously by most listeners, was neither widely recognized, exceedingly popular, nor considered an accepted musical style. There were a number of factors that served as catalysts around 1920 that helped to change this complexion and stimulate the growth of the new music.

The 1920s mark a rebellious period, especially for America's youth. Young Americans began to question the Victorian values that their European-bred parents tried to instill. These Victorian ideals were guided by basic principles: self-control, order, wholesomeness, and general decency. No longer was the younger generation content to adopt what they considered to be oppressive ideals regarding social behavior and other aspects of lifestyle. Young women shortened their skirts and began to show interest in those same activities that were in earlier years appropriate only for men's participation. Women began to frequent late-night establishments, sometimes unaccompanied by a male escort. Only a few years earlier, this behavior was considered the mark of a "loose woman" and inappropriate for upstanding ladies. The public display of affection, close embraces on the dance floor, public consumption of alcohol, and smoking had been frowned upon. Women and men together were now enjoying the sometimes naughty, late-night entertainment provided by dance halls, cabarets, speakeasies, and other such establishments. This growing sense of independence among women and youth in general would also lead to women's fight for the right to vote. The new morality would be identified with the emergence of a new music, jazz, the ideal symbol for freedom of choice and personal expression.

Immigrants and second-generation freed slaves migrated to major American cities in droves, all seeking jobs available as a consequence of the increasing industrialization of the United States. Rural populations dwindled, while the beginning of urban sprawl triggered a demand for housing, jobs, support services, and entertainment. These hard-working Americans who put in lengthy workweeks in steel mills; automobile, carpet, and clothing factories; and similar laborious jobs looked forward to enjoying their leisure time. Many peasants who had emigrated from Europe where similar ideals and lifestyles prevailed were used to hard work and played hard as well. This new attitude created a growing demand for various new forms of entertainment and leisure-time activities. Professional sports like football, baseball, and boxing helped fill leisure time, giving rise to new American heroes such as baseball legend Babe Ruth. As the number of theaters, speakeasies, cabarets, and other such establishments grew in response to American's zest for the less serious side of life, so did a new entertainment industry. Minorities were welcome in the entertainment business, explaining the great number of African-Americans and Jewish Americans who found work in this new industry, while unable to find work elsewhere. The entertainment industry as a line of work did not have the same appeal for more socially and economically well-established Americans; nonetheless they enjoyed the entertainment offered by these ethnically diverse groups.

No other modern culture can lay claim to fostering an entertainment industry on a scale equal to that which emerged in the United States concurrent with jazz in the 1920s. Music publishers, instrument manufacturers, booking agents and promoters, record companies, radio stations and networks, phonograph manufacturers, movie studios and theaters, performance rights organizations and unions, dance halls and ballrooms, and, of course, nightclubs, cabarets, and speakeasies complete the long list of entertainment-related businesses that sprang up in the 1920s as adjuncts to performers and composers, all satisfying the insatiable American appetite for entertainment. For example, by 1919 there were reportedly 295 piano-manufacturing companies compared to the two-digit number we have today. Scott Joplin's "Maple Leaf Rag" sold more than 1 million copies. While music publishers opened shops in major cities such as Denver, Chicago, and St. Louis, the Mecca for music publishers was New York City. Many of these New York publishers were concentrated in one area known as Tin Pan Alley and employed pianists by day to perform their latest publications in hopes of attracting sales. As music and dance became a significant part of American life, cabarets across the country were opened in cities such as Chicago, New York, San Francisco, Los Angeles, Kansas City, and, of course, New Orleans.

The 1920s also marked the beginning of innovative new technologies. Radio station KDKA began the first weekly broadcasts from Pittsburgh, Pennsylvania, in 1920 and broadcast the first live jazz performance by pianist Earl Hines in 1921. By 1922 there were 200 licensed radio stations throughout the country and 3 million radios had been sold, many of them running off battery power, since rural America had not yet been wired for home electricity. By 1924 the number of radio stations had increased to 694, networks had been formed, and households around the United States had purchased 10 million radios (the total population was about 114 million). Many of these radio stations employed musicians on a regular basis for live broadcasts, while also playing prerecorded 78-rpm records. The RCA Victor Company released its first one-sided record in 1903, and by 1916, there were 46 independent record companies in operation, an obvious response to America's taste for recorded music. By 1921 the recording industry reported about 100 million records sold. The Original Dixieland Jazz Band's first recording sold 1.5 million copies the first year (1917) at 75 cents each, and Paul Whiteman's recording of "Whispering" sold 2 million copies in 1922. Records in those days could be purchased in general stores, furniture stores, and the like. The motion picture industry also thrived in the 1920s and once talkies (motion pictures with sound) were developed, musicians discovered yet another form of employment. Many early cartoon films featured soundtracks that were obviously influenced by jazz.

Other arts and literature also reflected the new, more liberal attitudes associated with the "jazz age," the term used by author F. Scott Fitzgerald to describe the 1920s. Painters were less drawn to inanimate objects and sought to portray real-life experiences. Novelists were more apt to openly discuss sex and various aspects of the human condition that had been suppressed in earlier writings. In general, there was greater emphasis placed on freedom of expression, spontaneity, and human pleasures than ever before. Jazz soon became identified with this newfound freedom, representing a form of uninhibited personal expression. Through their writings, authors Langston Hughes and Alain Locke encouraged blacks to use education as a means to achieve political, social, and economic advancement and independence. They also urged black entertainers to capitalize on their unique brand of culture and its growing popularity.

There is no doubt that the U.S. entry into World War I in 1917 also had an impact on the American psyche. There was a new disillusionment never before experienced by this young country. Families grappled with the death or the potential death of loved ones while democratic thinking and personal freedoms were threatened. This sense of uncertainty about the future no doubt fueled young Americans' obsession with personal freedoms and zest for life. On the positive side, if there is one during war times, the U.S. war effort added to the growing new industrial economy.

Not all Americans applauded the arrival of jazz and the new morals associated with the jazz lifestyle. The conservative and self-righteous pushed for laws to regulate the sale of liquor, and in 1920 the **Prohibition Act** forbidding the public sale of alcohol was enacted. Prohibition was not repealed until 1933. In some ways Prohibition hurt the entertainment industry and jazz, though private clubs and cabarets somehow survived, often supported by the growing network of mobsters trafficking in illegal liquor, gambling, and prostitution. These illegal activities by the underground mob actually supported jazz music in many of their establishments in Chicago, Kansas City, and New York. For those who attended, looking for excitement and a chance to "slum" while enjoying their illegal liquor and musical spree, the illegal nature of these clubs added an element of daring.

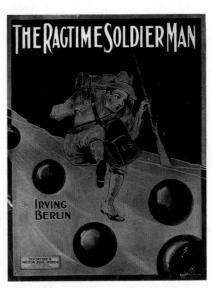

Composer Irving Berlin's song sheet cover is typical of many such World War I titles.

Clubs featuring black entertainers attracted white audiences seeking adventure and a glimpse of "uninhibited, barbaric" African life. These clubs were called "black and tans." The Cotton Club in New York City was just such a nightclub offering exotic floor shows.

The Storyville district, a 38-block area in New Orleans established through legislation passed in 1897, was lined with saloons and brothels. Until the Departments of the Army and Navy closed down Storyville in 1917, this district invited legalized prostitution, gambling, and other forms of late-night entertainment that called for music supplied by a host of early New Orleans jazz musicians. Through this association with the underworld, it is no small wonder that jazz in these early years was considered the "devil's music" and had little respect from morally conservative, "upstanding" citizens.

As modes of transportation improved through trains, and the growing automobile industry, musicians found travel from city to city less difficult. Musicians also traveled the Mississippi River on paddle wheel steamships with regular runs from New Orleans to ports throughout the Midwest. So what may have begun as a regional folk music became more widespread and universally practiced.

> **For more details about the History of Recording visit this section on the Online Learning Center.**

NEW ORLEANS—THE BIRTHPLACE OF JAZZ

The city of New Orleans and the surrounding Mississippi Delta reflect a rich cultural heritage. This area, one of the most active seaports for the transportation of goods to the nation's heartland via the Mississippi River, has been owned and inhabited by several nationalities including the French, Spanish, and British. While

New Orleans, Louisiana: Tom Anderson's cafe was a major musical center of Storyville on Basin and Iberville Streets.

this situation presented numerous political problems lasting through the first two decades of the 1800s, the cultural diversity provided by this mixture of residents and seafarers provided an environment that aided the creation of the earliest jazz styles. Many of the early jazz musicians who were **Creoles** of color, born of French and black parents, benefited from social and economic privileges not afforded to black descendents of slaves. As a result, many enjoyed some musical training and as adolescents likely attended concerts and operas in the New Orleans theaters. The surnames of many early jazz musicians such as Sidney Bechet, Kid Ory, Honrey Dutry, Johnny St. Cyr, and Ferdinand Joseph LaMothe reflect their French Creole backgrounds. Others such as the legendary cornetists Buddy Bolden, Bunk Johnson, Freddie Keppard, and Joe "King" Oliver were descendants of African slaves. They found that work as musicians, playing in traveling minstrel show bands, local New Orleans brass bands, brothels, and saloons in Storyville, provided an easier source of income than laboring at the docks or other menial forms of work open to nonwhites. In the early 1900s, New Orleans supported as many as 18 prominent bands sponsored by the fire department, police department, the Army, the Navy, and various fraternal lodges. Some bands were professional, while others were part-time organizations whose members practiced music as a sideline.

Among legendary New Orleans musicians, cornetist Buddy Bolden was never recorded and is remembered as somewhat of a mythological or Paul Bunyon–like character in the history of early jazz. Numerous tall tales about his amazing prowess as a musician have been told. Louis Armstrong, Sidney Bechet, and other early jazz artists have recalled Bolden in their memoirs as a powerful cornetist with a clear tone who was of great influence on the creation of early jazz. Bolden, who paraded the streets of New Orleans in various bands and performed in the Storyville district, was committed to a mental institution in 1907 for a brain disorder and he died there in 1931. His band, which later became known as the Eagle Band, became the training ground for many early jazz musicians including well-known clarinetist Sidney Bechet. Bechet remembered the Eagle Band as "much more of a barrelhouse band, a real gutbucket band, a low down band which really played the blues."[2]

Bunk Johnson, another early New Orleans cornetist, was undiscovered until historians began to try and piece together a history of early jazz. Johnson was not recorded until 1942, when he became a focal point of the Dixieland revival movement in the 1940s. Johnson apparently spun some rather tall tales and it was difficult for interviewers to separate the truth from the fiction invented by Johnson. There is, however, no doubt that in his prime, Johnson was an active musician performing in minstrel shows, theater orchestras, and circus and brass bands in and around New Orleans.

The only known photograph of Buddy Bolden and his orchestra, made in 1905. Notice the difference in instrumentation and size of this early New Orleans band compared to the Chicago band. Standing, left to right, William Warner, Willie Cornish, Buddy Bolden, James Johnson; seated are Frank Lewis and Jefferson Mumford.

Freddie Keppard (1889–1933), Joe "King" Oliver, and, of course, Louis Armstrong remain the only early New Orleans jazz cornetists whose careers eventually led to recordings that help to document this first early jazz style. Keppard led the Olympia Brass Band and performed in the Eagle Band earning the reputation as the most direct descendant of Buddy Bolden and "King" of the New Orleans cornetists. He traveled to California with the Original Creole Orchestra from 1912 to 1918 before settling in Chicago. It was in this city that his Jazz Cardinals band made its first recordings, but not until 1926. By this time though, his rough New Orleans Dixieland style had become eclipsed by that of more polished bands in Chicago, whose personnel included the likes of extraordinary improviser Louis Armstrong. Keppard played in Chicago and New York before the Original Dixieland Jazz Band's successful first recordings, and some say that Keppard turned down earlier offers to record because of his fear of being copied. His most representative recording is "Stock Yard Strut."

Dixieland Jazz Band Instrumentation

The classic New Orleans jazz band, many of which migrated to other cities such as Chicago and New York, and to the West Coast, was by no means standardized as photographs from the period testify. There were, however, some common instrumental configurations. The "front line," as it was called, typically consisted of a cornet, clarinet, sometimes violin, and trombone. This term originates from the New Orleans street parade bands, where the wind instruments marched in the front lines and the percussion followed in the "second line." The rhythm section in these early jazz bands might consist of some combination of guitar or banjo, string bass or tuba, and drums. The banjo, eventually replaced by the piano and/or guitar, and a bass instrument were optional in the early rhythm sections, but became standard members of the jazz band by the mid-1920s. The bass instrument could be a tuba (sometimes called "iron" or "brass" bass which again was a remnant of the brass marching bands), bass saxophone, or a string bass. String basses were not found in jazz bands on a regular basis until the mid- to late-1920s. There is much recorded evidence from as late as the early 1930s to indicate that the transition from tuba to string bass and banjo to guitar was very slow.

This instrumentation, as well as the roles these instruments played, is well exemplified by the recordings discussed throughout this chapter. The cornetist was often the star of the show, playing the syncopated main themes in brassy fashion. Gradually, the more brilliant trumpet replaced the cornet when jazz bands increased in size. The cornet, which came from the military and marching band traditions, does not produce as much volume as the trumpet. The clarinetist provided more rhythmically active embellishments and filigree, elaborately ornamenting the cornet melodies. These clarinet passages, often played as rapid 8th and 16th note scale-like patterns and **arpeggios** (chords outlined one note at a time), required technical mastery of the instrument. The trombone, which sounds below the cornet and clarinet, was used to outline the harmony by embellishing fundamental chord tones like the root, third, and fifth. The New Orleans Dixieland style trombonist perfected the "tailgate" technique by using the slide to smear, or **gliss** (short for glissando, meaning to slide from note to note in a very smooth, legato fashion), from one pitch to the next. Early New Orleans bands often paraded through the streets on a horse-drawn wagon ad-

Early classical music recording session showing use of acoustic horn and tiered seating.

vertising a minstrel show or the opening of a new shop or saloon, or participating in a funeral procession. The trombonist needed sufficient room to move his slide, which required that he sit on the tailgate of these wagons, hence the term **tailgate** trombone to describe this slippery style. Since many early jazz bands did not have a banjo, guitar, or bass, the pianist was required to maintain the harmony and rhythm of the piece. Early drummers had discovered ways to emulate the marching parade drum "second line" that typically required more than one player. By mounting a cymbal on a floor stand and creating a pedal arrangement to beat the bass drum with the foot, drummers were able to modify the marching configuration for indoor use by one player. Early drummers did little more than mimic the rudimentary techniques used by parade drummers and often employed gimmicky techniques and devices like temple blocks, spoons, and other novelty instruments. Early drummers did very little that resembles our contemporary impressions of jazz drumming and much of their performance consisted of antics like twirling and throwing their sticks in the air. Swing era bassist Gene Ramey referred to this as "showboating." In their defense, we have no accurate evidence of how drummers performed live since recording technology was still in its infancy in the early 1920s. Many trade-offs were made during the early recording process and especially by drummers since, prior to the advent of microphones and amplification, early acoustic recordings were unable to capture the same natural balance the bands achieved in live performance. One drummer or one loud cornetist could obliterate the sound of the other instruments and ruin a recording. These recording circumstances may also explain why early jazz cornet and trumpet players often used various mutes. We therefore do not know much about the performance practice of these early jazz drummers who often were relegated to playing temple blocks and other quiet accessories for recording sessions.

 It may be helpful to review the section about Instrumentation included in Chapter 3, Listening to Jazz, on the CD-ROM. This section contains recorded examples of the various instruments and mutes along with discussions about their construction and roles in a jazz band.

EARLY ARTISTS AND THEIR RECORDINGS

Original Dixieland Jazz Band

Despite the pioneering efforts made by black musicians in New Orleans and other parts of the South, the public's first widespread exposure to this new music would be through recordings made in New York by a white band calling themselves The Original Dixieland Jazz Band (ODJB). This band left New Orleans for Chicago in 1916 under the name Johnny Stein's Band from New Orleans and enjoyed a successful engagement at Schillers Café. The group was billed as "Stein's Dixie Jass Band." The band broke up because of a disagreement among its members and cornetist Nick LaRocca organized a new spin-off band he called the Original Dixieland Jasz [sic] Band. The success of Stein's band helped to encourage a gradual migration of New Orleans musicians to Chicago. In 1917 LaRocca took his new band to New York, where they were booked to perform one week at Reisenwebers for $1,000. They were an overnight sensation and changed the spelling of their name from "jass" to "jazz" to avoid having their advertisements defaced by erasing the letter "j." Columbia Records, which had been accustomed to recording light classical music and opera, rushed to record them. The company was ill equipped to deal with the raucous new sounds produced by this group and consequently made inferior recordings that went unissued until after the very successful recordings made this same year by the Victor label. The ODJB recorded its first successful sides for the Victor label on March 7, 1917, that subsequently sold over a million copies, breaking all previous sales records. Consequently, this band, which played its own version of New Orleans black-inspired jazz, made the first case for the commercial potential of recorded instrumental jazz. At this time, the band consisted of a cornet, clarinet, trombone, piano, and drums. Their music was not written down, but boasted little or no improvisation. Some of their numbers, like "Livery Stable Blues" and "Barnyard Blues," were novelty numbers featuring animal sounds imitated by the wind instruments. Some referred to this style as "nut" music. The balance of their repertoire consisted of rag- and blues-based numbers such as the popular "Tiger Rag" (which bears a resemblance to the "National Emblem" march), "Clarinet Marmalade," "Ostrich Walk," and "At the Jazz Band Ball." The ODJB's repertoire and style was created for dancing and entertainment and was often misunderstood by those who attempted to write about it. For example, the New York *American* tried to describe the ODJB style in a November 1917 article that read: "The peculiar, somewhat discordant melody is said to be produced by tuning each of the instruments at a different pitch; and to end some of the strains they occasionally play what we have termed a crazy cadenza."[3]

On the strength of their success in New York, the ODJB traveled to England in 1918 and performed at the ball celebrating the signing of the Treaty of Versailles that ended World War I. Cornetist Nick LaRocca was interviewed by the *Palais Dancing News* in England where he claimed that "jazz is the assassination, the murdering, the slaying of syncopation. In fact it is a revolution in this kind of music [syncopated dance music] . . . I even go so far as to confess we are musical anarchists . . . our prodigious outbursts are seldom consistent, every number played by us eclipsing in originality and effect our previous performance."[4] The band returned to New York, earning as much as $1,800 per week. It continued to perform and record and served as a model for many society dance bands that emerged in the 1920s. Like so many bands, the ODJB suffered from numerous squabbles, leading to various changes in personnel before they finally disbanded in 1938. In some ways, the ODJB's success at proving the commercial value of jazz became its own downfall as emerging bands quickly showed that the style could be performed far better.

The "Original Dixie Jazz Band One-Step," included on the accompanying CD anthology, is a classic example of the work produced by the ODJB when this group first shocked New Yorkers with their new brand of music. It was billed by Victor as "a jass band, the newest thing in cabarets . . . it has sufficient power and penetration to inject new life into a mummy, and will keep ordinary human dancers on their feet till breakfast time."[5] While there is no real spontaneously improvised music, or at least not any that is obviously improvised, the performance does feature a buoyant, swing rhythmic quality unlike any other recorded music of the time. Undoubtedly, the band reached this point through an improvisatory approach to developing the tune sometime prior to this recording. Their understanding of swing interpretation is proof that this aspect of jazz performance style

Original Dixieland Jazz Band: (left to right) Russell Robinson the pianist who succeeded Henry Ragas, Larry Shield, Nick LaRocca, Emile Christian (succeeded Eddie Edwards), and Tony Sparbarro; 1919.

was in practice in cities such as New Orleans and Chicago well before this recording was made. The ODJB was merely the first to capitalize on the new craze through the success of their early recordings.

The arrangement shows the typical New Orleans polyphonic style popular during this period. The multisectional, rondo-like thematic structure reflects the strong influence that the ragtime style exerted on early instrumental jazz. The four-measure introduction that is repeated during the statement of the initial "A" section is very similar to the beginning of many marches, while the two-measure solo breaks by clarinetist Larry Shields were also typical of most jazz band arrangements of the day. It was often during these solo breaks that most, if any, of the real improvisation took place. In this case, it appears as though Shields is merely playing the same material he has probably played many times before but may have originated through the process of improvisation. The outline and timeline that follows will help you to navigate through this historic recording and understand more clearly how the song is constructed.

It is obvious in this 1917 recording by the ODJB that the New Orleans street bands that played in a style similar to a marching parade band, left an impact on these white players who came from this same Delta city. The initial march-like introduction reoccurs numerous times throughout the piece. Many of the other characteristics associated with the early New Orleans Dixieland style are heard throughout this seminal recording including:

- sliding, tailgate trombone
- dense polyphonic style featuring all three wind instruments playing simultaneously
- florid, clarinet **obligato** (prominent accompanying melody secondary to primary melody) passages
- drummer playing in a march-like style including characteristic cymbal crashes and bass drum hits
- drummer's use of wood blocks, which were less distracting and invasive during this period of early recording technology
- **solo breaks** (a point in a piece of music lasting usually two to four measures when everyone in the ensemble stops playing except the soloist) for clarinet
- classic New Orleans instrumentation though lacking of any bass instrument such as tuba or string bass

Kid Ory (1890–1973)

While the ODJB may have been the first jazz band to record, they certainly were not the only band performing New Orleans style jazz during the late teens and early 1920s. Many black bands were performing music that historians consider far more authentic, original, and representative of the real jazz of the times. For example Edward "Kid" Ory, a black New Orleans trombonist had taken a band featuring his brand of New Orleans jazz to California in 1919. Ory's Sunshine Orchestra became the first black jazz band from New Orleans to record. They recorded in Los Angeles in 1922. These recordings feature Ory's band alone and as accompanists to blues singers from the vaudeville circuit. In 1925 Ory left California and moved to Chicago, where he participated in an early jazz radio broadcast in 1923. He later took part in some of the most historically significant recordings ever made as a

Listening Guide

Original Dixieland Jazz Band

Form: AABBAABB (8 bars of each theme) / Theme C (6 choruses of 16 bars each)

Keys: Theme A: B-flat Major
Theme B: E-flat Major
Theme C: A-flat Major

00:00–00:08	A theme
00:00–00:16	A theme repeated
00:16–00:23	B theme (change of key)
00:24–00:31	B theme repeated
00:31–00:38	A theme (return to first key)
00:39–00:46	A theme repeated
00:47–00:54	B theme (change of key)
00:54–1:002	B theme repeated
1:02–1:16	C theme (change of key again) "That Teasin' Rag" by Joe Jordan
1:17–1:31	C¹ theme varied slightly at second four-measure phrase
1:32–1:47	C theme
1:48–2:02	C¹ theme
2:03–2:18	C theme
2:19–2:35	Final C theme that includes a one-measure tag ending

"Dixie Jass Band One-Step" (ODJB) 2:35

Recorded 2/26/17, New York

(RCA Special Products)

Nick LaRocca: *cornet*

Larry Shields: *clarinet*

Eddie Edwards: *trombone*

Henry Ragas: *piano*

Tony Spargo: *drums*

member of Louis Armstrong's recording bands. Ory is considered to be the first important jazz trombonist in the long lineage of this instrument.

Joe "King" Oliver (1885–1938)

Perhaps the true "King" of New Orleans cornetists was Joe "King" Oliver. He became Louis Armstrong's mentor while playing in New Orleans brass bands around 1908. The closing of Storyville in 1917 was no doubt a factor in his choice to move to Chicago a year later, though many of the clubs that were closed in Storyville set up shop in other parts of the city. After establishing himself as a first-rate cornetist in various Chicago bands, Oliver formed his own Creole Jazz Band in 1920, eventually taking up residency at the Lincoln Gardens located at 459 East 31st Street. As the popularity of his band grew, he sent for Louis Armstrong, his young New Orleans protégé, to play second cornet. The recordings made by Joe Oliver's band in 1923 have become landmarks in the history of jazz for they not only displayed Oliver's prowess as an improvising soloist, but they served to introduce Armstrong who would soon revolutionize jazz by changing it from an ensemble style to a virtuosic solo art form. Perhaps the most famous recording made by this band was "Dippermouth Blues" aka "Sugarfoot Stomp." Oliver's solo on this recording became a model for many trumpet players to follow and was often quoted by other trumpet players who later recorded arrangements of this piece. Armstrong is barely identifiable in this recording; however, there are other significant works recorded by Oliver's Creole Jazz Band that do feature him in a more

Pianist Lilian Hardin Armstrong (1898–1971), ca. 1933.

prominent way and deserve mention. Armstrong cites "Chimes Blues" as a recording he was quite proud of for it features his first recorded solo. "Tears," a work co-composed by Armstrong and Creole Jazz Band pianist Lilian Hardin was also recorded by the band in 1923 and presents a glimmer of the great Armstrong solo style not yet fully developed, but showing that he was already far more advanced than most of his contemporaries.

Lilian Hardin deserves special mention as she was an exceptional pianist, composer, and arranger. She was also the most prominent woman to excel as a jazz instrumentalist at a time when this business was almost exclusively a man's world. A few women had become successful singers at this point, but it was rare to find a woman appearing as an instrumentalist in male-dominated jazz bands. The lifestyle of a jazz musician was considered inappropriate for women and remained so for many years. She played with bands led by Joe Oliver and Louis Armstrong, recording with the finest New Orleans and Chicago musicians of the day. Armstrong, who first met her when he joined Joe Oliver's Creole Jazz Band was taken with her instantly and commented that "it was startling to find a woman who had been valedictorian in her class at Fisk University [she never actually graduated] fall in line and play such good jazz."[6] She told the following story about her audition with Oliver: "When I sat down to play I asked for the music and were they surprised! They politely told me they didn't have any music and furthermore never used any. I then asked what key the first number would be in. I must have been speaking another language because the leader said, 'When you hear two knocks, just start playing.' It all seemed very strange to me, but I got all set, and when I heard those two knocks I hit the piano so loud and hard they all turned around to look at me. It took only a second for me to feel what they were playing and I was off. The New Orleans Creole Jazz Band hired me, and I never got back to the music store—never got back to Fisk University."[7] She married Louis Armstrong, a union that lasted until their separation and eventual divorce in 1938, and she was instrumental in encouraging him to strike out on his own and not remain a sideman in the shadow of other musicians.

To quote historian Martin Williams, "Dippermouth Blues" "[is a] sample of the dense polyphonic style of the New Orleans ensemble."[8] Unlike many songs from this period that erroneously used the term "blues" in the title but didn't follow this harmonic form, "Dippermouth Blues" is an authentic blues and follows the same I-IV-V chord scheme we found in Bessie Smith's "Lost Your Head Blues" and W. C. Handy's "St. Louis Blues." King Oliver's version of "Dippermouth Blues," aka "Sugar Foot Stomp," served as an inspiration and model for many other versions by other bands that followed. (Compare this version to Fletcher Henderson's larger band version, also found in the anthology.) Armstrong plays the lead cornet part during the ensemble section between the two solo choruses. The seminal solo is played by Oliver using a wah-wah style mute. This two-chorus solo was imitated by many trumpet players who followed. Oliver used a mute on this solo and many other recordings, and he is given much credit for introducing various brass mutes to add special color and dampen the brash sound of the cornet. It may have been out of necessity that Oliver often used mutes in his recordings in an effort to accommodate the limitations of early acoustic recordings that were easily overloaded

Joe "King" Oliver's Creole Jazz Band, 1923. Left to right: Honore Dutrey, trombone; Baby Dodds, drums; Joe Oliver, cornet; Lilian Hardin, piano; Bill Johnson, banjo; Johnny Dodds, clarinet; Louis Armstrong (kneeling), slide trumpet; Chicago, Illinois.

by loud sounds. Whatever the reason, the use of mutes by brass players in jazz became commonplace. Much like the ODJB recording included in the anthology, this drummer used wood blocks instead of the overpowering drums difficult to handle by early recording technology. The short vocal break is merely an interlude to precede the final full ensemble chorus and two-measure tag.

The listening guide that follows will help guide your listening experience.

King Oliver's Creole Jazz Band

Key and Form: 12-bar blues in C Major

0:00–0:04	Four measure intro featuring Oliver and Armstrong in harmonized duet
0:05–0:20	*First Chorus:* opening theme stated in polyphonic Dixieland style
0:21–0:35	*Second Chorus:* full ensemble continues in polyphonic style
0:36–0:50	*Third Chorus:* stop-time clarinet solo
0:51–1:06	*Fourth Chorus:* clarinet solo continues
1:07–1:22	*Fifth Chorus:* Full ensemble in polyphonic style Dixieland
1:23–1:37	*Sixth Chorus:* Oliver plays muted cornet solo while other instruments play simple, quiet background parts
1:38–1:52	*Seventh Chorus:* Cornet solo continues with background figures
1:53–2:06	*Eighth Chorus:* Last cornet chorus ends with two-bar vocal break
2:08–end	*Final Chorus:* Full ensemble in polyphonic style with extra two-bar tag

Listening Guide

"Dippermouth Blues" (Oliver) 2:32

Recorded 4/6/23, Richmond, Indiana

(Gennett 5132)

King Oliver, Louis Armstrong: *cornet*

Honoré Dutrey: *trombone*

Johnny Dodds: *clarinet*

Lil Hardin: *piano*

Bill Johnson: *banjo, vocal break*

Baby Dodds: *drums*

Jelly Roll Morton (1890–1941)

As recordings testify, the 1920s mark a period of tremendous growth and innovation in jazz and technology. Still a new music, jazz remained largely misunderstood and a controversial subject for hot debate. One of the reasons that jazz remained a mystery, shrouded in myth and misunderstanding, was that the musicians themselves were unwilling or unable to offer any meaningful explanations about it. The analysis was often left to those literary and classically trained writers who knew very little about it and were the least qualified to discuss it. This was largely the case until the 1930s, when scholars began to take greater interest in the music and its creators. World-famous anthropologist and folklorist Alan Lomax, working for the Library of Congress in 1938, took just such an interest in Jelly Roll Morton, who thought of himself as the inventor of jazz. He interviewed Morton, and an excerpt of these historic interviews appears on the CD-ROM.

Jelly Roll Morton, born as Ferdinand Joseph LaMothe (mistakenly referred to for many years as Lementhe) was one of the earliest pioneers of this new music, enjoying his success as a composer/arranger, pianist, and bandleader in the mid-1920s. Growing up in New Orleans, Morton was a Creole and took advantage of this stature. He studied piano with Tony Jackson, one of the very few musicians he ever praised, other than himself. Jelly Roll often lied about his birth date to substantiate his tales about inventing jazz, a bogus claim as jazz is the by-product of a collective spirit. To his credit, however, his recorded music does justify his claims as an innovator and early jazz stylist. He traveled the country performing on the West Coast, in Mexico, in the Midwest, and, of course, in New Orleans, often as a solo pianist and sometimes making a living as a pool shark, gambler, pimp, and hustler. His piano and composition style bears a remarkable resemblance to ragtime, but his own brand of invention labeled him as a transitional figure between the rag and stride piano styles. Ragtime and the blues served as his primary influences. His first published solo composition was entitled "The Jelly Roll Blues" and appeared in print in 1912. Many of his later compositions have become staples in the jazz repertoire. His unique piano style, which often resembled an entire band condensed to 10 fingers, led him to compose for a recording band that produced a series of sides considered his most historically significant works. His Red Hot Peppers recording band did not perform outside of Chicago, probably because all of the musicians featured on these recordings were the most prominent and in-demand musicians at the time in Chicago and did not need to travel to work steadily. Many were transplanted New Orleans residents, like trombonist Kid Ory. The arrangements recorded by this band earned Morton the reputation as the "first jazz composer/arranger." In these ensemble works, Morton demonstrated an unparalleled understanding (at least among early jazz musicians) of orchestration, form, balance, variety, and the importance of the soloists within the confines of a large group arrangement. Rather than follow the cluttered, polyphonic New Orleans style, he organized his material much more carefully by crafting composed duets and trios, interludes connecting main themes, key changes, and full ensemble choruses.

Morton's music, daringly advanced for its day by demonstrating sophisticated orchestration and arranging techniques, was actually outmoded almost the day it was recorded. His style, largely based on ragtime, was quickly becoming eclipsed in the mid-1920s by a newer style of jazz that spotlighted the soloist as much as the ensemble. Ragtime, the basis for much of his work, was passé, and he found himself competing with younger musicians playing in a newer style. Though his music swung more, his ragtime-derived syncopated rhythmic style was not enough to sustain his reputation. Some of his later works, only recently discovered, seem to reflect the work of big band composers like Duke Ellington, an ironic development since Morton never embraced the style and outwardly condemned the big band swing movement. Like so many early jazz performers, Morton was largely forgotten at the time of his death and found it difficult to earn a living in the field he helped to create.

Jazz pioneer Jelly Roll Morton at the piano.

The recording of "Black Bottom Stomp," included on the companion anthology, is considered to be the most seminal work by Morton and his Red Hot Peppers. While the work itself could have been better rehearsed, it nevertheless demonstrates not only the high level of his artistry as a composer/pianist, but also features excellent solos for the day by Mitchel, Simeon, St. Cyr, and Ory. This track uncommonly uses a trumpet instead of the typical cornet, but of even more interest is the inclusion of a string bass, which at times actually plays quarter-note walking lines. More typical for this period would have been a tuba or bass saxophone, so it is even more unusual to hear a **walking bass** line (ascending and descending scale-like bass lines where one note is played on each beat of the measure), not a common practice until many years later in the Swing Era. Also recognizable is the call–response format featured in the first repeated A section of Morton's original. This recording also showcases numerous solo breaks and riffs, two ingredients that Morton was adamant about when he discussed the qualities of good jazz with Alan Lomax. The outline and timeline that follows will help you to navigate through this historic recording and understand more clearly how the song is constructed.

You will find several recorded excerpts on the CD-ROM of trombone, trumpet, and clarinet parts extracted from this composition and rerecorded. Try to find where these excerpts appear in the original recording. The CD-ROM also contains a brief excerpt of the historic interview of Morton conducted by Alan Lomax.

Listening Guide

"Black Bottom Stomp" (Morton) 3:09

Recorded 9/15/26, Chicago

(Victor 20221)

Jelly Roll Morton: *piano*

George Mitchell: *trumpet*

Edward ("Kid") Ory: *trombone*

Omer Simeon: *clarinet*

Johnny St. Cyr: *banjo*

John Lindsay: *bass*

Andrew Hilaire: *drums*

Jelly Roll Morton's Red Hot Peppers

Key and Form: Theme A (16 bars in B-flat Major); Theme B (20 bars in E-flat Major)

0:00–0:07	8 measure intro (4 measures repeated) by full ensemble
0:08–0:21	A^1—8 measure section featuring call and response style; bass implies predominant 2-beat style with occasional 4-beat walking
0:22–0:36	A^2—Trumpet alternates 4 measure phrases with full ensemble question-answer style
0:37–0:51	A^3—Clarinet solo with banjo accompaniment
0:52–0:55	4 measure interlude and key change
0:56–1:14	B^1—6 measure ensemble phrase followed by short trumpet and trombone breaks; 12 measures of full ensemble follow for a total of 20 measures
1:15–1:32	B^2—Clarinet solo with 2 measure break and rhythm section accompaniment; another 20 measure section is unusual
1:33–1:50	B^3—Piano solo in stride-like style; section ends with full ensemble break that leads to next section
1:51–2:09	B^4—Trumpet solo in stop-time; rhythmic break figures resemble displaced habanera rhythm
2:10–2:28	B^5—banjo solo includes 2 measure break; bass occasionally shows more modern 4-beat walking style
2:29–2:47	B^6—Full ensemble returns to 2-beat style; 2 measure drum break followed by Dixieland ensemble style
2:48–end	B^7—Final chorus features strong drum back beat accents on 2 and; 2 measure drum break before final 12 measure ensemble section and 2 measure Coda or Tag

Louis Armstrong (1901–1971)

You will find no argument in describing Louis Armstrong as the first truly exceptional virtuoso jazz soloist. Even those early recordings with Joe Oliver show that there was something special not only about his rhythmic phrasing, but also about his choice of notes while improvising. His first encounter with the cornet came as a member of a band in a boy's school in New Orleans. (See the CD-ROM for excerpts of Armstrong discussing Buddy Bolden, Joe Oliver, and the early New Orleans traditions.) Growing up he worked menial jobs at the New Orleans docks and played in local bands. His first significant employment as a musician was with Fate Marable's Orchestra in 1919. Marable's small orchestra traveled up and down the Mississippi River on the S.S. *St. Paul,* a riverboat steamship that carried passengers and goods between New Orleans and Midwestern ports. This band included several of the musicians that would later team with him in Chicago to record his most influential early works. Armstrong stayed with Marable about 2 years before moving to Tom Anderson's cabaret band on Rampart Street in New Orleans. Soon after, he received word from his mentor Joe Oliver, now finding success in Chicago, to join his band as second cornet. It was

Armstrong's first recordings with Joe "King" Oliver that introduced him to the world, and, just like his mentor, he became widely known by several nicknames including "Satchmo" and "Pops." His success with Oliver led to a short stint as featured soloist with Fletcher Henderson's New York band that was pioneering the big band sound featuring more sophisticated arrangements for his larger band. Armstrong returned to Chicago in 1925 to form his most famous recording bands with his wife, pianist Lillian Hardin. These Hot Five and Hot Seven recordings are the most significant recordings made in the first 20 years of jazz history. These performances not only introduce a new way to structure jazz in order to highlight the improvising soloist instead of the collective ensemble, but they also mark a distinct change in the interpretation of eighth notes. Armstrong's style moved away from the stiff syncopations associated with earlier ragtime-based styles toward an uneven, buoyant, driving swing style. Armstrong's solos swing like no other from this period and serve to instruct not only future generations of wind players, but also drummers in the art of swing style playing. The following is a brief listing of those many aspects of Armstrong's style that characterize him as a true innovator.

- Armstrong demonstrated an ability to play higher notes than had previously been accomplished by other cornet players. He was one of the first musicians to discard the cornet in favor of the trumpet.

- Armstrong was a brilliant technician who demonstrated his dexterity and flexibility by playing **double time** solo breaks (16th notes and triplets instead of 8th notes, or playing notes twice as fast).

- Armstrong's choice of notes was also unique for the time. His solos feature chromatically altered tones at a time when most improvisations were largely **diatonic** (use of notes only from the basic chord or scale that relates to the chord).

- Armstrong's rhythmic style swung harder than that of any musicians of the day and consequently he influenced all instrumentalists—not just trumpet players.

- Armstrong's rhythmic phrasing was unique. He demonstrated the ability to treat a steady tempo in a more elastic manner by occasionally rushing, laying back slightly behind the beat, as well as implying polyrhythmic phrases (rhythmic groups of three against a 4/4 meter). (See Chapter 4, Example 4.3.)

- His tone quality was brilliant, immediately captivating the listener as he soared above the rest of the band.

- Armstrong used various embellishments to his advantage. Inflections such as rips up to high notes and varying **vibrato** speeds were used to full advantage to add special emotional quality.

- Armstrong was the first to popularize vocal improvisation using nonsense syllables—a style later described as **scat** singing.

In addition to his artistry as a trumpet player, Armstrong was the first to popularize scat vocal technique. He demonstrated this technique in his 1926 recording of "Heebie Jeebies." Armstrong's producer spread the rumor that he dropped the sheet music during the recording while others claimed he just forgot the lyrics, forcing him to vocally improvise using nonsense syllables instead of words.

The Hot Five, from left to right, were Louis Armstrong on cornet, banjoist Johnny St. Cyr, clarinetist Johnny Dodds, trombonist Kid Ory, and pianist Lilian Hardin.

Louis Armstrong's Hot Five, Exclusive Okeh Record Artists.

Whatever the case, this recording launched an entirely new style of vocal jazz, which has influenced jazz singers ever since.

Armstrong's popularity grew not only in the United States but also abroad, prompting him to tour worldwide. His ability as a charismatic entertainer, jazz trumpeter, and vocalist gave him the star power necessary for a minority person to achieve the stature and success that he enjoyed throughout his lengthy career. While he became involved at various times in his career with more commercial music ventures, he remained true to the art of jazz improvising, which he advanced further than anyone else had in this early jazz period.

There are so many outstanding recordings by Armstrong's Hot Five and Hot Seven bands that the inclusion of just one selection in the companion audio collection is difficult. "West End Blues" was chosen because it not only displays Armstrong's accomplishments as a trumpet and vocal soloist, but also displays the artistry of innovative pianist Earl Hines. Hines moved from his hometown of Pittsburgh to Chicago and became the first pianist to begin to discard the busy, two-hand ragtime and stride styles in favor of a more single-line approach similar to that of wind players. Count Basie during the swing era and the many bebop pianists in the mid- to late-1940s further honed this style. In this recording, Armstrong displays his clarion high register ability, technical command in executing double time solo breaks, and sense of rhythmic balance while playing streams of triplets yet at times purposefully lagging behind the beat. His vocal solo here is far from an example of his best work as a scat singer, but it does show how similar his vocal and instrumental styles were. The outline and timeline that follows will help you to navigate through this historic recording and understand more clearly how the song is constructed. Timings are approximate but will be helpful in delineating each section of this 12 measure blues.

Louis Armstrong and His Hot Five

Key and Form: 12-bar blues in E♭

"West End Blues"
(Oliver/Williams)

Recorded 6/28/28

(Okeh 8597)

Louis Armstrong: *trumpet, vocals*

Fred Robinson: *trombone*

Jimmy Strong: *clarinet*

Earl Hines: *piano*

Mancy Carr: *banjo*

Zutty Singleton: *drums*

Listening Guide

Introduction (0:00–00:15)	Armstrong plays a rubato **cadenza** (solo without accompaniment and sometimes without strict tempo) followed by a brief sustained chord played by the ensemble of accompanying instruments. This introduction is followed immediately by Armstrong's eighth-note pickups that establish the regular tempo and introduce the theme. These pickup notes (notes that anticipate the actual beginning of a phrase of music) establish a trend that is followed throughout the entire piece since each new section begins as an anticipation using pickup notes to begin each new chorus.
Main Theme (0:15)	The main 12-measure theme is played by Armstrong with accompaniment by clarinet, trombone, and rhythm section. Pianist and banjo player place strong chords on each beat.
Second Chorus (0:50)	This second 12-bar blues chorus features trombonist Robinson. It begins with a one-beat pickup at the end of the first chorus. Rhythmic accompaniment is provided by the drummer playing what sounds like spoons!
Third Chorus (1:24)	Clarinetist Strong trades phrases in call and response style with Armstrong in his scat vocal style. This chorus also begins with an anticipation at the end of the previous chorus.
Fourth Chorus (1:58)	Pianist Earl Hines is featured here in an unaccompanied solo, demonstrating why he is remembered as one of the most important pianists from this early period. His single-line right-hand melodies are reminiscent of those played by horn players. This more linear, hornlike style is in stark contrast to the busy, two-hand ragtime and stride piano styles reflected by most pianists from this period. His left-hand style in this solo does show the stride influence.
Fifth Chorus (2:32)	Armstrong returns to the spotlight for the first eight measures of this last chorus with a long sustained high C followed by repetitive triplets, which he rushes and drags to provide a dramatic climax to the close of this piece. The piece concludes with a short, rubato-style ending featuring solo piano followed by the entire ensemble. The drummer adds the final touch with his spoons!

Sidney Bechet (1897–1959)

While Sidney Bechet made significant contributions to jazz in the early years of its development, he remains a somewhat less prominent figure in its history. A New Orleans–born clarinetist, Bechet was largely self-taught, could not read music, and was known all his life as a somewhat discontent, migrant musician

Sidney Bechet plays soprano saxophone for a recording of "Summertime" in a Blue Note record label session, June 8, 1939.

constantly moving from one band and city to another. He never settled down with one band for any great length of time and consequently there are many diverse recordings available. After moving to Chicago where he performed with Freddie Keppard and King Oliver around 1918, he traveled to Europe with a large society orchestra led by Will Marion Cook. He stayed less than a year with Cook's Southern Syncopated Orchestra, but his travels to Europe with this group left an indelible mark on his career, for it was there that he discovered the soprano saxophone. He soon favored this instrument over the clarinet and he is now remembered as not only the first **woodwind doubler** (one who plays several different woodwind instruments proficiently), but also is given credit for introducing the soprano sax to the jazz world. Further advancement of this instrument beyond what Bechet had accomplished would wait until the 1960s and the artistry of John Coltrane. Bechet's travels to Europe were also rewarded by gaining recognition on both continents—no small claim for an early black jazz musician. Bechet's recordings with Clarence Williams' Blue 7 and the Red Onions bands, both of which also featured Louis Armstrong, are seminal and best show his blues and ragtime-derived style.

THE PIANISTS

The ragtime style served as a springboard for the creation of a looser, more swinging style that developed initially in the Harlem section of Manhattan. James P. Johnson, who was also a highly skilled ragtime pianist and composer, is considered to be the "father" of this new "stride" piano solo style. There were other pianists associated with this style and together they are remembered as the "Harlem pianists." This group included Eubie Blake, Willie "The Lion" Smith, Duke Ellington, Fats Waller, and Art Tatum, among others. The left-hand technique associated with this style is clearly related to the om-pah, two-beat style of ragtime, providing a steady regular rhythm while stating chord roots on strong beats and basic chord tones above the root on the weak beats. The left hand leaps in large "strides" across the keyboard. Rhythmically, however, the stride style is far more sophisticated with intricate cross rhythms, and a smoother sense of swing than the rather rigid syncopations associated with rags. There is a greater tendency toward improvisation, application of blues inflections, and generally faster tempos than in most classic rags that called for no improvisation and were not informed by the blues. In counterpoint to the regularity of the left hand, the right hand creates single-line melodies, as opposed to chords, and interacts with the regularity of the left hand in most unusual and irregular ways, setting up syncopations and polyrhythms. (The corresponding chapter on the CD-ROM provides a video example of stride piano.)

Many of these Harlem pianists earned their living supplying accompaniment for silent films and singers such as Bessie Smith. They also performed at cabarets, rent parties, and for Tin Pan Alley publishers to help market new music. Informal competitions, sometimes referred to as "cutting contests," were staged at a musician's home. A modest admission fee was charged and this income was used to help the tenant pay his rent. These rent parties became fairly commonplace not only in Harlem, but also in Kansas City and Chicago.

James P. Johnson (1891–1955)

The "father of stride piano" educated in the classical tradition and trained by Eubie Blake, James P. Johnson served as musical director for the black film "St. Louis Blues" and arranged some 16 musical reviews for Broadway. Despite his reputation among musicians as a superior pianist, composer, and accompanist, Johnson never enjoyed great commercial success. His popular tunes like "The Charleston" became standards, but were in sharp contrast to his love for more serious works in the stride style. These works include an opera, a symphony, a concerto, and a symphonic suite. Each of these major, multi-movement works was designed "to tell a story, the story of America's ethnic heritage, especially the distinctive role of his race."[9] Unfortunately, the white world of serious music was not ready to accept semi-serious, orchestral music by a black composer; consequently, much of his work in this vein was rejected by publishers. His work as a stride pianist nevertheless was of great influence on Fats Waller, Duke Ellington, and the bebop era pianist/composer Thelonious Monk.

Johnson's "Carolina Shout" is included on the companion CD anthology. It is truly one of the most inspired stride piano performances on record and shows a radical departure rhythmically from ragtime, which served as the immediate predecessor to this style. As the title implies, it is based on an old New Orleans ceremonial ring-shout featuring contrasting themes. The piano roll of this piece supposedly served to instruct a young Duke Ellington, who placed his fingers on the player piano keyboard to follow the piece note by note. This particular recording demonstrates Johnson's artistry regarding complete independence between left and right

Pianist James P. Johnson.

hands. The left hand creates shifting accents by deviating from the predictable, re-occurring om-pah pattern. Instead of always placing the root of a chord on strong beats 1 and 3, as was usually the case in earlier rag styles, he occasionally shifts these strong beat accents to 2 and 4, giving the false impression of a meter change. As you listen to this recording from the anthology, conduct a simple 4/4 pattern or count 1234, 1234, 1234, and so on, as this will help you to spot these situations and give you a frame of reference (a sample conducting pattern can be found in Chapter 2 on the CD-ROM under the section on rhythm). These shifting accents in the left hand and absence of repetitive om-pah rhythms provide an element of surprise and originality to this amazing performance. The shifting accents are most noticeable in the initial A sections and the D section of the form. While the multiple sections of this overall form seem to resemble a classic rag formula, the A section never repeats following its initial statement, which is the case in most rag compositions. The second A section in "Carolina Shout," unlike most rags, does not feature exact repetition but shows variation when compared to the initial statement of the A theme. A call–response between right and left hands is evident during the C sections. While there are similarities between sections, there are also significant differences, making it challenging to be precise about the form. Rhythm, rather than melody, seems to be the more predominant aspect of this classic recording. The listening guide that follows will help you to navigate through this historic recording and understand more clearly how the performance is constructed.

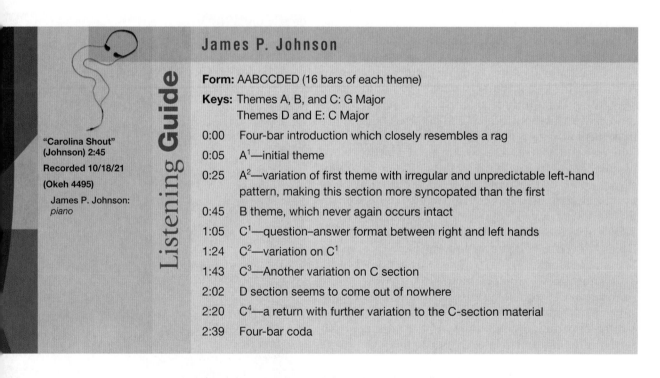

Listening Guide

James P. Johnson

"Carolina Shout"
(Johnson) 2:45

Recorded 10/18/21

(Okeh 4495)

James P. Johnson:
piano

Form: AABCCDED (16 bars of each theme)

Keys: Themes A, B, and C: G Major
Themes D and E: C Major

0:00	Four-bar introduction which closely resembles a rag
0:05	A^1—initial theme
0:25	A^2—variation of first theme with irregular and unpredictable left-hand pattern, making this section more syncopated than the first
0:45	B theme, which never again occurs intact
1:05	C^1—question–answer format between right and left hands
1:24	C^2—variation on C^1
1:43	C^3—Another variation on C section
2:02	D section seems to come out of nowhere
2:20	C^4—a return with further variation to the C-section material
2:39	Four-bar coda

THE RECEPTION OF EARLY JAZZ

Not everyone was receptive to this new music. For that matter, some black publications were even quick to disassociate themselves from this music. For example the New Orleans *Times-Picayune* in a 1918 issue came out strongly against the music that was attributed to their city. The writer of an article in this press disowned jazz saying that "it has been widely suggested that this particular form of musical vice had its birth in this city. . . . We do not recognize the honor of parenthood, but with such a story in circulation, it behooves us to be last to accept the atrocity in polite society, and where it has crept in we should make it a point of civic honor to suppress it. Its musical value is nil, and its possibilities of harm are great."[10] Black intellectuals fighting for freedom and respectability in the 1920s sometimes shunned jazz since it was considered by some to be a barbaric product of ghetto lowlife, produced by untrained and unsophisticated musicians who practiced their trade in saloons, whorehouses, and brothels. On the other hand, the *Chicago Defender*, another black press, applauded the music for it provided a symbol for black pride and offered the potential for upward mobility to its successful practitioners. An article that appeared in a 1919 edition of this publication stated "We hope the swing of Europe [referring to society orchestra leader James Reese Europe] and his band around the country will be nation wide. Europe and his band are worth more to our Race than a thousand speeches from the so-called Race orators and uplifters."[11] But Europe was not considered a jazz band leader.

To many, even those who were profiting from it, jazz was little more than a novelty, a fad that was often misunderstood. For example, in 1918 the Victor record catalogue issued the following statement: "A jazz band is a unique organization of which it may be said the worse it is, the better it is. If you have heard a jazz band before, and feel you already know the worst, try this record. Yet out of the mass of sounds there emerges tunes, and as the music proceeds you get order out of chaos. . . . One that not merely invites you, but almost forces you to dance."[12]

In 1921 *The Ladies' Home Journal* ran a series of articles that made it quite clear how some felt about the negative impact that jazz was having on youth and society in general. The title of one article in this series tells it all—"Unspeakable Jazz Must Go—It is worse than the saloon and scarlet vice."[13] Another entitled "Does Jazz Put the Sin in Syncopation"[14] attacked the music and its effect on young people's morals. The author Anne Shaw Faulkner wrote "that never in the history of our land have there been such immoral conditions among our young people, . . . and the blame is laid on jazz music and its evil influence on the young people of today."[15] The article attacked jazz that stimulated unwholesome dancing. She went on in this article to provide a misinformed definition of jazz and characterized it as "the accompaniment of the voodoo dancer, stimulating the half-crazed barbarian to the vilest deeds." She further described the music as symptomatic of a postwar culture and an "expression of protest against law and order."[16]

Jazz was clearly a controversial music right from the outset, creating a subject of great debate among intellectuals, conservatives, socialites, and young people. It seems that jazz received the most support from intellectuals and the classical music community both in the United States and abroad. *Etude* magazine, targeted largely for music teachers, conducted a survey among professionals from various aspects of the field to determine if there were any commonly agreed on perceptions about jazz. The responses were mixed. The editors, while careful not to take sides, did depict jazz as a music that "has been an accursed annoyance for years,"[17] while applauding the efforts of songwriters George Gershwin and Irving Berlin. John Alden Carpenter, a distinguished American composer, contributed his own thoughts about jazz to this article saying that: "I am convinced that our contemporary popular music (please note that I avoid labeling it "jazz") is by far the most spontaneous, the most personal, the most characteristic, and by virtue of these qualities, the most important musical expression that America has achieved. I am strongly inclined to believe that the musical historian of the year two thousand will find the birthday of American music and that of Irving Berlin to have been the

same."[18] (Berlin did compose a number of popular tunes that served as springboards for jazz renditions, but much of his work could not be considered jazz.) Other contributors to this survey labeled jazz a fad that exhibited the restless nature of wartimes and that "the problem would take care of itself through natural evolution." On the other hand, the "March King" John Phillip Sousa felt that there was "no reason, with its exhilarating rhythm, its melodic ingenuities, why it should not become one of the accepted forms of composition,"[19] and Leopold Stokowski, conductor of the Philadelphia Orchestra, stated that "Jazz has come to stay. It is an expression of the times, of breathless, energetic, super-active times in which we are living. The Negro musicians of America are playing a great part in this change. They have an open mind, and unbiased outlook. They are not hampered by traditions or conventions, and with their new ideas, their constant experiments, they are causing new blood to flow in the veins of music."[20] By 1919 the *Music Trade Review* proclaimed that "jazz music and jazz dancing are not novelties; they are accepted by the public at large. Their apostles run into the thousands."[21] Frank Peterson's 1922 article in the highly respected *Musical Courier* pointed out that "[Jazz] expresses our American nature—and as long as our nature is expressed by anything so simple and straightforward we will have no cause to worry. When our nature becomes so complex that we need the high art of Europe, or something similar to express it, it will then be time to realize that we are getting old and effete."[22]

As you can see and might expect, the reception of jazz in its earliest phase was very mixed though, according to jazz historian James Lincoln Collier, American magazines ran over 100 articles about jazz between 1917 and 1929 (still only about 8 a year) and "only a small minority of them" were hostile.[23] There were those that loudly applauded this new music and its creators, lauding these jazzmen as explorers of a new style of music that accurately represented contemporary society and could serve as an American emblem. Others just wanted it to go away, much like parents in the 1960s hoped that rock and roll and the Beatles would be a passing fancy. Fortunately the nay-sayers were wrong about jazz and at this point nothing could stop its progress.

Jazz in Perspective

The timeline that follows will put the developments of jazz discussed in this chapter into a larger historical context, providing you with a better sense of how landmark musical events may relate to others that match your personal areas of interest.

1917
- The United States enters World War I.
- Original Dixieland Jazz Band issues first 78-rpm recording that sells 1.5 million copies. Victor Records and New York press call it "jass."

1918
- Ironically, a New Orleans paper (the *Times-Picayune*) declared jazz "a musical vice" urging people of New Orleans to "be the last to accept the atrocity in polite society . . . and make it a point of civic honor to repress it."[24]
- War ends in Europe.

1919
- Signing of the Versailles Treaty officially ends World War I and Original Dixieland Jazz band plays at the signing party.
- Race riots mark "Red Summer" in Chicago.

1920
- Census shows growing urban population with rural figures dropping to only 30 percent of total. Illiteracy falls to 6 percent and life expectancy increases to age 54.
- Prohibition begins making production, sale, and transportation of alcoholic beverages illegal.

- Negro baseball league formed.
- Women's Suffrage Constitutional Amendment takes effect, winning them the right to vote.
- Radio station KDKA begins regular weekly broadcasts from Pittsburgh, Pennsylvania.

1921
- Jazz pianist Earl Hines makes the first live broadcast on KDKA radio.
- James P. Johnson records "Carolina Shout."
- The town of Zion, Illinois, bans public performance of jazz.
- America experiences worst economic depression since 1914.

1922
- The flapper marks end of Victorian age for U.S. women who now smoke and drink in public places, often wearing flashy clothing.
- Paul Whiteman's recording of "Whispering" sells 2 million copies.
- Kid Ory's Sunshine Orchestra becomes first black jazz band to record.

- Significant publications by authors James Joyce (*Ulysses*) and T. S. Elliot (*Waste Land*).

1923
- First jazz broadcast on radio live from Chicago.
- Russian inventor predicts television.
- Joe "King" Oliver records "Dippermouth Blues" with his Creole Jazz Band featuring Louis Armstrong.
- New Orleans Rhythm Kings become the first white jazz band to record with a musician of color.
- Officials around the country express concerns over teen dance marathons.

1924
- Paul Whiteman's "Experiment in Modern Music" features George Gershwin's *Rhapsody in Blue.*
- IBM is founded.
- Teapot Dome Scandal.

1925
- Composer/conductor Igor Stravinsky makes American debut conducting the New York Philharmonic in a program of his own music.

- Sinclair Lewis' *Arrowsmith* is published and F. Scott Fitzgerald releases *The Great Gatsby.*
- Florida State legislature requires daily Bible readings in all public schools.
- Tennessee passes law forbidding the teaching of any evolutionary theories that deny creationism.
- Attorneys William Jennings Bryan and Clarence Darrow fight court battle over legality of teaching evolution.

1926
- First liquid fuel rocket pioneered by Robert Goddard is launched.
- Hemingway authors first novel *The Sun Also Rises.*
- Langston Hughes publishes *The Weary Blues.*
- NBC is incorporated.
- Movies becoming most popular form of American entertainment, making Douglas Fairbanks, Greta Garbo, John Barrymore, and Charlie Chaplin national figures. A new era in pictures with sound begins.

CHAPTER SUMMARY

The 1920s represented a time of social, technological, and economic change in America that greatly influenced the growth of early jazz. The newly established recording industry, the advent of radio, a quickly growing music publishing industry, and improvements in transportation enabled this new music to spread quickly. Those rebelling against Victorian values embraced the freedom expressed by improvised music. Prohibition was a conservative reaction to this freedom, and since jazz musicians often played in clubs illegally selling alcohol, they became linked in the minds of conservatives to organized crime and general moral decay.

Early jazz groups were composed of a front line (most typically cornet, clarinet, and trombone) and a second line (the early rhythm section) since they evolved from street parade and funeral bands. The instrumentation of the second line varied considerably, but generally included a bass instrument (tuba, bass sax, or string bass), a chording instrument (banjo, or guitar, with or without piano), and drums. Because of limitations in the recording technology of the day, the drummer would often play wood blocks and other softer sounds to avoid distortion and balance problems. The groups tended to play in a very contrapuntal style (more than one important musical line played simultaneously).

The Original Dixieland Jazz Band (ODJB), a group of white musicians originally from New Orleans, made the earliest known instrumental jazz recording in 1917 in New York. Their music featured very little improvisation, but they enjoyed tremendous popularity. Cornetist Joe "King" Oliver, on the other hand, led an important early jazz band (Creole Jazz Band) that placed emphasis on improvisation. Jelly Roll Morton (Ferdinand LaMothe) was an early jazz pianist/bandleader and the first notable arranger who is known for his claim as the inventor of jazz.

Louis Armstrong is universally acknowledged as the first great jazz soloist. His technique, range, and rhythmic feel on cornet (later trumpet) were far beyond that of any of his contemporaries. More importantly, Louis Armstrong's improvisations showed an understanding of harmony and rhythm without peer. He also is recognized as the father of scat singing (improvising vocally using nonsense syllables). Having performed around the world, Louis Armstrong became an international star.

KEY TERMS

Important terms, people, places, and bands.

TERMS	PEOPLE	PLACES
Prohibition Act	Earl Hines	Tin Pan Alley
Creole	F. Scott Fitzgerald	Cotton Club
arpeggio	Langston Hughes	Storyville
gliss (glissando)	Alain Locke	
tailgate	Sidney Bechet	**BANDS**
obligato	Kid Ory	Original Dixieland Jazz Band
solo break	Buddy Bolden	Creole Jazz Band
walking bass	Joe "King" Oliver	Red Hot Peppers
double time	Louis Armstrong	Hot Five and Hot Seven
diatonic	Nick LaRocca	Blue 7
Vibrato	Lilian Hardin	Red Onions
scat	Jelly Roll Morton	
woodwind doubler	Fletcher Henderson	
	Clarence Williams	
	James P. Johnson	

REVIEW QUESTIONS

1. How was jazz perceived and received in the 1920s? Make sure that both opinions are presented.

2. New businesses and technologies in the '20s supported the growth, dissemination, and rapid spread of jazz. Discuss these innovations and how jazz was closely intertwined with them.

3. Where was Tin Pan Alley and what was its significance to early jazz?

4. Describe the social mood of the "jazz age."

5. Why was New Orleans such an ethnic, cultural melting pot?

6. What is meant by the term Creole?

7. What evidence supports the notion that many early New Orleans jazz musicians were Creoles, or at least had French ancestry?

8. Brass bands were popular in New Orleans in late 1800s and the earliest years of the twentieth century. What roles did they play?

9. What is meant by the second line?

10. What cities other than New Orleans supported the early growth of jazz?

11. What instruments might have filled out the rhythm section in an early New Orleans jazz band?

12. What were the usual wind instruments heard in an early New Orleans jazz band and what were their musical roles?

13. Why is it that we do not have a true picture of what early jazz band drummers sounded like?

14. What is the significance of the Original Dixieland Jazz Band?

15. Describe the style of music played by the ODJB.

16. Where and when was the first instrumental jazz recording made?

17. Who was one of the first successful women in jazz?

18. "Dippermouth Blues" bears some of the characteristics associated with many pieces from the period. What are they?

19. Where was most of the music recorded by transplanted New Orleans musicians?

20. Who is considered the first important jazz composer-arranger?

21. What aspects of Jelly Roll Morton's music made it unique and original for the times?

22. Who is considered to be the first great jazz soloist?

23. What characteristics made Louis Armstrong a true innovator?

24. What is scat and who was the first to popularize it?

25. What is the first recorded song to feature a scat solo and when was it recorded?

26. What jazz artist became the first significant international entertainer?

27. What is meant by the term woodwind "doubler" and who was considered the first?

28. What instrument did Sidney Bechet prefer over the clarinet?

29. Name some of the well-known "Harlem pianists."

30. What are the primary differences between the ragtime and stride styles?

31. What were rent parties and cutting contests?

32. Who is remembered as the "father of stride piano"?

33. Before the popularity of the trumpet, early brass men played the _____?

SUGGESTED SUPPLEMENTARY LISTENING

The abbreviation (iT) indicates that a particular recording cited in the text, or particularly demonstrative of the artist, is available from the Apple iTunes Web site. Other Web-based music distributors may also prove to be valuable resources. SCCJ indicates *Smithsonian Collection of Classic Jazz*.

The Complete Original Dixieland Jazz Band, Jazz Tribune No. 70
Paul Whiteman and His Orchestra Jazz Archives No. 37 157642
Kid Ory and His Creole Jazz Band 1922–1947 Document Records
  DOCD-1002.
James P. Johnson: Victory Stride, Musicmasters 01612-67140-2
James P. John Snowy Morning Blues GRP (iT)
King Oliver's Creole Jazz Band, Jazz Archives No. 13, 157462
Clarence Williams 1924–1926 I, Classics Records 695

Louis Armstrong

Milestone Classic Jazz: Louis Armstrong and King Oliver Milestone (iT)
  (includes "Chimes Blues" and several alternate takes for comparison)
Louis Armstrong—The Hot Fives Vol. I, Columbia CK 44049 (includes "Heebie
  Jeebies")
Ken Burns Jazz: Louis Armstrong Sony (iT)
Ken Burns Jazz: Sidney Bechet Sony (iT)
"Big Butter and Egg Man" SCCJ (iT)
"Potato Head Blues" SCCJ (iT)
"Struttin' With Some Barbecue" SCCJ (iT)
"Hotter Than That" SCCJ (iT)
"Heebie Jeebies" (iT)
"Weather Bird" SCCJ
"Sweethearts on Parade" SCCJ (iT)
"I Gotta Right to Sing the Blues" SCCJ (iT)
"Chimes Blues" (iT)
"Tears" (iT)

Sidney Bechet

The Complete Sidney Bechet, Jazz Tribune No. 10 RCA 66498-2
"Cake Walking Babies from Home" SCCJ
"Blue Horizon" SCCJ

Jelly Roll Morton

Jelly Roll Morton Library of Congress Recordings: Vol. 3 The Pearls Rounder (iT)
Jelly Roll Morton Library of Congress Recordings: Vol. 4 Winin' Boy Blues
  Rounder (iT)
Mr. Jelly Lord/Jelly Roll Morton, Tomato, 700692
Jelly Roll Morton 1923/1924 Milestone (iT)

"Dead Man Blues" SCCJ (iT)
"King Porter Stomp" SCCJ (iT)
"Grandpa's Spells" SCCJ (iT)
"Maple Leaf Rag" SCCJ (iT)
"The Pearls" (iT)

The Jazz Age
From Chicago to New York

"The first World War had been fought, and in the back-wash conventions had tumbled. There was rebellion then, against the accepted, and the proper and the old. . . . The shooting war was over but the rebellion was just getting started. And for us jazz articulated . . . what we wanted to say."[1]

HOAGY CARMICHAEL

While New Orleans was the epicenter of jazz, the aftershock was felt far and wide. Other cities that did most to support this new wave in American music were Chicago and New York. Both of these northern cities supported a tremendous influx of African-Americans between 1916 and 1930. About 500,000 sought a better way of life and moved from southern locations to northern cities between 1916 and 1919. More than 1 million more left the South in the decade that followed. Chicago and New York had become ethnic melting pots with a more diverse collection of European immigrants, blacks and whites, than any place in the world.

SOUTH SIDE OF CHICAGO

The south side of Chicago, known as the "vice district" or the "Levee," became the new home for many enterprising blacks during the 1920s. They launched business ventures catering to leisure time activities. Many of these establishments supported black entertainers and fostered a sense of racial pride in the south side. The cabarets and saloons were often referred to as **black and tans** since they catered to a mixed black and white clientele. In a 20-block area of Chicago's "vice district," one could find a staggering number of saloons, variety theaters, gambling houses, pool rooms, and bordellos.[2] It is no small wonder that the south side of Chicago in the 1920s was a magnet for black entertainers who found good-paying jobs plentiful. Many

The Carrol Dickerson band backs the floor show at Chicago's black-and-tan Sunset Café in 1922. When Louis Armstrong joined the orchestra four years later, Dickerson (center on violin) would be shunted aside in favor of the trumpet star.

transplanted New Orleans jazz musicians practiced their trade in the Levee District such as Freddie Keppard, Kid Ory, Joe Oliver, Louis Armstrong, Jelly Roll Morton, Lilian Hardin, Earl Hines, and Jimmy Noone, among others.

There was always a threat of police raids in the Levee District, which, as author William Kenney points out, "seemed to contribute just the right note of excitement to Chicago's jazz scene, mixing the new styles of personal liberation . . . [and] adding drama to the new music."[3] But if it wasn't the police, it was the Juvenile Protective Association (JPA) that was making life difficult for those who frequented the vice district. Essentially a temperance society, the JPA had made it their mission to curb the sins of Chicago's youth, whom they perceived as negatively influenced by the lure of the Levee District. The south-side "black and tans" were in the business of selling "suggestive African-American musical entertainment which helped customers to create an atmosphere of inter-racial sensuality," according to Kenny.[4] This atmosphere did draw a good deal of negative press from right-wing groups with conservative ideologies. For example, the New York published *American* issued the following warnings in its January 22, 1922, article entitled "Jazz Ruining Girls, Declares Reformer: Degrading Music Even Common in Society Circles, Says Vigilance Association Head."

Moral disaster is coming to hundreds of young American girls through patho-logical, nerve-irritating, sex-exciting music of jazz orchestras, according to the Illinois Vigilance Association. In Chicago alone the association's representa-tives have traced the fall of 1,000 girls in the last two years to jazz music. Girls in small towns, as well as the big cities, in poor homes and rich homes, are victims of the weird, insidious, neurotic music that accompanies modern dancing.

"The degrading music is common not only to disorderly places, but often to high school affairs, to expensive hotels and so-called society circles," de-clares Rev. Phillip Yarrow, superintendent of the Vigilance Association. The re-port says that the vigilance society has no desire to abolish dancing, but seeks to awaken the public conscience to the present danger and future conse-quences of jazz music.[5]

This New York press was not alone, as many other articles appeared in news-papers and music trade magazines that denigrated the increasingly popular new music. They often carried similar vigilante themes and rarely offered any real analysis or specific criticism of the music. For example, *Etude* ran an article in the January 1925 edition entitled "Is Jazz the Pilot of Disaster?" and *Metronome* printed the following in a 1923 article: "I can say from my knowledge that about 50% of our young boys and girls from the age 16 to 25 that land in the insane asylum these days are jazz-crazy dope fiends and public dance hall patrons. Jazz combinations—dope fiends and public dance halls—are all the same. Where you find one you will find the other."[6] While jazz was not without its critics in the 1920s, it also had its champions. Some writers about jazz made an effort to dis-criminate between "highbrow" and "lowbrow" jazz. In other words, they differen-tiated between good and bad jazz. The *Musical Quarterly* published an article in 1926 by Edwin J. Stringham in which he attempts to set the record straight about good and bad jazz. He said that "there are two sides to the Jazz question. This form of music . . . has been denounced far and wide as being of immoral charac-ter. I have in mind only the better type of jazz; that which is composed by under-standing musicians, that which is well conceived and written according to ordinary esthetical and technical standards."[7] Like so many early writers on the subject of jazz, Stringham failed to see that this music could not be judged and held to the same standards and practices associated with traditional European classical music and that it must be assessed by different criteria. His appreciation of jazz was ob-viously directed at the more symphonic style associated with Paul Whiteman. Re-gardless of the growing press and public debates inspired by jazz, the appeal and lure of the music was far too great for a few negative articles to abate its attraction to young Americans.

AND ON THE OTHER SIDE OF TOWN

The north and west sides of Chicago, inhabited by middle- and upper-class whites, offered dance halls and cabarets. A few even employed black performers though they were far from fully integrated. Many of these nightspots featured dance bands that included some jazz-like numbers as part of their repertoire, since this was the music that many young whites wanted to hear. Social dancing was a driving force of the entertainment industry in the 1920s and was a primary form of entertainment for upwardly mobile white audiences. By the 1920s, there was already a distinction between the ensembles that included orchestral instruments like strings and those that did not. Those ensembles featuring orchestral instrumentation and largely dance-oriented repertoire were categorized as "sweet" bands and the black south side bands were termed "hot" jazz bands. The sometimes-bitter debates that continue to rage among fans and critics advocating for one of these two sides actually began at the advent of instrumental jazz. Some gave little credence to those white bands that largely played sweet dance music with little improvisation but billed themselves as jazz bands. In order to appease both sides of this debate, many bandleaders like Isham Jones, who played popular dance halls in Chicago frequented by white clientele, employed a few jazz soloists so that they could respond to the growing request for hot jazz by the younger generation. These younger white patrons demanded music similar to what they had heard in the South side cabarets. "School dances, fraternity parties and the like became major venues for jazz and dance bands in the late 1920s. Many of the major college campuses gave birth to their own bands organized by students with or without the sanction of school officials. For example, Princeton, Harvard, Yale, Texas University and the University of Chicago all spawned jazz bands during the late 1920s."[8]

The Juvenile Protective Association (JPA) and other urban reform groups actively monitored many of the Chicago dance halls. They actually urged dance hall managers to speed up the tempos in order to encourage respectable dancing at arms length. There was a demand for fast paced dance music that was morally sterile. "Cooperation between dance hall entrepreneurs and urban reformers shaped the commercialization of the dance craze and created a demand for fast paced 'peppy,' but morally sanitary, jazz age social dance music."[9] Some say that these sanctions are largely responsible for the faster tempos that are generally agreed upon to be an identifying characteristic of Chicago jazz. According to New Orleans' banjoist Johnny St. Cyr, "the fastest numbers played by old New Orleans bands were slower than . . . the Chicago tempo."[10] Organizations like the JPA considered a night of dancing for their young people less harmful than a bout with liquor or associations with "people of color" on the south side.

Dance orchestras led by Paul Whiteman, known eventually as the "King of Jazz" thanks to his publicists, Guy Lombardo (Royal Canadians), Vincent Lopez, and Art Hickman who frequented Chicago hotel ballrooms and north side dance halls were paid thousands of dollars for a week-long engagement. This was no small sum considering the fact that an automobile could be purchased for well under $1,000! Those few "hot" jazz players who were hired to add spice to the dance repertoire played by these "sweet" bands often used this opportunity to refine their basic music reading skills and put good money in their pockets as they were often paid some of the highest salaries.

Young white Chicago musicians idolized the Black New Orleans musicians for their free spirit and ability to play unencumbered "real" jazz. To many of these young north and west side Chicago youth, jazz represented freedom and a breaking away from the authoritarian demands of their elders. "Jazz seemed to

Chicago's south-side Midway Gardens outdoor ballroom.

express artistic alienation from middle-class materialism,"[11] according to William Kenny. Some of these young white musicians, like clarinetist Mez Mezzrow, strove to emulate their black idols in every way—adopting their speech patterns and general lifestyles. Many young white Chicago musicians like Benny Goodman, the son of immigrant parents, and Bud Freeman, had a distinct advantage over the black New Orleans musicians. Being schooled musicians, able to read and execute difficult music as well as play jazz, their background opened up numerous opportunities that were unavailable to some black musicians who may have lacked formal training. These young white players nevertheless did everything they could to emulate the best of black jazz they had heard in the south side establishments.

THE CHICAGO SOUND

Bud Freeman, Jimmy McPartland, Frankie Teschemacher, and Dave Tough were all members of Chicago's white middle class and became known as the Austin High Gang. For some reason much has been made in the jazz history annals about the Austin High Gang, when in fact many of the musicians actually responsible for

The Wolverines in the Gennett recording studio in Richmond, Indiana, February 18, 1924. Left to right: Min Lelbrook (tuba), Jimmy Hartwell (clarinet), George Johnson (tenor saxophone), Bob Gillette (banjo), Vic Moore (drums), Dick Voynow (piano), Bix Beiderbecke (cornet), Al Gandee (trombone).

what became identified as the Chicago jazz sound had no relationship to this middle-class suburban high school. Many came to Chicago from elsewhere and many others actually became known only after leaving Chicago to perform and record elsewhere. It is these white musicians, regardless of their origins, who created the Chicago sound. As you will see in the following pages, the Chicago style serves as a transition to the big band swing era that follows and in some ways serves as a distant prelude to the "cool" jazz sounds of the 1950s. The following list of characteristics helps to define the Chicago jazz style.

- While there is some debate, there is evidence to support that the average tempo increased during the Chicago period as compared to the earlier New Orleans style.

- The saxophone appears as a regular, new member of the bands. By 1927 even first-generation New Orleans jazz cornetist Joe Oliver had added this new, emerging instrument to his band, and Armstrong fronted a large band with saxophones a year later.

- Most Chicago bands featured some New Orleans style polyphony, but the soloist begins to emerge, relegating other band members to more background roles during a solo.

- Chicago bands reflect a refinement of style and instrumental polish not associated with many early New Orleans bands.

- Individual musicianship appears to be on the rise in terms of technique, tone production, and the ability to read music.

- Further evidence of this polish and sophistication is that the ensembles seem less haphazard, with a greater emphasis placed on the arrangement and well-rehearsed ensemble performance.
- Rhythm sections are significantly more advanced and playing techniques have improved. The tuba gradually becomes replaced by the string bass and the guitar becomes favored over the banjo. This transition, however, is slow and the banjo and tuba can still be found in early 1930s big bands.
- The rhythm sections in some bands begin to create a new playing style. The earlier New Orleans two-beat style, reminiscent of the marches and rags that implied a 2/4 meter by emphasizing beats one and three (even if it was in 4/4 meter), was transformed by featuring walking bass lines and accents that imply 4/4 meter.
- The cornet is gradually phased out in favor of the trumpet.
- Some of the earlier white and black bands engaged in gimmicky, novelty music (using instruments to imitate animal sounds and the like), called "nut" music. The more sophisticated Chicago approach did not include this "nut" style.
- Motivated largely by Chicago's south-side black musicians, the new breed of white, Chicago musicians were more likely to pattern their playing after the refined and advanced techniques demonstrated by artists like Louis Armstrong and Jimmy Noone, rather than adopting the rougher, less polished early New Orleans style.
- Chicago bands began to expand in size and instrumentation.

NEW ORLEANS RHYTHM KINGS (NORK)

Perhaps the most influential group of white musicians to emerge in the early 1920s that helped define a new Chicago sound was the New Orleans Rhythm Kings (NORK). The pianist and arranger for this group was Elmer Schoebel, who composed "Bugle Call Rag" and "Prince of Wails." It was his influence on the NORK and his arrangements written for the NORK and other bands that helped to forge the new sound of jazz associated with the "windy city." The NORK based their sound in part on the black New Orleans style of polyphonic jazz, but their arrangements tended to favor a more sophisticated and organized sound. Their repertoire was similar to the New Orleans bands, but featured an amalgamation of blues, rag-based, and dance tunes. Some feel that many of the white bands like the NORK that emerged during the Chicago period were little more than dressed up, more polished, and in some cases, watered down versions of the New Orleans black style. Others viewed the new sound as a natural progression in refining what had come before.

The NORK in 1923 became the first white band to record with a musician of color, when it invited Jelly Roll Morton to record several sides with the group including his own "Mr. Jelly Lord" and "London Blues." Black and white musicians may have associated with one another in the black and tans of Chicago's south side, or for that matter in the Harlem district of New York, but it had been largely forbidden for people of color to mix publicly on the bandstand until Benny Goodman broke the unwritten ban on racially mixed bands in the late 1930s.

The NORK, first known as the Friars Society Club Orchestra, made its first recording in 1922, becoming the first Chicago based jazz band to record. Isham Jones' society, "sweet" dance band actually recorded a few months earlier, but their repertoire was more for dancing and not considered jazz. The original NORK included Paul Mares on cornet, George Brunies on trombone, Leon Ropollo on clarinet, Jack Pettis on C–melody or tenor saxophone, Schoebel on piano, Lou Black on banjo, Steve Brown on bass, and Frank Snyder on drums. As you can see, the NORK was a fairly large band sporting eight musicians.

The group's cornetist Paul Mares is quoted to have said "we did our best to copy the colored music we'd heard at home [New Orleans]. We did the best we could, but naturally we couldn't play real colored style."[12] Their influence was widespread and they made significant improvements in playing a smoother, more legato phrased style of jazz; however, as a group they never made a major impact at the time.

The first NORK recordings predated those made by Joe "King" Oliver by seven months, but there is no doubt that he, along with the New Orleans bands that had moved to Chicago, provided the primary inspiration for the formation of the Chicago jazz sound. The recordings made by Louis Armstrong's Hot Five and Hot Seven bands in the mid-1920s embodied both the spirit of earlier New Orleans bands and the new trend to spotlight the soloist more than had been the case in the earlier New Orleans groups. The white NORK and other Chicago-style bands followed this same path forged by Armstrong and other prominent black bandleaders.

The New Orleans Rhythm Kings (NORK) at the Friar's Inn, Chicago, in 1922. George Brunies plays trombone, Paul Mares is on cornet, and Leon Ropollo plays the clarinet.

A FEW AMONG MANY

Bix Beiderbecke (1903–1931) and Frankie Trumbauer (1901–1956)

Cornetist Leon Bix Beiderbecke and saxophonist Frankie Trumbauer are undoubtedly the most well-known Chicago era musicians. Ironically, neither Beiderbecke nor Trumbauer was a native Chicagoan. Beiderbecke was a transplanted Iowan, whose parents had sent him to a private academy in Chicago in hopes of bringing some discipline to their son and curbing his "unnatural obsession" with music. Beiderbecke had been a truant child in Iowa where he studied piano and became infatuated with jazz. Chicago was certainly the wrong city for him to learn about discipline and take his education seriously since the vibrant jazz atmosphere on the south side was a distraction and only encouraged him to further pursue his musical obsessions.

While Beiderbecke had access to formal music training, he largely rejected it in favor of his own, unorthodox style that was in part responsible for his unique tone quality and identity on the cornet. For example, he often used the wrong fingerings to produce certain notes on his cornet. He played both piano and cornet largely by ear and only learned to read music later in his career when the demands of reading written-out arrangements in large ensembles required it.

His first school band was The Rhythm Jugglers, but he was not heard around town until he joined the Wolverines. The Wolverines played at school dances and parties, imitating the sounds of black bands they had heard in the south-side cabarets, and white bands such as the NORK. Beiderbecke was actually never recorded in Chicago and in 1925 he left the Wolverines, moving to Detroit to take a job with the Jean Goldkette Orchestra. Goldkette commanded a large stable of society bands that performed throughout the Midwest and was based in Detroit. At one time he controlled as many as 20 bands, and his primary ensemble was

Bix Beiderbecke and the Wolverines, 1924. Bix is seated at the far right.

known to have squarely beaten the great Fletcher Henderson New York band in a battle of the bands. Beiderbecke's position with the Goldkette orchestra was merely a stepping stone before moving on to record with saxophonist Frankie Trumbauer's small group. The two had become acquainted in Goldkette's Orchestra and both joined the popular Paul Whiteman Orchestra along with a number of other renegades from the Goldkette outfit.

By the time Beiderbecke made the move to the Whiteman Orchestra, he had become known for his unique style that was in stark contrast to the hot players of the day like Louis Armstrong. Beiderbecke had a more lyrical sound that projected a sense of "subdued passion." In contrast to the flashy, double-timing Armstrong, his solo breaks might consist of only one note, repeated with slight shadings or inflections. Most consider Beiderbecke to be the first in a long line of "cool" style musicians that represented a departure from the "hot" school of playing associated with Armstrong. His long-time friend and popular songwriter Hoagy Carmichael (who composed "Stardust" and often booked Beiderbecke at Indiana University) described his sound as "pure, resembling a chime struck by a mallet."[13] You would never hear him adding a buzzing growl or thick wide vibrato to his sound as was the case with most black players of the day.

He had an obvious knowledge, or at least a keen natural sense of harmony, that he demonstrated in several piano compositions that reflect the popular 1920s French Impressionistic classical style of composition. His composition "In a Mist," notated for publication by Whiteman arranger Bill Challis since Beiderbecke was unskilled at such things, serves as an excellent example of this sophisticated, almost classical piano style which was never evident in his jazz cornet playing.

Ironically it is the recordings that Beiderbecke made with Frankie Trumbauer, and a few with Whiteman, that made him famous, but not until long after his untimely death in 1931 at age 28. Tuberculosis, alcoholism, and a generally reckless, bohemian lifestyle contributed to his poor health during the last several years of his life. While he was greatly admired by black and white musicians, he was not particularly well known by the general public during his lifetime. This obscurity may seem undeserved since his recordings, although not made in Chicago, have ultimately surfaced as those that help to signify and define the Chicago jazz sound. While Beiderbecke lives on in the annals of jazz history as the first great white performer, his band mate Frankie Trumbauer enjoyed a less illustrious career even though his contributions were significant. Frankie "Tram" Trumbauer (1901–1956) played the C-melody saxophone that was considered by many the black sheep of the saxophone family.

The C-melody saxophone sounds between the E♭-alto and the B♭-tenor, though its size more closely resembles the tenor sax. It was known for its unique tone quality, somewhere in between the alto and tenor. The C-melody was popular among amateurs because it did not require any music transposition. It was pitched in the key of C, enabling the performer to read from piano music, making it a good choice for at-home, family parlor sing-a-longs. The only other instrumentalist of note who played the C-melody saxophone was Rudy Wiedoeft who single-handedly popularized the saxophone in the United States from about 1917 to 1927. He was a popular radio and vaudeville performer who was perhaps the first to record a section of four saxophones in 1920. His technique and articulation was impressive, as were the flashy showpieces that he composed to showcase the instrument and his facility. Saxophone historian Ted Hegvik wrote that Wiedoeft "took the saxophone—an instrument without a style, a literature, or an artistic example—and, in supplying it with all of these, created the 'saxophone craze' of the 1920s."[14] It is only recently that historians have begun to realize the great influence that Wiedoeft, who was not a jazz saxophonist, exerted on early jazz players like Trumbauer.

Trumbauer recorded his first important solo in 1923 and through this recording became an immediate influence on black and white saxophonists. Like Beiderbecke, Trumbauer's sound was smooth, lyrical, and cool and his rhythmic phrasing rarely demonstrated much syncopation or thick, wide vibrato. He was a brilliant technician, following the path that Wiedoeft so deftly cleared. His solos were so well crafted they appeared premeditated and had a gracefulness that served as an antithesis to the hot school of jazz playing. Richard Sudhalter, author of *Lost Chords,* described his playing as "elegant and debonair."[15] He was of great influence on a future generation of jazz saxophonists like Lester Young who carefully studied and memorized his recorded solo on "Singin' the Blues," included on the companion audio anthology. This single solo turned the saxophone world on its ear and became the subject of future arrangements where the entire solo was quoted note for note. Every saxophonist, black or white, learned this solo and frequently quoted from it in their own solos. Most historians believe that Trumbauer's best work occurred during his four-year association with Bix Beiderbecke as members of the Goldkette and Whiteman Orchestras. The small group recordings that stemmed from these associations showed a unique musical kinship that Beiderbecke and Trumbauer shared. They not only complemented each other, but also seemed to feed off of the contrasts that they created.

"For No Reason At All in C" is another stunning Trumbauer performance that features an unusual trio of Beiderbecke on piano and Eddie Lang on guitar. Lang incidentally was one of the finest early jazz guitarists who came out of Chicago. Trumbauer ignores the theme in favor of improvising on the chord scheme of this old standard tune. While it is certainly not bebop, one could consider this recording an early predecessor of this style yet to come.

Following Beiderbecke's early death, Trumbauer left the Whiteman Orchestra in 1936 to strike out on his own. He performed and recorded briefly with the "Three T's," a group of Whiteman sidemen consisting of the Texas trombone sensation Jack Teagarden and his brother Charlie Teagarden, who played trumpet. Trumbauer's contributions to jazz, however, waned after Beiderbecke's death and he retired from the music business in 1940 for a career in aviation.

A number of features associated with the Chicago style are apparent in this classic Trumbauer-Beiderbecke recording, namely, the prominent use of the saxophone, greater solo space with less reliance on Dixieland style full ensemble, a clear four-beat emphasis that begins with Beiderbecke's solo, and the elevated role of the guitar as compared to the earlier use of banjo.

Saxophonist Frankie Trumbauer with guitarist Carl Kress.

Listening Guide

Frankie Trumbauer and His Orchestra

"Singin' the Blues"
(McHugh-Fields) 2:59

Recorded 2/4/27

(Okeh 40772)

Frankie Trumbauer:
C-melody saxophone

Bix Beiderbecke:
cornet

Bill Rank: *trombone*

Jimmy Dorsey: *clarinet,*
alto saxophone

Paul Mertz: *piano*

Eddie Lang: *guitar*

Chauncey Morehouse:
drums

Key and Form: E-flat Major; 32-bar theme divided into four 8-bar sections (ABA[1]C)

0:00–0:06	4-bar instrumental intro without rhythm section
0:07–0:20	*First Chorus:* Trumbauer solos on C-melody sax accompanied by piano and guitar (8 measures total)

0:21–0:34	Second Section; Trumbauer continues his solo ending the section with 2-bar solo break (8 measures total)
0:35–1:02	Final Section; Trumbauer continues in improvised style solo (notice how guitarist mimics fast sax triplet passage moments later); 2-bar break ends first chorus (16 measures total)

1:03–1:16	*Second Chorus:* Beiderbecke solos on cornet for 8 measures

1:17–1:31	Beiderbecke continues solo ending the section with 2-bar break, that begins with a double time phrase and ends with an Armstrong-like ascending rip to anticipate the last phrase of the chorus
1:32	Beiderbecke continues to solo for the final 16 measures of the form

2:00–2:13	*Final Chorus:* Dixieland polyphonic style full ensemble section

2:14–2:28	Dorsey plays clarinet solo quoting Hoagy Carmichael's famous "Stardust" (at 2:22–2:24)
2:29–2:42	Full ensemble Dixieland style
2:43–end	Full ensemble with a one measure guitar solo break.

Paul Whiteman (1890–1967) and Symphonic Jazz

In the words of jazz historian Marshall Stearns, "If the ODJB [Original Dixieland Jazz Band] made jazz a household word in 1917, Paul Whiteman made it semi-respectable in 1924."[16] When Paul Whiteman founded his orchestra in 1919 he wisely employed Ferde Grofé, stealing him away from Art Hickman's West Coast band. Pianist and arranger for Whiteman, Grofé is credited as a pioneer in developing concepts in arranging and composing for the large dance and symphonic orchestras. Both Whiteman and Grofé had similar backgrounds, having been schooled in the European classical tradition, so it is no surprise that this training became the basis of their style. Early writer and critic Henry Osgood referred to Grofé as "the father of modern jazz orchestration." While this might be a slight exaggeration, there is no doubt that he, along with Bill Challis, were largely responsible for the widespread success of Whiteman's orchestra. "Grofé's arrangements for Whiteman of "Whispering," "Japanese Sandman," "Avalon," and scores of other songs, became enormous sellers in 1920, and the years just after, and they made Whiteman the most celebrated bandleader of the period. An excerpt of "Whispering" is used on the CD-ROM. Perhaps the most acclaimed performance by the Whiteman Orchestra was his 1924 "Experiment in American Music" at which he premiered Grofé's orchestration of George Gershwin's "Rhapsody in Blue." In this concert, Whiteman dressed jazz in more respectable clothes, making it more appealing to the masses by shedding the barroom atmosphere and ragged musicianship that had been associated with some jazz of the times. Henry Osgood, who penned one of the first books about jazz in 1926, suggested that it was safer and less risky for the public to enjoy Whiteman's brand of jazz, and with his "experimental" concert he had taken "the very first step toward the elevation of jazz to something more than accompaniment for dancing."[17]

The overwhelming press that surrounded the premier of "Rhapsody in Blue," and Whiteman's syndicated book served to add some credence to the title "King of Jazz," coined by his publicist. Whiteman's orchestra, and others who followed his model, reported weekly payrolls in excess of $5,000 per week, a great deal of money in the twenties. (See the Whiteman payroll sheet found in the corresponding chapter on the CD-ROM.)

Historians have not always been kind to Whiteman and he has often been the brunt of criticism by jazz purists. For example, Robert Goffin described Whiteman's recordings as "essentially banal music, but played beautifully by first-rate musicians."[18] According to jazz scholar James Lincoln Collier, these criticisms are unfounded and unfair since about half of Whiteman's recordings featured jazz solos. Had it not been for Whiteman, Chicago artists like Beiderbecke, Jimmy Dorsey, Jack Teagarden, and Frankie Trumbauer, to mention a few, may never have received the widespread exposure that eventually proved to be important to the ongoing development of jazz. Collier also points out that it was Whiteman who introduced the idea of featuring vocalists along with symphonic, jazz-style arrangements, a concept that was capitalized on some years later during the peak of the big band swing era.[19] Both the idea of using singers and strings in the dance band context became a model, laying the groundwork for the success of jazz informed singers like Frank Sinatra who enjoyed great acclaim years later. Whiteman and his arrangers also demonstrated that jazz improvisation could coexist within the tightly arranged framework designed for the large, symphonic style ensemble. Though conservative compared to the authentic jazz combo, the Whiteman symphonic prototype has had a lasting impact on the history of jazz since the 1920s.

"Mississippi Mud" serves as an excellent example of the Whiteman style demonstrating an amalgamation of African-American jazz, popular music and a European style of orchestration. This particular tune also illustrates many of the

Paul Whiteman and his orchestra.

classic devices discussed previously and associated with this orchestra—the vocal solo and group, "scat" singing, the improvised "hot" jazz solo, and orchestrations inspired by the large, European classical-like ensemble.

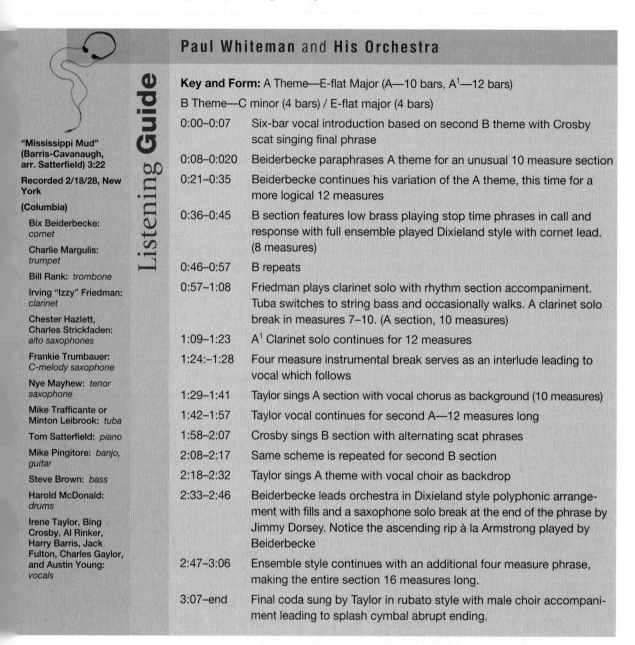

Listening Guide

Paul Whiteman and His Orchestra

"Mississippi Mud" (Barris-Cavanaugh, arr. Satterfield) 3:22

Recorded 2/18/28, New York

(Columbia)

Bix Beiderbecke: *cornet*

Charlie Margulis: *trumpet*

Bill Rank: *trombone*

Irving "Izzy" Friedman: *clarinet*

Chester Hazlett, Charles Strickfaden: *alto saxophones*

Frankie Trumbauer: *C-melody saxophone*

Nye Mayhew: *tenor saxophone*

Mike Trafficante or Minton Leibrook: *tuba*

Tom Satterfield: *piano*

Mike Pingitore: *banjo, guitar*

Steve Brown: *bass*

Harold McDonald: *drums*

Irene Taylor, Bing Crosby, Al Rinker, Harry Barris, Jack Fulton, Charles Gaylor, and Austin Young: *vocals*

Key and Form: A Theme—E-flat Major (A—10 bars, A¹—12 bars)

B Theme—C minor (4 bars) / E-flat major (4 bars)

0:00–0:07	Six-bar vocal introduction based on second B theme with Crosby scat singing final phrase
0:08–0:020	Beiderbecke paraphrases A theme for an unusual 10 measure section
0:21–0:35	Beiderbecke continues his variation of the A theme, this time for a more logical 12 measures
0:36–0:45	B section features low brass playing stop time phrases in call and response with full ensemble played Dixieland style with cornet lead. (8 measures)
0:46–0:57	B repeats
0:57–1:08	Friedman plays clarinet solo with rhythm section accompaniment. Tuba switches to string bass and occasionally walks. A clarinet solo break in measures 7–10. (A section, 10 measures)
1:09–1:23	A¹ Clarinet solo continues for 12 measures
1:24:–1:28	Four measure instrumental break serves as an interlude leading to vocal which follows
1:29–1:41	Taylor sings A section with vocal chorus as background (10 measures)
1:42–1:57	Taylor vocal continues for second A—12 measures long
1:58–2:07	Crosby sings B section with alternating scat phrases
2:08–2:17	Same scheme is repeated for second B section
2:18–2:32	Taylor sings A theme with vocal choir as backdrop
2:33–2:46	Beiderbecke leads orchestra in Dixieland style polyphonic arrangement with fills and a saxophone solo break at the end of the phrase by Jimmy Dorsey. Notice the ascending rip à la Armstrong played by Beiderbecke
2:47–3:06	Ensemble style continues with an additional four measure phrase, making the entire section 16 measures long.
3:07–end	Final coda sung by Taylor in rubato style with male choir accompaniment leading to splash cymbal abrupt ending.

BOOGIE-WOOGIE, EIGHT TO THE BAR

Solo pianists learned how marketable they could be in the 1920s since they had the advantage of being employable in almost any venue. The stride style, discussed in more detail in the preceding chapter, was the basis for much of the piano jazz, solo and ensemble, heard throughout the 1920s. Prior to the advent of talking motion pictures, many jazz pianists found employment in movie theaters, where they improvised accompaniments to silent films. In New York, the so-called "Harlem pianists" helped one another pay their rent by staging rent parties. These parties were essentially "cutting contests" where admission was charged to listen to local pianists do battle, one trying to outdo the other's performance. The admission charge collected was applied toward paying the host's rent, or one of the pianists, and the music played was stride and boogie-woogie.

Boogie-woogie was a solo piano style that initially surfaced, to no great attention, in the mid- to late-1920s. A rhythmically charged, blues-inspired style, early boogie-woogie first emerged around 1925. This gregarious, highly improvised style was spawned in roadhouses, barrooms, honky-tonks, and at rent parties. The style utilizes the basic 12-bar blues harmonic scheme and features a strong, repetitive left-hand motive that can resemble a walking bass line. This **ostinato** left-hand pattern usually consists of four pairs of eighth notes—hence the "eight to the bar" description often used (eight 8th-notes complete one 4/4 measure or bar). Pianists added elaborate right-hand melodies to this left-hand accompaniment pattern. Since one hand might imply a different meter than the other, this style requires much independence between right and left hands, as is the case with the stride style.

Pine Top Smith, who recorded "Pine Top's Boogie Woogie" in 1928, helped to popularize this style, which enjoyed a revival in 1938 and flourished well into the early 1940s. Chicago gave birth to several important second-generation contributors to this style—namely, Albert Ammons, Meade "Lux" Lewis, and Jimmy Yancey. Along with work by Pete Johnson and Joe Turner, the Lewis and Ammons recordings were successful enough to encourage the later adoption of this style by the big bands of Count Basie, Tommy Dorsey, and Charlie Barnet among others. The style was diluted during these years, though it was absorbed into the lasting Chicago blues tradition. Even today the blues tradition is maintained in clubs throughout this northern city.

> Time constraints did not allow the inclusion of a boogie-woogie recording on the companion CD audio anthology; however, a short video demonstration is found in the corresponding chapter on the CD-ROM.

THE DECLINE OF THE CHICAGO ERA

There are many factors that led to the steady decline of jazz in Chicago at the close of the 1920s. The most catastrophic economic event sending a shock wave through the entire nation was the stock market crash on "Black Tuesday," October 29, 1929, marking the beginning of the Great Depression. No single event in the history of the United States has eclipsed this economic disaster. The tremendous losses that effectively crippled Wall Street led to a run on banks with millions of Americans withdrawing their life savings for fear of losing it all. For many, it was too late, as banks and businesses across the country failed, leaving record numbers of Americans unemployed and concerned about the well-being of their families. A tremendous new industry had developed around the steady growth in popularity of jazz and much of it came tumbling down. Record and publishing companies, radio manufacturers and networks, cabarets, dance halls and speakeasies, theaters, booking agents, and, of course, musicians all suffered—none were insulated from this American economic tragedy. For example the Gannett record label, which at one

Depositors congregate outside the state-ordered closed doors of the Union Bank of New York City. This was a typical scene following Black Tuesday.

time had under contract many of the top performers, totally collapsed in 1929 as did a number of other labels.

But the Depression was not the only factor responsible for dimming the lights on Chicago's nightlife. By the late 1920s, musicians had begun to steadily migrate to New York, where more opportunities existed especially for recording, and recordings were perceived as a musician's ticket to mass popularity. For many musicians, New York was perceived as the place to be. There certainly were numerous opportunities for employment in dance orchestras that were taking advantage of the widespread dance craze. Some jazz musicians flocked to bands led by Isham Jones, Glen Gray, Jean Goldkette, Ben Pollack, Vincent Lopez, and of course Paul Whiteman among others.

Prohibition, politics, urban reform groups, movies with sound tracks, the closing of some cabarets, and police raids on mob-run speakeasies all contributed to musicians' desires to look for greener pastures. While the Chicago mob, with bosses like Al Capone, helped to provide an environment in the clubs that encouraged the music, their illegal activities also brought unending attention to many establishments that were raided on a regular basis. Some musicians found that the underworld could be your best friend one minute and turn into your worst enemy the next. Pianist Fats Waller was supposedly escorted under gun point from his dinner table to an awaiting car, driven to Al Capone's headquarters in East Cicero, and ordered to play at a surprise birthday party for the gangster. He was tipped handsomely for his trouble, but the money may not have outweighed the mental anguish. Joe Glaser, who eventually became Louis Armstrong's manager, had ties to the Chicago mob. The club that he managed was in reality run by the mob. It was raided so frequently that Armstrong's pianist Earl Hines claimed that he ran for the police paddy wagon at the first sign of a raid so that he could get a good seat![20] The Chicago underworld was then both a friend and a nemesis for the working musician. The government and the courts had closed many of the cabarets by 1928, and, as a result, many of the musicians were forced to look for work in larger dance bands or other cities. By 1928 "250 cabaret entertainers and 200 musicians had lost their jobs."[21]

The attraction to New York and the appeal of Kansas City, fast becoming a wild town in the image of Chicago, lured many away from the windy city. Larger dance-oriented bands and symphonic jazz-style orchestras began to win the battle for public attention in the mid- to late-1920s. There was still an audience for smaller, New Orleans and Chicago style groups, but the public's interest was in larger dance bands. The country was primed for the big band "Swing Era," but Prohibition would have to be repealed and the nation would need to recover from the economic ravages of the Depression before the climate would be right to encourage the most popular and lucrative times ever enjoyed by the jazz musician.

CHICAGO JAZZ IN RETROSPECT

Since the mid-1930s there have been a plethora of books written about jazz, each author with an individual take on the history of jazz. There is no doubt that the "longer view" offers a better perspective to historians and critics. The following viewpoints about F. Scott Fitzgerald's "Jazz Age" will provide some insight into the significance of this period.

Wilder Hobson published *American Jazz Music* in 1939. He offered the following opinions about the Chicago period.

> The Chicago jazz players, Negro and white, of the twenties were for the most part still, in effect, in a folk-musical environment, playing spontaneous music in obscure dance halls and moving on later for impromptu sessions in still more obscure speakeasies. Their music had a very limited white audience and little or no commercial value or publicity. By the late twenties fine jazz playing emerged somewhat into the commercial spotlight. But there was nothing which might have been called a public demand for, or recognition of, the jazz language.[22]

Hobson went on to describe Chicago jazz as "a blend of the 'negros' personal intensity and a linear economy suggestive of Bix Beiderbecke."[23] While some of Hobson's comments about the twenties are valid, many of his observations serve to show that he was out of touch with the reality of the 1920s and what it meant to the advancement of jazz. Hobson's book is, nevertheless, considered the first jazz criticism book of real value to be published by an American. French author Hugues Panassié first published *Hot Jazz* in America in 1934. The French author insisted that Chicago jazz was a "white appropriation"[24] of music created by black musicians. It is important to mention that Panassié never traveled to the United States to witness jazz firsthand prior to the writing of his first book on the subject. Author Rudi Blesh agreed with Panassié and referred to Chicago jazz as "white imitations of Negro jazz, sincere but not profound."[25] Blesh also felt that many good "Negro" musicians had been tainted and spoiled by the commercial influences of white jazz. Contemporary jazz scholar, composer, conductor, and author of *Early Jazz* Gunther Schuller classified the Chicago style as "commercial performances geared to a thriving mass market requiring a consumer's product."[26]

While it is interesting to look back on criticism written about jazz since this retrospective glimpse may help to give us a broader perspective on the music's reception, no artistic movement should be defused or devalued by critics and historians. When this occurs it is often due to the short-sighted perspective the writer has on the subject matter, missing the advantage of the longer view. Every new trend, regardless of its long-term effects, is valid and contributes to the on-going evolution of the art form—the continuum. No one has the right to interrupt this evolutionary process or the foresight to know where it may be going; but we must let it go there on its own natural course, unencumbered by criticism, and en-joy the ride—wherever it takes us.

NEW YORK AND THE HARLEM RENAISSANCE

While Chicago had its south side, New York City had Harlem, an area that served as a hot house for the germination of black intellectualism, cultural development, and community pride during the 1920s. On one hand, Harlem was the center of a growing sense of black pride, yet at the same time, conditions continued to de-teriorate as more and more blacks fled the south to this northern city in search of work and a better life. The influx of newcomers into this concentrated area grad-ually caused conditions that led to the creation of slums and ghettos.

While some black intellectual leaders like writer Langston Hughes were champions of jazz and reflected this attitude in their writings, other church-going black community leaders looked down on the music and its practitioners. This group considered the music to be "lowbrow," representing a part of black her-itage that should be repressed and forgotten rather than encouraged. Despite

Exterior view of the Cotton Club nightclub at night, its illuminated marquee presenting Cab Calloway and Bill Robinson, Harlem, New York City, cir. 1932.

these conflicts within the community, Harlem produced some of the finest jazz musicians of the day.

Aside from the "Harlem pianists," this area became the laboratory for early hot big bands led by Fletcher Henderson and Duke Ellington among others. More dance-oriented white bands, such as Ray Miller's, worked downtown and found ways to fuse elements of hot jazz with a more subdued, marketable dance style.

While it is not within the scope of this chapter to discuss in detail the careers of Henderson and Ellington, it should be pointed out that both leaders moved their music away from the older New Orleans tradition. Both men developed new concepts in arranging for larger bands and Henderson in particular paid heed to the popular dance craze that was sweeping the city. But he, like Ellington, was devoted first and foremost to "hot" jazz and sought out the best jazz soloists. Henderson, with the aid of saxophonist/arranger Don Redman, pioneered new ways to assemble written music for large bands consisting of sections of trumpets, saxophones, trombones, and rhythm. Louis Armstrong and tenor saxophonist Coleman Hawkins, as members of this band, had an inestimable impact on the creation of this new big band sound evolving in New York's Harlem.

Duke Ellington brought his "Washingtonians" band to New York from Washington, D.C., in 1923 in hopes of realizing his dream of achieving notoriety. While this first trip was not rewarding, his second engagement at the Kentucky Club, which lasted 4 years, proved to be his ticket to even more widespread recognition and exposure at the hottest spot in Harlem—the Cotton Club. The Cotton Club featured black entertainers and hired help catering to a white, high-class clientele. It was at this high-class club that Ellington honed his unique style capitalizing on his sidemen's special skills.

As had been the case in Chicago, ballrooms became popular haunts in New York for the young dance-crazed crowds. The popular Savoy Ballroom in Harlem opened its doors in 1926 and provided yet another opportunity for whites to partake of African-American culture. The Savoy employed both black and white bands and working there, as well as the Apollo Theater, was a goal for many of the new, young bands. This ballroom was integrated, much like the black and tans in Chicago, making it even more enticing to many whites.

The mob infiltrated New York nightlife, just as it had done in Chicago. The Cotton Club had close mob connections and during Prohibition provided bootlegged alcohol to its white patrons. (Ironically, marijuana was legal until 1937, while Prohibition laws banned alcohol from 1920 to 1933.) White aristocrats ventured into Harlem to get a glimpse of "barbaric, talented Negroes" who provided hints of deepest, darkest Africa, portrayed by exotic dancers and scenic design. In some ways, the Cotton Club was an African-American sideshow, the success of which was based on upper-class white patrons' curiosity and desire for black entertainment. Black entertainers and their managers (who were often white and of Jewish heritage) learned to capitalize on this white curiosity.

The Cotton Club kept Ellington and his men employed even through the dark depression years, a benefit not enjoyed by many of the struggling, emerging black or white big bands whose only recourse was to travel to find work where they could.

Harlem itself gradually deteriorated with clubs like the Cotton Club closing, driving the musicians and patrons downtown to seek a new nightlife. Harlem became overcrowded by poor, unemployed blacks and was left to the slumlords, only a shell of its former self.

Floor show at Small's Paradise Club in Harlem, New York City.

MARKETING JAZZ

The 1920s mark the first period of significant growth in the entertainment industry. The advances made in technology including the radio and record industries served to stimulate the popularization of jazz nearly overnight. There were many outlets for musicians in Chicago and New York. Musicians were paid well for their time and talents and typically earned $45 to $75 per week for a cabaret or dance hall engagement. Those more fortunate musicians who could read music, like Benny Goodman, supplemented this income with recording, radio, and theater work. Goodman in fact was one of the most in-demand musicians in Chicago at the time, well before his rise to fame as a big band leader. School dances, fraternity parties, and the like were also major sources of employment.

The OKEH recording label was the first to capitalize on **race records,** recording black blues singer Mamie Smith in 1920. These records were specifically targeted for the black audience selling for $1 to $2 a piece. Not only did they do as well as those other ethnically flavored recordings designed to capture the Irish, Polish, Yiddish, German, French, and Mexican immigrant markets, but they attracted many white buyers, which surprised the record companies specializing in these race records. Race records usually featured black, female blues singers who were often accompanied by jazz instrumentalists.

Warner Brothers produced the first Vitaphone talking picture in 1926. The end of the silent film era did some harm to jazz musicians who had previously provided music for silent films. Some live theater music still existed after the introduction of "talkies," because musicians were hired to provide music between feature films or newsreels. A very few fortunate musicians were either the subject of film or found work recording sound tracks for feature films, shorts, and cartoons, but these opportunities were few and far between in the 1920s.

The Amplivox, which was the predecessor of the juke box, was released in 1926, providing yet another opportunity for this music to be heard in public places that did not support live music.

A few of the most fortunate bands enjoyed the opportunity of regular exposure via weekly radio broadcasts sponsored by companies ranging from cigarettes to soap. Old Gold cigarettes sponsored a weekly broadcast by Paul Whiteman's orchestra and Camel cigarettes sponsored the Caravan of Stars featuring Glen Gray's Casa Loma Band and later Benny Goodman's orchestra. One of the first live radio broadcasts was made from Chicago in 1923, and the number of radio stations grew nationwide from 200 in 1922 to 694 in just 4 years. *Etude* magazine published an editorial in 1924 declaring "Listen on the radio any night. Tap into America anywhere in the air and nine times out of ten Jazz will burst forth."[27] The expansion of radio networks represented both an advantage and disadvantage to the jazz community. Radio stations that were controlled by white owners often overlooked black musicians, and the best engagements often went to white bands. The exception was black pianist/bandleader Earl Hines who did enjoy network coverage during his Chicago radio days. Dance and symphonic jazz became the lure and the most desirable outlet for many jazz musicians by the late 1920s. Radio networks took advantage of the dance craze and ran a wire to sites like New York's Savoy and Roseland Ballrooms so that they could broadcast live the performances of name bands. These broadcasts of course helped to publicize the bands and their latest recordings. According to a 1925 study by Maria Lambin and Larry Bowman: "The number of licensed dance halls in New York City grew rapidly in the early twenties, from almost 500 in 1920 to almost 800 in 1925. Approximately 10 percent of the female and 14 percent of the male population of New York attended once a week or oftener."[28] Bear in mind that the population of New York City in 1920 was approximately 5.6 million with 2.3 million living in Manhattan according to census polls. Given the growth in population that occurred between 1920 and 1925, it is conceivable that 1.3 million people attended one of these dances at least once a week. The dance hall and dance band business was clearly very lucrative while it lasted, which was nearly until the U.S. entry into World War II. *Billboard* magazine reported in 1925 that there were 600 jazz orchestras in New York. They went on to say that: "Any fellow in this line today who has the ability will not be able to accept all the work offered to him."[29] Jazz was quickly being elevated to America's popular music and it is no small wonder, given these statistics, why musicians were flocking to New York and other major cities in great numbers.

Despite the negative press leveled at jazz by some, as cited earlier, the twenties marked the beginnings of a new print industry devoted to the discussion of jazz. While stories about jazz both pro and con had circulated prior to 1926, no book on the subject had been published. It had taken nearly a decade for the music to become more that just a passing fancy and for authors to take the subject more seriously. Perhaps it was the growing acceptance of the music by whites or the enthusiasm that Europeans had shown for jazz that motivated Henry Osgood to publish the first book about jazz in 1926. For the most part, Osgood's scholarship was weak and he made misguided comparisons and analogies to classical music. He championed Paul Whiteman and the symphonic jazz movement, yet never mentioned the black creators of the art form. Armstrong, Morton, Bechet, Oliver—none of these jazz pioneers can be found in the pages of this early book about jazz. It was essentially a book selling white jazz. Osgood, who was critic and associate editor of *Musical Courier,* openly opposed real jazz and championed the "polished" jazz of Isham Jones, Whiteman, and Vincent Lopez. Osgood offered little substantive information or analysis of jazz.

Paul Whiteman's book *Jazz* was published with help from co-author Mary McBride that same year. The Whiteman book is essentially an autobiography and discussion of his highly acclaimed 1924 Aeolian Hall concert, billed as an "Experiment in Modern Music." The *Saturday Evening Post* serialized the book that added to Whiteman's growing popularity. In this book, the authors make several bold, and in retrospect, accurate predictions. For example, they predicted that one day, academia would embrace jazz, where it would be taught, studied, and analyzed much like European music. They also stated that: "Jazz is the spirit of a new country. It catches up the underlying life motif of a continent and period, molding it into a form which expresses the fundamental emotion of the people, the place and time so authentically that it is immediately recognizable."[30] Whiteman and his band were also the subject of a full-length film (*King of Jazz*) produced in 1930, a movie shoot that unfortunately Beiderbecke failed to make because of ill health. While the music and banter throughout is rather trite, the film does give us a glimpse into Whiteman's world of music circa 1930.

It was not until the 1930s that more serious efforts to write about jazz were persued in the form of books and periodicals, and until then the music remained much more engaging than the scholarship.

 To learn more about the early technologies that helped to promote jazz in the 1920s, find the corresponding chapter included on the CD-ROM. Here you can listen to a 78-rpm jazz recording on a 1925 radio and phonograph in much the same way and with the same quality experienced in the twenties.

Jazz in Perspective

The timeline that follows will put the developments of jazz discussed in this chapter into a larger historical context, providing you with a better sense of how landmark musical events may relate to others that match your personal areas of interest.

1922
- The flapper marks end of Victorian age for U.S. women who now smoke and drink in public places, often wearing flashy clothing.
- Paul Whiteman's recording of "Whispering" sells 2 million copies.*
- Kid Ory's Sunshine Orchestra becomes first black jazz band to record.

1923
- First jazz broadcast on radio live from Chicago.
- Russian inventor predicts television.
- Joe "King" Oliver records "Dippermouth Blues" with his Creole Jazz Band featuring Louis Armstrong.
- New Orleans Rhythm Kings become the first white jazz band to record with a musician of color.

---

* The Recording Industry Association of America (RIAA) established gold record (created in 1958) and platinum record awards (created in 1976) to recognize recordings with sales of 500,000 or more and 1 million or more respectively. In the case of Whiteman's 1922 recording, had the award been available he would have received platinum award for "Whispering." Comparatively, Elvis Presley's first three albums in the 1950s won only gold status. Michael Jackson won platinum records awards for *Bad* and *Thriller*.

1924
- Paul Whiteman's "Experiment in Modern Music" features George Gershwin's *Rhapsody in Blue.*
- IBM is founded.

1925
- Composer/conductor Igor Stravinsky makes American debut conducting the New York Philharmonic in a program of his own music.
- Sinclair Lewis' *Arrow Smith* is published.
- Florida state legislature requiring daily Bible readings in all public schools.
- Tennessee passes law forbidding the teaching of any evolutionary theories that deny creationism.
- "The Prisoner's Song" and "The Wreck of the Old '97" recorded by Vernon Dalhart becomes the first million selling country music recording.

1926
- First liquid fuel rocket pioneered by Robert Goddard is launched.
- Hemingway authors first novel *The Sun Also Rises.*
- NBC is incorporated.
- Movies became most popular form of American entertainment, making Douglas Fairbanks, Greta Garbo, John Barrymore, and Charlie Chaplin national figures. A new era in pictures with sound begins.

1927
- First public demo of TV.
- CBS is founded.
- Lindbergh makes first flight across the Atlantic from New York to Paris.

- Al Capone makes millions from illegal rackets in Chicago.
- Babe Ruth hits 60th home run breaking previous baseball records. His salary is $20,000.
- Ford launches Model "A."
- Bix Beiderbecke and Frankie Trumbauer record "Singin' the Blues (Till Daddy Comes Home)."
- Work begins at Mt. Rushmore of sculpture of four presidents.

1928
- Louis Armstrong records "West End Blues," which sells for 75 cents.
- Rise of Negro intelligentsia during Harlem renaissance (Langston Hughes and Alain Locke).
- Duke Ellington enjoys success at the Cotton Club.
- Pianist Pine Top Smith records "Pine Top's Boogie Woogie."
- "King of Jazz" Paul Whiteman records "Mississippi Mud."

1929
- Museum of Modern Art opens.
- Valentines' Day mob battle in Chicago.
- Beginnings of commercial passenger air travel.
- Black Tuesday—Wall Street Stock Market crash marks beginning of Great Depression.
- Author William Faulkner published *The Sound and the Fury.*

CHAPTER SUMMARY

With plentiful jobs available, including good paying jobs for musicians, Chicago became a destination for many black Americans migrating from the south in the 1920s. Many important New Orleans musicians, including Freddie Keppard, Joe Oliver, Louis Armstrong, and Kid Ory, made the move to Chicago. The Prohibition Act imposed by the government made the sale and manufacture of alcoholic beverages illegal. During Prohibition, nightclubs known as speakeasies illegally sold alcohol and were run by racketeers. Some conservative groups, notably the Juvenile Protective Association (JPA), sought to lessen the impact on youth of what they felt was sexually provocative music.

Jazz in Chicago in the 1920s served as a transition from the New Orleans jazz style to the swing of the 1930s. In addition to the transplanted Black New Orleans musicians, a generation of primarily white Chicago-based musicians became important contributors. One such group, the New Orleans Rhythm Kings (NORK), helped to define the Chicago sound by adding a saxophone and playing more sophisticated arrangements in a smoother, more connected style. In 1923 the NORK recorded with Jelly Roll Morton, becoming the first white group to record with a musician of color. Probably the most significant musicians of this new generation were Frankie Trumbauer and Bix Beiderbecke. Frankie Trumbauer was a stellar technician on the C-melody sax. Beiderbecke was accomplished as a pianist but is best known as a cornetist. He is generally considered the first great white soloist of jazz whose subdued approach served to foreshadow cool jazz of the 1950s. Sadly, an unhealthy lifestyle led to Beiderbecke's early death at age 28.

The jazz of Chicago tended to place more focus on the individual soloist compared to the collective improvisation of New Orleans jazz. The saxophone was much more commonly used, as was the string bass. Many of the white musicians were associated with "sweet" bands, which included strings and played primarily dance music. Some sweet groups, like the Paul Whiteman Orchestra, were immensely popular, sometimes selling in excess of 1 million copies of a single recording.

Around the same time, New York City's Harlem was becoming an important center of black culture. The Cotton Club, the Savoy Ballroom, and the Apollo Theater featured performers who would help shape the next style of jazz.

Boogie-woogie, a style of piano playing different from stride, developed not in Chicago but initially in the more rural areas in the mid-1920s. A key ingredient of this blues-inspired style was the ostinato rhythm in the left hand, often referred to as "eight to the bar." It became popularized in later years.

KEY TERMS

Your instructor should clarify which terms and aspects of this chapter are of primary importance. You should be familiar to some extent with the following terms, places, people and bands:

Important terms, places, people and bands:

TERMS	PEOPLE	Fletcher Henderson
black and tans	Paul Whiteman	Rudy Wiedoeft
boogie-woogie	Isham Jones	Eddie Lang
ostinato	Benny Goodman	Jimmy Dorsey
race records	Bud Freeman	Pine Top Smith
	Jimmy McPartland	Albert Ammons
PLACES	Frankie Teschemacher	Meade Lux Lewis
Levee District	Dave Tough	Pete Johnson
Harlem	Jimmy Noone	Earl Hines
Cotton Club	Bix Beiderbecke	Langston Hughes
Savoy	Frankie Trumbauer	Duke Ellington
Roseland	Jean Goldkette	

BANDS
Isham Jones
Guy Lombardo

New Orleans Rhythm
   Kings
Wolvereans

Jean Goldkette
Paul Whiteman

REVIEW QUESTIONS

1. What characteristics distinguish "hot" bands from "sweet" bands? Can you name some representative bandleaders in each style?

2. What features distinguish Chicago style jazz from its earlier New Orleans Dixieland predecessor?

3. Of what significance was the JPA to jazz in Chicago?

4. What was the first Chicago style white jazz band to record?

5. Bix Beiderbecke played what two instruments proficiently?

6. What Chicago style musician is often considered an early pioneer of the "cool" jazz sound?

7. What was the significance of Frankie Trumbauer?

8. What instrument did Frankie Trumbauer play?

9. Who was the first important guitarist to emerge during the Chicago period? What instrument did the guitar gradually replace?

10. What instrumentation changes or additions occurred in the Chicago jazz band?

11. What symphonic jazz bandleader introduced the notion of using vocalists with the jazz ensemble?

12. Describe the boogie-woogie style and name two premier artists associated with the style.

13. When and where was the first live jazz radio broadcast made?

14. Who authored the first book about jazz and in what year? Was it accurate in its discussions of jazz?

15. Was Paul Whiteman's book at all accurate in its predications about the future of jazz?

16. By the mid-1920s, what cities were considered to be the centers for jazz activity? Specifically, what areas within these two cities?

17. Jazz was widely criticized during this period. Why and what specifically were the stated objections?

18. What white band became the first jazz group to record with a person of color and who was he?

19. What early '20s classical saxophonist widely exposed on radio exerted a great deal of influence on early jazz saxophonists?

20. Name a few of the "Harlem pianists."

21. What affect did Prohibition, the Depression, new technologies, and the underworld have on jazz in the mid- to late-1920s?

22. In what ways did jazz become marketed during this period, helping to spread its popularity and serve to create a new industry?

23. What led to the decline of the Chicago jazz era?

SUGGESTED SUPPLEMENTARY LISTENING

The abbreviation (iT) indicates that a particular recording cited in the text, or particularly demonstrative of the artist, is available from the Apple iTunes Web site. Other Web-based music distributors may also prove to be valuable resources. SCCJ indicates *Smithsonian Collection of Classic Jazz.*

New Orleans Rhythm Kings and Jelly Roll Morton Milestone MCD-47020-2
Bix Beiderbecke, Singin' the Blues Vol. I Sony (iT) (Includes "In a Mist," "Riverboat Shuffle," and "For No Reason At All in C" among others)
Milestone Classic Jazz: Bix Beiderbecke and the Chicago Cornets Milestone (iT)
The Indispensable Bix Beiderbecke RCA Group (iT)
"Singin' the Blues" SCCJ (iT)
"Riverboat Shuffle" SCCJ (iT)
"Four or Five Times" (Jimmy Noone) SCCJ
Paul Whiteman and His Orchestra Jazz Archives No. 37 157642
The Isham Jones Centennial Album Viper's Next VN-156
"Stompin' At The Savoy" (iT)
Jean Goldkette: Victor Recordings: 1924–1928 TransAtlantic Radio CD 0011
Ben Pollack Vol. 1 1926–1928 Jazz Oracle BDW 8015
Ben Pollack Vol. II 1928–1929 Jazz Oracle BDW 8016

LIMITED ENGAGEMENT...
FULL LENGTH. NOTHING CUT BUT THE PRICE

DAVID O. SELZNICK'S
production of
MARGARET MITCHELL'S
Story of the Old South

GONE WITH THE WIND

IN TECHNICOLOR, starring
CLARK GABLE

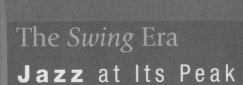

The *Swing* Era
Jazz at Its Peak

> "It is not very difficult to understand the evolution of Jazz into Swing. Ten years ago this type of music was flourishing, albeit amidst adverse conditions and surrounded by hearty indifference."[1]
>
> DUKE ELLINGTON 1939

THE DEPTHS OF THE DEPRESSION

By 1930 jazz had established itself as more than just a passing fancy, but the effects of the Depression were nearly devastating. Had it not been for the resilient spirit of the American people, there is little doubt that the musicians and their music would not have survived. By 1932 the Depression had left 15 million Americans unemployed, one quarter of the workforce. This depressed economic environment nearly eradicated the jazz and popular music movement, even though there was an increasing demand for inexpensive entertainment. Entertainment provided relief from stress and a chance to forget troubled times. The movie industry boomed during the 1930s since admission was only a nickel for the matinee and 10 cents for the evening show. For this modest admission, patrons were treated to live entertainment that could include singers, dancers, comedians, jugglers, and magicians in addition to a newsreel about current events, a serial (the predecessor of the TV series), and the feature film. The movie house was the logical successor to vaudeville, providing good entertainment for little money. The music industry, on the other hand, suffered during the Depression years. According to author Burton Peretti, record production, which had soared in the twenties, fell 96 percent in the early thirties. By 1932 even major labels such as RCA-Victor and Warner Brothers were close to bankruptcy.[2]

Americans' leisure time was occupied by inexpensive activities that they could afford—listening to the radio, parlor sing-alongs, movies, board games such as Monopoly, and, of course, inexpensive dance halls. Ballroom dancing was the craze and without this popular social ritual in the thirties and early forties there would not have been a big band Swing Era. The larger dance halls demanded larger bands capable of filling the room with the dynamic sounds dancers craved. The 1920s small groups would have been incapable of projecting enough volume to entertain dancers in the large dance halls and hotel ballrooms. While the move toward larger jazz bands began in the twenties, it took a complete economic recovery before the halcyon days of the big bands would be fully realized.

The Depression affected blacks more than whites, and racial unrest escalated in decaying ghetto communities of major cities throughout the United States. Civil rights grievances increased and the first major race riot occurred in Harlem in 1935. It is no wonder that a job in entertainment, even with its drawbacks, was an attractive alternative to more traditional employment where few opportunities were available, especially for blacks.

For big band musicians who were fortunate enough to continue to work through the Depression years, there were numerous hardships. The lives of traveling black musicians were especially arduous. They played successive one-nighters, traveling hundreds of miles between engagements, eating meals irregularly, and often encountering prejudices that required them to sleep in cars, busses, and local homes rather than the hotels at which they may have been performing. Gene Ramey recalls the hardships frequently endured by black bands in particular:

> Musicians didn't always like to travel especially a black musician. There were towns we had to avoid going close to. If they found out it was a Yankee band of blacks in town they'd find them and beat them. People would come out and throw rocks at a Negro car. We didn't have any hotels. When we hit town we had to try to find a rooming house. In Mobile, Alabama, I got there and went to the house where I'd been staying all the time and the lady says "all right go in and go to sleep." So I said "I'm not ready to go to sleep right now." She said "Well listen, three of you all sleep in that bed and if you stay past your shift and don't go to sleep now somebody else is going to have to get in that bed and you're just going to have to sit up to sleep." She didn't even change the sheets or nothin'.[3]

Even long after the Depression had subsided, popular white bands enjoyed plush accommodations at hotels where they were booked for extended engagements while black bands continued to tour. Popular black band leader Jimmy Lunceford is reported to have said that in 1942 his band logged "a couple of hundred one-nighters a year, 15–20 weeks of theaters [typically a week in each theater], maybe one four week location, and two weeks of vacation."[4] Needless to say, many of these musicians never enjoyed a normal home life, but it was something they were willing to sacrifice.

THE COUNTRY RECOVERS

Prohibition was repealed in 1933 and by 1935, thanks to the efforts of President Franklin D. Roosevelt and his "New Deal," the country saw economic recovery and began to experience a new sense of optimism about its future. Roosevelt's comprehensive "New Deal" provided numerous federal relief programs, created public works jobs, and offered farm credits and housing assistance—all designed to relieve the country from the effects of the economic Depression. His **WPA** (Works Progress Administration) even offered programs to help the arts by providing assistance for musicians, writers, and theater projects. The First Lady recognized the growing problems of racial inequality and publicly endorsed equal rights. This Civil Rights Movement would continue to escalate once the United States entered World War II.

The "common man," according to author Burton Peretti, became a central theme and spontaneously the country became focused on developing a new sense of nationalism. Classical composers such as Aaron Copeland (who composed "Fanfare For The Common Man"), Virgil Thompson, and Roy Harris created pieces that incorporated American folk songs, and authors such as John Steinbeck contributed books such as *The Grapes of Wrath* that underscored the "common man" theme.[5]

The Prohibition Act that prohibited the sale and consumption of alcohol until 1933 actually added some impetus in the early years to what eventually became known as the "Swing Era." Teens and young adults, until the repeal of Prohibition, freely attended dance halls across the "dry" American midland. It was the teenage and college crowds that created the first demand for swing music and were largely responsible for big band jazz becoming a lasting symbol of American society and culture. Even during the Depression years, bands maintained a working schedule by booking dances at high schools and college campuses. Alcohol during this period was not a factor in determining if young people could or couldn't attend popular venues. The music could therefore thrive in this benign environment, contrary to its beginnings in brothels, roadhouses, nightclubs, and cabarets where drinking was commonplace.

THE ANATOMY OF THE SWING ERA JAZZ BAND

By 1934, the groundwork for the success of big band swing style had been laid by the likes of Paul Whiteman, Glen Gray, Ben Pollack, Fletcher Henderson, Don Redman, and Duke Ellington. These early masters cultivated the jazz **arrangement** for larger bands, building on the accomplishments of Jelly Roll Morton and those arrangers in the employment of Whiteman, Gray, Art Hickman, and other sweet or symphonic bandleaders.

Armstrong's Hot Five and Hot Seven recordings, as well as his brief stay in New York with the Henderson band, revolutionized the way musicians began to think not only about improvisation but also about the swing rhythmic feel. Musicians followed Armstrong's lead during the Swing Era, smoothing out their articulation and producing less choppy, clipped phrases. Slurred passages became more practiced rather than the earlier staccato-tongued approach.

While establishing categories can be misleading in the clarification of any art form since exceptions always exist and artists frequently cross lines, it is safe to say that most of the many big bands could be generally categorized as follows:

- Sweet bands that made few attempts to play real jazz and focused on society dance repertoire. Guy Lombardo's Royal Canadians fits well into this category.
- Swing style dance bands featured a well-rehearsed repertoire performed by exceptional musicians playing arrangements informed by the swing style, but geared largely for the dance audience. Most of these bands featured

little improvisation and many of their leaders, like Glenn Miller, never laid claim to fronting a jazz band. These bands, such as the Jimmy and Tommy Dorsey and Glenn Miller bands were often the most popular with the general public as ranked in the graphic found in the following chapter.

- "Hot jazz dance bands" were successful at compromising by performing music that clearly captured the essence of hot jazz by featuring stellar soloists, while appeasing the dance crowd by including more tempered, danceable repertoire and vocalists. The great Benny Goodman and Artie Shaw bands are included in this group.
- "Hot" jazz big bands based their repertoires largely on pure hot, swing jazz with ample room for improvising soloists. Some of the arrangements grew out of an improvised process rather than stemming from a concerted effort by composers/arrangers. Jimmy Lunceford, Jay McShann and Count Basie led this type of band.

While a few bands like Duke Ellington's defied categorization, for the most part the bands could be placed in one of these four categories.

Instrumentation

The big bands all sported the same basic instrumentation as those early jazz bands that had preceded them—just more of them. Now, instead of just one each of the wind instruments, there were sections of them. By the mid-1930s the average big band had grown in size to include three or four saxophones, two or three trumpets, two or three trombones, and a three- or four-piece rhythm section. The saxophone, which first emerged in the mid-twenties, became the instrument of choice in most big bands and saxophonist Benny Carter perfected writing for a section of five saxophones. Gradually the saxophone eclipsed the clarinet in popularity, though many of the saxophonists were called on to play both instruments and may have started their careers as clarinetists. They were called woodwind doublers, or simply "doublers." The cornet players gradually converted to trumpet, a transition that started during the Chicago period. The trumpet delivered a more brilliant, powerful sound. The trumpet therefore lent itself more readily to the demands of the dynamic music performed by the powerful big bands. The single trombone, common to most New Orleans and Chicago jazz bands, was reinforced with the addition of one or more. The modern big band usually includes five saxophones, four or five trumpets, and three to five trombones. Most bands set up in three parallel rows with the saxophonists seated in the front row closest to the audience since they have the least ability to project. The trombones sit behind the saxophones, and the trumpets are in the back row. The brass section, the term often used to describe the collective trumpet and trombone sections, was often placed on tiered risers. The rhythm section is usually situated on the right side of the band (audience left). There are alternatives to this traditional seating arrangement, but often they were used to accommodate special circumstances.

Many of the big band leaders also fronted small groups, which became a necessity during World War II, when it was difficult to staff a full big band. Goodman, Shaw, and Basie, among others, had small groups as well as big bands. In some ways, the small group could be an enticement for the best soloists in the big band as it provided much more room for extended solos and additional recording opportunities. Most big band arrangements, particularly those by the popular white dance bands, included only short improvised solos, and the best soloists often felt this to be a confining, creatively stifling atmosphere. This limitation was particularly true

if the band recorded a hit that included an instrumental solo. In this case, audiences expected the soloist to duplicate in live performances the same recorded solo, defeating any sense of spontaneity or creativity. Even today, over a half a century after the popular big band hit "In the Mood" was recorded, audiences still expect to hear the same exact original solo even though it was initially an improvisation.

The rhythm section, which always seemed to be at the heart of major stylistic changes in jazz performance practice, was most responsible for the swing feeling associated with this style. It has always been somewhat confusing since the term "swing" in this case has a double meaning—it describes a certain rhythmic phenomenon associated with jazz interpretation and it is also a term used to describe this particular period in the history of jazz. When compared to the Chicago or New Orleans styles, the swing rhythm sections manifested several radical departures from earlier practices. First and foremost were the changes in instrumentation. Gradually rhythm sections embraced the string bass, moving away from using wind instruments like the tuba or bass saxophone. While the string bass was much quieter than its early counterparts, it was significantly more agile and capable of playing smooth, "walking" lines on all four beats and at fast tempos. The "walking" bass line is a performance practice still used today and first associated with the Swing Era. Amplification, a Swing Era innovation, later helped the acoustic bass to balance properly with the rest of the band.

The guitar eventually replaced the banjo, though, like the transition from tuba to bass, it was slow. It was not uncommon to see rhythm sections in swing bands as late as the early 1930s still using the tuba and banjo in their rhythm sections. The guitar was largely used as a rhythm and time-keeping instrument by strumming chords on the unamplified instrument on every beat of the measure.

By the 1930s, drum-set design and construction had significantly improved, as had recording techniques that enabled Swing Era drummers to play for recordings much as they did in live performances. As they developed more technique, dexterity, and independence of limbs, they began to create an approach to time keeping and rhythmic embellishment that more closely resembles what we hear today. Armstrong's rhythmic style did much to influence how drummers during this period played, since they eventually adopted his eight-note style, transferring it first to the **hi-hat** and later to the "ride cymbal" to create what we now identify as the classic swing style pattern. See Examples 7.1 to 7.3.

EXAMPLE 7.1
Approximation of the swing ride-cymbal pattern often played with variation.

Ding   Ding - ga Ding   Ding - ga   Ding   Ding - ga Ding   Ding - ga

EXAMPLE 7.2
A graphic representation of one measure in 4/4 meter showing alternation between a quartet-note of full value on beats 1 and 3, followed by even eighth note divisions of beats 2 and 4. This rhythm pattern does not swing.

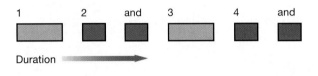

EXAMPLE 7.3
A graphic representation of one measure in 4/4 meter showing the uneven division of beats 2 and 4, causing a feeling of anticipation of the following beats. This was the typical pattern played by the drummer on the cymbals. This rhythm helps to create the basis of the "swing" feel. Horn soloists and pianists might also swing the eighth notes on every beat.

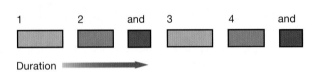

The bass drum was used on all beats to reinforce the bass line and the snare drum. Other drums were used to embellish and decorate the arrangement, highlighting certain rhythms played by the horns. A good drummer would play a brief improvised rhythmic figure described as a **fill** to set up a response played by the horns, or to underscore a particular high point in the arrangement (often termed **chart**).

Make sure that you review the sections about Performance Practice in Chapter 3, Listening to Jazz, found on the CD-ROM. It might also be helpful to view the short video entitled *Video Blues* paying particular attention to the rhythm section. If you haven't already done so, you should also examine the section on rhythm found on the CD-ROM in Chapter 2—The Elements of Jazz.

Since the bass and guitar players were playing on each beat, and the drummer was also emphasizing every beat, often embellishing in between major beats, pianists were forced to eventually create a new style of harmonic accompaniment. In earlier years, pianists had followed the earlier stride, boogie-woogie, and ragtime models that were best suited for solo performance or for bands that had no bass or guitar (banjo). Pianists found that these busy, early soloistic styles, centered around filling up every beat in every measure, were inappropriate for the swing style rhythm section since the other instruments had well-defined roles that duplicated much of what earlier jazz pianists used to play. Eventually, pianists developed a sparser style of harmonic accompaniment since it was no longer necessary to carry the added burden of keeping steady time, now the responsibility of bass and drums. The new piano accompaniment style to emerge from the Swing Era was termed **comping** an abbreviation of compliment. It was Count Basie's rhythm section that is given much of the credit for developing these more modern rhythm section techniques. Bassist Gene Ramey, who played with the Basie band and in Kansas City during the 1930s swing movement reminisced about this rhythm section phenomenon that revolutionized performance techniques:

> I started playing the bass violin in 1933 and in 1935 is when I started to hang around Walter Page. Although very little credit is given to him, he made the Basie rhythm section. Before that Basie rhythm section came into being all you ever heard of was a band that was swung by a "big foot" drummer. All you ever heard in the rhythm section was the drummer. And then, working with Basie, they figured out a way where the drummer wouldn't play so loudly. The piano and guitar would have a chance to be heard. All those instruments weren't amplified then you know. That's why you notice Basie played so few notes. That was the way for him to stay out of the way of the rest of the rhythm section. Imagine what it would be like if Basie was plowing through with his chord ideas and the guitar was playing his chords—there's bound to be a clash. So Basie and Walter Page worked that thing out and they started something that all musicians are using today. It gave the rhythm section freedom.[6]

Jazz pianist Teddy Wilson, ca. 1940, who performed with Gene Ramey, Benny Goodman, and Billie Holiday.

Repertoire and Arrangement

Throughout the history of jazz, each era has been responsible for contributing to a growing repertoire. This repertoire, along with established performance practices associated with the proper interpretation of this music, has resulted in what could be considered the "jazz canon." The first generation of jazz performers and composers contributed pieces to the canon like "Tiger Rag," "St. Louis Blues," "King Porter Stomp," and "Sugar Foot Stomp," to name just a few titles. The Swing Era gave birth to an astounding list of songs that were added to this expanding canon. One can view this repertoire, particularly from this period, as a list of works that fall into one of three basic categories: (1) the standard pop tunes that were readily adopted by jazz performers and arrangers; (2) **head charts** that were based largely on a series of improvised **riffs,** often in call–response style, that outlined a blues or "rhythm changes" ("I've Got Rhythm" model); and (3) the jazz standard written by jazz players and initially performed by them. This was the age of the great American popular song, written by composers such as Irving Berlin, Cole Porter, and George and Ira Gershwin. These songs were usually composed for the theater or film. Jazz arrangers and performers were quick to adopt

Bassist Gene Ramey as he performs for the recording of Sonny Rollins's "Sonny Rollins Volume I" album.

songs like Gershwin's "Lady Be Good" and "I've Got Rhythm" or Irving Berlin's "Blue Skies" and recast them in their own new molds. In addition to these Tin Pan Alley composers, Swing Era jazz composers also contributed immeasurably to the growing jazz repertoire. Duke Ellington of course was one of the most prolific, writing thousands of pieces during his lifetime. Ellington, sometimes with help from his band members, composed jazz standards such as "Perdido," "Don't Get Around Much Anymore," "Mood Indigo," and "In a Sentimental Mood." Ellington, like others, also borrowed from the earlier tradition, for example using portions of "Tiger Rag" as the basis for his new compositions. But Ellington was not the only composer contributing to the repertoire. Bix Beiderbecke's old friend Hoagy Carmichael, for example, wrote the timeless ballad "Stardust," and Benny Goodman composed "Stompin' at the Savoy," both of which serve as excellent examples of jazz standards that continue to be performed today.

All the swing bands had theme songs, many of which became charted by the trade journals that tracked record sales and other means of measuring a band's popularity. Fans immediately identified a theme song with the band that created it, for example, Count Basie's "One O'Clock Jump," Lionel Hampton's "Flying Home," and Duke Ellington's "Take the 'A' Train." Once a band popularized a song, it was not uncommon for other bands to create their own arrangements of it.

It has already been established that the arranger assumed a great deal of responsibility for developing a big band's particular sound. It was during this era that the jazz arranger first rose to high stature. This small select group gave each band its unique musical identity—its "DNA." It was the arrangers' job to promote the particular strengths of the bands they wrote for, showcasing the best soloists and capitalizing on special attributes that might be available to give the band its special musical signature. While some arrangers like Sy Oliver, Benny Carter, and Fletcher Henderson wrote for more than one band, they were able to adjust their writing style to suit the individual strengths of each band. Arrangers determined what key a piece should be in, the tempo, the style, which soloists and sections would be featured, how each section of the piece would be orchestrated and harmonized, and other details. A good arranger would not only find a unique way to **orchestrate** and harmonize the original tune, but might also add entirely new material that would appear as the introduction, coda, or even in the main body of the arrangement. While the big bands may have been relatively similar in terms of their instrumentation, the ways in which this repertoire was presented differed widely from band to band and the arrangers controlled the presentation.

SWING IN THE EAST

Since jazz music by the 1930s was so widespread that no single city served as a mecca, the Swing Era can be viewed geographically, examining the hot beds of musical activity throughout the country and the musicians associated with these areas. As discussed in Chapter 6, New York had become a mecca for jazz and the developments in big bands of the early 1920s. It is no surprise that this trend continued during the Swing Era when New York supported any number of swing and sweet dance bands both black and white. It was **gigs** at the Savoy and Roseland Ballrooms in New York, for example, that attracted bands from across the country as these engagements marked a level of accomplishment and achievement they all sought.

Fletcher Henderson (1897–1952)

The frequently told story about many black jazz pioneers is that many were simply street-trained musicians. This "noble savage" myth of unschooled, innate talent was perpetuated by many of the early jazz writers. To the contrary many of those jazz musicians like Fletcher Henderson, while not completing higher education degrees, sought training beyond high school. Admittedly his training as a mathematician and chemist may not have formally prepared him for the career path that he ultimately chose, but he was nevertheless an articulate, intelligent representative of the black arts community in Harlem. He initially found work in New York as a song peddler, working for W. C. Handy's jointly owned publishing company. This employment was supposed to be temporary until Henderson found work as a pharmacist. Whether it was a poor market for pharmacists or his initial success as a pianist that led to his career change is irrelevant, but he found himself in much demand as an accompanist for blues singers in race recordings and live performances. He recorded with Bessie Smith (see "Lost Your Head Blues" included on the Smithsonian Classic Collection of Jazz) and performed extensively with Ethel Waters. His first band was little more than an ordinary dance band, but it did earn him a local reputation as the "Black Paul Whiteman." When it became apparent that hot jazz was what was attracting public attention, particularly in Harlem, he began to employ more soloists who were exploring improvisation. In 1924 he brought in Louis Armstrong from Chicago. Armstrong stayed barely a year but left an indelible impression on Henderson's men and all New York musicians. Saxophonist Don Redman became Henderson's musical director about this same time, and together they began to develop a formula for big band arranging that became the archetype for many others to follow. Together, these arranging pioneers built upon devices that were pioneered by Whiteman and Jelly Roll Morton. Those characteristics and techniques that define this arranging style are as follows:

- Call–response style, setting brass and saxophones in opposition.
- Arranged by choirs, keeping like instruments together rather than mixing brass and woodwinds.
- Harmonized **soli** sections by composing a lead voice in an improvised style and creating parallel harmony by scoring secondary instrumental voices to follow the same melodic rhythm as the lead voice.
- Stock swing rhythmic patterns scored for wind players.

Henderson continued to improve his band, adding more top-flight soloists, but his rising star never reached a zenith. "A Study in Frustration" was the name that Columbia Records attached to their reissue of Fletcher Henderson big band recordings, and this title aptly defines much of his career. While he and his alto saxophonist Don Redman did much to establish the arranging formula that was followed for years to come, neither of these men ever enjoyed great success.

Fletcher Henderson's orchestra in New York, ca. 1924. The band features Henderson (seated at piano) and Louis Armstrong on trumpet (center, back). The saxophonists are (left to right): Coleman Hawkins, Buster Bailey, and Dow Redman.

Henderson was forced to replace Don Redman with Benny Carter when Redman left to work with McKinney's Cotton Pickers, eventually forming his own band. While Carter contributed top-flight arrangements to the band's library it was not enough to sustain the band as star soloist Coleman Hawkins also elected to leave. Hawkins had been with Henderson from the beginning, serving a 10-year apprenticeship before choosing to pursue lucrative opportunities in Europe. Hawkins' departure from the Henderson band was devastating and while many fine soloists came and went, no one seemed capable of elevating the band to its rather short-lived halcyon days. Henderson employed a long list of exceptional soloists, but nearly all had left by the early thirties. Perhaps it was his lack of business acumen, management skills, or general leadership qualities, but in 1934 Henderson was forced to break up his band. This was an unfortunate fate as the band had just begun to hit its stride, recording several hits including "Wrappin' It Up" (included on the *Smithsonian Collection of Classic Jazz*) and "Deep Down South Camp Meeting," which Henderson later sold to Benny Goodman. Even his last-ditch efforts to produce palatable, trivial arrangements of popular tunes failed to generate any real commercial success, and he succumbed to added pressure from a growing number of black and white bands. His attempt from 1936 to 1941 to revive his band featuring a stellar cast of soloists including Roy Eldridge on trumpet, tenor saxophonist Chu Berry and "Big" Sid Catlett was reasonably successful, enjoying regular employment and several hit records. Chu Berry, though he is often overlooked in general historical overviews, was a popular soloist who was winning critics' and readers' polls at the time. In the end though, it was Henderson's skill as an arranger that enabled him to sustain his career.

Fletcher Henderson and His Orchestra

Form and Key: 12-bar blues choruses (with variation), in B♭ major

0:00–0:04	*Introduction:* 4 bars.
0:04–0:15	*First Chorus:* 12-bar blues, 1st theme, saxes and rhythm.
0:16–0:26	*Second Chorus:* 12-bar blues, 2nd theme, trumpets and rhythm.
0:27–0:42	*Third Chorus:* 16 bars (8 + 8), 3rd theme, clarinets and rhythm.
0:43–0:53	*Fourth Chorus:* 12-bar blues, improvised trombone solo (C. Jones), with rhythm.
0:54–1:29	*Fifth, Sixth, and Seventh Choruses:* each 12-bar blues, improvised trumpet solo (R. Stewart), with rhythm and background riffs.
1:30–1:52	*Eighth and Ninth Choruses:* each 12-bar blues, improvised clarinet solo (R. Procope), with rhythm and background riffs.
1:53–2:28	*Tenth, Eleventh, and Twelfth Choruses:* each 12-bar blues, improvised trombone solo (B. Moten) with rhythm and background riffs.
2:28–2:52	*Thirteenth and Fourteenth Choruses:* 12-bar blues, and 10-bar blues with 2-bar drum break, improvised tenor sax solo (C. Hawkins) with rhythm and background riffs.
2:52–3:09	*Fifteenth Chorus:* 15 bars, 10-bar return of truncated 1st theme (like first chorus), with 5-bar repeat of Introduction as ending tag.

Listening Guide

"Sugar Foot Stomp"
(K. Oliver L. Armstrong)
2:50

Recorded New York City April 25, 1931

"The Father of the Big Band" Jazz Archives #137

"Connie's Inn Orchestra":

Russell Smith, Bobby Stark, Rex Stewart: *trumpets*

Benny Moten, Claude Jones: *trombones*

Russell Procope: *clarinet, alto sax*

Harvey Boone: *alto sax*

Coleman Hawkins: *clarinet, tenor sax*

Fletcher Henderson: *piano*

Clarence Holiday: *guitar*

John Kirby: *tuba*

Walter Johnson: *drums*

Coleman Hawkins—"The Father of Jazz Tenor Saxophone" (1904–1969)

Tenor saxophonist Coleman Hawkins had no idea that upon his return from a five-year stay in Europe, he would wax a recording that would catapult him to leadership status and earn him the title of the "father of jazz tenor saxophone." The impressive early sales of "Body and Soul" were astonishing. Pianist Thelonious Monk in talking to Hawkins about this phenomenon asked "how did these people, these old folks and everybody, go for your record of 'Body and Soul?' . . . 'Cause I've listened to the record, and I can understand if you played the melody, 'cause that's what they like, . . . they like melody. They sure won't listen to anything else that's jazz."[7] Monk was right in that the Hawkins' recording, which remained in jukeboxes well into the 1950s, is pure improvisation, making only vague references to the original melody. This recording helped to set the stage for the rebellious new music eventually described as bebop that featured performers in extended, improvised solos, rarely ever referring to the original melody. In some ways, Hawkins became an early mentor to many of the younger players he found in New York following his European hiatus. While big band swing was still the thing in 1940, this small core of New York musicians had begun to reach for something that had deeper artistic value for them and elevated the role of the improvising soloist.

Hawkins, or the "Bean" as he was nicknamed, was both an older style swing player deeply rooted in the blues tradition and an innovative upstart. He projected a huge, husky deep-throated sound and used a wide, thick **vibrato** that was associated with Swing Era players of his generation. His somewhat exaggerated swing rhythmic feel with an on-the-beat emphasis was somewhat predictable, at least by later-day standards, and gave away his roots in the "swing" style. But he also delivered **rubato**-like phrases, straying out of strict tempo, that were elastic, creating rhythmic tensions between the regular pulse of the rhythm section.

Like Louis Armstrong, whose brief membership in the Henderson big band overlapped with his own, Hawkins showed a penchant for demonstrating his ferocious technique through use of **double-time** phrases. It was no doubt Armstrong who also led Hawkins to take a smoother, more **legato** approach to phrasing and his **articulation** of notes (the way in which notes are attacked with the tongue). Hawkins' recordings in the early 20s with the Henderson band showed a very choppy, articulated style of tonguing (as did many early jazz players), but by the end of that decade, falling under Armstrong's influence, he showed the smoother phrasing evident in his 1939 recording of "Body and Soul." Hawkins was the first tenor saxophonist to bring this more modern approach to the instrument elevating its status from an earlier novelty role. He could well be considered the father of jazz saxophone for his significant contributions.

His understanding of music theory enabled him to create and negotiate elaborate chord progressions. He flaunts these impressive skills on "Body and Soul," included in the companion audio anthology. Throughout this improvised solo, he demonstrates his inventive and skillful use of chord substitutions and embellishments, replacing chords in the original progression with more harmonically colorful and rich alternates. Hawkins also introduced a new sense of **dissonance** (clash created by notes that do not fit a given harmony) and resolution by surrounding **chord tones** (notes that are part of a chord) with more dissonant neighbor tones (notes that are not part of the basic chord), eventually resolving them to **consonant** chord tones.

While it is limiting to place narrow, blanket descriptions on a soloist's improvisational style, it is generally agreed that Hawkins took a largely vertical, or arpeggiated rather than linear approach to improvising. Arpeggiated refers to the way a wind instrument plays a chord by playing each pitch, one at a time in ascending or descending order rather than playing them simultaneously, like a piano, to sound the chord. The arpeggiated approach is in contrast to a more horizontal, scalar or linear style associated with some other performers like Lester Young, Hawkins' most well-known counterpart (see Example 7.4.). No soloist conforms exclusively to either approach but uses a combination of both. Hawkins negotiated his way through chord progressions by outlining the chords, playing chord tones in ascending and descending sequences, creating **arpeggios**. He had attended Washburn

Tenor saxophonist Coleman Hawkins, ca. 1940s.

EXAMPLE 7.4

Vertical arpeggiated style

Linear, horizontal style

College in Topeka, Kansas, studying music theory and composition for two years, so it is no wonder that he excelled in his knowledge of harmony. As a result of these stylistic traits, his playing bore only slight resemblance to that of the instrument's early pioneers like Rudy Wiedoeft, Jimmy Dorsey, and Frankie Trumbauer.

In 1939 the *Down Beat* magazine reader's poll showed Hawkins in the top spot on his instrument enabling him to assemble fine big bands and small groups filled out with some of the most modern musicians of the day. This popularity led to his sponsorship of what many consider to be the first landmark bebop recording session in 1941 featuring young upstarts Dizzy Gillespie on trumpet, Oscar Pettiford on bass, and Max Roach on drums. Bebop, however, was not yet an established or recognized style.

Coleman Hawkins and His Orchestra

Listening Guide

Form and Key: 32-bar song form choruses (AA'BA''=chorus) D♭ major

0:00–0:09	*Introduction:* 4 bars, solo piano.
0:10–1:30	*First Chorus:* 32 bars, Tenor Chorus Melody and Solo.
0:10–0:29	*A section:* 8 bars, tenor plays chorus melody with simple, restrained piano, bass, and drums accompaniment.
0:30–0:50	*A' section:* 8 bars, tenor begins improvised virtuoso solo over chorus chord changes, only hinting at melody, with piano, bass, and drums.
0:51–1:10	*B section:* 8 bars, tenor improvises freely over bridge chord changes, with rhythm.
1:11–1:30	*A'' section:* 8 bars, tenor continues solo over chorus chord changes, with rhythm.
1:31–2:59	*Second Chorus:* 34 bars, Improvised Tenor Solo.
1:31–1:50	*A section:* 8 bars, tenor continues virtuoso improvisation over chorus chord changes, with sustained background chords in trumpets and saxes, simple rhythm section accompaniment.
1:51–2:11	*A' section:* 8 bars, similar to A section.
2:11–2:31	*B section:* 8 bars, tenor continues solo, trumpets and saxes tacit, continued simple rhythm.
2:32–2:59	*A'' section:* 10 bars, tenor climaxes improvisation over sustained chords in trumpets and saxes, short tenor solo cadenza followed by ending chord in trumpets and saxes.

"Body and Soul" (Green-Sauer-Heyman-Eyton) 2:59

Recorded 10/11/39 Bluebird B-10253

Reissued on The Smithsonian Collection A5 19477

Coleman Hawkins: *tenor saxophone*

Joe Guy, Tommy Lindsay: *trumpets*

Earl Hardy: *trombone*

Jackie Fields, Eustis Moore: *alto saxophones*

Gene Rodgers: *piano*

William Oscar Smith: *bass*

Arthur Herbert: *drums*

Elegant Ellington (1897–1974): Music Was His Mistress

As the title of John Edward Hasse's book implies, Edward Kennedy "Duke" Ellington was "Beyond Category." Ellington was more than a composer and bandleader; he became an institution and has been the subject of more books than possibly any other jazz musician. A prolific writer, Ellington is considered one of America's foremost composers whose catalogue contains approximately 2,000 works including film scores (*Anatomy of a Murder, Paris Blues,* with Louis Armstrong, and *The Asphalt Jungle*), musicals, sacred music, popular dance tunes, and episodic concert works. His work was and is recognized world wide, receiving France's highest award—The Legion of Honor—and the U.S. Presidential Medal of Honor for his contributions to the American art form. Four countries issued postage stamps to honor his accomplishments.[8]

Ellington followed a destiny instilled in him as a youngster by his family. He was the child of a proud black family who earned an honest living in Washington, D.C. As a youngster he was taught that he was special and should carry his head high so it is no surprise that he eventually earned the royal title of the "Duke" of jazz. In D.C., he studied piano and learned about the dance band business, performing with local bands and organizing his own which he called the Washingtonians. Ellington was articulate, sophisticated, witty, elegant, and most of all, had the self-confidence to believe in himself and his potential for greatness. He believed that, despite his blackness, he was heir to a throne. As a child, he showed talent as a painter, though he ultimately chose to follow another artistic calling. He continued, however, throughout his career to pursue painting as a form of relaxation while traveling with his band and performing

Duke Ellington and his orchestra at the Oriental Theater, Chicago, Illinois, 1934. Shown left to right are Wellman Braud, Otto Hardwick, Lawrence Brown, Tricky Sam Nanton, Rex Stewart, Arthur Whetsol, Sonny Greer, Harry Carney, Barney Bigard, Johnny Hodges, Juan Tizol, and Fred Guy.

in over 20,000 engagements, living out of a suitcase in hotels and backstage dressing rooms for most of his life. His visual mind clearly influenced his music and is evident in many of his impressionistic, moody works that often seem like tone paintings.

With his early success in New York at the famed Cotton Club (1927–1931), Duke Ellington continued to sustain a working big band for nearly 56 years until his death in 1974. His uncanny ability as a leader is a testament not only to his leadership, but also to his genius and charisma. Why else would some members of his band remain for over 40 years—virtually their entire careers? While he was a pianist, his real instrument became the band. Ellington developed a sound pallet comparable to no other composer or bandleader, learning to combine instruments in unusual ways, relying on the unique abilities of his band members. Even in the face of bebop and other stylistic trends in jazz following the Swing Era, Ellington stayed his course, following his own lead.

To fully appreciate Ellington's recordings, one needs to become more closely acquainted with the following characteristics that make the Ellington sound so unique.

1. The four years that Ellington spent at the Cotton Club represent what could be termed his workshop period. With an ever-changing floor show, often involving exotic choreography and singers depicting African scenarios, Ellington learned to create new music, or revise old music quickly, to accommodate the needs of new shows. He had to create moods that reinforced the jungle atmosphere by creating special, unique orchestrations and by using drums to provide a jungle-like scenario with African-American entertainers performing in exotic native-like costumes.

2. While the catalog of Ellington compositions is almost mind-boggling, it is not difficult to find pieces that are strongly influenced in some way by the blues. Another primary source of inspiration was train travel. Since Duke and his band often traveled by train, the sounds and rhythms associated with this mode of transportation permeate his scores. An early composition entitled "Daybreak Express" is an excellent example of his use of the train theme.

3. With the help of his outstanding musicians like trumpeter Bubber Miley and trombonist "Tricky" Sam Nanton, outstanding brass soloists who had developed unique performance techniques, he learned to make use of the special sounds of muted brass instruments.

4. Ellington's orchestration during the Cotton Club period began to demonstrate a special flare for orchestration, combining instruments from different families—termed cross-section orchestration—and using mutes to alter the open, unmuted sound of a brass instrument. In this way, he left an indelible and unique signature on every composition. Most bands followed the orchestration model made popular by Fletcher Henderson and Don Redman, who arranged by choir—keeping like families of instruments together in their statement of melodic and harmonic passages. Instead of following this already shopworn path, Ellington favored combining instruments from different families, carefully assigning notes to instruments in less-expected registers or ranges to achieve new sound colors. For example, in "Mood Indigo," he scores the clarinet in its lowest register sounding under the trombone, which usually plays under the higher pitched woodwind instrument.

5. Recognizing the strengths of his individual musicians, Ellington wrote specifically for them. His music never sounds quite the same when played by other bands because they lack the special musical personalities necessary to duplicate the Ellington sound. Over the years, other bands have performed arrangements of Ellington compositions, but none have been able to copy his unique sound, which relied so heavily on the musicians themselves.

6. Most music produced during the Swing Era, even by the most well-established and polished bands, never displayed much harmonic originality—if any at all. Ellington developed a harmonic style all his own, constructing unusual chord progressions that often broke the rules of convention that dictated which chords should precede and follow one another.

7. Harmonically speaking, Ellington also favored creating dissonances by adding tones outside the ordinary three-note triads, four-note sixth and seventh chords typically found in the run-of-the-mill swing band arrangements of the day. His penchant for dissonance was evident in both his piano and arranging styles. It is not uncommon to hear Ellington play closely grouped dissonant clusters of notes at the piano and this same harmonic sense found its way into his band arrangements. His dissonant piano style can be heard clearly in "Ko Ko," included on the accompanying audio anthology.

8. Duke's music frequently presented harmonically ambiguous introductions and interludes connecting main themes. These ambiguous sections defy a descriptive tone center and provide no clear sense of key, while breaking rules of functional harmony.

9. As discussed and illustrated in the section on form found in the Elements of Jazz chapter on the CD-ROM, most popular music follows a rather predictable structure based on phrase groups in multiples of 4 and 8 measures. For example, the A section of a typical jazz or popular song from this period is generally 8 or 16 measures in length. Ellington broke free of this stereotypical template, sometimes composing phrase groups of 5 and 10 measures, as is the case in his "Concerto for Cootie," included in the Smithsonian Classic Collection of Jazz.

10. Other big band composers were not particularly known for revising their work to create new, improved versions. Rarely did they extrapolate a section from one piece and use it as the basis for a new composition. Throughout his career, Ellington followed both of these practices. "East St. Louis Toodle-o" was later revised as "New East St. Louis Toodle-o" and is a good example of this Ellington practice. The more popular swing ballad "Do Nothin' Till You Hear from Me" was later extrapolated from "Concerto for Cootie." Ellington rarely performed anyone else's music, as was common practice in many other big bands from the period who often maintained a stable of arrangers and composers who contributed to their libraries. Other bands played arrangements of Ellington's music, but the reverse was rarely true.

While it is always dangerous to categorize art into neat cubbyholes, it does serve an instructional purpose. In the case of Duke Ellington, his prolific career offered him opportunities to compose for numerous occasions, people, and surroundings and to express his own beliefs and convictions. Categorization will help you to understand the depth and breadth of this man's talent and legacy. His music can be loosely divided into five categories: (1) jungle styles, (2) popular dance tunes, (3) atmospheric mood pieces, (4) miniature solo concertos, and (5) multimovement extended form concert works. Though he was not an active member of the civil rights movement or a militant, outspoken activist, Ellington was deeply committed to his race and proud to be black. As a result of this personal dedication, he often wrote on African-American themes including tributes to prominent members of the race. "Black, Brown, and Beige," "Black and Tan Fantasy," "Creole Rhapsody" and numerous others suggest this theme and attest to his commitment. A closer examination of the works in each of these five categories follows.

1. *Jungle Pieces* Ellington's first formative period as a composer/bandleader was during the band's Cotton Club engagement. During this time, he wrote a number of what are often classified as "jungle pieces." In these, he used drums, muted brass, and sometimes bizarre instrumental effects along with special orchestrations to project the jungle atmosphere depicted by the floor show. "Caravan," co-composed with his valve trombonist Juan Tizol, serves as a good example of this early style.

2. *Popular Dance Pieces* Perhaps in an effort to remain popular, Ellington composed a number of tunes designed to capture the attention of the dance-crazed public. Manager Irving Mills added words to some of Ellington's instrumental compositions. He had hopes that the recordings of these songs would become hits. Many of them did, but ironically other bands' arrangements of them were often more successful than his own recordings, which may have suffered because of the more extended improvised solos, of less interest to the general public. "In a Mellow Tone," "Don't Get Around Much Any More," "It Don't Mean a Thing if it Ain't Got That Swing," "Sophisticated Lady," and "Prelude to a Kiss" are fine examples of Ellington's more popular composition style. The somewhat angular, leaping melodies and wide range in the last two titles, along with their unusual chord progressions, were daring as far as pop tunes of the day went, making them less attractive to the casual listener, who liked best those melodies that were easily remembered.

3. *Mood Pieces* A number of Ellington's works are categorized as "mood" pieces. These compositions establish an atmospheric, pastel sense and often use the term "mood" in their titles, such as "Mood Indigo" or "In a Sentimental Mood."

4. *Solo Features* Ellington composed a number of miniature concertos to feature the various soloists in his band. Perhaps the most famous of these solo features is "Concerto for Cootie."

5. *Episodic, Concert Works* The final category of Ellington compositions is by far the most daring, as these works broke away from the established tradition of the big band serving a secondary function—providing music for dance or shows. While the two musicians were vastly different in many ways, Ellington followed Paul Whiteman's lead in believing that jazz and related American popular music could serve as the basis for more serious, concert or symphonic works that would establish a new, purely American tradition. There is evidence to support the idea that Ellington was so enthralled with the European high art that he worked to elevate his own music to the same stature. He was once asked what few recordings he would want if he were "fleeing from this or that wicker city." (The author Robert Goffin was a French-speaking Belgian who wrote his book about jazz during World War II when he had to flee, leaving behind thousands of records.) Ellington's initial response to Goffin's question included classical pieces by Ravel, Debussy, Delius, and Holst. Upon further consideration he

added six jazz works and his own composition "Something to Live For."[9] The technology of the time worked against his early efforts to create extended form, multimovement pieces that exceeded the typical three-minute established 78-rpm record model. His first effort, "Creole Rhapsody," was recorded in 1931 and broke new ground. Despite its innovations including unusual phrase lengths, the piece was marred by poor thematic structure and was not well received. We can only imagine that he was forced by the limitations of available recording technology to make certain compromises to this work that was nearly 6½ minutes long and occupied two sides of a 78-rpm record. His subsequent efforts were spotty; nonetheless the most important consideration was that he was making major strides in elevating his music to the level of art music, on par with multimovement classical works. Along these lines, he contributed numerous extended concert works, a dance suite, and three sacred concerts. A few of his many works in this category include the "Far East Suite," "Such Sweet Thunder" based on Shakespearean sonnets, "Suite Thursday," "Drum Is A Woman," the "Perfume Suite," "The River" commissioned by the Alvin Ailey Dance Company, "Togo Brava Suite," "The Liberian Suite," and the "New Orleans Suite." As is evident from many of these titles, his travels, along with people he had met, often inspired these lengthy compositions. While some of these works were criticized for their discontinuity and absence of sufficient jazz improvisation, there is little doubt that they helped to elevate jazz to a status on par with European concert music.

As pointed out earlier, categorization can be dangerous, and this is the case with two Ellington ballads recorded initially in the early 1930s. "Mood Indigo" and "Sophisticated Lady" can be considered as popular dance pieces but at least one falls into the "mood" or "blue" category of Ellington works. In the 1950s *Down Beat* magazine surveyed 50 celebrities and these two pieces tied for first place as their favorite Ellington tunes, and both were featured regularly at Cotton Club appearances. These ballads bear similar qualities though "Sophisticated Lady" is, as the title suggests, the more advanced of the two. Ellington favored chromatic harmonies and melodies, and it is a fact that his melodies, when stripped of their harmonic accompaniment, are often lifeless, lacking the definition and clarity they receive from the supporting harmony. This feature distinguished his tunes from the more typical popular big band tunes of the day. Like other Ellington ballads, "Sophisticated Lady" is most difficult to sing, especially at the tricky return to the final A section following the bridge. The A and B themes are contrasting in that the A section descends chromatically while the B section ascends diatonically. The introduction of this piece, which was the first highly successful popular piece for its composer, is short and quite ambiguous in the true Ellington fashion as he often struggled to compose convincing introductions and endings. Notice that neither the tempo nor key is well established before the solo trombone enters with the theme. "Sophisticated Lady" has been included for reference on the companion CD collection.

Ellington was an enigma without peer. He stands as somewhat of an anomaly since he was able to sustain a big band well beyond the years of its general popularity. Only a few other bands, some of which were latecomers, were able to continue beyond the true heyday of this great music. Count Basie, Woody Herman, Stan Kenton, Buddy Rich, and Maynard Ferguson are among the very few bandleaders who were able to keep their big bands touring and recording long after 1945 by adding new arrangements that captured current popular and jazz trends.

Elegant Ellington

Listening Guide

"Sophisticated Lady"
(Ellington, Hardwick, Brown, Mills, Parish)
3:09

Recorded New York, 5/16/33 on Brunswick 6600

Reissued on *Duke Ellington Reminiscing In Tempo* Columbia/Legacy CK 48654

Personnel

Trumpets: **Arthur Whetsol, Freddie Jenkins, Cootie Williams**

Trombones: **Joe "Trickey Sam" Nanton, Lawrence Brown, Juan Tizol** (*valve trombone*)

Saxophones and Clarinets: **Johnny Hodges, Otto Hardwick, Barney Bigard**

Rhythm Section: **Duke Ellington,** *piano;* **Freddie Guy,** *guitar;* **Wellman Braud,** *bass;* **Sonny Greer,** *drums*

Form and Key: AABA (32 bars, 8 per section), A♭ major

0–0:07	*Introduction:* 2 measures of piano followed by 2 measure instrumental quote from a Don Redman composition at a different tempo.
0:08–0:30	*A theme* stated by trombonist Lawrence Brown, woodwind backgrounds.
0:31–0:51	*Second A theme* embellished a bit by the trombone soloist.
0:52–1:13	Clarinet states the *B theme* with muted trombone backgrounds.
1:14–1:34	Muted brass with trumpet lead play *final A theme of first chorus.*
1:35–1:55	*Sax section soli on first A,* very chromatic much like original tune.
1:56–2:17	*Sax soli continues* on second A, notice coordinated vibrato and scoops.
2:18–2:36	Ellington plans stride style *piano solo on bridge.*
2:37–2:58	Hardwick plays *closing A theme on alto sax* using trills as embellishment.
2:59–end	Closing chords with sax obbligato brings piece to abrupt close.

On the other hand, Duke Ellington stayed on course, relatively unaffected by changing tastes and stylistic trends. Later, bebop, cool, and funk are all styles that passed him by, leaving no real impact on his own style. While other big bands of the day relied heavily on the popularity of their singers, many of whom went on to stellar solo careers, not one of Ellington's singers rose to such heights. Ellington never relied heavily on vocalists for popular appeal. He was his own master and is "beyond category."

Not only was he responsible for contributing a huge body of work to the jazz canon including pieces like "Sophisticated Lady," but also he was a leader who helped to introduce some of the most individualistic soloists to the world. These include the lyrical and bluesy alto saxophonists Johnny Hodges and Russell Procope; baritone saxophonist Harry Carney; trumpeters Bubber Miley, Cootie Williams, Clark Terry, Ray Nance (who also played violin), and Cat Anderson; drummers Sonny Greer and Louis Bellson, and trombonists "Trickey Sam" Nanton and Lawrence Brown. Many of these sidemen revolutionized the way in which their instruments were played, making people realize potentials that had never before been imagined. For example, one of the most important jazz bassists in the development of this instrument was Jimmy Blanton, who performed with Ellington's

Duke Ellington Orchestra performs "Take the A Train" with Singer Better Roche in the film Reveille with Beverly, *released January 1943.*

rhythm section in the early 1940s. As a soloist, Blanton was perhaps without peer at that time, consequently bringing the bass into the solo spotlight and out of its more obscure role as a member of the rhythm section. His strong walking bass lines, which can be heard on "Ko Ko," included in the accompanying anthology, provided the foundation for some of the finest recordings by this band. Baritone saxophonist Harry Carney was also often spotlighted as a soloist in Duke's arrangements and assigned colorful notes in **chord voicings** that would capture Carney's fat, luscious sound on the baritone. Prior to Carney's development on this instrument, the baritone sax had been relegated to playing tuba or bass-like parts usually emphasizing chord roots. Last and certainly not least was Ellington's alter ego, composer/arranger Billy Strayhorn. Strayhorn's first piece for Ellington was "Take the 'A' Train," written in haste to show Ellington what he could do. It not only became the band's theme song, but also marked the beginning of a lifelong relationship. Strayhorn so closely captured the Ellington sound that it became difficult to tell which of the two had actually written some of the music.

"Ko-Ko" is generally agreed to be one of Ellington's most outstanding showpieces, conceived and recorded during one of his prolific periods and by one of his best bands. This piece is one of many he based on a simple blues progression—in this case, in a minor key. While it is a commonplace blues, it is in the very unusual key of E♭ minor. His ability as a composer and orchestrator to develop a short three-minute masterpiece that transcends the simplicity of this simple, almost shopworn harmonic form, is a testament to his genius. According to Martin Williams, "Ko-Ko" "was originally dedicated to the drum ceremonies that centered in Congo Square in pre–Civil War New Orleans, survivals of African worship."[10] The tom-tom rhythm pattern stated in the introduction lays the groundwork for the rest of the piece and captures this old New Orleans scenario. Ellington also makes use of the timeless African call–response form with Juan Tizol stating the call on his valve trombone that invokes the response from the ensemble. This effect continues throughout much of the arrangement with different instrumental groups assuming the roll of the "caller" and "responder." Bassist Jimmy Blanton demonstrates clearly in this recording why he is considered to be an important link in the lineage of jazz bassists, providing strong, well-balanced walking lines and short solo fills throughout the arrangement.

Duke Ellington and His Famous Orchestra

0:00–0:11	*Introduction:* 8 measures featuring trombones over single bass note (pedal point) played by bass and baritone sax.
0:12–0:31	*First Chorus:* Theme played by muted trombone in call–response with sax section.
0:32–0:50	*Second Chorus:* Muted trombone solo (different from first mute) with sax line and brass syncopated brass punches as background texture.
0:51–1:07	*Third Chorus:* trombone soloist continues for another chorus.
1:08–1:25	*Fourth Chorus:* Ellington plays piano solo featuring dissonant chords and cascading lines over brass punches and sax unison line.
1:26–1:44	*Fifth Chorus:* Trumpet play melody with sax and trombone figures in contrast.
1:45–2:03	*Sixth Chorus:* 2–bar exchanges between full band and solo bass.
2:04–2:21	*Seventh Chorus:* Most climactic section termed the "shout chorus" when entire ensemble plays new material at high dynamic level.
2:22–2:33	Return of 8-measure introduction.
2:34–end	4-bar Coda.

Listening Guide

"Ko-Ko" (Ellington) 2:40

Recorded 3/6/40, Chicago

(Victor 26577)

Duke Ellington: *piano*

Wallace Jones, Cootie Williams: *trumpets*

Rex Stewart: *cornet*

Joe Nanton, Lawrence Brown, Juan Tizol: *trombones*

Barney Bigard: *clarinet, tenor saxophone*

Otto Hardwicke, Johnny Hodges: *alto saxophones*

Ben Webster: *tenor saxophone*

Harry Carney: *baritone saxophone*

Fred Guy: *guitar*

Jimmy Blanton: *bass*

Sonny Greer: *drums*

Be sure that you use the CD-ROM to review the high points of this chapter and access a wealth of supplementary material. There are some fascinating excerpts of interviews with Duke Ellington that are located in the corresponding chapter on the CD-ROM.

While Ellington may have been the "Duke" and the first to achieve many accomplishments cited in Table 7.1, someone else claimed the crown as "King" of swing. It is important to point out that none of the black bands captured the commercial spotlight and financial success to rival the best of the white swing bands. Benny the "King" Goodman led certainly one of the best of the white bands without overly compromising his standards to satisfy the dance-crazed public. His crown was earned only after many years of struggling and failing as a freelance musician and bandleader.

TABLE 7.1 Ellington Firsts

1. First black band to broadcast nightly on the radio
2. First composer to merge jazz with film to create the film short *Black and Tan Fantasy*
3. First black jazz band to appear in a full-length feature film—*Check and Double Check*
4. First black jazz composer to score a musical theater production and use his band in the production.
5. First jazz composer to create extended concerts pieces that required more than one side of a 78-rpm record to produce—*Creole Rhapsody* being the first
6. First jazz composer to compose for full-length feature films

Benny Goodman—The "King of Swing" (1909–1986)

A child of Russian-Jewish immigrants, Goodman was a product of the urban acculturation process in Chicago in the 1920s. Here he learned to borrow both accepted and unorthodox techniques from black and white musicians. Goodman associated with members of the Austin High Gang and sat in with the Blue Friars. He most likely learned the value of practice and maintaining a good work ethic from his parents. His efforts were rewarded with a polished and flawless technique along with a pure tone and vibrato that could at times be considered an anticipation of the "cool" sound developed years later in the 1950s. Because of his classical training, he developed a classical approach to the clarinet unlike many of the more free-wheeling, untrained jazz players of the day. This background no doubt led to his association with classical composers and performers later in his career.

His early Chicago experiences with society dance bands led by Ben Pollack and in recording studios as a freelance musician earned him a reputation as a consummate musician, comfortable in any number of musical situations. His solo work, as pointed out by historian Gunther Schuller, often sounded safe, or risk-free, lacking the tension and daring so often associated with great jazz performances. He was such a superior musician in every way that his music suffered at times from a lack of edge and urgency. In short, Goodman and his band were often just too perfect. His style was therefore contrary to the hallmark "hot" black soloists of the day.[11] As a result of this criticism, his early work is not considered to be profound or entirely original. This criticism, whether justified or not, followed him much of his life.

As Goodman's reputation as a recording soloist grew, he formed his own band in the early thirties to honor several recording contracts. While these early groups were not entirely successful, they did record several rewarding arrangements penned by Glenn Miller in 1931. Chicago drumming sensation Gene Krupa was instrumental in the success of the early Goodman band. This band also featured the brilliant Texas trombonist Jack Teagarden who would eventually take this instrument to new heights, away from the earlier tailgate style. But like most musicians, Goodman struggled through the effects of the Depression in the early 1930s. Since much of the recording work had disappeared during these years, he took to performing live for radio broadcasts. Since radio provided free entertainment, it became even more popular during these difficult economic times.

His first successful recordings were done with the English Columbia label. By then, he had formed an alliance with John Hammond, who was one of the most successful promoters and champions of jazz to emerge during this period.

Hammond, who was an active civil rights spokesman, convinced him to use the best possible talent for these recordings including the up and coming Billie Holiday. Holiday made her first recording with the Goodman band. It was also Hammond who exerted a major influence on Goodman for much of his career and who urged Goodman to strike an allegiance with Fletcher Henderson. Goodman hired Henderson as his chief arranger, which not only saved Henderson's decaying career, but also eventually attributed to Goodman's overwhelming success. Goodman, who had experienced more than one failure, had all but abandoned any hope of fronting a successful jazz band and was bored with the run-of-the-mill dance band arrangements. It was Hammond's commitment to Goodman, and Hammond's ability to secure engagements, including extended radio broadcasts, that kept his band working in the face of failure. Goodman employed some of the finest musicians and soloists of the day including Krupa, trumpeter Bunny Berigan, and pianist Jess Stacy.

The Goodman band struck out on what proved to be a lackluster tour across the country in 1935. By the time the band had reached Denver he was almost ready to abandon all hope for success. His "Let's Dance" radio contract had been dropped and he had succumbed once again to what he perceived as commercial pressures by playing more and more pedestrian arrangements of popular dance tunes. Most of these arrangements avoided improvisation and all sounded much the same. Something happened though when the band arrived at the Polomar Ballroom in Los Angeles, California. That night there was a young crowd on hand whose tastes had apparently caught up to the adventuresome Goodman and the more daring side of his band that featured "hot" arrangements by Fletcher Henderson. This young crowd craved Goodman's most demanding literature that featured more improvisation. The young crowd was enraptured by Goodman's set of "hot," danceable arrangements and their enthusiastic acceptance, which was broadcast nationwide on radio, inaugurated the beginning of the great Swing Era. It was ironic that these same Henderson "hot" arrangements that turned Goodman's career around had been recorded only a few years earlier by Henderson's band but failed at that time to generate any real notice. But on that particular night, Goodman and his band became an overnight success, capturing the title as "King of Swing." The differences between the Henderson and Goodman bands are obvious, but do not explain Goodman's overnight success. The Henderson band often featured more high-caliber soloists and swung harder, but it was difficult to match the level of precision and polish that Goodman, who was known as a taskmaster, had achieved.

Goodman and his band rode the crest of the wave that he had created until 1942 when he broke up his band. By then, he had posted an amazing list of accomplishments in the seven years since his overnight success at the Polomar.

Like many other big band leaders, Goodman found that he could also be successful surrounding himself with all-star casts in small group settings. His small groups that included Lionel Hampton on vibes, Charlie Christian on guitar, pianist Teddy Wilson, and Gene Krupa on drums may have actually contributed more to jazz in terms of a lasting influence than his big bands. Goodman's trios and quartets brought a chamber music element to jazz at a time when bombastic big bands were the thing. Throughout his career, Goodman showed a penchant for classical music, commissioning Igor Stravinsky and performing classical repertoire with the New York Philharmonic and the Budapest String Quartet. (Goodman's link to classical music is discussed in more detail in Chapter 17, found on the Online Learning Center.)

John Hammond, who eventually became Goodman's brother-in-law, recognized the growing importance of bringing the best soloists into Goodman's band. Motivated by his empathy for black musicians struggling for equality and recognition, he persuaded Goodman to become the first white bandleader to employ black musicians in public performance. Goodman's first historic trio formed in 1935 broke precedence by featuring black pianist Teddy Wilson, a native Texan, who one year later became a regular member of Goodman's small groups. Wilson was a polished pianist who had incorporated elements of Earl Hines' and Art Tatum's styles. The trio soon became a quartet with the addition of vibraphonist Lionel Hampton, another aspiring black musician. Hampton began his career as a drummer and had recorded with Louis Armstrong's big band. Hampton switched to vibes seeing more opportunity for notice on this unusual instrument. (Make sure that you become acquainted with the vibraphone that can be found on the CD-ROM in the instruments section of Chapter 3—Listening to Jazz.) Wilson left Goodman in 1939 to form his own band and for a time was singer Billy Holiday's musical director. Hampton, too, eventually left Goodman to form his own small and big bands and became one of the most important early innovators on his instrument. As a dedicated performer he was known for his showmanship and tireless energy.

Goodman's first step toward integrating his bands led other bandleaders like Charlie Barnet to follow. While jazz during this period did much toward improving race relations and can be viewed as one place in society where the concept of integration was beginning to work, some blacks viewed this step as perhaps more of a source of trouble than it was worth. Bassist Gene Ramey remembered all too well the price that was often paid for being a black man in a white band.

Benny Goodman quartet, featuring Lionel Hampton on vibraphone, Teddy Wilson on piano, and Gene Krupa on drums.

Jesse Price and I were supposed to be the first two blacks to go with Charlie Barnet. That was back in 1938. He was trying to steal us from Jay McShann and the money sounded good—$96 a week. But we had already heard from Teddy Wilson and Lionel Hampton about all the hardships they were having—the threats. Two weeks after we turned Barnet down they burned up his whole band—repertoire, horns and everything. It was a fire at the nightclub. He had announced that he was going to integrate.[12]

Ramey was convinced that the fire was a result of Barnet's public statements about his desire to integrate his band. As a black musician, Ramey encountered prejudices a few years later while traveling as the bassist with tenor saxophonist Stan Getz's first small group.

I went out with Stan Getz. It was Stan Levy, and myself and Al Haig and I'm the only black man. We got to the hotel there in St. Louis and that cat had a fit. "You got that Nigger. He can't play in this band. We'll let that Nigger play but we want him to come on in that back door, stay behind that curtain and I don't want him to come out here in this room at all. You've got a bathroom in the back." So I politely told Stan that I'd make tonight and give him time to call somebody. Give me my fare and let me go back. This was 1948 and the situations still weren't too kosher.[13]

The last great black performer to be added to Goodman's small group was the revolutionary guitarist from Oklahoma, Charlie Christian. Christian was a major talent by the time he hit New York at the age of 23. The blues background, which is apparent in his playing, reinforced the importance of this heritage at a time when it could easily have been forgotten amid the craze for popular big band

Record producer John Hammond (left) sits while Benny Goodman talks with guitarist Charlie Christian (second right) in a Columbia Records recording studio, New York, 1940.

dance tunes. Most importantly, Christian engineered a solo style on guitar that brought the instrument into a more prominent role in jazz. Prior to his work in jazz, the instrument had been largely relegated to playing chords, providing regular rhythmic accompaniment. Christian's father performed throughout Texas and Oklahoma in bands that could be described as the predecessors of the Western Swing style. Many of these players actually pioneered the use of amplified guitar, but Christian is justifiably given credit for bringing amplified guitar to widespread attention and use. The amplification helped him to break away from the traditional chording role and create a more linear, single-note solo style similar to that of saxophonists of the day. Jazz historian Gunther Schuller described his style as possessing "uncluttered lines, often arching shapes, flawless time, and consistently blues-inflected melodic/harmonic language."[14] Even today his solos sound as modern as if they were recorded yesterday. Christian died prematurely from tuberculosis in 1942, but not before leaving a heritage that revolutionized jazz guitar playing and continues to exert an influence on young guitarists. Up until his death, he had become a regular fixture at Minton's Playhouse, participating in after-hours jam sessions where the groundwork for the bebop revolution was being laid. As brief as his career was, he was considered to be one of the most advanced musicians of the day.

Listening Guide

The Benny Goodman Sextet

"Good Enough to Keep" 2:53, also known as "Airmail Special"

Recorded in Los Angeles, June 20, 1940, Columbia G.30779 Reissued on Columbia Jazz Masterpieces #45144

Benny Goodman: *clarinet*

Dudley Brooks: *piano*

Charlie Christian: *electric guitar*

Artie Bernstein: *string bass*

Nick Fatool: *drums*

Lionel Hampton: *vibraphone*

Form and Key: repeated 32-bar song form (AABA=chorus) in C major

0:00–0:34	*First Chorus:* 32-bar song form melody.	
	0:00–0:08	*A section:* 8 bars (verse), clarinet, vibes, guitar play song melody.
	0:09–0:17	*A section repeated:* 8 bars (verse), repeat of A section song melody.
	0:18–0:26	*B section:* 8 bars (bridge), clarinet, vibes, guitar play bridge melody.
	0:26–0:34	*A section:* 8 bars (verse), repeat of A section melody.
0:34–1:08	*Second Chorus:* 32-bar song form, Vibes freely improvise full chorus over chord changes with piano, bass, and drum accompaniment.	
1:09–1:43	*Third Chorus:* 32-bar song form, Guitar freely improvises full chorus over chord changes with piano, bass, and drum accompaniment.	
1:43–2:16	*Fourth Chorus:* 32-bar song form, Clarinet freely improvises full chorus over chord changes with piano, bass, and drum accompaniment.	
2:17–2:52	*Fifth Chorus:* 32-bar song form: "shout chorus" featuring variation on melody.	
	2:17–2:25	*A section:* 8 bars (verse), clarinet, vibes, guitar play "shout" variation of the melody.
	2:26–2:33	*A section:* 8 bars (verse), repeat of A theme.
	2:34–2:42	*B section:* 8 bars (bridge), clarinet, vibes, guitar play original (First Chorus) bridge melody.
	2:43–2:52	*A section:* 8 bars (verse), repeat of A to end.

Popular White Swing Bands

There were a select group of big bands in the late 1930s and through the '40s that topped the pop music charts for record sales and radio airplay. A high percentage of bands enjoying the limelight were white bands that catered more to the dance floor than they did to any higher aesthetic. In fact famous bandleader Glenn Miller made it clear that he never wanted to have a jazz band. Some of these bands, however, featured fine jazz soloists and excellent arrangements that provided redeeming qualities aside from those appreciated by the dance crowd. Benny Goodman successfully straddled the line that separated purely commercial dance music and music that offered both listener and performer greater challenges. Goodman was able to satisfy his best soloists' need for artistic challenge more through their small group work than with the big band, though his challenging big band arrangements often satisfied dancers, listeners, and musicians alike. Rival clarinetist Artie Shaw took a similar approach adding the Gramercy 5 small group to diversify his big band. Trombonist Tommy Dorsey followed the same path and his band within a band was called the Clambake Seven. Shaw also sought diversity by recording with strings, following in the footsteps of Paul Whiteman.

Artie Shaw (Arthur Arshawsky; 1910–2005) From the outset, Artie Shaw's approach to jazz was unique forming an early ensemble that included a string quartet, rhythm section, and clarinet. His fascination with modern classical composers no doubt explains the motivation to use strings throughout his career. Shaw's recording of "Begin the Beguine" was his first major hit in 1938, prompting the public to begin a long-time debate over who was the best clarinetist—Goodman or Shaw. Shaw was well known for his fluid technique, enabling him to spin long, flowing lines at any tempo as demonstrated by the track included on the companion anthology. His command of the instrument's high register is also evident on this recording that represents one of Shaw's million-sellers, "Traffic Jam." To quote noted swing era authority Gunther Schuller: "And in "Traffic Jam" . . . the Shaw band finally arrived at the level of virtuoso excitement and collective drive that Benny Moten had already attained in 1932."[15] It is a masterpiece in that so much variety has been packed into such a brief recording.

Artie Shaw

Listening Guide

"Traffic Jam" (Artie Shaw and Teddy McRae) 2:15

Recorded in Los Angeles, June 12, 1939

Reissued on *Artie Shaw the Centennial Collection*, RCA/Bluebird 82876260092-2.

Soloists: Artie Shaw, *clarinet;* Georgie Auld, *tenor sax;* George Arus, *trombone;* Buddy Rich, *drums*

Form and Key: repeated 32-bar song form (AABA=chorus)

0:00–0:03	Buddy Rich plays brief prelude to introduction on drums.
0:04–0:10	*Introduction:* played by full band culminating in long ascending clarinet gliss.
0:11–0:18	*First Chorus: A theme* stated by brass and saxes in call–response riff fashion while Shaw weaves improvised clarinet obbligato.
0:19–0:25	*Repeat of A theme;* Shaw continues soloing over top of ensemble.
0:26–0:33	*Tenor Sax solo* on bridge (B section of form).
0:34–0:40	*Repeat of A section* completes the first chorus.
0:41–0:44	*Interlude:* 4-measure trumpet section break in pyramid style; drums enter to lead into first solo.

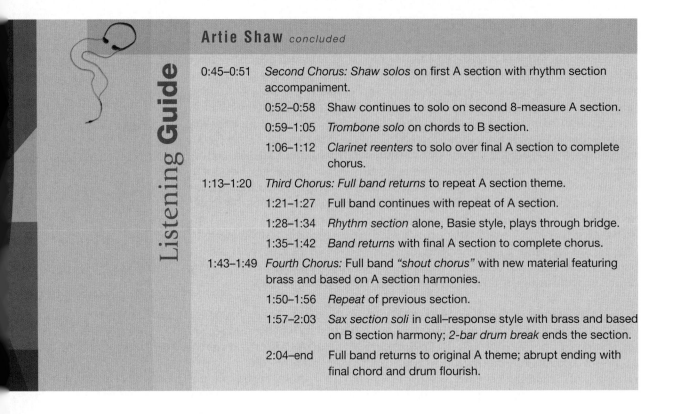

0:45–0:51	*Second Chorus: Shaw solos* on first A section with rhythm section accompaniment.
	0:52–0:58	Shaw continues to solo on second 8-measure A section.
	0:59–1:05	*Trombone solo* on chords to B section.
	1:06–1:12	*Clarinet reenters* to solo over final A section to complete chorus.
1:13–1:20	*Third Chorus: Full band returns* to repeat A section theme.
	1:21–1:27	Full band continues with repeat of A section.
	1:28–1:34	*Rhythm section* alone, Basie style, plays through bridge.
	1:35–1:42	*Band returns* with final A section to complete chorus.
1:43–1:49	*Fourth Chorus:* Full band *"shout chorus"* with new material featuring brass and based on A section harmonies.
	1:50–1:56	*Repeat* of previous section.
	1:57–2:03	*Sax section soli* in call–response style with brass and based on B section harmony; *2-bar drum break* ends the section.
	2:04–end	Full band returns to original A theme; abrupt ending with final chord and drum flourish.

Bandleader Artie Shaw in 1942; the drummer in the background is Buddy Rich.

Shaw, like Goodman, was an advocate for integration and racial equality, at one time featuring Billie Holiday, Roy Eldridge, and Orin "Hot Lips" Page in his bands. Provoked by racial attitudes, his own fame, publicity, and commercial pressures, Shaw left the music business in 1955, jaded about the music industry and bearing a distain for the average listener who would not support more thought provoking, artistic products. His own quest for artistry was so much at odds with the public's appetite for the commercial side of jazz that he was unable to continue in the business.

Goodman and Shaw weren't the only successful white bandleaders and there is a lengthy list of others who enjoyed lasting popularity during the swing era such as Glenn Miller, Artie Shaw, Tommy Dorsey, Jimmy Dorsey, Woody Herman, Les Brown, Charlie Barnet, Harry James, and Gene Krupa. Trumpeter James and drummer Krupa (who as a youth kept company with the "Austin High Gang" in Chicago) both made their mark while working as sidemen with Goodman's band. In each case, theme songs, featured vocalists, and popular recordings helped to secure enduring success for these bands. Some of the best selling hits have become timeless and are still recognized today even by younger generations far removed from the swing era heyday. Some of those most lasting tunes are listed in Table 7.2.

A few of these bands survived the transitional years, bridging classic and modern jazz when the war and bebop had a lasting effect on the music. The Herman and Kenton bands were most suc-

TABLE 7.2 Memorable Swing Era Hits and Associated Band.

Popular Hit Tune	Band Leader
"Let's Dance"	Benny Goodman
"Sing, Sing, Sing" (featuring Gene Krupa)	Benny Goodman
"In the Mood"	Glenn Miller
"Moonlight Serenade"	Glenn Miller
"String of Pearls"	
"Tuxedo Junction"	
"Stardust"	Tommy Dorsey
"I'm Getting Sentimental Over You"	Tommy Dorsey
"Opus No. One"	Tommy Dorsey
"Nightmare"	Artie Shaw
"Begin the Beguine"	Artie Shaw
"Stardust"	Artie Shaw
"Blue Flame"	Woody Herman
"Caldonia"	Woody Herman
"At the Woodchopper's Ball"	Woody Herman
"Artistry and Rhythm"	Stan Kenton
"Leap Frog"	Les Brown
"Cherokee"	Charlie Barnet
"Ciribiribin"	Harry James

cessful at adapting to change, bringing new young players into their bands and reflecting change through their arrangements. In both cases, these bands served as training grounds for many of the best jazz musicians of the twentieth and twenty-first centuries, some of whom are mentioned in Table 7.3.

In retrospect, not all the popular white bands during this period offered music that became timeless. Many leaders played to the popular dance crowd exclusively, unconcerned with a higher aesthetic or jazz improvisation. Some of these groups were described as "sweet," "Mickey Mouse," or just "mickey" bands. Bands led by Lawrence Welk, Guy Lombardo, Spike Jones, Kay Kaiser, Wayne King, Fred Waring, Freddie Martin, Lester Lannin, Horace Heidt, and the list goes on and on, fall into this category. None of these bands or sidemen, while enjoying widespread popularity and celebrity, had any significant impact on the development of jazz.

While big band jazz reigned in the 1940s, the vocalists, whose careers had been launched as members of the big bands, prevailed in the decade that followed and the top 40s record charts reflect this transition in American tastes. By the mid-1950s it was difficult to find a big band anywhere on the charts, but singers such as Frank Sinatra, Perry Como, Tony Martin, Doris Day, Kay Star, Jo Stafford, and Teresa Brewer were regular winners. Only Nat "King" Cole stands out as a jazz instrumentalist turned singer who enjoyed success in the '50s. Table 7.4 pairs some of these singers with the bands that gave them their initial exposure.

TABLE 7.3 Important Artists to Emerge from Woody Herman and Stan Kenton Bands.

Woody Herman Sidemen	Stan Kenton Sidemen
Nick Brignola, baritone sax	Art Pepper, alto sax
Stan Getz, tenor sax	Maynard Ferguson, trumpet
Zoot Sims, tenor sax	Peter Erskine, drums
Joe Lovano, tenor sax	Frank Rosolino, trombone
John Fedchock, trombone	Marvin Stamm, trumpet
Bill Chase, trumpet	Anita O'Day, vocalist
Neal Hefti, arranger	June Christy, vocalist
Ralph Burns, arranger	Pete Rugolo, arranger
Al Cohn, tenor sax	Kai Winding, trombone
Nat Pierce, piano	Mel Lewis, drums
Pete and Conti Candoli, trumpet	Gerry Mulligan, baritone sax
Dave Tough, drums	Bud Shank, alto sax
Sal Nestico, tenor sax	Tim Hagans, trumpet
Tom Harrell, trumpet	Conte Candoli, trumpet

TABLE 7.4 Popular Vocalists and Associated Bands.

Vocalists	Bandleader Affiliation
Jo Stafford	Tommy Dorsey
Rosemary Clooney	Tony Pastor
Billie Holiday	Benny Goodman, Artie Shaw
Helen Forest	Artie Shaw, Benny Goodman, and Harry James
Helen O'Connell	Jimmy Dorsey
Peggy Lee	Benny Goodman
Kay Star	Charlie Barnet
June Christy	Stan Kenton
Frank Sinatra	Tommy Dorsey
Anita O'Day	Gene Krupa
Bing Crosby	Paul Whiteman

By the mid-1950s the tide began to turn again, gradually diminishing the careers of all but the biggest of these stars with yet another new wave of American popular music—rock and roll.

While Benny Goodman may have worn the crown as "King of Swing," representing an East Coast brand of jazz, the Midwest and Southwest areas of the country found their own royalty to cradle their style of swing. Just as dialects within this vast country vary from region to region, so did swing music. Chapter 8 will explore Midwest swing in some detail in addition to a few of the singers and pianists from this period who left an indelible mark on this great music.

CHAPTER SUMMARY

In the first half of the 1930s, the Great Depression had a profound effect on life in America and on jazz. Twenty-five percent of the workforce was unemployed, with minorities being especially impacted. The recording industry slowed to a near standstill, as all but the most established record labels went bankrupt due to plummeting record sales. Looking for inexpensive forms of entertainment as a way to forget one's troubles, many Americans turned to radio, the movies, parlor games, and ballroom dancing.

As the popularity of ballroom dancing increased, so did the size and number of dance halls. At a time when sound reinforcement was still in its infancy larger musical groups were needed to fill these larger halls with music. Instead of the three-musician front line of the previous decade, bands expanded to have entire sections of trumpets, trombones, and saxophones, in addition to the three- or four-piece rhythm section. Fletcher Henderson and his arranger Don Redman are often credited with the standardization of big band instrumentation and arranging techniques still in use today.

Continuing the trend started in the 1920s by Louis Armstrong, most groups started playing in a more connected, less jerky fashion. For example, drummers began using the cymbals to indicate pulse rather than drums and the string bass gradually replaced the tuba and bass saxophone as the most common bass instrument. Bassists could play long lines without the need to stop for a breath, as had been the case with earlier wind instrumentalists playing low bass parts.

Duke Ellington was one of the great American musical geniuses. Throughout his long touring career, he composed more than 2,000 songs, many of which have become a part of the standard jazz repertoire. Ellington had a more sophisticated approach to arranging than did Fletcher Henderson and Don Redman, often effectively using very unusual combinations of instruments, longer forms, uneven phrase lengths, and more advanced chromatic harmonies.

During the Swing Era, jazz reached the height of popularity and was the popular music of the day. The most commercially successful groups were white big bands. Some, like the bands of Benny Goodman and Artie Shaw, featured hot jazz solos, while others, like Glenn Miller, contained few improvised solos. Benny Goodman is especially noted as the first white big band leader to integrate, featuring great black jazz artists like Teddy Wilson, Lionel Hampton, and Charlie Christian.

The solo work of Charlie Christian on amplified guitar and numerous other musicians indicated a new direction in improvisation yet to come. Probably the most important solo recording of the era was tenor saxophonist Coleman Hawkins' recording of "Body and Soul." This recording served as a model for the next generation of musicians, helping to foster the emergence of bebop.

KEY TERMS

Important terms, places, people and bands.

TERMS
WPA
arrangement
hi-hat
fill
chart
comping
head charts
riff
orchestrate
gig
soli
vibrato
rubato
double-time

legato
articulation
dissonance
chord tones
consonance
arpeggio
chord voicing

PLACES
Harlem
Cotton Club

PEOPLE
Duke Ellington
Benny Goodman

Don Redman
Coleman Hawkins
Johnny Hodges
Harry Carney
Jimmy Blanton
Billy Strayhorn
Gene Krupa
John Hammond
Lionel Hampton
Charlie Christian
Teddy Wilson

BANDS
Duke Ellington
Fletcher Henderson

REVIEW QUESTIONS

1. Can you describe the life of a traveling musician particularly during the Depression? How were things worse for the black performers?

2. How did the concept of swing change and what factors led to this important change from early jazz styles?

3. What characteristics distinguished "hot" bands from "sweet" bands? Can you name some representative bandleaders in each style?

4. Who was undoubtedly the most prolific jazz composer from the swing era?

5. Explain what arrangers do when they create music for a big band.

6. Describe the instrumentation of a Swing Era big band.

7. What was the specific contribution made by Jimmy Blanton?

8. What pioneering big band leader brought Louis Armstrong from Chicago to New York to join his band?

9. Benny Goodman's early success was based in part on music arranged by _____?

10. What pair of New York arrangers did much to establish certain models and norms for big band arrangements?

11. Who is remembered as "The Father of Jazz Tenor Saxophone"?

12. What was so special about Coleman Hawkins' recording of "Body and Soul?"

13. If Paul Whiteman was billed as the "King of Jazz," Benny Goodman was known as the "_____"?

14. What white bandleader was the first to hire black performers for public performances by his small groups? Who were these black musicians and what instruments did they play?

15. What jazz promoter played a role in integrating jazz bands during the Swing Era?

16. Where was the Cotton Club and what significance did it play in Ellington's career?

17. Were black or white big bands more popular? Of the two, which seemed to do more artistically to move the music forward?

18. Name three or four popular white swing bands.

19. What attributes made Duke Ellington's music so special?

20. Duke Ellington's music can be generally placed in several categories. Name these categories and name one tune that serves as an example.

21. How did changes in recording format eventually help Duke Ellington's quest to be a composer of more lengthy serious music?

Make sure that you also review material on the corresponding chapter of the CD-ROM.

SUGGESTED SUPPLEMENTARY LISTENING

The abbreviation (iT) indicates that a particular recording cited in the text, or particularly demonstrative of the artist, is available from the Apple iTunes Web site. Other Web based music distributors may also prove to be valuable resources. SCCJ indicates *Smithsonian Collection of Classic Jazz*.

Fletcher Henderson

A Study in Frustration: Fletcher Henderson Story Columbia Legacy
Fletcher Henderson and His Orchestra 1925/1927 Jazz Archives No. 137
"Copenhagen" (iT)
"Down South Camp Meetin' " (iT)
"Easy Money" (iT)
"Happy Feet" (iT)
"Henderson Stomp" (iT)
"King Porter Stomp" (iT)
"Rose Room" (iT)
"St. Louis Blues" (iT)
"Stampede"(iT) SCCJ
"Wrappin' It Up"(iT) SCCJ
"Hotter Than 'Ell" *Ken Burns Jazz*

Coleman Hawkins

Ken Burns Jazz: Coleman Hawkins Verve (iT)
"The Man I Love" (iT) SCCJ

Duke Ellington

"Mood Indigo" (iT)
"East St. Louis Toodle-Oo" (iT) SCCJ
"New East St. Louis Toodle-Oo" (iT) SCCJ
"Do Nothin' Till You Hear From Me" (iT)
"Rockin' In Rhythm"

"Jack the Bear" (iT)
"Concerto For Cootie" (iT) SCCJ
"Creole Rhapsody" (iT)
"Black and Tan Fantasy" (iT)
"Caravan" (iT)
"In a Mellow Tone" (iT) SCCJ
"It Don't Mean a Thing if it Ain't Got that Swing" *Ken Burns Jazz*
"Echoes of Harlem" *Ken Burns Jazz*
"Cotton Tail" *Ken Burns Jazz*
"Tourist Point of View" *Ken Burns Jazz*
"Don't Get Around Much Anymore" (iT)
"Sophisticated Lady" (iT)
"Prelude to a Kiss" (iT)
"In a Sentimental Mood" (iT)
"Diminuendo and Crescendo in Blue" (iT) SCCJ
"Solitude" (iT)
"Satin Doll" (iT)
"Take the 'A' Train" (iT)
"Blue Serge" (iT) SCCJ
"Queen's Suite" (iT)
Far East Suite BMG (RCA-Bluebird)
Ellington at Newport Columbia Legacy
And His Mother Called Him Bill BMG (RCA-Bluebird)

Benny Goodman

Benny Goodman Sextet Featuring Charlie Christian Columbia (Sony) CK45144
Benny Goodman: On the Air 1937-1938 Sony (iT)
Ken Burns Jazz: Benny Goodman Sony (iT)
Benny Goodman Small Groups Columbia Legacy
Benny Goodman Orchestra: Sing, Sing, Sing BMG (RCA-Bluebird)
"King Porter Stomp" *Ken Burns Jazz*
"Rose Room" *Ken Burns Jazz*
"Sing, Sing, Sing" *Ken Burns Jazz*

Charlie Christian

Charlie Christian: The Genius of the Electric Guitar Sony (iT)
"Breakfast Feud" (iT) SCCJ
"Solo Flight" (iT)
"Six Appeal" (iT)

Lionel Hampton

"When Lights Are Low" (iT) SCCJ

Gene Krupa

"Rockin Chair" (iT) SCCJ

Jimmy Lunceford
"For Dancers Only" *Ken Burns Jazz*

Artie Shaw
"Begin the Beguine" *Ken Burns Jazz*

Glenn Miller
"In the Mood" *Ken Burns Jazz*

Tommy Dorsey
"Well, Get It!" *Ken Burns Jazz*

Midwest *Swing* and a Few More Among Many

"No previous form of jazz had come even close to the immense popularity of the swing bands, which thoroughly dominated the hit charts during the years 1936 through 1945."[1]

BERNARD GENDRAN

While there are some similarities in terms of the nightlife and corruption, there are many differences that distinguish Kansas City and other Southwestern cities from New York in the 1930s. Remote Southwestern and Midwestern towns were less subject to the influences of New Orleans, and as author Ross Russell put it, musicians in these towns "were left to their own musical devices."[2] The Plains States were slow to absorb the more sophisticated musical styles evolving in Harlem and to participate in the growing music industry developing around Chicago and in these Eastern urban areas. Consequently, ragtime and blues styles continued to flourish during the Swing Era and exerted a strong influence on music in the Southwest. Many of the Eastern-based groups developed in ways that identified them with a more sophisticated approach as compared to the bands from the Midwest and Southwest. Bassist Gene Ramey who traveled to New York as a member of the Kansas City–based band led by Jay McShann was in a good position to assess the differences between bands from these two locales. He offered the following explanation:

> You'll notice another thing about the eastern bands. They were always writing arrangements that would lose somebody. "Man I wrote an arrangement and nobody could play it." The guy didn't know he was ruining his own career too. What he needed to write is something that everybody could play so they could express his arrangement better. So lots of those that came from the east were doing that—unnecessary interludes and modulations. If you're not going to have a vocalist or a soloist that likes

a certain key, then you didn't need to go through all the modulations. KC bands had a certain ruggedness, roughness that swung hard.[3]

The East Coast band with the most sophistication was of course Duke Ellington. Ramey also pointed out that eastern rhythm sections lacked the "laid-back," behind the beat "Baptist" beat that he associated with Midwestern and Southwestern bands. He felt that the eastern bands played with a very precise, "metronome beat."

MIDWEST AND SOUTHWEST SWING

Territory Bands

Since towns were many miles apart, musicians found it necessary to travel a great deal for work. Many of these bands traveled only within certain unofficial boundaries and became known as **territory bands.** These bands roamed the Southwest and Midwest often commanding salaries as high as $150 per week in the major cities like Dallas. Table 8.1 illustrates how far this weekly salary would go in terms of purchasing power in 1940.

TABLE 8.1 Cost of Living Index Circa 1940

Weekly Salaries Averages	Farmhand $10
	Factory worker $25
	Clerks $30
	White-collar employees no more than $60
Goods	Basic automobile $645
	Butter and bacon 35 cents per pound
	Loaf of bread 10 cents
	Whole chicken $2
	Dress shirt $2
	Worsted wool suit $25
	Woman's two-piece suit $15
	Blouse $3
	Shoes and socks or hose $6
Lodging	One-room New York apartment $40 per month
	House $6,000–$10,000
Entertainment and Luxuries	Restaurant dinner $2
	Movie ticket during prime time 25 cents
	Combination radio-phonograph $50
	Bottle of Scotch whiskey $1
	Cigarettes 15 cents per pack

SOURCE: www.audio-play.com/toodead/calif40.htm.

TABLE 8.2 Well-Known Territory Bands and Their Locales

Troy Floyd—Dallas	Milt Larkin—Texas
Alfonso Trent—Dallas	Black Aces—Colorado
Andy Kirk's 12 Clouds of Joy—Kansas City	Jesse Stone—Kansas City
Benny Moten Orchestra—Kansas City	Lawrence "88" Keys—Kansas City
Blue Syncopaters—Texas	Kansas City Rockets—Kansas City
Boots and His Buddies—Texas	Blue Devils—Oklahoma/Texas

Many Swing Era "territorial" musicians went their entire lives without being recorded, while some were recorded but with limited circulation and others, like Benny Moten and Jay McShann, became nationally known initially through their regionally produced records. Most of these bands were deeply rooted in a blues tradition and much of their repertoire was based on improvised **head** arrangements. Head arrangements came about as the result of musicians improvising simple riffs, usually blues based, that were memorized and eventually served to codify a particular arrangement. Many of these black performers came to jazz from a strong foundation in gospel and spiritual music as religion was an important part of their upbringing in this part of the country. Many of the greatest musicians of the Swing Era such as Ben Webster, Lester Young, Charlie Christian, Count Basie, and Mary Lou Williams apprenticed early in their careers with territory bands (See Table 8.2).

Mary Lou Williams (1910–1981)

With the exception of vocalists, the jazz profession remained largely a male-dominated world. Of course, there were exceptions like Ina Rae Hutton's Sweethearts of Rhythm and Phil Spitalny's "All-Girl" orchestra, but more often than not they were treated like novelty acts playing watered down jazz with window dressing. Some female orchestras became popular during wartime when many male musicians had been drafted. Mary Lou Williams was, however, an exception. Her accomplishments are even greater when you consider the general attitude towards women in jazz that was encouraged by the press. For instance, *Down Beat* Magazine, founded in 1934 on the strength of the growing enthusiasm for swing, ran an article in 1938 titled "Why Women Musicians Are Inferior." The author was coldly unsupportive of the "fairer sex" citing that "women should be able to play with feeling and expression and they never do." He went on to say that "women don't seem to be able to develop a lip to withstand the endurance required to play jazz on a wind instrument. The mind may be willing but the flesh is weak."[4] This same magazine printed rebuttals written by women in the field, but it was difficult to further their minority opinion. Other writers expounded that women were not hired for their musicianship as men were, but were employed because they were attractive to men. Women were "not well suited to the hard life of touring and playing in gin joints,'"[5] other writers claimed. The scales in the jazz gender battle have unfortunately always tipped on the side of the male musicians and only recently have women begun to be recognized for their artistic contributions to jazz. Consequently, it has taken decades for Mary Lou Williams' contributions to be fully appreciated and touted.

She was raised in Pittsburgh where she developed an early flare as a solo pianist and arranger. She was hired by Andy Kirk's Kansas City–based 12 Clouds of Joy and remained with Kirk from 1930 to 1942 before moving to New York. By this

Pianist/composer Mary Lou Williams, 1937.

time, her reputation as a first-rate arranger and composer earned her commissions from Benny Goodman, Earl Hines, Tommy Dorsey, and even Duke Ellington. In an unprecedented move, the New York Philharmonic Orchestra premiered in 1946 a portion of her *Zodiac Suite* in Carnegie Hall. The merging of jazz and symphonic styles in this work was by itself unique and groundbreaking, and the fact that the suite was composed by a woman added to the significance of its premier. In New York, Williams adapted her style as a pianist and composer/arranger to the new bebop idiom emerging in the mid-1940s, contributing works to Dizzy Gillespie's big band. Before her career came to a close, she had composed numerous jazz pieces, sacred works for chorus and orchestra, including three masses, and had made many recordings. She stands as an exceptional example of the highest accomplishments by women in jazz, claiming a list of awards of which any artist would be proud.

Kansas City

Kansas City, or "Kaycee" as the locals knew it, was the Midwestern big city hub for cattleman and wheat farmers selling their wares. They came to this city starved for the various forms of entertainment that were hard to come by in the more remote, rural plains. Cabarets, gambling houses, nightclubs and bars, opera houses, and dance halls were plentiful in this big city near the confluence of the Missouri and Kansas Rivers. "Kaycee" had its special brand of music, much of which was derived from blues and ragtime styles. As was the case in other big cities during this period, there was a shady side of Kansas City. After dark, nightlife activities were supported by gangsters who not only owned many of the establishments, but also saw to it that illegal alcohol flowed freely. Just as Al Capone controlled much of the Chicago scene, Kansas City flourished from dawn until dusk during the reign of political boss Tom Pendergast. Pendergast gained control of the rough-and-tumble immigrant district known as the First Ward. This appointment was a stepping-stone leading to his eventual control of much of the politics in the city, and eventually the entire state, until the federal government brought him down in 1938 on charges of tax evasion, among others. He enjoyed close ties to the gangster community. His demise came only after he did much to ensure the unencumbered operation of clubs selling illegal alcohol during Prohibition as well as every other imaginable vice. Much like Chicago and New York, there were the black and white sides of town in Kansas City, each supporting dozens of nightclubs and gambling houses. Kansas City, described as a "wild town" during these years, could satisfy any desire and was a magnet for musicians who willingly came to provide their brand of music. During the Depression years, the numerous clubs that supported live music sustained many of the Kansas City musicians. The ravages of the Depression years were too much for nearly all of the territory bands to overcome, since they relied so heavily on the ability to travel and for this reason many migrated to Kansas City seeking employment.

It was the popular Benny Moten band that is most associated with jazz in this city during the Pendergast reign. The Moten band captured much of the choice work, and when bookings became sparse and travel difficult for Walter Page's Blue Devils, many of Page's top bandsmen were lured to the Moten band. The Blue Devils out of Oklahoma City were a fine outfit that at one time employed Buster Smith and Lester Young on saxophones, Oran "Hot Lips" Page on trumpet, pianist William Basie, Walter Page on bass, Jimmy Rushing as vocalist, and Eddie Durham who contributed arrangements and played trombone and guitar. It was this Southwestern band, along with Moten's, that perfected the blues riff, head-style arrangement. By 1932, nearly all of these fine Blue Devils musicians including its leader had left to join the Moten band. Listen to Moten's recording of " Moten Swing" included on the *Smithsonian Classic Collection of Jazz* to hear this band at the top of its game.

In a radio interview with jazz radio DJ Art Vincent, bassist Gene Ramey made the following observations and comments about the scene in Kansas City.

A sample of Kansas City nightclubs popular in the 1930s.

It was back in 1932 when I came from Texas to Kansas City. At that time Benny Moten had his band. They had those fabulous battles of bands and I think that's the thing that impressed me the most about Kansas City. Those guys were dressed in the sharpest clothes. In those days it seemed like every big time musician owned a Hudson car. They were big like Cadillacs you know, and I think they were the first cars that I had ever seen that were painted green, purple and like that. I remember George E. Lee [Kansas City territory bandleader] had two of them. And they would have these battles of the bands . . . I can't name all of them . . . Andy Kirk's 12 Clouds of Joy, Walter Page's Blue Devils, Harlan Leonard's Rockets, Julius and Carl Banks, Clarence Love, and of course the mighty Benny Moten. On holidays, Labor Day or Christmas Eve, they'd have a ballroom battle of all those bands and it would start at 7 o'clock and go to about 5 o'clock in the morning. Just one band after another until whoever won that contest and of course Benny Moten always won.[6]

Benny Moten started his band in 1923, but at this point, the area was still heavily under the influence of ragtime, brass bands, and vaudeville style music. His first recording released in 1923, coinciding closely with those issued by King Oliver in Chicago and Fletcher Henderson in New York, featured a New Orleans–like instrumentation to project an arranged ragtime ensemble style. Over the years, Moten built his Kansas City–based band to be rivaled by no other from the area. He gradually expanded the instrumentation while moving away from the rag-based style. Up until the addition of Blue Devils' personnel, his band lacked the secure soloists that the Eastern bands boasted and he had difficulty producing arrangements that would adequately showcase his expanded band. The recruitment of those stellar Blue Devils' soloists, however, turned this situation around. Bill Basie, one of the first to leave the Blue Devils, replaced Moten at the piano, enabling the leader to concentrate on conducting and the business of running his band. Historian Ross Russell called bassist Walter Page "the single most important addition to the [Moten] band"[7] during this period. Fellow Kansas City bassist Gene Ramey agreed with Russell's assertion:

> I started playing the bass violin in '33 and in '35 is when I started to hang around Walter Page. Although very little credit is given to him, he made the [Moten] rhythm section. Before that rhythm section came into being all you ever heard of was a band that was swung by a big foot drummer. All you ever heard in the rhythm section was the drummer. And then, workin' with Basie they figured out a way where the drummer wouldn't play so loudly. The piano and guitar would have a chance to be heard. All those instruments weren't amplified then you know. That's why you notice Basie plays so few notes. That's the way for him to stay out of the way of the rest of the rhythm section. Imagine what it would be like if Basie was plowing through with his chord ideas and the guitar was playing his chords. There's bound to be a clash. So Basie and Page worked that thing out and they started something that all musicians are using today. It gave the rhythm section freedom.[8]

William "Count" Basie (1904–1984)

A tragedy struck Moten and his band in 1935 just as they were at the top of their game. Moten died on the operating table while undergoing a simple tonsillectomy. In short order, Bill Basie, capitalizing on his old friendships with members of the Moten and Blue Devils bands, brought together a new band under his leadership. At this point he declared himself the "Count." Basie's band was first dis-

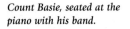

Count Basie, seated at the piano with his band.

covered by impresario John Hammond who heard a radio broadcast of the band. He was so impressed that he brought the band to New York in 1936.

It is doubtful at this point that Bill Basie, the "Kid from Redbank," New Jersey, realized that he had begun a legacy that would continue even today under the leadership of band alumni. With the exception of a brief two-year period from 1950 to 1952 when economics forced him to reduce his band to a smaller group, Basie maintained his career as a big band leader for 49 years. The Basie band brought together the finest musicians from this area and codified the relaxed, swinging blues-riff style that is associated with bands from the Southwest. The blues was at the core of this band's style and in these early years much of the arranging was accomplished by Eddie Durham who was gifted at constructing head-style arrangements based on riffs to serve as a framework for Basie's superb soloists. The arrangers who have provided "charts" for the band over the years have always maintained Durham's concern for economy of style. These arrangers utilized simple **motives** (short melodic phrases that can serve as the primary basis of a tune) often used as **riffs** (a short repeated musical phrase) that characterized a loose, improvised style. These motives and riffs were orchestrated for brass and saxophones and served both as **backgrounds** (secondary material that serves as accompaniment to a solo) behind soloists as well as primary material for the main themes. The various riffs were often tossed about from section to section in a call and response format. The arrangements also took advantage of the large dynamic range of a big band, contrasting quiet rhythm section moments with bombastic surprises in the form of full band blasts. The Basie band, while never specializing in sophisticated and elaborate compositions, attracted listeners who were caught up in the relaxed swing and simplicity that became the hallmark of this great band. Basie had eliminated all that was superfluous, leaving only those essential ingredients that appealed to man's basic instincts by creating an infectious brand of toe-tapping swing. Late in his career he was asked in a *60 Minutes* television interview to describe his music. After a brief pause he replied succinctly by saying, "tap your toe." His brief description was as streamlined and to the point as his music.

It was the Basie rhythm section that generated the undercurrent that attributed to a unique brand of swing. Known as the "All-American Rhythm Section," these four men revolutionized and modernized the approach to rhythm section playing by the late thirties. They were the first rhythm section to redefine the roles of their instruments to achieve a much-improved balance within the rhythm section. Page, who had already begun to assert himself as a fine bassist in the Blue Devils, perfected the **"walking" bass** line by playing ascending and descending quarter notes on each beat of the **measure.** These flowing lines gave impetus, power, and forward motion to the music. Guitarist Freddie Green, who spent his entire professional life with the Basie band, played an unamplified rhythm guitar, strumming dry, simple three and four note chords on each beat. Jo Jones, who had also played with the Blue Devils, joined Basie's rhythm section in 1934. He is credited with developing a more modern swing style of drumming by moving the emphasis away from the bass drum that could easily obscure bass lines. Jones focused on playing the uneven swing pattern on the hi-hat while using the bass drum more subtly and embellishing the basic beat using his free hand to chatter on the snare drum. Eventually this swing pattern was moved to the suspended ride cymbal. With each beat being well defined by bass, drums, and guitar, Basie was forced to abandon his

Left to right: drummer Joe Jones, Walter Page on bass, and Count Basie on piano comprising three-fourths of the All-American Rhythm Section from the Basie band.

earlier stride and boogie-woogie styles. These earlier piano styles were far too busy and duplicated the new roles established by Page, Jones, and Green. Basie developed a new economic approach to playing chords described as "**comping.**" It is a sparse, uncluttered technique as compared to earlier styles and allowed the music to breathe, giving the listener an opportunity to hear more clearly the bass and guitar. This new abbreviated, succinct accompaniment style is based on chords played often in short, rhythmically random and often syncopated gestures designed to punctuate other activities and provide harmonic accompaniment for soloists.

 The contrast between these styles is particularly evident when listening to the earlier stride approach as compared to the more modern comping style. Both styles can be found on the CD-ROM. A brief video example of the stride style is found in the section corresponding to Chapter 5, while an audio example of comping is found in the piano section of "Dissecting a Jazz Performance" located in Chapter 3—Listening to Jazz.

Basie also developed a sparse solo style based on simple motives consisting of single-note lines played in the upper register of the piano. This style became his easily recognized signature and arrangers always made sure to feature him in this way. While other bands on the East Coast, like those led by Ellington and Jimmy Lunceford, were perfecting a similar rhythm section concept, it is the Basie Band rhythm section that is justly given credit for initially advancing and perfecting it.

 Each of these specific rhythm section performance practice techniques is clarified through video and audio examples found in the Performance Practice tutorial of Chapter 3—Listening to Jazz—on the CD-ROM. These examples will enhance your understanding and recognition of comping, walking bass, and swing style drumming techniques.

The Basie band developed a reputation for featuring an endless parade of solos by the best players of the day, many of whom left other bands to join his ranks: trumpeters Harry "Sweets" Edison, Buck Clayton, and later Thad Jones who some years after forged his own modern big band; trombonists Lawrence Brown, Dickey Wells, Benny Morton, and Dan Minor; and saxophonists Hershel Evans, Earl Warren, Buddy Tate, Frank Foster, and, of course, the legendary Lester Young.

Lester Young (1909–1959)

Tenor saxophonist Lester Young, who began his career in music as a drummer in his touring family's territory band, offered an alternative to the bold, big sound asserted by Coleman Hawkins. (Refer to the interview excerpts found in the corresponding chapter on the CD-ROM.) Young's tone was often without obvious vibrato, light and airy, and much closer to the sound of the C-melody or alto saxophone. Young's sound was in stark contrast to that of Hawkins who began a long line of descendants who preferred his aggressive style with a husky sound and thick, wide vibrato. Because of his wispy sound, Young, along with Bix Beiderbecke and Frankie Trumbauer, is often considered an early pioneer of the "cool" sound not yet fully developed or defined. Even Young's posture was distinctive in that he cocked his head and held the saxophone at an odd angle, forcing him to play almost out of the side of his mouth. He also was rarely seen without his wide-brimmed porkpie hat, a trademark adopted by many Swing Era players.

There was at least one other obvious contrast between Hawkins and Young. Young tended to favor building improvisations by stringing together a series of simple melodic motives that consisted of pitches that were common to several consecutive chords in the progression. Hawkins, on the other hand, favored a busier harmonic style that engaged him in long phrases of endless arpeggiations (outlining of chords by playing one note at a time) as each chord changed. Young therefore favored linear melodic development regardless of changes in harmony, while Hawkins' solos were motivated by chord motion (see Chapter 7). Young's solos consequently often occupied a smaller range than Hawkins' improvisations. While he enjoyed success throughout his career, his style, particularly his sound, placed him in the minority and in some ways he lived bitterly in the shadow of the more robust tenor saxophonists who had followed in Hawkins' footsteps. Nicknamed the "President" or "Prez" for short, Young recorded with numerous small groups including vocalist Billie Holiday and pianist Teddy Wilson among others. He performed at festivals here and in Europe, but some say he never regained the "fire" in his playing after serving in World War II, when he was a victim of various forms of racial discrimination and harassment. He passed away only one month before his lifelong friend and kindred musical spirit, Billie Holiday.

Tenor saxophonist Lester Young plays with drummer Jo Jones.

"Every Tub," included on the companion CD anthology, provides an excellent glimpse of Lester Young as well as the Count Basie sound that has survived virtually unchanged, at least in basic stylistic concepts, for decades.

Count Basie

Form and Key: Song Form Choruses (AABA=chorus) B♭ Major

0:00–0:07　*Introduction:* 8 bars, tenor sax solo over stop-time band breaks.

0:08–0:30　*First Chorus:* 24-bar (abbreviated) Tenor Sax Solo (Young):

　　　0:08–0:15　*A section:* 8 bars, tenor sax solo over brass riffs, rhythm section.

　　　0:16–0:23　*B section:* 8 bars, tenor sax solo over bridge chords, with rhythm section only.

　　　0:24–0:31　*A section:* 8 bars, tenor sax solo over brass riffs, rhythm section.

0:31–0:54　*Second Chous:* 24-bar (abbreviated) Piano Solo:

　　　0:31–0:38　*A section:* 8 bars, piano solo with bass and drum accompaniment.

　　　0:39–0:46　*B section:* 8 bars, piano solo over bridge chords, with bass and drums.

　　　0:47–0:54　*A section:* 8 bars, piano solo with bass and drum accompaniment.

Listening Guide

"Every Tub" (Count Basie, Eddie Durham) 3:14

Recorded 2/16/38 New York City, Decca1728

Reissued by MCA and GRP records GRD-3-611

Count Basie: *piano*

Buck Clayton, Ed Lewis, Harry Edison: *trumpets*

Benny Morton, Dan Minor, Eddie Durham: *trombones*

Lester Young, Herschel Evans: *clarinets and tenor saxophones*

Listening Guide

Earl Warren: *alto saxophone*

Jack Washington: *alto and baritone saxophone*

Freddie Green: *guitar*

Walter Page: *bass*

Jo Jones: *drums*

0:55–1:21	*Third Chorus:* 36-bar Trumpet Solo (Edison):	
	0:55–0:58	*Interlude break:* 4 bars, trumpets play unison ensemble break with drums only.
	0:59–1:06	*A section:* 8 bars, trumpet solo (Edison) with sax section riffs, rhythm section.
	1:07–1:14	*A section:* 8 bars, trumpet solo continues with sax section riffs, rhythm section.
	1:14–1:21	*B section:* 8 bars, trumpet solo continues with rhythm section only
	1:22–1:30	*A section:* 8 bars, trumpet solo continues with sax section riffs.
1:30–2:01	*Fourth Chorus:* 32-bar Ensemble Shout Chorus, with saxes and brass in call and response pattern, alternating with piano solo:	
	1:30–1:38	*A section:* 8 bars, sax and brass play call and response riffs.
	1:38–1:46	*A section:* 8 bars, like A section above.
	1:46–1:53	*B section:* 8 bars, piano solo with rhythm.
	1:54–2:01	*A section:* 8 bars, like A section above.
2:02–2:33	*Fifth Chorus:* 32-bar Theme:	
	2:02–2:09	*A section:* 8 bars, saxes play theme with brass riffs and rhythm section.
	2:10–2:17	*A section:* 8 bars, like A section above.
	2:18–2:25	*B section:* 8 bars, tenor solo (Evans) over bridge chords, with rhythm section.
	2:36–2:33	*A section:* 8 bars, like A section above.
2:33–3:05	*Sixth Chorus:* 32 bar Varied Theme:	
	2:33–2:40	*A section:* 8 bars, saxes play varied theme with brass riffs and rhythm section.
	2:41–2:48	*A section:* 8 bars, like A section above.
	2:49–2:57	*B section:* 8 bars, trumpet solo (Edison) with sustained sax chords and rhythm.
	2:57–3:05	*A section:* 8 bars, like A section above.
3:05–3:14	Coda: 4-bar repeated brass riff, 2-bar tenor break (Young), 2-bar Dixieland style ensemble ending.	

Listen to the interviews with Lester Young and Billie Holiday found in the corresponding chapter on the CD-ROM.

THE SUCCESS OF BIG BANDS

For the first time in the history of American music, from 1935 until about 1945, popular music was in complete resonance with American society and thought. Whether one lived on the East Coast, the West Coast, or somewhere in between, swing was the thing. Attending dances was so much a part of the American way that it was often an important stage in the adolescent courtship ritual. Many young women and men met their lifelong partners on the dance floor. This is the only time in the history of jazz that the music was in sync with the American psyche. As the country came out of its worst Depression, Americans gained a sense of confidence and their renewed spirits yearned for the enjoyable things in life to occupy their leisure time. Never before, and never since, has jazz experienced such financial success, public acceptance, and worldwide acclaim. For almost 10 years, big band swing music was America's pop art and nearly any reasonably capable musician was working, and for good money. New magazine publications like *Down Beat* (which first hit the news stands in 1934), *Esquire*, and *Metronome* followed the music and its creators, sponsoring polls to determine the most popular musicians and bands of the day. Fans debated as to which was the best band or hottest soloist. Hot clubs sprang up in this country and abroad, formed for the sole purpose of providing a meeting ground for enthusiasts who collected and enjoyed listening to jazz recordings. Between 1937 and 1940 *Metronome* magazine posted nearly 300 big band entries for its readers to rank in their polls. This number represented only a portion of the number of working bands throughout the nation. They were to be ranked in one of three categories—"Swing," "Sweet," and "Favorite of All."[9] These same magazines also began ranking individual soloists and choosing "all-star" bands based on input from their writer-critics and readers. The critics and fans did not always agree, and as history proves, sometimes both parties were wrong in their selections, at least if we consider which musicians ultimately had a lasting impact on the music. Notice that the best-seller listing that follows shows only white bands or vocalists and at least three of these bands had no lasting impact on jazz. For that matter, it would be difficult to classify any of these top-10 hits as anything more than jazz influenced dance band numbers, yet these bands were considered jazz bands of the day.

During the peak years of the Swing Era (circa 1935–1945) it was not uncommon to see long lines of fans clambering to gain entrance to a dance where a name band was performing or crowding the bandstand or stage to get a closer look at their favorite band. Imagine being swept up in the frenetic enthusiasm of a throng of crazed fans rushing the stage to get a closer look at their swing idols, and struggling to get close enough to feel the throbbing pulse of the big band. This exchange of energy between musician and exuberant audience made the often difficult life of the big band musician all worthwhile. At times, these crowds were almost uncontrollable in their enthusiasm, much like those reactions in the 1960s to rock groups like the Beatles, Cream, or the Rolling Stones. New dances, like the shag, shim-sham, and big apple emerged overnight to become the next sensation. Dance marathons and contests, staged battles between bands, and "cutting contests" where soloists challenged one another on the bandstand were all familiar scenes during this era. Radio stations broadcast band battles live from ballrooms, adding to public exposure, helping to sell recordings, and promoting future engagements.

Successful leaders, particularly white bandleaders like Glenn Miller, Artie Shaw and Benny Goodman, became wealthy icons, enjoying reputations on a par with the most famous movie stars and much like those of pop, rock, or country

music headliners today. For that matter, some bandleaders married movie stars. Bandleader Artie Shaw married both Lana Turner and Ava Gardner, and the most successful bands were occasionally featured in films. The Swing Era also produced its share of bluebloods—even royalty, or at least their nicknames suggested such stature. Edward Kennedy Ellington, for example, was dubbed the "Duke," while Benny Goodman was known as the "King of Swing," William Basie was referred to as "Count," Billie Holiday was known as "Lady Day," and Lester Young was bestowed the title of the "President" or "Prez" for short.

A new cult language began to emerge during the Swing Era. Developed largely by the black jazz community, this new jargon was quickly adopted by white musicians. New words and expressions like "crib" (dwelling), "chick" (female), "hip" (wise, aware, and sophisticated), "bread" (currency or money), and "it was a gas" (impressive, satisfying, enjoyable) were born and helped to create an even more cultlike environment in which these musicians lived and worked.[10] Gene Ramey reminisces about some of the extra-musical slang expressions that developed particularly among jazz musicians:

> Now we always had lots of smoke signals that we used in conversation. Say you and your wife are sittin' over there and me and my wife are sittin' over here and you're talking in a different language. Now we can't understand what you're saying, but we can watch by the expression that you must be talkin' about us. So then I would say to her "You know, it's kind of drafty in here. Do you feel that draft." She's got the message right away. We started using anti-language. We would say

something was "bad" which really meant it was good. Lester Young and Cab Calloway had a whole bunch of those expressions. They really personalized it.[11]

The expression "feel a draft" was also coined as an expression of racial prejudice and
attributed to Lester Young. Jazz lingo has motivated American slang for decades, and
it is not unusual to find more than one meaning associated with a particular word.

Many of the successful star soloists left the employment of one band to strike
out on their own forming a new band under their leadership. One successful band
often led to several other spin-offs. For example, Gene Krupa, Teddy Wilson, Lionel Hampton, Cootie Williams, Harry James, Jack Teagarden, and Bunny Berigan
formed their own bands after serving apprenticeships with Duke Ellington, Benny
Goodman, Count Basie or others. It was not uncommon for those most in-
demand soloists to move from one band to another, following the best wage, best
working conditions, and best public exposure. The most in-demand musicians
were bartered and traded from band to band almost like athletes.

There were several factors that were responsible for the success or failure of
a big band during the Swing Era.

- Arrangers and musical directors established a band's identifiable sound.
  Their particular treatment of a song gave the band its unique sound. Fans
  could often identify a particular band after listening to only a few
  measures of music.

- Soloists contributed significantly to the overall success of a band,
  explaining why bandleaders typically paid them the highest salaries.

- The leader's personality, stage presence, and charisma also contributed to
  the band's public appeal, and for that matter, a few leaders like Cab
  Calloway did not play an instrument, though most did.

- Vocalists added an extra element of popular appeal since everyone could
  appreciate a lyric even if they did not understand or relate to the more
  involved instrumental arrangements. Consequently, every band had at
  least one vocalist and they might feature two—a male and a female. In
  some ways, the overwhelming success of some of these singers, like Frank
  Sinatra, actually contributed to the gradual downfall of big band jazz.

- Businessmen, booking agents, and promoters helped bandleaders make
  their careers. Without them, a great band would languish, unknown in its
  quest for notoriety.

- The quality of the band's dance music attracted fans.

- The band's exposure on radio, on record, and in major venues helped
  immeasurably to popularize a band.

While these factors promoted a band's success, any one factor could also
lead to its demise. For example, bassist Gene Ramey, along with many black musicians, was very much against many of the white managements and their business
practices, feeling that they placed too many conditions on employment and often
worked against a band's success.

> Moe Gale was intent on breaking up the [Jay] McShann band after he found
> he couldn't bring us into his fold. You see Moe Gale owned the Savoy [ball-
> room] and he owned the Golden Gate and he had control of the Rockland
> Palace, Apollo Theater, and Audubon Ballroom. I remember they had us set
> up to be one of the first black bands to play in a white hotel. That hotel was

down on 43rd and Broadway. I forget the name of it but it's nothing but a dump now. Anyway, this was the come-on, now the stipulation they came up with—McShann would give them complete authority over the band [including] hiring and firing. This was the thing they tried to do when they got rid of Charlie Parker. We were a band with only one record out and I was making $16 a night and the other guys were making $13. They even sent us out with phony booking agents who would run away and we would have to pay for the dance hall, bouncer, ticket-takers and everything. That happened to us in Georgia, Virginia and South Carolina. They had that attitude: "We can help you and without us you're nothing. We can do whatever we want to do with you and if you don't like it we won't help you." We had lots of that sort of thing happening, so the musician who went to New York expecting to really make it found that he was at their mercy—somebody else was the master of his fate.[12]

The record industry, which had all but collapsed during the Depression years, made a tremendous rebound during the peak years of the Swing Era. For example, 10 million records were sold in 1933 and by 1938 that figure climbed to 33 million. By 1941 the record industry boasted sales in excess of 127 million! In only one year during the swing peak the number of jukeboxes (a term for coin operated record players derived from "juke joint," a slang expression for black brothel) in use soared from 25,000 to 300,000, serving to promote black artists at a time when there were few featured on radio broadcasts. This music had truly captured the attention of most Americans and was no longer the brunt of harsh criticism. Swing music had in fact become impossible to ignore and to some degree the popular singers had much to do with the record industry's rebound.[13]

A FEW MORE AMONG MANY: THE SWING ERA SINGERS AND PIANISTS

Since the Basie band's style was molded largely by the blues, it stands to reason that the band would feature blues singers. A long line of exceptional blues singers, mostly males, performed with the Basie band during its lengthy history. Jimmy Rushing and Joe Williams best exemplify this style. One of the most famous of all jazz singers worked with the Basie band early in her career, though her stay was brief, and commenced what became a lengthy relationship with Lester Young. Her name was Billie Holiday.

Billie Holiday (1915–1959)

Lester Young gave her the nickname, "Lady Day," but Lester called everybody "Lady" even the men. Gene Ramey, who performed and recorded with Lester Young and worked with "Lady Day," offered the following insight into these two compatible and compelling artists:

> Louis Armstrong showed us that you could play a melody and not actually play the melody. You could play the harmonic structure of a melody which made it more pleasing. I think she [Billie Holiday] got some from Louis Armstrong—the idea of how to make songs, even the worst songs, so appealing. And along with that you'll notice that Lester Young got his idea from that, so I would say that Billie Holiday kept the thing going, the sound that was actually created by Armstrong; but she is the only one to this day that put it through with the voice like that. She would sing a note with so much appeal. She was the greatest singer with the worst voice. If you'll notice her voice—it sounded like nothing, but she had

so much control of the way to put a song over. It would sound like, as they would say, a bluesy singer. It was appealing—she was begging. She would take a half-ways good song and make it wonderful. I was one of the pall bearers at Prez's funeral and the last time I saw her was about three or four months before he died.[14]

Ramey was both complimentary and a bit harsh in his assessment of Holiday, but another bassist John Levy who worked with Holiday seemed to confirm Ramey's opinions: "Billie was a complete stylist. When you listen to her sing, you feel she has lived that experience and she is telling a story about it. I don't think anyone can express a story better than Billie. She didn't have great range or any of that stuff, but most of the tunes she sang had good melody lines and good stories, and they're not easy to sing or play."[15]

Information about her early life is somewhat obscure and blurred by inaccuracies, but we do know that Billie Holiday's father played guitar with Fletcher Henderson's band. While her life was clouded with problems, including prostitution and drug and alcohol addiction which eventually led to her arrest, her talent should not

Billie Holiday sings with an unidentified big band.

be obscured by these details. Like other black performers, she owed her initial discovery and subsequent first recordings with Benny Goodman to John Hammond. It was through this association that Holiday met Teddy Wilson who served as musical coordinator for her outstanding recordings from the mid-1930s. Her long association with Lester Young, whose wispy, light sound complemented Holiday's, is well known as is her fairly short stay with Artie Shaw's big, band, which followed her even shorter stay with the Basie band. She joined the Shaw band in 1938 to become one of the first black singers to appear with a white band. This arrangement was not without problems, and there is evidence that Shaw, who stood by Holiday, became frustrated and disgusted with racially prejudiced attitudes. Her best work is considered to have been accomplished from about 1939 to 1944, before her life was turned to chaos by drugs, alcohol, and ensuing legal problems. While the movie about her, *Lady Sings the Blues*, gives one the impression that she was primarily a blues singer, much of her repertoire does not confirm this. She claims Louis Armstrong as a significant influence, and preferred popular tunes and love songs. Her style was certainly informed by the blues style and she was a fine blues singer, though she might be more accurately labeled a torch singer. Her untrained voice projected a certain plaintive cry, a forlorn quality that went beyond the accomplishments of most singers of the day. She became quite popular as a singer who could deliver passionate, poignant performances. She phrased much like an improvising instrumentalist and rarely interpreted the melody strictly as it was written—so one could say in this way she improvised; however, she is not known for scat singing or straying completely away from the melody. Holiday always took great liberty in reinterpreting the rhythm of a melody so as to find just the right way to give the lyric its greatest impact. Listen to her rendition of "Body and Soul," included on the accompanying anthology, and pay particular attention to the way in which she accents or emphasizes certain words, syllables, and phrases to give the lyrics special meaning and maximum impact.

She is accompanied by an all-star cast including some members of the Basie band, including Roy Eldridge who was the most important trumpet soloist to serve as a link between Louis Armstrong and the more modern Dizzy Gillespie.

You should go back and listen to the Coleman Hawkins recording of this same song paying particular attention to how radically Hawkins departs from the original melody which is more closely adhered to by Holiday. Hawkins' version is considered to be an instrumental *arrangement* of the original.

Listening Guide

Billie Holiday

"Body and Soul"
(Heyman-Sour-Eyton-Green) 2:57

Recorded 2/29/40 Vocalion 5481

Reissued on Columbia Legacy K 65757-S1

Roy Eldridge: *trumpet*

Jimmy Powell, Carl Frye: *alto saxophones*

Kermit Scott: *tenor saxophone*

Sonny White: *piano*

Lawrence Lucie: *guitar*

John Williams: *bass*

Jo Jones: *drums*

Form and Key: 32-bar song form choruses (AA'BA"=chorus), A♭ major

0:00–0:11	*Introduction:* 4 bars, trumpet solo over sustained chords in saxes, rhythm section accompaniment.
0:11–1:44	*First Chorus:* 32 bars, Vocal Chorus Melody:
0:11–0:34	*A section:* 8 bars, vocal chorus melody over sustained sax section lines, rhythm accompaniment.
0:35–0:57	*A' section:* 8 bars, similar to A.
0:58–1:21	*B section:* 8 bars, vocal chorus bridge over long moving trumpet and sax section lines.
1:22–1:44	*A" section:* 8 bars, vocal chorus melody over moving sax section lines.
1:45–2:57	*Second Chorus:* 24 bars, Trumpet Solo (Eldridge), Vocal Bridge and Chorus:
1:45–2:07	*A' section:* 8 bars, improvised trumpet solo, over moving sax section lines, rhythm section
2:08–2:30	*B section:* 8 bars, vocal bridge over moving sax section lines, rhythm section
2:31–2:57	*A" section:* 8 bars, vocal chorus over trumpet and sax section sustained moving lines, rhythm section.

Holiday's performance of "He's Funny That Way," included on the *Smithsonian Collection of Classic Jazz,* also serves as an excellent illustration of her uncanny ability to deliver a lyric with an impact even greater than any composer or lyricist could imagine or hope for. This particular recording, as Martin Williams indicates, also reveals the rapport that Holiday enjoyed with Lester Young who weaves beautiful counterpoint to her emotionally charged lyricism. Her life was ultimately overcome by the effects of her substance abuse, which eventually took over her life, leaving her nearly destitute in her final days. Fortunately her music has stood the test of time, transcending this tarnished aspect of her life.

Make sure that you review the corresponding chapter on the CD-ROM that includes several short interviews with Billie Holiday and Lester Young.

Ella Fitzgerald (1918–1996): The "First Lady of Song"

A case can be made that Coleman Hawkins and Lester Young served to represent two contrary sides of jazz playing during the Swing Era—hot and cool, respectively. Of equal contrast were singers Billie Holiday and Ella Fitzgerald. Holiday represented the cool, lyrical, and melancholy plaintive cry of the era, while Fitzgerald represented the hot, boisterous, gregarious macho side of jazz singing. Orphaned as a child, she moved to New York, where she was initially discovered at a talent contest sponsored by the Apollo Theater. Black bandleader and drummer Chick Webb hired her and she became a near overnight success with her 1938 recording of "A-Tisket, A-Tasket." Her popularity enabled her to assume the leadership of Webb's band when he died in 1939, a position which she held for three years before striking out on her own. Her partnership with promoter Norman Granz in the years to come is legendary and led to a series of "songbook" recordings featuring the repertoire of America's finest popular songwriters. Fitzgerald also became a headline attraction in Granz's Jazz at the Philharmonic tours, and recordings helped her to achieve international stature as a performer. It didn't hurt that she was accompanied by some of the very best instrumentalists of the day.

Fitzgerald was a consummate performer who never failed to astound her audiences with her amazing range, vocal flexibility, and sense of rhythmic swing. As was the case with Holiday, she has served as a model for all future jazz singers to follow, particularly those who improvised in the **scat** style (an improvised jazz singing style using wordless syllables), unlike Holiday's style which did not favor significant improvisation or scatting. Armstrong no doubt served as her influence in this regard (and they recorded more than once together), but she elevated the art of scat singing to new heights. Her improvisations were as sophisticated as those of instrumentalists who admired her ability to interact with them using a similar, hornlike language. Fitzgerald was equally skilled at improvising lyrics as

Ella Fitzgerald performing in 1948.

illustrated by the track included on the accompanying anthology. She enjoyed a long and very productive career performing in every imaginable setting world-wide. Once again, trumpeter Roy Eldridge is showcased.

Listening Guide

Ella Fitzgerald

"Honeysuckle Rose"
(Fats Waller-Andy Razaf) 4:32

Recorded live July 1964 at Juan-Les-Pins, France

Ella Fitzgerald Live
Verve Compact Jazz 833 294-2

Ella Fitzgerald: *vocal*

Roy Eldridge: *trumpet*

Tommy Flanagan: *piano*

Bill Yancey: *bass*

Gus Johnson: *drums*

Form and Key: repeated 32-bar song form (AA'BA=chorus) in F major

0:00–0:07	*Introduction:* 4-bar piano solo.	
0:07–0:54	*First Chorus:* 32-bar song form: Vocal Chorus:	
	0:07–0:18	*A section:* 8-bar vocal verse, original melody, with trumpet improvisation.
	0:19–0:30	*A' section:* 8-bar vocal verse, with trumpet continuing "ad-lib" improvisation.
	0:31–0:42	*B section:* 8-bar vocal bridge, with trumpet improvisation.
	0:43–0:54	*A section:* 8-bar vocal verse, with trumpet improvisation.
0:55–1:42	*Second Chorus:* 32-bar song form: Improvisation:	
	0:55–1:06	*A section:* 8-bar vocal improvisation, repeated scat musical ideas or "riffs," with trumpet and rhythm section accent answers.
	1:07–1:18	*A' section:* 8-bar vocal improvisation, repeated scat "riffs," with band answers.
	1:19–1:30	*B section:* 8-bar vocal free scat improvisation, with rhythm, trumpet drops out.
	1:31–1:42	*A section:* 8-bar vocal scat mimicking rapid "trumpet-like" melodies.
1:42–2:29	*Third Chorus:* 32-bar song form: Improvisation:	
	1:42 1:53	*A section:* 8-bar vocal improvisation, bluesy scat "riffs," with band accents, trumpet reenters.
	1:54–2:05	*A' section:* 8-bar vocal scat, repeated "riffs," with rhythm and trumpet accents.
	2:06–2:17	*B section:* 8-bar vocal and trumpet free simultaneous improvisation.
	2:18–2:29	*A section:* 8-bar vocal free scat, also using words, trumpet drops out.
2:29–3:15	*Fourth Chorus:* 32-bar song form: Shout Chorus:	
	2:29–2:40	*A section:* 8-bar vocal and trumpet "shout" melody, with band accents.
	2:41–2:52	*A' section:* 8-bar vocal and trumpet "shout" melody repetition with variation.
	2:52–3:03	*B section:* 8 bars (bridge), vocal and trumpet trade 1 bar improvisations.
	3:04–3:15	*A section:* 8-bar vocal and trumpet "shout" melody as in previous A section.

3:16–4:25　*Fifth Chorus*, 32-bar song form with tag: Vocal Verse:

　　3:16–3:27　　*A section:* 8-bar vocal verse variation, improvised words and new melody, trumpet fills.

　　3:27–3:38　　*A' section:* 8-bar vocal verse variation, more improvised words.

　　3:39–3:50　　*B section:* 8-bar vocal bridge variation, improvised words, new melody, trumpet fills.

　　3:51–4:25　　*A section:* 8-bar vocal verse variation, extended 15-bar vocal tag, trumpet improvisation.

Art Tatum (1909–1956)

Art Tatum was an anomaly among pianists. The art of solo piano playing, while certainly not disappearing, had at the very least become less prominent during the "swing" years. The focus had shifted away from solo pianists, most of whom, like Earl Hines, had joined the bandwagon and formed their own big bands in hopes of riding the popularity wave. Tatum was truly an exception and is considered to represent the epitome of solo jazz piano in the 1930s and 1940s. Legally blind, Tatum concentrated on developing a solo and trio style during the Swing Era that was without equal. While he received some early formal schooling in music, his impaired vision made formal training less practical, while his self-taught approach seemed more appropriate. His early inspiration was Fats Waller, though he showed more of a penchant for classical music than his elder. Idolized by critics and musicians, Tatum never gained widespread popularity with fans or in the magazine readers' polls probably because he strayed away from the Swing Era mainstream. His most striking recordings in the solo and trio format show his total mastery of the keyboard and illustrate an unparalleled technique that awed both jazz and classical pianists. He was in total control with unprecedented facility, a rich sense of harmony, an uncanny ability to improvise long lines, and a grasp of the earlier stride tradition. While he was a masterful improviser, he was sometimes criticized for repeating himself, working out arrangements and improvisations in advance, and often duplicating his recordings in live performance. Whether performing solo or with his famous trio that included Tiny Grimes on guitar and bass specialist Slam Stewart, he preferred to perform arrangements rather than original material and his arrangements were incredibly intricate. His style was unique and in many

Pianist Art Tatum performs at the Cafe Society, New York City, December 11, 1940.

ways chameleon-like, featuring frequent shifts from one mood to another; frequent chord substitutions; rhythmic, metric, and tempo shifts; thematic variation and counterpoint between left and right hands. Consequently he was difficult to play with as observed firsthand by bassist Gene Ramey.

> I worked with Tatum, though I never did satisfy him. Tatum wanted a bass player to stay at home [play simply, outlining the basic harmony]. He would really rather have you play 2-beat (only 2-notes out of every 4-beat measure) no matter how fast the tempo. He had a thing where he would play one song with his right hand and another song with his left. I might get carried away with what he was playing with his right hand and go right along with that and he would get so mad . . . Slam Stewart took my place with him. No bass player should be playing with Tatum. He's a solo player. A solo pianist can go any where he wants to.[16]

One cannot overemphasize how far Tatum raised the bar, influencing future generations of jazz pianists like Bud Powell, Lennie Tristano, and more contemporary pianists like Oscar Peterson and Herbie Hancock to mention but a few. His sheer virtuosity and technical mastery of his instrument, though, had an impact on many instrumentalists of the day, not just pianists. The recorded example included on the companion CD anthology provides evidence of his incomparable virtuosity and illustrates why he had such an impact on so many pianists who followed. An additional listening guide through his performance of "Tiger Rag" can be found in the corresponding chapter on the CD-ROM.

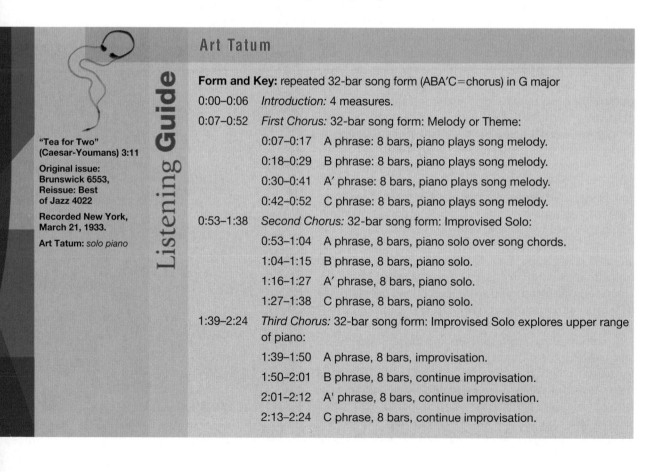

Listening Guide

Art Tatum

"Tea for Two"
(Caesar-Youmans) 3:11

Original issue:
Brunswick 6553,
Reissue: Best
of Jazz 4022

Recorded New York,
March 21, 1933.

Art Tatum: *solo piano*

Form and Key: repeated 32-bar song form (ABA'C=chorus) in G major

0:00–0:06	*Introduction:* 4 measures.	
0:07–0:52	*First Chorus:* 32-bar song form: Melody or Theme:	
	0:07–0:17	A phrase: 8 bars, piano plays song melody.
	0:18–0:29	B phrase: 8 bars, piano plays song melody.
	0:30–0:41	A' phrase: 8 bars, piano plays song melody.
	0:42–0:52	C phrase: 8 bars, piano plays song melody.
0:53–1:38	*Second Chorus:* 32-bar song form: Improvised Solo:	
	0:53–1:04	A phrase, 8 bars, piano solo over song chords.
	1:04–1:15	B phrase, 8 bars, piano solo.
	1:16–1:27	A' phrase, 8 bars, piano solo.
	1:27–1:38	C phrase, 8 bars, piano solo.
1:39–2:24	*Third Chorus:* 32-bar song form: Improvised Solo explores upper range of piano:	
	1:39–1:50	A phrase, 8 bars, improvisation.
	1:50–2:01	B phrase, 8 bars, continue improvisation.
	2:01–2:12	A' phrase, 8 bars, continue improvisation.
	2:13–2:24	C phrase, 8 bars, continue improvisation.

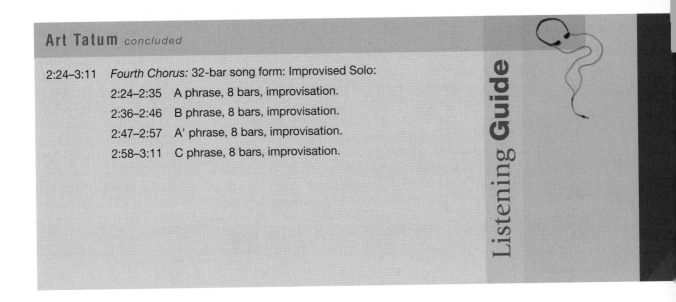

Art Tatum *concluded*

2:24–3:11   *Fourth Chorus:* 32-bar song form: Improvised Solo:

   2:24–2:35   A phrase, 8 bars, improvisation.

   2:36–2:46   B phrase, 8 bars, improvisation.

   2:47–2:57   A' phrase, 8 bars, improvisation.

   2:58–3:11   C phrase, 8 bars, improvisation.

TRADITIONAL JAZZ REVIVAL

While swing reigned supreme during the late 1930s and early 1940s, it was not without contenders. There were some who spoke out against what they thought was overly commercialized, stagnant dance music and expressed their support for the "authentic," "hot" jazz styles of the twenties. The nostalgic rebirth of interest in New Orleans and Chicago style jazz led to the establishment of two record labels devoted to recreating this earlier tradition. H.R.S. and Commodore along with other established labels such as RCA Victor and the newly formed Blue Note rushed

Special edition of Jazzmen produced by the Armed Services and designed to fit in soldiers' knapsacks.

to record Bunk Johnson, Sidney Bechet, Johnny Dodds, Jelly Roll Morton, Kid Ory, and other nearly forgotten artists who had forged early instrumental jazz. The Yerba Buena Jazz Band from the San Francisco Bay area also contributed to what became an international revival movement.[17] Perhaps it was new books on the subject of early jazz such as Frederick Ramsey's *Jazzmen* issued in 1939, or the numerous articles in upscale magazines such as *Esquire* that helped to spark this revival.

Benny Goodman and John Hammond sponsored the landmark "From Spirituals to Swing" concert at Carnegie Hall in 1938 featuring a lineup of blues, spiritual, boogie-woogie, and New Orleans performers offering a jazz retrospective that kindled interest in historic jazz and the roots of swing. The concert was also unique because jazz and related forms were presented for the first time in a hallowed concert hall that had previously showcased only classical music. For nearly eight years, a sometimes-bitter feud waged between traditionalist jazz fans, labeled **Moldy Figs,** the swing crowd, and the new modernists who sided with the newer music challenging swing for attention and described as bebop.

CONCLUSION

As is the case with any fad, "swing" spawned its own industry that revolved around the making and marketing of this music. By 1940 there was for the first time a clear jazz tradition, a developmental timeline that could be examined, dissected, and debated among journalists, historians, critics, and fans. As a result, numerous articles about jazz ran in trade magazines, journals, and newspapers. Magazines devoted to jazz began to flourish, drawing the attention of jazz fans lured to the print debates and encouraged to participate in reader's polls. A new generation of writers contributed several new books on the subject and as one would expect, each offered their own views on jazz—some optimistic and some less so about the future of jazz. For example, English-born critic and historian Leonard Feather wrote that there was an obvious differentiation between commercial and authentic jazz. For example, in 1945 he asserted that "Among the outright commercial bands, Tommy and Jimmy Dorsey and Harry James and the rest of them, there were the customary assortment of good jazz, bad jazz and music that does not pretend to be jazz by my standards or anyone else's." In this same article, he cited the young Woody Herman and Billy Eckstein bands as exciting surprises for the year. He closed the article saying that: "By the time the musicians in uniform come marching home [from World War II], the music business will be ready, both artistically and commercially, to hit a new all-time high in jazz history."[18] If this was a prediction about the decline of "swing" bands and the upsurge of a new kind of jazz, he was right. If he was predicting ongoing health for the big bands and the jazz business in general, then he was wrong.

There was a false sense of security that surrounded the big band movement, but not everyone was lulled into believing that they could ride the crest of this commercial wave indefinitely. Some critics took a hard line on many of the swing bands that made little effort to challenge the listener. Author Wilder Hobson called swing a fad that had been encouraged by the repeal of Prohibition. Like so many writers on the subject, he was concerned about overcommercialization. He said in his 1939 book *American Jazz Music* that the bands "follow the usual practice of mixing many compromise arrangements of popular songs with its jazz orchestrations; this is undoubtedly a necessity if a band wishes to maintain such an extraordinary wide popularity as Goodman has had. It is no small wonder that talented jazz musicians in general regard their playing as a livelihood and make their best music in small, impromptu sessions. As working men, they may appreciate the swing fad, but as musicians they dislike it intensely."[19] The rapid changes that had occurred in jazz styles throughout its relatively short history had already led critics to expect periodic change to occur, and, at this point, some were becoming impatient. But Hobson agreed that "in the midst of the 'swing' salesmanship a good deal of excellent music [had] been made," citing Goodman's small groups and the best of the black bands as high points. He added though that, "The swing fad has encouraged just about every imaginable kind of commercialization of the jazz language."[20] Even Duke Ellington recognized that by 1940 the fad had run its course and he too publicly expressed concerns about the music's future. It had clearly become shopworn and at least with many bands, too predictable.

By the mid-1940s big band swing in most cases had become a cliché, a caricature of itself. While there were a few new bands that arrived on the scene during this time, most of the bands began to dissolve, leaving only a few led by Count Basie and Duke Ellington in particular to carry on the tradition. The new younger bands led by Stan Kenton and Woody Herman had embraced the newer style of jazz emerging from New York along with the Afro-Cuban forms that are discussed in great detail in Chapter 16. While they never flourished as they had in the 1930s and early 1940s, the big band tradition would be carried forward into the next century, at least in terms of the general sound and instrumentation, but this discussion will be delayed until a future chapter. By the mid-1940s it was time for a change, and there was a line of young musicians in New York waiting to forge a new path for jazz that was radically different than the big band swing brand of jazz. The big band Swing Era, while not forgotten, was destined to become a lasting but faded memory.

Jazz in Perspective

The timeline that follows will put the developments of jazz discussed in Chapters 7 and 8 into a larger historical context, providing you with a better sense of how landmark musical events may relate to others that match your personal areas of interest.

1929
- Museum of Modern Art opens.
- Valentine's Day mob battle in Chicago.
- Beginnings of commercial passenger air travel.
- Black Tuesday—Wall Street Stock Market crash marks beginning of Great Depression.

1930
- The planet Pluto is discovered.
- George Gershwin's musical *Girl Crazy* opens featuring "I Got Rhythm" that serves a role as important to jazz as the blues.

- Nancy Drew books about teenage female sleuth become popular with young female readers.

1931
- More bank failures create an even more unstable economy.
- "Star Spangled Banner" declared national anthem.
- Empire State Building completed as world's tallest.
- Dick Tracy cartoon begins.
- George Washington bridge completed— longest suspension bridge.

1932
- Roosevelt elected president on "New Deal" promises.
- Radio City Music Hall opens as largest theater in world.
- Amelia Earhart becomes first woman to fly solo across the Atlantic in a small plane.
- Greta Garbo and John Barrymore star in *Grand Hotel.*

1933
- *Newsweek* and *Esquire* magazines founded.
- Chicago Exposition showcases "Century of Progress."
- Twenty-first Amendment repeals Prohibition after nearly 14 years.
- Jazz pianist Art Tatum records "Tea For Two."
- Adolph Hitler becomes Chancellor of Germany.

1934
- Cole Porter's musical *Anything Goes* opens.
- F. Scott Fitzgerald publishes *Tender is the Night.*
- Comic strip "Li'l Abner" makes debut.
- John Dillinger, Bonnie and Clyde, "Pretty Boy" Floyd, and "Baby Face" Nelson all killed by lawmen.
- Legendary blues singer Leadbelly is pardoned from prison term.
- Securities Exchange Commission and Federal Communications Commission are established to regulate stock market and communications.
- Disney character Donald Duck is born.
- *Down Beat* magazine, dedicated to jazz, founded.

1935
- George Gershwin's American opera/musical *Porgy and Bess* opens.
- W (Works) P (Progress) A (Administration) formed in an effort to put America's 11 million jobless back to work. Affects ¼ of American families.
- President Roosevelt established Rural Electrification Administration to electrify rural America.

- Dancer Martha Graham gains notice as pioneer of modern dance.
- Social Security Act becomes law.
- Germany imposes anti-Semitic laws.

1936
- American morals loosen as *Fortune* magazine poll shows 67 percent favor birth control.
- Babe Ruth and Ty Cobb named to newly founded Baseball Hall of Fame.
- F.D.R. wins reelection in landslide vote.
- Child actor Shirley Temple is box office smash.
- First artificial heart pump is displayed.
- Margaret Mitchell's book *Gone With the Wind* sells record 1 million copies in 6 months.
- Benny Goodman enjoys hit with "Goody-Goody."

1937
- Mitchell wins Pulitzer Prize for *Gone With the Wind.*
- First NBC Orchestra performance with Toscanini conducting.
- *Look* magazine is launched.
- General Motors gives in to striking workers and union demands. Union also wins victory at U.S. Steel.
- Dirigible *Hindenburg* bursts into flames in Lakehurst, New York.
- Amelia Earhart disappears in single engine airplane.
- Golden Gate Bridge in San Francisco opens.
- Right wing political movements attract some American interest because of Depression.
- Dale Carnegie publishes *How to Win Friends and Influence People.*
- Walt Disney releases film *Snow White and the Seven Dwarfs.*

1938
- Benny Goodman and racially mixed all-star band perform at Carnegie Hall.
- Dupont Company makes first products with Nylon, Teflon, and fiberglass introduced same year.
- Austria falls to Nazi Germany.

- Minimum wage law established along with 40-hour workweek. Same law prohibits wage discrimination based on sex.
- H.G. Wells radio hoax has millions of Americans believing in Martian invasion.
- Ella Fitzgerald launches her career with successful recording of "A-Tisket, A-Tasket."
- Count Basie's band records "Every Tub."
- "Superman" introduced as an action comic.

1939
- United States hosts 60-nation World's Fair.
- War erupts in Europe as United States attempts to remain neutral.
- Einstein reports on atomic power potential for weapons.
- Negro performers, athletes, writers, politicians, continue to fight for equality.
- First baseball game televised to only 400 viewers with TV sets.
- As depression fades, Hollywood capitalizes on renewed American spirit making 388 films. These included:
  - *Gone with the Wind* with Clarke Gable and Vivian Leigh
  - *The Wizard of Oz* with Judy Garland
  - *Stage Coach* with John Wayne
  - *Wuthering Heights*
  - *Goodbye Mr. Chips*
  - *Mr. Smith Goes to Washington* with Jimmy Stewart
  - *Pinocchio*
  - *Gunga Din* with Cary Grant
- Dance team of Ginger Rogers and Fred Astaire become popular on stage and screen.
- Radio dramas, soap operas, comedies, and variety shows becomes popular with *Search for Tomorrow, Burns and Allen,* and *The Jack Benny Show.*

- Author Frederick Ramsey publishes *Jazzmen.*
- Author John Steinbeck publishes *The Grapes of Wrath.*

1940
- Hattie McDaniel becomes first Black woman to win an Oscar for her performance in *Gone with the Wind.*
- First recipient of Social Security.
- John Steinbeck wins Pulitzer Prize for *The Grapes of Wrath.*
- American Negro Exposition in Chicago celebrates Emancipation.
- Bugs Bunny cartoon debuts.
- Hemingway authors *For Whom the Bell Tolls.*
- War in Europe escalates with fall of France.
- Draft lottery created to bolster U.S. armed services. Males 21 to 36 must register for draft.
- CBS demonstrates color TV.
- Billie Holiday records "Body and Soul."

1941
- Automakers cut production to aid war effort.
- President Roosevelt establishes Fair Employment Practices Commission to end discriminatory practices.
- NBC and CBS compete on commercial TV.
- Pearl Harbor is invaded by Japanese air strikes on December 7 prompting United States to declare war.
- Orson Wells writes, directs, produces and stars in film *Citizen Kane.*
- President Roosevelt wins unprecedented third term.
- Band Leader Glenn Miller records timeless hit "In the Mood."

1942
- Large numbers of women enter U.S. workforce to aid war effort and replace men drafted.
- Automobile production halted for 3 years as a consequence of World War II; rationing of petroleum products, sugar, meat and other products.

- Singer Frank Sinatra becomes new king of American pop music, though wartime hits by the big swing bands still selling.
- Jackson Pollock has one-man art show.
- Movie industry vows to no longer restrict blacks to comic and menial roles.
- *Casablanca,* all time American film hit, stars Ingrid Bergman and Humphrey Bogart.
- Bing Crosby, Bob Hope, and Dorothy Lamour star in *Road to Morocco.*
- Bing Crosby records *White Christmas* for the movie *Holiday Inn.*

1943
- War death toll reaches 60,000 Americans, though United States turns tide in Pacific, Africa, and European fronts.
- Rodgers and Hammerstein enjoy hit with Broadway musical *Oklahoma.*
- Racial tensions lead to riots in New York, Los Angeles, and Detroit.
- T.S. Elliot publishes *Four Quartets.*

1944
- *Esquire* magazine publishes first jazz poll and sponsors all-star concert at the Metropolitan Opera House.
- Cost of living escalated almost 30 percent in 12 months.
- Playwright Tennessee Williams publishes *The Glass Menagerie.*
- Americans salvage discardable goods for war effort.
- D-Day: American troops storm beaches at Normandy forcing Germans to retreat from France.
- American composer Aaron Copeland premiers *Appalachian Spring*, while Sinatra continues to woo young audiences with popular vocal stylings.
- FDR wins record fourth term as U.S. president.
- Major Glenn Miller, popular swing band leader, lost in apparent plane crash. He was known for "In the Mood," "Moonlight Serenade," and "Tuxedo Junction."

CHAPTER SUMMARY

Being a bit isolated from Chicago, New York, and the other main population centers, big bands developed somewhat independently in Kansas City and the Southwest. Groups performing primarily in this territory tended to rely on the blues and ragtime as a basis for their repertoire. Head arrangements made up primarily of various riffs (repeated phrases) were much more common in this region than the more sophisticated arrangements of East Coast groups. Using some key players from these southwestern territory bands like the Blues Devils and Benny Moten's band, William "Count" Basie formed his band that rose to national and international notoriety, surviving well beyond the life of its founder. The rhythm section of the Basie band of the late 1930s, sometimes referred to as the All-American Rhythm Section, helped to redefine the roles of the rhythm section instruments, not only for the Swing era but for future jazz styles.

In the 1930s, Kansas City was a hub for farming and ranching communities and also offered opportunities for musicians beyond those of many other cities due, in part, to political boss Tom Pendergast. Under his control, clubs were able to operate openly, serving alcohol during Prohibition and offering many other forms of daring entertainment. This situation made Kansas City a wild town with many clubs featuring some of the area's top groups including the bands of Jay Mc-Shann, Andy Kirk, Benny Moten, and Count Basie.

Tenor saxophonist Lester Young was probably the most influential of the many great soloists in the Basie band of the 1930s. His light, airy sound and linear improvisations were in sharp contrast to the assertive and angular solos of Coleman Hawkins. Just as Coleman Hawkins' approach had an important impact on bebop, Lester Young's approach influenced many cool jazz musicians of the 1950s.

The styles of vocalists Billie Holiday and Ella Fitzgerald paralleled those of Lester Young and Coleman Hawkins. Billie Holiday was not known as an improviser, but created interpretations of melodies that hardly resembled the originals, and made even more compelling by her understated voice. Fitzgerald, on the other hand, had magnificent technique and was an exceptional improviser. Her assertive approach would align her more with Coleman Hawkins' style.

The Swing Era was a golden age for jazz in that big band music was the popular music of the day; however, not all big bands placed emphasis on hot jazz solos. Generally, the most popular of the big bands were dance bands, precisely performing arrangements that left little space for improvisation.

KEY TERMS

Important terms, people and bands.

TERMS	PEOPLE	BANDS
territory bands	Benny Moten	Jay McShann
head	Lester Young	Benny Moten
motives	Mary Lou Williams	Andy Kirk
riffs	Walter Page	Blue Devils
walking bass	William "Count" Basie	Count Basie
measure	The Prez	Artie Shaw
comping	Billie Holiday	
scat	Ella Fitzgerald	
Moldy Figs	Art Tatum	

REVIEW QUESTIONS

1. Was there a discernable difference between Midwest, Southwest, and East Coast bands? If there was a difference what was it?

2. Who was Tom Pendergast and what was his significance to jazz and where?

3. Why did jazz flourish in Kansas City just as it had in New York and Chicago?

4. What Midwest band is said to have perfected the blues riff, head-style arrangement associated with this regional brand of swing?

5. Describe the musical character of the Basie style.

6. What does the "All American Rhythm Section" refer to and what was its significance to jazz?

7. Compare and contrast the styles of Lester Young and Coleman Hawkins.

8. Who was "Lady Day"?

9. Can you describe Billie Holiday's style?

10. Can you explain how Louis Armstrong influenced two female jazz singers?

11. Perhaps the most famous band to emerge during the peak of jazz activity in Kansas City was led by ___. The band was later reformed under the leadership of ___.

12. What was a territory band? Can you name several?

13. Who is considered "the first lady of song"?

14. Compare and contrast Ella Fitzgerald's and Billie Holiday's styles.

15. What was so amazing about Art Tatum and what more modern day pianist did he influence?

16. What is the significance of the "Moldy Figs"?

17. What is meant by the "shag" and "shim-sham"?

Make sure that you also review material on the corresponding chapter of the CD-ROM.

SUGGESTED SUPPLEMENTARY LISTENING

The abbreviation (iT) indicates that a particular recording cited in the text, or particularly demonstrative of the artist, is available from the Apple iTunes Web site. Other Web based music distributors may also prove to be valuable resources. SCCJ indicates *Smithsonian Collection of Classic Jazz.*

Benny Moten

"Moten Swing" SCCJ

Count Basie

Count Basie: The Complete Decca Recordings (iT)
Verve Jazz Master 2: Count Basie (iT)
The Essential Count Basie, Vols. I, II, III Sony (iT)
"Lester Leaps In" (iT) SCCJ
"Doggin' Around" (iT) SCCJ
"Taxi War Dance" (iT) SCCJ
"April in Paris" (iT)
"Shiny Stockings" (iT)

Jay McShann

"Swingmatism" (iT)
"Hootie's Blues" (iT)
"Sepian Bounce" (iT)

Mary Lou Williams

"(Keep It) In the Groove" (iT)
Mary Lou Williams: The Zodiac Suite Vintage Jazz Classics

Art Tatum

"Willow Weep for Me" (iT) SCCJ
"Too Marvelous for Words (iT) SCCJ

Art Tatum Solo Masterpieces Vol. 7 and 8 (iT)
"Humoresque" (iT)
Best of Jazz, The Swing Era: Art Tatum Best of Jazz

Ella Fitzgerald

Compact Jazz: Ella Fitzgerald Verve
"You'd Be So Nice to Come Home to" SCCJ
Ken Burns Jazz: Ella Fitzgerald (iT)
The Complete Ella Fitzgerald Song Books (iT)
At Newport: Ella Fitzgerald and Billie Holiday (Live) (also with Carmen McRae)
  Verve (iT)

Billie Holiday

Billie Holiday Greatest Hits Columbia Legacy
"These Foolish Things" (iT) SCCJ
"He's Funny That Way" (iT) SCCJ
The Complete Billie Holiday On Verve (iT)

"Moldy Figs"

Bunk Johnson and His Superior Jazz Band Good Time Jazz (iT)
Bunk and Lu: Bunk Johnson and Lu Watters Good Time Jazz (iT)

The **Bebop** Revolution

> "It is the repetition and monotony of the present-day Swing arrangements which bode ill for the future. Once again it is proven that when the artistic point of view gains commercial standing, artistry itself bows out, leaving inspiration to die a slow death."[1]
>
> DUKE ELLINGTON, 1939

THE END OF AN ERA

No single event or action was responsible for the gradual decline in big band popularity. This music had succumbed to the pressures of entertainment, and had become a commodity—a business that relied on basic principles of supply and demand. There was an astounding demand for this music just prior to the U.S. entry into World War II and there were hundreds of bands ready to supply the popular music. Once the United States was drawn into the war with the bombing of Pearl Harbor on December 7, 1941, both the demand and supplies necessary to sustain the big band swing movement were cut off, or at the very least, the supply lines were dramatically reduced. An examination of the specifics of this decline around 1944 will help you to understand the complexities of the situation that caused the downfall of the most successful times for jazz.

1. The music became one of the many casualties of wartime and for less than obvious reasons. While to many fans, the life of a jazz musician may have seemed glamorous, it wasn't. Long hours spent traveling in between gigs, and a generally unstable and irregular lifestyle tended to discourage a normal family life. Consequently, many big band musicians were young, single, and very vulnerable to the armed services draft. Many

were drafted and others voluntarily enlisted. Successful bandleader and arranger Glenn Miller enlisted, as did many of his bands members. Their duty was to entertain the troops in the Great Britain area. His plane disappeared in flight over the English Channel and was never found. The assumption is that the plane was shot down by enemy or friendly fire, ending Miller's exceptional career. Bandleaders who did not join the armed services were left with the difficult task of staffing their bands. Some leaders formed small combos, or ultimately gave up, disbanding their bands until after the war, while others never regrouped. Dances became less popular because of the reduced male population, and women were recruited into the workforce to help stimulate the wartime economy and contribute to the war effort. "Rosie the Riveter," portrayed in posters and movie newsreels, served as an example to women across the country of women's capabilities, doing what previously was considered men's work in factories. With such a shortage of men, and women's leisure time curtailed by their new work-a-day lives, it is obvious why dance halls began to close their doors. Even the famous Cotton Club fell victim to these circumstances and was gradually forced to close. Since dance halls became scarcer, it was difficult for the bands to maintain a reliable, steady work schedule. If they had released a new record, it would sell only on the strength of their personal appearances and it became more and more difficult to book the necessary number of engagements to sustain the bands and the sale of their recordings. In some cases, promoters could not fill engagements because they could not find a band to book, or the band was unable, due to the transportation crisis, to travel to the engagement. In the summer of 1942, *Variety* magazine reported that there was a shortage of bands available to fill bookings. As a result, musician's salaries escalated, making it even more difficult for bandleaders to employ those most in-demand musicians.

2. Petroleum and its by-products were key to the war effort. Gasoline, oil, and rubber were much in demand as these precious resources were essential for a successful campaign abroad and at home. Consequently, travel became much more difficult, and many of the swing bands relied on automobile or bus transportation to get from one engagement to the next. The rationing of petroleum products particularly hurt the black bands. According to author and historian Scott DeVaux, the NAACP (National Association for the Advancement of Colored People) complained after the Department of Defense banned the use of buses for travel not related to the war effort. For a short time, the government conceded, allowing five buses for the transportation of 45 bands. This arrangement failed for obvious reasons and was curtailed in 1943, leaving the traveling black bands in the lurch.[2]

3. In 1940 James Petrillo was elected president of the American Federation of Musicians (A.F. of M.). Petrillo rose to this position as national union head after serving as chief of the Chicago local musicians union. By 1942, Petrillo determined that musicians had been selling themselves short in terms of their payment for recordings. Recordings, for which musicians were paid only once, were played countless times on the radio and the popularity of jukeboxes that provided no return to musicians provided Petrillo with a convincing argument. His claims that the record companies were getting rich at the musician's expense were not unfounded. In 1942, claiming that recording musicians were "playing for their own funerals,"[3]

Petrillo called for a ban on all recording by union members. The timing in some ways was good in that record companies had been forced to reduce their production since records were made from a petroleum by-product that was in short supply. The only records made for nearly two years, aside for bootlegged sessions, were "V-Discs" made exclusively for U.S. troops abroad and sanctioned by the Defense Department. Gradually, the major record companies succumbed to Petrillo's pressure and signed the union agreement which established a royalty structure. Monies paid by the record companies to the A.F. of M. were used to establish the Music Performance Trust Fund, a fund that is still in existence and is used to subsidize free public performances by union musicians. Not all of the union members supported the spirit of this strike, however. In a conversation with this author, bassist Gene Ramey explained how Jay McShann's Kansas City–based band had made their way across half the country to seek their fame in New York. No sooner had they arrived in New York than the recording ban was imposed. Many of the members of this band, including Ramey and bebop pioneer Charlie Parker, felt they had been deprived of their chance at the gold ring—the chance to record and become rich and famous musicians at the peak of their careers. For Parker, things did work out, at least in terms of being noticed, but for others, careers were definitely stalled or even halted by Petrillo's actions.

4. As previously discussed, the presence of vocalists became increasingly important to the success of a big band (see sales information included at the close of this chapter). It stands to reason that the general public would warm to the good-looking male and female singers that delivered heart-rending ballads and uplifting swing tunes. People untrained to appreciate instrumental music are quick to follow and appreciate the universality of a lyric—something everyone can understand and enjoy without any special knowledge of music. It was this widespread appeal of the vocalist and their success with popular songs that eventually contributed to the steady decline of big band jazz. Singers were less affected by the A.F. of M. recording strike, since they were not members and consequently were offered some limited recording opportunities during the strike. Frank Sinatra, for instance, issued a record that featured his vocal solos with choral accompaniment. If they used union musicians to back them, they didn't dare give credit to them on the record for fear of repercussions from the union for breaching the ban—in effect crossing the picket line. At this point in the history of American music, the pop singer begins to take the lead, gradually eclipsing the popularity of the swing big band. Sinatra is a good example of a singer who started his career as a big band singer/sideman rising to fame following the recording strike. While he is often considered in discussions of jazz vocal styles, he is more a pop singer than a jazz singer. He could be considered a pop singer whose phrasing and overall style is informed and influenced by the jazz, swing style. This is certainly apparent in many of his recordings since he was often surrounded by jazz style big bands and arrangements. In the mid to late 1940s, jazz moved in one direction while the popular singers moved in another.

5. A growing artistic unrest among some of the more prominent soloists and younger musicians like Coleman Hawkins, Dizzy Gillespie, and Charlie Parker began to manifest itself concurrently with the U.S. entry into World War II. Big band arrangements, particularly those designed for recordings,

rarely left very sufficient room for the improvised solo. These 78-rpm records supported only about 3 minutes of music per side, which left only 8 to 16 measures on the average for a solo. Many of the fine soloists spotlighted in these bands began to enjoy the musical freedom provided by the after-hours jam session more than their regular salaried position with a big band. In the eyes of some of the musicians, a few fans, and some critics, jazz had strayed off the path pioneered by its first great soloist—Louis Armstrong. A desire for more musical freedom of expression made way for the beginning of a return to small group jazz in the mid-1940s, and eventually labeled bebop.

6. Immediately following the end of World War II, the future of big band jazz seemed questionable at best. By the end of the '40s, jazz had endured a second recording strike and faced the growing onslaught from rhythm and blues performers vying for popularity. The number of outlets for big band swing entertainment had substantially diminished, and a new social paradigm seemed to be taking root. Men had returned from the war eager to start families; reclaim lives that had nearly been lost; and in many cases, take advantage of the GI bill, which provided government financial assistance to those who wanted to pursue a higher education degree or specialized vocational training. A new focus on family, planning for the future, and buying a house took precedence over partying, dancing, or club hopping. There was much less room in this generation's lives following World War II for the music they had so loved and left to defend democracy. They grew up in the face of war and at its conclusion, found themselves engendered with new goals and dreams. The music of the big band Swing Era just didn't fit in any more.

Gene Ramey, who serves as a good example of a jazz musician who lived through the transition from swing to bebop, provides firsthand insight into those extra-musical factors that began to discourage the big band swing era.

> Bop [small groups] closed up all the ballrooms. That and the wage price scale. There was a time you could take a band on the road and if you had ten men in the band $200 would pay for that night. . . . Now you take a five-piece band out you're not going [for less than] $350, especially if you're going to travel. Plus another thing, musicians didn't want to travel, especially a black musician. These were some of the reasons why the guys were glad that bop came in and you could play in small groups and when you did you'd go some place on location.[4]

Summary of the Decline
The economic trappings of maintaining a big band during the war years created insurmountable hurdles for many bandleaders and promoters. There could be no missing link for the success of this era to continue, and there were suddenly many. In the end, the big band era fell victim to devices of its own design and creation—overcommercialization. It became too successful at a time when the country was on the verge of entering into a world war. The ultimate downfall of the era did not occur until after the war. To quote Scott DeVaux, "The artificial stimulation of a wartime economy temporarily disguised the structural problems in the music industry and postponed the inevitable collapse of the Swing Era until after the troops returned in 1945."[5]

The musicians' own rejection of what some of them viewed as an artistically stifling atmosphere also contributed to the decline of this most successful period in jazz. While the results of the A.F. of M. recording ban paid off in the long run, at the time, it drove another nail in the coffin of a jazz style that was facing one too many obstacles to endure. All of these issues attributed to the gradual decay of this style and encouraged many younger players to establish jazz as a serious art form, a style that stood on its own and did not serve at the pleasure of some other popular entertainment form. Critic Roger Pryor Dodge said in 1945 that "the demands of the listening public could never create an art. Its demands are not creatively inciting to the musicians."[6] By the close of World War II, the younger generation of jazz musicians who may have begun their careers in the ranks of big bands were tired of being second-class citizens subservient to dance. The end of World War II opens the door for this new sound, bebop, the first modern jazz style.

While there were more musicians working as sidemen than any other time in the history of jazz during the big band Swing Era, many of these musicians were left behind by the new bop style. Many musicians were unable to cope with the innovations associated with the bop style and were quick to criticize it. They did not possess the skills necessary to confront the demands of this complex new style. While some musicians were left behind by bop, so too were many fans. Fans that had followed the more listenable, danceable big band style were shocked to find after the A.F. of M. recording ban that the music had so radically changed. Some fans felt that it had become a self-indulgent music for "insiders" and no longer related to the masses. In many cases, they were right. You had to be "hip" to understand it and willing to hang out in the small clubs where it was played. Despite this controversy, it is safe to say that the bebop style has had a lasting influence on jazz as even today it serves as the basis for studying and teaching the language and craft of jazz improvisation.

THE LIFESTYLE AND MUSICAL CHARACTERISTICS

An underground, cultlike, rebellious music, bebop, or "rebop" as it was first called, lacked the commercial appeal of the big dance band. Instead, its appeal was based on new challenges for listeners and practitioners who strove to create a new form of jazz that demanded the attention of its listeners and was not subservient to any other form of entertainment. While there were several big bands that played danceable bop-like music, bop music was largely played by small bands and made no effort to pander to the dance-hungry public, as had been the case during the previous decade. The new younger-generation black musicians sought to reclaim their music, reshaping it as an art-music through a combination of experimentation and repackaging of certain aspects of the earlier jazz tradition.

Some thought bebop was a frantic music and reflected the chaos associated with war times and the beginnings of the modern atomic age. In every way, this new modern music challenged the old ways and traditions much as the earliest forms of jazz had done. Even the dress, mannerisms, speech, and general bohemian (someone in the arts who disregards conventional behavior) lifestyle of the bebop musician worked against the old ways and accepted norms. The bop musicians were well dressed, often sporting dapper suits, berets, and goatees. Their demeanor on stage often projected a more detached, aloof attitude toward their audiences. For example, dark sunglasses hid their eyes from full view and musicians often left the stage after their solo. This behavior was often considered arrogant by the uninitiated public but more often than not was merely a gesture of respect for the other musicians who were subsequently featured. Bebop jazz was an insider's music, played initially by musicians for musicians in a jam session atmosphere.

Thelonious Monk, Howard McGhee, Roy Eldridge, and Teddy Hill at Minton's Playhouse, New York City, circa September 1947.

There were other aspects of this new style that unfortunately served to attract a good deal of negative press. Beboppers seemed to have a reputation for loose sex with racially mixed partners and for a wide array of alcohol, drug stimulants, and depressants. While mild drugs such as marijuana had been in use years before, bebop musicians turned to more deadly, addictive drugs that ruined the careers of some of the music's greatest innovators. For the first time in jazz, we see black and white musicians resorting to heroin and other illegal substances as a form of escape from the everyday discriminations or in an attempt to reach new heights of artistic creativity. For some, drugs seemed to offer a false sense of confidence, and a euphoric relief from the trials of their everyday existence. Drug use for many became a badge of hipness and a talisman of their lifestyle, and many young musicians felt that in order to play like their heroes, they must act like them in every way, including the use of addictive drugs. Saxophonist Stan Getz in an interview with National Public Radio's *Fresh Air* host Terry Gross spoke candidly about drug use among musicians.

As I look back on it, musicians used drugs and alcohol for two reasons. One is the same reason why doctors use morphine, because when you get tired morphine is a work drug. As long as you don't take too much of it, it will keep you going. Alcohol is a temporary stimulant before it is a depressant. I think that was one reason because we traveled and worked very hard. I didn't look to any idols as a reason to take drugs or [because] it would make me play better. That's nonsense. The other reason is that there is a state of mind that you need to do anything in the art forms. It's called the alpha state. . . . Alpha is the state of mind [that you need] to create something. It's sort of thinking off the top of your head—relaxed concentration, and when you can't get that naturally, you're too tired or something, you might resort to alcohol, drugs, chocolate, food—anything that will give you a chance to get into alpha—to relax and think but not like an accountant would think. Think in the artistic sense. That's the reason I used stuff.[7]

Bop musicians were sometimes labeled as communists, anti-American, and unpatriotic, but it was racism, economic exploitation, poverty, and other forms of discrimination that they protested, not a political ideology. Some turned to religion, particularly Islam for solace, as it seemed that Muslims saw no difference in the color of their comrades. Bebop to some was the expression of a newfound militancy by black musicians and one that would prove to escalate in the years ahead.

Bebop, not for "squares" or the unhip, created a civil war in the music scene. For the first time in the history of jazz, there was no one single popular style. A few swing bands based on a now shopworn tradition still existed alongside a handful of more modern new big bands led by Billy Eckstine, Dizzy Gillespie, Stan Kenton, and Woody Herman. These musicians along with beboppers and traditional jazz musicians such as Louis Armstrong all vied for attention from the industry and public. Musicians and critics were outspoken in their assessments of bebop declaring that its creators Dizzy Gillespie and Charlie Parker were either jazz music's saviors or destroyers. For example, Norman Granz, a well-known promoter, producer, and jazz entrepreneur, initially said in a 1945 *Down Beat* magazine interview that "Jazz in New York stinks,"[8] referring to the small clubs that had sprung up on 52nd Street that supported small bebop bands. Granz went on to criticize Charlie Parker's sets at the Three Deuces club as rigid and repetitive. Some years later Granz embraced this music and its associated artists and packaged successful tours featuring all-star casts including bop figures Parker and Gillespie. Louis Armstrong, whose own brand of jazz in the mid-1920s was revolutionary, criticized bop in a 1948 *Down Beat* magazine article entitled "Bop Will Kill Business Unless It Kills Itself First." Here he described bop as "crazy mixed-up chords that don't mean nothing at all" and attacked bop musicians as "young cats who want to carve everyone because they're full of malice, and all they want to do is show you up . . . [At] first people get curious about it because it's new, but soon they get tired of it because it's really no good and you got no melody to remember and no beat to dance to."[9] Some years later, Armstrong made peace with the younger generation, appearing on the same stage with Gillespie and other younger generation musicians. Other more traditional jazz and swing musicians like Chicago's Mez Mezzrow called bebop "frantic, savaged, frenzied, and berserk"[10] while swing era bandleaders like Benny Goodman were equally harsh. Goodman for example initially accused bop musicians of "faking it," but later employed them in his band and hired arrangers to write in the bop style.[11]

THE BIRTH OF BEBOP: THE FIRST RECORDINGS

While it is true that Charlie Parker and Dizzy Gillespie are considered the founding fathers of bebop, the birth of this new style was actually encouraged, supported, and embraced at a few New York clubs by several older musicians during the A.F. of M. recording ban. Uptown Harlem nightspots like the Club Onyx, Clark Monroe's Uptown House, and Minton's Playhouse became the staging ground for jam sessions attended by guitarist Charlie Christian, bassists Oscar Pettiford, and tenor saxophonists Don Byas and Coleman Hawkins. Younger upstarts like trumpeters Dizzy Gillespie and a young Miles Davis, drummer Kenny Clarke and pianist/composer Thelonious Monk also frequented these clubs, particularly Minton's, which many consider to be the most important laboratory for the creation of this new music. These loose jam sessions allowed for experimentation, unencumbered by the demands of an audience wanting to dance. Old melodies were discarded in favor of creating new ones, using their associated chord progressions as a springboard for lengthy improvisations. Against the musician's union, club owners charged an admission to those curious patrons who wanted to enjoy the fruits of these experimental jam sessions. Only the most exceptional musicians dared to participate and sit in at these sessions, since the music presented challenges that demanded virtuosic command of their instruments and a thorough understanding of music theory. Musicians frequented these clubs after they

Club Onyx in New York City.

finished their more sedate big band dance jobs in search of a more challenging, artistic stimulus. The popularity of these few uptown clubs opened up opportunities for new clubs downtown on 52nd Street, which became know as "Swing Street" or just "the street." These clubs offered steady, good-paying employment for many small groups in the mid to late-1940s once the idea of a small, intimate club to showcase jazz for listening caught on.

Characteristics of the Style

Bebop, the onomatopoetic (a word or use of a word that sounds like what it is meant to describe) term that was eventually used to describe the scat sung rhythms associated with this new music, was a radical departure from big band swing jazz. These characteristics can be summarized as follows:

- Bebop featured smaller combos (trios, quartets, and quintets) rather than large ensembles.
- While swing emphasized arrangements for large bands of 10 or more with little improvisation, bop arrangements were simple following a predictable scheme: theme-solo-solo-solo-theme that allowed ample space for improvised solos. The theme may have been preceded by an introduction and a brief coda or tag at the end might follow the final repetition of the theme.
- The emphasis therefore returned to improvisation, as it had been when Louis Armstrong recorded his Hot Five and Hot Seven disks.
- Bebop showed little concern for the dancing public and was intended to challenge both the serious listener and musician.
- Bebop repertoire was based on:

    1. Blues forms.
    2. The George Gershwin "rhythm changes" model derived from his popular song "I've Got Rhythm" featured in his 1930 Broadway show *Girl Crazy*.
    3. New melodies composed over chord progressions borrowed from other songs (described as **contrafacts,**) which enabled bebop musicians to make additional royalties from their recordings. (Copyright laws do not protect chord progressions.)

 An excellent example of a bebop "contrafact" composed and recorded during the bebop period can be found in the corresponding chapter on the CD-ROM.

    4. New tunes designed on the new style and vocabulary by composers such as Charlie Parker, Thelonious Monk, and Dizzy Gillespie.

- When bebop artists did perform a popular tune, they often completely disregarded the original melody, sacrificing it in the interests of improvisation. As historian Martin Williams once said, "Bop made a practice of featuring variations upon melodies that were never stated."[12]
- The saxophone surpassed the clarinet in terms of popularity and the clarinet began to fall out of favor, in sharp contrast to earlier decades and jazz styles.
- The guitar became a less essential instrument in the bop combo. While excellent soloists began to develop during this period, as long as there was a pianist, the guitar was a nonessential ingredient in small bop groups.

- Bebop music was virtuosic in its musical demands on the performer in that it often featured: (1) fast tempos and very slow ballads, (2) technically difficult "heads" (jazz lingo for tune), and (3) more sophisticated and challenging chord progressions.

Bebop Performance Practice and Instrumental Roles Redefined

When compared to earlier styles, bebop shows obvious and subtle differences in performance techniques attributed to all the instruments associated with this style. For example,

- The horn players used noticeably less vibrato than had previous generations. Lester Young can be considered the model for this lighter, smoother sound and smaller vibrato.

- There was less obvious and predictable swing or unevenness in the melodic lines that typically consisted of strings of eighth notes, triplets, and double-time sixteenth note phrases. The de-emphasis on exaggerated swing was no doubt due to the faster tempos that made it more difficult to facilitate an exaggerated swing eighth note emphasis. Try skipping fast; the faster you go, the more difficult this uneven gait becomes.

- Horn players demonstrated increased technical facility, enabling them to improvise complex, fast passages.

- In some cases, bebop instrumentalists pushed the upper, useful range of their instruments. Trumpeter Dizzy Gillespie serves as a good example of pushing this envelope.

- Bebop instrumentalists became more aware of music theory that enabled them to negotiate the more advanced harmonies and dissonances associated with the style.

As was the case with every major stylistic innovation throughout the history of jazz, changes in rhythm section performance practice lie at the heart of advances during the bebop era. The bass, which had largely been relegated to the role of time keeping and outlining harmonies, begins to emerge during the bop period as an instrument that, in the hands of a master, was capable of creating meaningful improvised solos. The groundwork for the bass to emerge as a solo instrument had been laid by the previous generation swing players such as Jimmy Blanton with the Ellington band, Slam Stewart with Benny Goodman and Art Tatum, and, of course, Walter Page with the Count Basie band.

By the close of the Swing Era, drummers had begun to move the well-defined swing pattern from the hi-hat to the ride cymbal and were occasionally featured in solo spots. Their solos, however, were usually predictably rudimental in construct and more rhythmic than melodic. Bebop drummers began to shape their solos in a more melodic fashion, even though the drums are not considered to be melodic instruments. Using saxophonists and trumpet players as their model, they approached the drum set in a more melodic manner than had ever been done before. Bebop drum set innovators Kenny Clarke and Max Roach also discarded the use of the bass drum on every beat in favor of using it only for occasional punctuation and to prod the soloist. The earlier concept of playing the bass drum on every beat not only masked the bass player's walking lines, but it became impossible to play with any regularity at the faster bop tempos. Clarke is given much of the credit for this modern innovation, claiming that it was a technique he happened on by accident when he realized he could not maintain the fast tempos for any length of time.

Pianists followed the comping style that had been pioneered by Count Basie and singer/pianist Nat "King" Cole, who played sparse chord accompaniments in nonrepetitive and unpredictable rhythmic gestures. The intent of this comping style was to accompany and complement the soloist and not be distracting by over playing. This style was a radical departure from the busy earlier stride and ragtime styles. Bebop pianists developed their right-hand single-line technique enabling them to play long improvised lines in the same style of bebop horn players. In some cases, pianists only occasionally played left-hand chords to accompany their right-hand improvisations.

Table 9.1 provides a quick reference and comparison of swing and bebop styles, serving to summarize the aforementioned discussion.

TABLE 9.1 Comparison of Swing and Bebop Styles

Swing Style Characterisics	Bebop Style Characteristics
Big bands personified the Swing Era and style.	Bop bands were small combos of three to five pieces.
The elaborate arrangement brought attention to the ensemble rather than the soloist. Solos were often brief, especially on recordings.	Arrangements were not elaborate. Bop combos placed the emphasis on the improvising soloist. Consequently, the greatest percentage of recordings was dedicated to improvisation.
Swing Era soloists at times were required to play the same solo that they played on recordings.	Bop soloists prided themselves in spontaneous creativity, striving to be different each time they played a tune.
Vocalists became prominent during the Swing Era.	Vocalists were rarely featured with bebop bands.
Swing bands were often subservient to commercial pressures aimed at entertainment—dancing.	Bop bands played music for artistic reasons. Bop was aimed at listeners not dancers.
The bass plays walking lines, fulfilling a time-keeping role in the rhythm section.	The bass continues to maintain a time-keeping roll, but emerges as a solo instrument.
Drummers emerge as soloists, but still rely on technical, rhythmic rudiments. Responsibility is largely time keeping, using bass drum on all beats.	Drummers become more melodic in their approach and further develop as soloists. Bass drum is reserved for explosive punctuation rather than used on all beats.
Guitar often used in big bands but largely in rhythmic, chording contexts.	Guitar is infrequently used in bebop bands. A few performers advance the instrument's soloistic potential.
Performances always placed emphasis on presenting recognizable and memorable melodies.	Melodies were often obscured beyond recognition in favor of fresh variation and improvisation.
Repertoire was based on arrangements of pop and show tunes of the day.	Repertoire placed emphasis on blues and "rhythm changes," formats that inspired the composition of new tunes.
Clarinet is popular instrument especially in the hands of bandleaders.	The saxophone eclipses the clarinet in bop. No prominent bop innovators were known for their clarinet playing.
Swing is the popular music of the day, leading record sales and radio play.	Bop did not enjoy the mass appeal of swing.
Performers could be good musicians and work in a big band without ever soloing.	Bop bands featured only the best virtuosic soloists.
Vibrato was usually obvious.	Vibrato became less emphasized, especially as tempos increased.
Uneven eighth-note swing was quite noticeable.	Uneven eighth-note swing becomes deemphasized, especially as tempos increase.

Consult Chapter 3—Listening to Jazz—on the CD-ROM and explore the Performance Practice subsection. Here you will learn to recognize many of the concepts that relate to the bebop style. Specifically the sections to be reviewed under Performance Practice are Piano, Bass, Drum Set, Interpretation, Dissecting a Jazz Performance, and Improvisation.

A FEW AMONG MANY

While there were many outstanding musicians associated with the bebop movement, only a few have ultimately been considered real innovators who pushed the boundaries to new heights. The following section will focus primarily on those instrumentalists who made significant contributions to the evolution of their particular instruments in the jazz continuum.

The Horn Players

Dizzy Gillespie and Charlie Parker are considered to be the founding fathers of the bebop style. Their first meeting was as members of the Earl Hines big band before it was taken over by singer Billy Eckstine. Unfortunately the recording ban is responsible for no lasting evidence of their work together in this band. While musically there were similarities that brought these two artists together, there were as many contrasts, particularly in lifestyle, that ultimately sent them in different directions. Despite their differences, both musicians left an indelible imprint on the future of jazz.

John Birks "Dizzy" Gillespie (1917–1993) Gillespie was born to a large family in South Carolina. He left school at age 18 to join his family in Philadelphia and it was here that he met his first mentor, trumpeter Charlie Shavers. Shavers, like Gillespie in his early years, closely followed the Roy Eldridge model. Gillespie, who was known for his practical jokes and clownish behavior, became known in the Philly area as "Dizzy," a nickname that stayed with him the rest of his life. Gillespie made the move to New York in 1937 and, like most of the bebop artists, found employment in big bands. In his case, Teddy Hill and Cab Calloway provided big band opportunities for Gillespie to travel to Europe and to record. He met Cuban musician Mario Bauza in Calloway's band and this lasting relationship spawned Gillespie's deep interest in Afro-Cuban music. The Latin and Afro-Cuban rhythmic influences that permeated many of Gillespie's compositions are the direct result of his close relationship with Bauza. To quote from Gillespie's autobiography, "My own contributions to the new style of music at this point were rhythm—Afro-American and Latin—along with harmony. I built most of the harmonic structure [of bebop] and showed the piano players how to play comp with the soloists."[13] Gillespie is the first modern jazz artist to embrace the marriage of jazz with Afro-Cuban and Afro-Latin styles. His compositions "Manteca," "A Night in Tunisia," and "Con Alma," among others, serves as examples of the many offsprings of this marriage. (See Chapter 16 for more discussion of "Cubop" and Gillespie's role in Afro-Cuban Jazz).

Gillespie began to surpass the influences of Eldridge by the early 1940s. He met Charlie Parker at Minton's jam sessions and they both became members of the Billy Eckstine big band. The Eckstine big band became a home for many of the younger generation bop players. In addition to Parker and Gillespie, it included at one time saxophonists Gene Ammons and Sonny Stitt, Fats Navarro on trumpet, and vocalist Sarah Vaughan. Gillespie contributed many arrangements to this band and served as its musical director. The band was short-lived, however, and failed to provide the kind of danceable entertainment that was appealing to most fans. Despite the appealing vocals by Eckstine and Vaughan, the band's repertoire was too modern at a time when dance audiences and large ballrooms were dwindling.

It was perhaps Gillespie's relationship with Coleman Hawkins in the early 1940s that is most significant to his own advancement and to the birth of bebop as a new style. The early 1940s collaborations of these two artists, immediately following the A.F. of M recording ban, led to recording sessions that produced the first bop records and served to introduce listeners to the new style. The overwhelming and unexpected success of Hawkins' "Body and Soul" (released in 1939), which boldly presented improvisations without ever stating the original melody, no doubt served to inspire and give hope for commercial success to the next generation of younger bebop artists.

Gillespie and Parker formed their history-making quintet in 1945, shortly after the Hawkins sessions. It fizzled, in part due to Parker's personal battles with drug and alcohol addition, and in no time at all Gillespie returned to the big band format, while Parker continued to struggle developing his reputation as a small group performer. This situation underscores two major differences between these two artists: (1) though economics often encouraged him to work in smaller bands, Gillespie favored big bands throughout his life while Parker always favored small groups, and (2) Parker struggled with drug addiction and alcoholism most of his life, which drove him and Gillespie (the more clean living of the two) apart more than once.

Dizzy Gillespie fronts his big band that includes Miles Davis, John Lewis, Cecil Payne, and Ray Brown on bass.

Gillespie's bebop big band included some of the best musicians of the day including Art Blakey on drums, John Lewis, and Milt Jackson (pianist and vibraphonist, respectively, who would later found the Modern Jazz Quartet), along with bassist Ray Brown in the rhythm section. During the band's four-year lifetime other luminaries featured included saxophonists John Coltrane, Sonny Stitt, and James Moody as well as the first modern bebop jazz trombonist J. J. Johnson. Cuban percussionist Chano Pozo was recruited to satisfy Gillespie's appetite for Afro-Cuban rhythms and Gillespie's big band was at the epicenter of the Cubop jazz movement in the late 1940s.

Dizzy Gillespie and His Orchestra

Form and Key: Repeated 40-bar song form chorus (AABCA=chorus) in B♭ major, Latin Big Band arrangement

0:00–0:37   *Introduction:* 28 bars. Afro-Cuban Latin Groove, Trumpet Solo:

     0:00–0:18   *Section 1:* 14 bars, staggered entrances of conga drums, bass, drums, baritone sax, trumpets, and trombones set up Latin groove, with "Manteca" chanted vocals.

     0:19–0:31   *Section 2:* 9 bars, improvised "bebop" trumpet solo (Gillespie), over continuing Latin groove, concluded by 1-bar ensemble triplets with "fall."

     0:31–0:37   *Section 3:* 5 bars, conga, bass, and drum groove.

0:38–1:47   *First Chorus:* 50-bar Theme:

     0:38–0:48   *A section:* 8 bars, repeated riff melody in saxes, answered by brass, followed by ensemble variation of brass riff, with conga fills.

     0:49–0:59   *A section:* 8 bars, similar to first A section.

     1:00–1:10   *B section:* 8 bars, saxes play sustained bridge melody, with brass answer, swinging rhythm section accompaniment.

     1:11–1:22   *C section:* 8 bars, trumpet (Gillespie) plays remainder of bridge melody, with sustained ensemble chords, Latin rhythm section accompaniment.

     1:22–1:33   *A section:* 8 bars, similar to A section.

     1:34–1:47   *Solo-Send-off:* 10 bars, break down to rhythm section groove similar to Introduction (section 1), followed by 4-bar ensemble "shout" send-off to tenor solo.

1:48–2:42   *Second Chorus:* 40-bar Tenor Solo, Trumpet Solo:

     1:47–1:58   *A section:* 8 bars, improvised tenor solo (Nicholas) over chorus chord changes, with ensemble accents and riffs, swinging rhythm section accompaniment.

     1:59–2:09   *A section:* 8 bars, tenor solo continues, ensemble tacet, with swinging rhythm section.

     2:10–2:20   *B section:* 8 bars, ensemble "shout" variation of theme bridge melody, with swinging rhythm section.

Listening Guide

"Manteca" (Gillespie, Fuller, Pozo) 3:06

Recorded 12/30/47, New York City, RCA Victor Vi20-3023

Reissued "The Complete RCA Victor Recordings" Bluebird 07863 66528-2

Dizzy Gillespie: *trumpet*

Dave Burns: *trumpet*

Elmon Wright: *trumpet*

Lamar Wright Jr.: *trumpet*

Benny Bailey: *trumpet*

William Shepard: *trombone*

Ted Kelly: *trombone*

John Brown: *alto saxophone*

Howard Johnson: *alto saxophone*

Joe Gayles: *tenor saxophone*

"Big Nick" Nicholas: *tenor saxophone*

Cecil Payne: *baritone saxophone*

John Lewis: *piano*

Al McKibbon: *bass*

Kenny Clark: *drums*

Chano Pozo: *conga drums, bongos*

2:21–2:32	*C section:* 8 bars, improvised trumpet solo (Gillespie), with sax sustained backgrounds, swinging rhythm section.
2:32–2:42	*A section:* 8 bars, ensemble theme similar to first chorus A sections, with "Manteca" vocals.
2:43–3:06	*Coda:* 15 bars, ensemble Latin groove similar to introduction, with "Manteca" chants, staggered instrumental "exits," drum figure.

Gillespie's big band enjoyed some success during its career but by 1950, its future was extinguished by the ever-encroaching popular music trends. Despite his best efforts and those of the U.S. State Department who sent him on several world tours as an ambassador of American good will, he found himself without a recording contract. He was proclaimed the "Crown Prince of Bebop," and in his later years served as mentor to many aspiring young black and white jazz musicians like trumpeter Jon Faddis and saxophonist Phil Woods. Later in life, his appearances on the Cosby and Muppets television shows added to his celebrity. Comparing profiles with Kermit the Frog, he showed off the same enormous, balloon-like cheeks known in medical books as "Gillespie Pouches."

Like Armstrong and Eldridge who had preceded him, Dizzy Gillespie was an innovator. Many of the characteristics that define his style as a composer and performer became the heart and soul of the bebop style. He claimed his signature up-turned trumpet was the result of an accident when a birthday party guest sat on it. He liked its newfound acoustical properties, so he had future instruments designed with an up-flared bell. All innovators are known for very specific contributions and Gillespie is no exception:

- He further developed the extremely high register of the trumpet, executing improvised lines in the stratosphere.

- He fused bebop and swing style jazz with Afro-Cuban rhythms.

- Gillespie possessed a blinding technique that, along with his high register abilities, made him one of the flashiest performers on the instrument.

- He was a ferocious trumpet player, but despite his high notes and fast technique, he was known to invoke shocking surprises by sudden changes in dynamics and range, and by slowing down or speeding up his technique. His style was dramatically captivating and dynamic, based on contrasting extremes—soft to loud and high; subtle, simple melodies to long bursts of rapidly played notes.

- There was a new element of harmonic sophistication in Gillespie's compositions as well as his improvisations. He began to incorporate notes from the blues scale (flatted thirds and fifths) into chords, and composed unusual chord progressions to accompany his sometimes exotic melodies. These notes were considered dissonant before the bebop period.

- Many of his compositions are now important landmarks in the repertoire, for example, "Woody N' You," "Bebop," "Manteca," "A Night in Tunisia," "Groovin' High," and "Con Alma."

Gillespie's discography indicates that he lived a great deal longer than Parker. Once again in contrast, Parker with his voracious appetite for life somehow compressed at least one full lifetime of creativity into a significantly shorter lifespan. On the other hand, Gillespie's durability, showmanship, musicianship, and resilience earned him countless honors and awards and his legacy will live for years to come.

Dizzy Gillespie performing at the Meridien Hotel in Paris, France.

Charlie Parker (1920–1955) Parker was nicknamed "Yardbird," which became simply "Bird." He earned the nickname while traveling by car through the Ozarks with a local territory band. The car swerved and hit a chicken crossing the road and Parker insisted they retrieve it for dinner! From that moment on he was known as Yardbird or Bird for short. That is at least one of the several explanations of his nickname.

Born in Kansas City, Parker's life was in stark contrast to that of Gillespie, who had experienced a normal childhood and upbringing. For most of his life, Parker knew no father and his male role models were those traveling jazz players who passed through Kansas City. Parker hung out whenever he could to get a glimpse of his heroes like Lester Young whom he claimed as one of his influences. By fifteen, Parker had switched from the baritone horn to the alto saxophone, had become involved with various addictive drugs, and had married his first wife. In contrast to Gillespie, who was raised in an upstanding family more privileged by educational opportunities, Parker learned only the basics in school and was largely a self-taught musician. He nevertheless developed an innovative style that was to become the model and inspiration for generations of players. For years after his premature death at age 35, subway walls and billboards were painted with the words "Bird Lives," the title of Ross Russell's captivating Parker biography. Parker became a cult hero and was idolized by the many young musicians that were inspired by his new, modern approach to improvising.

Parker's first recordings were made with Jay McShann's Kansas City swing style big band. Like most bands from the Midwest, the McShann band was deeply rooted in the blues tradition and Parker's style was based in part on this tradition throughout his career. Germs for at least one of his later small group compositions can be heard in these early McShann recordings, but his mature style did not gain widespread exposure until the small group recordings made in 1945–1946 with Dizzy Gillespie surfaced. Following a nervous breakdown in California brought on by family problems and drug abuse, Parker resurfaced with his second quintet featuring the young trumpeter Miles Davis, whom he hired to replace Gillespie. While still in the very early stages of development, Davis' style was in many ways radically different from the bravado style of Gillespie. Parker

Portrait of Jay McShann's Kansas City Orchestra in Dallas, Texas, 1941. Charlie Parker stands third from left with vocalist Walter Brown on his right. Bassist Gene Ramey is at the far right and McShann is seated at the piano.

enjoyed great success throughout the late 1940s and early 1950s, earning awards in various jazz magazine polls and increased record sales. He enjoyed a fertile period of recording and live performances with his own small groups, Afro-Cuban bands, string ensembles, and various all-star bands. His recording of *Just Friends* with a small chamber ensemble of strings, woodwinds, and rhythm was his biggest selling record. He looked back on this series of recordings as one of his proudest accomplishments. Despite what appeared on the surface to be a successful career, his life was always in a state of chaos, living on the edge both musically and personally. His reputation as a known drug user, however, cost him deeply, and in 1951, the New York authorities revoked his cabaret card, banning him from performing in the city's nightclubs. Until several years later he could not even perform in Birdland, the club that bore his name. Parker attempted suicide several times and was nearly always in debt to friends or the pawnshop, where more than once he hocked his alto for quick cash. His last engagement was at Birdland, only seven days before his death. He was a tormented artist who never fulfilled many of his dreams, not the least of which was to study classical composition.

Parker's style, while based in great part on the blues, was entirely unique and one that redirected the path of jazz for decades to follow. As a composer and performer, he charted a new course for many to follow. His style and contributions can be summarized as follows:

- Like Gillespie, Parker patterned many of his new compositions off of the chord progressions and formal schemes of old standard tunes and 12-bar blues; that is "Anthropology" (Gershwin's "I Got Rhythm"), "Ornithology"

("How High the Moon"), "Scrapple from the Apple" ("Honeysuckle Rose"), "Now's the Time," and "Billie's Bounce" (Blues).

- Parker eliminated or severely curtailed the use of vibrato in comparison to Swing Era styles. His lean tone had an edge.

- Like Gillespie, Parker possessed a blazing technique that enabled him to negotiate complex chord progression at very fast tempos and gave him the ability to play fast, double-time lines.

- Parker played in a more legato style (less articulation or tonguing of notes) than most players from the previous generation of saxophonists.

- Parker's improvisations were newly created complex melodies that rarely bore any resemblance to the tune. Each improvised chorus was a newly created masterpiece, often with little repetition or reference to previous material.

- Parker had a gift for improvising lines that outlined the fundamental harmony through ornamentation, disguising the basic chord tones as shown in Example 9.1.

Bassist Charles Mingus, drummer Roy Haynes, pianist Thelonious Monk, and saxophonist Charlie Parker perform at the Open Door in New York City, September 13, 1953.

EXAMPLE 9.1

Notice that each chord tone is preceded by its upper or lower neighbor serving to embellish and disguise the chord itself. Chord tones from G major chord are highlighted.

The concept illustrated in this example can be more easily grasped by playing the same example found in the corresponding chapter on the CD-ROM.

- As an improviser, Parker had a rare gift that enabled him to render two completely different solos from performance to performance as demonstrated by the two takes of "Embraceable You" featured on the *Smithsonian Classic Collection of Jazz*. These solos were recorded only moments apart but are entirely different.

- Parker was particularly gifted at taking simple chord progressions, like the 12-bar blues or an old standard tune, and embellishing it by adding chords to link the original skeletal framework. (Listen to "Blues For Alice"as an example of a complex blues approach.)

- Parker introduced the improvisational possibilities that existed beyond using basic, fundamental chord tones (1,3,5,7). He often introduced chromatically altered tones to connect chord tones and played lines using upper extensions to basic four-note chords (notes beyond the 7th, such as 9ths, 11ths, and 13ths) as illustrated in Example 9.2.

EXAMPLE 9.2

In each measure, Parker favors upper extensions (9th and 13th) and altered tones (♭13, ♯11, ♯9, ♭9) as circled to enhance the basic D7 chord. The basic chord is shown on the bottom staff. None of these altered tones are part of the basic chord.

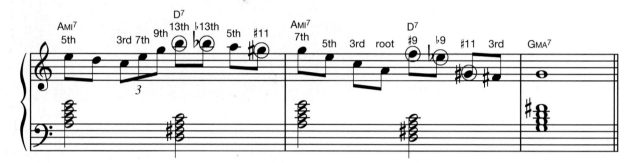

Despite his untimely death in 1955, his music exerted a major force for the next several decades. Young musicians hung on every phrase he played and sought to emulate him in every way. Bassist Charles Mingus told *Down Beat* magazine at the death of Parker, "Most of the soloists at Birdland had to wait for Parker's next record to find out what to play next. What will they do now?"[14] They not only copied his playing note for note, but also sought to follow his lifestyle, leading many to experiment with drugs in an effort to reach the same creative state. His improvisations remain at the core of jazz musicians' education even today. The Los Angeles group Supersax revitalized his music in the midst of the jazz-rock fusion movement in the 1970s, recreating his improvisations by harmonizing them for five saxophones. Parker and Gillespie stand alone as the major forces behind the bebop movement and are responsible for developing a new and innovative musical language through improvisation.

Parker's recording of "Koko," which had no relationship to Ellington's "Ko-Ko," was based on the chord progression to "Cherokee." It is therefore a fine example of a "contrafact." "Cherokee" was an old tune that predated the bebop period and served as the theme song for Charlie Barnet's swing band. It was also a tune that was often played at jam sessions. Parker claims it was this tune that prompted his discovery of a new, modern approach to improvising that eventually defined the essence of bebop. (See the CD-ROM for an audio example.)

Other bebop horn players of note who contributed to the advancement of this style and their respective instruments are trombonist J. J. Johnson, tenor saxophonists Dexter Gordon and Sonny Rollins, and trumpeter Fats Navarro. Rollins and Navarro can be heard along with bop pianist Bud Powell on the audio anthology track entitled "52nd Street Theme," that will be discussed in more detail later in this section.

J. J. Johnson (1924–2001) Johnson is considered the first trombonist to absorb the new harmonic and melodic language fostered by Parker and Gillespie. His fluid technique, ability to negotiate the faster bop tempos, rhythmic inventiveness, fast articulation yet light tone, and reserved vibrato accommodated the new postwar style. The trombone is perhaps the most difficult of the wind instruments to master from the technical standpoint and Johnson's technique enabled him to master the new bebop style. His first important recorded solo was as a member of Parker's small group on a 1947 recording of "Crazeology." In the 1950s, he collaborated with trombonist Kai Winding to form an unusual small group that featured the trombone duo. Johnson eventually also became as well known for his arrangements and compositions, spending many years in Hollywood composing for film and television before returning to the jazz scene as a performer in his later years. He was a key figure in the Miles Davis/Gil Evans historic "Birth of the Cool" recordings, and a

Trombonist J. J. Johnson at a recording session at WOR Studios for a Miles Davis album.

major force as a composer and performer in the third stream jazz movement in the late 1950s and early 1960s. Third stream jazz, discussed in detail in Chapter 10 (and Chapter 17 on the Online Learning Center), was a termed coined by Gunther Schuller to describe the merging of jazz rhythmic styles and improvisation with European-based composition techniques associated with classical music.

Dexter Gordon (1923–1990) Like many American jazz artists from this period, Gordon found working conditions for black jazz artists better in Europe. He is known as the first tenor saxophonist to incorporate Bird's bop alto style, though in many ways the younger Sonny Rollins is perhaps a better example of the first modern postwar tenor saxophonist to take this instrument to new heights in later years. Gordon's career throughout the 1940s included stints with Fletcher Henderson, Billy Eckstine, Dizzy Gillespie, and Tadd Dameron. "Bikini," an excellent recording by Gordon that is reflective of his work during the bebop period and before he left for Europe, can be found on the *Smithsonian Collection of Classic Jazz*. On the surface, Gordon appears to be productive during this period, but it was marred by his struggles with drug addiction. He managed to conquer these problems by 1960 and contributed as an actor, musician, and composer to the West Coast production of Jack Gelber's play *The Connection* about drug addiction. Following a lengthy stay in Europe, his much lauded return to the United States in 1976 helped to announce the nostalgic rebirth of acoustic, bop-flavored jazz that had all been erased from memories by the rock-influenced jazz of the 1970s. His robust tone projected a hard edge and thicker vibrato than Parker employed. He shared with many others from this era a penchant for quoting other tunes, some as humorous as "Happy Birthday" or "Here Comes the Bride" in the midst of his improvisations. *Down Beat* magazine readers voted him musician of the year in 1980 and he received an Academy Award nomination for his seminal role in the feature film *Round Midnight* in 1986. Gordon served as an important link between swing style and more modern tenor saxophonists like John Coltrane and Sonny Rollins who were influenced greatly by him.

Sonny Rollins (b 1930) Tenor saxophonist Rollins is often mentioned in discussions of the hard bop style (Chapter 11) that was the 1950s outgrowth of bebop, although he first rose to critical acclaim in the latter days of the bop era. His recordings with Parker, the Modern Jazz Quartet, J. J. Johnson, Fats Navarro, Miles Davis, and the Clifford Brown/Max Roach Quintet put him at the center of the bebop and hard bop explosion. In later years Rollins, or "Newk" as he was nicknamed, preferred the trio setting in the 1950s. With the absence of piano or guitar in his trios, he followed the same path as those pianoless groups led by "cool" style saxophonist Gerry Mulligan and the subsequent free-jazz experimentalist Ornette Coleman. In recent times, Branford Marsalis has followed this same model, preferring the melodic freedom encouraged by the absence of chord playing instruments. Rollins is recognized by his fat sound reminiscent of Dexter Gordon and the elder

Tenor saxophonist Dexter Gordon during the recording session for his GO *album.*

statesman Coleman Hawkins. According to Gunther Schuller, he was the first of the modern improvisers to create long-winded solos that consisted of a series of logically developed motives. Unlike most soloists from this period who based their solos on a series of unrelated ideas guided solely by the progression of chords, Rollins in contrast developed solos that were based on thematic developments of his improvised ideas. His improvisations could be considered more melodically driven in the style of Lester Young, rather than directed by Coleman Hawkins' style geared more to harmony.

By the late 1950s, following a long list of outstanding collaborations, recordings, and compositions, Rollins was heralded as the leading tenor saxophonist in the post-bop tradition. He contributed a number of compositions now considered as staples in the jazz repertoire including "Valse Hot," "Blue 7," "St. Thomas," "Oleo," "Airegin," and "Doxy." Of particular interest are his "Valse Hot" for its 3/4 meter (an unusual digression for the times from the predictable 4/4 meter) and "St. Thomas," which featured a calypso rhythmic feel.

Sonny Rollins plays the tenor saxophone during the recording session for his Newk's Time *album.*

Fats Navarro (1923–1950) Born in Florida in 1923, trumpeter Navarro played in territory bands as a teenager, often doubling on tenor saxophone. He later toured with Andy Kirk's band before joining the Billy Eckstine big band where he replaced Dizzy Gillespie who had left to form a smaller band with saxophonist Charlie Parker. While settled in the New York area, he recorded with many of the musicians that made bebop an important style, most notably Bud Powell, Kenny Clarke, Coleman Hawkins, and Tadd Dameron. He became a key solo voice in Dameron's outfits and was considered to be the most important new trumpet player on the East Coast scene. Had he not contracted tuberculosis, there is no way to estimate the impact he undoubtedly would have had. This disease, not nearly as well checked then as it is today, coupled with his heroin addiction led to his untimely death in 1950 at the young age of 27. His most impressive recordings, which display his fat full sound, range, uncanny ability to pace a solo, and melodic inventiveness, were those with the Dameron outfit and recordings made with Bud Powell, as illustrated by the track included on the companion audio anthology.

The Rhythm Section Players

"The Amazing Bud Powell" (1924–1966) To borrow the title of his multivolume set of recordings on the Blue Note label, Powell is considered the most eminent of bebop pianists, known for his incredible right-hand technique and sparse left-hand comping style that was rhythmically freer than that of earlier pianists. Like so many artists from this period, he struggled with racial prejudices, various addictions, and mental disorders. Powell jammed at Minton's Playhouse where he met and was influenced by pianist Thelonious Monk. Ellington trumpeter Cootie Williams was first to employ Powell as his pianist from 1942 to 1944, and it was this band that lay claim to being the first to record a Monk composition ("Epistrophy" in 1942).

Powell suffered a severe head injury in 1945 as the result of a racial incident during which he was beaten. Coupled with his already quirky personality, this injury led to a series of emotional breakdowns, alcoholism, and numerous stays in

Bud Powell during a recording session at WOR Studios for the Bud Powell's Modernists group.

medical institutions where he even underwent electric shock treatments. Poor physical and mental health plagued Powell for much of his adult life, hampering his career and causing erratic performances. Eventually Powell moved to Paris, where audiences were more accepting of black performers and very receptive to jazz. There he teamed with another expatriate Kenny Clarke, who had been the house drummer at Minton's, and French bassist Pierre Michelot. While his recordings from this period tend to be spotty compared to his earlier standard, he was still capable of displaying the virtuosic talent that had earned him a reputation as the best of the bebop pianists.

Powell's style was original, yet based on a synthesis of Art Tatum's technique and Teddy Wilson's lyricism. He preferred to play rapid, Parker-like right-hand lines in counterpoint and contrast to a sparse, rhythmically jagged and irregular, low-register, and often dissonant left-hand chordal accompaniment that resembled Monk's style. His technique enabled him to play fast, double-time lines at will. Like Earl Hines had done decades before in copying Armstrong, Powell preferred a style that was more akin to the single-note, improvised lines associated with the bop horn players. While Powell had a penchant for the trio setting, he often performed and recorded with the prominent bop horn players of the day including Charlie Parker, Dizzy Gillespie, J. J. Johnson, and of course Fats Navarro and Sonny Rollins, as is the case with the recording included in the companion audio anthology. Like most bop innovators, Powell's legacy includes a catalogue of compositions that are now standard repertoire, including "Tempus Fugue-it," "Dance of the Infidels," "Budo," "Bouncing With Bud," and "Un Poco Loco."

Powell's recording of Monk's "52nd St. Theme" is a classic, particularly because it includes exemplary solos by young Sonny Rollins and Fats Navarro. The analysis that follows corresponds to this recording included on the audio anthology.

Listening Guide

Bud Powell

"52nd St. Theme" (Thelonious Monk) 2:49

Recorded 8/8/49, Blue Note, "The Amazing Bud Powell, Vol. 1" Reissue: The Complete Blue Note Recordings, B21 Y-81503

Bud Powell: *piano*

Fats Navarro: *trumpet*

Sonny Rollins: *tenor saxophone*

Tommy Potter: *bass*

Roy Haynes: *drums*

Form and Key: Repeated song form choruses (AABA=chorus), in C major

0:00–0:03   *Introduction:* 4 bars, *Trumpet Solo*, trumpet plays varied melody from end of each A section, with ensemble accents.

0:04–0:30   *First Chorus:* 32 bars, *Song Form:*

       0:04–0:10   *A section:* 8 bars, trumpet and sax play melody with piano answering fills, rhythm section swinging accompaniment.

       0:10–0:16   *A section:* 8 bars, melody as in the "A" section.

       0:17–0:23   *B section:* 8 bars, piano plays bridge melody, trumpet and sax tacet.

       0:24–0:30   *A section:* 8 bars, melody as in "A" section.

0:31–0:57   *Second Chorus:* 32 bars, *Sax Solo:* Tenor sax solo (Rollins) over chorus chord changes, with trumpet/piano riff in first two "A" sections, swinging rhythm section accompaniment.

0:58–1:23	*Third Chorus:* 32 bars, *Trumpet Solo:* trumpet solo (Navarro) over chorus chord changes, with swinging rhythm section accompaniment.
1:24–1:49	*Fourth Chorus:* 32 bars, *Piano Solo:* piano solo (Powell) over chorus chord changes, with swinging rhythm section accompaniment
1:49–2:15	*Fifth Chorus:* 32 bars, *Piano Solo:* continued piano solo.
2:15–2:55	*Sixth Chorus:* 32 bars, *Ensemble Riff/Drum Solo/Melody:*

2:15–2:21	*A section:* 8 bars, trumpet, sax and piano lead ensemble riff.
2:21–2:27	*A section:* 8 bars, variation on first "A" section ensemble riff.
2:28–2:34	*B section:* 8 bars, improvised drum solo, all others tacet.
2:34–2:49	*A section with ending tag:* 10 bars, trumpet and sax play melody as in first chorus "A" sections, with short tag repeating and varying last 2 bars of melody.

Thelonious Sphere Monk (1917–1982) Monk was perhaps the most enigmatic personality to gain attention as a pianist and composer in the late 1940s. Monk became the house pianist at Minton's, where he performed with Parker, Gillespie, Charlie Christian, Kenny Clarke, and many of the other pioneers of the new bop style. Ironically, however, Monk's own piano style eventually became the antithesis of what bop represented and encouraged—fast, flashy, notey passages. While his harmonic concepts were very advanced for the day, his style was deeply rooted in the older stride tradition, and he did not seem to possess the right-hand technique required to play the fast lines typically associated with the bop style of improvisation. Everything about Monk, his music, and persona was unorthodox and eccentric, from his hand position at the keyboard to the way he dressed. Monk's style was rhythmically driving, percussive, harmonically rich, and quirky to say the least. Bassist Gene Ramey who participated in early Monk recording sessions theorized that Monk purposely sought to create a style that was less easily mimicked since by the mid-1940s most of the younger musicians on the scene were overtly copying the Parker-Gillespie-Powell style. Improvisational clichés were quickly becoming common practice and it is no wonder that Monk's more obtuse, almost avant-garde style caused the jazz world to initially overlook him. Consequently he is often referred to as a rediscovery figure not widely recorded or recognized until the 1950s and 1960s. It was difficult for Monk to get work in his early years because of this unique style that was contradictory to the current trends. His sparse accompanying style and unusual chord voicings comprised a style that was often criticized by horn players looking for the ideal accompanist. Monk never wasted a note and his solos were often masterful understatements, sounding like an edited improvisation in which all extraneous material had been omitted. He used the entire range of the keyboard and often approached the instrument in a percussive fashion.

Ex-Ellington trumpeter Cootie Williams was the first to record an arrangement of a Monk composition, though it seemed out of character to be performed by this swing style big band. Monk also performed and recorded with tenor saxophonist Coleman Hawkins. Monk's most significant compositions from this bebop period were collected on two LPs for Blue Note Records. Each tune illustrates a perfect marriage between melody, harmony, and rhythm, making the whole better than the sum of these individual components. Monk's compositions are very difficult to perform, as the musicians must completely

Pianist Thelonious Monk during a recording session at WOR Studios.

internalize the composition, being willing to give up a certain amount of themselves in order to project the essence of the tune through their improvisations. His later recordings for the Prestige and Riverside labels, while not big sellers at the time, were later identified as landmark recordings. Some believe that his much touted 1957 "Brilliant Corners" release planted further seeds for the not yet realized avant-garde movement in jazz. A favorite recording is the double CD reissued by Columbia entitled *Monk: Big Band and Quartet in Concert*. In addition to the big band and quartet tracks, Monk contributes a solo piano rendition of the old, forgotten standard "Darkness on the Delta," during which his stride roots and trademark piano orchestrations with the cascading descending scales are evident.

Monk was one of the few jazz artists to be pictured and written about in *Time* magazine and after his death was the subject of more than one film. His legacy, which includes compositions like "Straight No Chaser," "Ruby My Dear," "'Round Midnight," "Criss Cross," and "Well You Needn't" among others, can be summed by his own quotation from *Harper's* magazine: "Maybe I've turned jazz another way. Maybe I'm a major influence. I don't know. Jazz is my adventure. I'm after new chords, new ways of syncopating, new figurations, new runs. How to use notes differently. That's it. Just how to use notes differently."[15] He chose his own path and was unaffected by the press or current trends, passing this attitude and uncompromising ethic on to those like avant-garde pianist Cecil Taylor who would follow.

"Well You Needn't" was chosen as an example of Monk and his music for several reasons. This particular track was featured on his earliest recording as a leader for the Blue Note label. It also includes Gene Ramey on bass, the subject of numerous interviews found throughout this book and on the accompanying CD-ROM.

Listening Guide

Thelonius Monk

"Well You Needn't" (Monk) 2:56

Recorded 10/24/47 New York City, Blue Note 543

Reissued: Blue Note "The Blue Note Years" 7243-4-95698-2-9

Thelonious Monk: *piano*

Gene Ramey: *bass*

Art Blakey: *drums*

Form and Key: Repeated 32 bar song form choruses (AABA=1 chorus) in F major

0:00–0:04	*Introduction:* 3 bars, *Piano Solo.*
0:04–0:44	*First Chorus:* 32 bars (AABA), *Piano Plays Theme,* with bass and drum accompaniment.
0:45–1:24	*Second Chorus:* 32 bars (AABA), improvised *Piano Solo,* with bass and drum accompaniment.
1:25–2:04	*Third Chorus:* 32 bars, (AABA), improvised *Piano Solo,* with bass and drum accompaniment.
2:05–2:45	*Fourth Chorus:* 37 bars, (AABA), improvised *Piano Solo,* with bass and drums (AAB). Last A: 8-bar *Theme* statement, followed by 5-bar tag; final theme is repeated.

Tadd Dameron (1917–1965) Pianist/composer Dameron began his career as a singer, which may explain why he had limited pianistic skills. He worked in a band led by a relatively obscure trumpeter Freddie Webster, frequently cited by Miles Davis, Clark Terry, and others as an advanced player from the Midwest who had a significant influence on the formation of the new bop style. When the band's pianist quit, Dameron took over. While he possessed an advanced understanding of harmony and chord construction, he is most remembered as a composer and accompanist who never developed a solo style on the level of Bud Powell or other major forces in the bop piano world. He composed a fine collection of tunes now considered significant contributions to the repertoire including "Good Bait," "If You Could See Me Now," "Our Delight," "Lady Bird," "Hot House," and others. Aside from his contributions as a composer, he is known as the bandleader who nurtured trumpeters Fats Navarro and Clifford Brown along with other important bebop and hard bop instrumentalists. In many ways, he is considered a catalyst for the next generation of musicians who advanced bebop to become the mainstream hard bop of the next decade.

Oscar Pettiford (1922–1960) Pettiford was the first modern bassist to serve as a link between swing era bassists Slam Stewart and Jimmy Blanton and the more modern demands of bebop. Pettiford, who was first schooled as a pianist, toured with a family band as a teenager. His first major positions were held in swing bands led by Charlie Barnett (1942), becoming the first black musician to join this band, and Roy Eldridge (1943). It was Coleman Hawkins' important transitional recordings that brought Pettiford to the center of attention in terms of the new bop movement and he soon found himself co-leading a quintet with Dizzy Gillespie in 1944. He returned to working with big bands, holding down the bass chair in Duke Ellington's band from 1945 to 1948 and a year later with the Woody Herman Band. Throughout the next decade, he recorded with most of the significant personalities of the bebop era including Monk, Art Blakey, Stan Getz, and Bud Powell. Later in his career, he adopted a jazz playing technique for the cello. He passed away suddenly in Copenhagen, his home away from home, as a result of a polio-like virus. Pettiford is remembered for bringing the bass into a more well-defined solo role and is considered the first modern jazz bassist.

Kenny Clarke (1914–1985) Clarke is considered the true father of the modern bebop style of drumming. Clarke was the first of this new breed of bop drummers to disregard the regular use of the bass drum. Drummers in the earlier styles played in a chunky, less flowing style than what evolved in the mid-1940s thanks to the efforts of Clarke, Roach, and Art Blakey (Chapter 11). The most immediate predecessors of this new modern style were Jo Jones (with Basie's band), Cozy Cole, and Sid Catlett. Both Cole and Catlett had cut some of the first early bop sides with Gillespie and Parker. Bop drummers, along with bass players, still carried the burden of maintaining the steady pulse and time feel; what changed was how they maintained the time. Swing style drummers used the bass drum on every beat and often very aggressively, while Clarke and his followers transferred this every beat pulse from the bass drum to the lighter, more flexible ride cymbal where it was easier to achieve more variety. Clarke, who also played piano and vibes, which may explain his more melodic approach to the drums, is credited as the first drummer to overtly avoid using the bass drum on every beat. He claimed to have developed this approach by accident when playing the faster bop tempos, which made it tiring to use the bass drum on every beat and slowed the tempo down on extended tunes with long solos. He developed a more independent, less rigid style of drumming where all limbs were free to embellish the basic beat and inherent rhythms of the melody. This new style is akin to the punching and jabbing of a boxer who continues to move in a flowing rhythm around the ring. Teddy Hill, who once fired Clarke from his big band for playing in this wilder style, took over the management of Minton's Playhouse where he later hired Clarke as house drummer. It was here in the years that followed that Clarke perfected this new style. Max Roach elaborated on it by adding even more complex syncopations and cross-rhythms. Hill described this new accented approach to playing, using the bass drum only to "drop bombs" as musical punctuation marks, as "Klook-mop music," a name that stuck and Clarke earned his new nickname—"Klook."

Before taking up permanent residence in Paris in 1955, Clarke became a dominant figure in the New York scene performing with Miles Davis, Monk, Tadd Dameron, Ella Fitzgerald, Gillespie, and many others. After serving time in the Army, Clarke returned to the States to become a regular member of Gillespie's big band before leaving to help found the Modern Jazz Quartet with pianist John Lewis (Chapter 10). Clarke was less intrigued by Lewis's new brand of "cool" jazz and termed it "too bland and pretentious." He left New York for Paris where he cofounded the Kenny Clarke—Francy Boland big band. Clarke was a well-rounded musician who brought his knowledge of composition and melodic instruments to the drum set to create a new way of playing time by engaging in a dialogue with the performers in ways that had never been done before.

Max Roach (b 1924) Drummer Roach represents one of the newer breeds of schooled musicians that surfaced during the bebop period. By day he studied percussion and composition at New York City conservatories and by night he sat in at Minton's and Monroe's Uptown House. Roach and Kenny Clarke, his mentor, are considered to be the best representatives of the explosive new drumming style that emerged in the mid-1940s and complimented what the bop horn players were doing melodically and rhythmically. Roach is considered the earliest and most fluent member of the modern school of drumming less concerned with mere time keeping and more concerned with a melodic approach to drumming and rhythmically complimenting the tune and soloists. Roach was the first to approach the drums in a more melodic fashion.

Roach replaced Clarke at Minton's, later recording with Hawkins, Gillespie, and Parker where he showed off the new style of drumming. At home in small groups and big bands including those led by Ellington, Benny Carter, and Gillespie, Roach co-led the famous hard bop group in the mid-1950s with trumpet virtuoso Clifford Brown (Chapter 11). Since then he has performed and recorded with most noted jazz soloists of the past several decades. In the 1970s and 1980s he pursued composition with more fervor, writing for new and interesting amalgamations of instruments including string quartets and choirs while always maintaining true to the basic tenets of the jazz tradition. Roach, a vocal spokesman for equal rights, also explored more fringe styles of jazz in the '60s and '70s with artists such as pianist Cecil Taylor and saxophonists Archie Shepp and Anthony Braxton, all movers and shakers in the avant-garde jazz style. His *We Insist—Freedom Now* suite, recorded

Max Roach sits behind his drum set during a 1950 Metronome All-Stars recording session.

in the 1960s, showed his awareness and deep commitment to the civil rights movement with which he was actively involved. The claims that there is little relationship between sociopolitical issues and the arts are clearly mistaken. Currently his career may have slowed, but he continues to compose, perform and teach, exerting an influence on young drummers as he has for nearly seven decades.

Sarah Vaughan: The "Devine One" (1924–1990)

One of the many talented musicians to perform with Dameron was vocalist **Sarah Vaughan**. Vaughan was one of several singers, along with Carmen McRae and Betty Carter, to fall under the influence of the bop generation of instrumentalists and serve as an example of the vocalist's side of this movement. A contralto, she earned the nickname the "Devine One" because of her incomparable vocal technique and mastery often compared to that of the best of opera singers. She negotiated her exceptional four-octave range with ease, and her signature swoops from the height of her range to the extreme low register and back are legendary and hallmarks of her individualistic style. Vaughan used her rich, resonant vocal quality, strong controlled vibrato, sudden changes in dynamics, and flare for the daring and dramatic to advantage, bringing her praise from vocalists and instrumentalists. In contrast to Billie Holiday, her incredible vocal technique at times inspired her to ignore the interpretation of a lyric in favor of exploring and flaunting her vocal talent; but if doing the unexpected with utmost sincerity and virtuosic artistry is the mark of a truly great performer, then Sarah Vaughan earned her reputation. Vaughan's talent shined on sultry ballads and, like Fitzgerald and Holiday, she did not favor blues but did enjoy a romping, swing, or bop style tune.

Sarah Vaughan began her love affair with music as a child, singing and playing organ and piano in a Newark, New Jersey, Baptist church. Like Ella Fitzgerald had done eight years earlier, she won a competition at an Apollo Theater Amateur Night and captured the attention of pianist/bandleader Earl Hines. Hines put her to work serving as second-string pianist and vocalist in his band, sharing that spotlight with baritone Billy Eckstine. It was here, and later with Eckstine's own bop oriented band that splintered off from the Hines band, that she encountered the horn players that would write the new bebop language including its finest authors Charlie Parker, Dexter Gordon, Dizzy Gillespie, Fats Navarro, and others. Gillespie called her, along with Carmen McRae, a "musician's singer. Both of them can play the piano and accompany themselves. They know all the flat fives and modern progressions and can do them vocally."[16] As a scatting improviser, something she did with less abandon or flash than Ella Fitzgerald, Vaughan took full advantage of her training as a pianist, enabling her to not only embrace the melodic side of improvisation, as is the case with most singers, but also to get inside the complex bebop harmonies in much the same way as the horn players. "You had to sing within whatever the chords were they were playing. You had to know a little about music or have a hell of a good ear" according to Vaughan. [17]

In 1944 she became one of the first singers to record in the bop vein immediately after the A.F. of M. recording strike was settled. *Down Beat* magazine recognized her in their polls from 1947

Sarah Vaughan singing "Black Coffee" at a recording session.

to 1952 and she won top vocalist in 1950. Her most exceptional recorded work is undoubtedly those sides preserved on the Mercury/Emarcy label and those made later in life for the Mainstream and Pablo labels. Despite these successes in the 50s, recording with the likes of the Count Basie Band, Miles Davis, saxophone hard bopper Cannonball Adderley, and trumpeter Clifford Brown, she found herself jumping from label to label and producer to producer. She was trying her hand at becoming a more mainstream popular success at a time when the general public had lost track of jazz in favor of following pop trends. Her volatile, diva-like personality earned her a second nickname, "Sassy," and this may partially explain her label/producer hopping. For the most part, even amid the backdrop of overproduced orchestral arrangements, or in lavish productions of pop tunes including Beatles tunes of later years, she remained true to her roots as a jazz singer, emerging later and throughout her career to record exceptional jazz. Along with Bessie Smith, Billie Holiday, Ella Fitzgerald, Betty Carter, and Carmen McRae, Sarah Vaughan stands as one of the most original and identifiable jazz singers, serving as an important model for the younger generation of singers to follow.

"Easy Living," included on the companion CD anthology, is an example of Vaughan in the later stage of her career but still in impeccable form, demonstrating her flare for slow ballads and operatic-like technique. Some of the finest rhythm section players of the twentieth century, each in their own right noted soloists, provide exquisite accompaniment on this Pablo recording produced by jazz impresario Norman Granz.

Listening Guide

Sarah Vaughan

"Easy Living" (L. Robin/ R. Rainger) 4:36

Recorded 4/25/78 in Hollywood, CA, Pablo PACD-2310-821-2

Sarah Vaughan: *vocals*
Oscar Peterson: *piano*
Joe Pass: *guitar*
Ray Brown: *bass*
Louie Bellson: *drums*

Form and Key: 32-bar song form (AABA), A♭ major.

0:00–0:16	*Introduction:* Pianist Oscar Peterson provides rubato introduction.
0:17–0:56	Chorus begins with *first A section* sung in tempo with rhythm section accompaniment.
0:57–1:35	*Repeat of A section.*
1:36–2:12	*Bridge* or B section of form.
2:13–2:40	Return to *final A section* to complete first full chorus; bass and drums drop out (2:41–2:49) in final bars of chorus as tempo deteriorates to rubato.
2:50–3:31	Piano and voice in duet *return to bridge*, breaking from expected form by eliminating first two A sections.
3:32–4:02	Band reenters in tempo to state final A section.
4:03–end	Vaughan improvises a short rubato coda; listen for bowed bass.

THE DECLINE OF BEBOP

It would be unfair and misleading to say that bebop has ever really declined in terms of its influence. It was a new music in the mid-1940s that quickly was noticed in the downtown Harlem and Village clubs like Minton's and Clark Monroe's Uptown House and nearly overnight moved to successful uptown establishments like the Onyx, Spotlite, and The 3 Deuces. 52nd Street, eventually referred to as "The

Street," was the new home for jazz in the small clubs that nightly packed in curious audiences. While some critics initially questioned its value and condemned it, most quickly rose to champion the bop practitioners and even the naysayers eventually changed their tune. The novelty for most fans who were looking for entertainment had worn off and most bop performers were ill prepared to sell themselves or their art. Bop placed too high a demand on listeners who found that they couldn't dance to it; couldn't talk over it; and couldn't find, hear, or understand its melodies and harmonies. As early as 1946, the Street began to suffer from bad press causing clubs like the Onyx to close because of stories about conmen, hipsters, and junkies who were frightening away some fans. Many of the great clubs on the Street turned into strip joints and the music moved to new clubs on Broadway, but even those (Birdland and The Royal Roost) closed their doors in 1949. It appeared that bebop had burned out as quickly as it ignited, but the style would prove to have a much longer life span and range of influence than anyone anticipated.

Jazz in Perspective

The timeline that follows will put the developments of jazz discussed in this chapter into a larger historical context, providing you with a better sense of how landmark musical events may relate to others that match your personal areas of interest.

1945
- FDR dies—Harry Truman sworn in as president.
- House of Representatives establishes Committee on un-American Activities.
- Fuel shortages due to World War II.
- J. Steinbeck publishes *Cannery Row.*
- John Hersey wins Pulitzer Prize for *A Bell For Adano.*
- Germany surrenders.
- United States drops atomic bomb on Hiroshima—Japan surrenders.
- Americans begin social and economic recovery from World War II.
- Charlie Parker and Dizzy Gillespie record "Koko."

1946
- American industry readjusts to peacetime economy.
- United States begins space exploration.
- "Iron Curtain" signals beginning of "Cold War" conflict between democracy and communism/socialism.
- United States begins atomic testing at Bikini Atoll (Island).
- Irving Berlin premiers new musical *Annie Get Your Gun.*
- ENIAC computer ushers in new age.
- Popular films include *The Postman Always Rings Twice,* and *Best Years of Our Lives.*
- Richard James invents a new toy "Slinky" by accident.

1947
- Robert Penn Warren wins Pulitzer Prize for *All the King's Men.*
- Author James Michener publishes *Tales of the South Pacific.*
- Tennessee Williams premiers *A Streetcar Named Desire.*
- GI Bill provides housing, education, and business opportunities for former armed services members in an attempt to infuse postwar rebuild.
- Jackie Robinson becomes first African American to play professional baseball.

- Growing concerns about communist activities in the United States—10 Hollywood personalities blacklisted.
- Television grows in popularity.
- Tape recorder is produced for home use.
- Dizzy Gillespie's bebop big band records Afro-Cuban tinged "Manteca" defining the Cubop style.
- Thelonious Monk's trio records "Well You Needn't."

1948
- Toscanini conducts first NBC Orchestra concert on TV.
- The transistor is developed by Bell Labs to replace vacuum tube.
- Supreme Court rules that race may not be used to consider law school admissions at University of Oklahoma.
- James Michener wins Pulitzer Prize for *Tales of the South Pacific.*
- Supreme Court forbids prayer in schools.
- *Candid Camera* and *Milton Berle* top list of popular new TV shows.
- President Truman attempts to halt racial discrimination in the military.

1949
- Rodgers and Hammerstein create Broadway musical *South Pacific.*
- Harry S. Truman wins presidential election.

- *Lone Ranger* debuts on TV.
- Arthur Miller's play *The Death of a Salesman* wins Pulitzer Prize.
- Pianist Bud Powell records Thelonious Monk's "52nd St. Theme."
- Miles Davis and company launch the cool jazz style.
- General Electric engineer invents "silly putty."

1950
- Senator McCarthy denounces communism and begins efforts to purge the United States of all members of this party, blacklisting 205 well-known personalities.
- United States backs South Korea against North Korea and war with Korea begins.
- William Faulkner wins Nobel Prize for Literature and Ralph Bunch wins the Peace Prize.
- U.S. Census indicates 150 million people.
- Beginnings of Cold War.

1951
- United States detonates H-bomb.
- UNIVAC electronic, digital computer unveiled.
- *I Love Lucy* is instant TV success.
- Author J. D. Salinger's *Catcher in the Rye* is tale of teenage alienation.

MILLION-SELLING RECORD ALBUMS

This table indicates million-selling record albums produced during the peak swing years and leading up to the decline of big bands. The (V) indicates a vocal recording and (I) represents an instrumental recording. It is clear that the tide seems to shift around 1944 to 1945, when the number of million-selling vocal recordings surpasses instrumental sales. From this point on, jazz begins to decline in widespread popularity as it moves closer to art music while being taken over by new popular music styles.

Year	Title	Artist
1937	"Bei Mir Bist Du Schoen"	Andrews Sisters (V)
(2-V and 1-I)	"Sweet Leilani"	Bing Crosby (V)
	"Marie"	Tommy Dorsey Orchestra (I)

Year	Title	Artist
1938	"Boogie Woogie"	Tommy Dorsey Orchestra (I)
(4-I)	"Begin the Beguine"	Artie Shaw Orchestra (I)
	"Nightmare"	Artie Shaw Orchestra (I)
	"Back Bay Shuffle"	Artie Shaw Orchestra (I)
1939	"Traffic Jam"	Artie Shaw Orchestra (I)
(8-I and 4-V)	"That Silver Haired Daddy of Mine"	Gene Autry (country vocal)
	"Jumpin' Jive"	Cab Calloway Orchestra (V)
	"Over the Rainbow"	Judy Garland (V)
	"Body and Soul"	Coleman Hawkins (I)
	"Woodchoppers Ball"	Woody Herman (I)
	"Ciribiribin"	Harry James Orchestra (I)
	"One O'Clock Jump"	Harry James Orchestra (I)
	"All or Nothing at All"	Frank Sinatra with H. James Orch. (V)
	"Little Brown Jug"	Glenn Miller Orchestra (I)
	"Moonlight Serenade"	Glenn Miller Orchestra (I)
	"In the Mood"	Glenn Miller Orchestra (I)
1940	"Pennsylvania 6-5000"	Glenn Miller Orchestra (I)
(5-I and 1-V)	"Tuxedo Junction"	Glenn Miller Orchestra (I)
	"Frenesi"	Artie Shaw Orchestra (I)
	"Stardust"	Artie Shaw Orchestra (I)
	"Summit Ridge Drive"	Artie Shaw Orchestra (I)
	"San Antonio Rose"	Bob Wills and his Texas Playboys (country vocal)
1941	"San Antonio Rose"	Bing Crosby (V)
(4-I and 4-V)	"Amapola"	Jimmy Dorsey Orchestra (I)
	"Green Eyes"	Jimmy Dorsey Orchestra (V)
	"Maria Elena"	Jimmy Dorsey Orchestra (V)
	"You Made Me Love You"	Harry James Orchestra (I)
	"Chattanooga Choo Choo"	Glenn Miller Orchestra (I)
	"Dancing in the Dark"	Artie Shaw Orchestra (I)
	"Rose O'Day"	Kate Smith (V)
1942	"There Are Such Things"	Tommy Dorsey Orchestra (I)
(8-I and 5-V)	"Why Don't You Do Right"	Benny Goodman Orchestra (I)
	"I Had the Craziest Dream"	Harry James Orchestra (I)

continued

Year	Title	Artist
	"I've Heard That Song Before"	Harry James Orchestra (I)
	"Easter Parade"	Harry James Orchestra (I)
	"Kalamazoo"	Glenn Miller Orchestra (I)
	"American Patrol"	Glenn Miller Orchestra (I)
	"Praise the Lord and Pass the Ammunition"	Kay Kyser Orchestra (V)
	"Strip Polka"	Kay Kyser Orchestra (I)
	"Who Wouldn't Love You?"	Kay Kyser Orchestra (V)
	"Jingle Jangle Jingle"	Kay Kyser Orchestra (V)
	"White Christmas"	Bing Crosby (V)
	"Silent Night"	Bing Crosby (V)
1943*	"Besame Mucho"	Jimmy Dorsey Orchestra (I)
(3-I and 1-V)	"Artistry in Rhythm"	Stan Kenton Orchestra (I)
	"Is You Is or Is You Ain't?"	Louis Jordan Orchestra (V)
	"Cow-Cow Boogie"	Freddie Slack Orchestra (I)?
1944	"White Christmas"	Frank Sinatra with H. James Orch. (V)
(7-V and 5-I)	"You Always Hurt the One You Love"	Mills Brothers (V)
	"Begin the Beguine"	Eddie Haywood Orchestra (I)
	"Cocktails for Two" (novelty)	Spike Jones Orchestra (I)
	"Opus No. 1"	Tommy Dorsey Orchestra (I)
	"On the Sunny Side of the Street"	Tommy Dorsey Orchestra (I)
	"Swingin' On a Star"	Bing Crosby (V)
	"Don't Fence Me In"	Bing Crosby (V)
	"Too-Ra-Loo-Ra-Loo-Ra"	Bing Crosby (V)
	"Sentimental Journey"	Les Brown Orchestra (I)
	"Rum and Coca Cola"	Andrews Sisters (V)
	"Into Each Life Some Rain Must Fall"	Ella Fitzgerald (with the Ink Spots) (V)
1945	"Till the End of Time"	Perry Como (V)
(7-V and 3-I)	"If I Loved You"	Perry Como (V)
	"Dig You Later"	Perry Como (V)
	"Temptation"	Perry Como (V)
	"I Can't Begin to Tell You"	Bing Crosby (V)
	"Cottage for Sale"	Billy Eckstine (V)
	"Prisoner of Love"	Billy Eckstine (V)

*In 1943 the recording industry was hit hard by the A.F. of M. recording ban, hence the fewer million-selling hits, most of which were recordings issued from archived, previously unreleased stock.

MILLION-SELLING RECORD ALBUMS concluded

Year	Title	Artist
	"Laura"	Woody Herman Orchestra (I)
	"Tampico"	Stan Kenton Orchestra (I)
	"Shoe-Fly Pie"	Stan Kenton Orchestra (I)
1946	"Prisoner of Love"	Perry Como (V)
(13-V and 3-I)	"I'm Always Chasing Rainbows"	Perry Como (V)
	"South America, Take it Away"	Bing Crosby (V)
	"McNamara's Band"	Bing Crosby (V)
	"Alexander's Ragtime Band"	Bing Crosby (V)
	"To Each His Own"	The Ink Spots (V)
	"The Gypsy"	The Ink Spots (V)
	"April Showers"	Al Jolson (V)
	"Rockabye Your Baby"	Al Jolson (V)
	"You Made Me Love You"	Al Jolson (V)
	"Sonny Boy"	Al Jolson (V)
	"Anniversary Song"	Al Jolson (V)
	"Glow-Worm"	Spike Jones Orchestra (I)
	"Humoresque"	Guy Lombardo Orchestra (I)
	"Christmas Island"	Guy Lombardo Orchestra (I)
	"Choo Choo Ch' Boogie"	Louis Jordan and His Tympani 5 (V)
1947	By 1947 nearly every million-seller was either a vocal, novelty number, or instrumental by a "sweet" dance band bearing no resemblance to jazz aside from instrumentation. The big band era had clearly come to a close at least in terms of capturing the attention of throngs of Americans as it had only a few years earlier.	

SOURCE: Information is based on statistics cited in Peter A. Soderbergh's *Old Records Price Guide 1900–1947* (Des Moines: Wallace-Homstead Book Company, 1980), pp. 176–180.

CHAPTER SUMMARY

In the early 1940s, numerous factors combined to cause the demise of many of the big bands. America's entry into World War II necessitated a military draft that claimed many big band musicians. Others, wanting to do something for their country, enlisted. Those still in the United States had to cope with the rationing of petroleum related products including gasoline and tires, making travel very difficult. Even records depended on petroleum products that were being reserved to support the war effort. On the home front, with so many men away fighting the war, women took on many of the jobs traditionally held by men, leaving them very little leisure time. Add to this situation the recording ban of the early 1940s imposed by the musicians union and it becomes clear that big bands could no longer thrive as they had.

At the same time, top jazz soloists continued to seek more artistically rewarding avenues to express themselves beyond the confines of the big band. At after-hours clubs like Minton's Playhouse, where musicians could play music for themselves, rather than for the public, a return to the early jazz ideal emphasizing improvisation fostered a new music—bebop. Although older musicians (notably, Coleman Hawkins) were important in helping to bring about this new style, trumpeter Dizzy Gillespie and alto saxophonist Charlie Parker are considered the true founders of bebop. Typically a bebop group was small (three to five performers), enabling each member to have ample time to solo. As a music for musicians, bop tended to use much more complex harmonies and could be played at very fast tempos since dancers were no longer a consideration. Pianist Bud Powell, tenor saxophonist Dexter Gordon, and trombonist J. J. Johnson all made significant contributions to developing the bop language on their instruments and only the very best musicians were capable of playing this music.

Pianist/composer Thelonious Monk contributed a sophisticated and original harmonic approach to bop. Although he served as the house pianist at Minton's, participating in many important bop sessions, his quirky, unorthodox style does not fit the bop ideal. At the time, his music and performance style defied classification and mainstream trends.

Not all of the bebop innovations involved solo styles. Changes took place in the rhythm section to accommodate this new style. Drummers used primarily the ride cymbal to maintain pulse rather than the hi-hat and bass drum since at some of the fast tempos it became physically impossible for drummers to maintain a steady pulse with the bass drum. Bop drummer Kenny Clarke is normally credited with this development. He and Max Roach were the trend setting bebop drummers. Pianists abandoned the timekeeper role in favor of a punctuated style known as comping, and the guitar was often omitted from bop rhythm sections. Bass players still frequently played walking bass lines but some, notably Oscar Pettiford, used the bass more and more as a solo instrument. This new approach gave the rhythm section a more open, less cluttered feel.

Bebop-rooted vocalist Sarah Vaughan was an exceptionally talented singer, possessing the technique and range equal to top performers of any style of music. Also an accomplished jazz pianist, she was the first vocalist to apply a more advanced harmonic approach to her interpretations and improvisations.

Bebop never actually ceased being influential. Another generation of bop players would be important in the 1950s playing hard bop. Bebop lives on today serving as the basis for study and teaching improvisation.

KEY TERMS

Important terms, places, people and bands:

TERMS
Contrafact

PLACES
Onyx Club
Clark Monroe's
  Uptown House
Minton's Playhouse
Birdland
Swing Street

PEOPLE
James Petrillo
Charlie Parker
Dizzy Gillespie
Oscar Pettiford
Kenny Clarke
Thelonious Monk
Max Roach
Nat "King" Cole
Mario Bauza

J. J. Johnson
Chano Pozo
Yardbird
Dexter Gordon
Sonny Rollins
Fats Navarro
Tadd Dameron
Bud Powell
The "Devine One"

REVIEW QUESTIONS

1. Cite the reasons for the gradual decline of swing style popularity.
2. Compare and contrast bebop with swing style.
3. Describe the social atmosphere that surrounded the bebop style.
4. Can you name some of the older swing musicians who helped to develop and promote the earliest forms of small group bebop?
5. What changes occurred in the bass's role and performance style during the bebop period?
6. What three earlier bassists had laid the groundwork for a more modern style that emerged during the bebop period?
7. Bebop drummers initiated what significant changes in their playing during the bebop period? What two drummers were most instrumental in making these changes?
8. Who are the two pianists given much of the credit for modernizing the jazz pianist's accompaniment style?
9. Who was the first trombonist to embrace the more modern bebop style?
10. What was Cubop and who was largely responsible for it?
11. List the musical characteristics that define Dizzy Gillespie's unique style.
12. List the musical characteristics that define Charlie Parker's revolutionary and unique style.
13. Who are considered the originators of the bebop style?
14. Who was the tenor saxophonist given much of the credit for incorporating Parker's bebop alto style?
15. What tenor saxophonist was heralded as the leading tenor saxophonist of the postbop school?
16. Who was the preeminent bebop pianist?
17. What kind of repertoire did bop bands concern themselves with?
18. Describe the typical bebop tune in terms of the overall form or architecture of its presentation.
19. What eccentric bop era pianist was equally recognized as a composer?

20. In what ways did Monk's style make him an anomaly in the bebop period?

21. Who was the bassist that served as a link between swing style bassists Jimmy Blanton and Slam Stewart and the more modern, soloistic demands of the bebop style?

22. What two drummers are considered to be the best representatives of the explosive new drumming style that emerged in the mid-1940s and complimented what the bop horn players were doing melodically and rhythmically? In what ways did these two drummers modify their playing as compared to earlier Swing Era drummers?

23. Who is considered the true father of the modern bebop style of drumming?

24. Name one preeminent vocalist from this period and describe her style.

25. Were there any bebop style big bands? If so, who were their leaders?

26. How can the decline of bebop be explained?

27. Was bebop an art music or music that supported entertainment?

> **Make sure that you also review material on the corresponding chapter of the CD-ROM.**

SUGGESTED SUPPLEMENTARY LISTENING

The abbreviation (iT) indicates that a particular recording cited in the text, or particularly demonstrative of the artist, is available from the Apple iTunes Web site. Other Web-based music distributors may also prove to be valuable resources. SCCJ indicates *Smithsonian Collection of Classic Jazz.*

Coleman Hawkins

Coleman Hawkins—Rainbow Mist with Dizzy Gillespie, Ben Webster, Georgie Auld Delmark
Ken Burns Jazz: Coleman Hawkins Verve (iT)

Dizzy Gillespie

Shaw' Nuff Dizzy Gillespie and his Sextets and Orchestra Musiccraft
Dizzy Gillespie The Complete CA Recordings Bluebird
Groovin' High Savoy Jazz
Ken Burns Jazz: Dizzy Gillespie Verve (iT)
"Con Alma" (iT)
"A Night in Tunisia" (iT)
"Woody 'N' You" (iT)
"Bebop" (iT)
"Groovin' High" (iT)
"Anthropology" (iT)

Charlie Parker

Ken Burns Jazz: Charlie Parker Verve (iT)
"Billie's Bounce" (iT)
"Now's the Time" (iT)
"Ornithology" (iT)
"Just Friends" (iT)
"Blues for Alice" (iT)

J. J. Johnson

"Alone Together" (with Kai Winding) (iT)
"Bernie's Tune" (with Kai Winding) (iT)
Stan Getz and JJ Johnson at the Opera House Verve (iT)
The Eminent JJ Johnson Vols. I and II Blue Note
JJ Johnson's Jazz Quintet's Savoy

Dexter Gordon

The Chase! Gene Ammons and Dexter Gordon Prestige (iT)
Our Man in Paris Blue Note (iT)
Homecoming Sony Music (iT)
The Jumpin' Blues Prestige (iT)

Sonny Rollins

"Doxy" (iT)
"St. Thomas" (iT)
"Oleo" (iT)

Fats Navarro

"Fat Girl" (iT)
The Complete Blue Note and Capital Recordings: Fats Navarro and Tadd Dameron
  Blues Note (iT)

Bud Powell

"Dance of the Infidels" (iT)
"Bouncing with Bud" (iT)
"Tempus Fugue-It" (iT)
"Un Poco Loco" (iT)
The Amazing Bud Powell Vols. I and II Blue Note (iT)
The Amazing Bud Powell—The Scene Changes Blue Note

Thelonious Monk

"'Round Midnight" (iT)
"Criss Cross" (iT)
"Straight, No Chaser" (iT)
"Ruby My Dear" (iT)

"Well, You Needn't" (iT)
"Brilliant Corners" (iT)
"Epistrophy" (iT)

Tadd Dameron

"Our Delight" (iT)
"If You Could See Me Now" (iT)

Sarah Vaughan

Live in Japan, Mainstream
"All Alone" and "My Funny Valentine" from SCCJ
"Mean to Me" (iT)
"Lover Man" (iT)
Ken Burns: Sarah Vaughan Verve (iT)

Max Roach

Clifford Brown and Max Roach Verve/EmArcy (iT)
Brown and Roach, Inc. Verve/EmArcy (iT)

Kenny Clarke

"The Squirrel" (iT)

Be Cool

Fifties and Early Sixties Cool, Intellectual, and Abstract Jazz

> "The first time in history that a jazz drummer's solo was so soft that you had to whisper or be conspicuous."[1]
>
> RALPH GLEASON

On the surface, the 1950s appeared to be a period of great prosperity and tranquility in the United States. In many ways, this was true. Americans had survived the ravages of World War II. Those who returned to a normal life were realizing the American dream—starting families; owning a TV, a car, and a house in suburbia; and perhaps profiting from a college education funded by the GI bill for those who had served in the armed forces. But beneath this rosy surface lay the beginnings of a cold war, essentially a battle between democracy (the United States) and Communism, represented by Russia and the Iron Curtain communist bloc countries. Not only was there increasing political tension between the United States and Russia, but the race to stake out new frontiers in space eventually found these two superpowers even more at odds. The National Aeronautics and Space Administration (NASA) was formed in 1958 and the United States launched the first artificial, unmanned earth satellite that same year. Extraterrestrial activity and science fiction were in the minds of many Americans, and some jazz performers reflected this new obsession in their record titles such as the Riverside release *Clark Terry in Orbit* and George Russell's *Jazz in the Space Age.* The atomic bombs dropped on Hiroshima and Nagasaki to end World War II launched the nuclear age, causing great concern for many Americans. The University of Chicago developed the first nuclear power plant in 1956, resulting in the realization that the same tool that had provided peace through destruction was now also the key to new scientific discoveries. This new reality caused many Americans to reassess the very nature of life itself.

Racial tensions, while largely nonviolent during the 1950s, continued to escalate, though some progress was made toward desegregation of schools and public places. Young people once again found the need to reevaluate life and look inwardly for solutions to living in a world that was becoming increasingly stressful. No longer were their parents' values always desirable models. In some ways, a new cycle much like the 1920s had begun, especially with the under 30 generation. Some turned to Eastern philosophical teachings and the offbeat writings of poets, who represented the new beat generation. Langston Hughes, for example, became identified as the poet laureate of the late 1940s and 1950s, while other writers also emerged and found a kinship with the spontaneity of improvised jazz. For many, it became increasingly important to learn how to "stay cool" and find new ways to enjoy life while controlling their emotions.

CHARACTERISTICS OF COOL JAZZ

If bop was hot, muscular, and macho, then cool was the subtler, more romantic, more feminine reaction. While vivid reds, yellows and orange shades might best represent bebop, a painter might use light pastel shades to represent the sound of much cool jazz. The following musical attributes are typically associated with this 1950s restrained, more intellectual style:

- Cool jazz featured toned-down dynamics accomplished through a variety of means including drums that were often played by brushes instead of sticks. Bands played more quietly, brass players often added mutes, and trumpet players might choose the mellower flugelhorn.

- Tempos were often, but not always, slower than bop tunes.

- More emphasis was placed on improvising listenable melodies rather than playing fast, technical passages.

- Trumpet players placed less emphasis on playing screaming high notes and focused on playing mellow, middle-register sounds.

- Vibrato is a useful device in expressing emotions and cool horn players often projected a steely, colder emotional style by discarding or nearly removing vibrato from sustained note values. Bop players had already significantly reduced the amount of vibrato as compared to the previous swing generation.

- While cool musicians didn't abandon the previous repertoire and forms, the blues was nearly forgotten in favor of experimenting with new forms. Compositionally speaking, they stretched boundaries by mixing meters within a song (going from four beats a measure to three) and using unusual phrase lengths. (Most songs up until this time were constructed of typical patterns where melodies were grouped in two- or four-measure subdivisions).

- Arrangers and bandleaders began to make use of instruments that had not been previously associated with jazz—for example, French horn, tuba, flute, and oboe. In other instances, instruments like the piano that had previously been considered indispensable were omitted.

- The influence of European derived composition devices such as counterpoint associated with J. S. Bach's music is increasingly noticeable in cool style jazz.

- While the ensembles were never larger than 9 or 10 players, tightly defined arrangements even for trios and quartets became very important, much as they had been during the big band period.

- General experimentation was the motto of many cool jazz instrumentalists.

Cool jazz in the 1950s reflected a complete reexamination of what had come before. Without being so radical as to throw the baby out with the bath water, the musicians associated with this school broke new ground. Predictable rhythmic patterns and forms were dismantled and reassembled in new ways. While improvisation was still important, and integral to jazz, in the cool sound, it sometimes occupied an equal role with composition and arrangement, as had been the case in the big band era. It was a musical style that was practiced by more white performers than black. It may be that white performers were subconsciously trying to get back in the game by producing a new brand of jazz that was more destined for the concert hall, more polished and sophisticated, and less intrusive than bop. White musicians, who had enjoyed such a prominent role in the big band swing era lost their place in the starting lineup during the bebop period to black artists who refocused jazz as an art, not as entertainment. Cool served to bring white musicians back into the foreground by offering a menu of jazz that in some cases was more accessible to the casual listener. Jazz historian Joe Goldberg described cool as offering "all the pleasures of being involved without paying the inevitable price of true involvement."[2]

The images displayed on the covers of many of the cool recordings sent a different message as well, depicting beautiful women, beaches, men and women posed with fast cars, and the general sunny California beach vibe. This cool jazz imagery was in stark contrast to that shown on recordings released by black artists of the period who continued to follow the bebop tradition. These musicians were portrayed with sweat pouring off their brows in dimly lit nightclub scenes, surrounded by cigarette smoke. Cool jazz, therefore, projected a much cleaner image to the consumer.

The terms "cool" and "West Coast" jazz have been used interchangeably, causing some confusion and misunderstanding about this period. While it is true that many of the musicians associated with the new 50s style were based on the West Coast, this should not give the impression that all cool jazz originated here. For that matter, the West Coast at this time was simultaneously a source for the hotter bop style of jazz. Easterners also became involved in the cool sound and approach. It is important to note that many musicians who were associated with

Cool jazz album cover.

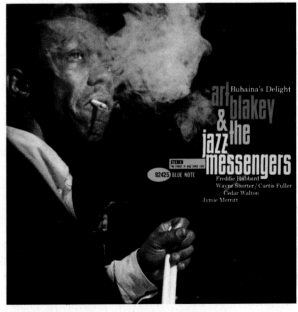

Hard bop album cover.

TABLE 10.1 Comparison of Bebop and Cool Styles

Bebop Style Characteristics	Cool Style Characteristics
Aside from ballads, bop was a garish, flashy, dynamic, "in your face" music.	Cool was softer dynamically and less intrusive than bop.
Drummers were aggressive and primarily used sticks.	Drummers popularized brushes to help inspire a more mellow, relaxed approach.
Bop tunes often featured fast tempos and technically demanding "heads."	Tempos were generally slower with greater emphasis placed on listenable melodies.
Trumpet soloists developed macho, technical flare, exploring the extreme upper register.	Trumpeters were less concerned with playing high notes and toned down their approach by using mutes and the more mellow flugelhorn.
Heavy vibrato was less popular with bop soloists than it had been with previous generations.	Vibrato became even less predominant in the cool style with some players nearly discarding it completely.
Bop style was dominated by black musicians.	The cool style was popularized largely by white musicians.
Experimentation in terms of composition, orchestration, and instrumentation was of little significance and takes a back seat to the soloist	Innovative compositions featuring experimentation with orchestration and instrumentation became increasingly important.
Bop bands were usually small combos.	Cool bands, with a few exceptions, were usually small combos.
The blues continued to dominate the bop repertoire.	The blues is much less important to the cool repertoire.
European classical influences were virtually nonexistent in bebop.	European classical influences became embraced including compositional techniques like counterpoint.
In its day, bebop did not prove to be commercially viable.	Cool was more commercially successful than bop. One artist who emerged from this period was featured on the cover of *Time* magazine.

cool jazz were not devoted to it exclusively. It was a time of experimentation and unlike the earlier periods of jazz where one or two styles dominated, musicians in the 50s often moved freely from one style to another, and perhaps even within the confines of one recording. This chameleon-like activity becomes commonplace in jazz from this time on. For example, tenor saxophonist Stan Getz contributed several burning bop recordings in the late 1940s, but is often considered in discussions of cool jazz. Pianist Bill Evans, discussed in this chapter, also defies categorization in any one single style.

A summary of the fundamental characteristics that define cool jazz along with a direct comparison to the bebop style is presented in Table 10.1. The table offers a quick reference, making clear how these two styles served to contrast with one another.

WEST AND EAST COAST MUSICIANS WHO DEVELOPED THE COOL SOUND

It was Gil Evans and Miles Davis on the East Coast and Dave Brubeck, Chet Baker, and Gerry Mulligan on the West Coast who are said to be the progenitors of this new direction in jazz. San Francisco became the center for their activities and was the city that also harbored the Moldy Figs revival of traditional early jazz styles. Many new record labels were formed to capitalize on the new West Coast artists and their experimental music.

Miles Davis and Gil Evans: The Birth of the Cool

Gil Evans grew up on the West Coast where he started his own swing band that never quite made the leap to star status. He actually used progressive big band leader Stan Kenton as an occasional subpianist in this early band. Just before and after World War II, Evans worked as an arranger for the most influential of the "Johnny come lately" East Coast big bands led by pianist Claude Thornhill. Thornhill encouraged his arrangers to experiment. Evans and other arrangers like Gerry Mulligan, who also wrote for Thornhill's band, were the first to add French horns and tuba to the standard big band, often juxtaposing this rich brass sound with the dark, reedy sound of a section of clarinets instead of saxophones. These orchestrations laid the groundwork for the innovations that soon followed, serving as the catalyst for the first major cool style recording.

Evans moved to New York, taking up residence in an apartment that became a hangout in the late 1940s for trumpeter Miles Davis, baritone saxophonist Gerry Mulligan, and others who were instrumental in forming the nonet that would define the new cool sound. They collectively decided to form a band with an unusual instrumentation designed to emulate the Thornhill sound, but with only nine players. Their new ensemble would have one of each member of the brass family (French horn, trumpet, trombone, and tuba), alto and baritone saxes, and a three-piece rhythm section. The group's pianist John Lewis, along with trumpeter Miles Davis, arranger Johnny Carisi, Evans, and Mulligan contributed arrangements to this historic series of recordings eventually issued as the *Birth of the Cool* by Capitol Records. No other movement in jazz was announced so abruptly with the release of a single recording, as was the case in 1949 and 1950. This band defined the cool style, but without abandoning all that had come before. Their music projected an air of sophisticated, "restrained chamber music" to the astute, well-prepared audience. Mulligan, altoist Lee Konitz, and Davis served as the prominent soloists and they all sought to shed the trappings and licks that had become bebop's clichéd language. Mulligan was a gifted soloist and arranger who was the first noted baritone sax soloist to come forward since Ellington's Harry Carney. As an earlier member of the Thornhill band, Konitz had already displayed his willingness to blaze new trails as an improviser, emerging from Bird's long shadow. Davis had been somewhat of a misfit in Parker's bop bands as he lacked the aggression associated with the Gillespie trumpet style and seemed to prefer a more mellow, minimalist approach as he matured. The band performed live in New York for only a short time, but the impact they had on the future of jazz, particularly the cool style, was immeasurable. Davis' association with Evans would spark even greater collaborations in the future. Most of the cool players who followed captured the essence of this first model including trumpeters Shorty Rogers and Art Farmer, saxophonists Paul Desmond, Art Pepper, Stan Getz, and Warne Marsh, and pianists Lennie Tristano, Russ Freeman, and Dave Brubeck.

 Listen to the interviews with Miles Davis and Gerry Mulligan who discuss the *Birth of the Cool* sessions. They can be found on the corresponding chapter on the CD-ROM.

While "Moon Dreams," one of several contributions by Evans to the *Birth of the Cool* sessions, is not representative of every song on this landmark recording, it does exemplify Evans' flare for orchestration and personifies many aspects of the cool sound. His ability to cast moody tone paintings through unusual instrumental textures defied earlier arranging doctrines practiced by most large ensemble arrangers. Solos by Davis, Konitz, and Mulligan are very characteristic of the cool sound, often vibratoless, stark, and spare in technique. Other pieces on the recording, such as "Boplicity," are clearly more upbeat, offering a renewed look at the bop influences still omnipresent.

Listening Guide

Miles Davis

"Moon Dreams"
(MacGregor-Mercer)
3:17

Recorded 3/9/50 in New York City

Reissued on Capitol Jazz "Birth of the Cool" CDP 7 92862 2

Miles Davis: *trumpet*

J. J. Johnson: *trombone*

Gunther Schuller: *French horn*

John Barber: *tuba*

Lee Konitz: *alto saxophone*

Gerry Mulligan: *baritone saxophone*

Al McKibbon: *bass*

Max Roach: *drums*

Form and Key: 32-bar song form (ABA'C=chorus) in D major, with extended Coda in B minor

0:00–0:25	*A section:* 8 bars, *Theme:* played by ensemble with trumpet lead
0:25–0:50	*B section:* 8 bars, *Theme:* 4 bars, alto sax plays theme with background chords and answering lines in ensemble
	0:25–0:36 4 bars, ensemble plays theme with trumpet lead
0:51–1:16	*A' section:* 8 bars, *Theme:* played by ensemble with trumpet lead (2 bars), then trombone lead (6 bars)
1:17–1:43	*C section:* 8 bars, *Theme:* 4 bars, alto sax plays theme with background chords and lines in ensemble
1:17–1:29	4 bars, trumpet lead over moving parts and lines in ensemble
1:44–2:12	*C' section:* 9 bars *Bari Sax Solo, Ensemble:* 4 bars, bari sax solo with moving background ensemble lines
	1:44–1:57 4 bars, ensemble with trumpet lead, bari and alto sax fills
2:13–3:17	*Coda:* trumpet leads overlapping, cascading, descending ensemble lines

Gerry Mulligan (1927–1996) and Chet Baker (1929–1988)

Baritone saxophonist Gerry Mulligan and West Coast native son Chet Baker on trumpet are justifiably also given much credit for sowing the seeds of cool jazz on the West Coast. Mulligan was a stylistically versatile baritone saxophonist who could mix comfortably, jamming with musicians from any era. He played an unusual instrument mastered by very few and, coupled with his gift as a composer/arranger, left an indelible mark on jazz history. Pianist/composer George Russell called him "the most important innovator of the 1950s."[3] Like so many musicians from the 1950s, Mulligan cut his teeth as a member of numerous big bands. He met Gil Evans as a result of his employment as an arranger for the Thornhill band after a stint with Gene Krupa's mid-1940s big swing band. Following his collaborations with Evans on the *Birth of the Cool* sessions, Mulligan moved to sunny California where he conceived of the piano-less quartet. His first quartet featured the young Chet Baker, recently discharged from the armed services. Baker had sat in with Charlie Parker earlier in his career, but had begun to formulate a more lyrical, wistful style than that associated with bop. Baker's romantic, abbreviated vocal and instrumental style helped to define the new cool style while also serving to make him and the quartet very popular. Baker, who struggled through life with drug addiction, could be compared to James Dean, the young, good-looking 1950s actor who played the youthful, troubled soul on the silver screen. The resemblance between the two was remarkable, and both pro-

jected the misunderstood, rebellious, brooding, sensitive image that represented the antiestablishment ideals of the younger generation. Many lived on the fringe, as did Baker. Baker's success as a trumpet player and vocalist prompted him to strike out on his own, performing and recording in Europe and the United States with a number of different partners and rhythm sections. He was replaced in the Mulligan quartet by valve trombonist/composer Bob Brookmeyer and later flugelhornist Art Farmer. Brookmeyer has distinguished himself since as one of the foremost modern jazz composers, frequently working in Europe and teaching in his later years.

The Mulligan-Baker quartet was unique in that there was no piano or guitar, leaving only single-line performers. Mulligan felt that the absence of a chording instrument freed the soloists to become more melodically inventive, since they would not be slaves to the pianist's chords. The result was pure melody in counterpoint between bass and the two horns. Their style was relaxed, detached, and rhythmically subdued. It is also worth noting that much like the work of Brubeck's quartet, melodic clichés that had become associated with the bop style were almost completely absent in the Baker-Mulligan quartet's performances. Mulligan described his music to *Down Beat* magazine as "Pipe and slipper music. I like jazz that is easy

Baritone saxophonist with trumpeter Chet Baker.

and quiet with a subtle swing. Lester Young used to get a sound on his horn that I would like to get with my whole group. Jazz is an art of many emotions; ours is to relax and build from a comfortable position."[4]

Listen to the interviews with Gerry Mulligan who talks about Chet Baker and the famous piano-less quartet. These excerpts can be found on the Library of Congress Web site at http://memory.loc.gov/cocoon/ihas/htms/mulligan/gm-home.html.

"Line for Lyons," included on the companion CD anthology, was composed as a tribute to West Coast jazz entrepreneur and festival promoter Jimmy Lyons. The performance on this track is exemplary of the improvisational style associated with this period of jazz where the **contrapuntal** dialogue between the two instrumentalists almost makes the listener forget that there is no piano or guitar accompaniment. Their improvisations are reserved, lyrical, and not overbearing.

Listening Guide

"Line For Lyons"

Recorded 9/2/52,
Fantasy EP 4028

Reissued on OJC,
OJCCD-711-2

Gerry Mulligan:
baritone saxophone

Chet Baker: *trumpet*

Carson Smith: *bass*

Chico Hamilton: *drums*

Gerry Mulligan Quartet with Chet Baker

Form and Key: Repeated 32-bar song-form choruses (AA'BA''=chorus), in G major

0:00–0:22	*First Chorus:* 32 bars, *Melody:*	
	0:00–0:11	*A section:* 8 bars, trumpet plays melody, with accompanying sax counterline and swinging bass and drums
	0:11–0:22	*A' section:* 8 bars, trumpet plays slightly varied melody, with sax and rhythm similar to "A" section
	0:23–0:34	*B section:* 8 bars, trumpet plays bridge melody with answering sax counterline and swinging bass and drums
	0:35–0:46	*A'' section:* 8 bars, trumpet plays slightly varied melody, with sax and rhythm similar to "A" section
0:46–1:33	*Second Chorus:* 32-bar *Sax Solo/Trumpet Solo:*	
	0:46–0:57	*A section:* 8 bars, sax improvises solo over chorus chord changes, with swinging bass and drums, trumpet tacit
	0:58–1:09	*A' section:* 8 bars, sax continues improvised solo
	1:10–1:21	*B section:* 8 bars, trumpet improvises solo over bridge chord changes, with sustained descending sax counterline, swinging rhythm section
	1:22–1:33	*A'' section:* 8 bars, trumpet continues solo, with long sax counterline
1:34–2:30	*Third Chorus:* 35-bar *Sax/Trumpet Solo and Melody with Tag:*	
	1:34–1:45	*A section:* 8 bars, sax and trumpet improvise solo together, using fragments of the melody
	1:45–1:57	*A' section:* 8 bars, sax and trumpet improvise, similar to previous "A" section

1:57–2:09   *B section:* 8 bars, trumpet plays bridge melody similar to first "B" section, with answering sax counterline and swinging bass and drums

2:10–2:30   *A'' section:* 8 bars, trumpet plays melody as in first "A" section, with accompanying sax counterline and swinging bass and drums; 3-bar ending tag repeats last line of melody

Mulligan appeared in several movies including *I Want to Live* (1958) and the1960 beatnik flick *The Subterraneans*. By the early 1960s, Mulligan abandoned the small group and founded the Concert Jazz Band that played challenging, big band compositions featuring some of the finest New York musicians of the day including trumpeters Clark Terry and Doc Severinsen of television's *Tonight Show* fame. He also appeared on record with numerous pairings including record dates with Ben Webster, Stan Getz, Thelonious Monk, Johnny Hodges, and Paul Desmond. The *Two of a Mind* recording with Paul Desmond is one of the finest examples of improvised duet playing in a piano-less quartet setting.

Dave Brubeck (b 1920)

While it is true that many of the players who became involved in the cool movement were based on the West Coast, Mulligan, Davis, J. J. Johnson, and others involved in the *Birth of the Cool* sessions were part of the New York scene and key players in the bop trend a few years earlier. Unlike these Easterners, Dave Brubeck was a West Coast native son. Born and raised in the northern farmlands of California, Brubeck attended the University (then College) of the Pacific in Stockton, studying classical composition and piano. This is where his archives now reside and where he formed his first groups. Very few recordings of his early octet exist, but we do know that their style was the precursor of what Brubeck eventually became famous for—merging jazz with "classical" techniques. Perhaps no one is more closely associated with the West Coast style, and no one was more successful and controversial at the same time. Critics have either loved or despised his brand of jazz, but it was all this publicity, pro and con, that helped to catapult him to fame in the mid-1950s. Not many other jazz artists can lay claim to being on the cover of *Time* Magazine—an honor bestowed on Brubeck in 1955. In retrospect, his music was more important then than it is now, but he nevertheless served as an important link in the history of jazz. Most of those who leveled criticism at his quartet claimed that it did not swing and had not assimilated the roots of jazz. His critics felt that his music was too compositionally derived and lacked the improvisational spontaneity of the jazz jam session atmosphere. Such criticism is of-

ten directed at new jazz that breaks from mainstream traditions, as was the case with Brubeck and many later avant-garde artists.

When Brubeck was praised, it seemed almost begrudgingly, but it is irrefutable that his quartet was rhythmically charged, producing unexpected accents, heavy-handed piano accompaniments and experiments in odd meter signatures. For example, he was known to play in one meter and tempo while the rhythm section forged ahead in another, creating mesmerizing polymetric tensions. His piano style was very chordal, using big blocks of chords rather than fast, single line passages associated with the bop pianists. In contrast, Brubeck's quartet avoided the now cliché-ridden bop style, favoring modern "classical" composition devices such as contrapuntal interplay, and he relied on saxophonist Paul Desmond to help inspire improvisational dialogue. They resorted to blues tunes later in their careers, but Brubeck's earlier music was harmonically rich and fresher, drawing from a contemporary "classical" pallet, which he used to influence arrangements of standard tunes. He studied "classical" composition with renowned French composer Darius Milhaud, who himself had been influenced by jazz, so the influences went full circle. (See the supplementary chapter included on the CD-ROM for additional information about the marriage of jazz and classical music. Third stream jazz is discussed later in this chapter.)

Like other white bands before him led by Beiderbecke, Trumbauer, and Goodman, Brubeck's quartet brought jazz out of the urban taverns that had spawned it, developing a marketable niche on the college concert circuit. His success encouraged others to follow suit including the important cool style black combo the Modern Jazz Quartet. The campus market for jazz grew in large numbers during the 1950s and Brubeck's quartet cashed in before the market was swept away by the rock and roll phenomenon of the 1960s.

The tune that served to make Brubeck and his quartet familiar to households worldwide was "Take Five," composed by his long-time associate, alto saxophonist Paul Desmond. Contemporary pop artist Billy Joel is reputed to have said that this tune was as important to him as "Sergeant Pepper" was to the Beatles and rock and roll nearly a decade later.[5]

Paul Desmond was an anomaly in the continuum of jazz saxophonists. His playing was in direct opposition to the trend of creating an edgier, harsher, and more aggressive, brittle tone. Instead, he chose to model his serene, demur, lyrical, and dry sound after earlier black tenor saxophonist Lester Young. A would-be writer, Desmond was intelligent, well read, and witty, often poking fun at his own playing. He once said that he was "unfashionable before anyone knew who he was. I wanted to sound like a dry martini,"[6] he said. While to some degree he may have been right in his self-assessment and criticism, he influenced at least one generation of young players and has never really been copied. Writer Gene Lees described him as "the loneliest man [he] ever knew"[7] and at times you can hear a melancholy in his playing. His high register is unmistakable in its crystalline, almost classical sounding purity, which in some ways made him the perfect partner for Brubeck, counterbalancing his own flowing, perfectly developed melodic lines with the pianist's rhythmic, chordal, and percussive style.

Listen to the interviews with Dave Brubeck included on the CD-ROM in the corresponding chapter.

Despite their unconventional approach to jazz, the Brubeck quartet, collectively and as individuals, soared in popularity, releasing a new record every four months or so and winning polls in *Down Beat*, *Metronome*, and *Playboy* magazines. It is amazing to realize that the quartet not only survived the 1960s, but also flourished despite the rock and roll sensation that had begun to take the country by storm.

Dave Brubeck Quartet

Listening Guide

Form and Key: 24-bar song form melody (ABA), with open tonic chord solos, in E♭ dorian minor, 5/4 time

0:00–0:22	*Introduction:* 12 bars, *Drums, Piano, Bass:* 4-bar staggered entrances of drums, piano, and bass set up 5/4 groove	
0:22–1:06	*Opening Melody section:* 24-bar *Melody:*	
	0:22–0:36	*A section:* 8 bars, alto sax plays melody in two similar 4-bar phrases, with continuing swinging 5/4 piano, bass, and drum groove on vamp
	0:37–0:51	*B section:* 8 bars, alto sax plays bridge melody in two similar 4-bar phrases
	0:52–1:06	*A section:* 8 bars, alto sax plays melody similar to opening "A" section

"Take Five" (Desmond)
2:52 (Short Version)

Recorded July 1959, New York City, "Time Out," Columbia

Reissued on Sony Legacy Records

Dave Brubeck: *piano*

Paul Desmond: *alto saxophone*

Gene Wright: *bass*

Joe Morrello: *drums*

Dave Brubeck Quartet *concluded*

1:07–1:58   *Solo section:* 28-bar *Alto Sax Solo:* Improvised sax solo over tonic (E♭) chord, and swinging 5/4 rhythm section accompaniment

1:59–2:18   *Solo section:* 11-bar *Drum Solo:* Improvised drum solo, with continuing piano and bass 5/4 swinging groove

2:19–2:33   *Closing Melody section:* 8-bar *Melody:* Sax plays "A" section of melody, similar to opening A section

2:33–2:52   Ending Tag: 9 bars, sax repeats last melody fragment over 5/4 tonic chord groove in rhythm section

"Take Five" represents the more popular side of the Brubeck Quartet and the track was released as a longer LP version and an edited, ready for radio, shorter 45-rpm record. While some critics may not have accepted this track as great jazz, millions of listeners, some who may not have been aware of jazz, turned on to the tune's memorable melody and rhythm vamp that served as a bed for improvisations by Desmond and drummer Joe Morello. What makes the success of this song even more phenomenal is that it was written in 5/4 meter rendering it a nondanceable form of jazz. Desmond was as surprised as anyone that it was so widely acclaimed, since his only goal had been to compose a simple tune to serve as a canvas for a drum solo feature.

Bill Evans (1929–1980)

Pianist Bill Evans, one of a long line of pianists who served with Miles Davis' bands, revolutionized the jazz trio of piano, bass, and drums. In addition, his innovations as a pianist served to influence future generations of pianists including Herbie Hancock, Chick Corea, and Keith Jarrett among others. His first important collaboration was as a member of composer George Russell's small groups where he premiered Russell's famous "Concerto for Billy the Kid." In 1958 he joined the Miles Davis Quintet during the pivotal years when the new modal approach (discussed in Chapter 12) was being developed. It was with this quintet, and in his prior work with Russell, that Evans began to demonstrate a mastery of the keyboard, technically and harmonically unique in the development of jazz piano styling. While he had the facility to "burn" like Bud Powell at fast tempos, he also favored a sensitive touch in the ballad tradition. No one could play a ballad as slowly, lushly, or sensuously as Evans. His trios featured a revolving collection of bassists and drummers over his lifetime, setting a new standard in modern jazz. They developed a sense of improvised interplay by liberating the bassist from playing walking bass lines to involvement in a more melodic dialogue with the pianist. Evans' technique was refined and fluid, though he varied his right-hand melodic approach with a more rhythmic, close block chord solo style known as **locked hands** style. This more rhythmic, chord style of playing, along with his penchant for juxtaposing one meter or tempo against another, showed a certain kinship with Brubeck's work, though Brubeck tends to have a heavier touch at the keyboard. Evans favored the tension created by long lines of triplet patterns over the relentless 4/4 meter laid down by bass and drums. Try tapping your feet in a regular pulse while saying *mer-ri-ly, mer-ri-ly, mer-ri-ly, mer-ri-ly,* as shown in Examples 10.1 and 10.2.

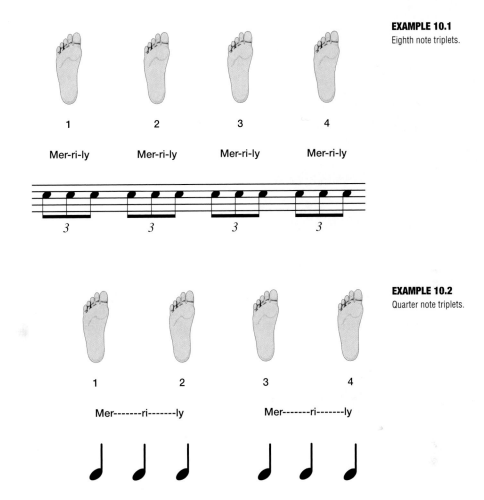

EXAMPLE 10.1
Eighth note triplets.

EXAMPLE 10.2
Quarter note triplets.

The space that Evans left in his improvised phrases was purposeful, allowing the drums and bass to provide their own musical commentary. The lines were often blurred, and at times it was difficult to tell who the featured soloist was. The titles of Evans' recordings not only reflected his musical style, but also captured his muse by projecting his forward-looking, introspective, experimental, and cerebral creative process. Titles like *Explorations, Interplay, Intuition, Quintessence,* and *Moonbeams* are good examples, along with the popular solo recording *Conversations with Myself,* where Evans took advantage of new multi-track recording technologies, enabling him to improvise in counterpoint with his previously recorded tracks, the result sounding like three pianists playing simultaneously.

The Evans trio style developed to its most advanced stage with young bassist Scott LaFaro. With LaFaro and drummer Paul Motian, Evans' trio developed a sense of free rhythmic and melodic interplay that was truly telepathic—like three minds thinking as one. The polyphonic, contrapuntal dialogue between Evans and LaFaro's irregular, non–walking bass lines illustrated a unique collaboration never before achieved. LaFaro, with his classical training, was perhaps the most important new voice since he brought to focus an entirely new concept of bass playing that was more melodic and hornlike. While the walking style had been the most important innovation to occur during the Swing Era, LaFaro's more liberated soloistic style is viewed as the next most important change in jazz bass performance practice.

Pianist Bill Evans performs in Copenhagen, 1964.

The CD-ROM includes an excellent audio example that exemplifies the interactive dialogue improvised style developed by pianist Bill Evans and bassist Scott LaFaro. This example is the last example under the discussion of the bass in the Performance Practice section of the chapter Listening to Jazz on the CD-ROM.

Listening Guide

Bill Evans Trio

"Witchcraft" (Leigh-Coleman) 4:30

Recorded 12/28/59 New York City,CD: Riverside 12-315

Bill Evans: *piano*

Scott LaFaro: *bass*

Paul Motian: *drums*

Form and Key: Repeated 40-bar song form choruses (ABCDA') in F major. Note similar arrangements in each chorus

0:00–0:52   *First Chorus:* 40 bars, *Song Melody:*

      0:00–0:10   *A section:* 8 bars, piano plays song melody in block-chord style, with improvised bass fills and swinging groove with brushes on drums

      0:11–0:21   *B section:* 8 bars, piano continues song melody in block-chord style, with bass fills and swinging drums

      0:21–0:31   *C section:* 8 bars, piano plays melody in single-note style, with syncopated repeated pattern in bass, swinging groove in drums

      0:31–0:41   *D section:* 8 bars, piano plays melody in single-note style, bass walks with swinging drums

0:42–0:52 *A' section:* 8 bars, piano returns to block-chord style melody, with improvised bass fills

0:52–1:44 *Second Chorus:* 40 bars, *Piano and Bass Solo:*

    0:53–1:02 *A section:* 8 bars, piano and bass solo together over song chord changes, creating interweaving lines in conversational style, with swinging drums

    1:03–1:13 *B section:* 8 bars, continues as in previous "A" section

    1:14–1:23 *C section:* 8 bars, piano continues improvised solo, with repeated bass pattern similar to first chorus "C" section

    1:24–1:34 *D section:* 8 bars, piano continues solo, with walking bass and swinging drums similar to first chorus D section

    1:34–1:44 *A' section:* 8 bars, piano and bass solo continues as in previous "A" section

1:45–2:36 *Third Chorus:* 40 bars, *Piano Solo:*

    1:45–1:55 *A section:* 8 bars, piano continues solo with walking bass and swinging drums

    1:55–2:05 *B section:* 8 bars, piano continues solo with walking bass and swinging drums

    2:06–2:15 *C section:* 8 bars, piano continues solo with repeated syncopated bass pattern similar to previous "C" sections

    2:16–2:26 *D section:* 8 bars, piano solos with walking bass and swinging drums, similar to previous D sections

    2:26–2:37 *A' section:* 8 bars, piano solos with walking bass and swinging drums

2:37–3:29 *Fourth Chorus:* 40 bars, *Bass Solo:* Bass improvises with occasional piano "comments," swinging drums

3:29–4:32 *Fifth Chorus:* 47 bars, *Song Melody:*

    3:29–3:39 *A section:* 8 bars, piano plays varied melody in block-chord style, similar to first chorus "A" section

    3:40–3:50 *B section:* 8 bars, piano plays melody in single-note style, with walking bass

    3:50–4:00 *C section:* 8 bars, piano continues single-note melody with repeated syncopated bass pattern, similar to previous "C" sections

    4:01–4:10 *D section:* 8 bars, piano continues single-note melody, with walking bass

    4:11–4:32 *A' Section with ending tag:* 15 bars, piano plays varied melody in block-chord style, with improvised bass fills, similar to first chorus A' section; added 7-bar ending tag

Drummer Marty Morrell who performed and recorded extensively with Evans' trio in the mid-1960s recently commented:

> Bill was a complete musician, totally immersed in his music and deeply committed to it. He was incredibly organized and planned his sets very carefully to insure that one tune flowed into another so the performance was as musical an experience as possible. He was not the least bit arrogant and you could consider Bill to be a humanitarian of the highest order. Bill's music was the perfect projection of his personality—sensitive and highly emotional. Nothing about his music was superfluous. Each solo was well paced, never too long and with every note perfectly placed within each phrase making for a perfectly balanced and organized improvisation. He played like a painter—every stroke had special meaning and contributed to the whole picture.[8]

In terms of repertoire, Evans, like most cool style musicians, avoided the blues and focused on original material coupled with reworked, obscure standards not usually performed. Outside the trio context, his collaborations with Getz, guitarist Jim Hall, and singer Tony Bennett represent the highest level of performance. Evans continued to play a significant role in jazz up until his premature death in 1980 at the age of 51. While he may not be the classic cool artist, he emerged during this period and his music reflects some of the characteristics of this style. Bill Evans never produced a mediocre recording, maintaining the highest level of musical integrity throughout his short career.

Listen to the interview with Bill Evans included on the companion CD-ROM and found in the corresponding chapter.

Stan Getz (1927–1991)

Stan Getz was a tenor saxophonist who, like Mulligan, was at home in many different jazz styles. Perhaps it is his musical connection to Lester Young's melodic style and sound that explains why Getz is so often considered in discussions of the cool sound. Young and Bix Beiderbecke are often considered the earliest forefathers of the cool sound, offering an alternative to the Coleman Hawkins and Louis Armstrong hot heritage. Getz first appeared on the scene, however, in the midst of the bebop revolution, gaining widespread exposure initially through his association with the more modern Woody Herman big band. It was here that he helped to establish the famous "Four Brothers" Herman saxophone section. His hit solo on Herman's recording of "Early Autumn" served as the necessary springboard to leader status, recording his first quartet sides in the late 1940s. Like so many white, cool era players, Getz had learned to create a style that was fresh and free of many of the clichéd bopisms associated with Parker and his crowd. What makes Getz somewhat difficult to classify is his chameleon-like style for he could comfortably play hot, swinging solos, yet was equally at home in the more subdued cool style of the fifties. He was fairly inactive for much of the 1950s as he struggled to conquer drug addiction and it was his ingenious recording of Eddie Sauter's *Focus*, a suite for strings and rhythm, that helped to restart his career.

Perhaps the greatest, most lasting contribution made by Stan Getz was the marriage of jazz with the Brazilian bossa nova. He always had a penchant for romantic ballads and was drawn to this same sultry, romantic quality in Brazilian music. (Additional information about the bossa nova style is found in Chapter 16.) The style is played at various tempi, but rarely very fast. While at times there can be an almost subliminal similarity between the clavé rhythm pattern and the bossa nova, the bossa nova is actually a discretely different rhythmic style, as shown in Examples 10.3 and 10.4.

EXAMPLE 10.3

Traditionally, the guitar maintains the fundamental and highly syncopated bossa nova rhythm pattern, reinforced by the drummer. The Getz recording included in the companion anthology follows this scheme. While the pattern can vary as shown below and heard on the recording, the essential syncopated rhythms that serve as the foundation of this style continue without interruption helping the music to glide along.

Foot tapping each 8th note.

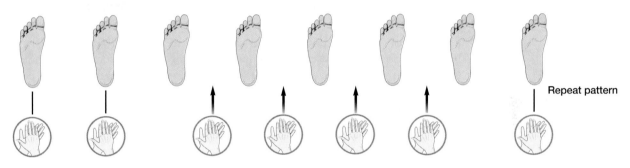

Repeat pattern

Hand clapping syncopated bossa nova rhythm – syncopated tensions occur when hands clap between the foot taps.

EXAMPLE 10.4

This example illustrates some of the standard rhythmic variations of the basic bossa nova rhythm. They can be strung together in many different ways as is evident on the Getz/Gilberto recording.

Suffice it to say that Getz was instrumental in launching the bossa nova jazz craze, initially with his recording of "Desafinando" and later the "The Girl From Ipanema" featuring Brazilian singer Astrud Gilberto. This recording also introduced

Saxophonist Sten Getz and Astrud Gilberto during their historic Cafe Au Go Go engagement in 1964. Sitting in on guitar is Brazilian composer Antonio Carlos Jobim.

a number of Brazilian musicians and composers to American audiences. Getz's light, airy sound was a wonderful compliment to the wispy, vibrato-less sound of the Brazilian vocalists. An analogy could be made to the musical rapport that also existed between Lester Young and Billie Holiday, whose two sounds were symbiotic. The jazz bossa nova recordings released by Getz, and a host of others who capitalized on the "easy listening" nature of this music, were a huge success in the United States selling millions of records. Even AM radio stations aired 45-rpm single versions of these hits. It is difficult to achieve commercial success without compromising artistic integrity, but Getz did just this with his immensely popular bossa nova recordings. Getz, in a 1990 interview with Terry Gross on her NPR syndicated *Fresh Air* program, explained why he was drawn to this Brazilian style: "[The bossa nova] is very beautiful music with suggestive, laid back rhythms. The melodies are beautiful, sad and romantic. It's a folk music and all folk music is beautiful and it goes perfectly with jazz."[9]

Use the CD-ROM to listen to several interviews with Stan Getz where he speaks about the essence of jazz. These can be found in Chapter 1—The Nature of Jazz. To listen to a typical bossa nova drum style, go to the section on the CD-ROM about Instrumentation located in Chapter 3—Listening to Jazz.

In the following song, included on the accompanying CD audio anthology, Getz demonstrates his ease at improvising in this genre and is accompanied by the famous Brazilian guitarist/singer João Gilberto. While the title suggests that it is a samba, the guitar and drum patterns more closely resemble the rhythmic style of a medium fast bossa nova. The bossa nova and samba are Brazilian folk dance rhythms. Getz's solo is certainly one of the happiest on record in this style, demonstrating his facility in improvising complex double-time phrases tempered by sultry blues derived lines. Also of note on this session is the participation of pianist Antonio Carlos Jobim who is undeniably the most recognized composer of Brazilian bossa novas and sambas.

Listening Guide

"So Danço Samba"
(DeMoraes, Jobim)
2:33 (excerpt)

Recorded New York
City, 3/18-19/1963,
Verve LP 8858651

CD reissue, Verve
810 048

Stan Getz: *tenor
saxophone*

Astrud Gilberto: *vocals*

João Gilberto: *guitar,
vocals*

Milton Banana: *drums*

Tommy Williams: *bass*

Antonio Carlos Jobim:
piano

Form and Key: Repeated song form choruses (AABA=chorus) in D major, F major, A♭ major, Bossa Nova jazz

0:00–0:05   *Introduction:* 4-bar guitar and piano sets up bossa nova groove

0:06–0:51   *First Chorus:* 32-bar *Vocal Melody*:

> 0:06–0:16   *A section:* 8 bar vocal (João Gilberto) in Brazilian Portuguese, with guitar, bass, and drums accompaniment

> 0:17–0:28   *A section:* 8 bar vocal, similar to "A" section

> 0:28–0:39   *B section:* 8 bar vocal bridge, similar to "A" section

> 0:40–0:51   *A section:* 8 bar vocal, similar to previous "A" sections

0:52–1:38   *Second Chorus:* 32-bar *Tenor Sax Solo:* Improvised tenor sax solo with bossa nova rhythm section accompaniment, key change to F major

1:39–2:25   *Third Chorus:* 32-bar *Tenor Sax Solo:* Continued tenor sax solo, key change to A♭ major

2:25–2:33   *Fourth Chorus:* (fades out) Tenor Sax returns to *Melody* (in A♭ major)

A FEW MORE AMONG MANY

Modern Jazz Quartet

No discussion of the cool, West Coast style would be complete without including the Modern Jazz Quartet, the longest running group in jazz with the fewest personnel changes. The original members of this quartet served as the nucleus of Dizzy Gillespie's big band rhythm section in 1947. The quartet became known for their polished chamber jazz approach, counterbalanced by Milt Jackson's more aggressive, blues influenced style on the vibes. First known as the Milt Jackson Quartet, they changed their name in 1953 to the more co-op sounding MJQ. Their first recording as the MJQ in that year showed an early penchant for an arranged sound, contrary to the freewheeling nature of most bop-influenced groups. They avoided the theme-solo-solo-solo-theme predictability and favored a more structured, at times classically influenced light sound. Improvised counterpoint in the tradition of European classical music composers became the MJQ's hallmark, as was their dapper attire in smartly styled, tailored suites—an influence, no doubt, years later on Wynton Marsalis and his cohorts in the 1980s. "I am an American Negro," pianist John Lewis said, and "I'm proud of it and want to enhance the dignity of that position."[10] Duke Ellington and Lewis were similar bedfellows in this regard and both produced dignified jazz suitable to the most elegant concert halls. "Django," dedicated to the Belgian guitarist, is one of the best-known works by the MJQ and it appeared on their second recording. "Django" is included in the *Smithsonian Classic Collection of Jazz*. Their dignified, refined, and polished brand of jazz made them attractive to wide-ranging audiences and performance venues. On the other hand, some felt their music was pretentious, but under the musical leadership of John Lewis the Quartet broke new ground for many years. Lewis, Gunther Schuller, and

J. J. Johnson were all serious in their efforts to elevate jazz to the same high plateau as European art music. All three of these musicians were at the center of the third stream movement, born in the mid-1950s, to bring together elements of jazz and aspects of European concert music. At the time this style had little impact, influence, or following and it was not until years later that its repercussions would be of value. Third stream jazz is discussed in more detail later in this chapter.

Lennie Tristano (1919–1978)

Blind pianist Tristano is perhaps the most overlooked and misunderstood artist from this period. While jazz fans bought Brubeck, Mulligan, Baker, Davis, and the MJQ, they largely ignored the cerebral music that Tristano created along with his colleagues Billy Bauer on guitar, bassist Arnold Fishkin, and protégés Warne Marsh and Lee Konitz on saxophones. Cool was one thing, but Tristano's music, described by some as "chilly," was too much for most listeners. "Why don't they leave me alone," said Tristano in a *Down Beat* article. "I'm told my music is supposed to be cold, over-intellectual. If what I play were intellectual, it would have to be all premeditated and it isn't."[11] His 1949 Capitol Records recordings of "Digression" and "Intuition" should be strong proof of his statement since both are completely free improvisations—pure spontaneous dialogue between the musicians with no preconceived ideas about harmonic structure, melody, or form.

Pianist Lennie Tristano, bassist Eddie Safranski, and guitarist Billy Bauer in a recording session, circa 1955.

These experimental works were so progressive that the record company failed to issue them until years later. Tristano's work predates the much-praised free jazz recordings by Cecil Taylor and Ornette Coleman (discussed in detail in Chapter 12) by nearly a decade, but very few knew about it!

"Intuition," included on the companion CD collection, features a series of ever-changing textures, changing tempi, and improvised gestures. Listening to it can be compared to viewing an abstract painting where the depth of field, or foreground and background, are in a constant state of flux. The instrumentalists are not bound by traditional guidelines or role expectations. The musician's contributions to the group sound are more important to this style than their role as individual soloist. Apparently the only preconceived aspect of the performance was the order of instrument entrances. Alto saxophonist Lee Konitz's individuality is particularly remarkable in view of the bebop firestorm that surrounded him at this time. His unique tone quality can only be compared to that of Paul Desmond. It is obvious that the entire group on this track has completely shed any clichés attributed to earlier or mainstream jazz styles.

Tristano was praised as *Metronome* magazine's "musician of the year" in 1947, but his recordings were largely unsuccessful from a commercial standpoint and Tristano turned to

Lennie Tristano and **Warne Marsh**

Listening Guide

Form and Key: Free form—no set key, harmony, or form

0:00–0:20	*Solo piano* establishes a tempo
0:21–0:33	*Alto sax* enters in improvised dialogue with piano
0:34–0:41	*Bass* enters walking, but quickly adopting style to more gestural-like exchanges
0:42–1:07	*Guitar* enters texture, varying style between single-note solo style and playing chords rhythm style
1:08–1:46	*Tenor sax* enters; entire group is now engaged in improvised dialogue
1:47–end	Tempo begins to erode, gradually slowing down and continues to decay to the end as instruments drop out

"Intuition" 2:27

Recorded 5/16/49 New York City

CD: Capital Jazz (Blue Note) CDP 72438 8 52771 2 2

Lennie Tristano: *piano*

Lee Konitz: *alto saxophone*

Warne Marsh: *tenor saxophone*

Billy Bauer: *guitar*

Arnold Fishkin: *bass*

teaching. His music was an anomaly in the midst of bebop and cool. His style was based on long improvised lines often played without swing and devoid of any reference to bop clichés. His tunes were sometimes harmonically complex, forcing the soloists to radically depart from the well-trodden path laid by the bop generation. Much like Art Tatum, Tristano and his music defied categorization though he is generally associated with this period of intellectual and cool jazz.

THIRD STREAM JAZZ

The fact that significant jazz and classical composers as well as performers (Miles Davis, J. J. Johnson, John Lewis, Duke Ellington, Charles Mingus, and Gunther Schuller) were attracted to the idea of merging certain aspects of the jazz tradition with classical composition techniques and instrumentations, lends credibility to the third stream jazz movement. While the product of this movement in the mid- and late-1950s through early 1960s was not particularly attractive to the general public nor for that matter to many of the jazz musicians, it was a movement that has endured, had lasting influence, and gained some momentum as time passed. The most definitive recording of works in the third stream style was produced by Columbia Records in two 1950s recordings—*Music For Brass* (1956) and *Modern Jazz Concert* (1957), which featured a collection of four compositions commissioned for premier at Brandeis University's Festival of the Arts. Compositions from these two recordings were later included in an LP compilation entitled *Outstanding Jazz Compositions of the 20th Century.* It fell out of print for many years until the long awaited reissue by Columbia on compact disk entitled appropriately *The Birth of Third Stream.* These landmark recordings which serve to document the work of crossover composers J. J. Johnson, Gunther Schuller, John Lewis, 12-tone serial composer Milton Babbit (omitted from the most recent reissue), Charles Mingus, Duke Ellington, and George Russell represent the wide range of possibilities for composers who are open to the influences of both music styles. It was Schuller, a true Renaissance man in this age of specialization, who participated in the movement and coined the term "third stream" to describe it. As European classical art music is labeled the first stream, American jazz the second, the term third stream seemed appropriate to describe a style of music that combined elements of both traditions. It was a logical direction for jazz composers to pursue since by the late 1950s jazz had developed a strong tradition with an identity and repertoire that could now withstand the risk of affiliations with the music from which its founders had initially sought distance. Jazz pianist composer John Lewis described it as a "hybrid," while Schuller used the term to include music that "attempts to fuse the essential characteristics of jazz and so called 'classical' music."[12] While third stream jazz was far more structured and organized from the compositional standpoint than any other style of jazz, composers who work in this style seek to create pieces that present the illusion or impression of spontaneity that is so essential to good jazz. The problem these composers faced was in creating music that was tightly controlled while also allowing the important elements of jazz—rhythmic vitality, spontaneity and the essential element of improvisation—to rule. As many of the pieces from the heart of this period show, this union was a tall order and one that often went unsatisfied. Consequently much of the original music labeled third stream was not well received by either the jazz audience or the classical crowd. In Schuller's own words:

> A fair amount of controversy did, of course, surround this kind of music in the 1950s and early 1960s, primarily in the professional magazines and journals. Great fears were expressed on both sides of the stylistic fence that, in coming together, the two musics would seriously damage each other. Jazz critics were worried that the "spontaneity" of jazz would be severely affected with alleged "stiffness," "straightness," "abstractness"—what was deemed the "academicism"—of modern "classical music." Conversely, critics on the "classical" side either considered these "experiments" as simplistic and naïve, or were concerned that the sacred precincts of modern music would be contaminated by the populist "vulgarities" and/or "simple-mindedness" of jazz.[13]

Some of the best work found on the aforementioned Columbia recording are those pieces by MJQ pianist John Lewis, composer/conductor/author Gunther Schuller, bebop trombonist J. J. Johnson, classical composer Milton Babbitt who contributed the 12-tone piece "All Set," George Russell with his three-movement "All About Rosie," and, of course, Duke Ellington.

John Lewis as composer and musical director of the popular Modern Jazz Quartet (MJQ) is considered one of the most convincing leaders of the third stream movement. The MJQ did more than any organized group to promote this movement, no doubt because of its commitment to the "cool," restrained style of jazz and Lewis' education in classical composition techniques. It was then a natural marriage of style for the MJQ personnel. Their initial recording in this vein, *MJQ and Orchestra*, featured works by Lewis, French composer/author André Hodeir, Werner Heider's "Divertimento," and Schuller's adventuresome three-movement "Concertino for Jazz Quartet and Orchestra." Hodeir had studied at the Paris Conservatory with Oliver Messiaen while the German Heider encountered jazz as a member of GI combos during the war years. He later worked as an arranger for German radio orchestras. Some years later in 1987 the quartet issued *Three Windows*, featuring its collaboration with the New York Chamber Symphony for which Lewis functioned as composer, conductor, and pianist.

It would be remiss not to mention the efforts by pianist/composer Dave Brubeck. Brubeck, who studied composition with Darius Milhaud in the 1940s, considers himself a composer who happens to play the piano. The press has

The Modern Jazz Quartet performs in concert, circa 1956. Shown (left to right) are bassist Percy Heath, drummer Connie Kay, pianist John Lewis, and vibraphonist Milt Jackson.

focused primarily on his work as leader of the popular jazz quartet, though his classical background in composition is obvious when one considers his entire output. Brubeck has composed ballets, a musical, an oratorio, four cantatas, a Mass, and various works for jazz quartet and orchestra. His most widely performed works from this third stream catalogue are those of religious nature and he should be considered in this discussion of crossover jazz artists.

Father Time is often kinder in assessing new art forms than are initially skeptical critics because the new movements gradually become more widely accepted and respected as time passes. The marriage of classical music and jazz in this third stream tradition is an example of just such a development, for more recent efforts such as Wynton Marsalis' *All Rise*, though not necessarily labeled third stream, have become more widely accepted as composers learn how best to marry what on the surface appears to be two polar opposites.

WHO WAS POPULAR?

Others who contributed to the West Coast, cool sound included alto saxophonists Art Pepper and Bud Shank, trumpeter and arranger Shorty Rogers, drummers Shelly Manne and Chico Hamilton, and Brazilian guitarist Laurindo Almeida. Many of these musicians found that being based in the Hollywood area led to more lucrative careers in film and television studios and ended their careers as part-time jazz musicians. The popular poll winners throughout this decade were Dave Brubeck, the Modern Jazz Quartet, Miles Davis, Paul Desmond, J. J. Johnson, Shelly Manne, Gil Evans as arranger, Stan Getz, Gerry Mulligan, and the progressive, adventuresome big band fronted by Stan Kenton. In the vocal categories, Ella Fitzgerald continued to capture the attention of fans and critics along with Frank Sinatra whose style and demeanor wowed the women and sold millions of records in the 1950s. The pianists, who attracted the most attention during the 1950s, at least in terms of the polls, were oddly enough the hotter style players,

Canadian Oscar Peterson, who patterned his blazing technique in the Art Tatum tradition, and Errol Garner who wrote the popular tune "Misty."

STAYING COOL WITH JAZZ IN THE 1950s

By the mid-1950s, jazz had not only become an art, it had become a way of life, and to some a science with a unique subculture somewhere to the left of mainstream society. Not everyone supported the new cool, intellectual jazz movement. Some felt that jazz was running parallel to what had happened to classical music when the serial 12-tone composers took over, applying too many formulas for music to be enjoyable. Jazz in the hands of these so called "mathematicians" (referring to the third stream crowd and Lennie Tristano's early free jazz experiments) had become more of a science than an art, and it was this criticism from those who appreciated more mainstream black jazz from the same period that served to chill some of the cool experimentalists.

The new more abstract attitude could be seen in other artistic arenas as well. Painters like Jackson Pollack no longer cared to portray lifelike objects, preferring to drip paint on his canvas in more spontaneous, abstract gestures, often improvising as he created. Architects began to use more functional designs that were sometimes criticized for their tendency to be too stark and pessimistic. The titles of some jazz recordings seemed to capture this mood and project a sense of moving forward into uncharted territory. Stan Kenton, who for a time called his band the "Innovations Orchestra," featured works like the "City of Glass" (composed by Robert Grettinger) or "Opus in Abstract." Keeping with the more intellectual, academic trend among the new breed of 1950s jazz musicians was composer George Russell who in 1953 published the first major theoretical treatise about jazz harmony and melody. He called it his *Lydian Chromatic Concept of Tonal Organization*. Perhaps it was the more intellectual jazz known as third stream that combined elements of jazz improvisation and rhythm with European art music, or the more cerebral, sedate, and sophisticated sound of cool jazz, or simply the now 40 years of jazz tradition that explains the steady flow of more scholarly publications like Russell's that emerged in the 1950s. Serious efforts by Marshall Stearns, *The Story of Jazz*, and French author/composer André Hodeir, *Jazz, Its Evolution and Essence*, marked the beginning of more informed writings about jazz than ever before.

The literary world reflected similar attitudes and many closely allied themselves with jazz—both bebop and cool. In 1957 Jack Kerouac wrote the novel *On the Road* about the wanderings of itinerate jazz musicians, often at loose ends and out of sync with mainstream society. His representation of the West Coast scene though depicted a more carefree, relaxed, and affluent lifestyle. For that matter, the names of new jazz record labels like Fantasy, Contemporary, and Pacific Jazz helped to reinforce the California "la-la land" stereotype. The Walt Disney, Hollywood, expansive beach images helped to sell millions of newcomers on the opportunities available in the sunny state with a mild climate. As a result, the state's population nearly doubled during the 1950s. Allen Ginsberg, Norman Mailer, William Burroughs, and Lawrence Ferlinghetti, who, like Kerouac, known to perform with jazz musicians, all latched on to the jazz subculture. Some labeled this group of artists, musicians, and writers as deviants, but their freer ideas about race, religion, and sexuality were resonant with the younger generation's modern, "hip" new attitudes. Thespians used the jazz performer as a metaphor to represent the struggling, repressed, minority viewed as second-class citizens by respectable society, and caught in an anguished struggle to gain acceptance and respectability. It is no small wonder that a bebop-derived score was used as a backdrop for the film version of Tennessee Williams' *A Streetcar Named Desire*. Many actors, along with this same group of performers, writers, and artists were victimized for their freethinking ideas and blacklisted by the radical conservative Senator Joseph McCarthy. The growing cold war fueled anticommunist sentiments and McCarthy was the most vocal advocate for democracy. He single-handedly led a crusade to rid the country of all suspected communists, or worse, anyone who spoke of liberal ideas freely. Many artists, actors, and writers were blacklisted because of mere accusations about communist sympathies and McCarthyism ran unchecked, ruining careers for some time.

The U.S. State Department, however, saw in jazz the perfect counteroffensive to thwart communism and the cold war. Construction on the Berlin Wall began in 1961 and was designed to separate communist East Germany from the free world. The Bay of Pigs incident between Cuba and the United States underscored the growing tensions between communist block countries and the free world. Communism was painted to represent repression, oppression, and rigid structure, while jazz was cast as the perfect weapon—the Western embodiment of democracy, freedom of choice, and expression. Tours abroad were sponsored by the State Department, making use of Louis Armstrong and Dizzy Gillespie as jazz ambassadors. Willis Conover hosted a regular jazz program targeted at the iron curtain countries by the Voice of America radio station operating on shortwave frequencies. Ironically, African Americans, who continued their quest for equality in the United States more earnestly than ever before, had still not earned the very democratic freedoms they were asked to promote. Despite the 1954 Supreme Court ruling against school segregation, President Eisenhower was reluctant to send federal troops to Arkansas to enforce the high court's ruling. Louis Armstrong, who rarely took his political views public, openly criticized the president and was so unnerved that he canceled an upcoming State Department goodwill trip to Russia. Armstrong stated publicly that: "The people over there ask me what's wrong with my country. What am I supposed to say? It's getting almost so bad a colored man hasn't got any country."[14] Two years later, Miles Davis, stepping outside Birdland in New York for a smoke, was assaulted and bludgeoned by the police. (A photo of this incident can be found on the CD-ROM). The NAACP was forced to activate its forces against the courts again in 1956 and Reverend Martin Luther King rose to be the most effective leader and spokesman for the growing civil rights movement.

Home entertainment and rock and roll had a negative effect on jazz popularity. Television became the center of family entertainment and the improved "Hi-Fi" stereo recordings that could be enjoyed in the confines of one's living room often became a reasonable substitute for live, late-night entertainment. The "baby boomer" generation was cradled during the 1950s, and home entertainment was a must in order to stay close to the nest after a hard day's work. The younger set turned on to emerging rock and roll and folk, a rage that began to sweep the nation in the 1950s, but not without protest from the more mature generation who reacted to it in the same way their parents had to jazz decades earlier. Rock and roll represented immoral, sexual behavior as jazz had in the 1920s. The Coasters, Little Richard, Fats Domino, Jerry Lee Lewis, The Platters, Bill Haley and the Comets, Chuck Berry, and, of course, Elvis Presley rose to star status while jazz began to take more and more of a back seat. Television also had a direct impact on record sales. A survey of 50s hits shows a direct relationship to television exposure. For example, Tennessee Ernie Ford with his country brand of religious tinged music, Jackie Gleason, Pat Boone, Perry Como, Mitch Miller, the Kingston Trio, Rick Nelson, Harry Belafonte, and Johnny Mathis enjoyed gold record sales and were simultaneously regular TV personalities.

Somehow, amid the slump in live entertainment and despite the popular rock and roll phenomenon, the jazz festival concept was successfully born at this same time, serving to salvage many jazz careers. In 1954 George Wein produced the successful Newport Jazz Festival, which started a new trend. Even some of the older jazz acts were rejuvenated by such festivals. For example, Duke Ellington made headlines at this festival in 1956 at a time when he was being accused of becoming passé. Norman Granz began his Jazz at the Philharmonic series and successfully booked all-star groups on tours throughout Europe and Japan. Both promoters were champions of racial equality and insisted that people of all races be permitted to attend these performances. Many of Granz's Philharmonic concerts were recorded and are still available in CD reissues.

Sadly, the 1950s marked the end of a number of brilliant jazz careers and left fans looking for new heroes. Charlie Parker, Fats Navarro, Billie Holliday, Lester Young, Art Tatum, the Dorsey Brothers, Frankie Trumbauer, James P. Johnson, W. C. Handy, Walter Page, and the great young trumpeter discussed in Chapter 11, Clifford Brown, all passed on in the 1950s, leaving room for new voices and new directions in jazz. But before we look too far into the next decade, it is important to examine the other side of jazz in the 1950s, the African-American mainstream jazz that stemmed from the bebop tradition in the previous decade.

Jazz in Perspective

The timeline that follows will put the developments of jazz discussed in this chapter into a larger historical context, providing you with a better sense of how landmark musical events may relate to others that match your personal areas of interest.

1949
- Rodgers and Hammerstein create Broadway musical *South Pacific.*
- Harry S. Truman wins presidential election.
- *Lone Ranger* debuts on TV.
- Arthur Miller's play *The Death of a Salesman* wins Pulitzer Prize.

1950
- Senator McCarthy denounces communism and begins efforts to purge the United States of all members of this party, blacklisting many well-known personalities.
- United States backs South Korea against North Korea.
- William Faulkner wins Nobel Prize for Literature and Ralph Bunch wins the Peace Prize.

- U.S. census indicates 150 million people.
- Beginnings of cold war.
- Miles Davis and cohorts record famous *Birth of the Cool* sessions.

1951
- United States detonates H-bomb.
- UNIVAC electronic, digital computer unveiled.
- *I Love Lucy* is instant TV success.

1952
- *Mad Magazine* first published.
- Dwight "Ike" Eisenhower elected 34th president.
- Gerry Mulligan and Chet Baker record "Line for Lyons" with their piano-less quartet.
- Author Ralph Ellison's *Invisible Man* presents the black man's underworld.

1953
- The beginning of McDonald's fast-food hamburger chain.
- McCarthy and House Committee on Un-American Activities continues to persecute many artists, poets, writers, actors, and other intelligensia.
- After 3 years, Korean war draws to a close, but not before 3 million casualties.
- Marilyn Monroe becomes film sex symbol.
- Modern Jazz Quartet asserts its new name.
- Jazz composer George Russell publishes first major treatise on jazz theory—*Lydian Chromatic Concept of Tonal Organization.*

1954
- *Brown* vs. *Board of Education* decision by courts is key victory for NAACP and desegregation movement—Supreme Court rules against school segregation.
- Ernest Hemingway wins Nobel Prize for Literature.
- McCarthy and communist witch hunt are condemned.
- The first Newport Jazz Festival is a success.

1955
- United States begins involvement in Vietnam.
- Minimum wage set at $1.
- African-American Rosa Parks is arrested in Alabama for not giving up her bus seat.

1956
- Civil rights advocate Martin Luther King has home bombed.
- *Peyton Place* by Grace Metalious becomes best seller.
- Musical *My Fair Lady* hits Broadway.
- Top films include *Invasion of the Body Snatchers*, *The Ten Commandments*, and *Bus Stop.*
- University of Alabama sued for banning blacks from enrolling.
- Elvis Presley becomes rock and roll idol.

- Bus segregation declared unconstitutional.
- University of Chicago develops first nuclear power plant.

1957
- John F. Kennedy awarded Pulitzer Prize for *Profiles in Courage.*
- Nuclear arms race heats up.
- Count Basie band becomes first black band to perform at New York's Waldorf-Astoria Hotel.
- Vocalist Pat Boone enjoys popularity.
- President Eisenhower sends federal troops to assist integration of Little Rock, Arkansas, schools.
- Race with Russia in space exploration.
- Leonard Bernstein enjoys hit musical *West Side Story.*
- Beat author Jack Kerouac publishes *On the Road.*

1958
- Texan Van Cliburn wins Tchaikovsky Piano Competition.
- NASA created to bolster U.S. position in space race against U.S.S.R.
- Kingston Trio, Everly Brothers, Little Richard, Rick Nelson, and Chuck Berry are pop music successes.
- Texas Instruments engineer invents the microchip.

1959
- Coast-to-coast flight becomes a reality along with passenger flights to Europe.
- Richie Valens, Texan Buddy Holly, and "Big Boppper" die in plane crash.
- Jazz singer Billie Holiday dies at age 44.
- Integrated schools open in Little Rock, Arkansas.
- Ill-fated Ford Edsel hits market.
- Dictator Fidel Castro takes control of Cuba.
- Dave Brubeck Quartet becomes popular with recording of "Take Five."
- Alaska and Hawaii become the forty-ninth and fiftieth states, respectively.
- *Some Like It Hot* and *Ben Hur* are popular films.
- Bill Evans trio records "Witchcraft."

CHAPTER SUMMARY

The 1950s was a time of prosperity but also unrest in America. The space race, the cold war, the first nuclear power plant, and court rulings in favor of school desegregation all mark the 50s. Advances in technology with the huge growth of television and hi-fi audio equipment gave parents of the baby boom generation more reasons to stay home in their leisure time rather than going out to clubs. These factors and the birth of rock and roll increasingly diverted the public's attention from jazz. One development that served to renew interest in some of the more established jazz groups was the jazz festival, notably the Newport Jazz Festival that began in 1954 and became an annual event.

Although Miles Davis' *Birth of the Cool* album signaled the beginning of cool jazz, the majority of important cool jazz artists/groups were white. California was home to a number of influential cool jazz musicians, leading to the somewhat inaccurate term "West Coast," which, for many, was synonymous with cool jazz. This style, in comparison with bebop, tended to be more subdued and delicate, with few instances of especially loud, high, or fast playing. Other differences contrasting with earlier styles included the use of instruments not normally associated with jazz (French horn, tuba, flute, etc.), very little use of the blues form, mixed meters, and in some cases a return to emphasizing the arrangement and ensemble playing.

The quartet featuring baritone saxophonist Gerry Mulligan and trumpeter/vocalist Chet Baker gained much popularity in the 1950s. This group used no piano or other chording instruments, deriving harmony instead from the counterpoint between the bass and two wind instruments. The Dave Brubeck Quartet achieved worldwide fame, especially for selections in odd meters including "Take Five" (in 5/4 meter) and others. The Modern Jazz Quartet was an important black cool jazz group, which remained virtually intact for many years. Lenny Tristano led groups in the late 1940s and 1950s that, in addition to playing in a cool style, also recorded the first examples of free jazz, "Intuition" and "Digression," in 1949. Tenor saxophonist Stan Getz was a contributor to numerous styles of jazz but is best known for his part merging the bossa nova, a Brazilian style, with jazz. Defying classification, Bill Evans' influence as a pianist and leader is undeniable. His trios explored a new concept in rhythm section playing in which interaction was more important than the traditional roles of piano, bass, and drums.

The term "third stream," coined by Gunther Schuller, refers to a music combining elements of the European classical tradition and jazz. It was a music that lacked much popular appeal and emerged during this period of greater intellectualism in jazz.

KEY TERMS

Important terms, people, and bands:

TERMS	Bill Evans	John Lewis
contrapuntal	Gil Evans	Lee Konitz
locked hands	Miles Davis	Shorty Rogers
	Dave Brubeck	Paul Desmond
PEOPLE	Chet Baker	Art Pepper
Stan Getz	Gerry Mulligan	Warne Marsh

Lennie Tristano
Bob Brookmeyer
Scott LaFaro
Antonio Carlos Jobim
Milt Jackson

BANDS
Dave Brubeck Quartet
Modern Jazz Quartet
  (MJQ)
Bill Evans Trio

REVIEW QUESTIONS

1. What new and unusual instruments not typically associated with jazz were sometimes heard in cool style bands?

2. What was the first cool recording and when was it made? What was unique about its instrumentation? Who were the principal musicians including arrangers involved in creating this new sound?

3. Describe the "Moon Dreams" recording found on the accompanying anthology.

4. What was unique about the Mulligan/Baker quartet?

5. What cool, West Coast style artist was so popular that his picture appeared on the cover of *Time* magazine?

6. Did cool style jazz attract primarily black or white musicians?

7. Describe and characterize the cool jazz sound.

8. In what way did Bill Evans change the approach to jazz trio performance?

9. What Chicago-style musicians are credited as early pioneers of the more cool approach to jazz?

10. What is the significance of the MJQ?

11. Describe the political, social, and literary climate during the 1950s and how there was a parallel to what transpired in the jazz community.

12. Who coined the term "third stream" and what is meant by this term?

13. Name an artist or two who is associated with this style.

14. Was third stream jazz popular in its time?

15. What great arranger partnered with Miles Davis to contribute some of jazz's most serious concert works?

16. Why was Lennie Tristano important to jazz?

17. What jazz artist is identified with the bossa nova jazz movement?

18. What Dave Brubeck Quartet recording sold over a million records to become one of the most widely recognized instrumental jazz recording of all time? Can you explain this success?

Make sure that you also review material on the corresponding chapter of the CD-ROM.

SUGGESTED SUPPLEMENTARY LISTENING

The abbreviation (iT) indicates that a particular recording cited in the text, or particularly demonstrative of the artist, is available from the Apple iTunes Web site. Other Web-based music distributors may also prove to be valuable resources. SCCJ indicates *Smithsonian Collection of Classic Jazz.*

Dave Brubeck

Jazz Goes to College (1954) Sony (iT)
The Dave Brubeck Octet (1956) Fantasy (iT)
Ken Burns Jazz: Dave Brubeck Sony Music Entertainment (iT)
Dave Brubeck's Greatest Hits Sony (iT)

Chet Baker

Young Chet Pacific Jazz (iT)
Chet Baker (1959) Riverside (iT)
Chet Baker Quartet with Russ Freeman Capital (iT)
Chet Baker Sings (1954) Pacific Jazz (iT)

Gerry Mulligan

Two of a Mind: Gerry Mulligan and Paul Desmond Classics/Windham (iT)
Gerry Mulligan Tentet and Quartet Gnp Crescendo (iT)
Concert Jazz Band Live at the Village Vanguard Verve (iT)
Konitz Meets Mulligan (1953) Pacific Jazz (iT)
Mulligan Meets Monk (1957) Riverside (iT)

Bill Evans

Conversations with Myself Verve (iT)
Everybody Digs Bill Evans (1958) Riverside (iT)
The Tony Bennett Bill Evans Album Fantasy (iT)

Stan Getz

Focus Verve (iT)
Verve Jazz Master 53: Stan Getz Bossa Nova Verve (iT)
Dizzy Gillespie and Stan Getz Verve (iT)
Cal Tjader Stan Getz Sextet Fantasy (iT)
Stan Getz and Bill Evans Verve (iT)

Modern Jazz Quartet

Django (1955) Prestige (iT)
The Modern Jazz Quartet Savoy (iT)

Miscellaneous

Jazz in the Space Age: George Russell and His Orchestra GRP (iT)
The Complete Birth of the Cool Capitol (iT)
Intuition: Lennie Tristano and Warne Marsh Capitol (iT)
Wow: Lennie Tristano Sextet (iT)

Third Stream

The Birth of Third Stream Columbia
The Modern Jazz Quartet and Orchestra Atlantic
Three Windows: The Modern Jazz Quartet with the New York Chamber Symphony Atlantic Jazz
Stan Kenton—City of Glass by Bob Graettinger Capitol Jazz
Stan Kenton Conducts the Los Angeles Neophonic Orchestra Capitol Jazz

11

Tradition Meets the Avant-Garde
Moderns and Early Postmoderns Coexist

> "Fire! That's what people want. Music is supposed to wash away the dust of everyday life. . . .You're supposed to make them turn-around, pat their feet. That's what jazz is all about. . . . I think you should play to the people."[1]
>
> ART BLAKEY

Among his many discoveries and theories, Sir Isaac Newton is known best for his three laws of physics. One of these principles often applies to the arts. He said that "for every action there is an equal and opposite reaction."[2] Newton's principle is sometimes referred to in the arts as the pendulum theory, implying that styles swing radically as a reaction and in opposition to one another. This principle is quite applicable to the jazz of the 1950s and 1960s. Cool had been a reaction to bebop. Hard bop, referred to at the time as mainstream jazz, was a reaction to the predominantly white jazz of the cool school, serving as a continuation of the bop tradition. Hard bop featured somewhat more aggressive horn and rhythm section playing, with driving rhythm section grooves and an overall harsher sound with heavier articulation from the horn players. The term "mainstream" is often used to define jazz from the 1950s and 1960s. Critic Stanley Dance first coined the term and, while the definition of this term is somewhat murky, it is usually applied to describe jazz that embraces key aspects of the jazz tradition. Mainstream usually refers to jazz based on typical harmonic schemes that follow tightly organized formal schemes.[3]

If fans had trouble grasping what the term jazz meant in the early years, then the waters became even more muddied in the 1950s and 1960s. There was the "mainstream" and so many other currents and eddies, making it easier than ever before to be confused about what jazz meant. On the other hand, this was a healthy situation as it afforded fans many choices. The 50s and 60s represent a time of all-out war, with critics and fans defending their own preferences

273

Drummer Art Blakey during a performance at The Cork & Bib on Long Island, New York.

outing at Birdland in 1954 produced a two-volume recording entitled *A Night at Birdland with the Art Blakey Quintet*. The quintet featured the amazing young trumpeter Clifford Brown, and this landmark recording set the tone for at least the following decade. Later that year, Blakey and Silver reorganized the band bringing in seasoned Texas born trumpeter Kenny Dorham and Philadelphia tenor saxophonist Hank Mobley. This group's first recording for the Blue Note label bore their new name on the cover—*Art Blakey and the Jazz Messengers*—and included Silver's gospel-tinged "The Preacher" along with other toe-tapping, rhythmically driving pieces. While the personnel stayed intact for only a year, they served their purpose, establishing Blakey as the leader of a dynasty that would reign for four decades. Silver struck out on his own and accomplished similar success with his own quintets. Both leaders are considered as head masters of prep schools for many of the most influential performers and composers in the years that followed. The list of players who carried Blakey's message into the future is as long as it is impressive including trumpeters Clifford Brown, Kenny Dorham, Bill Hardman, Donald Byrd, Lee Morgan, and Freddie Hubbard; saxophonists Lou Donaldson, Hank Mobley, Benny Golson, Johnny Griffin, Jackie McLean, Bobby Watson, and Wayne Shorter. The Blakey sphere of influence has been far-reaching, as this list of protégés also includes contemporaries Wynton and Branford Marsalis and trumpeter Terrance Blanchard.

The group's music was always fresh and original, dictated by these strong horn players and pianists like Silver and Bobby Timmons, who also composed material for the band. It was Silver and Timmons who are justifiably given credit for developing a major current within the hard bop mainstream known as funky jazz, or soul-jazz. The Messengers' seminal 1958 recording featuring Timmons' title track "Moanin'" capitalized further on groundwork already established by Silver in his "The Preacher." Listen and follow the analysis of this classic tune included in the accompanying anthology. Its three salient features: (1) a call and response using a church-like amen response, (2) a very definite and aggressive rhythmic style that encourages the listener to tap the beat, and (3) an apparent blues roots—typifying the "funky" style. While it is not Silver's composition, it does fit his personal criteria (or as he put it "guidelines to musical composition") and summarizes the hard bop style:[5]

1. Melodic beauty
2. Meaningful simplicity
3. Harmonic beauty
4. Rhythm
5. Environmental, hereditary, or spiritual influences

Lee Morgan's trumpet solo on "Moanin' " is dripping with soulful, bluesy gestures, smears, and half-valve techniques that add to the greasy appeal of his solo.

Art Blakey and the Jazz Messengers

Listening Guide

"Moanin'" (Bobby Timmons) 3:02 (excerpt)

Recorded 10/30/58, Blue Note BST 84003

Reissued: "The Blue Note Years" 7243-4-96375-2-8

Lee Morgan: *trumpet*

Benny Golson: *tenor saxophone*

Bobby Timmons: *piano*

Jymie Merritt: *bass*

Art Blakey: *drums*

Form and Key: Repeated song form choruses (AA'BA-chorus), in F major

0:00–0:59   *First Chorus:* 32 bars, *Theme*

      0:00–0:14   *A section:* 8 bars, piano plays melody theme (call), answered by stop-time response

      0:15–0:29   *A' section:* 8 bars, trumpet and saxophone play melody theme, answered by stop-time band response

      0:30–0:43   *B section:* 8 bars, trumpet and saxophone play bridge melody over rhythm section, no stop-time

      0:44–0:59   *A section:* 8 bars, piano plays "A" theme melody answered by stop-time band responses

1:00–1:59   *Second Chorus:* 32 bars (AABA), *Trumpet Solo,* with rhythm accompaniment, in straight 4/4 shuffle style time

2:00–3:01   *Third Chorus:* 34 bars (AABA), *Trumpet Solo*, with rhythm accompaniment. First two measures of fourth chorus sets up tenor sax solo at fade

Once you have listened to this track, go to Chapter 3—Listening to Jazz—found on the CD-ROM and explore the section about trumpet and trombone technique. This section will help to acquaint you with some similar effects used by Lee Morgan in his stirring solo. Go back and listen to "Moanin'" again to see if you can identify Morgan's use of these techniques.

The Messengers

It would be unfair not to acquaint you with the work of a few of Blakey's outstanding Messengers who left their own legacy as leaders following their association with the drummer. Horace Silver (b 1928) is undoubtedly one of the most noted not discussed in later chapters. He formed his own stable quintets and even now, in semiretirement, continues to resurface periodically with a new recording. His own brand of jazz has relied heavily on strong and often repetitive bass lines, blues-influenced chord progressions, and musical influences from outside the United States, in particular his native Cape Verde. Through his compositions, Silver's recordings often gave the listener a sense of continuity from track to track, for example, *Cape Verdian Blues* and his most popular recording, *Song For My Father.* The titles of many of his other fine recordings used word plays based on his name that suggested musical continuity throughout such as *Silver and Wood, Silver and Brass*, and *Silver and Voices.* Like Blakey, he relied heavily on the strengths of outstanding sidemen, a list of which is a who's who of contemporary jazz. For instance, saxophonist Joe Henderson and trumpeter Tom Harrell, two of the most influential improvisers of the late twentieth century, recorded with Silver as did saxophonist Bob Berg and the Brecker Brothers—saxophonist Michael and trumpeter Randy, both of whom have exerted an immense impact on recent jazz. "Jazz had a little better shot [then] than today," Silver said, "precisely because they would take a jazz tune and put it on the jukebox where it had more potential for people hearing it. Also because [the tunes] had that danceable thing."[6]

"Strollin,' " the Silver track included on the companion audio anthology, is a fine representation of the hard bop sound. The chord progression is quite sophisticated and far more complex than his blues- and Latin-influenced tunes. The tune is based on two contrasting eight-measure phrases that, for analysis purposes, will be labeled A and B. Each of these eight-measure phrases can be furthered divided into two, four-measure sections—the first serving as the antecedent, and the second as the consequent response. The body of the tune is a good illustration of the older "two-beat" swing style with the drummer playing the signature open-closed hi-hat cymbal pattern, while the bass emphasizes primarily beats one and three—hence the "two-beat" identification. It isn't until the solos begin that the bassist begins walking a four-beat line more typical of this era. The relaxed gait, as the tempo suggests, and infectious melody make "Strollin' " one of the many unforgettable Silver tunes.

Listening Guide

Horace Silver

"Strollin'" (Silver) 4:57

Recorded New York City July 8, 1960

Blue Note Records CDP 7 84042 2

Blue Mitchell: *trumpet*

Junior Cook: *tenor saxophone*

Horace Silver: *piano*

Gene Taylor: *bass*

Roy Brooks: *drums*

Form and Key: 32-measure tune in four, eight-measure phrases—ABAB'; key of D♭ Major

0:00–0:01		Begins with short bass pickup
	0:02–0:15	*First Chorus:* Trumpet and tenor sax state *first theme (A)* in harmony; rhythm section plays in 2-beat style
	0:16–0:30	*B theme* stated in similar fashion
	0:31–0:44	Return to *first theme (A)* with exact repetition
	0:45–0:59	*B' Second Theme*, second four-measure entirely different than earlier B
1:00–1:56		*Second Chorus:* Blue Mitchell's *trumpet solo* on entire form
1:57–2:53		*Third Chorus:* Junior Cook's *tenor sax solo* on entire form (notice lack of vibrato; quotes tune at close of solo (2:40) ending with a bluesy descending line
2:54–3:49		*Fourth Chorus:* Silver's *piano solo* begins; aggressive left hand low register jabs are similar to Thelonious Monk's style; quotes from Sonny Rollins' "St. Thomas" at 3:36-3:40
3:50–4:45		*Fifth Chorus:* Trumpet and sax return to state tune with rhythm section 2-beat style accompaniment
4:46–end		Coda is additional 2 measures

Listen to the interviews with Horace Silver that can be found in the corresponding chapter on the CD-ROM.

Trumpeters Lee Morgan and Freddie Hubbard also enjoyed success and widespread popularity following their association with the Messengers. Morgan's aggressive style and funky brand of hard bop found commercial success with his *Sidewinder* recording for the Blue Note label. Morgan was also a major voice on the seminal *Blue Trane* recording on the same label under saxophonist John Coltrane's leadership. Hubbard was active on numerous sides of the fence, performing in avant-garde settings with Ornette Coleman, no-nonsense hard bop sessions, and more commercial offerings. While he contributed a number of high caliber recordings, his most influential are no doubt *Red Clay* and *Hub Tones*.

Saxophonist Wayne Shorter, another important Blakey alumnus, will be discussed in more detail in future chapters.

More About Funky, Soul-Jazz and the 50s and 60s

Funky jazz, or soul-jazz as some call it, is a style that united jazz with the down-home qualities of the black community and popular music: rhythm and blues, gospel and sanctified, holy-roller music. It was a time for black musicians to reconnect with a heritage that had in some ways been previously shunned because of memories of repression and slavery. Time had provided some distancing and black musicians could once again be proud of their rich culture and history. It was particularly significant that their efforts to renovate these musical roots came in the midst of the biggest push for civil rights since the emancipation. Funky jazz raised the black communities' awareness of their cultural heritage, while white audiences appreciated it for its memorable melodies, slower tempos, and strong rhythmic basis, which rendered some of the material almost danceable.[7] The more popular and danceable recordings found their way into jukeboxes across the country.

The titles of hard bop recordings and tunes often gave away the funky punch line even before a first playing as in, for example, Horace Silver's "The Jody Grind," "Sister Sadie," "Serenade to a Soul Sister," and "The Preacher"; Cannonball Adderley's album *Them Dirty Blues*, featuring "Work Song" and "Dat Dare," *Mercy, Mercy, Mercy*, and *Why Am I Treated So Bad*; Jimmy Smith's *The Sermon, Home Cookin'* and *Back at the Chicken Shack*, and in the 60s, Herbie Hancock's popular "Watermelon Man." The themes of these titles all relate to "soul foods," religious activities, black slang, or comments on their earlier years of slavery and repression. Other titles invoking black slang terms or hip language such as Blue(s), Dig, Boss, Funky, Mojo, Workin', and Cookin' were also commonplace.[8] This music, some of which was marketed on the 45-rpm record designed for the popular music market, reached a large audience through jukeboxes and radio play. Alto saxophonist and Blakey alumni Jackie McLean referred to the popularization of this style of jazz as "a banner of racial self-affirmation."[9] Musical values for black and white musicians as well as audiences had changed radically by the mid-1960s, caused largely by the surge in popularity of commercially viable pop groups like the Beatles, Rolling Stones, Cream, Jimmy Hendrix, and others. Since the earliest recordings by the Original Dixieland Jazz Band, the recording industry has shown interest in promoting white popular styles that are imitations or renditions of black music

While funky jazz was popular with many fans that accepted it as an honest effort to make an artistic endeavor commercially palatable, many critics felt differently. For example, Martin Williams felt that the movement was largely "regressive, self-conscious, monotonous, and even contrived."[10] But the musicians fought back. Saxophonist Cannonball Adderley, well known for his commercially successful funky recordings in the early 1960s, countered with his own rebuttal: "we just played music we enjoyed. There was nothing calculated about it. However, I feel a responsibility to the man who's paying the freight, and I try to be reasonably entertaining by playing music I think they want to hear—and music I think they should hear. In addition to this responsibility to the audience, you have a responsibility to yourself, the band, [and] your art. I see no reason why jazz

Julian "Cannonball" Adderley on alto saxophone and his brother Nat on trumpet perform at Randall's Island Jazz Festival.

musicians should not live well simply because they're jazz musicians and artists. Responsibility to the art doesn't mean you have to be hungry."[11]

This brand of jazz sold records, engaged audiences and was commercially viable. It resurfaced in the 1990s as the basis for what has been termed "acid jazz." Many of the early recordings in this new genre were little more than facelifts of tunes from the late 1950s and 1960s.

The Guitar and Organ Trios

Two instruments emerged as powerful forces in jazz during the 1950s and 1960s and collaborated to capitalize on the jazz-soul movement. While the guitar had been a standard member of the rhythm section through the swing years, it wasn't until Charlie Christian arrived on the scene, along with modern amplification technology in the 40s, that the instrument became viable as a solo instrument. The organs used by Count Basie and Fats Waller in earlier years were of older design and remnants of silent film theaters. New electronic technologies enabled this instrument to become more viable in contemporary settings.

Wes Montgomery (1923–1968)

Guitarist Wes Montgomery was raised in Indianapolis, where he worked with his brothers and other local musicians. His first opportunity for more widespread exposure was as a member of Lionel Hampton's band. Hampton is remembered for giving many young, unknown musicians their first opportunity for broader exposure.

Guitarist Wes Montgomery at the Newport Jazz Festival.

Riverside records enabled Montgomery to strike out on his own, and his first recording for that label quickly established him as one of the leading innovators on this instrument. It seems that self-taught musicians, as was the case with Montgomery, often discover revolutionary new techniques, as they are not bound by accepted conventions. This was the case with Montgomery, who employed thumb picking, chord soloing (in contrast to single note), and octave techniques (two notes an octave apart played simultaneously) that had never before been used. These techniques are evident in the recording found on the accompanying anthology. He quickly became known as the most important guitarist since Charlie Christian and was signed by Verve records. While this label offered better exposure, their producers favored slicker, popish, commercial productions, framing Montgomery with lush string backup arrangements of pop tunes of the day like "California Dreamin'" and "Goin' Out of My Head."

The other important aspect of Montgomery's brief career that was significant to the development of jazz styles was his organ trio sessions, the basis of his first recordings for the Riverside label. Organ trios, coupling the instrument with guitar or saxophone and drums became a popular configuration in the late 50s, since they were easy to record and inexpensive to book. The organ's bass pedals eliminated the need for a bass player. The sound of the electronic Hammond organ, with its large dynamic range and versatile tone quality, resonated with the new wave of pop music stemming from the R & B and rock and roll community. To quote author David Rosenthal: "There was something raucous, something down and dirty in its array of electronic growls, wails, moans, and shrill ostinato tidal waves that immediately appealed to black ears,"[12] and many white followers of mainstream jazz. The organ is considered the immediate predecessor of the synthesizer that rose to popularity in the 1970s.

Jimmy Smith (1925–2005)

Montgomery's first recordings paired him with organist Melvin Rhyne, but Montgomery's overnight success led to a recording partnership with another rising star—organist Jimmy Smith (1925–2005). Smith, who began his career as a Philadelphia area pianist, was influenced by contemporary blues organists Wild Bill Davis and Bill Doggett and ultimately found more success as an organist. He developed a ferocious right hand and can be recognized by his rapid-fire bursts of notes. He used the instrument to full advantage, playing it like a powerful orchestra capable of projecting a wide range of moods from electrifying to more subtle. Like other black artists from the period, Smith rode the crest of the popular funky-soul tidal wave, releasing numerous recordings that featured secular, modern versions of sanctified, down-home, and dirty blues. The organ was a natural for this style, since it was so often a part of worship in the sanctified churches. Other organists followed Smith's lead capitalizing on the new trend. They included Richard "Groove" Holmes; "Brother" Jack McDuff; and the queen of jazz organ, Shirley Scott. In addition to his work with Montgomery, Smith recorded with other solid guitarists like Kenny Burrell and Quentin Warren, who earned popularity during this era. The organ trios from this period can be considered as the genesis of many of the more modern "groove" bands popularized in the late 1990s and early part of this new century by guitarists John Scofield, the group Medeski Martin & Wood, and second-generation Philadelphia organist Joey DeFrancesco.

Guitarist Kenny Burrell accompanies organist Jimmy Smith during a recording session at the Manhattan Towers.

The "James and Wes" excerpt from a critically acclaimed recording that is included on the companion audio anthology features Smith and Montgomery in a straight-ahead, swinging blues tune, demonstrating their muscular style as soloists, showing off the aforementioned personal stylistic traits. Notice that in this trio, there is no bass instrument and Smith's feet, playing bass lines on the organ bass pedals, fulfill this role.

"James and Wes"
(excerpt) (Smith) 2:48

Recorded 9/28/66,
Verve "Jimmy and Wes:
The Dynamic Duo"
SVLP 8678

Reissued Verve Master
Edition Series

Jimmy Smith: *organ*

Wes Montgomery:
guitar

Grady Tate: *drums*

Listening Guide

Form and Key: Repeated blues 12-bar blues choruses in F Major

0:00–0:16   *First Chorus:* 12-bar *Melody:* Organ plays riff melody with guitar, organ bass pedal, and drum accompaniment

0:17–0:33   *Second Chorus:* 12-bar *Melody:* Organ repeats riff melody with similar accompaniment

0:34–0:50   *Third Chorus:* 12-bar *Guitar Solo:* Improvised guitar solo with organ and drums accompaniment

0:51–1:08   *Fourth Chorus:* 12-bar *Organ Solo:* Improvised organ solo with guitar, organ bass pedal and drums accompaniment

1:08–1:25   *Fifth Chorus:* 12-bar *Guitar Solo:* Improvised guitar solo with organ sustained chords, organ bass pedal and drums accompaniment

1:26–1:42   *Sixth Chorus:* 12-bar *Organ Solo:* Improvised organ solo with organ bass pedal and drums accompaniment, guitar tacet

1:42–1:59   *Seventh Chorus:* 12-bar *Guitar Solo:* Improvised guitar solo (octaves), with organ sustained chords, organ bass pedal and drums accompaniment

2:00–2:17   *Eighth Chorus:* 12-bar *Melody:* Organ plays riff melody with guitar, organ pedal bass and drum accompaniment, octave guitar fills at end

2:18–2:48   *Ninth Chorus:* 12-bar *Melody:* Organ plays riff melody with guitar, organ pedal bass and drum accompaniment, octave guitar fills at end

Clifford Brown (1930–1956) and Max Roach (b 1924)

Critics in some cases were more prone to write favorably about hard bop musicians that did not cater to commercial tastes. For better or worse, critics have always sided with music that is less influenced by public taste and more likely to have an impact on the long-range artistic development of the music. To be commercially successful as a jazz artist is often, but fortunately not always, the kiss of death when it comes to critical favor.

Clifford Brown (1930–1956) was critically acclaimed for his uncompromising work in elevating the hard bop style to a new high level. He was lauded as the next Dizzy Gillespie—the torch bearer for the next generation of jazz trumpeters and he most likely would have had an even more lasting impact had he not died in an automobile accident at the age of only 25.

After brief apprenticeships with bands led by Lionel Hampton, Tadd Dameron, and Art Blakey, Brown joined up with drummer Max Roach to form the Clifford Brown–Max Roach Quintet in 1954, etching their first recordings in California. This recording is evidence that more than just the "cool" sound was emanating from the West Coast during

Clifford Brown at a rehearsal for the Lou Donaldson and Clifford Brown Quintet recording session.

the 50s. Roach, who was a veteran drummer from the bebop generation, had impeccable credentials, never swaying from the straight and narrow artistic path and always uncompromising in his social and political doctrines. As an artist, he did what he could through music to express dissatisfaction with the black man's status in America's society.

The first generation of the Roach/Brown Quintet featured Richie Powell, Bud Powell's younger brother, and West Coast tenor saxophonist Harold Land. The few recordings that this band made, and the 1956 version with saxophonist Sonny Rollins replacing Land, stand alone as some of the best that hard bop had to offer. Brown's musicianship was unparalleled, with flawless technique and a trumpet sound that was controlled and fat, flowing like warm butter from his bell. His style was based in part on Fats Navarro, but his improvisations show originality and an uncanny ability to play long, meaningful improvised lines that make so much sense one has to wonder how they could have been created spontaneously. Land was an able counterpart, but Rollins was more his equal. "Daahoud," the track included on the companion audio anthology, along with "Joy Spring," "Jordu," "Sandu," and "Pent-Up House" from the *Smithsonian Classic Collection of Jazz* provide some of the most memorable moments from this great trumpeter. While the version of Brown's tune on the companion anthology features a larger West Coast band than his quintet with Roach, Brown is in his usual fine form.

Clifford Brown

Listening Guide

"Daahoud" (Clifford Brown) 4:14

Recorded Los Angeles, 7/11 or 7/12/54

Clifford Brown: *trumpet*

Stu Williamson: *valve trombone*

Zoot Sims: *tenor saxophone*

Bob Gordon: *baritone saxophone*

Russ Freeman: *piano*

Joe Mondragon: *bass*

Shelly Manne: *drums*

Jack Montrose: *arranger*

Form and Key: Repeated song form choruses (AABA′ = chorus) in E♭ major. Solos based on 32-bar form.

0:00–0:03	Short ensemble introduction
0:04–0:43	*First Chorus*
	0:04–0:12 A section begins with pickup phrase; melody played by trumpet (Brown) with horn ensemble accompaniment
	0:13–0:21 A section repeats with drums and bass implying Latin feel
	0:22–0:29 B section featuring full ensemble, swing feel with breaks
	0:30–0:41 Final A section to close form features trumpet and extended tag
	0:42–0:43 2-measure trumpet solo break
0:44–1:17	*Second Chorus:* 32 bars, *Trumpet Solo*
	AABA trumpet solo over theme chord changes with rhythm section accompaniment
1:18–1:51	*Third Chorus: Trumpet Solo* continues
	AABA trumpet solo over theme chord changes with rhythm section accompaniment
1:52–2:24	*Fourth Chorus: Tenor Saxophone Solo*
	AABA tenor saxophone solo over theme chord changes with rhythm section accompaniment
2:25–2:59	*Fifth Chorus: Valve Trombone Solo*
	Not often heard valve trombone solo for one chorus over AABA chord changes with rhythm section accompaniment

3:00–3:31   *Sixth Chorus: Piano Solo*

AABA piano solo over theme chord changes with bass and drums

3:32–3:48   *Seventh Chorus:* Full Ensemble *Final Chorus*

3:32–3:48   Abbreviated, punctuated version of both A sections serves to frame solo drum breaks

3:49–3:55   Full ensemble plays B section of tune

3:56–4:03   Last A section played by full ensemble to complete the form

4:04–4:14   *Tag* or *Coda* culminating in final sustained chord

DEFINING POSTMODERNISM

While much of the 1950s and 1960s was consumed with modern mainstream jazz, at the close of the 1950s Ornette Coleman stood the jazz world on its ear, signaling with much fanfare a new age of postmodern jazz. It isn't exactly clear when postmodernism began, nor is there unanimous consensus about what the term means. There are some generalities that can be made in an effort to clarify how the term can be applied to the jazz that follows Coleman's path and emerges in other forms in the mid to late-1960s and beyond. Typically, postmodernism refers to art that features a mixture of historical styles and new approaches, warped through various forms of reinterpretation and purposeful misrepresentation. The result is considered unconventional and sometimes produces what could be considered a parody. Such performances are not governed by the same rules used to create the original art, and as such are not subject to analysis by applying familiar, traditional criteria. Instead, postmodern artists attempt to force the development of entirely new sets of criteria by creating works that defy analysis by traditional means. These artists develop new processes for the making of art by bringing diverse elements together in new and different ways. In some situations, the creative process can be more important than the product.[13] Postmodern art also tends to reflect the influences of new techniques and technologies particularly those associated with electronics and the information age. The postmodern age stands as a time of great diversity when no singular trend is evident but instead many different directions are being pursued simultaneously. Diversity is an important trend to remember as we progress through the 1960s and beyond, tracing further developments in jazz.

POSTMODERN JAZZ COMES OF AGE WITH ORNETTE COLEMAN AND HIS DISCIPLES

California-based alto saxophonist Ornette Coleman, a transplanted Texan with a strong grounding in bebop and rhythm and blues, turned the jazz world upside down causing international debate and controversy in 1958–1959 with the release of his first recordings on the Contemporary and Atlantic labels. He delivered an entirely new kind of jazz that was well suited to the new postmodern age.

A native of Fort Worth, Texas, Coleman kicked around his home area and nearby states playing in R & B and circus bands. As a saxophonist he was largely self-taught and preferred to play a plastic alto sax. One of his band mates claimed that "it [had] a drier, warmer sound without the ping of the metal."[14] He also used a special mouthpiece and reed combination that "enabled him to develop his tone so that he can control it. He has real control of pitch and the pitch is so important to him."[15] The result was a vocal quality that at times simulates crying, shouting, and moaning that is akin to early blues and African vocal styles. "You can always reach into the human sound of a voice on your horn if you're actually hearing," Coleman said, "and [trying] to express the warmth of the human voice."[16] Not everyone was impressed with his originality, however, and he endured unimaginable abuses simply because he chose to play in a nontraditional manner. Some found his sound and sense of pitch to be offensive, annoying, unschooled, and inappropriate. He suffered beatings and had his horn destroyed because of his quest for individuality.

He left Texas for Los Angeles, where he hoped to find a more supportive environment, but found it necessary to sustain himself by working odd jobs as a houseboy, porter, babysitter, and similar low-paying day jobs that enabled him to seek out nightly jam sessions. The local musicians found Coleman to be eccentric, brazen, and without any inhibitions, and most refused to let him sit in, often asking him to leave the bandstand. In time, however, Coleman encountered a small group of kindred spirits who recognized that he offered something entirely new, not based on the laws laid down by the bebop crowd that everyone was bound to at the time. For example, trumpeter Bobby Bradford cited Coleman's penchant for playing "outside the harmony." (The term "outside" is often used to refer to avant-garde, free jazz that denies most prescribed rules of functional harmony, form, and melody.) "I was very impressed that he had the courage and audacity to test Charlie Parker's law," Bradford said. "That's when I began to think of him as a genius."[17]

So what made Coleman and his music so controversial and different than what had come before? For the jazz neophyte or newcomer to experimental free jazz, Coleman's music presents a challenge, for it is difficult to draw relationships to other familiar musical experiences. His music defies predictability. Aside from occasional reoccurring melodic and rhythmic fragments that are composed and serve as springboards for improvisation, nothing can be labeled as formulaic. There are several important aspects of Coleman's legacy to become acquainted with before hearing his music.

- His compositions, while often folksy in quality, frequently introduced shifting meters, changing tempos, and odd phrase groupings.
- Bass and drums sometimes played in different, opposing tempos.
- While Coleman's composed themes may imply a tone or key center, his improvisations were polytonal in that they constantly shifted from one tonality to another.
- Coleman and Don Cherry, his longtime trumpeter, did not adhere to conventional ideas of intonation. By traditional standards, they often played out of tune.
- Their improvisations did not rely on prescribed chords or formal structure and were based solely on melody and melodic development.
- While his main themes were composed and often demonstrated a sense of form, his improvisations were often free of any allegiance to the form and were rather unpredictable departures from his theme.

- Coleman's group concept was revolutionary from the standpoint of liberating the rhythm section from their earlier roles. The bassist was free to follow his own muse rather than playing rigid, walking bass lines that implied specific chords in a progression. The drummer was equally free to interact in a free-form dialogue with the other members of the quartet.

Coleman's music could be compared to **aleatoric** classical music, since the outcomes of his quartet's improvisations were based somewhat on chance and total spontaneity without premeditation. On the other hand, there is an intentional dialogue in Coleman's performances, though unrestrained by traditional guidelines. Such planned group interchange does not exist in aleatoric, "chance" music. Coleman said: "When our group plays, before we start out to play, we do not have any idea what the end result will be. Each player is free to contribute what he feels in the music at any given moment. . .I don't tell the members of my group what to do. I let everyone express himself just as he wants to."[18]

Gunther Schuller, along with MJQ pianist John Lewis, was an early champion of Coleman, describing his improvisations as "little motives attacked from every conceivable angle, tried sequentially in numerous ways until they yield a motivic springboard for a new contrasting idea, which will in turn be developed similarly, only to yield to another link in the chain of musical thought, and so on until the entire statement has been made."[19] Since his tunes are based on melody for its own sake without reference to prescribed harmony, his improvisations, too, were melodically derived with no concern for chords or a set harmonic progression. Consequently, and like no other jazz before, each performance of a tune was radically different and comprised of a higher degree of pure improvisation than ever before. Coleman termed the theory that drove his music "harmolodics," but it is a term more widely known than it is understood. In essence, it was his way of describing the ever-shifting relationships that can occur when freely improvised melodies interact with one another, implying different accidental harmonies and tonalities. Shifting key centers helped to ensure that any harmonic relationships that might exist between melody and bass line were strictly accidental. Imagine the result of a three-voice vocal group, all singing the same song but each singer changing keys at will. A melody, or a melodic phrase, can be set to any number of different chords, and he wanted his bassists to be free and sensitive to any of the possible relationships that they could help imply. To ensure that harmony never influenced his player's decisions, he did not use a pianist. In many ways, Coleman's seminal quartets demonstrated a further extension of earlier works by (1) Gerry Mulligan's pianoless quartets, (2) Bill Evans' trios that sought to liberate the bass from its time-keeping responsibilities, (3) early New Orleans jazz that often featured improvised counterpoint between instruments, (4) Thelonious Monk's free-spirited compositions and performance style, and (5) Lennie Tristano who pioneered free jazz in 1949.

Coleman's improvisations, and those of his other quartet members, were almost entirely unpredictable, though based in part on the more conservative and predictable rhythmic style of Charlie Parker. Coleman's

Ornette Coleman with his alto saxophone during a rehearsal for his Empty Foxhole *album.*

rhythmic style was more irregular than earlier beboppers and kept the listener constantly off balance. There were no traditional signposts to guide the listener, just pure emotion. Some critics and musicians criticized him for being a charlatan who had no training and couldn't play. In the 1958 *Down Beat* reader's poll, the year Brubeck Quartet saxophonist Paul Desmond won, Coleman received only 21 votes following the release of his first two recordings on the Contemporary label. Many other critics and musicians, on the other hand, like Nat Hentoff, Amiri Baraka, Schuller, and Lewis, felt that Coleman was making a "unique and valuable contribution to tomorrow's music."[20]

As a true postmodern, Coleman forced the listener to abandon old standards and means of comparison and evaluation. His music made it necessary to reevaluate the way jazz was judged. Coleman and his producers were convinced that his new brand of jazz was a beacon for those looking for a new direction and his first album titles illustrate his commitment to predicting and pioneering the future—*Something Else, Tomorrow Is the Question, The Shape of Jazz to Come*, and *Change of the Century*.

Listen to "Mind and Time," included on the companion anthology. See if you can identify the unusual characteristics of Coleman's quartet style. This track is from his second release on the Contemporary label and was the first recording to demonstrate the true essence of his style, which led to a contract from the major New York–based Atlantic label. Despite its freshness, the tune itself adheres closely to a standard riff-like call and response format. Trumpeter Don Cherry described it as a 10-bar form,[21] but it is actually 11 and a half measures in all, divided into an initial six-and-a-half measure phrase followed by a five-measure phrase in 4/4 meter. The entire 11-and-a-half-measure tune is repeated before improvised solos begin.

Ornette Coleman

Listening Guide

"Mind and Time" (Coleman)

Recorded 1/16/59, Contemporary 7569

Reissued on OJC OJCCD-342-2

Ornette Coleman: *alto sax*

Donald Cherry: *trumpet*

Percy Heath: *bass*

Red Mitchell: *bass*

Shelley Manne: *drums*

Form and Key: 11½-measure melody, and solos without chord structure or bar structure in F# major

0:00–0:22	*Melody*	
	0:00–0:06	*A section:* 6½ bars, alto sax and trumpet play melody in unison, with rhythm section accompaniment
	0:06–0:11	*B section:* 5 bars, sax and trumpet play melody in unison, with rhythm section accompaniment
	0:11–0:17	*A section:* 6½ bars, sax and trumpet repeat A section melody in unison, with rhythm section accompaniment
	0:17–0:22	*B section:* 5 bars, sax and trumpet repeat B section melody in unison, with rhythm section accompaniment
0:23–1:52	*Open "Free" Alto Sax Solo*, exploring the melodic and harmonic material of the melody section, with bass and drum swinging accompaniment	
1:52–2:36	*Open "Free" Trumpet Solo*, exploring the melodic and harmonic material of the melody section, with bass and drum swinging accompaniment	
2:36–end	*Melody with 3-bar Ending Tag*, Sax and trumpet play melody in unison, similar to opening melody section, with ending tag inverting last phrase of melody	

White Light, *by Jackson Pollock was featured on the Ornette Coleman* Free Jazz *record jacket.*

Coleman's greatest accomplishment is perhaps the 1960 Atlantic Records recording entitled *Free Jazz* (an excerpt of which is included on the *Smithsonian Collection of Classic Jazz*), which featured two quartets playing 36 minutes of uninterrupted, improvised music. Coleman chose an appropriate painting by abstract expressionist painter Jackson Pollock for the cover of this landmark recording. Pollack's postmodern painting offered a perfect visual association with Coleman's music.

Aside from a few composed, but loosely played, ensemble passages that serve as interludes between solos, the balance of *Free Jazz* features entirely improvised dialogues between the two quartets—(1) Coleman, Don Cherry (trumpet), Charlie Haden (bass), Ed Blackwell (drums); (2) Freddie Hubbard (trumpet), Eric Dolphy (bass clarinet), Scott LaFaro (bass), and Billy Higgins (drums). All except LaFaro, Hubbard, and Dolphy had been regular members of Coleman's quartets. The result is a mind-boggling stream of consciousness mosaic of ever-changing textures. It can be compared to a group of people at a party, all having conversations, interacting, some voices sounding more predominant at times than others. While some of the rhythm instruments essentially fulfill traditional roles as timekeepers, others are free to interact, comment, and react to the horn players' gestures. The horn players, in turn, based their background riffs on ideas that began as improvisations stated by the primary soloist at the moment. *Down Beat* magazine played it safe when they reviewed this recording, electing to straddle the fence by printing opinions that represented both camps. For example, Pete Welding gave the recording a five-star rating—the highest possible. He said that the recording "does not break with jazz tradition; rather it restores to currency an element that has been absent in most jazz since the onset of the swing orchestra—spontaneous group improvisation."[22] Welding went on to say that Coleman's music was "relentless in its re-examination of the role of collective improvisation, and this is, in many respects, where the work is most successful."[23] Critic John Tynan, who had been one of Coleman's cheerleaders contributing rave reviews following the release of his first two recordings, had a different impression of Coleman's *Free Jazz*. He wrote: "'Collective improvisation'? Nonsense. The only semblance of collectivity lies in the fact that these eight nihilists were collected together in one studio at one time and with one common cause: to destroy the music that gave them birth. Give them top marks for the attempt."[24] Tynan's refusal to give any stars in his review of *Free Jazz*, the recording that coined the term and set a new course for jazz also known as the "new thing," will no doubt continue to be disputed. It cannot, however, be disputed that Coleman's music exerted a magnetic force that attracted and influenced many young jazz musicians. Bassists Charles Mingus, Charlie Haden, and Scott LaFaro; saxophonists John Coltrane, Eric Dolphy, Dewey Redman, Jackie McLean, Albert Ayler, Pharoah Sanders, Archie Shepp; modern pianists Cecil Taylor and Keith Jarrett; the more contemporary World Saxophone Quartet, Anthony Braxton; and modern guitarists James "Blood" Ulmer and Pat Metheny all credit Coleman with changing the way in which they thought about playing jazz. Many of these saxophonists shared with Coleman a common background in rhythm and blues that spilled over into their music. Coleman and his music laid the foundation for the formation of the non-profit AACM (Association for the Advancment of Creative Music) centered in Chicago and devoted to supporting black, avant-garde jazz. Muhal Richard Abrams founded the organization in 1965, following a landmark series of sold-out concerts the year before organized by Bill Dixon and billed as "The October Revolution in Jazz." The AACM can be directly linked to the formation of such contemporary avant-garde bands as the Art Ensemble of Chicago and Anthony Braxton's various ensembles. A similar organization in St. Louis known as the Black Artists Group, formed in 1968 in the image of the AACM, later helped to foster groups like the World Saxophone Quartet.

Coleman and his 1983 band Prime Time continued to exert influence on the jazz scene with its brand of electrified free jazz. By this time Coleman was also playing trumpet and violin and the band included two electric guitarists, two electric bassists, and two drummers—following the double quartet model he established two decades earlier. It is safe to say that, while demonstrating an interesting fusion of electronic/rock influences with free jazz improvisations, this band has had less of an impact on jazz than his earlier efforts.

The less-informed listener often finds free jazz difficult to understand or appreciate for its practitioners took so many liberties, breaking away from well-established traditions. Any new art form or style becomes difficult to understand when there is no frame of reference, causing one to lose the ability to relate it to something that is understood. Free jazz therefore threw many listeners off balance, as it continues to do even today. Table 11.1 should help to put this style in sharper focus, making the juxtaposition and contrast of styles and approaches clearer.

TABLE 11.1 A Study in Contrasts: A Comparison in the Characteristics of Free Jazz and More Traditionally Grounded, Modern Mainstream Jazz Styles

	Free Jazz	Modern Mainstream
Repertoire	New compositions, often lacking chord progressions. Based more on melody and rhythm than harmony. If supporting harmony is used, rules governing functional harmony are ignored, much like African music. Form and structure may be less obvious or completely absent.	Blues, tunes based on "rhythm changes" harmonic scheme, contrafacts, recreations of standard pop and show tunes, and newly composed tunes by jazz artists. Melodies clearly derived from harmonies. Form and structure fairly obvious, frequently based on modern song form.
Instrument Roles	*Bass*—Freed from walking bass lines derived from prescribed chords. Not always in sync with drums. Instrument emerges with equal stature as potential soloist. *Piano*—At times absent from ensemble altogether, or freed from traditional comping roles defined by traditional chord progressions. *Drums*—Played in unconventional ways, sometimes out of time, out of sync with bass, and without traditional swing style. Solos in a more melodic fashion and often not bound by tempo or form.	Bass—walking bass lines derived from prescribed chord progression and in sync with drums. Instrument emerges with equal stature as potential soloist. *Piano*—Bound by prescribed chord progression. Supplies harmonic backdrop to melody. Comping technique employed to accompany soloists. Drums—Played in conventional synchronized fashion. Along with the bassist, defines steady tempo and style. Modern drummers begin to solo in a more melodic fashion. Often bound by tempo and form of composition.

(continues)

TABLE 11.1 (Concluded)

	Free Jazz	Modern Mainstream
Instrument Roles	*Horns*—Statement of melody, if one exists, followed by improvisations often not bound by traditional chord progressions, or any chords whatsoever.	Horns—Statement of melody followed by improvisations. Improvisations bound completely by prescribed chord progression.
Performance Practice	Horn players redefine traditionally accepted standards in intonation, phrasing, sound and articulation. Use of bop-inspired rhythms, but free of melodic clichés.	Intonation and overall sound derived from traditionally accepted European performance practice, but with ample room for personal expression.
	Performance practice less bound by the jazz tradition and reflecting past practices.	Performance practice heavily influenced by the jazz tradition and past practice.
	Impromptu, seemingly ragged, or under-rehearsed performances as compared to traditional standards.	Cohesive, well-rehearsed performances.
	Overall performance presentation is less prescribed and expected. Focus on group textures—soundscapes—rather than consistently well-defined individual solos. (There are exceptions to this in free jazz, however.)	Performance presentation is well defined, prescribed by past practice. Clearly defined sections with each instrument fulfilling a well-understood role including that of soloist.
	Simultaneous dialogue, like the many conversations of a crowd, and similar to the collective polyphonic improvisations heard in early New Orleans jazz but less governed by traditional harmonies and bass lines. Individual instrument voices often blurred.	Clearly defined musical dialogue where main characters are well defined and individual instrument voices easily separated.

Charles Mingus (1922–1979)—The Underdog

Many artists were profoundly influenced by Coleman's work, though they may have been more careful in pushing the envelope beyond what had become the accepted mainstream. One such artist was indisputably one of the most important pioneers and bandleader-composers of the late modern and early postmodern era—Charles Mingus. Much like Monk, Mingus was an enigma on and off stage. His passionate, volatile, unpredictable, and highly expressive music was a true refection of his personality. Mingus was a powerfully commanding bassist who hailed from Watts, the Los Angeles equivalent of New York's Harlem. He set out to be a classical performer and composer, studying trombone, cello and bass in the European classical tradition, but at this time Mingus found that a career as an orchestral musician was an unattainable dream for black men and women. Mingus chose a career in jazz, despite his concerns about the way in which he felt black artists were taken advantage of by the largely white dominated music industry. He said in his autobiography *Beneath the Underdog* that "Jazz is big business to the white man and you can't move without him. We just work-ants."[25] He was outspoken about who held the rightful deed and title to this music and that despite all the primary innovations stemming from black artists' innovations, jazz had been largely usurped by white entrepreneurs.

The most innovative jazz artists throughout its history have defied categorization and Mingus can be added to this group along with Duke Ellington, Miles Davis, Ornette Coleman, John Coltrane, and a few others. While his contributions as a bass soloist were significant, it was his work as a composer that has stood the important test of time. His music was chameleon-like in reflecting roots that ranged from the blues, gospel, hollers, and work songs to free jazz and European classical music. In many ways, he serves as an early example of a jazzman not particularly rooted in one style, as has been the case with most of his predecessors. While he comes out of a hard bop tradition, there are many signs of a more postmodern approach that surface. He participated in the third stream movement, contributing works like "Abstractions" which bear little resemblance to jazz but bearing more similarities to contemporary classical trends. In every Mingus composition, whether Ellingtonesque in its episodic format, or blues drenched with religious overtones, any number of the following attributes can combine to characterize his music:

- A loose, unrehearsed, and improvised atmosphere.
- Riffs, often layered in antiphonal fashion, some composed and some improvised.
- A penchant for 6/8 and 3/4 meters, unusual for jazz up until this time.
- Hard-driving swing from the rhythm section propelled by Mingus's own forceful, aggressive bass lines.
- Backgrounds arranged for the horn section as a backdrop to the soloist, often strong compositional statements on a par with the main theme.
- Shifting moods, meters, and tempos as explosive as his personality.
- Blues often the basis for the compositions and a preference for minor tonalities—characteristics shared by many hard bop bands.
- A reverence and loyalty to the jazz tradition, yet the impact of Coleman's free jazz is eventually felt, loosening it up even more.

Mingus's ensembles were always a harbinger for exceptionally innovative soloists who were encouraged to go out on a limb, experiment and express their blackness. While mixed about Coleman's "new thing," Mingus was clearly intrigued by it. After hearing a Coleman recording among a group of more traditional recordings he commented later that, "his [Coleman's] notes and lines are so fresh. It made everything else he was playing, even my own record that he played, sound terrible. I'm not saying everybody's going to have to play like Coleman. But they're going to have to stop playing like Bird."[26] This was an important revelation considering Mingus had begun his career playing traditional jazz with Louis Armstrong and Lionel Hampton and bop with masters like Parker, Powell, and Gillespie.

To capture the looseness and improvised feel and ensure that members of the band could contribute their own personal sounds and emotions, Mingus preferred to teach the musicians their parts rather than write them down. He even referred to his bands as the Jazz Workshop. He was public in showing his respect for the jazz tradition and especially for Jelly Roll Morton, Monk, and Ellington. His compositions bore some resemblance to Ellington's in that each composer shared a similar flaw—Mingus's more lengthy compositions were at times fragmented and lacked continuity, but this was a common trait (some considered blemish) of much postmodern art and in some ways helps to define it.[27]

Like Monk, Mingus is considered a rediscovery figure in that his music has gained more respect and popularity in the years following his death than during his lifetime. Pop star Joni Mitchell completed a project that was intended as a collaboration with Mingus but ended as a tribute recording following his death. Some years later, composer Gunther Schuller recreated from Mingus's sketches a two-hour,

Bassist Charles Mingus in 1964.

multimovement concert work entitled *Epitaph*. The bass line that begins Mingus's famous "Haitian Fight Song" became the backdrop for a 2001 automobile TV commercial, though it is doubtful that most viewers were aware of the origins. The contemporary Mingus Big Band tribute band, formed years after his death, has been most successful in recreating his music while capturing recent polls and public attention in the process. They have established themselves as one of the most significant big bands of the early twenty-first century and are helping to keep this great tradition alive.

Mingus's brand of loose, driving hard bop is well defined by "Boogie Stop Shuffle" included on the companion CD audio anthology. It is classic Mingus in that it draws on important aspects of the black tradition—in this case boogie-woogie, blues, and a riff style associated with bands from the earlier years of jazz. As the title implies, the piece is built on a foundation of boogie-woogie style riffs. Mingus had a penchant for also using ensemble riffs to accompany soloists and this particular piece is no exception.

Listen to the interviews with Charles Mingus that are included on the CD-ROM and found in the corresponding chapter.

Listening Guide

Charles Mingus

"Boogie Stop Shuffle" (Charles Mingus) 3:41 (Original truncated LP release)

Recorded 5/5/59 New York City

Columbia CS 8171

Charles Mingus: *bass*

Danny Richmond: *drums*

Horace Parlan: *piano*

John Handy: *alto saxophone*

Booker Erwin: *tenor saxophone*

Shafi Hadi: *tenor saxophone*

Willie Dennis: *trombone*

Jimmy Knepper: *trombone*

Form and Key: Repeated 12-bar blues choruses in E♭ major

0:00–0:12	*First Chorus:* 12 bar *Riff*: Tenors, trombones, piano, bass, and drums play blues bass riff
0:13–0:23	*Second Chorus:* 12 bars, *Varied Riff*: Piano and bass continue blues bass riff, saxes and trombones play accents and last 4 bars of Theme 1 melody
0:24–0:34	*Third Chorus:* 12 bars, *Theme 1*: Piano and bass continue blues bass riff. Saxes, trombones play Theme 1
0:35–0:45	*Fourth Chorus:* 12 bars, *Theme 2*: Piano and bass continue blues riff. Saxes, trombones play Theme 2
0:46–0:57	*Fifth Chorus:* 12 bars, *Theme 2* repeated in saxes and trombones. Piano and bass now quit blues bass riff and swing hard
0:57–1:08	*Sixth Chorus:* 12 bars, *Tenor Sax Solo* (Erwin) with backgrounds in saxes and trombones, rhythm section swinging hard
1:09–1:19	*Seventh Chorus:* 12 bars, *Tenor Sax Solo* continues with backgrounds
1:20–1:30	*Eighth Chorus:* 12 bars, *Riff and Piano Solo*, blues bass riff returns in saxes and trombones as piano solo background
1:31–1:42	*Ninth Chorus:* 12 bars, *Riff and Piano Solo* continues
1:42–1:53	*Tenth Chorus:* 12 bars, *Piano Solo,* with bass and drums
1:53–2:04	*Eleventh Chorus:* 12 bars, *Piano Solo* continues
2:05–2:15	*Twelfth Chorus:* 12 bars, *Riff, Alto Sax, and Drum Solo:* Tenors, trombones, piano, and bass play blues bass riff behind alto and drums solo

Charles Mingus *concluded*

2:16–2:26	*Thirteenth Chorus:* 12 bars, *Drum Solo*
2:27–2:37	*Fourteenth Chorus:* 12 bars, *Drum Solo* continues
2:37–2:48	*Fifteenth Chorus:* 12 bars, *Varied Riff* (like second chorus)
2:48–2:59	*Sixteenth Chorus:* 12 bars, *Theme 1* (like third chorus)
3:00–3:10	*Seventeenth Chorus:* 12 bars, *Theme 2* (like fourth chorus)
3:11–3:21	*Eighteenth Chorus:* 12 bars, *Theme 2* repeated (like fifth chorus)
3:21–3:30	*Tag 1: "Free" Solos:* all players solo freely without time
3:31–3:41	*Tag 2: Drum Solo,* all others tacet

THE END OF MODERN JAZZ HERALDED BY THE BEGINNING OF THE POSTMODERNS

There were two stylistic strata moving in parallel during the 1950s and 1960s and it is important to realize that both modern jazz and emerging postmodern styles coexisted and will continue to do so for quite some time (see Example 11.1).

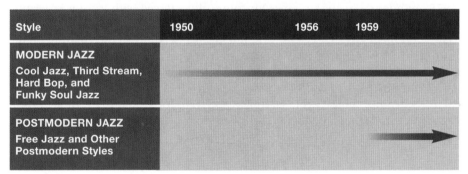

Style	1950		1956	1959
MODERN JAZZ Cool Jazz, Third Stream, Hard Bop, and Funky Soul Jazz				
POSTMODERN JAZZ Free Jazz and Other Postmodern Styles				

EXAMPLE 11.1
Modern and postmodern jazz coexist.

There seems to be no single reason why hard bop became of less interest, any more than there is a reason why any popular art form falls out of favor. Styles inevitably decline for any number of reasons. Hard bop was designed to attract and hold black and white audiences at a time when attentions were being drawn toward new emerging pop styles such as rhythm and blues and rock and roll. Television had also become affordable and along with movies and musicals became frequent leisure time activities. For example, recordings of TV personalities, Broadway musicals, and movie themes contributed to nearly half of the top 50 gold (sales of 500,000 copies or more) and platinum (sales of 1 million copies or more) recordings produced in the 1950s. The balance of these hit recordings are attributed to Elvis Presley, Frank Sinatra, Johnny Mathis, Nat King Cole, Harry Belefonte, and two jazz artists—Dave Brubeck for *Time Out* (with "Talk Five") and Miles Davis for *Kind of Blue* (Davis' *Kind of Blue* has sold over 5 million copies worldwide since its release, but at the time of its release in 1959 was not even charted by sales polls).

Numerous problems plagued the performers of this time, not the least of which was their highly publicized drug use. Jazz journalist Leonard Feather pointed out that "of the 23 *Down Beat* poll winners, nine were known narcotics users and five had arrests and convictions on record."[28] An alarmingly high percentage of hard bop artists were junkies, causing many to ask why. Saxophonist and Blakey alumnus Jackie McLean suggested that drugs were a "form of self-medication-trying to cool yourself out. It's the pain of being so creative and not having avenues to express it, or having your work considered less than important that could drive a man to many things."[29] Saxophonist and convicted drug user Stan Getz talked with National Public Radio's Terry Gross in 1990 about his own drug use. Quoted previously, Getz described his drug use as an avenue to the artistic alpha state.[30] Not all artists felt this way, however. Pianist Oscar Peterson offered an alternative view: "I have seen how players can succumb to this false crutch, especially when their careers seem stagnated or suspended. I have observed the raft of famous but misguided players follow their idols into drug-abuse, and often into death as a result. . .If I had to advise any young musician, I'd say that your instrument should be your needle, and music your addiction. It is mine."[31]

For many musicians participating in the hard bop scene, notoriety was fading by the early 1960s, losing their battle for acceptance by young audiences to the rock and roll bands. *Down Beat* magazine reviewer John S. Wilson gave Blakey's Messengers recording *Big Beat* a lackluster review stating that it was nothing more than a repetition of "material that has been gone over time and time again."[32] In 1978, author and historian James Lincoln Collier agreed with Wilson in writing that "the hard bop style was exhausted [by 1960], worn out by overuse. . . . The central problem was a lack of musical intelligence, a failure of imagination on the part of the players in the style."[33] Dave Brubeck and Miles Davis are examples of two exceptionally successful musicians who survived the transition from modern jazz to the postmodern era. Since Davis, a successful hard bop musician, spanned so many decades, all the while serving as a steward for so many new directions in jazz and introducing along with them new young artists, his career will be discussed in detail in the upcoming chapter.

Jazz in Perspective

The timeline that follows will put the developments of jazz discussed in this chapter into a larger historical context, providing you with a better sense of how landmark musical events may relate to others that match your personal areas of interest.

1954
- *Brown* vs. *Board of Education* decision by courts is key victory for NAACP and desegregation movement—Supreme Court rules against school segregation.

- Ernest Hemingway wins Nobel Prize for Literature.
- McCarthy and communist witch hunt are condemned.

- The first Newport Jazz Festival is a success.
- Clifford Brown/Max Roach Quintet records "Daahoud."

1955
- United States begins involvement in Vietnam.
- Minimum wage set at $1.
- Rock and roll craze is launched by success of "Rock Around the Clock" recorded by Bill Haley and the Comets.

1956
- Civil rights advocate Martin Luther King has home bombed.
- *Peyton Place* by Grace Metalious is best seller.
- Musical *My Fair Lady* hits Broadway.
- Top films include *Invasion of the Body Snatchers, The Ten Commandments,* and *Bus Stop.*
- University of Alabama sued for banning blacks from enrolling.
- Elvis Presley becomes rock and roll idol with release of *Heartbreak Hotel.*
- Bus segregation declared unconstitutional.

1957
- John F. Kennedy awarded Pulitzer Prize for *Profiles in Courage.*
- Nuclear arms race heats up.
- Count Basie band becomes first black band to perform at New York's Waldorf-Astoria Hotel.
- Vocalist Pat Boone enjoys popularity.
- President Eisenhower sends federal troops to assist racial integration of Little Rock, Arkansas schools.
- Race with Russia in space exploration.
- Leonard Bernstein enjoys hit musical *West Side Story.*
- Beat poet-writer Jack Kerouac publishes *On the Road.*

1958
- Texan Van Cliburn wins Tchaikovsky Piano Competition.
- NASA created to bolster U.S. position in space race with Russia.
- Kingston Trio, Everly Brothers, Little Richard, Rick Nelson, and Chuck Berry are pop music successes.

- Art Blakey's Jazz Messengers records the funky jazz tune "Moanin'."

1959
- Coast-to-coast flight becomes a reality along with passenger flights to Europe.
- Richie Valens, Texan Buddy Holly, and Big Bopper die in plane crash.
- Jazz singer Billie Holiday dies at age 44.
- Integrated schools open in Little Rock, Arkansas.
- Ill-fated Ford Edsel hits market.
- Alaska and Hawaii become the forty-ninth and fiftieth states.
- *Some Like It Hot* and *Ben Hur* are popular films.
- Avant-garde jazz artist Ornette Coleman records "Mind and Time."
- Racial incidents in Alabama of the period inspired jazz composer Charles Mingus to compose *Fables of Faubus*, recorded in 1959.

1960
- Protests, sit-ins, and other forms of nonviolent protest against segregation and discrimination.
- Martin Luther King becomes prominent civil rights leader.
- Free jazz artist Ornette Coleman records the revolutionary *Free Jazz.*
- The *Fantastics,* written by two University of Texas grads is hit on New York stage.
- Birth control pill is approved.
- Cold war tensions escalate following U2 spy plane incident. Tension mounts in Cuba.
- J.F. Kennedy defeats Richard Nixon for presidency by narrow margin.
- *Camelot* opens on Broadway.
- Charles Mingus records "Boogie Stop Shuffle."

1961
- Rock and roll is a hit with teenagers. *American Bandstand* TV show and Chubby Checker's "The Twist" are hot with teens.
- Fear of armageddon as missile race and atomic testing escalate.
- Harper Lee wins Pulitzer Prize for *To Kill a Mockingbird.*

- United States continues assistance to South Korea, defending democracy against communism.

- Freedom riders attacked as they tour the South to evaluate compliance with desegregation acts.

- American astronauts Shepard and Grissom are first to explore space, helping the United States to catch up with Russia in space race.

1962
- Astronaut John Glenn orbits earth.

- Hollywood starlet and silver screen sex symbol Marilyn Monroe dies.

- John Steinbeck wins Nobel Prize for *The Winter of our Discontent.* Other best sellers included Helen Gurley Brown's *Sex and the Single Girl* and *One Flew Over the Cuckoo's Nest* by Ken Kesey.

- United States sends small force to Laos.

- Popular films include *Lawrence of Arabia, Dr. No, The Days of Wine and Roses, To Kill a Mockingbird, What Ever Happened to Baby Jane, Long Day's Journey into Night, The Manchurian Candidate,* and *How the West Was Won.*

- Russia agrees to withdraw missiles from Cuba.

1963
- Violent demonstrations in Birmingham, Alabama, lead to desegregation of lunch counters and integration of schools.

- Four young girls killed in Birmingham, Alabama, church bombing.

- Martin Luther King jailed for his civil disobedience actions.

- President Kennedy lends support to racial equality.

- First blacks graduate from the University of Mississippi.

- Popularity of folk music soars through work by singers Bob Dylan, Joan Baez, Pete Seeger, and Peter, Paul & Mary.

- Martin Luther King addresses largest ever civil rights rally and declares "I have a dream."

- Pop artists like Andy Warhol gain popularity for controversial art breaking traditional barriers.

- JFK assassinated in Dallas, Texas; Lyndon Baines Johnson (LBJ) sworn in as president.

- William Faulkner wins Pulitzer Prize in fiction.

- James Baldwin publishes *The Fire Next Time.*

1964
- British rock group The Beatles widely accepted by American youth.

- Folk musicians like Dylan continue to express themes of social injustice and horrors of war in lyrics.

- Congress passes Civil Rights Act prohibiting racial discrimination.

- Race riots in New York lead to deaths and arrests.

- Student unrest on Berkley campus.

- Julie Andrews stars in *Mary Poppins*; other popular films include *The Pink Panther* and The Beatles' *A Hard Days Night.*

- Martin Luther King wins Nobel Peace Prize.

- LBJ wins presidential election handily.

1965
- United States takes offensive in Vietnam despite divided public opinion.

- Dances like the Frug and the Watusi are popular along with minidresses and go-go boots.

- Black Muslim sect leader Malcolm X shot by member of opposing sect.

- 25,000 blacks organize march on Montgomery, Alabama, to affirm right to vote.

- Astronaut walks in space.

- President Johnson signs voting rights act favoring African Americans.

- Racial tension explodes in the Los Angeles Watts district.

- Timothy Leary advocates use of drugs to "tune in, turn on, and drop out."

- War in Vietnam escalates amid waves of antiwar protests.
- Race riots erupt in Chicago and Atlanta.
- Pop music matures with The Beatles, Bob Dylan, Beach Boys, the Byrds, and Motown groups the Supremes and Miracles.

- LBJ launches war at home on urban decay, awarding grants to cities for reconstruction.
- Top films include *Blow Up, A Man For All Seasons,* and *Who's Afraid of Virginia Woolf.*

CHAPTER SUMMARY

In the 1950s, fans had numerous jazz listening options. While the cool reaction to bebop was taking place, most notably on the West Coast, a new generation of musicians continued the development of the bop tradition creating hard bop. Within the hard bop movement was a smaller faction playing not only bop-inspired jazz, but also a more commercial, sometimes danceable music. Influenced by gospel music and rhythm and blues, this brand of jazz was labeled "funky jazz" or "soul jazz." By the mid-1950s important early third stream works were recorded, and by the end of the 1950s free jazz took listeners to entirely new destinations, while other groups continued to play cool jazz and hard bop.

Art Blakey, Horace Silver, Clifford Brown, and Max Roach led important early hard bop groups. Originally drummer Blakey and pianist Silver worked together forming the Jazz Messengers. Horace Silver later went on to lead his own groups and both leaders had a knack for finding and developing young talents who became important contributors to jazz. Young trumpet sensation Clifford Brown teamed with bop veteran drummer Max Roach to form the Clifford Brown–Max Roach Quintet. Brown would tragically die in an automobile accident at age 25. Outstanding hard bop alto saxophonist Cannonball Adderley was better known to the general public for his funky jazz hits, as was guitarist Wes Montgomery for his renditions of pop tunes. Selections by both artists could be heard on the radio and on jukeboxes throughout the country.

The postmodern movement is probably best illustrated by free jazz alto saxophonist Ornette Coleman. His 1960 recording "Free Jazz" announced the dawn of a new era in jazz, just as Miles Davis' "Birth of the Cool" had done 10 years earlier. In a way, free jazz reestablished the emphasis on group or collective improvisation, important in early New Orleans jazz. Unlike early jazz, however, free jazz did not rely on meter, melody, or chord changes. A free jazz performance might contain some basic kind of theme statement, but beyond that, the performers were welcome to add comments to the improvised conversation as they see fit. Free jazz artists also frequently treat pitch/intonation in a completely different way, resulting in what sounds out of tune by traditional standards. It should come as no surprise that, in general, free jazz has enjoyed the least commercial appeal of any jazz style.

Bassist/composer Charles Mingus, an important pioneer of late modern and postmodern jazz defies categorization. His diverse background includes work with Louis Armstrong, serving as bassist for the important bebop concert of Charlie Parker and Dizzy Gillespie at Toronto's Massey Hall, and performing and composing third stream works. Mingus's reputation gained more notoriety in the years following his death. Much of his music lives on in the work of the Mingus Big Band.

KEY TERMS

Important terms, people, places, and bands.

TERMS	Horace Silver	PLACES
pendulum theory	Bobby Timmons	Watts
mainstream	Max Roach	
aleatoric	Clifford Brown	BANDS
	Wes Montgomery	Jazz Messengers
PEOPLE	Jimmy Smith	
Ornette Coleman	Don Cherry	
Cannonball Adderley	Charles Mingus	
Art Blakey		

REVIEW QUESTIONS

1. How would you describe the hard bop style?

2. What size bands are associated with hard bop and what is the typical instrumentation?

3. Name the various styles of jazz that could be heard during the 1950s.

4. What cities seemed to be the strongholds for hard bop bands and musicians?

5. Name some of the stable small groups that emerged during the hard bop period.

6. Who is given credit for developing the funky style of hard bop jazz?

7. Discuss the essence of the funky jazz style.

8. What guitarist, who is known as the most important player of this instrument since Charlie Christian, teamed up with organists and in what ways did he make his playing style unique?

9. What electronic instrument became an important new centerpiece in trios and quartets during the 1950s and 1960s?

10. What was unusual about the instrumentation of Ornette Coleman's revolutionary bands and how did this instrumentation help him to forge a new style?

11. While Ornette Coleman's style attracted a great deal of attention in the late 1950s, many characteristics of his music were not entirely new or unique. What artists paved the way and followed similar musical paths?

12. What was so unique about Charles Mingus's music?

13. Compare and contrast the hard bop style to free jazz including a discussion of instruments' roles.

14. Discuss the meaning and implications of the term "postmodern."

15. What is the significance of Isaac Newton's "pendulum theory" to jazz at this point in time?

16. What kind of music had become popular with the American public in the 1950s gradually eclipsing jazz and why?

Make sure that you also review material on the corresponding chapter of the CD-ROM.

SUGGESTED SUPPLEMENTARY LISTENING

The abbreviation (iT) indicates that a particular recording cited in the text, or particularly demonstrative of the artist, is available from the Apple iTunes Web site. Other Web-based music distributors may also prove to be valuable resources. SCCJ indicates *Smithsonian Collection of Classic Jazz.*

Cannonball Adderley

African Waltz Riverside (iT)
Why Am I Treated So Bad Capitol
Mercy, Mercy, Mercy Capitol

Art Blakey

The Freedom Rider Blue Note (iT)
A Night In Tunisia Blue Note (iT)
The Messengers Sony (iT)
Ugetsu Riverside (iT)
Jazz in Paris (iT)

Clifford Brown

The Complete Blue Note and Pacific Jazz Recordings Blue Note (iT)
Brown and Roach, Inc. Verve (iT)
Clifford Brown and Max Roach at Basin Street Verve (iT)
Clifford Brown and Max Roach Verve (iT)

Ornette Coleman

Something Else: The Music of Ornette Coleman Original Jazz Classics (iT)
Tomorrow is the Question Original Jazz Classics (iT)
This is Our Music Atlantic
The Shape of Jazz to Come Atlantic
Change of the Century Atlantic
Free Jazz Atlantic
Skies of America Sony (iT)

Tadd Dameron

Mating Call with John Coltrane Prestige (iT)
Fontainebleau Prestige (iT)

Andrew Hill

Black Fire Blue Note (iT)

Freddie Hubbard

Red Clay Sony (iT)
Hub Tones

Jackie McLean

Let Freedom Ring Blue Note (iT)

Charles Mingus

Mingus Ah Hum Sony (iT)
Let My Children Hear Music Sony (iT)
"Slop" (iT)
"Better Get It in Your Soul" (iT)
"Fables of Faubus" (iT)
"Mood Indigo" (iT)
"Gunslinging Bird" (iT)

Lee Morgan

Cornbread Blue Note (iT)
Sidewinder Blue Note (iT)

Wes Montgomery

Bags Meets Wes Riverside (iT)
Portrait of Wes Riverside (iT)
Verve Jazz Masters 14: Wes Montgomery Verve (iT)

Horace Silver

The Best of Horace Silver Vol. 2 Blue Note (iT)
Blowin' the Blues Away Blue Note (iT)
Cape Verdian Blues Blue Note (iT)
Song for My Father Blue Note (iT)
The Jody Grind Blue Note (iT)

Jimmy Smith

Home Cookin' Blue Note (iT)
Roots of Acid Jazz: Jimmy Smith Verve (iT)
Jazz Masters 29: Jimmy Smith Verve (iT)

Miles and Miles of **Miles**
Miles Davis and His Sidemen
Redefine Postmodern Jazz

> "I don't want to sound like nobody but myself.
> I want to be myself, whatever that is."[1]
> MILES DAVIS

THE 1960S: AN AGE OF PEACE, LOVE, AND WAR

The 1960s were tumultuous times in America when jazz experienced many changes and vied for attention with new trends in popular music. This decade is perhaps the most unsettled, at least on home soil, of any on record, and the music in many ways reflects the tension and restless atmosphere. Political and social unrest was sparked and fueled by the war in Vietnam (1965–1973), the missile and space race with the Soviet Union, a soft and sagging economy, a volatile civil rights movement, the rock and roll music explosion, and the rise and eventual assassinations of two of America's greatest leaders and orators—President John F. Kennedy (1963) and Reverend Martin Luther King (1968).

In retrospect, Stanley Kubrick's film *2001: A Space Odyssey* may have done more to summarize the 1960s than may have been apparent at the time. His 1968 episodic film, complete with dramatic special effects, is a study in contrasts of mankind's frailties and accomplishments. A year later U.S. astronaut Neil Armstrong became the first human to set foot on the moon, where he announced to the world that his was "one small step for man" but a "giant leap for mankind." While this may have been true in terms of scientific advancements and outer space exploration, on earth it seemed like mankind was taking backward steps at an alarming rate. The U.S. involvement in the war between North and South Vietnam drew mass protest, inspiring musicians like Bob Dylan to perform political commentary at his concerts and on recordings. Peace marches to protest the war and young males burning their draft cards were common occurrences. Some radical college students who were enraged by the war, the draft, social injustices, and racial inequalities joined the Students for a Democratic Society (SDS) organization. Other young people tried a less volatile means of protest, marching 50,000 strong one summer to San Francisco for a "love-in." Dressed in their tie-died clothing with males sporting hairdos that made The Beatles look conservative, these young men and women sought both to escape from the harsh realities of life and to end political and social injustices with peaceful solutions. Their peaceful demonstration at the 1968 Chicago Democratic convention against the war in Vietnam, however, turned to bloodshed with 700 injuries and 650 arrests.

During these same years the civil rights movement escalated, bringing new focus to racial prejudices. The famous phrase "I have a Dream," spoken by civil rights champion Reverend Martin Luther King who preached nonviolent resistance, was intended to incite peaceful protest for equal rights, but public gatherings often led to violence in American cities and on college campuses. Riots in Watts lasted five days leaving behind a charred community that saw 34 dead, 1,000 injured, and 4,000 arrested. Riots erupted in other major cities across the country including Birmingham, Philadelphia, Boston, Chicago, and Detroit where 38 died in 1967. King, who was awarded the Nobel Peace Prize in 1964, was assassinated only four years later. Other black leaders, like Black Muslim Malcolm X, led more violent demonstrations following his civil disobedience credo, but he, too, was struck down by an assassin's bullet in 1965. Women, led by spokespersons such as author Gloria Steinem, were also vocal in the 60s, demanding equal treatment. The women's liberation movement was born in the 60s and encouraged the symbolic burning of bras to make a case for an end of male supremacy.

The 1960s was a time when drugs, sex, and rock and roll seemed to permeate college campuses, breeding a new sense of social unrest and revolution, much as had been the case about 40 or 50 years earlier when Victorian ideals were put on trial and rejected by the younger generation. Just as jazz became the theme song for this earlier generation, rock and roll was adopted as the anthem of 60s youth. Beatlemania struck American youth in 1964 when the British pop group first appeared in 73 million homes via the *Ed Sullivan Show* on TV. Young people experimented with LSD, marijuana, and other mind-expanding hallucinogenic drugs as they listened to Janis Joplin's "Women Is Losers," The Beatles' John Lennon's "Give Peace a Chance," or guitar sensation Jimi Hendrix's "Are You Experienced." For many teens and college age students, it was the "age of Aquarius," peace and love, flower people, hippies, nonconformity, and a time to drop out from an intolerant, flawed society. It was impossible for the jazz world to go untouched by such significant developments in the evolution of American society and thought.[2]

THE MUSIC

The jazz purists felt that the three Ms, referring to Monk, Mingus, and Miles (Davis), kept "real" jazz alive through the 1950s and early 1960s in the midst of soulful, funky jazz, cool jazz, and third stream fads. The jazz world had lost its spiritual leader and guiding light with the death of Charlie Parker in 1955, and many were waiting, looking for the next messiah to show them the way. The "three Ms" created original, adventuresome forms, harmonies, rhythms, and new compositions not forged merely by borrowed chord progressions stolen from earlier compositions, as had been the case with much of the bebop repertoire. These new approaches challenged soloists to dig out of the predictable ruts left by those who had sculpted the modern bebop style. Mingus and Monk were both significant bridges linking past jazz traditions to the artist soon to be recognized as the new messiah. In 1955 no one yet knew that Miles Davis, the child of an East St. Louis dentist, who had first come to New York to study classical music at the Juilliard School of Music, would ultimately be the one to achieve such recognition. He cultivated or made significant contributions to seven periods of jazz developments including bebop, hard bop, cool, modal, third stream, progressive, and jazz-rock fusion. No other jazz artists can lay claim to such an accomplishment and contribution. His music was as provocative as his stylish, at times flamboyant dress, and his elusive, sometimes militant behavior only fueled his rise to notoriety, adding to the mystique that will always be a part of his legacy. In time, Davis would transcend his status as just a preeminent musician to become a cultural icon, a man whose art never remained static and always reflected the current state of an ever-changing American culture.

THE EARLY MILES

Without the advantage of the broader perspective that we now enjoy, Miles Davis' career could easily have ended, or been doomed to relative obscurity by the early 1950s and he might have been remembered as just another trumpet player. In many ways, his less-flamboyant trumpet style, as compared to the macho Gillespie, Navarro, or Brown approaches, characterized many of his earliest recordings where he was featured as the youngest member of Parker's late 1940s bebop band. These early solos were often undeveloped and lacked the virtuosic traits that were the hallmark of bebop. His technique was at times unsteady, his sound small by comparison, and he rarely played bravado-like high note passages, preferring the middle to lower register of the instrument. He was no doubt preoccupied with finding his own voice while feeling pressure to conform to the accepted style at the time. There was an element of insecurity and inconsistency in many of these early solos, yet they also possessed an austere melodic beauty that was often absent in bop. While it is true that he did not demonstrate a commanding, in your face style compared to notable bop artists, Davis did demonstrate in these early solos a desire to be different, following his own path and muse. Historian Martin Williams aptly described Davis' first entry into the jazz scene as Parker's sideman: "Davis was an effective foil for Parker's technical and emotional exuberance."[3] Davis was preoccupied with finding a lyrical, more subdued approach to improvisation, caressing the harmonies rather than setting fire to them, as was the case with Parker, Gillespie, and the other hot bop soloists. In his autobiography, comparing bebop artists' approach with his different cooler style, Davis described Gillespie and Parker's music as "this hip, real fast thing, and if you weren't a fast listener, you couldn't catch the humor or the feeling of their music. Bird and Diz were great, fantastic, challenging—but they weren't sweet. The *Birth of the Cool* was different because you could hear everything and hum it also."[4]

The cooler side of Davis, exposed briefly in the 1949 *Birth of the Cool* recordings and short-lived nonet club engagements, served to launch the cool style, a movement that many artists devoted entire careers to exploring. The music recorded by the nonet seemed to frame Davis in a much more comfortable setting, as illustrated by his exceptional solos throughout these recordings. His solos were as revolutionary as the arrangements and compositions.

The *Birth of the Cool* was just a way station and Davis kept moving, always in search of something new and more in sync with his own personal feelings about jazz. Everything about his playing, particularly his sound and attack, was different than what had come before. While one hears the earlier tradition in his playing, there is also a very clear new message being given. The very fact that his style didn't fit well into the bebop context provided a framework for him to emerge as perhaps the most influential jazz artist of the postmodern era. But Davis' career was nearly derailed by an addiction to heroin, a four- or five-year habit that he eventually conquered only through his own perseverance and abstention. During the early 1950s, he was under contract with the Prestige label and recorded a number of fine disks, but he was with no real established group. In every case, these recordings featured headline performers from the era, including the MJQ. The Prestige recordings all offer some shining examples of brilliant playing. Miles' solos during this period, particularly those on "Walkin'" and "Blue n' Boogie," showed a new-found maturity, a new personalized trumpet sound, and a sense of pacing and confidence where the element of space was becoming as valuable if not more so than a rapid burst of notes à la Gillespie. He had effectively learned to edit out all the unnecessary notes from the bebop style, simplifying improvisations down to the most essential melodic ingredients. The result was a poignant and to-the-point musical statement. Economy of style, along with his frequent use of the metallic harmon mute, became his trademarks as he developed a more mature style. Additional characteristics associated with Davis' sound that separated him from dozens of trumpet players were his unique attack and preference for a straight tone with no vibrato. In his autobiography, he said that: "People tell me that my sound is like a human voice and that's what I want it to be."[5]

Without a band he could call his own, and with a bad habit that was consuming much of his life, it was difficult to see Davis in the early 1950s going much further, despite his unique approach to the instrument. By 1955 both became nonissues as Davis found new freedom from his drug addiction and formed his first stable quintet including John Coltrane on tenor saxophone (who replaced Sonny Rollins), Red Garland on piano, Paul Chambers on bass, and Philly Joe Jones at the drums. From this point on, Davis never looked back and each personnel change to the quintet added a new dimension and often inspired him to pursue an entirely new musical direction. Perhaps his greatest attribute of all was his uncanny ability as a leader to identify and nurture new, young talent, in a sense returning the favor many times over that Parker had done for him. "I have always said that what the group does together is what makes music happen," he said. "My gift [was] having the ability to put certain guys together that would create a chemistry and then letting them go; letting them play what they knew and above it."[6] The list of alumni from Miles Davis' bands includes the most significant innovators in the past four decades of jazz. Topping this list are John Coltrane, Cannonball Adderley, Bill Evans, Wynton Kelly, Philly Joe Jones, Jimmy Cobb, Herbie Hancock, Ron Carter, Tony Williams, Wayne Shorter, Chick Corea, John McLaughlin, Dave Holland, Joe Zawinul, Keith Jarrett, Jack DeJohnette, Bob Berg, Mike Stern, John Scofield, Dave Liebman, and Kenny Garrett.

THE FIRST GREAT QUINTET

Miles' first great quintet followed the pattern established by the all-star dates he had fronted or participated in earlier in the decade. This repertoire included a balance of original jazz compositions and transformations (and at times abstractions) of standards like "I'll Remember April," "Easy Living," "Alone Together,"

"The Man I Love," and "There is No Greater Love." By the mid-50s, however, Davis' own quintet was devoting more and more attention to creating new works, and typically over half of the pieces included on these recordings were jazz compositions as opposed to face-lifts of older standards. The group hit its stride during their performance at the 1955 Newport Jazz Festival. Their performance at Newport of "Walking," a composition Davis had recorded two years earlier with J. J. Johnson, Horace Silver, and Kenny Clarke, brought the group long-overdue recognition. This successful performance served to mark the rebirth of Miles Davis and earned him a top spot in the *Down Beat* magazine's critics' poll that same year. He relinquished the top spot in this annual poll for only two years during the next 17 years.

Modal Jazz

Several personnel changes at the close of the 50s added more depth to Davis' quintet and brought a more modern sound to the group. These changes included Bill Evans, the replacement for the older style pianist Red Garland, and the addition of Cannonball Adderley to the front line, making the quintet a sextet. The two saxophonists—Adderley on alto and Coltrane on tenor—were stylistically different enough that they served to complement one another. Adderley was deeply rooted in the blues and hard bop traditions projecting a wonderful, bouncy, and happy sound, while Coltrane was the more contemporary player who shunned vibrato making his sound more metallic, brooding, and coldly passionate. The late 50s also marked the beginning of a longtime relationship Davis enjoyed with Columbia Records, which successfully cataloged nearly every major innovation in his career from this point on. The new sextet recorded two significant albums in 1958 and 1959 that served to revolutionize both the compositional and improvisational sides of jazz, and in many ways led Davis down a path that he would walk for the balance of his career. The new concept displayed on these recordings was labeled "modal" and was first introduced by the title track of the quintet's 1958 recording *Milestones* (though the original title was just "Miles"). While this track was the only modal composition included on the *Milestones* recording, it established new concepts that would revolutionize future generations of jazz players and composers, and served as the central theoretical basis behind Davis' next landmark 1959 release, *Kind of Blue*. Over time, this album sold more copies than any other Davis recording totaling more than 5 million worldwide. "I wanted the music this new group would play to be freer, more modal, more African or Eastern and less Western,"[7] he said. The modal concept was not new, but it was certainly new in terms of its applications to jazz in 1958. The theory of **modality** originated with the Greeks and medieval church music where entire pieces were based on one or two scales, also called modes. There are seven modes that can easily be seen by relating them to the white notes of the keyboard (see Example 12.1).

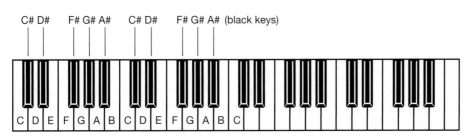

EXAMPLE 12.1
The keyboard helps to visualize the sequential nature of scales, modes, and chromatically altered notes.

The modal eight-note scale that begins on C and ends on C is called the Ionian mode. It is also called the C major scale. If one begins on D and plays all the same white notes ascending to the next D, this is the Dorian mode. If we began on E then we would construct the Phrygian mode. The Lydian mode begins on F, Mixolydian on G, Aeolian on A, and Locrian on B. Each of these seven "church modes," as they were called in ancient times, can begin on any of the 12 different notes (C, C#, D, D#, E, E# and so on) on the keyboard—so one could begin any of the seven modes on a black key or a white key by following the same pattern of half and whole steps.

Traditional tunes are constructed of melodies derived from a progression of different chords. The progression of chords is created by the tendency of one chord to move to another. Each different chord dictates a different relative scale and has a somewhat different quality. The chords in such a progression often feature notes that are chromatic in that they don't adhere to the given key signature or scale that serves as basis for the overall tune. Modal music, on the other hand, lacks these typical harmonic sequences and exists when melodies and harmonies are derived from pitches contained in a single scale that usually lasts for long periods (eight measures or more). Modal tunes center around one or two tones or key areas (D Dorian for example), occasionally shifting from one key center, or mode, to another (D Dorian to Eb Dorian as is the case in Davis' "So What"). Tunes of this nature establish a sense of tonality through long durations of one mode. The harmonies played as accompaniments to solos on modal tunes are all constructed exclusively from the notes found in the particular mode, even though there is an illusion of the pianist changing harmonies or chords (see Example 12.2). It is easier to grasp this concept and hear a modal tune when you focus on the bass that is rather static.

EXAMPLE 12.2

By using colors to represent sound, it is possible to differentiate between modal and functional harmony as shown in these illustrations.

Visual representation of a modal texture—the horizontal line represents the often static bass tone or pedal point in modal music, while the horizontal color bars represent shifting chords, all bearing some relationship to one another by sharing notes from the same scale or color palette.

Visual representation of functional harmony shown above—each different color bar represents a chord of different quality, often bearing no resemblance to the preceding or following harmony.

By taking jazz in an entirely new modal direction, away from what had become dominated by increasingly complex chord progressions, Miles Davis and his sextet made a bold statement in the late 1950s that provided newfound freedom to the improvising soloist. Improvisations became freer and were driven more by the importance of spinning out endless melodic lines through constant variation rather than concern for adhering to ever-changing chords. No longer were soloists confined by chord progressions that presented harmonic signposts to help guide or map them in specific directions through a maze that represented the form of the piece. Without fixed, repetitive chord progressions, modal tunes presented more uncharted maps, lacking fixed repetitive chord progressions and encouraging the soloist to go in any number of directions, forcing them to place more emphasis on melodic invention. One entire section of a modal tune might dwell on one mode for 16 measures before changing to another mode or key. One structural similarity between more traditional and modal tunes exists, however, in that both are often based on the song form architectural plan (AABA or ABA).

If necessary, review the sections about harmony and melody found on the CD-ROM in Chapter 2—The Elements of Jazz—to further clarify your understanding of these concepts. There is an example to further clarify the difference between modal and functional harmony found in the section about harmony.

The classic song form, defined as AABA, was the model that Davis used for his first two modal jazz pieces—"Milestones" (1958) and "So What" (1959). Either tune serves as an excellent example of this new style and "Milestones" is included in the companion audio anthology because it was the first of this style and offers some of the finest listening from this period of the Davis group's development. The overall scheme is classic bebop or hard bop in that there is a song form theme presented once and without introduction, followed by a series of improvised solos based on the form, before a predictable return to the theme. The thematic material is simple, yet beautifully concise and contrasting. The A theme may have originated from a background riff to become the central theme of this song. It is a series of ascending and descending short notes generated by the mode (scale). The B section is in stark relief, while still following a rise-and-fall contour, since now the scale-like pattern is played in a smooth, legato, and lyrical manner before returning to the crisp, punctuated A theme. All three soloists perform masterfully on this classic recording and each soloist has his own unique approach to improvising on the form, each showing how skillfully they can develop a melodic

(Left to right) Saxophonists John Coltrane and Cannonball Adderley join Miles Davis and pianist Bill Evans in a 1958 recording session.

idea before moving on to a new one. While each soloist has a somewhat different approach to the improvisation, each logically follows the preceding soloist by taking the last phrase of the previous improvisation as a starting point for a new improvisation. This tag team practice was typical of hard bop bands. The entire piece then evolves much like a coauthored story with each musician contributing his own paragraphs that relate the central themes. The rhythm section's accompaniment to each soloist is fairly consistent and based largely on the tune itself.

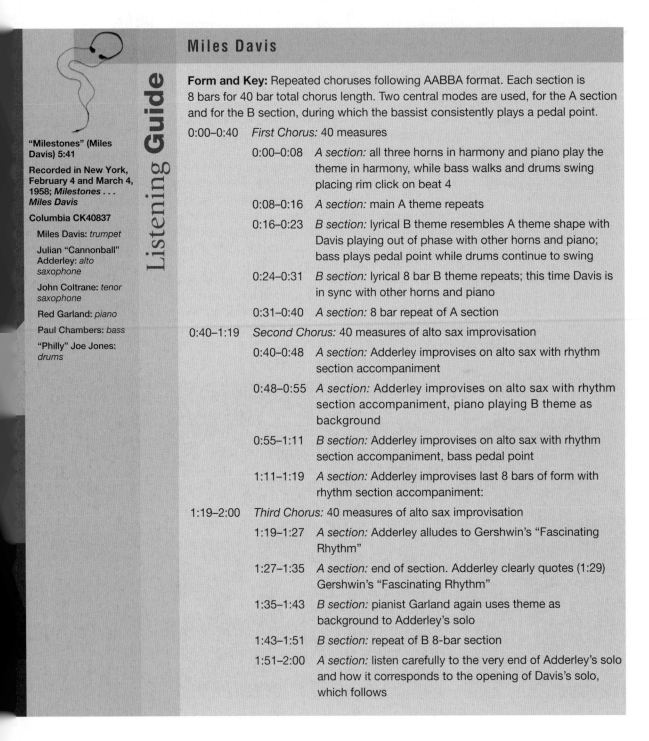

Miles Davis

Listening Guide

"Milestones" (Miles Davis) 5:41

Recorded in New York, February 4 and March 4, 1958; *Milestones . . . Miles Davis*

Columbia CK40837

Miles Davis: *trumpet*

Julian "Cannonball" Adderley: *alto saxophone*

John Coltrane: *tenor saxophone*

Red Garland: *piano*

Paul Chambers: *bass*

"Philly" Joe Jones: *drums*

Form and Key: Repeated choruses following AABBA format. Each section is 8 bars for 40 bar total chorus length. Two central modes are used, for the A section and for the B section, during which the bassist consistently plays a pedal point.

0:00–0:40	*First Chorus:* 40 measures	
	0:00–0:08	*A section:* all three horns in harmony and piano play the theme in harmony, while bass walks and drums swing placing rim click on beat 4
	0:08–0:16	*A section:* main A theme repeats
	0:16–0:23	*B section:* lyrical B theme resembles A theme shape with Davis playing out of phase with other horns and piano; bass plays pedal point while drums continue to swing
	0:24–0:31	*B section:* lyrical 8 bar B theme repeats; this time Davis is in sync with other horns and piano
	0:31–0:40	*A section:* 8 bar repeat of A section
0:40–1:19	*Second Chorus:* 40 measures of alto sax improvisation	
	0:40–0:48	*A section:* Adderley improvises on alto sax with rhythm section accompaniment
	0:48–0:55	*A section:* Adderley improvises on alto sax with rhythm section accompaniment, piano playing B theme as background
	0:55–1:11	*B section:* Adderley improvises on alto sax with rhythm section accompaniment, bass pedal point
	1:11–1:19	*A section:* Adderley improvises last 8 bars of form with rhythm section accompaniment:
1:19–2:00	*Third Chorus:* 40 measures of alto sax improvisation	
	1:19–1:27	*A section:* Adderley alludes to Gershwin's "Fascinating Rhythm"
	1:27–1:35	*A section:* end of section. Adderley clearly quotes (1:29) Gershwin's "Fascinating Rhythm"
	1:35–1:43	*B section:* pianist Garland again uses theme as background to Adderley's solo
	1:43–1:51	*B section:* repeat of B 8-bar section
	1:51–2:00	*A section:* listen carefully to the very end of Adderley's solo and how it corresponds to the opening of Davis's solo, which follows

2:00–2:40   *Fourth Chorus:* Miles Davis improvises first of 2 choruses on trumpet

       2:00–2:08   *A section:* Davis begins with opening phrase similar to Adderley's closing phrase

       2:08–2:16   *A section:* Davis plays more lyrically than either saxophonist and uses more space between ideas

       2:16–2:24   *B section:* Davis shows lyrical approach to bridge

       2:24–2:32   *B section:* continues lyrical approach while pianist uses thematic material for background

       2:32–2:40   *A section:* final 8 bars of chorus

2:40–3:21   *Fifth Chorus:* Davis' second 40 bar chorus with rhythm section accompaniment

       2:40–2:48   *A section:* Davis develops new idea; rhythm section swings with rim click on drums on every 4th beat

       2:48–2:57   *A section:* continues lyrical approach while piano continues to base comping on A theme

       2:57–3:05   *B section:* excellent example of thematic repetition and development

       3:05–3:13   *B section:* development of simple ideas continues

       3:13–3:22   *A section:* Davis plays just past the end of the chorus; listen carefully to his last phrase (3:20–3:21)

3:21–4:02   *Sixth Chorus:* John Coltrane's first chorus on tenor sax with rhythm section accompaniment

       3:23–3:30   *A section:* Coltrane begins by repeating Davis's last phrase but at another pitch level (called sequencing)

       3:30–3:38   *A section:* a "sheet of sound" gesture is evident at 3:33–3:34

       3:38–3:46   *B section:* Coltrane less lyrical about improvising on bridge than Davis

       3:46–3:54   *B section:* piano accompaniment again based B theme

       3:54–4:02   *A section:* solo culminates at altissimo note (4:00) followed by "sheet of sound"—like gesture (4:01–4:04) that carries Coltrane seamlessly from the end of chorus 6 to beginning of 7

4:02–4:45   *Seventh Chorus:* Coltrane's second chorus with rhythm section accompaniment

       4:02–4:11   *A section:* continuation of fast, sound sheet idea begins chorus

       4:11–4:19   *A section:* Coltrane plays very bop-like lines

       4:19–4:27   *B section:* uses fast sound sheet toward end of 8-bar phrase

	4:27–4:36	*B section:* additional fast sound sheet phrases again (4:31–4:32) that do not swing in traditional sense
	4:36–4:45	*A section:* finishes chorus by nearly playing too long into return of head
4:45–5:26	*Last Chorus:*	Repeat of the entire form AABBA before fading out
	4:45–4:52	*A section:* all three horns in harmony and piano play the theme in harmony while bass walks and drums swing
	4:52–5:01	*A section:* repeat of A theme in similar manner
	5:01–5:09	*B section:* alto, tenor, and piano play lyrical theme with Davis playing behind them, out of sync
	5:09–5:18	*B section:* same approach as in first B section, bass continues pedal point
	5:18–5:26	*A section:* final repetition of A theme
5:26–end	*Fade Out:*	tune ends with fade on opening A section

Coltrane and Adderley left Davis' quartet after the recording of *Kind of Blue* to pursue their own careers as leaders. The competent tenor saxophonist Hank Mobley replaced Coltrane who, along with other personnel rotated into the quintet's lineup, served during this transitional phase that linked Davis to perhaps his greatest, most prolific years with the second stable quintet. This quintet as well as the significant careers of Davis' sidemen will be discussed later in this chapter.

MILES AND GIL

Miles Davis had many interests and at times he was involved in more than one artistic direction at a time. "I met Gil Evans for the first time when he approached me about arranging 'Donna Lee.' I told him he could do it if he got me a copy of Claude Thornhill's arrangement of 'Robbins Nest' . . . I liked the way Gil wrote music and he liked the way I played."[8] Miles was particularly found of the lush orchestrations that Thornhill favored. Evans and Thornhill parted ways in 1948 and it was during this time that Evans and Davis began formulating a plan that led to the *Birth of the Cool.* "Gil and Gerry [Mulligan] had decided what the instruments in the band would be before I really came into the discussions," Miles said. "But the theory, the musical interpretation and what the band would play was my idea."[9] This collaboration would not be the last and in 1957, while John Coltrane was off serving his year informal apprenticeship with Thelonious Monk, they collaborated again to produce the first of several critically acclaimed recordings. These recordings established Evans as the new Svengali (ironically an anagram based on Gil Evans) of the arranging world, a title he still holds long after his death in 1988. The Davis-Evans partnership is perhaps the best known in jazz history and comparable to that of Duke Ellington and Billy Strayhorn. The 1957 project for the Columbia label was titled *Miles Ahead* and, like the *Birth of the Cool* sessions, featured an unusual combination of instruments and adventuresome arranging of an eclectic group of pieces. The orchestra included a full compliment of brass including

French horns and tuba in the Thornhill tradition; but in place of the traditional saxophone section Evans substituted flutes, clarinets, bass clarinet, and oboe—all instruments more closely associated with a classical music setting. This instrumentation created a tone pallet that became the Evans trademark for years to come. Evans, much like Ellington, hand-crafted each part with the knowledge that exceptionally gifted musicians would interpret them. In the case of the Evans-Davis collaborations, these musicians were the best studio musicians in New York, comfortable in classical and jazz idioms. Only such training would enable them to meet the challenges that Evans presented in his scores. Evans, once again like Ellington before, demonstrated a gift for mixing brass and woodwinds in unusual and previously untried combinations. The result was wonderful sonic pastels in which all of the individual sounds of the instruments lost their identity while contributing to the creation of an entirely new sound color. Evans biographer Stephanie Stein Crease stated that "Evans [had the ability] to orchestrate a mood." And Davis had an uncanny ability "to respond to the ambiance Gil created for him."[10] There was a special symbiotic relationship between this black soloist and white arranger, which first bloomed with the *Miles Ahead* project. This recording was based on a carefully sequenced group of pieces that represented an integrated suite or musical panorama as compared to the typical jazz recording that was often nothing more than a random collection of unrelated pieces.

The episodic suite became the foundation for two additional collaborations that followed—*Porgy and Bess* in 1958 and *Sketches of Spain* in 1959. Each project became more adventuresome. *Porgy*, George Gershwin's seminal work that premiered in 1935, was in some ways a misfit as it was neither an opera nor a Broadway musical. *Porgy* fit somewhere in the middle and could best be described as a purely American opera. Gershwin had already established himself as a somewhat controversial composer of symphonic jazz who blended together elements of jazz, blues and classical traditions. *Porgy* was Gershwin's most daring work, at least in terms of crossing boundaries. The Jewish born Gershwin composed a pseudo-opera *Porgy and Bess* that was based on black themes and set in a ghetto wharf known as "Catfish Row." What could have been more controversial in 1935? *Porgy* did survive the controversy and enjoyed successful revivals in 1943, 1952, and again in 1959 when Hollywood made the film version featuring Sidney Poitier, Dorothy Dandridge, Sammy Davis Jr., Pearl Bailey, and Diahann Carroll. "The film's production and release (June 1959) coincided with the rapidly growing Civil Rights movement" that was gaining momentum, and "once again, *Porgy* attracted criticism in the black community due to increasing sensitivity to racial stereotyping [and exploitation]."[11] The Davis-Evans remake of *Porgy* could not have been better timed and Davis' brooding, plaintive, vocal-like trumpet sound was the perfect instrumental sound to substitute for the traditional vocals in the original opera. *Porgy* is a masterpiece in terms of arranging, orchestration, and melding of soloist to ensemble. Davis used a complete arsenal of instruments including the trumpet, flugelhorn, and trumpet with a harmon mute—the sound that became his signature throughout his career. Some critics, though, openly objected to the lack of swing and presence of jazz tradition in Evans' arrangements. They felt that it was too orchestral to be real jazz.

Miles Davis with arranger Gil Evans during one of their collaborative recording sessions.

If necessary, reacquaint yourself with the sound of the harmon mute. This mute, along with examples of other brass instrument mutes, can be found on the CD-ROM in Chapter 3—Listening to Jazz. Excerpts of interviews with Evans and Davis among others who discuss their collaboration are also included on the CD-ROM in the corresponding chapter.

Both *Miles Ahead* and *Porgy* are also significant from a technological standpoint since both made use of stereo recording and the overdub process, at this point still a new technique. Overdubbing allowed Davis to play his solo parts after a polished recording of all the underlying instrumental accompaniments were recorded. This technique marked the beginning of a new era in recording. *Porgy and Bess* sold more copies immediately surrounding its release than any other Miles Davis recording until his *Bitches Brew* release in 1970 that quickly sold 400,000 copies. (*Kind of Blue* continues to break sales records, selling over 5 million copies worldwide to date and 5,000 more are sold daily in the United States.) *Miles Ahead*, *Porgy and Bess*, and the 1959 release of *Sketches of Spain* established Miles as a crossover artist, attracting many non-jazz record buyers. "Summertime"

Listening Guide

Miles Davis/Gil Evans

"Summertime"
(G. Gershwin,
I. Gershwin,
D. Heyward) 3:17

Recorded 8/18/58, New York, *Porgy and Bess*, Columbia CL 1274, Reissued Columbia CK 40647

Miles Davis: *trumpet*

Louis Mucci, Ernie Royal, John Coles, Bernie Glow: *trumpets*

Jimmy Cleveland, Joseph Bennett, Richard, Hixon, Frank Rehak: *trombones*

Julian Adderley, Daniel Banks: *saxophones*

Willie Ruff, Julius Watkins, Gunther Schuller: *French horns*

Philip Bodner, Romeo Penque: *flutes*

Bill Barber: *tuba*

Paul Chambers: *bass*

Philly Joe Jones: *drums*

Arranged by Gil Evans

Form and Key: Repeated 16-bar song choruses (A-A'), B♭ major in swinging 4/4, with ending tag

0:00–0:35	*First Chorus:* 16 bars, *Theme played by muted trumpet*, with repeated ascending French horn line, answering trombone, and woodwind descending lines, swinging rhythm section
0:35–1:10	*Second Chorus:* 16 bars, *Muted Trumpet Solo*, with continuing repeated ascending French horn line (add flutes), answering trombone and woodwind descending lines, swinging rhythm section
1:11–1:46	*Third Chorus:* 16 bars, *Muted Trumpet Solo* continues, with repeated ascending line now played by flutes and muted brass, answering trombone and woodwind descending lines, new closing ensemble melody (mm.15–16) based on ascending brass line, swinging rhythm section
1:46–2:21	*Fourth Chorus:* 16 bars, *Muted Trumpet Solo* continues, with backgrounds similar to Second Chorus, closing ensemble melody (mm.15–16) similar to Third Chorus, swinging rhythm section
2:22–2:57	*Fifth Chorus:* 16 bars, *Muted Trumpet Solo* continues, with repeated ascending line woodwind, answered by new tuba figure, trombone and saxophone descending lines, swinging rhythm section
2:58–3:17	*Tag:* 4 bars, bass tacit, *Trumpet Closes* on long note over first repeat of ascending line, with answering tuba; second repeat slows down to final ensemble chord

is no doubt the most famous track from the *Porgy* recording and this Evans arrangement has been the source for many other imitations since. The lush orchestrations using combinations of instruments that at times lose their individual identity and, when mixed together, represent an entirely new tone color.

THE SECOND GREAT QUINTET

Just as was the case in the formation of Miles Davis' first stable quintet, personnel for his second and most adventuresome group did not take shape immediately. His *Seven Steps to Heaven* recording from 1963 features two different pianists, two drummers, as well as a new saxophonist and bassist. *Seven Steps* is therefore a transitional recording and includes only two original compositions yet serves to introduce his new trio that will become the nucleus of this revolutionary new quintet—Herbie Hancock on piano, Ron Carter on bass, and the amazing young drummer Tony Williams. Tenor saxophonist George Coleman rounds out the quintet that followed with two additional recordings before Davis makes one final personnel change. These two live recordings—*My Funny Valentine* and *Four and More* show enough of the new band to indicate that a significant change in performance practice is underway, but it is not until Davis replaces the less adventuresome Coleman with Wayne Shorter that the quintet begins to soar in an entirely new direction. Davis recruited Shorter from Art Blakey's Jazz Messengers where Shorter had earned the title of musical director, shaping much of the Blakey band's repertoire. Pianist Hancock was also already a seasoned player with a recording contract for Blue Note Records and a modern approach to harmony and melodic invention. His recordings with hard bop trumpet ace Freddie Hubbard, another Blakey alumnus, have become legends on their own. *Maiden Voyage* in particular is a must for every serious jazz collector as is his *The Prisoner* and *Empyrean Isles*, where he combined funky tunes with very modern repertoire. All three new youthful rhythm mates were not afraid to go out on a limb and all were keenly aware of the importance of developing telepathic communication to attain the

Miles Davis Quintet with Wayne Shorter, tenor saxophone, Herbie Hancock, piano, Ron Carter, bass, and Tony Williams on drums.

cohesive, yet seemingly loose, free sound they were searching for. They sought to go on an entirely new journey each time they performed a piece and they took their listeners with them. This quintet revolutionized small group improvisation and ensemble playing. Drummer Tony Williams, only 17 years old when Davis hired him, had developed an entirely new way of playing that relied on total independence of each limb so that he could interject a constant barrage of polyrhythmic jabs, playing all around the fundamental beat but without interfering with the regularity of it. As a protagonist in the group he introduced constant interplay and dialogue. He didn't just play time as had been the tradition with all drummers before him, he played around the pulse without destroying it and could always rely on the steady bass lines played by Ron Carter to provide the necessary glue to keep things together. Williams was the first contemporary drummer to utilize the sock cymbal (hi-hat) on all four beats, as had been done years earlier with the bass drum. By this time, most postmodern drummers had elected not to use the bass drum on every beat. Each member of this rhythm section became recognized as the next important player in the jazz developments of their instruments.

The quintet's initial repertoire in 1964 was based largely on blues, Gershwin's "rhythm changes" model, and standards in the AABA song form. But this new quintet was destined to push the envelope much farther, challenging the old traditions and breaking entirely new ground. The group recorded six albums together, focusing more and more on original compositions that broke away from predictable chord sequences that for years had been appropriated from the Tin Pan Alley repertoire. Each band member contributed to the repertoire, creating tunes that destroyed old models and stereotypes by introducing unusual chord progressions that often seemed to have no beginning or ending. Shifting meters and changing tempos, as had been the case in much of Ornette Coleman's music earlier in the decade, also made this new repertoire unique and challenging. These tunes were almost always abstract and cerebral, serving a higher goal of freer group interplay and improvisations, the length of which was less dictated by the form and guided largely by the soloist. Some labeled this new direction "progressive" jazz, but whatever the label, the quintet was made up of explorers traveling new ground.

E.S.P., their first major release as a quintet, came in 1964 and the title track could be interpreted as their new group motto or higher goal. The subtle, intense level of improvised group interaction demonstrated on this and the five subsequent recordings up until 1969 was without equal at the time and marks the beginning of what most agree to be Davis' most creative period. Bassist and jazz historian Todd Coolman offered the following comments in his notes that accompanied the reissue of these historic recordings:

> The second great quintet combined elements that encompassed the entire history of jazz, including group improvisation and interaction reminiscent of early jazz groups from the 1920s, new compositional forms that revolutionized the relationship between jazz composition and improvisation, and phenomenal presence of a prodigy, drummer Tony Williams, whose revolutionary and unprecedented polyrhythmic approach served as a catalyst for the extraordinary creative expression that only the greatest jazz musician of that era could have produced.[12]

"Tony Williams was a phenomenon," said Herbie Hancock, the quintet's pianist. "Nobody was playing like him. He was creating a whole new approach to drumming and we actually clicked."[13]

The quintet's five additional recordings that followed *E.S.P* were *Miles Smiles*, *The Sorcerer*, *Nefertiti*, *Miles in the Sky*, and *Filles De Kilimanjaro*. Each recording featured primarily new compositions by band members, yet the quintet continued to perform the old, time tested repertoire ("Stella by Starlight," "Round About Midnight," "All of You," and "I Thought About You") in live concerts and not the daring new repertoire being recorded. The *Live at the Plugged Nickel* recordings are outstanding proof of this observation and show how each time Davis' quintet performed an "old chestnut," it became an entirely new and imaginative renovation compared to any earlier rendition. It is quite likely that Davis knew his recorded material was too demanding and esoteric for the general public and sought to make his live appearances more palatable.

"Orbits," the Wayne Shorter recording included on the companion audio anthology, appeared on the *Miles Smiles* recording and serves to exemplify this quintet's revolutionary new style. "Orbits" demonstrates Shorter's prowess as a composer who refined his craft with Davis' second great quintet. While on the surface this tune may appear to be quite simple, its true complexity nearly defies conventional analysis. The opening nine-bar introduction, divided into three, three-bar phrases, is stated in a very free, loose tempo, almost rubato that seems to imply a 3/4 meter rather than the more common 4/4 meter. Davis and Shorter then present the main thematic material in unison. This main theme, now in 4/4 meter, is repeated at the end of the recording following improvised solos, and can be described as three related phrases, each comprised of melodic fragments that rise and fall. These fragments are built largely on two intervals—the perfect fourth and the minor second (also described as half step). The three primary phrases that comprise the main melody are constructed in unusual lengths of six measures (with one measure in 3/4 meter to complicate matters at the end of the phrase), four measures, and 10 measures. Like Ornette Coleman's music, which clearly serves as an inspiration, this tune is presented without any well-defined harmonic structure. The melody implies chords, even though none are ever played, and an interesting chord progression can be constructed in which a juxtaposition of major and minor relationships is explored. Hancock is never heard until his single-line piano solo three-quarters of the way through the performance. Instead of being bound to chords, each soloist relies on melodic gestures from the main tune for improvisational inspiration and guidance. In some ways, this theme and variation approach to improvisation harkens back to the earliest days of jazz. Soloists use fragments of the tune to signal the end of their solos. Carter's bass lines remain rock solid throughout the performance, which is no easy task since the soloists and drummer Williams are constantly darting around rhythmic sign posts sometimes ignoring references to expected beat emphasis. While in constant dialogue, the group seems to do everything they can to play against the grain, rhythmically erasing any sense of regular meter or bar lines in favor of creating a free flowing pulse without regular accent. The title, like many progressive jazz performances of the times, alludes to being "far out," "spacey," experimental, and of another world. Aspects of this performance that make it unique can be summarized as follows:

1. Drummer Tony Williams does not play a traditional swing pattern until Herbie Hancock's piano solo, and even then it is not a clear swing pattern.
2. Williams seems to be playing a pattern that resembles a fast bossa nova beat.
3. No chords are played throughout the entire piece.
4. The improvised solos are short and concise.
5. The entire piece is based on the ongoing development of the initial melody. Melody exists in this piece for its own sake, to inspire improvisation, and with no real reference to prescribed chord changes.

6. Pianist Hancock is completely silent until his solo, during which he never plays a chord—only single note lines.
7. Each soloist makes significant use of and references to snatches of the original melody and always ends his improvisations with a reference to it. This seems to signal the end of their solo.

The outline that follows will help you to navigate through the performance of this challenging, somewhat abstract tune and performance.

Miles Davis Quintet

Listening Guide

"Orbits" (Wayne Shorter) 4:38

Recorded New York City 1966

Originally issued on *Miles Smiles* Columbia CS 9401

Miles Davis: *trumpet*

Wayne Shorter: *tenor saxophone*

Herbie Hancock: *piano*

Ron Carter: *bass*

Tony Williams: *drums*

Form and Key: Introduction followed by 20-measure, three-part form primarily in 4/4 meter and around G minor, but no clearly established key center.

00:00–00:09	*Introduction:*	Trumpet and tenor sax play opening gestures without strict tempo or meter, drums and bass loosely accompany for about 9 measures
00:09–00:15	*First Phrase:*	Trumpet and tenor sax play unison first phrase in clearer 4/4 meter but with implied 3/4 meter in next to last measure of phrase, bass and drums drop out at close of phrase
00:15–00:18	*Second Phrase:*	Trumpet and tenor sax play second short phrase of melody, bass walks implying more traditional 4/4 swinging time with drums
00:19–00:28	*Last Phrase:*	Horns complete statement of melody with a four-measure phrase repeated followed by a repeated two bar tag
00:28–1:38	*Trumpet Solo:*	Davis improvises freely accounting fragments of the main melody, bass and drums accompany
1:38–2:41	*Tenor Sax Solo:*	Shorter improvises freely using fragments of the main melody, bass and drums accompany
2:43–4:03	*Piano Solo:*	Hancock improvises freely using only his right hand to play single line melodies while bass and drums accompany
4:03–4:10	*First Phrase:*	Trumpet and tenor sax return to first phrase of melody played in unison while bass and drums continue to play time
4:10–4:13	*Second Phrase:*	Trumpet and tenor sax play second short phrase of melody with bass and drums swinging
4:13–4:38	*Last Phrase:*	Horns complete statement of melody with a four-measure phrase repeated followed by a two bar tag played two additional times before bass and drums trail off to end

The second quintet represented a "celebration in individuality,"[14] as Wayne Shorter put it, but without sacrificing the benefits of a collective product. The quintet completely shed bebop, the omnipresent influence throughout the 1950s and early 60s. Forms of tunes changed from night to night, each time being stretched to suit the needs dictated by each soloist.

With personnel changes to this stable quintet, following the recording of *Filles De Kilimanjaro* in 1968, a predictable change in musical direction gradually became evident and was manifested by three tunes in particular—"81" from the quintet's first recording *E.S.P.*, "Freedom Jazz Dance," a composition from *Miles Smiles* by an outsider, and "Tout de Suite" from the quintet's last recording *Filles De Kilimanjaro*. In each case, we begin to hear the following characteristics:

Straight rather than swung eighth notes

Repetitive bass lines or **pedal points** implying a modal approach more reflective of rock trends than jazz

Use of electric bass and piano

More rock, less swing style approach to the drum set by Tony Williams

These tracks clearly indicate that Miles Davis was headed in yet another new direction largely influenced by his earlier modal approach and the new popular music. This new style became more solidified with his next recording, *In a Silent Way* (1969), which boldly announced on the LP cover that Miles was once again charting new ground. The album cover included these words: "New Directions in Music." It is important to note that he did not label this new music as "jazz." Davis had now added an electric guitar (played by George Benson and later John McLaughlin), a predominant voice in popular rock and roll, and three electronic keyboards played by Herbie Hancock, Joe Zawinul, and Chick Corea who was to become his next regular band mate. The music on this recording is atmospheric, pensive, at times funky, and filled with layered electronic textures, a by-product of three keyboard players all improvising simultaneously. This recording is considered pivotal and marks Davis' transition from acoustic jazz, still influenced by traditional jazz roots, to his final stylist period.

THE ELECTRONIC JAZZ-ROCK FUSION PERIOD

"A lot of people started saying jazz was dead," said Miles in his autobiography, "and blaming the way-out free thing."[15] The way-out free thing wasn't what most people wanted to hear, however, and suddenly rock and roll was in the forefront. According to Davis, "White rock 'n' roll [was] stolen from black rhythm and blues people like Little Richard and Chuck Berry and the Motown sound."[16] Miles was interested in music coming from the pop side of black culture in the 1960s and was most intrigued by what musicians like Sly Stone and Jimi Hendrix were doing. Both of these pop artists were exponents of the rhythm and blues tradition. "Nineteen-sixty-nine was the year rock and funk were selling like hot-cakes," Miles told autobiography co-author Quincy Troup, "and all this was put on display at Woodstock. There were over 400,000 people at the concert. It was the first time in a long time that I didn't sell out crowds everywhere I played . . . we played a lot of half-empty clubs in 1969."[17] Davis had lost his appeal to his own people.

Columbia Records signed Blood, Sweat & Tears in 1968 and Chicago in 1969. Each group fused a jazz style horn section with the electric, rhythmic aspects of rock and roll and rhythm and blues styles. By this time jazz had become more distanced from mainstream popular culture than ever before. Jazz musicians found themselves totally out of sync with the younger audience, and the gap had never been quite so wide, except perhaps at the dawn of bebop. Rock and roll had not only captured white audiences' attention, it had driven young black musicians away from their jazz heritage. In the past, Parker, Ellington, Gillespie, and Monk had been heroes and inspirations to young black musicians, but now they abandoned their interest in jazz, choosing to side with a pop style that was hot and would make money—Hendrix, and the Motown sounds of The Four

Tops and the Temptations, Marvin Gaye, Sly Stone, and other black pop artists. Miles Davis and Columbia Records were primed to develop some new direction that would once again attract the attention of younger audiences and critics. The genesis of Davis' jazz-rock fusion period dates back to his *Filles De Kilimanjaro* recording where songs like "Tout De Suite" and "Stuff" introduced electronic keyboards, repetitive ostinato bass lines, and rock influenced straight eighth note drum styles. "I wanted to change course, had to change course for me to continue to believe in and love what I was playing,"[18] Miles said. Davis was a student of popular culture, and during the late 60s and early 70s he earned a grade of A+. He became the first in a long line of contemporary, postmodern jazz artists who found it necessary to periodically step back and reevaluate their music and become recharged by new trends in popular culture. In every case, Davis' sidemen have followed suit in that many of them have worn different stylistic hats throughout their careers, unlike earlier generations of jazz artists who largely specialized in one style.

Davis commented that, "When I went into the studio in August 1969 [to record *Bitches Brew*], besides listening to rock music and funk, I had been listening to Joe Zawinul and Cannonball [Adderley] playing . . . 'Country Joe' and 'The Preacher.'"[19] Miles Davis developed *In Silent Way* (1968) and *Bitches Brew* (1969–1970) from only a concept and brief sketches. He involved the musicians in spontaneous creativity, or as he put it, a "living composition,"[20] by taking his sketches and elaborating on them. He likened these sessions to the old-time jam sessions at Minton's. He wanted a feeling of spontaneity—a looseness that could only be the result of a group process, not some preordained, prearranged and composed exercise. "[The *Bitches Brew*] session was about improvisation, and that's what makes jazz so fabulous,"[21] he said. Once again, overdubbing allowed Miles and producer Teo Macero to go back and layer additional parts on top of what had already been recorded—in a sense to recompose. *Silent Way* and *Bitches Brew* were both heavily modal in quality and, while some motives, repetitive bass lines, and basic harmonies had been preconceived by Davis, the final composition and in some cases the final form of each composition on these recordings was left up to chance, spontaneous creativity, and editing on the part of the leader, his sidemen, and producer. It is clear that the free school's ideas about collective improvisation and the need for increased freedom in jazz had not gone unnoticed by Davis. His return to dance-oriented tempos, rhythms, and strong melodic content in later albums catapulted him once again to widespread fame, playing to large crowds in huge pop music venues like California's Fillmore East and West. His band, now augmented by electronic keyboards, percussion, and a host of electronic effects, opened for such popular rock groups as the Grateful Dead. Following the release of *Bitches Brew,* Davis won the *Down Beat* magazine Readers' and Critics' Polls for Record of the Year and Artist of the Year. That same year his pianist Herbie Hancock won the piano category and Wayne Shorter won the soprano saxophone category.

The following excerpt from *Bitches Brew*'s "Spanish Key" is a good illustration of the kind of music included on this landmark album that many point to as marking the dawn of the fusion, jazz-rock movement. (Tony Williams' own bombastic fusion trio with organist Larry

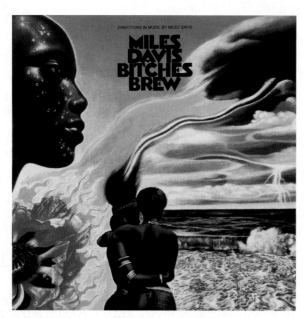

Miles Davis' landmark Bitches Brew *album cover.*

Young is often overlooked in such discussions.) The original recording of "Spanish Key" is 17½ minutes in its entirety, and at times is analogous to a crowded room of people at a party with many conversations providing the basic fabric, but with occasional more prominent voices coming to the foreground. There is a similar ebb and flow to this music as each soloist reaches a climax before passing on to the next soloist. There were striking similarities to Ornette Coleman's *Free Jazz* from nearly 10 years earlier. Both recordings (1) utilize two rhythm sections, (2) juxtapose one ensemble against another, and (3) feature precomposed, brief motives as mere springboards to lengthy improvisations. The principle differences that separate these landmark albums is that the Davis recording (1) makes use of electronic instruments, (2) features a straight eighth-note rock-influenced rhythmic pulse, (3) gravitates to a clear tonality, and (4) distinguishes the soloist from the crowd. The length of solos in "Spanish Key" was determined by Miles and the soloist during the performance, and with each solo a new key, mode, and tonality was launched. The outline that follows will help to guide you in listening to the "Spanish Key" excerpt included on the companion audio anthology.

Miles Davis

Form and Key: Essentially formless and through composed. Short precomposed motives link lengthy solos, each soloist marking a new modal key shift, 4/4 meter, jazz-rock rhythmic style

0:00–0:35	*Introduction:* 34 bars drums, then bass set up jazz-rock groove, joined by percussion, drums, guitar, bass clarinet, electric piano
0:36–1:16	*First section:* 38 bars, repeated 6-note *Trumpet Theme*, surrounded by bass clarinet, electric pianos, guitar, with repeated bass E pedal figure, drums, and percussion jazz-rock accompaniment
1:17–2:40	*Second section:* 78 bars, *Trumpet Solo,* surrounded by electric pianos, guitar, and bass clarinet, with repeated bass D pedal figure, drums, and percussion jazz-rock accompaniment
2:40–3:16	*Third section:* more intense *Trumpet Solo,* surrounded by more active and intense bass clarinet, guitar and electric pianos, with repeated bass E pedal figure, drums, and percussion jazz-rock accompaniment. Ensemble electric piano figure (3:11) closes section and moves to new key of G
3:17–5:21	*Fourth section:* trumpet solo gives way to *Guitar/Electric Piano dialogue,* surrounded by continuing bass clarinet, electric piano, with repeated 4-note bass figure in G, drums and percussion jazz-rock accompaniment. Ensemble electric piano figure (5:16) closes section
5:21–excerpt end	*Fifth section:* repeated 6-note *Trumpet Theme* as in First Section, surrounded by electric pianos, with repeated bass E pedal figure, drums and percussion jazz-rock accompaniment; serves as segue to next soloist

Listening Guide

"Spanish Key" (M. Davis) (excerpt) 5:30

Recorded New York, August 21, 1969 (released 1970), *Bitches Brew,*

Columbia BP 26, reissued Columbia Legacy C2K 65774

Miles Davis: *trumpet*

Wayne Shorter: *soprano saxophone*

Bennie Maupin: *bass clarinet*

John McLaughlin: *guitar*

Chick Corea: *electric piano*

Joe Zawinul: *electric piano*

Larry Young: *electric piano*

Dave Holland: *bass*

Harvey Brooks: *electric bass*

Jack DeJohnette: *drums*

Lenny White: *drums*

Charles Don Alias: *drums and percussion*

Jumma Santos: *percussion*

"Fewer and fewer black musicians were playing jazz and I could see why, because jazz was becoming the music of the museum. . . . They were only playing the same musical licks that we played way back with Bird, over and over again, along with some of the things Coltrane introduced, and maybe Ornette [Coleman]."[22] The jazz scene as seen through Davis' eyes had become stagnant and was certainly not engaging black audiences because it no longer was a mirror of popular culture as it always had been during its most successful years. Davis recorded another powerful rock influenced album in 1970 that could be considered the precursor of "heavy metal." The music for *Jack Johnson* was designed as a sound track for a film about the first black prizefighter to rise to supremacy despite threats from the Ku Klux Klan. Not unlike Miles, who was an amateur boxer, Johnson loved fancy clothes, flashy cars, and fast women. This recording perhaps even more than *Bitches Brew* marks the dawn of a new era for the jazz guitarist, for in this recording the instrument is elevated to new heights. John McLaughlin's screaming and distorted electric guitar wails its way through the entire recording, leaving space for cameo appearances by Davis. McLaughlin's dominant voice on this recording paves the way for his significant work yet to come in the 1970s.

By 1972, when Davis recorded *On the Corner*, his dress and his music mimicked the latest street culture—platform shoes, flashy colors, tight leather pants, headbands, vests, and so forth. Not only was he musically playing to the people but in his own creative way, he was visually playing to them as well. His concerts, like those by popular rock bands of the day, were as much happenings as they were concerts. He made use of tape loops, various electronic devices, and driving "minimalist" rhythm grooves long before the style and word was made popular in the world of twentieth-century classical music. "What I was playing on *On the Corner* had no label. It was actually a combination of some of the concepts of Paul Buckmaster, Sly Stone, James Brown and Stockhausen, some of the concepts I had absorbed from Ornette's music, as well as my own. The music was about spacing, about free association of musical ideas to a core kind of rhythm and vamps of the bass line."[23] Davis and his other soloists then layered their improvisations on top of what was an often rather simplistic, dance oriented rhythm section accompaniment. But focal points and the depth of field in his musical paintings were constantly changing (curiously like Ellington, Miles was a painter in his spare time). Borrowing the most innovative aspects of rock and roll (rhythm, bass ostinatos, vamps, and new electronic instruments and effects) and fusing these ingredients with free form improvisation, Davis single-handedly created the next stylistic wave in jazz that had a significant impact on its future.

Miles Davis summarized his own views on jazz musicians and the question of popularity by saying that: "As a musician and as an artist, I have always wanted to reach as many people as I could through my music. And I have never been ashamed of that. I always thought I should reach as many people as I could, like so-called popular music, and why not? . . . Jazz was never meant to reach just a small group of people, or become a museum thing locked under glass like all other dead things that were once considered artistic."[24]

Miles Davis making his typical 1989 fashion statement.

By 1974, numerous health problems forced Davis into retirement, but like the phoenix, he was resurrected in 1981 with the release of *The Man with the Horn*. But it was his second effort during this final period, *We Want Miles* released in 1982, that showed he still had what it took. This live recording featured a catchy nursery rhyme tune entitled "Jean Pierre" that took the jazz world by storm. "Hip," informed soloists in small jazz groups around the nation were quoting from this simple tune. "Jean Pierre" became the rage and was evidence of Davis' continued ability to be musically charismatic.

During his final years, Miles performed a mixed repertoire that even included an arrangement of pop artist Cyndi Lauper's "Time After Time." His most successful performances during these final years were the result of collaborations with guitarists Mike Stern and John Scofield along with bassist/composer/producer Marcus Miller. Often sophisticated, this modern repertoire still showed roots in the jazz tradition. For instance Scofield's title track from *You're Under Arrest* (perhaps referring back to the illegal bust in front of Birdland in the 1940s) was based essentially on the time tested Gershwin AABA "I've Got Rhythm" model. Davis' *Tutu*, produced in collaboration with Marcus Miller, is reminiscent of the highly orchestrated, textural style of Gil Evans, only in this case achieved not by acoustic instruments but with layers of orchestrated electronic sounds.

Davis' final studio 1992 recording *Doo Bop* once again proved that he had his ear to the street. This collaboration with rapper Easy Moe Bee bears all the signs of street music with infectious, machine-like and throbbing bass and drum grooves providing the landscape for Davis' improvisation. Dance grooves permeate the recording, along with a few more seductive tempos. While Davis was in good form, the repetitive vamps and sampled drums that surround him are a bit tiresome and lack the spontaneity that lie at the heart of good jazz and earlier work by Davis.

No other instrumentalist in the history of jazz had such a presence and lasting impact on this music. Davis ranks with a select few including Armstrong, Ellington, and Parker as a true innovator. But unlike any of these icons who had preceded him, Davis was a chameleon, always changing his course and updating his approach. Davis was always on the move, never so deeply rooted in one particular tradition that he was not able, willing, and eager to change. In many ways, this one man's career represents the essence of what jazz was and should be—music in constant transition and evolution, borrowing from the past, but not stuck in it.

MILES DAVIS SUMMARY

Miles Davis

1. Was active in seven different styles—bebop, cool, third stream, modal, hard bop, progressive or post–hard bop, and fusion.
2. Preferred the middle and low register rather than the extreme high register, though at times spikes and flares into the high register were used as an element of surprise and tension.
3. Employed an economy of style where space was often favored over long, notey passages.
4. Often used the harmon mute.
5. Developed a unique and identifiable sound and attack. His sound could change like the weather and varied from dramatic to passionate, cold, and militant.

6. As a melodic improviser, was less concerned about harmony and often played phrases of unusual length.
7. Avoided bebop clichés, though vocal-like blues influences can be found in his playing.
8. Had a lyrical tone that frequently lacked noticeable vibrato.
9. Preferred a linear, scalar approach instead of the vertical, arpeggiated style.
10. Demonstrated an element of angularity and preference for chromatic, more dissonant passages as his style matured.
11. Was ever evolving, never resting on prior accomplishments—the most significant innovator in the postmodern jazz era.

THE DAVIS SIDEMEN BECOME MAJOR FORCES

John Coltrane (1926–1967)

Tenor saxophonist John Coltrane was as important to the development of jazz in the postmodern period as Parker was to the moderns. Every player who followed Coltrane, or "Trane" as he was nicknamed, has been significantly influenced by the repertoire he created and his new approaches to the instrument. Like Parker, he was equally comfortable with blues, ballads, standards, and up-tempo repertoire. He added to this older cannon a new repertoire that included complex, fast-paced tunes, harmonically fresh ballads, free-form atonal pieces, modal music, and cross-culturally influenced works that moved jazz in several new directions.

Coltrane was born in North Carolina but began to mature as a saxophonist while playing in the Philadelphia area with blues and dance bands. While his roots were in blues and hard bop, he was destined to be a major voice in the later developments of modal and free jazz. Coltrane rose to prominence as a member of Miles Davis' first great quintet. At this point in his development he was considered a disciple of bop saxophonists Sonny Stitt and Dexter Gordon but with more technique and a tendency towards more jagged phrases. He left the Davis quintet in 1957 to take up with pianist Thelonious Monk for a period that proved to be one of the most rewarding experiences in his training. Monk taught him more about harmony and melodic development. "Working with Monk," Coltrane said, "brought me close to a musical architect of the highest order. Monk was one of the first to show me how to make two or three notes at the same time [multiphonics]."[25] Their live recordings together from the Five Spot are now considered significant in the documented evolution of both careers.

Coltrane first encountered the modal style upon his return to the Miles Davis band in 1958 and subsequently participated in both recordings that served to introduce the style to the world—*Milestones* and *Kind of Blue*. Perhaps it was these encounters with modal music that led him to develop a new technical approach to improvising on a harmony. Ira Gitler, writing for *Down Beat* magazine, was the first to describe this technique as "sheets of sound."[26] Coltrane played such rapid bursts of notes (usually ascending) that each individual note was indistinguishable and the by-product was as close to the sound of a chord as a saxophone was capable of producing. Chords can be played on a keyboard instrument, guitar or vibes, but wind instruments are nearly incapable of playing more than one note at a time (aside from multiphonic techniques). Coltrane's "sheets" of notes, always played as a rapid gesture, are as close as one can come to sounding a complete harmony on the instrument. The effect is very akin to running your thumb up the strings of a harp or piano keyboard. Another striking aspect of these gestures is that they did not swing, since the notes were played so fast, and this was a very new concept to jazz since previously it was thought that everything one played should swing and fit within the context of the rhythm section's steady pulse. One could say that he played against the time or pulse, or simply ignored it. These techniques became part of Trane's musical signature—his style. His **sheets of sound** led to explorations of other new devices, many of which became adopted by serious, contemporary classical saxophonists and composers. Later in his career, for example, Coltrane began utilizing both harmonic fingerings and **multiphonics.** Harmonic fingerings enabled him to produce an unusual **timbre** (tone quality) on certain notes by using unorthodox fingerings to produce them. The principle relates to simple laws of physics that govern the vibration of a string. When a string is set in vibration and then divided at certain points, different higher pitches above the fundamental pitch established by the string length will result. These pitches above the fundamental note are called **harmonics.** All musical instruments make use of this basic principal. Multiphonics are produced by special fingerings that enable the instrument to sound more than one note at a time. It was a logical progression for Coltrane to move from his "sheets of sound" effect to multiphonics.

Even before he left Davis' group, Coltrane had secured the interest of major record labels. In Miles' own words: "The group I had with Coltrane made me and him a legend. It also brought me great critical acclaim because most of the critics really loved this band."[27] "Trane" recorded two landmark recordings under his own name while still performing with Miles—*Blue Trane* (Blue Note 1957) and *Giant Steps* (Atlantic 1959). Ironically, both of these recordings are the antithesis of the modal style he had been introduced to by Davis at this same time. These recordings mark the culmination of Coltrane's involvement in the post–hard bop style and are considered to be the penultimate conclusion of his immersion in tunes that presented complex harmonic progressions. In both recordings, most notably *Giant Steps*, he explores complex chord changes derived by substituting new chord sequences for more typical, expected ones. He was clearly concerned at this time with developing total control of his instrument, practicing obsessively to develop a virtuosic technique that allowed him to address any challenge, harmonic or technical. Both the title track from *Giant Steps* and "Countdown" from the same recording are excellent examples of this advanced period in Coltrane's development. While neither tune is a beautiful work of art since both served as technical exercises for Coltrane, both tunes continue to be important yardsticks in measuring saxophonists' progress, prowess, and level of achievement. The ability to improvise on "Giant Steps" and "Countdown" has become a necessary rite of passage for all saxophonists. In stark contrast to this complex harmonic style, Coltrane includes "Naima," which is far more static and modal in conception, featuring pedal point bass lines with slow moving harmonies. *Down Beat* magazine awarded five stars to this recording and a retrospective review pointed out several significant factors: it was his first recording to include completely original tunes; he introduced the pedal point (repetitive bass tone with changing harmonies above) as an effective compositional device in jazz; and he reached a new plateau of virtuosic control that has taken nearly 30 years to equal and surpass.[28] With these two recordings at the close of the 1950s, Coltrane took hard bop to the brink in terms of harmonic complexity, and sheer virtuosity. "Lazy Bird," a Coltrane composition included on the companion CD anthology, is a fine example of this complexity and the ease with which Coltrane negotiated challenging chord progressions at brisk tempos. The sidemen on this record date are in good form representing some of the finest hard bop soloists of the day, and two-thirds of the rhythm section (Chambers and Jones) had worked with Coltrane as members of Miles Davis' quintets so there was good chemistry. Trombonist Curtis Fuller clearly descends from the earlier J. J. Johnson bebop trombone style.

Listening Guide

John Coltrane

"Lazy Bird" (Coltrane) (excerpt) 4:31

Recorded in New York, 9/15/57

Blue Note Records reissued on CDP 7243 8 53428 0 6

John Coltrane: *tenor sax*

Lee Morgan: *trumpet*

Curtis Fuller: *trombone*

Kenny Drew: *piano*

Paul Chambers: *bass*

Philly Joe Jones: *drums*

Form and Key: Repeated 32-bar song-form (AABA = chorus), in G major

0:00–0:07	*Introduction:* 8 measures featuring piano
0:08–0:15	*First Chorus:* A section theme played by trumpeter Lee Morgan
0:16–0:23	Trumpet repeats A theme
0:24–0:31	Bridge or B theme played by trumpet with tenor sax/trombone counterline in call–response style with trumpet
0:32–0:38	Trumpet ends first chorus with repeat of A theme
0:39–1:08	*Second Chorus:* Improvised trumpet solo on entire AABA form with rhythm section accompaniment
1:09–1:39	*Third Chorus:* Trumpet solo continues on form with rhythm section
1:40–2:10	*Fourth Chorus:* Trombone solo featuring Curtis Fuller with rhythm section accompaniment
2:11–2:40	*Fifth Chorus:* Trombone solo continues
2:41–3:11	*Sixth Chorus:* Coltrane enters with first of several choruses
3:12–3:42	*Seventh Chorus:* Tenor sax continues solo
3:43–4:14	*Eighth Chorus:* Coltrane plays final solo chorus
4:15 to end	Excerpt ends with beginning of piano solo

Coltrane eventually left Davis to strike out on his own, abandoning the dense, complex harmonic web in which he had become entangled and immersing his new quartet in a steady diet of modal music. He pursued this new style as if it were a religion, seeking more and more freedom to express new emotions. With pianist McCoy Tyner, drummer Elvin Jones, and bassist Jimmy Garrison, they popularized modal jazz to an extent that undoubtedly surprised even the record label executives. *My Favorite Things*, the quartet's first highly acclaimed 1960 recording, featured Coltrane on soprano saxophone as well as tenor. Sidney Bechet had been the only other jazz instrumentalist to use the soprano with any regularity. The soprano had become little more than a footnote until this recording revived interest in the instrument. Improvements in its design made it more acceptable and since the 1960s the instrument has become standard in the saxophonist's arsenal. Coltrane's sound on this instrument was as unique and personal as it was on tenor. He evoked an eastern or North African flavor on the soprano, at times producing a sound similar to the nasal quality of Indian reed instruments or the oboe developed centuries earlier in Europe to perform classical music.

The intensity of this quartet, with Coltrane on soprano sax and tenor, Tyner and Jones in the rhythm section, is remarkable—spellbinding in its intensity and without comparison at the time, at least for a small group. The "Afro Blue" excerpt included on the companion CD collection is no exception, comparing favorably to his other modal work at the time. He seemed to prefer up-tempo 3/4 meters for the lengthy soprano sax excursions, and this live recording along with "Inch Worm" and "My Favorite Things" all share this quality. Drummer Elvin Jones is explosive, constantly prodding pianist Tyner and Coltrane, dropping salvos with bass drum and cymbals while injecting machine gun-like chatter with his other hand. The excerpt begins at the close of Tyner's solo, propelled by the trio to a fevered pitch that requires Coltrane to begin his solo at this precipice and build from there. Since the excerpt begins in midtrack, you may want to first listen to the return of the tune from 3:08 to 4:34 before listening to the entire track.

John Coltrane

Form and Key: Two contrasting phrases each 8 measures (AB Improvised Interlude A'B); modal in F minor

0:00–0:28	Pianist McCoy Tyner builds the end of his solo to a climax
0:29	Coltrane enters in the extreme high register of the soprano sax
3:08	Coltrane returns to the first section of the original melody
3:22	Coltrane begins improvising again
4:19–4:34	Coltrane plays the second portion of the main theme
4:35	Quartet begins to wind down dynamically
5:46	Group states last phrase of tune in dramatic rubato style

Listening Guide

"Afro Blue" (Mongo Santamaria) (excerpt)
6:00

Recorded live at Birdland in New York, 10/8/63

Impulse Records IMPD-198

John Coltrane: *soprano sax*

McCoy Tyner: *piano*

Jimmy Garrison: *bass*

Elvin Jones: *drums*

The modal repertoire and recordings that followed, including the highly touted *A Love Supreme*, demonstrated a growing spirituality in its leader. Many of the pieces on these recordings, including the originally released version of "Impressions," were long incantations—lengthy improvisations that kept building in hypnotic intensity much like "Afro Blue." Critics and listeners were captivated, awarding him Jazzman of the Year, record of the year, first place in the tenor saxophone category and electing him to the *Down Beat* Hall of Fame, all following the release of *A Love Supreme* in 1965. This recording was one of his most compelling and lasting works, selling a million copies by the close of the 1970s, 20 years after it was recorded.[29] Supplemental listening guides to "Acknowledgement" from *A Love Supreme* and "Impressions" are provided in the corresponding chapter on the CD-ROM.

Following an all too familiar bout with drug and alcohol addiction, Coltrane had turned toward religion and philosophy to seek inner peace and to help him on his personal and musical journey. He is the first jazzman to overtly present his music as a religious offering, as was the case with *A Love Supreme*. The music on this recording, and others that followed, borders on meditations or prayers such as "Alabama," his elegy for four small girls who lost their lives in the 1963 Birmingham church bombing. "Alabama" is a riveting testament to the mood of the

Tenor saxophonist John Coltrane in New York, 1961.

times, when the eyes of the nation were riveted on individuals like Governor Faubus who sent National Guard troops to keep young black school children from attending school. This situation and many others like it were reflected in the music of many black artists during this time. His search for spirituality led him to the study of Indian music and he also showed an interest in Latin, Arabic, and African music. Hence, Coltrane is often considered the first jazz musician to seriously pursue world music styles and consciously weave them into his new brand of American jazz. These influences are most evident in *Africa Brass*, *Olé Coltrane*, and "India" among others. One gets the impression after hearing Coltrane's performances from this modal period and beyond, that he is searching, at times desperately reaching and crying out with his distinctive vocal-like wails for something that was unattainable. With its folk-like quality, there is a sense of both deep passion and inner torment in his music. His tone was unique, often lacking vibrato, projecting a steely quality and a vocal-like primordial cry as if he were in pain. The metal mouthpiece he used instead of the hard rubber or plastic variety no doubt contributed to his ability to deliver his unique and identifiable tone. His sound has been described as hard-edged, metallic, and brittle. As Wayne Shorter once said, "he had a sense of urgency like he couldn't get everything he wanted out."[30] At other times, as shown on his *Ballads* recording, he could be more caressing, rarely straying far from merely interpreting the beautiful melodies of these tunes.

Coltrane's quartet continued to push the boundaries in the early 60s and in 1961 he added multireed player Eric Dolphy to the quartet. While Dolphy played flute and alto saxophone, he is most remembered for unleashing the potential of the bass clarinet, an instrument that had rarely been explored for its potential as a jazz solo instrument. Now a quintet, their performances became more and more abstract, featuring relentless, long solos. One tune could last an entire set in a live performance or occupy the entire side of a recording. Some labeled the group's new direction, and that of other black experimentalists, as "the new thing" or "outside" jazz. Coltrane defended their long solos: "they're long because all the soloists try to explore all the avenues that the tune offers. They try to use all their resources."[31] But many audiences became alienated and turned off by what they perceived as a self-indulgent attitude. After attending a live club date, a *Down Beat* correspondent wrote: "I heard a good rhythm section . . . go to waste behind the nihilistic exercises of the two horns . . . Coltrane and Dolphy seem intent on deliberately destroying swing. They seem bent on pursuing an anarchistic course in their music that can be termed anti-jazz."[32] Dolphy expanded his possibilities with the flute, sometimes deriving his inspiration from birdcalls and the 1/4-tone whistles that they sometimes sing. Both instrumentalists seemed to want to begin with a blank easel that could be totally open and responsive to their feelings and surroundings. Their music was about finding new ways to communicate with their instruments in an effort to convey their innermost feelings to the listener. "The main thing a musician would like to do is to give a picture to the listener of the many wonderful things he knows of and senses,"[33] Coltrane said. The "new thing" put off some critics and listeners and some were openly critical, accusing the artists of abandoning the tradition including "swing." "It's kind of alarming to the musician," Dolphy said, "when someone has written something bad about what the musician plays but never asks the musician anything about it."[34]

Coltrane continued to push the boundaries of jazz and by 1965 it seemed that he had exhausted the possibilities that modal jazz presented, just as he had several years before with harmonically complex hard bop. The only logical alternative for Coltrane was to venture into completely unknown and unpredictable territory as Ornette Coleman had done several years earlier. "In the early 60s he was studying with me," Coleman said. "He was interested in non-chord playing, and I had cut my teeth on that stuff."[35] The work he had done with Coleman and the new breed of black musicians experimenting with the "new thing" no doubt all had a major impact on Coltrane, moving him toward his final phase of exploration—free jazz. Perhaps it was the sense of chaos that everyone who lived through the 60s felt that also motivated Coltrane to move further outside of tradition, motivating him to assemble one of the most important recordings in this history of jazz—*Ascension*. In this recording, Coltrane abandoned predictability as Coleman had done with his *Free Jazz*. The roles of meter, pulse, melody, harmony, and form were redefined since they were nearly nonexistent. Ironically it was released the same year that he was awarded Jazzman of the Year for his work on the *Love Supreme* recording, but *Ascension* was far less accessible to the average listener. Listeners often have more difficulty appreciating recorded free jazz, regardless of the artist, as compared to the energy of the live experience. *Ascension* featured four saxophonists, two trumpets, two bassists, one drummer, and a pianist. Nothing was pre-composed aside from the opening five-note melody introduced by Coltrane. What follows is 38 minutes of unstructured improvisation, an orgiastic free-for-all that portrays the contrast between group chaos and free form solos by the individual instrumentalists. The solos, like that of saxophonist Pharaoh Sanders, were at times streams of shrieks, squawks, screams, squeaks, shouts, hollers, cries, moans, yells, wails, and occasional blues-inflected melodies. The soloists were not bound by any prescribed or accepted syntax, making them free of melodic, rhythmic, harmonic, and structural conventions. It was this blatant attack on accepted standards and the very tradition itself that enraged many. The nonmusical effects served to turn off many listeners and incited their "anti-jazz" allegations. The release of this recording was the most controversial event in jazz since Coleman's *Free Jazz*, eliciting such criticism as "unattractive" and the result of Coltrane "going off the deep end."[36] But the jazz community was polarized since others felt *Ascension*, and the other free jazz works that followed, were inspirational and challenging, elevating jazz to a new plateau of art music. Tenor saxophonist Archie Shepp who performed on *Ascension* described Coltrane as a great musical scientist "merging black art with black science."[37] *Down Beat* magazine in 1966 came out in favor of the recording describing it as "possibly the most powerful human sound ever recorded."[38]

John Coltrane lived only two more years, passing away as the result of liver cancer in 1967. His death shook the jazz world much as the loss of Parker had.

Saxophonist Eric Dolphy during the recording session for his Out to Lunch *album, his last American recording before his unexpected death four months later.*

His candle had burned quickly and perhaps that is why he had been so compulsive and obsessive about accomplishing so much in such a short time. His influence has been pervasive in much of the jazz produced after 1960 and he continues to exert a significant influence on contemporary saxophonists like Branford Marsalis, Michael Brecker, James Carter, Kenny Garrett, Joshua Redman, and Chris Potter among others.

John Coltrane Summary John Coltrane

1. Was active in three different phases of jazz—hard bop, modal, and free.
2. Had a penchant for lengthy improvisations.
3. Produced a highly original tone quality that often lacked vibrato, projecting a plaintive quality.
4. Reintroduced and popularized use of the soprano saxophone.
5. Discarded long improvised lines in favor of developing smaller motives or melodic cells.
6. Was one of the first jazz musicians to overtly incorporate music of other cultures, Western and non-Western.
7. Played music that was deeply inspired and informed by the blues tradition.
8. Developed new saxophone performance techniques including "sheets of sound," multiphonics, and harmonic fingerings in addition to extending the range of the instrument into the altissimo register.
9. Sometimes played purposefully dissonant lines that were outside the given key (chord). This practice is often referred to as "side-stepping" or playing "outside."
10. Significantly raised the bar for all future performers through his sheer virtuosity and challenging compositions.
11. Established a new approach to freer, open modal playing.
12. Openly used music to express his religious and social beliefs.
13. Was the most important postmodern tenor saxophonist.

Wayne Shorter (b 1933)

Born in Camden, New Jersey, Wayne Shorter pursued and completed a BA degree in music education at New York University before joining the armed forces. By the time Shorter made his first appearance with Miles Davis in 1964 he had already established himself as an important voice working with Horace Silver, Maynard Ferguson, and Art Blakey. Like so many saxophonists in the early 60s, Shorter was profoundly influenced by Coltrane, but also bore similarities to both Lester Young and the more contemporary Sonny Rollins in terms of his gift for melodic development. In comparison to Coltrane, his tone was softer and lighter, more in the Young tradition, and somewhat broader. Shorter, like Coltrane, used vibrato only sparingly, which made it that much more poignant when he did. The most unique aspect of Shorter's style was his sense of rhythm. While he could lock into the groove of a rhythm section and swing with the best of them, he often chose not to, floating over the top of the regular pulse and upsetting the listener's equilibrium with a sense of unanticipated expectation. His preference for long tones and space over blinding bursts of notes often gives one the impression that he is playing "slower than the rhythm sections that accompanied [him]."[39] In contrast to Coltrane's earlier hard bop style and more in resonance with his later approach, Shorter rarely quoted anyone except himself and his improvisations are barren of any clichés. Much like Miles Davis, Shorter tended to spin melodies that were grouped in odd numbers of measures and his choice of notes also contributes to his unique and original approach. He was a guiding force as a saxophonist and composer in the famous Davis quintet of the mid-60s, just as he had been with Art Blakey's Jazz Messengers in prior years. "Wayne was the idea person, the conceptualizer of a whole lot of musical ideas we did,"[40] Miles said. "Wayne has always been someone who experimented with form instead of someone who did it without form [referring no doubt to the free jazz movement]. That's why I thought he was perfect for where I wanted to see the music I played go. He understood that freedom in music was the ability to know the rules in order to bend them to your own satisfaction and taste. That's why I say he was the intellectual musical catalyst for the band."[41] His compositions often broke rules when compared to Tin Pan Alley standards. Unusual forms and chord progressions, dictated more by melody and improvisation than functional harmony, are his trademarks. His tunes often do not adhere to simple and predictable architectures, but take the shape of 14, 18, and 20 measures. He sees composition and improvisation as closely intermingled and consequently it is not unusual when a Shorter composition flows freely and seamlessly between written and improvised material, blurring the lines between composition and improvisation. "Paraphernalia" (*Miles in the Sky*), "Dolores" (*Miles Smiles*), and "Masqualero" (*Sorcerer*) serve as excellent examples of this approach. An intellectual artist, Shorter's compositions are often motivated by nonmusical occurrences. For example, his 1964 *Speak No Evil* recording was inspired by folklore, black magic, and legends. Shorter says, "I was thinking of misty landscapes with wild flowers and strange, dimly seen shapes—the kind of places where folklore and legends are born. I'm getting stimuli from things outside of myself. Before I was concerned with . . . my ethnic roots, but now I'm trying to fan out, to concern myself with the universe instead of just my own corner of it."[42] His improvisations are as thoughtful as his compositions and are always perfectly conceived in terms of their reference to the original tune. In contrast to Coltrane who played obsessively long, self-indulgent solos, Shorter was the master of the understatement, producing short compositions and even more abbreviated solos with each note thoughtfully placed.

Shorter left Davis's quintet at the close of the decade to enable a more focused pursuit of his own career. You will see when we examine his impact throughout the 1970s, discussed in more detail in Chapter 13, why Wayne Shorter is considered one of the most influential jazz musicians of the late twentieth century.

Herbie Hancock (b 1940)

Herbie Hancock was the most important jazz pianist to hit the scene following Wynton Kelly and Bill Evans. The bond between all three was not only stylistic, as Hancock borrowed from both artists who preceded him, but also because each performed with Miles Davis. His stylistic diversity, another characteristic he shares in common with many of the Davis sidemen, has earned him fans from the pop, jazz, and to some degree classical worlds since as a child prodigy he performed with the Chicago Symphony. Since then, Hancock somehow managed to maintain multiple careers, freely moving between solo piano performances, producing and recording in pop and jazz worlds, film scoring, experimenting with the latest electronic technology, and performing with cutting edge jazz groups both mainstream and avant-garde.

Hancock was already an established musician when he signed on with the Miles Davis Quintet. While working with Davis he continued to maintain a profile as a leader on records and as a highly sought after sideman. It would be difficult to find a pianist who has participated on more recordings and in more diverse settings than Hancock, listing collaborations on his discography with, among others

Lee Morgan, Freddie Hubbard, Donald Byrd, Hank Mobley, Eric Dolphy, Kenny Dorham, Blue Mitchell, Wayne Shorter, Jackie McLean, Paul Desmond, Wes Montgomery, Quincy Jones, and Stanley Turrentine.

His pianistic style is derived from two distinct genealogy lines—the harmonically rich style associated with Bill Evans and the right-hand technical approach fostered by a long line of pianists including Bud Powell, Oscar Peterson, and Wynton Kelly. Hancock's comping style is also highly personal and identifiable for its crispness and rhythmic agility. Hancock's solos are often contrasting in terms of dynamics, density, and texture, juxtaposing dense harmonic passages with single-note lines. One can often sense his classical training, which provides him the facility to perform the most difficult passages with ease.

Hancock's first recording as a leader in 1962 featured the funky, gospel-tinged "Watermelon Man," one of the most widely performed pieces from his repertoire along with the modal "Maiden Voyage" from his 1965 recording by the same name. "Watermelon Man" and "Cantaloupe Island" from his 1964 release entitled *Empyrean Isles* were revived and became part of the foundation of the acid jazz movement of the later 1990s. Other compositions by Hancock that were penned in the 1960s and have since become part of the jazz canon include "Dolphin Dance," featured on his *Maiden Voyage* album, and "Speak Like a Child," the title track from his 1968 release. Hancock was a major force in shaping jazz over the next several decades, particularly the 1970s during which time his Jekyll and Hyde musical personality was difficult to track.

One should not underestimate the contributions Miles Davis' sidemen made in reshaping jazz during and after their apprenticeships with the great master. Chapter 13 will look more closely at these and other Davis sidemen who continued to exercise a significant influence on shaping jazz through the end of the twentieth century.

Jazz in Perspective

The timeline that follows will put the developments of jazz discussed in this chapter into a larger historical context, providing you with a better sense of how landmark musical events may relate to others that match your personal areas of interest.

1958
- Texan Van Cliburn wins Tchaikovsky Piano Competition.
- NASA created to bolster U.S. position in space race.
- Kingston Trio, Everly Brothers, Little Richard, Rick Nelson, and Chuck Berry are pop music successes.
- Miles Davis' Sextet records the modal composition "Milestones."
- Miles Davis collaborates with Gil Evans to create *Porgy and Bess* featuring the popular "Summertime."

- 20 million hula-hoops are sold in the United States in just 6 months.

1959
- Coast-to-coast flight becomes a reality along with passenger flights to Europe.
- Richie Valens, Texan Buddy Holly, and "Big Boppper" die in plane crash.
- Jazz singer Billie Holiday dies at age 44.
- Integrated schools open in Little Rock, Arkansas.
- Ill-fated Ford Edsel hits market.
- Alaska and Hawaii become the forty-ninth and fiftieth states.

- *Some Like It Hot* and *Ben Hur* are popular films.
- Barbie doll is released, inspiring comic strip *Kathy.*

1960
- Protests, sit-ins, and other forms of nonviolent protest against segregation and discrimination.
- Martin Luther King becomes prominent civil rights leader.
- The *Fantastics,* written by two University of Texas graduates, is hit on Broadway.
- Birth control pill is approved.
- Cold war tensions escalate following U2 spy plane incident; tension mounts in Cuba.
- JFK defeats Nixon for presidency in narrow margin.
- *Camelot* opens on Broadway.
- Etch-a-Sketch becomes popular toy.

1961
- Rock and roll is a hit with teenagers; *American Bandstand* TV show and Chubby Checker's "The Twist" are hot with teens.
- Fear of armageddon as missile race and atomic testing escalate.
- Harper Lee wins Pulitzer Prize for *To Kill a Mockingbird.*
- United States continues assistance to South Korea, defending democracy against communism.
- Freedom riders attacked as they tour south to evaluate compliance with desegregation acts.
- Astronauts Shepard and Grissom are first to explore space helping the United States to catch up with Russia in space race.

1962
- Astronaut John Glenn orbits earth.
- Hollywood starlet and silver screen sex symbol Marilyn Monroe dies.
- John Steinbeck wins Nobel Prize for *The Winter of Our Discontent;* other best sellers include Helen Gurley Brown's *Sex and the Single Girl,* and *One Flew Over the Cuckoo's Nest* by Ken Kesey.

- United States sends small force to Laos.
- Popular films include *Lawrence of Arabia, Dr. No, The Days of Wine and Roses, To Kill a Mockingbird, What Ever Happened to Baby Jane, Long Day's Journey into Night, The Manchurian Candidate,* and *How the West Was Won.*
- Russia agrees to withdraw missiles from Cuba.
- Early "women's lib" author Betty Friedan writes *The Feminine Mystique.*

1963
- Violent demonstrations in Birmingham lead to desegregation of lunch counters and integration of schools.
- Martin Luther King jailed for his civil disobedience actions.
- President Kennedy lends support to racial equality.
- President John F. Kennedy assassinated in Dallas, Texas—Lyndon B. Johnson (LBJ) sworn in as president.
- Lee Harvey Oswald in custody for murder of JFK is killed by Jack Ruby.
- First blacks graduate from the University of Mississippi.
- Popularity of folk music soars through work by singers Bob Dylan, Joan Baez, Pete Seeger, and Peter, Paul & Mary.
- Martin Luther King addresses largest ever civil rights rally and declares: "I have a dream."
- Pop artists like Andy Warhol gain popularity for controversial art breaking traditional barriers.
- William Faulkner wins Pulitzer Prize in fiction.
- James Baldwin publishes *The Fire Next Time.*
- The Beatles release their first album.

1964
- British rock group The Beatles widely accepted by American youth after appearance on TV.
- Folk musicians like Dylan continue to express themes of social injustice and horrors of war in lyrics.

- Congress passes Civil Rights Act prohibiting racial discrimination.
- Race riots in New York lead to deaths and arrests.
- Student unrest on Berkley campus.
- Julie Andrews stars in *Mary Poppins;* other popular films include *The Pink Panther* and The Beatles' *A Hard Day's Night.*
- Martin Luther King wins Nobel Peace Prize.
- John Coltrane records his ever popular *A Love Supreme.*
- LBJ wins presidential election handily.
- Young boys intrigued with new GI Joe toy.

1965
- United States takes offensive in Vietnam despite divided public opinion.
- Dances like the Frug and Watusi are popular along with minidresses and go-go boots.
- Black Muslim leader Malcolm X assassinated by member of opposing sect.
- 25,000 blacks organize march on Montgomery, Alabama, to affirm right to vote.
- Astronaut walks in space.
- President Johnson signs Voting Rights Act, guaranteeing blacks the right to vote.
- Racial tension explodes in Los Angeles' Watts district—five days of riots.
- Timothy Leary advocates use of drugs to "tune in, turn on, and drop out."

1966
- War in Vietnam escalates amid waves of antiwar protests.
- Race riots erupt in Chicago and Atlanta.
- Pop music matures with The Beatles, Bob Dylan, Beach Boys, The Byrds, and Motown groups the Supremes and the Miracles.
- Miles Davis Quintet records "Orbits."
- LBJ launches war at home on urban decay awarding grants to cities for reconstruction.

- Top films include *Blow Up, A Man for All Seasons,* Who's Afraid of *Virginia Woolf.*
- Black Panthers organization is founded.

1967
- Sports fans enjoy first football Super Bowl—Packers against the Chiefs.
- Race riots in Detroit are worst in U.S. history.
- Free love, flower people, psychedelic drugs, communes, love-ins, sit-ins and Eastern religious philosophies reflect new youth's alternative and reactionary lifestyles.
- Long hair (males), hippies, and rock bands such as Otis Redding, The Beatles, Mamas and the Papas, The Byrds, Jefferson Airplane, Grateful Dead, The Who, Janis Joplin, Jimmie Hendrix, and the Doors create music that represent the times.
- College enrollments show 100 percent increase since 1960.
- Bare skin and miniskirts reflect growing hedonist attitudes with American youth.
- Public Broadcasting Networks established.
- Growing antiwar sentiment.
- *The Graduate* is top film.

1968
- Growing antiwar sentiment influences LBJ's decision not to run for reelection.
- Civil rights leader Martin Luther King is assassinated.
- Robert Kennedy is assassinated.
- Government issues report exposing trend toward a two-society nation divided by race.
- Rock musical *Hair* reflects times.
- 5,000 radical student members of SDS (Students for a Democratic Society) take over Columbia University campus.
- Riots at Democratic national convention in Chicago.
- Stanley Kubrick's movie *2001: A Space Odyssey* reflects nation's infatuation with space travel.

- Supreme Court orders end to all school segregation.
- Top films are *Midnight Cowboy, Easy Rider,* and *Butch Cassidy and the Sundance Kid.*
- Norman Mailer wins Pulitzer for *The Armies of the Night.*
- President Richard Nixon takes steps to pull the United States out of Vietnam amid continued antiwar rallies.
- Astronaut Neil Armstrong walks on the moon.

- Woodstock event is largest rock concert ever; thousands of youth enjoy music, sex, and drugs in a peaceful display for peace.
- Miles Davis records landmark *Bitches Brew*, recording released the following year.
- Campus demonstrations against the war in Vietnam become heated.

CHAPTER SUMMARY

The 1960s was a decade of both tremendous challenges and achievements for America. Wars often unify a country, but military involvement in Vietnam instead polarized Americans, causing both peaceful and deadly protests against the war. Civil rights and women's rights issues came to the forefront, sparking yet more protests and demonstrations. U.S. president John F. Kennedy was assassinated as was civil rights leader Martin Luther King and presidential hopeful Robert F. Kennedy. The Cuban missile crisis, another chapter in the continuing cold war with the Soviet Union, may have nearly started a third world war. In science, man first set foot on the moon, while in the world of music British rock and roll bands, most notably The Beatles and The Rolling Stones, changed the American popular music scene. The turmoil of the 1960s is also reflected in the many concurrent new approaches to jazz that developed in the 60s and through the styles that continued along paths established years earlier.

Miles Davis stands apart from all other great innovators in jazz who preceded him in that, unlike Louis Armstrong or Charlie Parker, Davis was an important contributor to more than one single style of jazz. After playing his version of bebop with Charlie Parker, Miles announced the arrival of cool jazz with his 1949 *Birth of the Cool* album. Had Miles been like most of the other great jazz innovators, he would have continued to play and refine cool jazz for the balance of his career. To the contrary, Miles Davis continued to change, identifying and nurturing young talent while pioneering new styles of jazz. The group described as Davis' "first great quintet," later a sextet, featured John Coltrane (tenor sax), Cannonball Adderley (alto sax), and Bill Evans (piano), brought a new modal approach to hard bop. This group's *Kind of Blue* album (1959) has sold more than 5 million copies since its release. During this time, Davis also worked with arranger Gil Evans, recording three third stream albums with large ensembles. When Coltrane, Adderley, and Evans departed to form their own groups, personnel in Davis' group became unsettled, finally stabilizing with the group known as the "second great quintet." This group featured Wayne Shorter (tenor sax), Herbie Hancock (piano), Ron Carter (bass), and Tony Williams (drums). This quintet produced a more progressive jazz, often playing music that used odd phrase lengths, disguised meter, and unconventional chord changes and forms. Many feel that this was Davis' most creative period. As the group matured, the music became less structured, influenced by the free jazz approach of Ornette Coleman, but sometimes played with a straight eighth-note feel rather than a more traditional swing feel. By the late 1960s, the group expanded, adding guitar and using as many as three electronic keyboard players. This music, combining the instruments and grooves of rock with jazz, became known as fusion and reflected a more postmodern spirit. Many of Davis' sidemen went go on to become leaders of important fusion groups. For health reasons, Davis went into retirement in 1974. Coming out of retirement in 1981, he formed a new group that continued to play in a pop-influenced fusion style. His final project was a hip hop–jazz album produced by rapper Easy Moe Bee.

John Coltrane pushed the tenor saxophone to new limits in technique and improvisation and also reintroduced the soprano saxophone to the jazz world. His use of multiphonics (playing more than one note at a time), rapid-fire runs (described as sheets of sound), facility in the extreme high register, and his ability to navigate complex chord changes set a new standard against which saxophonists today still measure themselves. Coltrane played with Miles Davis in the late 1950s, but also served as leader for recordings during that time. After leaving Davis, Coltrane assembled a quartet that played primarily modal jazz. With his spiritual awakening, Coltrane incorporated more eastern elements into his music. In his final years, Coltrane's music became much freer and was clearly influenced by Ornette Coleman's work.

Wayne Shorter and Herbie Hancock both were members of Miles Davis' second great quintet. Shorter's importance is not just as a saxophonist, but also as a composer. He brought new, unconventional ideas to Davis' group before leaving to co-found the very important fusion group Weather Report. Herbie Hancock, well established before joining the Davis group, has continued to play in a diverse range of settings from mainstream to pop.

KEY TERMS

Important terms and people.

TERMS	Red Garland	John McLaughlin
modality	Paul Chambers	Joe Zawinul
pedal point	Philly Joe Jones	Keith Jarrett
sheets of sound	Cannonball Adderley	Hank Mobley
multiphonics	Bill Evans	George Coleman
timbre	Herbie Hancock	"Trane"
harmonics	Ron Carter	
	Tony Williams	
PEOPLE	Wayne Shorter	
John Coltrane	Chick Corea	

REVIEW QUESTIONS

1. The 1960s was a tumultuous time in the United States and it was perhaps the most productive and innovative decade for Miles Davis. What was the social, political, and cultural mood of the times and what issues dominated American thought?

2. Miles Davis first surfaced as a visible performer as a member of whose small group and playing what style of music?

3. How did Davis' style contrast to that of Dizzy Gillespie?

4. Discuss Davis' involvement in the "cool" style.

5. Who were members of Miles Davis' "first great quintet" and what kind of music did they play?

6. When were the first modal jazz recordings made and what were the titles?

7. Describe the difference between modal jazz and more traditional jazz based on functional harmony.

8. What was the formal scheme of the first modal tunes recorded by Davis?

9. What impact did modal jazz have on the improvising soloist?

10. What mute became synonymous with Davis' sound?

11. Who was the arranger that collaborated with Davis to create some of the most significant works in the history of jazz? Name some of these important recordings.

12. Who was the earlier swing era bandleader that had some influence on Gil Evans and the concepts presented on the *Birth of the Cool* recording?

13. Name the Davis recording that remains as the leading selling album in the history of jazz.

14. Name the musicians that became members of Davis' "second great quintet." What instruments did they play?

15. Who became one of the most significant composers to contribute to Davis' second quintet?

16. Did Ornette Coleman show any influence on the original music produced by Davis' second quintet?

17. Davis' *Filles De Kilimanjaro* recording marks the beginning of his adventures in incorporating aspects of popular music in forming a new direction in jazz. What are several new characteristics apparent on this recording that point to pop music influences?

18. The merging of popular music elements with jazz marked a new style of jazz called _____.

19. What popular rock bands or artists served as inspiration to Miles Davis and Herbie Hancock?

20. What two Davis recordings mark the beginning of the last period of Davis' musical growth?

21. What are the similarities and differences between Davis' music heard on *Bitches Brew* and Ornette Coleman's *Free Jazz*?

22. Why did Davis chose to merge jazz with popular rock styles of the time?

23. Miles Davis participated or was at the forefront of what seven jazz styles?

24. What was so unique about Miles Davis' style and remained a constant throughout his career?

25. Which member of the saxophone family was popularized by John Coltrane?

26. What two members of the saxophone family is Coltrane noted for?

27. Describe the term "sheets of sound" and what was unique about this technique?

28. Coltrane left Miles Davis briefly to join what pianist's group?

29. Could John Coltrane be classified as one who was interested in world music? Explain and defend your answer.

30. Did Coltrane's music reflect the racial tensions of the times? Explain and defend your answer.

31. Coltrane was essentially involved in three styles or approaches to jazz. What were they and name one recording associated with each approach.

32. Who was the significant free jazz woodwind player who recorded with Coltrane?

33. Was Coltrane influenced by Ornette Coleman? Explain your answer and provide evidence.

34. Summarize John Coltrane's accomplishments and contributions to jazz.

35. Describe Wayne Shorter's style and how it may have differed from Coltrane's.

36. Herbie Hancock is one of the most important jazz pianists of the late twentieth century. Describe his performance style and indicate the style of jazz that he has been associated with.

37. Aside from Hancock, name three other important contemporary pianists who performed with Davis in the late 1960s and early 1970s.

38. What social blemishes, landmark innovations, or discoveries mark the landscape that parallels Miles Davis' musical development throughout the 1960s?

> **Make sure that you also review material on the corresponding chapter of the CD-ROM, including interviews with Miles Davis, John Coltrane, and others.**

SUGGESTED SUPPLEMENTARY LISTENING

The abbreviation (iT) indicates that a particular recording cited in the text, or particularly demonstrative of the artist, is available from the Apple iTunes Web site. Other Web-based music distributors may also prove to be valuable resources. SCCJ indicates *Smithsonian Collection of Classic Jazz*.

Miles Davis Quintets

Cookin' with the Miles Davis Quintet Prestige (iT)
Kind of Blue Sony (iT)
E.S.P. Sony (iT)
Nefertiti Columbia
Miles Smiles Sony (iT)
Miles in the Sky Sony (iT)
Sorcerer Sony (iT)
Filles De Kilimanjaro Sony (iT)
Live at the Plugged Nickel Sony

Highlights from the Plugged Nickel Sony (iT)
In a Silent Way Sony (iT)
Bitches Brew Sony
A Tribute to Jack Johnson Sony
The Complete Jack Johnson Session Sony (iT)
Tutu Warner Jazz (iT)
The Essential Miles Davis Sony (iT)
Jazz Profile: Miles Davis Blue Note (iT)
Miles Davis: Greatist Hits(Legacy) Sony (iT)
"Jean Pierre"(iT)

Miles Davis and Gil Evans

Miles Ahead; Porgy and Bess
Sketches of Spain
Miles Davis and Gil Evans: The Complete Columbia Studio Recordings
   Columbia (iT)

John Coltrane

Thelonious Monk with John Coltrane Prestige (iT)
Monk's Music Riverside (ois) (iT)
Blue Trane Blue Note (iT)
Coltrane's Sound Atlantic
Giant Steps Atlantic
Impressions Impulse!
My Favorite Things Impulse!
"Naima" (iT)
Coltrane Deluxe Edition! Impulse! (iT) includes version of "Impressions"
   discussed on the CD-ROM
Coltrane Live at Birdland GRP (iT)
Ascension Impulse!
The Very Best of John Coltrane Impulse! (iT)

Eric Dolphy

Out to Lunch Blue Note (iT)
Out There Prestige (iT)
Live at the Five Spot Vols. I and II Prestige (iT)

Wayne Shorter

Speak No Evil Blue Note (iT)
Ju Ju Blue Note (iT)
Schizophrenia Blue Note (iT)
Night Dreamer Blue Note (iT)
The Blue Note Years: The Best of Wayne Shorter Blue Note (iT)
V.S.O.P. Quintet Live Sony (iT)
Footprints Live Verve (iT)
Alegría Verve (iT)

Herbie Hancock

Maiden Voyage Blue Note
The Prisoner Blue Note (iT)
Empyrean Isles Blue Note

Mwandishi Herbie Hancock Warner Jazz (iT)
Head Hunters Sony (iT)
Thrust Sony (iT)
Herbie Hancock: A Jazz Collection Sony (iT)
Gershwin's World Verve (iT)
"Maiden Voyage" (iT)
"Watermellon Man" (iT)
"Dolphin Dance" (iT)

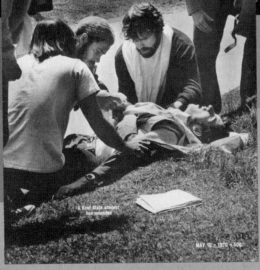

LIFE

TRAGEDY AT KENT

Cambodia and Dissent:
The Crisis of
Presidential Leadership

A Kent State student
lies wounded

MAY 15 · 1970 · 50¢

The Electric 1970s and 1980s

Up until the 1950s, jazz had followed a traceable, linear progression of developments with only one or two being predominant at any given time; but by 1970, the rich tradition that now included numerous styles and influences seemed to yield to no single musical direction. The 70s was an age of synthesis on all levels and, in the true spirit of postmodern culture, performing artists drew from all available sources for new inspiration. The tremendous amalgamation of styles was emblematic of an ever-increasing multicultural society posting growing immigrant populations from Asia and south of the border. This expanding minority population no doubt appreciated jazz's willingness to embrace and absorb musical influences from non-Western cultures, many of which counted improvisation as a key ingredient in their native music. Rhythm sections also evolved and were augmented by the addition of percussionists during the 70s. While a few groups during the Cubop days of the late 40s had made use of Afro-Cuban drummers, most jazz bands until this period carried only a drum set player. Additional percussion instruments enabled these new 70s bands to absorb and reflect Brazilian, Afro-Cuban, Indian, and other world music styles. Jazz became a more global music in the last decades of the twentieth century due in part to improved means of communication and because of the postmodern jazz artist's quest for new ways to express themselves. Jazz from this point on was a fractured, splintered genre. It became increasingly difficult to tell what was meant by the application of the word "jazz" to describe music. The menu for fans in the 70s and 80s included:

- Electric, jazz-fusion bands in the Miles Davis *Bitches Brew* tradition—Mahavishnu Orchestra
- Soul, rhythm, and blues style jazz inspired by the African-American tradition—Grover Washington, Jr.
- The first wave of instrumental pop, easy listening, or smooth jazz artists—George Winston, Spyro Gyra, and Chuck Mangione
- A new European sound pioneered by the German ECM label—Jan Garbarek and Keith Jarrett
- Rebirth of forgotten mainstream hard bop artists, some of whom had become expatriates in Europe, now returned to the United States playing what was termed neo- or progressive bop—Phil Woods and Dexter Gordon
- Emerging young black artists eventually labeled as the "Young Lions" and led by an amazing trumpeter Wynton Marsalis. Most of these newcomers follow the progressive or neo-bop course
- Free jazz patterned after earlier work by Ornette Coleman, Eric Dolphy, and John Coltrane—Art Ensemble of Chicago and Anthony Braxton
- Modern big bands likened to Count Basie and Duke Ellington but representing all that had happened in jazz since the 40s necessitating an update of the older model—Toshiko Akiyoshi and Thad Jones
- The beginnings of world music–influenced jazz styles—Herbie Hancock, Pat Metheny, and Weather Report

After considering this menu there is no wonder that listeners, critics, journalists, and promoters were more confused than ever by the "jazz" label. Following the deaths of Albert Ayler, John Coltrane, and Eric Dolphy, and the retirement of Miles Davis in mid-decade, the jazz world was at a loss for a single guiding force. There was no single beacon to light the way, and consequently the music that is practiced throughout the final decades of the twentieth century moves in many different directions simultaneously, with no single trend or leader outstanding. This chapter presents the electric and more popular trends and artists who have contributed to the jazz tradition during the 1970s and 1980s.

JAZZ AND ROCK: THE TWO-WAY CONNECTION

By 1970, jazz was suffering from the widespread popularity of a new wave of rock bands, some of which incorporated certain aspects of jazz. Even *Down Beat* magazine proclaimed as early as 1967 that, while they would continue to cover jazz, they would also cover rock music.[2] Pop bands, just like the Swing Era big bands of the 1930s and 1940s, captured the attention of the public at large by featuring vocalists. Major record labels like Columbia dropped acoustic jazz artists like Charles Mingus, Ornette Coleman, and Keith Jarrett because the average younger listener disconnected from established more traditional instrumental jazz and were attracted to the new "fusion" brand. Older fans felt disenfranchised from the bop and swing styles they had grown up enjoying. The word "fusion," most often used in association with a style of hybrid electric-jazz-rock music, actually had a much broader application during the 70s, including new fusions of world and classical music styles with jazz.

Many of the 70s rock bands found success by adding jazz style horn sections to the usual collection of electric guitars, bass, drums, keyboards, and vocals. For the most part, these horn bands could be placed in one of two categories—those that were essentially rock bands but played music featuring horn arrangements that were sometimes informed by certain aspects of the jazz tradition, and those that employed authentic jazz-trained horn players, performing repertoires that harkened back to jazz and rhythm and blues canons. Chicago Transit Authority (CTA), or Chicago as they became know, fit into this first category, never claiming much in the way of a jazz heritage. Blood, Sweat & Tears (BS&T) and Chase, on the other hand, often featured improvisation and swing grooves in their presentation of original material as well as remakes of classic jazz pieces like Billie Holiday's "God Bless This Child." BS&T's trumpet star Lew Soloff, remembered for his stratospheric bop-influenced solo on "Spinning Wheel," left the band to become one of the most important jazz players on the New York scene, a position that he still enjoys. He was a mainstay of the later Gil Evans Orchestras and many other New York–based jazz groups. There was a free exchange of players from both camps, for example, jazz tenor saxophonist Joe Henderson played with BS&T, as did revolutionary electric bassist Jaco Pastorious but briefly, and pianist George Duke left Frank Zappa's band to join jazz saxophonist Cannonball Adderley and his quintet. Other bands like the Flock and Dreams were short-lived, amounting to valiant experiments featuring players like Michael and Randy Brecker and electric violinist Jerry Goodman, who would go on to greater heights some years later. While it is difficult to generalize, these and other rock-inspired bands from this period absorbed and reflected one of two fundamental traditions, but rarely both—white English rock groups or black R & B bands and the Motown sound. The rock bands, whether or not they sported jazz-like horn sections, rarely based their music on the kind of spontaneity associated with jazz. The jazz-rock fusion bands, on the other hand, often featured some element of spontaneity.

Popular jazz-rock fusion group Blood, Sweat & Tears with (left to right) Steve Katz on guitar, Bobby Colomby on drums, Jim Fielder on bass, Fred Lipsius on soprono saxophone, Jerry Hyman on trombone, Chuck Winfield on trumpet, and Lew Soloff on trumpet.

While John Travolta's film *Saturday Night Fever* and the public's craving for disco style dance music swept the nation, jazz was morphing into new styles rooted in Miles Davis' music of the late 60s and early 70s. The overriding texture in this new brand of jazz was electronic. The synthesis of electronic and acoustic sounds provided the perfect sound track for an ever-changing American society. Jazz tenor saxophonist Eddie Harris popularized the electronically modified sax and the octavider and varitone were electronic gadgets that enabled wind instrumentalists to compete in a landscape increasingly dominated by electronic instruments. The electronic piano, the electric guitar with all the possible special effects gadgets, and the electric bass became ever present. For that matter, the acoustic bass became nearly forgotten, eclipsed by its electric cousin, a less-expensive and more easily played instrument. Even many well-established acoustic jazz bassists found it necessary to add this new instrument to their arsenal. Being a good acoustic bassist was not enough in the 70s.

The music world was rocked in the 1980s by the digital revolution, a tremor brought on by the increased accessibility of desktop computing, the compact disk, and the release of the MIDI standard—a new way for musical instruments to be controlled and information distributed using a simple binary computer code. The music industry may not have realized in 1983 when they first unleashed the MIDI standard that this invention would have as sweeping an impact on the industry as had the phonograph, tape recorder, LP, electric guitar, and bass in earlier years. MIDI implementation allowed computers to control instruments, amplified acoustic instruments to control electronic ones, and permitted computer generated music to interact with live musicians. "It's a whole new ballgame," said guitarist Pat Metheny in a 1985 *Down Beat* magazine interview. "Now my guitar can be a harp, it can be vibes, it can be anything. It's unlimited in the sense that it's up to your imagination."[3] The guitar came of age in the 70s fusion bands, no doubt due to the focus on this instrument in rock and roll styles. Since then, the instrument has become a major voice and enjoys a role in the jazz ensemble as important as any other instrument. It took time for musicians to learn how best to take advantage of the new tools and influences, just as it took time for new technology to evolve beyond the gimmickry stage to a point where they could be used creatively and sensibly.

Like most jazz and pop styles, the electric fusion jazz style began to short-circuit by the late 70s as the market became saturated with clones of the artists and bands that had pioneered the style. Eventually, even the pioneers became caricatures of themselves. Raw fusion became more and more sanitized and the watered-down versions at the end of the decade and into the 80s and 90s became known by various names—"happy jazz," "hot tub jazz," "fuzak," and most recently, "smooth jazz" and "acid jazz." Whatever the name and while there are differences that are addressed more thoroughly in Chapter 15, all of these different breeds are related to similar seeds cultivated first in the late 60s and early 70s. Record companies began to give up the quest to cast jazz into some easily marketed formula. The 70s was an era when nonconformists preached the importance of individuality, yet there was a certain homogenization in terms of dress and music. Blue jeans became the uniform for those under 30, while record companies began to behave like fashion designers, using huge marketing budgets to package and promote bands that seemed to offer a formula for success. First it was electric jazz-rock fusion bands, then it was the newcomers from Europe who offered a new slant on improvised music, then the nostalgic rebirth of older artists who once again captured a brief period of limelight, and then, at the end of the decade, came the pride of young black artists dressed smartly in suits and labeled the "Young Lions." Nearly all of these artists and trends can in some way be traced back to the influences of Miles Davis, who had cut a wide path leaving a large wake.

MILES BEYOND: LIVING IN THE SHADOW OF MILES DAVIS

Miles Davis sidemen continued to impact jazz trends in the 70s leading bands like Weather Report, Return to Forever, the Mahavishnu Orchestra, and Headhunters. While there were others like guitarist and fusion pioneer Larry Coryell with his Eleventh House and Tony Williams' Lifetime, these bands exerted the most influence on the new wave of electric jazz. A second wave of fusion groups hit in the later part of the decade, and included groups like Spyro Gyra, Auricle (a young band of Eastman School of Music students including smooth jazz star Rick Braun), Seawind, and Caldera, but by this time the movement had stalled and become shopworn in the eyes of media and many fans. *Down Beat* magazine's best review of any of these groups' efforts was 2½ stars on a scale of 5.[4]

A significant difference between leaders of the fusion movement and their mentor Miles Davis is that while Davis had moved jazz forward by initiating numerous stylistic changes, he generally pursued only one or two styles at a time. To the contrary, this new breed of 70s Davis protégés wore many hats, and often simultaneously.

Weather Report

Two Davis sidemen founded this groundbreaking group—keyboardist Joe Zawinul (b 1932), who had first come into the spotlight as a member of Cannonball Adderley's Quintet in the 1960s, and Davis alumnus Wayne Shorter (b 1933) on soprano and tenor saxophone. Following his stint with Adderley, during which time he composed the popular funky hit "Mercy, Mercy, Mercy," Zawinul composed the title track for Davis' *In a Silent Way* and added his electronic keyboard voice to *Bitches Brew*. The genesis of Weather Report dates back to 1970 and the release of their initial recording entitled *Weather Report*. While there were many personnel changes throughout the group's 16-year career, they remained true to several important doctrines:

- Spontaneity and invention
- Improvisation as a paramount virtue in achieving spontaneity
- Deviation from predictable AABA forms and melodic phrase lengths
- Percussion in addition to the drum set as an important ingredient
- Application of electronic sound textures to promote an entirely new sound pallet, while providing a contemporary sound[5]

This was the first time bands used names that more closely resembled rock bands, even though their music was the furthest thing from "commercial" during the early years.[6] Many other jazz groups followed Weather Report's lead, using names such as Headhunters, Return to Forever, Prime Time, and the Yellowjackets rather than the name of the leader as had been the case for decades before.

Like so many jazz-fusion bands from this period, their jazz roots were most apparent in the group's initial recordings (*Weather Report* and *Sweetnighter*), but as time passed, they became more drawn to those characteristics closely associated with black popular music of the period as well as non-Western influences and electronic instrumental effects. As co-leader Zawinul put it, "It's Weather Report because that would allow us to change, just like the weather so the scope is limitless."[7] And so they did, gradually incorporating popular dance rhythms, memorable melodies, and throbbing rhythm sections that all served to draw the attention of more and more listeners, helping Weather Report to effectively cross lines between jazz and popular music. The group's first album was named record of the year by *Down Beat* magazine. Zawinul described it as "a soundtrack for the imagination."[8] This recording predated the group's affinity for electronic synthesizers, at this point rather large and cumbersome instruments, so the group utilized a fairly traditional instrumentation, but in very free, less-structured forms and in less conventional ways. Interactive gestures and reactions wove a lattice of varying textures, where the roles of the instruments were always changing. Collective improvisation was often more important in their recordings than individual cameo solos, much as had been the case years earlier in early New Orleans jazz. Subsequent recordings became more structured and improvised solos became less apparent, though improvisation continued to be a paramount feature in much of their music. Saxophonist Wayne Shorter spoke about the stream of consciousness undercurrent in the band's music and their attempt to break new ground: "Let's do music without capitalization and paragraphs and periods and semi-colons and colons. Then we found out what those capitalizations and indentations were, what we were talking about when we knew we were approaching something new. We didn't want to approach those things that have already been done."[9]

One can trace the impact, evolution, and maturation of the synthesizer as well as the musician's ability to make artistic use of the new instrument by listening to the progression of Weather Report recordings from *Sweetnighter* (1973) on. Zawinul has always felt that original and unique rhythmic grooves should be paramount and feels that his groove on *Sweetnighter*'s "Boogie Woogie Waltz" was the immediate predecessor of the 1990s hip-hop style. Like the astronaut in his ship exploring space, Zawinul pioneered new frontiers using the electronic synthesizer as his vehicle for exploration. Zawinul learned during the 70s how to use like a sculptor all the modern studio electronic tools and production techniques that Miles Davis and producer Teo Macero had pioneered in recordings like *In a Silent Way* and *Bitches Brew*. The group's efforts were rewarded in 1972 by winning the Best Jazz Combo category in *Down Beat* magazine.

Perhaps one of the most important personnel changes came in 1976 when the band added flamboyant electric bassist Jaco Pastorius to its roster. Anyone who has played the electric bass since this time has fallen under his influence. Pastorius' amazing technique, pointed articulation, pulsating bass lines, and improvisational skill along with his stage appeal helped to catapult Weather Report to even more widespread popularity. It was Pastorius who advanced the fretless electric bass by removing the frets from the fingerboard, enabling a more connected and sustained style. His lyrical, singing quality on the bass and his ability to play bass lines in octaves and even multinote chords and harmonics was astounding. Pastorius' technique was particularly revolutionary considering the electric bass had emerged largely from the rock and roll side and had not been considered capable of virtuosic flare or been entirely accepted by the jazz community. "He had that magical thing about him," said Zawinul, "the same kind of thing Jimi Hendrix had. He was an electrifying performer and a great musician . . . Before Jaco came along we were perceived as a kind of esoteric jazz group . . . but after Jaco joined the band we started selling-out concert halls everywhere."[10] *Down Beat* magazine agreed stating, "Pastorius' rock sensibility steered the group away from the mattress-on-the-floor, Indian-bedspread-on-the-walls mentality of the earlier recordings toward a more aggressive rock-funk path."[11] The group's surprise popular smash hit "Birdland" appeared on their 1977 *Heavy Weather* release. Every modern big band, marching band, and pop band copied this AM radio hit, and the vocal group Manhattan Transfer added lyrics to their version, keeping the hit in the public's ear for more years than the average instrumental hit. With the success of "Birdland," Weather Report was assured more than a footnote in future histories of jazz. *Heavy Weather* was voted album of the year, and a year later, *Down Beat* readers voted Weather Report Best Jazz Combo for the ninth consecutive year.

The track included on the companion audio anthology is taken from the award-wining recording that featured "Birdland" and shows that each track on this landmark recording was as infectious as another. "Palladium" bears all the trademarks of the polished and sophisticated sound that popularized Weather Report and introduced numerous listeners to a new electric brand of jazz.

Electric bassist Jaco Pastorius.

Weather Report

Listening Guide

"Palladium" (Wayne Shorter) 4:47

Recorded in California, 1977; *Heavy Weather*, Columbia CK 65108

Wayne Shorter: *soprano and tenor saxophone*

Joe Zawinul: *Arp 2600 syntheziser, Fender Rhodes electric piano*

Jaco Pastorius: *electric bass and steel drums*

Alex Acuña: *drums*

Manolo Badrena: *percussion*

Form and Key: Lengthy introduction followed by an elastic AB form repeated with extended C section or Coda. 4/4 meter and D and F serve as primary key centers. What makes this tune particularly interesting are the phrase lengths, which are uneven and never the same twice ranging from 15½ bars to 18, 19, and 22 bars long. All the while, the bass plays a complex ostinato line against a nearly regular 2-bar keyboard chord progression.

0:00–0:23	*Introduction:* Unison rhythm section line for 2 bars is followed by a 2-bar vamp featuring conga drums; tenor sax enters for 2 additional repeats of the vamp
0:24–0:25	*Grand Pause:* entire band pauses for 2 beats and a bar
0:26–0:35	*Vamp:* prominent bass line serving as the underpinning to entire tune anchors another 2-bar vamp played twice as intro to main melody
0:35–1:16	*A section:* tenor sax enters with primary *theme*. This theme and series of chords centers around D and the melody serves as the basis of nearly the entire tune
1:16–2:00	*B section:* electric piano featured for first 4 bars of this new section in the new key center of F, tenor sax enters with variation on A thematic material, electric piano solos in between melodic statements

Weather Report *concluded*

2:00–2:37	*A section:* tenor sax enters with *primary theme*
2:37–3:07	*B section:* electric piano fills featured for first 4 bars of this new section in the new key center of F, tenor sax enters with variation on A thematic material, electric piano solos in between melodic statements
C or Coda	New simple, catchy tune serves as background first for Shorter's tenor improvisations and then for Zawinul's synthesizer solo. Breakdown of entrances is as follows:
3:07–3:23	rhythm section plays tune
3:23–3:39	tenor improvises
3:39–3:55	band plays tune
3:55–end	sax and rhythm section play tune while synthesizer improvises until abrupt and unresolved ending

Both Zawinul and Shorter have had a major impact on modern jazz composition. Shorter has been described as a poet for not only his saxophone improvisations, but also his compositions. There was, however, a vast difference between the two in terms of their creative process as composers: Zawinul's compositions were based on a very spontaneous, improvisational process, while Shorter's were the result of painstaking analysis and reworking of ideas with a discipline akin to Thelonious Monk. These co-leaders offered a new approach to an age-old challenge—the integration of improvisation and composition. Each was able to seamlessly mask the boundaries between these two techniques.

Though their last recording *This Is This* was released in 1986, for all practical purposes Weather Report pulled the plug in 1985, ending their nearly 16-year run. The band had run its course and both Zawinul and Shorter yearned to devote more time to their own projects. Zawinul continues to explore the fusion of non-Western music and jazz in his Syndicate band whose 2002 recording received a Grammy nomination. While Shorter did not maintain a regular band during the closing years of the twentieth century, he continues to be reasonably prolific, recording in recent years with a host of artists including folk/pop singer Joni Mitchell, Herbie Hancock, Chick Corea, bassist Stanley Clarke, pianist Michael Petrucciani, Renee Rosnes, and female drum sensation Terri Lynn Carrington. His twenty-first-century recording *Footprints Live* was the first major recording released under his own name in quite some time and received excellent reviews. His follow-up recording *Alegria* captured critical acclaim, winning a Grammy in 2003 and once again demonstrating his prowess as both a composer and performer.

Herbie Hancock and the Headhunters

Herbie Hancock (b 1940), as previously discussed, has moved in many different musical directions following his departure from Davis, but his work in the early 70s was a logical continuation of his earlier efforts to merge certain aspects of jazz with pop. "I wanted to explore my roots and pop music of today," he said. "I wanted to see if I could make a record that was at the heart of rock."[12] *Mwandishi*, his sextet record issued in 1970, was a step in this direction. The compositions on this record were African influenced and the members of the band adopted Swahili names—Hancock calling himself "Mwandishi" meaning composer. "I wanted to recognize my African ancestry,"[13] and the music with its odd time signatures, prominent percussion, modal openness, repetitive bass lines, and free forms that inspired improvisation all served to provide an African flavor. On some levels the experiments were successful, though *Down Beat* described it as "sub-par Miles Davis electric jazz."[14] While *Mwandishi* may not have captured large audiences, it did serve as a prelude to more accessible efforts to follow. "[We are] influenced by things that are happening in rock and roll and we've found ways to use some of the things we've heard in more commercial aspects of black music to expand our horizons,"[15] Hancock said at the time. His most successful post–*Bitches Brew* effort, *Crossings*, followed *Mwandishi*. Highly motivated by percussion, electronics, and new synthesizer technology, working to create spacey African-like grooves, this recording also failed Hancock's hopes to reach large audiences. The music was still too improvised, too free form and cerebral for most pop-oriented listeners. Hancock regrouped with a new band he called The Headhunters and a new repertoire that drew heavily on those salient features of commercially popular black music being produced by such artists as Sly Stone; Stevie Wonder; Marvin Gaye; Earth, Wind & Fire; and the "Godfather of Soul," James Brown. Layered rhythm vamps played cleanly and tightly atop repetitive ostinato bass lines punctuated by funky drum grooves supplied the foundation for Hancock's new band and repertoire. Looking back on this period, Hancock said in a 1996 interview that, "I began to feel that I had been spending too much time exploring the upper atmosphere and the more ethereal kind of far-out, spacey stuff. Now there was this need to take some more of the earth and to feel a little more tethered."[16] The new band's first recording gave birth to a new brand of funk that combined blues, soul, and earlier black funky jazz roots (a style that Hancock had found some success with in earlier years with tunes like "Watermelon Man" and "Cantaloupe Island") with while laying the groundwork for the "hip-hop" and "acid jazz" styles of later years. This first Headhunters recording was immediately successful because of its danceable simplicity and featured the memorable hit "Chameleon," as well as Hancock's personal tribute to Sly Stone entitled simply "Sly." This album became one of the biggest selling jazz records of all time, reaching platinum status (1 million or more record sales) and, much like Weather Report's *Birdland* (an album that went gold with 500,000 sales) was quickly arranged for every imaginable medium including marching bands and big bands that also enjoyed hits with their arrangements. "Miles had a major influence on Head Hunters," Hancock said. "There was a very open approach in the improvisations and in the structures of the tunes that allow for a lot of rhythmic, harmonic and melodic freedom." The melody is very simple he observed, and is "based on a two-note motif . . . actually it's one note repeated. That's how you get complexity over to the general public . . . put it in simple form."[17] You can't help but move to the danceable rhythms and infectious repetitive bass lines of "Chameleon." The introduction of this tune included on the audio anthology has been edited and condensed from the original, but still represents the essence of Hancock's layered approach—placing one brick at a time to build the funky foundation until the saxophone enters with the melody. Hancock used only electric keyboards including ARP synthesizers and the Hohner clavinet to create the funky, staccato comping figures. What made this popular record even more unique was the absence of screaming guitars (the clavinet and keyboard synthesizers were used instead) contrary to most other electric-jazz-fusion groups of the day.

Herbie Hancock in 1983 playing a portable, strap-hung synthesizer keyboard giving him the mobility of a guitarist.

Head Hunters was followed by *Thrust* in 1975. It and each succeeding Headhunters' recording featured more and more infectious dance-oriented music that began to draw sharp criticism from the traditional jazz community, who accused Hancock of selling out. *Future Shock*, released in 1983, was his most successful pop effort and included the hit single "Rockit," for which he won a Grammy and five music video awards. It was Hancock's "Rockit" video along with Michael Jackson's video productions during this same time that broke open MTV and expanded this market for black entertainers.

While The Headhunters may have accomplished Hancock's goal of achieving widespread popularity, the music disenfranchised him from the jazz crowd. To counteract this alienation Hancock formed the acoustic jazz group V.S.O.P. (Very Special One-Time Performance) including his old bandmates from the Davis quintet years and additional headliners like commanding trumpeter Freddie Hubbard and eventually the young Marsalis brothers. Throughout the 70s and 80s Hancock was busy in the studio, collaborating with other artists such as Milt Jackson, Wayne Shorter, Quincy Jones, Jaco Pastorius, Chick Corea, Bobby McFerrin, and Joe Farrell in various projects, some fusion and others more traditionally based. He was a frequent addition to CTI recordings, a new label created by Creed Taylor in the 70s that produced albums as rapidly as Detroit produced new model automobiles. These products were often jazz, pop, Latin, and R&B laden instrumentals that promoted artists such as arranger Emir Deodato, Freddie Hubbard, Joe Farrell, and amazing flutist Hubert Laws as well as more traditional performers such as Paul Desmond and Milt Jackson. Many of these recordings included Hancock in some capacity. Hancock also collaborated with South American percussionist Milton Nascimento during the late 80s, serving to document and reaffirm his interest in world music and particularly the music of Latin America and Africa. As if these accomplishments were not enough, Hancock has contributed several successful film scores during his career including *Blow Up*, *Death Wish*, and the 1986 award-winning film staring saxophonist Dexter Gordon, *Round Midnight*.

Hard bopper Art Blakey and Hancock were instrumental in launching Wynton Marsalis' successful career, and the overwhelming success of Marsalis served to once again validate the significance of acoustic jazz, rooted in the tradition that Hancock helped to forge. Hancock's more recent work in a trio format with drummer Jack DeJohnette and bassist Dave Holland, his solo performances and recordings, as well as tribute and thematic recordings like *Gershwin's World* and *Double Rainbow* with saxophonist Joe Henderson have more than reestablished Hancock as one of the most important, gifted, and diversely productive artists of the late twentieth century.

Listen to the Herbie Hancock interview clips found in the corresponding chapter of the CD-ROM.

"Chameleon" (Hancock)
(excerpt) 4:40

**Recorded San
Francisco, CA, Fall,
1973; *Herbie Hancock
Headhunters*, Columbia
CK 65123**

Herbie Hancock:
*Fender Rhodes electric
piano, Hohner D6
Clavinet, ARP Odyssey
and ARP Soloist
synthesizers*

Bennie Maupin:
*soprano and tenor
saxophones, saxello,
bass clarinet*

Paul Jackson: *electric
bass and marimbula*

Harvey Mason: *drums*

Bill Summers:
percussion

Listening Guide

This track is not available on the companion CD anthology, but can be found on the Apple iTunes Web site.

Form and Key: Introductory Vamp A B Vamp, B♭ major, 4/4 meter

0:00–1:00	*Introduction:* long introduction serves as a funky prelude to the main melody:
	0:00–0:12 4 bars synthesized bass
	0:12–0:22 add drums for 4 more bars
	0:22–0:32 add high register electric bass for 4 more bars
	0:32–1:00 add keyboards
1:00–1:37	*A section:* tenor sax enters with first melodic statement which is played four times:
1:37–2:13	*B section:* second theme is played four times, the last time somewhat truncated for drum solo break:
	2:13–2:48 *Vamp Interlude:* similar vamp to introduction
	2:13–2:22 4 bars synthesized bass and drums
	2:22–2:31 add high register electric bass for 4 more bars
	2:31–2:48 add keyboards
2:48–fade	*Synthesizer Solo:* Hancock improvises on keyboard synthesizer over the rhythm section vamp until the track fades

John McLaughlin (b 1942) and the Mahavishnu Orchestra

The Englishman John McLaughlin added an important voice to those keystone Davis recordings that marked the beginnings of the electronic jazz-rock fusion movement. As author Stuart Nicholson pointed out: "What is immediately striking is McLaughlin's technical facility and his tone, which was hard, cutting, and metallic in a way favored by rock guitarists. Along with Larry Coryell he was responsible for bringing the sound of rock guitar to the jazz mainstream."[18] The Mahavishnu Orchestra, as McLaughlin called it, provided an expressive panorama of sound that was driven by sheer volume but with a wide range of dynamic contrast. McLaughlin had studied Eastern religion with guru Sri Chinmoy. The guitarist was one of a new breed of jazz musicians who took their cue from Coltrane and sought to use spiritual enlightenment rather than narcotics as a means of achieving higher levels of creative freedom and inspiration. McLaughlin had been profoundly influenced by Jimi Hendrix and had jammed with him in the late 1960s. McLaughlin recruited Rick Laird to play electric bass, Jan Hammer on keyboards (Hammer later became involved in television and film scoring, providing the music for the hit TV show "Miami Vice"), Jerry Goodman on electric violin (formerly of the group Flock), and Billy Cobham, the ambidextrous drummer who used two bass drums. The band premiered in New York in 1971 and quickly became know for its

- Odd time signatures (7/4 and 14/8)
- Changing time signatures

Guitarist John McLaughlin (Mahavishnu) performing with the jazz-fusion group Mahavishnu Orchestra at the 1975 Orange Rock Festival.

- Tempo changes
- Fast tempos
- Complex yet cohesive ensemble passages

McLaughlin established himself through the work with this band as the most important new guitarist since Wes Montgomery. The band's 1971 release *Inner Mounting Flame* featured a new concoction of rock and jazz with an eastern flavor. Like many of Chick Corea's compositions, these were complexly structured works propelled by a driving rhythm section emphasizing blinding, virtuosic lines played in unison by guitar, violin, and keyboard. This particular record paved the way for many groups that followed, the most successful of which was Corea's Return to Forever. The group's subsequent 1973 album *Birds of Fire* (a takeoff on Stravinsky's *Fire Bird Suite*) was charted at the 15th slot by *Billboard* magazine, an amazing accomplishment for an instrumental jazz recording at this time. According to *Melody Maker* magazine, "Speed had become all important. [There] were many, many moments of punishing pace, abrupt gear changes, and the acceleration almost crushed the breath from your lungs."[19] The group was relentless in their quest for musical intensity.

The Mahavishu Orchestra, despite its rapid rise to the top of the charts, broke up due to various disagreements in 1973. A tour and recording with Carlos Santana kept McLaughlin in the spotlight, however, before he eventually turned away, as did Corea and Hancock, from loud jazz. He formed Shakti as a strictly acoustic group and some years later, after a revival of Mahavishnu, toured with an acoustic guitar trio including Paco deLucia and Al diMeola. The short-lived 1974 reincarnation of Mahavishnu featured the extraordinary French violinist Jean-Luc Ponty who had previously performed with progressive rocker Frank Zappa.

McLaughlin returned to record with Miles Davis in the 80s, and numerous other projects have kept him in sight, but not in the limelight he enjoyed in the early '70s when he broke entirely new ground with the aggressive, experimental Mahavishnu Orchestra drawing audiences to jazz who had never before listened to it.

Chick Corea (b 1941) and Return to Forever

Less drawn to pop music initially, Chick Corea was more attracted to freer jazz after leaving the Miles Davis group. The adventuresome trio, which he called Circle, including Dave Holland on bass and drummer Barry Altschul, played more abstract jazz, and the group became even more cerebral with the addition of avant-garde saxophonist/composer Anthony Braxton. While Corea was interested in experimental jazz, Braxton's lack of traditional jazz grounding served to discourage Corea from further pursuit of Circle. His work on *Piano Improvisations Volumes I and II* (recorded in 1970) led him to rediscover the importance of melody and harmony. With this new ideal in mind, Corea joined forces with drummer/percussionist Airto Moreira, vocalist Flora Purim, Joe Farrell on saxophone and flute, and bassist Stanley Clark to form a new band that became one of the most influential groups of the decade. They called themselves Return to Forever and it was actually saxophonist Stan Getz who served as an important catalyst for the first version of Corea's new band. Getz, who had pioneered the jazz styled Brazilian bossa nova, commissioned Corea to compose new pieces for him and hired Corea's group to serve as his backup band. Corea's finest work from the period was recorded on Getz's *Captain Marvel* recording. Many of the same compositions featured on this recordings were later recorded by Return to Forever and released on their first solo recordings by the same name. Tunes like "500 Miles High," "La Fiesta," "Times Lie," "Captain Marvel," and "Crystal Silence" all remain today as significant contributions to the repertoire. In all of these pieces, Corea shows a love of strong melodies, Spanish and Brazilian attributes, Brazilian samba rhythms, and a light, airy group sound that was promoted by Joe Farrell's soaring flute and the wordless, vibrato-less vocals of Brazilian singer Flora Purim. Keeping with the electric times, Corea used the electric piano exclusively with the early Return to Forever band.

Corea veered off in yet another new direction when he added an electric guitarist to replace Farrell. Like Hancock, Corea became increasingly concerned about making his music appealing to the average listener acquainted more with pop music. As Corea pointed out, "the guitar seems like a very modern instrument of communication."[20] By the time the group recorded *Hymn of the 7th Galaxy* in 1973, additional personnel changes had occurred, new material had been composed, and the group was headed on a more rock-influenced course. From this point on, Corea has habitually moved from an acoustic, more traditional viewpoint to the more electrified jazz-rock and Latin-rock sound. In later years, it became difficult to track from one minute to the next whether he would appear in his electric or acoustic mode. By his own admission, it was guitarist John McLaughlin's band and its success that inspired him to turn his own band's volume up, adding guitar and penning more aggressive, in-your-face music. Corea's compositions by comparison, were even grander in scale, often heavily orchestrated in multiple movements. Musical characteristics often included a series of complex themes comprised of highly technical lines and complex rhythms. The five-note pentatonic scale frequently inspired his melodies and improvisations from this period, and his use of this scale started a new trend among jazz soloists.

Like Hancock, Corea employed the latest electronic synthesizer keyboards, giving the band an even richer electrified sound. The electric version of Return to Forever reached its zenith with the addition of the 19-year-old guitar sensation Al DiMeola. DiMeola was a technical wizard who was able to deftly negotiate Corea's most demanding lines. In 1975 the band issued an impressive release entitled *No Mystery* with original music of near epic proportions. To quote author Stuart Nicholson, "the similarities [to progressive rock created by Rick Wakeman and Keith Emerson] were unmistakable: pompous themes, a preoccupation with speed of execution for its own sake, a reliance on the latest electronic hardware, and a shared spiritual and/or cosmic preoccupation."[21] (Corea had been drawn to Scientology and the teachings of L. Ron Hubbard some years earlier.) By comparison, Corea's music bears a closer resemblance to works by these rock composers and the Mahavishnu Orchestra than to Headhunters. Corea's music during this period also shows an infatuation with Spanish music and music of Latin America, in particular the samba rhythms. The example track included in the companion audio anthology clearly demonstrates the many facets of Corea's style at this time— highly arranged and electronically orchestrated compositions, sometimes of episodic length, and with a range of heavy rock, Latin American, and Spanish influences. The acoustic piano introduction is very colored by Spanish music.

Listening Guide

Chick Corea and Return to Forever

"Excerpt from the First Movement of Heavy Metal" (Corea, Clarke, White, DiMeola) 2:45

Recorded January 1975, *No Mystery* Polydor 827149-2

Chick Corea: *keyboards, snare drum, marimba*

Stanley Clarke: *electric and acoustic bass*

Lenny White: *drums, percussion, marimba, congas*

Al DiMeola: *electric and acoustic guitar*

Form and Key: Arch-shape overall form; Rubato (out of strict) tempo piano Introduction and Coda surround hard-driving band ostinato rock-style 4/4 sections in E minor (Dorian)

0:00–0:24	*Introduction:* no tempo, *Acoustic Solo Piano* with *Spanish* fantasy-like melody in right-hand octaves and arpeggios, answered by left-hand sustained piano "power chords," ending on arpeggiated dominant harmony
0:24–0:42	*First section:* 12 bars, *Acoustic Solo Piano* sets 4/4 *tempo* and ABA (4+4+4 measure) melodic vamp featuring call–response format between right hand and left hand during A sections
0:43–0:59	*Second section:* 10 bars, *Electric "Wah-Wah" Guitar* enters with 2-bar Jimi Hendrix–influenced repeated part; drums and bass enter last 4 bars with crescendo
1:00–1:19	*Third section:* 12 bars, *Full Band Rock Vamp:* "Wah-Wah" Guitar part continues, joined by bass, drums, and electric keyboard each playing complementary repeating 2-bar parts
1:19–1:32	*Fourth section:* 8 bars, ad-lib *"Wah-Wah" Guitar Solo*, drums, bass, and electric keyboard change from repeating ostinato to free "ad-lib" E minor rock groove
1:33–1:46	*Fifth section:* 8 bars, *"Wah-Wah" Guitar Solo* continues over repeating 2-bar "stop-time" pattern in drums, bass, and electric keyboard
1:47–2:00	*Sixth section:* 8 bars, *"Wah-Wah" Guitar Solo* continues with return of 2-bar repeating bass part of third section, hard-driving drums, and electric keyboard accompaniment

2:01–2:13 *Seventh section:* 8 bars, *"Wah-Wah" Guitar Solo* continues over ascending chromatic bass line. Acoustic piano returns and gradually replaces 'Wah-Wah' Guitar solo

2:13–2:30 *Eighth section:* drums and bass fade out, *Acoustic Piano Solo* returns material similar to first section

2:30–2:45 *Coda section:* no tempo, *Acoustic Solo Piano* briefly returns to E minor Introduction material

Listen to excerpts of interviews with Chick Corea that are included in the corresponding chapter found on the CD-ROM.

Corea's recording *Leprechaun* was released in 1976 and was awarded two Grammy awards along with a five-star review in *Down Beat* magazine. Orchestral instruments in addition to a battery of synthesizers makes this recording even more dynamic. Like Hancock, Corea sought to do what was necessary to get the uninformed listener to take notice. In a 1974 interview Corea told *Down Beat* writer John Toner that "A project of ours is familiarizing people with what we do. If we play as an opening act to a well-known rock group, 80 percent of the audience doesn't know us from Adam, and doesn't know anything about John Coltrane, Miles, and jazz. All they are familiar with is the sound of our instruments, the electric instruments; and that we have a beat."[22]

Like so many bands from the electric phase of the 1970s, Corea's Return to Forever ran out of creative rope in their efforts to create popular crossover music that also satisfied the musician's creative sides. But by the time he disbanded Return to Forever (RTF), Corea had left an important legacy and indelible mark on jazz. His creations constitute the best examples of the fusion of jazz, electronics, rock, classical, Brazilian, and Spanish elements.

All of these former Miles Davis sidemen share one thing in common: they never stood still and Corea was no exception. Following the demise of RTF, Corea returned to his early love for acoustic jazz, partnering with vibraphonist Gary Burton in a series of duo recordings as well as duets with Herbie Hancock and a threesome adding Keith Jarrett, another Davis keyboard alumnus. Additional collaborations with the amazing saxophonist Michael Brecker led to their inspiring *Three Quartets* recording. Throughout the 80s, Corea recorded in all-star settings with Freddie Hubbard, vocal phenomenon Bobby McFerrin, Pat Metheny, and Joe Henderson. As if these outings were not different enough from his earlier fusion years, Corea has also recorded Wolfgang Mozart's *Double Piano Concerto* and other classical piano pieces. Almost simultaneously he moved from outings with his

Chick Corea performing with his band Return to Forever.

Akoustic and Elektric bands, confusing his fans to no end. Corea stands as one of the most important and influential jazz musicians of the late twentieth century.

SOUL AND POP INSTRUMENTAL JAZZ

David Sanborn (b 1945)

A new wave of R&B, blues, and gospel inspired musicians swept through the 1970s and into the 1980s, offering listeners a milder dose of instrumental jazz than the aforementioned Davis sidemen. While the style seems to personify black music, it was not limited to black musicians. For example, alto saxophonist David Sanborn represents one of the most influential, soulful and identifiable voices from this era. He initially received widespread exposure through his membership in the *Saturday Night Live* TV band, frequently spotlighted on camera during one of his passionate, sometimes screaming, high-octane solos. Additional cameo solo performances on recordings by James Taylor, David Bowie, and Stevie Wonder helped him become one of the most copied players during this time. There is always an intense, gospel quality to his solos, and it was his unique sound, musical mannerisms, well-paced solos, and unusual "harmonica-like phrasing"[23] (perhaps inspired by Stevie Wonder) that brought him widespread recognition and popularity. His Grammy award in 1981 in the rhythm and blues category is evidence of his success and popular appeal; but Sanborn was, and still is a fine improviser whose exceptional work can be heard on Gil Evans' *The Priestess* and on recordings with the Brecker Brothers. With this recognition came the idolatry of a new crop of young saxophonists, all rushing to purchase the unusual metal mouthpiece Sanborn used on alto sax and making every effort to copy his musical mannerisms.

The Brecker Brothers

Brecker brothers Michael and Randy have been protagonists in pop and jazz circles since their pioneering efforts to fuse elements of both traditions in the 1960s. In 1975 they regrouped to establish The Brecker Brothers band as a sequel to earlier bands they had been involved with, such as Dreams and drummer Billy Cobham's band. There were a number of pop bands that included horn sections along with vocals in the mid-1970s that may have helped to inspire The Brecker Brothers' band sound along with influences from jazz groups like John McLaughlin's Mahavishnu Orchestra and Tony Williams' Lifetime. Tower of Power, Average White Band, James Brown, and of course the *Saturday Night Live* TV band, founded in 1975, all captured certain elements of soul, funk, and other black-influenced styles that became part of The Brecker Brothers' sound. All of these groups shared several musical characteristics: (1) hard-driving rhythm sections and rock-like grooves that frequently emphasized back beats (beats two and four), (2) complex "heads" featuring intricate, busy, and jagged 16th note melodic lines; (3) melodies that were largely based on syncopated rhythms; (4) heavily articulated, short staccato lines; and (5) ballads often reminiscent of the Motown black pop tradition. The Brecker Brothers band stood out from the field of pop bands, distinguishing itself with more adventuresome compositions featuring angular melodies, unusual harmonies, odd meters, and rapid-fire virtuosic solo improvisations out of the jazz tradition. Randy Brecker experimented with various electronic devices to alter the sound of his trumpet, helping him to compete with the era's electronic sound of synthesizers and guitars that had drawn listeners away from acoustic instruments. A long list of important studio session and pop musicians from the period, including David Letterman's Paul Schaeffer, David Sanborn, and Frank Zappa drummer Terry Bozzio, augmented the core band, helping to establish the Brecker Brothers sound. The band enjoyed a seven-year run recording six albums for Arista Records until the group disbanded in 1982. Their efforts were rewarded with seven Grammy nominations, confirming the crossover appeal to pop and young jazz fans. The GRP label celebrated the nostalgic rebirth of The Brecker Brothers band in 1992 with the release of *Return of The Brecker Brothers*. The band's second recording for GRP *Out of the Loop* came in 1994 and was recognized with two Grammy awards. Both Randy and Michael (see Chapter 15) continue to be important forces on the contemporary jazz scene.

Popular soul and rhythm & blues–influenced saxophonist Grover Washington, Jr., playing the soprano saxophone.

Grover Washington, Jr. (1943–1999)

Philadelphia tenor saxophonist Grover Washington, Jr., could be considered a new breed of transplanted Texan, as his soulful brand of jazz can be traced back to the school of "Texas Tenors," a group of saxophonists from the 1940s well oiled by the Southwest blues tradition. Organ trios were his preference along with R&B groups that kept him working regularly through the mid-1960s. His first major recording date took place in 1971 when he released *Inner City Blues*. His subsequent 1975 *Mister Magic* recording was charted as the number one record on several polls. A number of other gold and platinum records followed, each offering his unique blend of jazz and soulful blues while often featuring other prominent studio musicians of the day. Like other pioneers of the "smooth jazz" movement, Washington was an accomplished musician, who was capable of playing jazz with more substance than required by the soulful style he popularized.

Chuck Mangione (b 1940)

Not all those artists who enjoyed popular success for their palatable brand of instrumental jazz were saxophonists. Call him a sell-out, call him the creator of "smooth jazz," describe his music as instrumental pop, whatever the rhetoric, trumpeter/flugelhornist Chuck Mangione enjoyed pop-star status from the mid-70s through the early 80s. Most fans that followed his career then had no idea of his earlier achievements—tours and/or recordings with Art Blakey's Jazz Messengers, trombonist Kai Winding, and high-note trumpeter/band leader Maynard Ferguson. His earlier Jazz Brothers combo included his brother Gap, tenor titan Sal Nestico, Jimmy Garrison (one-time Coltrane bassist), and Roy McCurdy (long-time Cannonball Adderley drummer). Most listeners are more familiar with the lyrical, catchy melodies, pleasing harmonies and memorable Latin-inspired grooves that were the hallmark of Mangione's '70s hits like "Land of Make Believe," "Bellavia," "Chase the Clouds Away," and of course, the hugely successful "Feels So Good" that reached number 2 in the 1977 pop charts—no small accomplishment for a jazz-inspired instrumental recording. Mangione's commercial success was confirmed by the Grammy he received in 1977. His successful score for the unreleased film *The Children of Sanchez* brought him a second Grammy award in 1978 and a Golden Globe nomination. His large scale orchestral collaborations produced the 1970 recording *Friends and Love* and *Together* in 1971, both unique for the time. It was during this time that Mangione became identified with the flugelhorn, and he is given much credit for the instrument's popularity in years that followed.

Flugelhornist/composer Chuck Mangione fronting a large orchestra.

Mangione's gift for composing memorable, sometimes romantic melodies, paired with jazz-inspired harmonies and rhythms, served as a bed for his bebop-grounded improvisations on flugelhorn, the instrument that helped him to develop his signature sound. Often criticized for selling out by the purist jazz community, Mangione countered, defending his music by pointing out how critics had a predictable track record of attacking anything that was successful. He used Adderley's "Mercy, Mercy, Mercy," guitarist George Benson's "This Masquerade," as well as popular hits by Hancock and Grover Washington, Jr., to make his point. "I think that categories are becoming meaningless," Mangione said in a 1977 interview, "because of the boundaries that are being crossed. People who get into the artists that are popular now will go back and check out other records they've made in the past."[24] It would be tempting, but misleading, to declare Mangione as the pioneer of twenty-first-century "smooth jazz." The glaring difference between Mangione, Washington, Sanborn, Corea, Hancock, or Benson and the smooth jazz performers is that the popular smooth artists have no recordings from the past to check out as Mangione suggests doing. They often have no heritage for fans to trace back—no roots in the jazz tradition.

The featured example recording is classic Mangione in that it is strongly influenced by Latin American rhythmic styles, features a memorable melody over pleasant infrequently changing harmonies, simple repetitive bass line serving as an ostinato, and bebop style improvisations. Our example is one of many versions of a primary theme Mangione used in his award winning film score *The Children of Sanchez*.

Listening Guide

Chuck Mangione

Form and Key: AABBAA, each section represents 8 bars in 4/4 time for a total chorus length of 48 bars

0:00–1:19	*First Chorus:*

	0:00–0:13	*A section:* Mangione plays the main A section melody on flugelhorn with only slight variation
	0:13–0:27	*A section repeated:* Mangione improvises around the A theme
	0:27–0:40	*B section:* original melody from film theme is never played here and improvisation is used instead
	0:40–0:53	*B section repeated:* once again, Mangione continues to improvise rather than play the melody
	0:53–1:06	*A section:* two-measure phrase from initial melody is played in call and response style with drum/timbales solo breaks
	1:06–1:19	*A section repeated:* two-measure phrase from initial melody is played in call and response style with drum/timbales solo breaks
	Interlude:	high register electric piano (almost sounding like a toy piano) plays Latin-style vamp

"Market Place" (Mangione) 3:11

Recorded in California, 1978; *Children of Sanchez* A & M Records 82839 6700 2

Chuck Mangione: *flugelhorn and electric piano*

Grant Greissman: *guitar*

Charles Meeks: *electric bass*

James Bradley, Jr.: *drums and timbales*

Chuck Mangione *concluded*

1:31–2:48 Second Chorus:

    1:31–1:44   *A section:* Mangione plays main A section melody

    1:44–1:56   *A section repeated:* Mangione plays main A section melody

    1:57–2:10   *B section:* while it appears coming out of the previous section that Mangione will continue to stay close to the original themes, he doesn't and improvises around the B theme

    2:10–2:23   *B section repeats:* improvisation continues

    2:23–2:35   *A section:* once again the theme is used as a basis for improvised departures

    2:35–2:48   *A section:* Mangione continues to improvise around the original melody

2:48–end *Third Chorus:*

    2:48–3:00   *A section:* improvisation continues

    3:00–end   *B section:* this section seems to occur sooner than it should if the AABBAA structure were to be adhered to; at this point, however, Mangione begins to finally state the B section theme just before the track fades

Mangione left the scene in 1989, a hiatus from music that lasted about five years before announcing his return in 1994. His more recent recordings on the Chesky label prove that he still writes melodies that are "hard to resist"[25] according to *Down Beat'*s John McDonough.

Steps Ahead

Jazz-rock fusion and pop instrumental jazz were not the only games in town during the 1970s and 1980s and there were several nonelectrified, or partially unplugged, paths taken by artists who strove to stay closer to the acoustic roots of this music. For example, a band that flew under the popular radar at the end of the decade and into the 80s was Steps. For musicians and fans in the know, however, Steps Ahead, as they became known, stood as a bright beacon influencing many musicians. The band performed a uniquely original repertoire that had a post-bop edge, successfully fusing elements of the tradition with a hip, current sound using primarily acoustic instruments, and embracing Latin and jazz-rock fusion styles. They never enjoyed commercial success though, and early recordings were available only as imports from Japan, making them rare coins for American buyers. Even now and despite the success of its individual musicians, Steps' recordings are challenging to find since a small American label (NYC Records) with little retail distribution has reissued them. Fortunately, the talented founding members of Steps including Michael Brecker (tenor saxophone and EWI—electronic wind instrument), Mike Mainieri (electric vibraphone), Don Grolnick (piano), Eddie Gomez (former Bill Evans bassist), and drummer Steve Gadd all received significant exposure through other projects and record labels. Over time the personnel changed and the group sound veered off in a more jazz-rock fusion direction. While many artists like those in Steps practiced jazz based on the acoustic tradition during these years, widespread attention for their brand of jazz was difficult to achieve, particularly in light of the popular fusion movement. The next chapter will examine the other more acoustic styles of jazz vying for attention during these two decades.

Jazz in Perspective

The timeline that follows will put the developments of jazz discussed in Chapters 13 and 14 into a larger historical context, providing you with a better sense of how landmark musical events may relate to others that match your personal areas of interest.

1970
- Jean Stafford wins Pulitzer for *Collected Stories.*
- American Medical Association votes in support of abortions in some cases.
- *Patton, M*A*S*H*,* and *Woodstock* are popular films.
- Kent State University student riots protesting war end in four deaths.
- Students strike for peace in 450 U.S. colleges.
- Women march for equality in New York.
- Drug culture rock stars Jimmy Hendrix and Janis Joplin die of drug overdoses.
- The Beatles break up.

1971
- Disney World opens.
- Busing supports integration of schools.
- 26th Amendment allows 18 year olds to vote.
- Andrew Lloyd Webber's rock musical *Jesus Christ Superstar* creates a stir.
- Astronauts further explore lunar surface.

1972
- Liberated women publish *Ms.* magazine.
- Cigarette advertisements banned from airwaves.
- Senate ratifies Equal Rights Amendment.
- Movies of the year include *The Godfather, Cabaret, Last Tango in Paris,* and *Play It Again Sam.*

- Nixon reelected amid Watergate affair.

1973
- Francis FitzGerald awarded Pulitzer for *Fire in the Lake.*
- United States ends role in Vietnam following approximately 55,000 deaths.
- Courts allow abortion in *Roe* vs. *Wade* case.
- Watergate conspirators convicted; Nixon declares innocence.
- Herbie Hancock enjoys success with Headhunters band and recording of *Chameleon* is popular hit.

1974
- Robert Lowell wins Pulitzer Prize for *The Dolphin.*
- Jazz composer and bandleader Duke Ellington dies.
- Courts rule that schools must teach English.
- President Nixon forced to resign over role in Watergate; Gerald Ford assumes presidency.
- School busing continues to incite protest.
- Pianist Keith Jarrett records *The Windup* for the German ECM label.

1975
- President Ford declares Vietnam era officially over.
- *The Wiz* wins awards as new musical sensation.

- VCR becomes common home appliance.
- President Ford saves city of New York from bankruptcy.
- Top films include *One Flew Over the Cuckoo's Nest* and *Jaws*.
- Chick Corea's band Return to Forever records *No Mystery*.

1976
- Hit films are *Rocky* and *Network*.
- Apple Computer begins with only $1,300 capital.
- Sunbelt attracts many new businesses.
- Americans celebrate bicentennial.
- Stagnant economy hampers and frustrates U.S. citizens and government.
- Jimmy Carter elected president.
- Satirist Tom Wolfe declares the 1970s as "Me Decade."
- Anthony Braxton records *Creative Orchestra Music 1976*.

1977
- Alex Haley wins Pulitzer award for *Roots*.
- Space shuttle *Enterprise* makes test flight.
- President Carter declares energy crisis.

- Detroit car makers feel pinch from Japanese competition.
- American rock idol Elvis Presley dies.
- John Travolta's *Saturday Night Fever* helps to popularize discos.
- Other pop films include *Star Wars, Annie Hall,* and *Close Encounters of the Third Kind.*
- Weather Report records "Palladium" along with "Birdland" on their *Heavy Weather* album.

1978
- Retirement age is raised to 70.
- Carl Sagan awarded Pulitzer Prize for *Dragons of Eden*.
- Hannah Gray becomes first woman university president at the University of Chicago.
- Economic malaise continues and President Carter announces anti-inflation plan.
- Jonestown cult mass suicide shocks nation.
- Chuck Mangione records Grammy winning film score for *Children of Sanchez* including "Market Place."

CHAPTER SUMMARY

In the 1970s and 1980s the term "jazz" continued to encompass more and more substyles, some representing further development of previous styles and some exploring new directions. The line between jazz and rock became blurred with the advent of rock bands that included jazz-like horn sections (Chicago or Blood, Sweat & Tears), and jazz bands that featured rock rhythm sections (Chase). The development of electronic instruments, notably synthesizers, led to a vastly expanded sound palette. Five former Miles Davis sidemen continued to explore the heavily electronic approach that served as the foundation of the *Bitches Brew* album in the formation of four significant jazz-fusion groups—Weather Report, Return to Forever, The Headhunters, and the Mahavishnu Orchestra.

Weather Report, founded by keyboardist Joe Zawinul and former Miles Davis saxophonist Wayne Shorter, was a major contributor in jazz fusion for

16 years. A perennial *Down Beat* magazine award winner, the group initially played with a jazz-inspired freedom similar to that heard on the Miles Davis *Bitches Brew* album. Over time, however, the group developed a more commercial approach. In 1976, fretless electric bass phenomenon Jaco Pastorious was added to the group. Weather Report then recorded "Birdland," its biggest hit. This tune has been arranged for, and performed by countless big bands, marching bands, and drum corps.

Pianist Herbie Hancock first gained widespread recognition for his 1962 funky jazz hit "Watermelon Man." After working with Miles Davis he tried other different settings before forming the fusion group The Headhunters who recorded the hit "Chameleon" in 1973. In 1983 his hit "Rocket" won a Grammy award and five music video awards. In addition to film scoring, Hancock continues to be involved with the commercial side as well as the bop inspired mainstream of jazz.

Bitches Brew guitarist John McLaughlin founded the Mahavishnu Orchestra in 1971, adding electric violin to the typical fusion instrumentation. The band was known for their very complex music including changing odd time signatures.

After playing in free and mainstream jazz settings, former Miles Davis keyboardist Chick Corea founded the group Return to Forever (RTF). Initially, RTF played Latin- and Spanish-inspired jazz, some of which had been commissioned by saxophonist Stan Getz. The group eventually replaced the saxophone with electric guitar enabling a repertoire with more commercially appealing rock grooves, many of which featured very complex, tight orchestrations and sophisticated large scale forms. Since the breakup of RTF, Corea has played both in fusion settings, notably his "Elektric Band," and numerous mainstream neobop settings including his own "Akoustic Band."

A number of other jazz artists have continued to cross and blur the line separating jazz and rock. Saxophonist David Sanborn was highly visible on television and copied by many young players. The Brecker Brothers (Michael and Randy) produced complex funk influenced jazz with innovative soloists. Grover Washington, Jr., gained much popularity playing a soulful predecessor of smooth jazz. His 1975 recording *Mr. Magic* was a huge hit. Trumpeter Chuck Mangione at one time played burning hard bop with Art Blakey and the Jazz Messengers. In later years, he became better known for his easy listening flugelhorn hit "Feels So Good," which in 1977 reached number 2 on the pop charts. The group Steps Ahead (Steps) began as a mainstream acoustic group featuring top soloists. Over time and with personnel changes, the group gradually moved from its mainstream beginnings toward a more electric fusion approach.

KEY TERMS

Important people and bands.

PEOPLE
Grover Washington, Jr.
Chuck Mangione
Herbie Hancock
Jaco Pastorious
Michael Brecker
Randy Brecker

Joe Zawinul
Wayne Shorter
John McLaughlin
David Sanborn

BANDS
Mahavishnu Orchestra

Weather Report
Chicago
Blood, Sweat & Tears
Return to Forever
The Headhunters
The Brecker Brothers
Steps Ahead

REVIEW QUESTIONS

1. Jazz became fractured in the 1970s and 1980s in part because of the prevalence of so many different styles—name them.

2. What style of jazz seemed to take the lead during much of the decade and why?

3. Name two popular rock bands that featured jazz-like horn sections.

4. Electronics and new technology exerted significant influences on jazz during this period. Discuss these innovations in some detail and what influences they had on the music, specific jazz groups, or individual artists.

5. What are some of the key characteristics that describe Weather Report's style?

6. Who was the electric bassist that brought this instrument to the attention of the jazz community? What was so unique about his approach to the instrument?

7. What was Weather Report's biggest selling recording?

8. Herbie Hancock explored the funky side of jazz in the 1960s with what hit tunes?

9. Several failed attempts at bringing jazz to the masses by Hancock followed his relationship with Miles Davis. These recordings relied less on influences of popular music and more on what kind of ethnic music?

10. Hancock's The Headhunters band released what hit recording that changed the sound of jazz in the 1970s?

11. What popular music artists helped influenced Hancock's The Headhunters band sound?

12. Like so many former Miles Davis sidemen, Hancock has worn many musical hats since the early 70s. Discuss some of his other stylistic adventures aside from the fusion style expressed by The Headhunters.

13. What two guitarists during this period were responsible for bringing the sound of rock guitar to jazz?

14. How would you characterize the music of Mahavishnu?

15. Like Herbie Hancock, Chick Corea has explored many different styles of jazz. Discuss this aspect of Corea's musical split personality.

16. Some of Corea's compositions for Return to Forever are episodic in nature. Can you name one?

17. Certain aspects of non-American music permeate the music produced by Corea's Return to Forever band. What world music influenced this band?

18. What instrument in the 1970s became one of the prominent voices of fusion jazz?

19. What saxophonist explored the soul-pop side of jazz, showing roots in the Texas-tenor R&B tradition?

20. What style of jazz is associated with the Brecker Brothers band and what instruments did its leaders play?

21. What importance does Chuck Mangione have to the popular instrumental side of jazz?

22. What is an EWI and who is known for his use of it?

SUGGESTED SUPPLEMENTARY LISTENING

The abbreviation (iT) indicates that a particular recording cited in the text, or particularly demonstrative of the artist, is available from the Apple iTunes Web site. Other Web-based music distributors may also prove to be valuable resources. SCCJ indicates *Smithsonian Collection of Classic Jazz*.

Blood, Sweat & Tears Sony (iT)
Blood, Sweat & Tears 3 Sony (iT)
The Very Best of Chicago: *Only the Beginning* Rhino (iT)

Weather Report

Weather Report Sony (iT)
Black Market Sony (iT)
Heavy Weather Sony (iT)
I Sing the Body Electric Sony (iT)
Sweetnighter Sony (iT)
Mysterious Traveler Sony (iT)
Tale Spinnin' Sony (iT)
Night Passage Sony (iT)

Mahavishnu Orchestra

Birds of Fire Sony (iT)
Inner Mounting Flame Sony (iT)
Apocalypse Sony (iT)
Love, Devotion and Surrender (with Carlos Santana) Sony (iT)

Herbie Hancock

V.S.O.P Live Sony (iT)
Herbie Hancock Quintet (with Wynton Marsalis) Sony (iT)
Headhunters Sony (iT)
Mwandishi Warner Jazz (iT)
Crossings Wea International
Thrust Sony (iT)
Gershwin's World Verve (iT)
An Evening with Chick Corea and Herbie Hancock Sony (iT)
New Standard Verve (iT)

Chick Corea

Light as a Feather GRP (iT)
Now He Sings, Now He Sobs Blue Note (iT)
Hymn of the Seventh Galaxy Polydor (iT)
My Spanish Heart Verve (iT)
The Leprechaun Verve (iT)
Three Quartets (with Michael Brecker) Stretch (iT)
Solo Piano Originals Part I and II Stretch (iT)

David Sanborn

The Best of David Sanborn Warner (iT)
Backstreet Warner (iT)
Change of Heart Warner (iT)
Close-Up Warner (iT)
Heart to Heart Warner (iT)
Hideaway Warner (iT)

Grover Washington

Mr. Magic Motown (iT)
Inner City Blues Motown (iT)
Soulful Strut Sony (iT)
Live at the Bijou Hip-O (iT)

Chuck Mangione

Buttercorn Lady (with Art Blakey and the Jazz Messengers) Verve (iT)
Live at Hollywood Bowl Hip-O (iT)
Chase the Clouds Away A&M (iT)
Chuck Mangione: Greatest Hits A&M (iT)

Steps (Ahead)

Smokin' in the Pit NYC Records
Steps: A Collection NYC Records

The Brecker Brothers

The Brecker Brothers Collection Vols. I and II RCA (Novus) (iT)
Return of the Brecker Brothers GRP (iT)
Out of the Loop GRP (iT)

The Unplugged, Eclectic 1970s and 1980s

"[I'm] almost thinking of retiring and waiting for the '80s. There's such a sense of stagnation and a lack of direction now, a shying away from possibilities rather than an embracing of them."[1]

PAT METHENY

LONG LIVE ACOUSTIC JAZZ

The voice of acoustic musicians was nearly drowned out by the omnipresent electric jazz style of the 70s. These two decades appear to be the most fractured period in the history of jazz where "anything goes" was the unspoken motto. The deaths of many earlier jazz pioneers made this an even more uphill struggle for the jazz musician who was more informed by the acoustic tradition. The 1970s saw the passing of Duke Ellington, Johnny Hodges, Albert Ayler, Paul Desmond, Lee Morgan, Charles Mingus, Louis Armstrong, Bobby Timmons, Gene Krupa, Lennie Tristano, Oliver Nelson, Harry Carney, and Cannonball Adderley to name but a few. While the work of those who clung to this tradition was somewhat eclipsed by fusion-style jazz, there were several other trends and significant artists that did not go unnoticed or without lasting influence.

The ECM Sound

German classical bassist and part-time production assistant Manfred Eicher launched the independent label ECM in 1969, initially specializing in recordings by free jazz artists such as Paul Bley and Marion Brown. ECM (Editions of Contemporary Music) established a new trend in independent labels, eventually serving as a successful model for the many "indies" that would follow. Free of commercial restrictions and contractual obligations, ECM artists found freedom to follow their creative muse. ECM promoted quiet, chamber jazz at a time when volume had been increased to rock level decibels by the electronic jazz-fusion movement. In Eicher's words,

European saxophonist Jan Garbarek's ECM album Dis.

"people had to learn to listen again. We tried to channel the chamber music esthetics of written classical music into the improvisational aspect."[2] Consequently, "ECM was not recognized as a jazz label only, but as a stream of music [notice he uses Gunther Schuller's term appropriately here since much of the ECM music merged jazz with classical styles] where we combined improvisational fields with written fields—of course with the jazz tradition."[3] Eicher wanted to duplicate the efforts of the finest European classical record labels by providing the same high-quality sonic reproduction for jazz and he successfully set a new standard in recording. "I wanted to get that element of transparency."[4] The music captured by the label soon became described as "the ECM sound." This sound is characterized by pastel, modal melodies that are often folk-like in quality. Improvisation was abundant on ECM recordings as was the absence of swing since even, nonswung eighth-note rhythm grooves were more commonplace than the more traditional jazz swing style.

Even the artwork on ECM record jackets promoted a quiet, pensive, and introspective quality. Unlike U.S. labels that typically featured portraits or photos of the artists in action, ECM covers presented landscapes, abstracts, and other panoramas. "We try to capture much more atmospheric waves than any title,"[5] said Eicher.

The label became known for its uncompromising releases and, contrary to large American labels, artistic freedom for their artists. This freedom lured some of America's finest artists, along with a growing pool of European artists experimenting with jazz and improvised music. Guitarists Pat Metheny and Ralph Towner along with pianists Chick Corea and Keith Jarrett and drummer Jack DeJohnette helped the label to grow. Jarrett's success almost single-handedly brought ECM into the global market. Both Corea and Jarrett recorded solo albums for the label and the success of these recordings breathed new life into the art of solo jazz piano playing, once again extending a long tradition that had enjoyed an earlier rebirth through the work of Bill Evans.

Once again, however, some jazz purists criticized the label for its "classical-music sentimentality" and for abandoning the real roots of jazz. Thanks to Eicher's label though, a number of American and European artists were afforded widespread exposure throughout Europe, Japan, and the United States at a time when their efforts could have easily gone unnoticed because of the emphasis on jazz-rock fusion. In addition to those American musicians previously mentioned, ECM served to launch the careers of a new, emerging breed of European musicians profoundly influenced by jazz like saxophonist Jan Garbarek, pianist Bobo Stenson, guitarist Terje Rypdal, and bassist Eberhard Weber. ECM continues to be a source of interesting music that crosses many boundaries and more recently the label has also focused on issuing pure twentieth-century classical music.

The CD-ROM includes an interesting assessment and discussion of European jazz that began to emerge with some direction in the 1970s. This discussion with a former member of Amsterdam's Willem Breuker Kollektief as well as interviews with Tim Hagans can be found in the corresponding chapter on the CD-ROM.

Keith Jarrett (b 1945)

A child prodigy determined to have a genius IQ before entering public school, Keith Jarrett was an important force in the sunset years of the twentieth century. Jarrett, like Hancock, is a classically trained pianist. He gave his first full-length concert performance, complete with original compositions, at age 6. His intense interest in jazz and improvisation did not bloom until he was a teenager, and by this time he had already demonstrated amazing technical facility and musicianship. Discovered by Art Blakey at a New York jam session, Jarrett joined Blakey's Jazz Messengers, sharing the stage with Chuck Mangione. He was quickly catapulted to public prominence after joining saxophonist Charles Lloyd's quartet. Jarrett gained widespread recognition for his amazing solo performances on Lloyd's most successful recording, *Forest Flower* (1966). Jarrett left Lloyd to work with his own trio that included ex-Coleman bassist Charlie Haden and former Bill Evans drummer Paul Motian. An awareness of these associations is important to understanding Jarrett's somewhat "outside," free trio music from this period that also featured saxophonist Dewey Redman who was an Ornette Coleman disciple.

Jarrett, yet another alumnus of the Davis band's keyboard chair, initially turned down Miles' first offer to join his band in favor of continued pursuit of his own trio. He eventually did join the Davis group at the height of his electronic-funk phase, serving alongside Chick Corea as a second electronic keyboard player and later occupying the sole keyboard chair. Jarrett, a dedicated purist and committed acoustic musician, later commented that there was only one person he would ever have played an electronic instrument for—Miles Davis. There was a mutual respect between these two great musical forces, despite Jarrett's lack of respect for Davis' 70s band sound. "I thought the band was the most egocentric band I had heard musically . . . except for Miles. Miles was still playing nice, beautiful things, and the rest of the band was in boxes [not listening to one another or communicating]. I just wanted to do a little bit to change the feeling,"[6] said Jarrett. A man of few words, Davis once asked Jarrett, "Keith, how does it feel to be a genius?"[7] and years later Miles characterized Jarrett as "the best pianist I ever had."[8] This was no small compliment given the others under his consideration.

Jarrett's mind is a sponge, absorbing every kind of music he ever encountered, and his tonal memory enables him to recall things in an instant. Consequently, he often amazes listeners by the full range of his eclectic creative process. He can instantly shift gears from playing bebop one moment to romantic Bill Evans style the next, with European classical devices and bombastic avant-garde gestures lurking to emerge at any moment. Jarrett has always been motivated by folk music, something he shared with Davis and a commonality that no doubt drew them together.

Jarrett left Davis following the loud, electric Fillmore years in order to pursue musical directions that couldn't have been more contrasting—his progressive acoustic trio as well as his works for solo piano. It was Jarrett's partnership with Manfred Eicher and the ECM record label that had jump-started his unparalleled success as an acoustic jazz musician at a time when nearly everyone else was focused on fusion. *Facing You*, his first successful ECM solo piano release led to his overwhelmingly successful *The Köln Concert* (1975) that sold 600,000 copies in the first five years and continues to sell consistently. Jarrett approached the keyboard with a completely blank slate, nothing performed with premeditation, much as he does today with his trio that rejects rehearsing. He used improvised folk-like melodies, rhythmic riffs, and down-home gospel-like vamps in improvisations that typically lasted 30–45 minutes without pause. Never once does he falter, totally immersing himself in the physical and spiritual aspect of piano playing and the creative process itself. In Jarrett's own words, "The ideal state to be in, just

Pianist/Composer Keith Jarrett.

before I make a sound, would be a state where there is nothing to gain, no ideas to purge. You can only make music when there isn't anything first."[9] His blazing technique is unparalleled, and, coupled with his lyrical romanticism, produces a captivating performance that leaves audiences breathless. Jarrett's technique has been compared to that of Art Tatum and Oscar Peterson, but with a more modern sensibility that puts him in a category by himself. Some say that the genesis of pianist George Winston's "New Age" style began with Jarrett, which is an unfortunate comparison as Jarrett's music is so much richer, intellectually more challenging, and dynamic.

The unexpected success of his solo, trio, and quartet recordings was proof that an audience still existed for acoustic, adventuresome jazz that challenged the listener and found a universality with the folk tradition. Jarrett rekindled the art of solo jazz piano playing and he helped to expose in his ECM trio and quartet recordings a number of emerging European artists. Jarrett's discography is more diverse than one could imagine including chamber works (*In the Light*), works for soloist and orchestra (*Luminescence* and *Celestial Hawk* commissioned by the Boston Symphony), and of course, more recent recordings of classic standards by his second regular combo known simply as the Standards Trio with Gary Peacock on bass and Jack DeJohnnette on drums. This group has dedicated itself to keeping a tradition and great repertoire alive. Their performances and recordings are completely impromptu—no rehearsals, no set lists, and only one take for recordings, preserving the live and spontaneous aspect of the performance. Many consider his trio to be one of the best, rivaling those led by the great pianists he has been compared to—Bill Evans and Oscar Peterson.

"The Windup," found in the accompanying collection, is an excellent example not only of Jarrett's unique personal style from this period, but also of the kind of company he kept with an emerging breed of new European musicians. The track begins with Jarrett's signature—a syncopated gospel, folksy vamp that serves to introduce the melody played with soprano saxophonist Jan Garbarek. The loose rhythmic feel and placement of accents in the melody provide an illusion that the meter is changing, but in fact the piece is not that unusual metrically. A simple 4/4 meter is nearly consistent throughout with only one 2/4 measure occurring just prior to the second theme. While the piano solo may imply harmonies, much as was the case with Ornette Coleman's free jazz, there are none whatsoever for Jarrett to follow. Drums and bass are added, yet there is still no set form or chords, which makes his solo completely improvised, inspired by the flow of thought and motivated solely by his improvised melodic direction. His solo could be compared to stream of consciousness creative writing including some modern poetry.

Since Jarrett's music offers such a wide range of features, the summation of characteristics in Table 14.1 might help you to identify and appreciate what his music is all about. See if you can identify any of these characteristics in "The Windup."

TABLE 14.1 Distinguishing Characteristics of Keith Jarrett's Music

- Unusual chord progressions in trio tunes
- Use of *pedal points* (a sustained or reoccurring bass pitch around which harmonies change)
- Free form solos, sometimes with no clear tonality
- Chromatic harmonies that avoid predictable functionality
- Down-home, gospel-like vamps and syncopations
- Rock- and Latin-tinged straight-eighth-note tunes in the 1970s
- Unusual phrase groupings and lengths in composed and improvised melodies that cause meter and form to often sound unconventional even if they are not
- Spectacular, flawless, virtuosic technique and execution
- Penchant for folk-like melodies especially in solo repertoire
- Minimalist aspect of some solo music where lengthy sections are dependent on repetitive or ostinato figures that often serve as underpinning to more elaborate improvisations
- Emotionally charged, romantic, and classically influenced passages
- Athletic and physical performances—rising off the bench, groaning, and singing along with his improvisations
- Occasionally reaching inside the piano to play the strings directly
- Ventures into free jazz

Keith Jarrett

Form and Key: AABA' C in C major and 4/4 meter

0:00–0:39	*Introduction:* gospel-like vamp with staggered entrances by piano, bass and drums; bass and left hand piano play repetitive ostinato figure
0:39–1:22	*First Chorus:*

    0:39–0:47 *A section:* soprano sax enters with A theme

    0:47–0:55 *A section:* soprano sax repeats A theme

    0:55–1:01 *B section:* contrasting theme yet still surrounding the pitch C

    1:01–1:06 *A¹ section:* soprano restates a theme that closely resembles the first A theme

    1:06–1:13 *C section:* rhythmically punctuated melody

    1:13–1:22 *Vamp:* much like intro but trio repeats figure for only 8 bars

1:22–1:56 *Second Chorus:*

    1:22–1:30 *A section:* soprano sax returns with A theme

    1:30–1:37 *A section:* soprano sax repeats A theme

    1:37–1:42 *B section:* contrasting theme yet still surrounding the pitch C

Listening Guide

"The Windup" (Jarrett) (excerpt) 4:57

Recorded in Oslo, Norway, 4/24-25/74; *Belonging* ECM 1050 422 829 115-2

Keith Jarrett: *piano*

Jan Garbarek: *soprano saxophone*

Palle Danielsson: *bass*

Jon Christensen: *drums*

1:42–1:47	*A¹ section:* soprano restates a theme that closely resembles the first A theme	
1:47–1:56	*C section:* rhythmically punctuated melody	
1:56–	*Piano Solo:* free, unaccompanied piano solo, not based on any preconceived chord progression	
2:30–4:36	*Piano Solo Continues:* joined by bass and drums in free flowing, almost timeless playing; bass does not walk nor does drummer play in a strict tempo	
4:36–4:42	*B Section:* piano solo seamlessly returns to B theme	
4:42–End	*C Section:* soprano sax plays final C theme before abrupt end (original, unedited recording includes a soprano sax solo before the group returns to play the entire tune)	

Chronic fatigue syndrome struck Jarrett in 1996 and at times he felt he would never leave his house again let alone perform, but he struggled back to record with his trio, performing to date as much as his health allows. His solo recording *The Melody, At Night, With You* was made at his home in 1999 and served to announce his return and road to recovery. His trio, also once again working and recording, has collaborated for three decades.

Jarrett continues to be one of the most outspoken public critics of the new wave of young musicians in "designer suits," new age music, electronic music, and the record industry as a whole.

RETURN OF EXPATRIATES UNLEASH A REBIRTH OF ACOUSTIC JAZZ

Dexter Gordon's triumphant return to the United States in 1976 was heralded by the two-record set *Homecoming* recorded live at New York's famed jazz club the Village Vanguard. His no-nonsense, hard bop–derived band featured one of the bright lights of postmodern trumpeting—Woody Shaw. Shaw introduced a new vocabulary to jazz trumpet playing, borrowed from contemporary pianists like Corea, but his unfortunate early death interrupted the natural conclusions and potential of his innovative style. Gordon's follow-up studio recording *Sophisticated Giant* sold an amazing 100,000 copies during this time when acoustic, mainstream jazz was poorly marketed amid the fusion boom. Gordon's successful repatriation was followed by the return of two other saxophone titans who had sought refuge in Europe from fusion and pop disco trends—Johnny Griffin and Phil Woods.

Dexter Gordon, the tenor saxophonist credited in the 40s for adopting Parker's bop style, was public about his distaste for the rock and roll craze at jazz's expense. He was also uncomfortable with the political and social strife during the time, so he left for Paris, eventually setting up shop in Copenhagen. "There was no racial discrimination or anything like that [in Europe.] And the fact that you're an artist in Europe means something, they treat you with a lot of respect."[10] While there was significant attention paid to these rediscovered musicians, the buzz was loudest not over the rebirth of older, established musicians like Gordon, but over the young trumpet prodigy who first gained widespread exposure through his work with Art Blakey's Jazz Messengers—Wynton Marsalis. The successful return of the older expatriates and acceptance of their music (the same they had played years before when people stopped listening) no doubt had a great deal to do with paving the way for the success of what eventually became described as the "Young Lions." Marsalis and a large, new crop of outspoken, well-trained, impeccably dressed, and bountifully talented young black performers came to be known as the Young Lions, following the title of the 1982 Marsalis recording. Giving new life to progressive bop, neobop, postbop, or whatever label you choose for the move- ment, his success is undeniable and has changed the jazz landscape. Wynton Marsalis and his sax-playing brother Branford drew much attention in the 80s, paving the way for a steady stream of other young black and white artists. Bran- ford toured with British pop artist Sting and served for a time as musical director for Jay Leno's Tonight Show band. Other newcomers (black and white) that fol- lowed closely, taking advantage of the Marsalis wake, were drummer Jeff "Tain" Watts, pianists Marcus Roberts and Cyrus Chestnut, trumpeters Terrence Blan- chard, Wallace Rooney, Ryan Kisor, and Nicholas Payton, saxophonists Donald Harrison, Chris Potter, Ravi Coltrane (yes, John's son), and Joshua Redman, and a host of others helped, to rekindle what some felt was an old flame dressed up in new clothes. Marsalis dismissed free jazz and electric-jazz-rock fusion styles, claiming that many of the artists associated with these styles were little more than carnival barkers, ungrounded in the important roots of jazz and strayed too far from the tree. The die had been cast and these artists signaled a full-scale, suc- cessful revival of acoustic jazz firmly rooted in the bop tradition and the sound of Miles Davis' mid-1960s progressive quintet. Their champions applauded them for reclaiming the rich jazz heritage and bringing it back to the rightful owners—the black artists who had largely created it—while their detractors criticized them for embalming jazz, stagnating its progress and curating it for the museum.

Wynton Marsalis (b 1961) and the Young Lions

Despite some negative press brought about in part by Marsalis' own outspoken convictions and preferences, he has single-handedly done more to raise an inter- national awareness of the importance of jazz than anyone in the past 20 or 30 years. He has been tireless in the pursuit of his own convictions and has succeeded where many have failed in securing significant support and visibility for jazz.

Born in the birthplace of jazz, his training as a youth in New Orleans pre- pared him for study at the world-renowned Juilliard School of Music in New York. Art Blakey was impressed by the young upstart and, before Marsalis turned 20, hired him and his saxophonist brother Branford to form the front line of his ac- claimed Jazz Messengers. Aside from Miles Davis' small groups, Blakey's band had given birth to more leaders in the field than any other. Before long, Marsalis was fronting his own band and made his recording debut as a leader in 1982 with an exciting, young quintet. His group at that time was known for their adventure- some new compositions and reinterpretations of standards that often ended in obscuring the original form beyond recognition. Modeled in many ways after Davis' second great quintet in the mid-1960s, Marsalis' musicians played on the edge, with drummer Jeff "Tain" Watts doing everything he could to build on the

EXAMPLE 14.1
Metric Modulation from 3/4 to 2/4.

Start by tapping your right or left foot in a steady tempo. Clap your hands beginning with beat 1 of the 3rd measure (second line). Continue the layered rhythm pattern until the 5th measure. At this point stop the foot, but continue clapping your hands without changing pace. You will notice that the tempo has now slowed significantly compared to the pace of your foot tap, and you have changed from 3/4 to 2/4 meter.

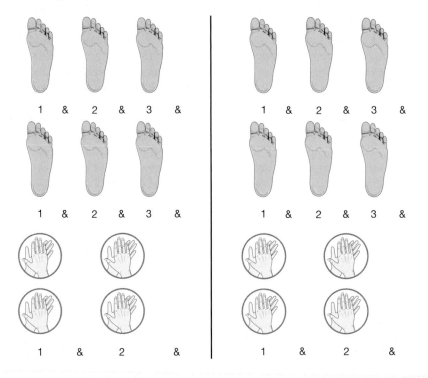

Tony Williams tradition of metric modulations (using a rhythmic gesture to subtly move from one meter and tempo to another as in Example 14.1), power playing, and unparalleled intensity.

The group shared a telepathic sense of communication much like Davis' classic mid-1960s quintet, capable of playing at any tempo and seamlessly shifting gears from one tempo to the next. Marsalis is a gifted trumpeter with flawless technique, warm, liquid, buttery sound, a sense for dramatic contrast, strong background in the tradition including the skillful use of various mutes, and the unusual ability to perform classical music as well as jazz. He never fails to demonstrate his complete and total command of the instrument enabling him to control his sound much as a vocalist does to interpret a lyric. His brother, saxophonist, Branford Marsalis, is an extension of Wayne Shorter and is equally equipped on the soprano saxophone. Drummer Watts, with his prize fighter–like punching and jabbing, keeps things heated up in "Delfeayo's Dilemma," the track included on the companion anthology, and is guilty of being a constant sparkplug in this quintet.

Since the early 1980s, Marsalis has been a powerful and articulate spokesman for jazz, backing up an overconfident attitude and opinions by producing an astounding catalogue of 40 jazz and classical recordings and nine Grammy Awards at this writing. In 1983 he became the first and only artist to win a Grammy Award in both jazz and classical categories, an amazing accomplishment which he duplicated two years later. Perhaps his most treasured accomplishment was the coveted Pulitzer Prize in music composition, bestowed upon him in 1997, the same year he was named Artistic Director of Jazz at Lincoln Cen-

Wynton Marsalis

Listening Guide

"Delfeayo's Dilemma"
(Wynton Marsalis) 6:46

**Recorded in New York,
January, 1985;** *Black
Codes (From the Underground)*

Columbia CK40009

Wynton Marsalis:
trumpet

Branford Marsalis:
tenor saxophone

Kenny Kirkland: *piano*

Charnett Moffet: *bass*

Jeff "Tain" Watts:
drums

Form and Key: repeated choruses (ABC) in the key of G predominantly in 4/4, varying in length from 23 to 28 bars (section C always includes one 3/4 bar even during solo sections). Each section (A, B, and C) of the *Theme* choruses is divided in half, with the first half presenting thematic material, and the second half an improvised (ad-lib) solo.

0:00–0:27	*First Chorus:* 27 bars (includes a 3/4 bar), *Theme*
	0:00–0:11 *A section:* 11 bars: 5-bar *Quartal* (notes progressing by intervals of a 4th) *Theme* played by trumpet, sax, piano, with bass and drums tacit; then 6 bars of swinging bass and drums, with piano ad-lib solo
	0:11–0:19 *B section:* 8 bars: 4-bar *Modulating Theme* played by trumpet and sax, with rhythm section accompaniment; then 4 bars of swinging bass, drums, with piano ad-lib solo
	0:19–0:27 *C section:* 8 bars: 4-bar *Unison Theme* (the fourth bar here is 3/4), played by trumpet, sax, over bass "C" pedal; then 4 bars of swinging bass and drums, with ad-lib piano solo
0:27–0:52	*Second Chorus:* 25-bar *Theme* similar to First Chorus, but last four bars of C section are abbreviated here to two bars
0:53–1:20	*Third Chorus:* 28 bars, *Trumpet Solo,* following chorus (ABC) solo form (A = 12 bars, B = 8 bars, C = 8 bars), with swinging rhythm section accompaniment
1:21–3:07	*Fourth-Seventh Choruses:* 28 bars each, *Trumpet Solo* continues
3:08–3:34	*Eighth Chorus:* 28 bars, *Tenor Sax Solo,* following chorus solo form, with swinging rhythm section accompaniment
3:34–4:26	*Ninth and Tenth Choruses:* 28 bars each, *Tenor Sax Solo* continues
4:27–4:52	*Eleventh Chorus:* 28 bars, *Piano Solo,* following chorus solo form, with swinging rhythm section accompaniment
4:53–5:45	*Twelfth and Thirteenth Chorus:* 28 bars each, *Piano Solo* continues
5:45–6:11	*Fourteenth Chorus:* 27 bars, *Theme* similar to First Chorus
6:12–6:46	*Fifteenth Chorus:* 23+ bars, *Theme* similar to Second Chorus, but last four bars are a closing sustained G-Lydian chord

ter. Marsalis became the first jazz composer to receive the Pulitzer that was awarded for his massive three-hour *Blood on the Fields.* This work almost defies classification but most closely resembles a cantata since it involves big band, vocal soloists, and narration to tell the story of slavery in America. In size and breadth alone it was a Herculean accomplishment, brilliantly performed and recorded by Marsalis' Lincoln Center Jazz Orchestra. This orchestra now tours regularly, carrying its musical message to large and small communities alike worldwide. The orchestra has also served as a catalyst for numerous commissions and collaborations, primarily with dance companies and choreographers including Alvin Ailey's American Dance Theater, the New York City Ballet, Garth Fagan, Twyla Tharp, and the New York Philharmonic. His most recent episodic work parallels an Ellington Sacred Concert in that the underlying message is one of

Trumpeter/composer Wynton Marsalis at a recording session.

religious overtones. Entitled *All Rise*, it may be Marsalis' best effort yet at least in terms of concert jazz. The work, which seamlessly interweaves jazz and various styles of classical music, is in 12 parts composed for orchestra, big band, chorus, and vocal soloists. To completely appreciate this work one must be at least casually acquainted with some of the most important twentieth-century classical works by Igor Stravinsky, Charles Ives, and Paul Hindemith as well as aspects of the Ellington tradition. Marsalis has clearly studied the many facets of music in order to absorb and reflect all of these traditions in something that is altogether new. *All Rise* is the culmination of intensive study and it is clear that Marsalis is a highly motivated, still youthful artist who has already left an indelible mark on the history of jazz. *The New York Times* as part of its review of *Blood on the Fields* accurately summarizes Marsalis' style of composition, which is also evident in *All Rise*: "Mr. Marsalis' ensembles bristle with polytonality, dissonance and jagged, jumpy lines and countermelodies, but the rhythm section pushes them along as if they were dance music. . . . He comes up with elaborate structures and [musical] abstractions, but he also encourages old fashioned jazz pleasures; snappy riffs, strutting syncopations, repartee between sections, competitive solos and the bedrock of the blues."[11]

Marsalis' artistic output is equal to that of at least several artists especially when one realizes his additional commitment to the production of educational programs, fund-raising for Jazz at Lincoln Center, TV specials like the Ken Burns epic documentary, and the publication of an array of instructional materials. It is not difficult to understand why *Time* magazine named him one of "America's 25 Most Influential People."[12] There seems to be no end to Marsalis' capability to accomplish seemingly insurmountable projects, but it would be foolish to underestimate or predict his potential for amazing future feats. Perhaps most important to this discussion is Marsalis' apparent realization that it will be through composition and the new challenges presented to performers and listeners that jazz will advance to new unknown vistas in the century that lies ahead.

The Freedom Fighters Take Risks

While it was Thelonious Monk, Lennie Tristano, Ornette Coleman, and John Coltrane along with Chicago bandleader Sun Ra and pianist Cecil Taylor who pioneered the free jazz movement, new faces arrived on the scene in the 70s who joined in continuing to push the envelope. Some of these artists emerged from the Jazz Composers' Orchestra Association like organizers Carla Bley and her husband Mike Mantler, bassist Steve Swallow, trombonists Roswell Rudd and Grachan Moncur III, and saxophonists Pharoah Sanders and Archie Shepp. Shepp used his music to make personal statements about civil rights, delivering his message in albums such as *Things Have Got to Change, Cry of My People*, and *Attica Blues*. The new breed of adventuresome performers and composers were deconstructionists in the true spirit of the postmodern ethic. The deconstructionists took earlier styles of music and tore them apart, salvaging certain aspects that served as the basis for their own redesigned renditions. These artists borrowed from old and new forms ranging from marches and polkas to punk rock, R & B, Monk, Mingus, Morton, Joplin, blues, and Ellington, forming a new music that put a different spin on these earlier traditions. At times these artists seemed as much concerned about process as they were about product and were sometimes accused of being irreverent in their reinterpretations of earlier styles. They had no fear of exploring new ground and were immune to the possible outcome of their efforts—it was the creative process and what it led to that counted most.

John Zorn, David Murray, Roscoe Mitchell, Anthony Braxton, and the World Saxophone Quartet were all saxophonists who were profoundly influenced not only by the early jazz tradition, but also by the more recent work of Eric Dolphy, John Coltrane, and, of course Ornette Coleman. In many ways, their new slant on jazz could be viewed as parodies or satires on what had already transpired in jazz. In the case of many of these new artists, no two projects were the same. Artists like Murray have been known to pursue more than one direction at a time, using different ensembles to satisfy their various creative musings. Not all of the new pioneers were saxophonists and guitarist Bill Frisell along with pianist Ronald Shannon Jackson offered their own work based on combinations of diverse styles of music. Some of the active avant-garde jazz artists in the 70s and 80s were not so new to the scene as was the case with Sun Ra whose Astro Intergalactic Infinity Arkestra had been exploring the outer rim of the jazz universe for some time, but only discovered by a few devoted fans.

The New York loft scene was a bastion of experimental, risky music that pushed jazz in new directions, though some of the music born in these loft performances did not stray far off paths already forged by pianist Cecil Taylor, or saxophonists Ornette Coleman and John Coltrane. Those artists who stand out as unique individuals to emerge from the New York loft scene include Henry Threadgill, Arthur Blythe, and Sam Rivers' Studio Rivbea, once again, all saxophonists.

Chicago was another hothouse of creativity during this period, germinating a number of cutting edge artists. The Art Ensemble officially formed in 1969 best exemplified the Chicago avant-garde style. This collective transformed the expected concert into a musical happening, a theatrical event at which, to the shock of some audiences, the musicians sported tribal African garb, face paint, and masks. In contrast trumpeter Lester Bowie wore a medical lab coat. Their music, in some ways much like the older Chicagoan Sun Ra, represents a mosaic of numerous styles of music and at times bordered on the comical and absurd. Ra served as the mentor, model, and instigator of the Art Ensemble's own unique style. To see them live, as is the case with many free styles of jazz, is far more meaningful than listening to recordings, which is often the downfall of much new, experimental jazz. It is so much in the moment, about process, group interaction, and theatrics, that much is lost in the translation to a solely audio medium. Fringe artists also risked being labeled "charlatans" by many traditional artists and critics who expressed the opinion that "the emperor has no clothes." On the other hand, other critics came forward to support the efforts made by experimental artists and placed more hope in their efforts than they did in the new traditionalists—the Young Lions obsessed with recreating what in their opinions had already been done. These critics may also have been reluctant to admonish a new trend since some had been burned in their past negative assessments of early bebop and other innovations in jazz. Many had lived to eat their words, retracting earlier negative reviews about Parker and Coleman.

While the new brand of experimental jazz did draw on familiar traditions and often was based on discernable forms, the ways in which these traditions were warped often left listeners confused about the value of this new music. For example Anthony Braxton's *In the Tradition* featured the multireed artist in performances of traditional bebop tunes but recreated with odd instruments like the contrabass clarinet. This deconstructionist approach often left listeners with too little that was familiar, and unfamiliarity in the arts often breeds discontentment.

Anthony Braxton (b 1945) Of all the fringe performers to surface in the 70s and 80s, The Art Ensemble, the World Saxophone Quartet (WSQ), and Anthony Braxton undoubtedly left the most lasting impression. For example, the Art Ensemble's ECM release *Nice Guys* was awarded four and a half stars, a near perfect assessment, by *Down Beat* critics. The WSQ can take much of the credit for introducing the notion that jazz could be performed by ensembles that do not resemble a jazz band, at least in terms of typical instrumentation. They often performed without a rhythm section, and in doing so paved the way for many other groups to follow, for instance the Kronos and Turtle Island String Quartets.

Anthony Braxton's *Creative Orchestra Music 1976* is another recording that has stood the important test of time. This particular recording continues to be a favorite of many critics and demonstrates that the traditional big band could be dressed in an entirely new wardrobe to provide a fresh new look at this very traditional ensemble. Braxton's pieces on this recording were not titled in the traditional manner, nor were they conceived in any standard form or harmonic basis. Each was described with numbers and graphic shapes. His deconstructionist approach featured throughout this recording is classic postmodern in approach. He draws on many unimaginable traditions, even utilizing a march as the basis of one piece. In some ways, his approach could be compared to that of contemporary classical American composer Charles Ives. It is important to point out that more and more, jazz composers began crossing the borders between jazz and contemporary classical music, a topic discussed in more detail on the supplementary chapter included on the CD-ROM.

Braxton's "Piece 1," or "W-138" as his alternate title suggests, is less abstract than many free jazz works from this period since there is some form and shape, though any reoccurring themes are certainly difficult to identify. It is difficult to determine, without access to a score, whether the soloists are bound by any harmonic conventions, or if there are changing meter schemes throughout the piece. It is safe to say that the harmonies in this piece are nontraditional and nonfunctional. The reoccurring, insistent rhythmic vamp presented throughout the piece could be described as a call and response gesture and implies a meter change from the predominant 4/4 to 3/8. The melodic lines are written in an obtuse, postbop style creating a complex, sometimes frantic web throughout the piece. The instrumental counterpoint between sections of instruments, soloist, and ensemble also create an air of tension as the piece develops. Many of the shapes created by Braxton's fairly traditional ways of orchestrating and arranging for the big band—combining instruments by families and using opposing instruments as backgrounds to improvised solos—harken back to

1 **Piece One** (5:10)

Graphic used by composer Anthony Braxton to represent the first track on his Creative Orchestra Music 1976 *album (included in the companion anthology).*

the 1940s. The harmonic and melodic language he uses, however, is right out of the postmodern Ornette Coleman clan. Listen to this complex piece found on the companion anthology and listen to it more than once to fully appreciate the artistry, homage to tradition, and complexity.

Anthony Braxton

Listening Guide

"Piece 1" (Anthony Braxton) 5:11

Recorded New York City February 1976

Issued *Creative Orchestra Music* RCA Bluebird 6576–2-RB

Anthony Braxton: *alto saxophone*

Seldon Powell: *alto saxophone*

Bruce Johnstone: *baritone saxophone*

Ronald Bridgewater: *tenor saxophone*

Kenny Wheeler, Ceçil Bridgewater, Jon Faddis: *trumpets*

Leo Smith: *conductor*

George Lewis, Garrett List: *trombones*

Earl McIntyre: *bass trombone*

Jonathan Dorn: *tuba*

Muhal Richard Abrams: *piano*

Dave Holland: *bass*

Warren Smith: *drums and percussion*

Form and Key: Three-part orchestral jazz composition predominantly in 4/4

Part 1: Introduction, Theme Chorus, Ensemble Vamp, and Ensemble Chorus

Part 2: Solo Choruses (Bari, Trumpet, Alto), Ensemble Vamp, and Ensemble Chorus

Part 3: Drum Break, Solo/Ensemble Chorus, Ensemble Vamp, and Ending Section

0:00–0:14   *Introduction:* 14 bars, *Vamp and Ensemble:*

    0:00–0:07   *First section:* 7 bars: 3 bars of repeated brass ensemble chord vamp followed by 4 bars of saxophone section unison melody—rhythm section tacit

    0:07–0:14   *Second section:* 7 bars: 3 bars of repeated brass chord vamp as above, followed by 4 bars of different saxophone section unison melody—rhythm section tacit

0:14–0:43   *Theme Chorus:* 32 bars (AABA, 8+8+8+8), post-bebop *Theme* played by saxophone section, with swinging rhythm section

0:43–0:50   *Ensemble Vamp:* 8 bars, repeated brass ensemble chord *Vamp* similar to Introduction with swinging rhythm section

0:51–1:22   *Ensemble Chorus:* 32 bars: *Ensemble:*

    0:50–0:57   *Ensemble I:* 8 bars: 4-bar trumpet melody over sustained trombone chords, followed by 4-bar brass "shout" phrase

    0:58–1:22   *Ensemble II:* 24 bars, unison trumpet section and sax section lines over ostinato bass, trombone and snare drum rhythm

1:22–1:51   *Solo Chorus:* 32 bars, *Baritone Saxophone Solo,* with swinging rhythm section

1:52–2:21   *Solo Chorus:* 32 bars, *Trumpet Solo,* with sax section and trumpet section background lines and swinging rhythm section

2:22–2:51   *Solo Chorus:* 32 bars, *Alto Saxophone Solo* with long ensemble background lines

2:51–3:02   *Ensemble Vamp:* 12 bars (6+6), *Alto Saxophone Solo* continues over chord vamp similar to Introduction:

3:03–3:19   *Ensemble Chorus:* 16 bars, interweaving unison trumpet and sax section lines over ostinato bass, trombone and snare drum rhythm, similar to Ensemble II above

3:20–3:25   *Drum Break:* 8 bars, *Drum solo*

Anthony Braxton *concluded*

3:26–4:27   *Solo/Ensemble Chorus:* 64 bars (AABA, 16+16+16+16)

  3:26–3:41   *First section:* 16 bars, *various instruments trade solos*, with long ensemble background line, and swinging rhythm section

  3:41–3:56   *Second section:* 16 bars, various solos continue, with repeat of long ensemble background line of first section, and swinging rhythm section

  3:56–4:11   *Third section:* 16 bars, various solos continue, with new trumpet section background line and swinging rhythm section

  4:12–4:26   *Fourth section:* 16 bars, various solos continue, with long ensemble line from first two sections, and swinging rhythm section

4:27–4:42   *Ensemble Vamp:* 12+ bars, short fragmented *alto, trumpet, and baritone sax solos* over brass chord vamp similar to Introduction and previous Ensemble Vamp sections

4:43–5:12   *Ending Section:*

  4:42–5:02   Short fragmented, free, *alto, trumpet, and baritone sax solos* continue, out of time, no rhythm section

  4:54–5:04   Ensemble tacit until *sustained chord*

  5:05–5:11   Trumpet, baritone sax and alto sax play last *sustained chord*

Cecil Taylor (b 1929) Pianist Cecil Taylor's career in some ways followed Monk's in that, while he had an impact in the early stages of his career, he was far better received in later years. Taylor, caught up in the wake of a new wave of experimental artists who were receiving more press in the 70s and 80s than ever before, was rediscovered and appreciated for his obtuse, abstract style. He studied serious music and jazz at the New England Conservatory, where he fell under the influence of black and white, classical and jazz artists such as pianists Horace Silver, Thelonious Monk, Dave Brubeck, and Lennie Tristano along with composers Duke Ellington and Igor Stravinsky. Taylor developed an awesome piano technique that was as much percussive as it was pianistic. His amazing technique and facility has impressed both jazz and classical pianists. He uses his fists, forearms, elbows, and palms to create dense, dissonant clusters of sounds that defy analysis and for some listeners are like fingernails on a blackboard. *Down Beat* magazine awarded him "Best New Star" in 1962, but there was no significant support for his odd brand of jazz that placed "unrelenting demands . . . on the listener"[13] according to pianist, educator Bill Dobbins. His music is more about texture and rhythm, sound and organization than it is about European derived harmonies and recognizable melodies. While Taylor described his music as an "extension of period music—Ellington and Monk,"[14] and tried to "imitate on the piano the leaps and space a dancer makes,"[15] his style more closely resembles European avant-garde classical music than jazz, and he was virtually unemployed through much of the 1960s. As audiences began to catch up to the avant-garde in the 1970s, Taylor's career was rejuvenated along with other older fringe artists. His abstract music has been more widely accepted since then and his 1974 solo recording *Silent Tongues* received much critical acclaim.

Ornette Coleman Ornette Coleman, who had been a godfather to most of the new breed of jazz fringe artists, also enjoyed a second wind in the 80s. Fueled by the electric, jazz-rock fusion years, Coleman's new Prime Time band featured two electric basses, two drummers, and two electric guitarists in multilayered dialogues. The group's record debut, *In All Languages*, captured a live 1987 performance in his native Fort Worth, Texas. The sound was different but the "harmolodic" approach, a theory with no precise explanation, was similar to that used by his earlier bands. Musical democracy was important to both bands, with each instrument being equally important and free to take a dominant role at any given moment.

OLD BOTTLES, NEW WINES— BIG BANDS ARE FOREVER

As more and more educational institutions began to embrace the study of jazz throughout the 70s and 80s, the market became saturated with young players looking to establish careers. Many of the more fortunate ones found spots in bands led by graying big band leaders that had somehow survived the Beatles, Janis Joplin, Jimi Hendrix, and the jazz-fusion movement.

Buddy Rich (1917–1987)
Drummer Buddy Rich (1917–1987), who started his career in vaudeville as a youngster and played with Artie Shaw and other swing bands, started his own big band in 1966 and attracted a host of young players. Despite the band's success, he dissolved it in 1974, only to regroup in the 80s, touring once again until his death in 1987. Rich did his best to keep his repertoire in sync with popular music and constantly upgraded his book with arrangements of songs like "Norwegian Wood," popularized by the Beatles, Weather Report's "Birdland," and an epic rendition of Leonard Bernstein's "West Side Story."

Woody Herman (1913–1987)
The resilient saxophonist, clarinetist, and bandleader Woody Herman (1913–1987) led his Thundering Herd into the postmodern age by also keeping his band freshly stocked with vital young musicians and modern arrangements. Herman had taken over Isham Jones' dance band in 1936 and maintained a working band until his death in 1987. His roster claims an amazing list of alumni over a 50-year span including many of the most important contemporary musicians including saxophonist Joe Lovano, trumpeter Tom Harrell, and trombonist and contemporary big band leader John Fedchock (an important big band leader and composer/arranger of the twenty-first century).

Maynard Ferguson (b 1928)
The Woody Herman alumni band continues to tour and record sporadically as does another popular 70s and 80s big band led by stratospheric trumpeter Maynard Ferguson (b 1928). Ferguson, who began his career in the late 40s with

several swing bands rose to attention through his work with Stan Kenton's progressive 50s big band. The trumpeter's unusual gift as both an amazing, screaming high-note specialist and respectable jazz improviser enabled him to start his own contemporary big band in the 1960s. Like the previously mentioned bands, Ferguson survived the 70s by keeping his book of arrangements as fresh and young as his sidemen. His arrangements of popular hits like "MacArthur Park," "Gonna Fly" from the film *Rocky*, the Beatles' "Hey Jude," and Weather Report's "Birdland" enabled the band to keep working, even though big bands had largely fallen out of favor by the 70s. While now in semiretirement, Ferguson continues to record and tour with a high-energy, but scaled-down band of fresh-out-of-college young stars of tomorrow.

Stan Kenton (1911–1979)

Another progressive bandleader, known for his commitment to jazz education, survived the onslaught of pop music and did his best to keep big bands in the public's ear and eye. Pianist and arranger/composer Stan Kenton (1911–1979) first surfaced in the late 1940s leading his own band that was labeled "progressive" even for those times. He not only incorporated the influences of be-bop and Cubop, but also ventured into the realm of contemporary classical music (see the supplemental chapter included on the CD-ROM). Much as had been the case with all the aforementioned bands, Kenton helped to launch the career of a host of notable jazz performers and arrangers. The list includes cool-style saxophonists Art Pepper, Lee Konitz, Lennie Niehaus, Stan Getz, and Zoot Sims (the latter two who also played with Herman). Additionally, brass men Frank Rosolino, Carl Fontana, and Maynard Ferguson among many others did tours of duty with Kenton's band. Kenton was a champion in the 1960s of the still young jazz education movement, sponsoring camps and clinics throughout the United States and employing exceptional young college graduates. Kenton passed on in 1979 and his will prohibited the formation of "ghost bands" to recreate his music.

Thad Jones (1923–1986) and Mel Lewis (1929–1990)

The two most important big bands to emerge in the late 1960s and mid-1970s, at least in terms of advancing a new standard, were the New York–based Thad Jones/Mel Lewis Jazz Orchestra and the West Coast Toshiko Akiyoshi/Lew Tabackin Jazz Orchestra. The Jones/Lewis organization began as a rehearsal band, driven by an interest among New York's finest studio recording and theater musicians to play more challenging music than they typically encountered in the recording and TV studios. The band's first book consisted of a group of 10 originals that Count Basie had commissioned his former trumpeter Thad Jones (1923–1986) to score. Basie's band found them too modern and out of character so they were rejected. The band's first performance came on Monday night, February 6, 1966, at the Village Vanguard. Word had spread about this stellar collection of New York's finest and people were lined up for blocks to hear the new band. Audiences were quickly impressed by Jones' arrangements that brought together the Basie band's sense of swing with a more modern harmonic palette and plenty of fine soloists. His arrangements also highlighted challenging saxophone section work carved out of the modern bebop vocabulary. The woodwind section showcases made

Thad Jones, playing a flugelhorn, fronts the jazz orchestra he co-led with drummer Mel Lewis, shown at far right.

use of the exceptional abilities of these studio saxophonists who also played flutes and clarinets. The band eventually performed music by other writers including its trombonist Bob Brookmeyer and saxophonists Jerome Richardson and Jerry Dodgion. Unlike so many big bands before, Jones' writing placed equal emphasis on improvised solos. Jones acted as a traffic cop in live performances, waving out the rhythm section, or part of it, to allow the soloist to stretch out even further and to ensure that no two performances were the same. Jones' direction ensured that the group had both the power of a big band and the subtle spontaneity of a small group. Jones' writing demonstrated Ellington-like clusters and close, dense chord voicings, bop sensibilities, and a sly sense of humor. Drummer Mel Lewis (1929–1990) served as the band's protagonist and was the linchpin of its many spectacular rhythm sections including Gerry Mulligan's Concert Jazz Band.

The band's initial success at a time when New York jazz clubs were in a serious slump prompted Vanguard owner Max Gordon to book the band for a regular Monday night gig—a perfect night since the theater district was dark on Mondays. The band members were paid only $17 each, so their commitment was one of love for the music and respect for Jones and Mel Lewis who handled the band's business affairs.

The band did not tour regularly, as had been the case with earlier big bands, but they did stay together under "Thad and Mel" for 13 years. Thad suddenly and with no warning mysteriously left for Europe where he took up residence in 1979 as leader of the Danish Radio Orchestra. Lewis kept the band alive at the Vanguard and recorded new charts by Bill Holman, Jim McNeeley, Bob Mintzer, Bob Brookmeyer, and others. While the band's influential work began in the late 60s with some of their seminal recordings, the impact of this cohesive unit and Jones' repertoire stretched well into the 70s and continues into the twenty-first century under its new name—The Vanguard Jazz Orchestra. While Jones and Lewis have both passed on, their legacy continues at the Village Vanguard every Monday night. Most historians agree that it was Jones' writing, realized by his exceptional band, that revitalized the big band, breathing new life into it so that it could survive beyond the twentieth century.

Toshiko Akiyoshi (b 1929)

Who could ever imagine that a female Japanese jazz pianist would also play a significant role in the 70s revival of the sleeping giant—the big band that some had pronounced a dead dinosaur years earlier. Educated at Boston's Berklee College of Music, pianist Toshiko Akiyoshi (b 1929) was inspired by the late Bud Powell. Promoter Norman Granz was instrumental in advancing her career in the 50s when she became the first Japanese jazz musician to be recorded by an American record company. She and her husband, saxophonist and flutist Lew Tabackin, took up residency in Los Angeles in 1972, where she formed her first big band to perform her own music. The band was recorded in 1974–1975 by RCA who released the band's first U.S. recording *Long Yellow Road* in 1976. Akiyoshi's band was staffed with highly skilled LA studio musicians and brilliant jazz soloists. They had to be the best musicians available, since Akiyoshi's charts were incredibly demanding as she broke away from many accepted writing conventions. Her writing esthetic has often been compared to that of Duke Ellington who found his unique sound in part by ignoring conventions and allowing the special talents of his bandsmen to influence the way in which he composed and arranged. Akiyoshi's featured soloist Lew Tabackin was significantly influenced by tenor saxophonists Sonny Rollins, Don Byas, Coleman Hawkins, and Ben Webster. He had been a member of Doc Severinsen's *Tonight Show* TV band and became Akiyoshi's husband and co-bandleader. To quote Tabackin, "Toshiko is never afraid to try devices that haven't been used. The woodwind aspect [flutes and clarinets] is particularly noteworthy; her saxophone voicings have a heavier sound than most reed sections; like Thad Jones she uses five-part harmony [there are usually five saxophonists in a big band] rather than let two instruments double the same note [as had been the standard rule up until Jones and Akiyoshi]."[16] Tabackin continues to point out how his wife "draws so much on her own culture, not fighting it like so many foreign jazz musicians who try to prove themselves by being ultra-Americans."[17] Her ethnic background brought an entirely new viewpoint to big band composition as shown by "Children in the Temple Ground," "Kogun," and "Tanuki's Night Out." Akiyoshi's music also shows her own unique sense of rhythm and phrasing, no doubt an additional result of her Asian descent. The Akiyoshi/Tabackin big band was the rage in the late 70s, winning Grammy nominations from 1976 to 1994. *Down Beat* magazine named her Best Composer for four straight years in the early 80s and she won the Best Arranger category in 1984. She has also been the recipient of numerous other awards, commissions, and prizes both in this country and abroad. In the early 80s, she relocated her band to New York, where she and her husband continue to create, though she retired the big band with a final Carnegie Hall performance in 2003. Aside from vocalists, no woman in jazz had captured so much attention prior to Akiyoshi's rise to popularity.

Pianist/composer Toshiko Akiyoshi leads her big band with co-leader tenor saxophonist Lew Tabackin, seated far left.

SIGNS OF THE TIMES

Political corruption in the 1970s surrounding President Nixon's Watergate affair and subsequent resignation, a lost war in Vietnam that left scars on the government, American families, and democracy itself, an ever growing drug culture, rising inflation, and a level of unemployment that rivaled that of the1940s created an air of doubt, cynicism, and suspicion among all classes of Americans. Society as a whole became more bifurcated and as the 70s gave way to the 80s, the economic gap between classes widened. More subgroups formed particularly as the United States offered a safe haven and land of opportunity for numerous ethnic minority groups who emigrated. With each subgroup came a uniquely different brand of culture that encouraged a more fractured American music scene. Perhaps the only area that showed progress and improved by the 1980s was racial relations. Blatant segregationist policies had been all but eliminated and through new equal opportunity and affirmative action programs, more African Americans were seeking and completing educations beyond high school. Consequently, an increasing number of blacks entered the workforce in various professional roles, including science, medicine, law, and politics. African Americans became mayors of major cities and visible leaders in other aspects of public service. The study of black history and culture was suddenly elevated to a new high level of importance. Black artists in all fields including television, theater, literature, and music were making greater strides than ever toward achieving equal footing with other groups in the United States. There was a noticeable increase in TV shows starring all black casts. Isaac Hayes became the first black composer to win an academy award for his score to the film *Shaft* and a record number of Americans watched Alex Haley's

TV mini-series *Roots,* depicting the struggles of a black family in America over many generations. These trends had a positive effect in raising the awareness of jazz, paving the way for a new wave of young black artists who reclaimed their birthright to this music and gave it a greater degree of respect than ever before.

The debate that surrounded the renewed interest in jazz, however, occupied most of the 1980s and cast a long shadow into the next millennium. The controversy wasn't about whether jazz should be nurtured; it was more about which kind of jazz should receive our support. Two factions emerged—those who championed imitation and those who represented innovation. Wynton Marsalis became the mouthpiece and chief advocate for the preservation of those elements he deemed most important to jazz—swing and the blues. Yet some accused Marsalis and his Young Lions of merely shoplifting music that had already been patented by the mid-1960s. Meanwhile, artists such as John Zorn, David Murray, Henry Threadgill, Anthony Davis, Anthony Braxton, and others tried to steer jazz away from what they saw as stale, shopworn traditions. They were the postmodern renegades who found nothing sacred and borrowed freely from any musical style they felt worthy. Eclecticism became this group's motto.

New Technologies, Changing Business Models, Lost Artists, and High Art: The Changing Jazz Landscape as the Millennium Comes to a Close

The digital revolution occurred in the last decades of the twentieth century, brought about by the miniaturization of electronic components and less costly production processes. It enabled and encouraged the creation of lengthy concert recorded works and the marketing of voluminous chronological reissue packages. The impact of these new technologies can be roughly compared to that of electrification in the early 1920s. Apple pioneered the small personal computer when they first unveiled the Apple II computer in 1977. A few years later, new technologies that had already been available for high-end professional users were brought to the average household in the form of the VCR. The first units cost about $1,000, and blank videotapes averaged $15 each. While the cassette format dominated the audio marketplace in the 1970s, this format was eclipsed by the compact disk, which first hit the consumer market in 1982. This new format did much to encourage reissue campaigns of treasures that had been in some cases locked in vaults for years, tragically unavailable to a new, younger generation of jazz enthusiasts. Major labels began reissue campaigns that brought about a renewed interest in standards, classic jazz repertoire, and the piano trio format with artists like McCoy Tyner and Keith Jarrett, and the rediscovery of artists like saxophonist Frank Morgan, who had, in some cases, nearly been forgotten. Unfortunately major labels focused more on inexpensive reissues that guaranteed sales and incurred minimal production costs rather than taking risks with new artists. The only new artists to receive major media attention at the end of the decade were those Young Lions who essentially played music similar to that heard on older reissued material. As the cost of CD production fell, some of the best music was issued by a growing number of small, independent U.S. and European labels, all trying to cash in on the new marketable CD format with newly discovered artists. Many of the small "indie" labels, however, lacked widespread distribution and marketing tactics, so great music was often lost in a sea of unknown releases.

By the close of the 1980s, jazz had lost an even greater number of important artists including big band leaders Thad Jones, Woody Herman, Count Basie, Benny Goodman, Gil Evans, Buddy Rich, and Harry James. Other innovative performers and composers who passed on during the decade included Thelonious Monk, Woody Shaw, Joe Farrell, Jaco Pastorius, Chet Baker, Mary Lou Williams, Bill Evans, Philly Joe Jones, and Kenny Clarke. *Down Beat* magazine columnist Art Lange wrote in a retrospective column about the 80s that "If jazz is the home of the individual, the repository of the unique, and personal expression is to be prized above all else, the music lost a measure of authenticity that will be hard to replace."[18]

While some moaned that jazz was dying a slow death, some progress was being made. Despite the raging debates in the press between Marsalis and his Young Lions and the opposition that included other musicians along with some critics, jazz musicians began to achieve what they strove for since the beginning—respectability and equality with high art. Since Scott Joplin and James P. Johnson, Jelly Roll Morton and Duke Ellington, W.C. Handy and James Reese Europe, efforts to elevate jazz to the same high plateau as classical music had succeeded. Much like classical music, jazz had become institutionalized. The growing jazz education movement corresponds to the rekindled interest in what jazz composers and arrangers had brought to the tradition, and what new inspiration could be torched by a modern generation of composers like Kenny Wheeler, Toshiko Akiyoshi, Vince Mendoza, Jim McNeeley, Kenny Werner, Bob Mintzer, Wynton Marsalis, and Maria Schneider. There was a renewed interest, in part inspired by jazz educators and the Young Lions, in the music of Duke Ellington, Charles Mingus, Tadd Dameron, Gil Evans, and Thelonious Monk. The jazz education movement, spearheaded by the International Association for Jazz Education, gained significant ground in the 70s and 80s as music programs nationwide jumped to employ specialists to deliver instruction in a wide array of courses. Even U.S. government legislators stood up to recognize jazz in 1987 when they passed a resolution designating jazz as a "rare and valuable national American treasure to which we should devote our attention, support, and resources to make certain it is preserved, understood, and promulgated." The resolution's sponsor, Michigan State Representative John Conyers, Jr., sited jazz as "a unifying force, bridging cultural, religious, and age differences." Conyers also pointed out that jazz "makes evident to the world an outstanding artistic model of individual expression and democratic cooperation within the creative process thus fulfilling the highest ideals and aspirations of our republic."[19] The National Endowment for the Arts along with state and private foundations awarded major grants to promote jazz festivals, composers, and touring ensembles. New ensembles were created for the specific purpose of perpetuating earlier jazz by recreating the works of Ellington, Henderson, Mingus, and others. But, once again, these efforts were criticized by some who felt that by concentrating on the preservation of the past, a stranglehold was put on the music's continued growth and it would be doomed to the same fate as classical music in the 80s and 90s. Perhaps that which was fought for so long—the elevation of jazz to a stature of high art—in the end would not prove to be worth the fight, since, along with classical music sales, jazz began to hit a serious slump. The unanswered question appeared to be—would the 1990s and the new millennium offer anything better for jazz, its practitioners and listeners?

Jazz in Perspective

The timeline that follows will put the developments of jazz discussed in Chapters 13 and 14 into a larger historical context, providing you with a better sense of how landmark musical events may relate to others that match your personal areas of interest.

1970
- Jean Stafford wins Pulitzer for *Collected Stories*.
- American Medical Association votes in support of abortions in some cases.
- *Patton, M*A*S*H*,* and *Woodstock* are popular films.
- Kent State University student riots protesting war end in four deaths.
- Students strike for peace in 450 U.S. colleges.
- Women march for equality in New York.

1971
- Disney World opens.
- Busing supports integration of schools.
- 26th Amendment allows 18-year-olds to vote.
- Andrew Lloyd Webber's rock musical *Jesus Christ Superstar* creates a stir.
- Astronauts further explore lunar surface.

1972
- Liberated women publish *Ms.* magazine.
- Cigarette advertisements banned from airwaves.
- Senate ratifies the Equal Rights Amendment.
- Movies of the year include *The Godfather, Cabaret, Last Tango in Paris,* and *Play It Again Sam.*
- Nixon reelected amid Watergate affair.

1973
- Francis Fitzgerald awarded Pulitzer for *Fire in the Lake*.
- United States ends role in Vietnam following approximately 55,000 deaths.
- Courts allow abortion in *Roe* vs. *Wade* case.
- Watergate conspirators convicted; Nixon declares innocence.

1974
- Robert Lowell wins Pulitzer Prize for *The Dolphin*.
- Jazz composer and bandleader Duke Ellington dies.
- Courts rule that schools must teach English.
- President Nixon forced to resign over role in Watergate; Gerald Ford assumes presidency.
- School busing continues to incite protest.
- Pianist Keith Jarrett records *The Windup* for the German ECM label.

1975
- President Ford declares Vietnam era officially over.
- *The Wiz* wins awards as new musical sensation.
- VCR becomes common home appliance.
- President Ford saves city of New York from bankruptcy.
- Top films include *One Flew Over the Cuckoo's Nest* and *Jaws.*

1976
- Hit films are *Rocky* and *Network.*
- Apple Computer begins with only $1,300 capital.
- Sunbelt attracts many new businesses.
- Americans celebrate bicentennial.
- Stagnant economy hampers and frustrates U.S. citizens and government.
- Jimmy Carter elected president.
- Satirist Tom Wolfe declares the 1970s as "Me Decade."
- Anthony Braxton records *Creative Orchestra Music 1976.*

1977

- Alex Haley wins Pulitzer Prize for *Roots*, the most watched TV mini-series in TV history.
- Space shuttle *Enterprise* makes test flight.
- President Carter declares energy crisis.
- Detroit car makers feel pinch from Japanese competition.
- American rock idol Elvis Presley dies.
- John Travolta's *Saturday Night Fever* helps to popularize discos.
- Other pop films include *Star Wars, Annie Hall,* and *Close Encounters of the Third Kind.*

1978

- Retirement age is raised to 70.
- Carl Sagan awarded Pulitzer Prize for *Dragons of Eden.*
- Hannah Gray becomes first woman university president at the University of Chicago.
- Economic malaise continues and President Carter announces anti-inflation plan.
- Johnstown cult mass suicide shocks nation.
- First test tube baby is born.
- Disco is hugely popular dance/music craze.

1979

- Ronald Reagan declares liberalism a problem, not an answer.
- Forty-six percent attend segregated schools.
- Divorce rates continue to escalate.
- Nuclear disaster at Three Mile Island power plant.
- Carter says the United States is a nation of lost confidence and self-doubt as a result of energy crisis, assassination of JFK, Vietnam war, Watergate, and inflation.
- Ninety-nine percent of Americans own a TV set says *Washington Post* poll.
- Award winning films include *Kramer vs. Kramer, Norma Rae, All That Jazz, Manhattan, Star Trek,* and *Apocalypse Now.*

- Iran seizes U.S. embassy taking 80 hostages.

1980

- Government admits to recession.
- Race riots erupt in Miami.
- Auto and steel industries continue to lose money.
- Prime rate soars to 21.5 percent.
- Popular *Pac Man* video game launches new trend in leisure time activity.
- Ted Turner launches all news CNN network.
- The Beatles' John Lennon is murdered.

1981

- Ronald Reagan takes office.
- Iranian hostages released.
- *Columbia* shuttle flight orbits earth.
- IBM makes first-generation personal computers available.

1982

- John Updike wins Pulitzer Prize for *Rabbit Is Rich.*
- Andrew Lloyd Webber's *Cats* is Broadway musical hit.
- Recession sets industry back to lowest levels in 34 years.
- National debt reaches all-time high.

1983

- Sally Ride becomes first woman in space.
- National committee determines United States at risk due to mediocre education performance.
- Poverty in Mexico and Central America causes increase in illegal immigrants.
- Alice Walker wins Pulitzer Prize for *The Color Purple.*
- Musical Instrument Digital Interface (MIDI) binary language is developed by electronic musical instrument manufacturers—creates boom in electronic instrument sales.

1984

- 1984 Democrats pick woman for vice presidential candidate.
- Most American bank failures since 1938.
- Reagan wins reelection.
- Top films include *Ghostbusters, Amadeus,* and *Beverly Hills Cop.*

1985
- Madonna, new pop singing sensation, performs in pop concert Live-Aid to benefit African relief efforts.
- Wynton Marsalis' quintet that includes brother Branford records "Delfeayo's Dilemma."
- Hit movies include *Out of Africa* and *Kiss of the Spider Woman.*
- Continued efforts to relieve national debt and stimulate economy.
- British scientists discover hole in the ozone layer above Antarctica.

1986
- Chernobyl nuclear reactor incident in U.S.S.R. alerts world to dangers of nuclear energy plants.
- Space Shuttle *Challenger* explodes killing all astronauts on board.
- United States bombs Libya.
- Secret mission to send arms to Iran (Iran Contra Affair) is revealed.
- FOX created as fourth TV network.
- Nintendo video games are introduced.
- Grammy song of the year is "We Are the World"—USA for Africa.

1987
- Author Toni Morrison publishes *Beloved*, a story about slavery.
- Stock market plummets on Black Monday.
- Nuclear arms treaty reached between U.S.S.R. and the United States.
- Madonna and Bon Jovi top pop music charts.
- *Dirty Dancing* and *Beverly Hills Cop III* are top movies.

- August Wilson's *Fences* wins Pulitzer Prize in drama.
- *Les Miserables* wins Tony award for best musical.
- Grammy record of the year is Paul Simon's African-inspired "Graceland."

1988
- For the first time, CDs outsell vinyl records.
- Pan Am Flight 103 explodes over Scotland; Libyan terrorists suspected.
- Jazz singer Bobby McFerrin enjoys hit with "Don't Worry, Be Happy."
- Prozac introduced as drug to treat depression.
- Les Chunnel, the world's largest undersea tunnel, is completed connecting France with the United Kingdom.
- Soviet Union withdraws troops from Afghanistan.

1989
- George Bush elected U.S. president.
- The Berlin Wall separating East and West Germany falls, signaling the end of the cold war.
- *Exxon Valdez* oil tanker disaster near Alaska.
- Thousands of Chinese student protestors killed in Tienanmen Square.
- Pan Am Airlines files Chapter 11.
- Arsenio Hall, Oprah Winfrey, and Colin Powell forge new ground for black entertainers and politicians.

CHAPTER SUMMARY

While the jazz-rock-fusion music received much public attention and air play in the 1970s and 1980s, a core of musicians continued to play and develop various aspects of acoustic jazz. With the popularity of fusion, major record labels dropped many lower-selling acoustic jazz artists. Fortunately for a few musicians, the German independent label ECM was established in 1969, primarily as an alternative to fusion featuring quiet, acoustic jazz. Pianist Keith Jarrett who had played hard bop with Art Blakey in the mid-1960s, and later electrified jazz with

Miles Davis, went on to become one of ECM's most important artists. Jarrett is both a technician and improviser of the highest order, performing primarily in solo piano and small group settings.

The 1970s also saw the return of some jazz masters to America. Dexter Gordon had opted in earlier years, along with other more senior performers, to live overseas in order to make a living playing the music they enjoyed rather than give in to commercial pressures. Their return to the United States in the 70s rekindled interest in mainstream jazz, focused not only on returning jazz giants, but also on a new young generation of bop-inspired players often referred to as the Young Lions. Trumpeter/composer Wynton Marsalis became the spokesman for the very talented and well-trained musicians representing this movement. Marsalis is not only an expert improviser but is also an outstanding classical trumpeter. In an amazing feat he won Grammy Awards in both jazz and classical categories in the same year—and he did that twice (1983 and 1985)! Additionally, Marsalis became the first jazz composer to be awarded the Pulitzer Prize. As director of the Lincoln Center Jazz Orchestra, Wynton Marsalis has also committed himself to jazz education.

Some view the work of the Young Lions as "imitation" of mid-1960s progressive jazz, and look to the free jazz work of Ornette Coleman and other free jazz experimentalists as the "innovation" of 1970s and 1980s in jazz. Anthony Braxton, Sun Ra, The Art Ensemble of Chicago, and the World Saxophone Quartet represent a few of the many contributors to this style. Pianist Cecil Taylor, an active free jazz artist for five decades, may be one of the most underappreciated of these performers.

A few big bands from previous eras (including the bands of Buddy Rich, Woody Herman, Stan Kenton, and Maynard Ferguson) continued to perform in the 1970s and beyond. These groups were able to continue because they changed with the times, adding arrangements of current tunes and by hiring talented young sidemen. Two outstanding new big bands, the Thad Jones/Mel Lewis Big Band and the Toshiko Akiyoshi/Lew Tabakin Jazz Orchestra emerged during the late 1960s and 1970s. Both bands featured fresh new approaches to big band writing, tight ensemble work, and outstanding soloists.

The many "schools" and events of jazz of the 1970s and 1980s may, in some ways, reflect other events and developments of the time. During the 1970s President Richard Nixon resigned as a result of the Watergate cover-up, the United States continued waging war in Vietnam and eventually withdrew without victory, inflation and unemployment grew at alarming rates, and the personal computer was introduced. In the 1980s the development of the VCR, the compact disk, and the Musical Instrument Digital Interface (MIDI) made a tremendous impact on the entertainment industry. Some of the great jazz legends died, while the Young Lions emerged on the scene to provide momentum in preserving and advancing their rich jazz heritage.

KEY TERMS

Important people and bands.

PEOPLE	Dexter Gordon	Young Lions
Manfred Eicher	Wynton Marsalis	Ornette Coleman
Keith Jarrett	Branford Marsalis	Sun Ra

Cecil Taylor Stan Kenton BANDS
Anthony Braxton Thad Jones World Saxophone
Buddy Rich Mel Lewis Quartet
Woody Herman Toshiko Akiyoshi Prime Time
Maynard Ferguson

REVIEW QUESTIONS

1. Discuss this significance of the ECM label on jazz.

2. Name a few artists who were important to establishing the ECM sound.

3. Describe what became known as the ECM sound.

4. While pianist Keith Jarrett has been involved in several different jazz styles, he has an individual approach that can be characterized by what traits?

5. Who was the older tenor saxophonist that is in part responsible for rekindling interest in acoustic, modern jazz?

6. Who was the hard bop bandleader that provided a training ground for many of the important young artists of the 1980s?

7. Name at least two other expatriates who, like Dexter Gordon, left the United States to take up residence in Europe, eventually returning in the 70s.

8. Who became the unofficial ringleader of a group of acoustic jazz musicians who in the 80s were determined to rekindle interest in mainstream jazz?

9. Name four important Young Lions.

10. Who became the first jazz musician to win the Pulitzer Prize? What composition won him this unprecedented distinction?

11. In what ways has Wynton Marsalis been compared to Duke Ellington?

12. What six artists are given credit for pioneering free jazz in the earlier decades?

13. Name several artists who carried the torch for free jazz in the 1970s and beyond.

14. Why in some cases has it been difficult for free jazz to gain supportive listeners in any significant numbers?

15. Can you name several resilient big band leaders who maintained large groups through the 1970s and in some cases beyond?

16. What were the two more contemporary big bands to gain some exposure in the 1970?

17. In what ways did new recording technology and changing business models change the landscape for the jazz musician?

Make sure that you also review material on the corresponding chapter of the CD-ROM.

SUGGESTED SUPPLEMENTARY LISTENING

The abbreviation (iT) indicates that a particular recording cited in the text, or particularly demonstrative of the artist, is available from the Apple iTunes Web site. Other Web-based music distributors may also prove to be valuable resources. SCCJ indicates *Smithsonian Collection of Classic Jazz*.

Keith Jarrett

Expectations Sony (iT)
The Impulse Years GRP Records (iT)
Köln Concert ECM
Solo Concerts: Bremen & Lausanne ECM
Gary Burton and Keith Jarrett Rhino
Luminessence ECM
Chick Corea, Herbie Hancock, Keith Jarrett, and McCoy Tyner Atlantic
My Song ECM
Belonging ECM

Dexter Gordon

Homecoming Sony (iT)
Sophisticated Giant Sony (iT)

Phil Woods

Song for Sisyphus Compact Classics (iT)
Phil Woods Live, Vol. 1 Clean Cuts

Wynton Marsalis

Black Codes from the Underground Sony (iT)
Marsalis Standard Time Vol. 1 Sony (iT)
Hot House Flowers Sony (iT)
J Mood Sony (iT)

Branford Marsalis

Crazy People Sony (iT)
Random Abstract Sony (iT)
Trio Jeepy CBS Records, Inc. (iT)

David Murry

Conjure: Music for the Texts of Ishmael Reed American Clave (iT)

Ornette Coleman

Song X Geffen Records

Cecil Taylor

Conquistador! Blue Note (iT)
Unit Structures Blue Note
Silent Tongues 1201 Music
"Enter Evening" SCCJ

Buddy Rich

Buddy and Soul Pacific Jazz (iT)
Mercy, Mercy, Mercy Pacific Jazz (iT)
Big Swing Face Pacific Jazz (iT)
Keep the Customer Satisfied Pacific Jazz (iT)
The Best of Buddy Rich Capitol (iT)

Woody Herman

Giant Steps Fantasy (iT)
The Raven Speaks (iT)

Maynard Ferguson

The Blues Roar Mainstream (iT)
Chameleon Sony (iT)
This Is Jazz No. 16: Maynard Ferguson Sony (iT)

Thad Jones

Central Park North Blue Note (iT)
Consummation Blue Note
One Night: Thad Jones/Mel Lewis Big Band at the Village Vanguard February 7, 1966 Alan Grant Productions

Toshiko Akiyoshi

Long Yellow Road BMG/RCA
Kogun BMG/RCA
March of the Tadpoles BMG/RCA

Stan Kenton

Journey to Capricorn Creative World (iT)
Kenton '76 Stan Kenton and His Orchestra Creative World (iT)

World Saxophone Quartet

Experience Justin Time (iT)
"Steppin" SCCJ
W.S.Q. Black Saint

Art Ensemble of Chicago

Nice Guys ECM

Anthony Braxton

Creative Orchestra Music 1976 RCA
In the Tradition Steeplechase
New Jazz from the 70s Dunya

Sun Ra

Love in Outer Space Leo Records (iT)
Helocentric World Vol. 1 ESP Disk
Space Is Place: Sun Ra and His Astro Intergalactic Infinity Arkestra Impulse! (iT)
Stardust from Tomorrow Leo Records (iT)

Jazz at the Close of the Century

> "The ultimate achievement for any culture is the creation of an art form."[1]
>
> WYNTON MARSALIS
>
> "The student has to absorb, and make discriminating choices about what he thinks is good or bad, and not let somebody else tell them."[2]
>
> KEITH JARRETT

The eclecticism prevalent throughout the 80s and the absence of any single jazz style foreshadowed the future, as the 90s are even more difficult to grasp in terms of pinpointing developments in jazz that would have any lasting significance. We are too close to enjoy a good perspective, and there has not been sufficient time for us to fully realize the outcomes of recent trends in jazz. While jazz is certainly not dead, it seems that we can no longer expect regular change or single trends, as was the case in the early decades. As in the previous two decades, there seems to be no single style or movement, but a number of trends simultaneously pursued in the final years of the twentieth century. It is safe to say that women instrumentalists are now becoming more noticed than ever before, exerting a more noticeable impact on the music than in earlier decades.

Table15.1 summarizes recent trends, and it is quite a list, especially when we realize that the same four-letter word we started out with in Chapter I is used to describe all of the styles listed. It is clear that there is a strong tendency toward straight-ahead jazz, since so many musicians and record labels seem concerned with the reevaluation and reinvention of past traditions. Some jazz practitioners are doing their best to renew the music by retreading older styles, rebuilding audiences that appreciate and understand it; but in doing so, some feel the music is in danger of homogenization (in part due to the jazz education movement), which puts at risk the very spirit of individuality that has always been a cornerstone of jazz.

TABLE 15.1 Late-Twentieth- and Early-Twenty-First-Century Movements in Jazz

- Tribute bands
- Contemporary big bands and composition for larger forms
- Reissue campaigns of historically significant and sometimes obscure, earlier recordings
- Repertoire ensembles specializing in historic works, new music, or compositions by a single composer
- Increased activity and awareness of well-established artists who emerged in the 70s or 80s and matured in the 90s
- The not so young, Young Lions
- Experimental jazz
- "Smooth jazz," aimed at mass-market appeal
- A renaissance for new and established vocal artists
- World-influenced or ethnically influenced jazz, including Asian, African, Caribbean, and Middle Eastern
- Jam jazz (also described as "acid jazz," "groove music" and "bass 'n' drums")
- Rock- and Latin- (especially Cuban-) influenced jazz

THE MUSICAL TRENDS

Each of the aforementioned directions will be summarized in this chapter. While no one has a crystal ball, the more lengthy discussions address those aspects of twenty-first-century jazz that are more apt to have a long-lasting impact on the future.

Large Ensemble Composition

A new emphasis on composition began to take shape just prior to the 1990s. To quote author Lewis Porter, this new generation of jazz composers (some of whom are not so young) are "well-schooled, often in both jazz and the classics; they take virtuosity for granted. They organize bands that draw on . . . the entire sweep of jazz—from African roots to swing to free-form."[3] In contrast to the traveling big bands in the 30s and 40s, many of the modern big bands do not tour on any regular basis, so their music is most often accessible only through recordings and occasional live performances. Composers like Bob Brookmeyer, Jim McNeely, Maria Schneider, John Fedchock, David Murray, Bob Mintzer, Kenny Wheeler, Dave Holland, Andrew Hill, Gordon Goodwin, Don Sebesky, Vince Mendoza, and, of course, Wynton Marsalis have shown in their recent work that much new ground remains to be explored in the form of large ensemble jazz composition. In his or her own way, each of these writers has pushed the boundaries of the big band, making it do things that would have amazed even Ellington. Some of the best of this new repertoire has been commissioned and recorded by European Radio Orchestras, making it less accessible to American audiences. Getting access to some of this inspiring new music is like looking for buried treasure: you know it's there but need a map to find it. The Internet is a most useful tool in leading us to these pots of gold. Composers Bob Brookmeyer, Maria Schneider, Jim McNeely, Bob Florence, and Vince Mendoza offer the best of the best and Schneider has achieved much acclaim for her work in the United States and abroad, winning a Grammy in 2005 for a recording that can be purchased only on the Internet. Despite the important and ever-expanding legacy of these groups, their complete absence from the Apple iTunes and other Internet MP3 format vendors is a testament to the unfortunate and ever-increasing obscurity of large ensemble jazz.

The Mingus Big Band deserves mention here as well, since it has received numerous awards for its efforts to recreate a rich body of music created by the famed bassist/composer. This exciting big band is well armed with potent soloists, and their live performances are even more rewarding than their recordings. They should be credited with not only reviving the Mingus tradition, but also with keeping the big band in the spotlight, be it ever so narrowly focused. The Carnegie Hall Jazz Orchestra under the direction of Dizzy Gillespie protégé trumpeter Jon Faddis was an unfortunate failure in terms of its ability to become self-sustaining, but Marsalis' Lincoln Center Jazz Orchestra has done its share in keeping the big band tradition alive in the twenty-first century. Aside from his long list of musical conquests, Marsalis and his benefactors have accomplished what no one who preceded them could in creating a new state-of-the-art venue in New York for Jazz at Lincoln Center. Opened in 2004, this complex is fit for the kings, counts, ladies, and dukes of jazz's past, providing performance and showcase facilities equal to those enjoyed by classical musicians for decades.

Rediscovery Figures, Reissues, and Tributes

The end of the twentieth century was also marked by renewed interest in what could be termed rediscovery figures—artists who had been on the scene for many years, but had somehow been forgotten by the recording industry during the fusion and postelectronic years. Tenor saxophonist Joe Henderson is an excellent example of a mainstream jazz player who enjoyed attention in the 90s that he should have received through his entire career. His final recordings in the late 90s were like aged wine, tempting new listeners to seek out his earlier work from the late 60s and 70s. Henderson was caught up in the tribute trend, recording songs by Brazilian composer Antonio Carlos Jobim to celebrate his life and mark his passing in 1994.

Andrew Hill, a progressive pianist who Blue Note Records promoted heavily in the late 60s and early 70s, had completely vanished from the scene until the turn of the century, when he made a dramatic comeback with an edgy, adventuresome new band. Horace Silver, another graying artist who had enjoyed great success during the heyday of hard bop and funky jazz, released two new recordings in the 90s, the first to be issued in quite some time. Herbie Hancock, who had certainly not been forgotten, also capitalized on the thematic or tribute concept, winning favor for his *Gershwin's World* recording and *The New Standard*, which features new renditions of this generation's hits by pop artists Don Henley, Stevie Wonder, Simon and Garfunkel, Prince, Kurt Cobain, and others. Just as jazz in the early years borrowed from popular Tin Pan Alley music of the day, Hancock put new clothes on tunes born in and parented by the postmodern culture. Wayne Shorter, Hancock's associate with Miles Davis in the mid-1960s, has also enjoyed renewed exposure in recent years, partnering again with Hancock and releasing well-received live and studio recordings.

Composer/bandleader Maria Schneider accepts a 2005 Grammy Award for her big-band recording "Concert in the Garden," the first recording not marketed by retail stores to receive such an award.

While record sales gradually declined during the 90s, the still fairly new CD format and a new listener base encouraged major labels to reissue vast numbers of out-of-print LPs. Reissue packages required very low overhead to produce and offered new and old collectors an exceptional opportunity to enhance their libraries. A survey of those CDs awarded 5 stars in *Down Beat* throughout the decade shows that slightly more than one third were not new recordings but reissues. The percentages are a bit better in the 4½-star category, which shows that only 25 percent were actually reissues. There has been no better time in the history of jazz to build a collection and gain easy access to even the most obscure artists' materials recorded perhaps many years earlier. Retrospective and tribute recordings, concerts, and bands were all common throughout the decade.

Preservationists

The coincidence of the recording companies' reissue campaigns of historically significant jazz that coincided with the emergence of Marsalis and his Young Lions, dedicated in part to recreating older styles, is a phenomenon that should not go unmentioned. Much lip service was given to those preservationists coming out of the 80s who became absolutely dogmatic about those essential characteristics that define real jazz, and the debates continued into the 90s. In their minds, jazz was illegitimate if it did not possess large doses of what they viewed as essential ingredients—swing, blues, and improvisation. Qualified young players continued to emerge from the halls of distinguished music schools throughout the country, but much of what they had to say had been heard, or played, before and there was (and is) concern that jazz has exhausted itself—run out of rope—and is in danger of choking itself in a sea of clones. Marsalis and his Lions, in their efforts to preserve the past, had a profound impact, changing the course, if not the sound, of jazz away from the pull of popular music in the 80s. Their efforts, however, did not go unchallenged. Peter Watrous wrote in *The New York Times* that "the danger is that if looking backward becomes jazz's prime activity, the music becomes embalmed, lifeless,"[4] and there is grave danger that jazz will become a slave to its past tradition. Pianist Marcus Roberts, who was a first-generation Lion, performing with Marsalis' quintet, is a good example. Much of his recorded output as a solo pianist is studies of earlier jazz artists' work or medleys of old standards—for example, *The Joy of Joplin, Cole* [Porter] *After Midnight, Gershwin for Lovers, Deep in the Shed, In Honor of Duke,* and *Alone with Three Giants.* According to Keith Jarrett, "You need to be aware of everything that came before, but to say that you are reviving a tradition, or to school people in the revival of a tradition, which is a tradition of a certain time, takes potential away from those players."[5] But the Lions did what needed to be done, at least in terms of rekindling an interest in the jazz tradition. Marsalis rejuvenated interest in great masterworks by Ellington and Fletcher Henderson. The Smithsonian Masterworks Jazz Orchestra co-led by Gunther Schuller and David Baker also did much to spark new interest in the preservation of important landmark works throughout the tradition of composed jazz. The not so "young" Lions, including Marsalis, may just now be coming into their own after a decade or more of exploitation by record companies who saw an opportunity to clone successful 50s and 60s artists by packaging recordings of a younger generation at an early stage in their development. Marsalis' most recent work shows innovation and is his most adventuresome to date. Second-generation "new Lions" like Joshua Redman, Jason Moran, Chris Potter, Avashi Cohen, Roy Hargrove, Terrance Blanchard, Brad Mehldau, Jackie Terrasson, and Danilo Pérez, to name a few, are now exhibiting the potential to reach beyond the work of their forbearers.

Post–Avant-Garde Experimentalists

The most recent wave of postmodern experimentalists challenges every aspect of the tradition while at the same time embracing it. Some of these musicians have tried to reconcile jazz with the classical music ethos by composing for the orchestra, the string quartet (The Kronos and Turtle Island Quartets); chamber groups experimenting with unusual instrumentations (most notably The World Saxophone Quartet); and collaborations with poets, visual artists, filmmakers, and choreographers, all in an effort to guide jazz down a new path without forsaking its tradition. Take for example Anthony Davis who was trained at Yale University's School of Music in the techniques of classical composition. According to author Lewis Porter, he is "probably the most abstract and classical-sounding composer among his peers,"[6] and his work could easily be compared to the 60s chamber works of Cecil Taylor. Davis' music effectively blurs the boundaries between written and improvised music and he tends to work more from an earlier twentieth-century classical slant. In 1986 he premiered his unorthodox opera based on the life of freedom fighter Malcolm X. "I came to the realization that I wasn't concerned whether people looked at my music or not," he said. "I'm writing American music, and it draws on a whole spectrum of influences in all kinds of traditions."[7]

Ornette Coleman continued to cast a long shadow into the twenty-first century. Coleman's own Prime Time band recorded *Tone Dialing*, Coleman's 60s bassist Charlie Haden formed the Liberation Orchestra, and crossover guitarist Pat Metheny broke his own mold by recording the adventuresome *Song X* album with Coleman, Haden and drummer Jack DeJohnnette. Other artists who have done their best to stretch the envelope were pianists Geri Allen (another Coleman disciple) and Carla Bley, saxophonists David Murray, Greg Osby, and Steve Coleman whose M-base collective also advanced a new brand of funk featuring odd and changing time signatures, guitarist Bill Frisell, saxophonist John Zorn, trumpeter and composer Paul Smoker, and clarinetist/composer Don Byron, who was *Down Beat* magazine's "Jazz Artist of the Year" in 1992. There are no lines that Byron hasn't crossed in his efforts to reflect in his music the complex cultural fabric that makes up the most multicultural nation in the world. He has borrowed from rap, hip-hop, funk, blues, classical, Jewish klezmer, bebop, salsa, and swing—nothing is immune to Byron's eclectic mixes.

The popular rap, DJ mix, bass 'n' drums, hip-hop, and urban electronic styles have exerted influences on twenty-first-century jazz musicians just as Sly Stone and Jimi Hendrix provided new motivation to an earlier generation of jazz musicians. Trumpeter Tim Hagans and composer/arranger/saxophonist Bob Belden teamed to record *Animation-Imagination* and *Re-Animation Live*, which offered unique fusions of the latest esoteric electronic pop and a full dose of improvisation a là Miles Davis, post 70s. Hagans' imaginative live band adds splashes of freely improvised bass, drums, and keyboard to electronic samples, DJ mixes, drum loops, funky electronic dance grooves, and various other soundscapes. Hagans and Belden improvise in a very free, unencumbered style on top of these shifting aural landscapes. There is absolutely no commercial compromise about either recording

Trumpeter/composer Tim Hagans.

and both represent the finest in cutting edge, twenty-first-century jazz. Tim Hagans discusses his work on "Trumpet Sandwich" included on the companion audio anthology.

> Trumpet Sandwich is a through-improvised composition. Each phrase is 16 bars containing smaller subdivisions of 4 bars each. The first three subdivisions present improvised melodic material that builds and weaves, as do traditional melodies. The last segment, usually simpler, is the summation of the 16-bar phrase.

> The piece stresses the importance of meaningful melodic construction whether supported by traditional harmony or not. One can improvise over the chords of a tune or, on a deeper level, one can improvise over the emotions generated by those chords. Here, I am improvising over the emotions of a non-existent chord progression with the emphasis on a standard melodic form.

> The original version, on *Animation/Imagination*, was an improvised jam with Billy Kilson (drums) and David Dyson (bass) during a session lunch break, hence the title. With no plan in advance, we turned the lights out, Dave started playing the bass line and the rest is . . . [open to chance].

> In order to keep my mind totally free, I avoided figuring out the key Dave was playing in. That prevented me from assigning scale numbers and traditional emotions to the notes I used.

> After the initial studio recording, the tune's basic concept was established but with this group of freethinkers, the direction and vibe was new and fresh every time. This version closed our set at the Montreal Jazz Festival in 1999.[8]

An excerpt of "Trumpet Sandwich" is included on the companion audio anthology.

The European experimental jazz scene became increasingly active at the close of the twentieth century giving even more credence to American experimental efforts. Artists such as the Vienna Art Ensemble, Willem Breuker Kollektieff, Kenny Wheeler, Jan Garbarek, Graham Haynes, Evan Parker, and John Taylor

Listening Guide

Tim Hagans and Bob Belden

"Trumpet Sandwich" (Hagans/Belden) 3:29

Recorded October 2000, Blue Note Records B00004YLJM, *Re-Animation Live*

Tim Hagans: *trumpet*
Bob Belden: *saxophones*
Scott Kinsey: *synthesizer*
DJ Kingsize: *electronic effects, loops*
David Dyson: *bass*
Billy Kilson: *drums*

0:00–0:27	Random, improvised electronic and DJ sounds
0:28–0:49	Electronic drums begin with various electronic distortions added to soundscape
0:50–1:10	Electric bass enters; various electronic distortions of trumpet (1:00)
1:11–2:15	Hagans begins trumpet improvisation; electronic keyboard comps from 1:20, conversing with trumpet
2:16–3:07	Hagans begins ferocious double time improvisation, expanding into the upper register as solo builds in intensity; electronic effects continue to provide soundscape backdrop.
3:08–3:12	Notice how drummer and trumpeter play off one another
3:13–to fade	Hagans winds down his trumpet solo before passing it on to keyboard soloist who follows

brought their own tradition to be reconciled with the roots of jazz. For example, saxophonist Jan Garbarek has issued recordings where he improvises with an a cappella vocal ensemble singing somber Renaissance music in a grand European cathedral. Though this music could certainly not be considered avant-garde, what better way to combine two Western music traditions in order to realize something altogether new?

While more critics than ever at the close of the twentieth century became champions of the new avant-garde, some writers like *Down Beat*'s John McDonough agreed with Marsalis and felt that too many charlatans were hiding behind the "mantra of progress." Referring to the avant-garde, McDonough said that: "It [is] not an advancement of musical law. It [is] a rejection of it. Total freedom cast jazz backward into a primal lawlessness, an emotional state of nature."[9] While there are certainly those who disagree with McDonough, it is safe to say that this music continues to live on the fringe, offering its own counterculture and with a relatively small but growing audience. Champions of the new avant-garde believe just as strongly that they are saving jazz from the jaws of banality otherwise known as "smooth jazz" or "jazz-lite."

Jazz-Lite—Popular Instrumental Jazz

Saxophonist Kenny G became both a controversial performer and popular success story in the 90s. G's overwhelming success justifiably branded him as the leader of the 90s smooth jazz movement and gave rise to a host of other instrumentalists who sought to promote an easy listening style of jazz that would be accepted by the masses. Also described as contemporary jazz, Boney James, Rick Braun, Shadowfax, Dave Koz, Larry Carlton, Acoustic Alchemy, Lee Ritenour, Walter Beasley, David Benoit, Richard Elliot, Marc Antoine, and Chris Botti are all representatives of this popular style. Their melodically memorable music (almost like pop vocals without the lyrics) is typically derived from simple harmonic progressions with easy, danceable grooves and an unobtrusive sound popular with AM radio stations who had all but banned jazz from their play lists. Some of these stations have been known to sponsor smooth jazz festivals and sampler compact disks. To be branded as a smooth jazz artist, at least in the eyes of the well-bred, die-hard jazz connoisseur, however, is the kiss of death. Criticized as meaningless pabulum, mindless, sanitized pulp designed for a generation on Prozac, smooth jazz critics also object most to the absence of any real challenge or controversy presented to the listener, and the absence of any apparent jazz roots in the performers. The critics of this music cannot find in it the range of emotion that is a cornerstone of all good jazz.

"Acid Jazz," another 90s variation on a pop-jazz theme, was a term coined by London DJ Gilles Peterson. Acid jazz grew out of London dance clubs where groovy, electronic remakes of funky 60s jazz were popular. Its success encouraged a new music that was the result of a bond between soul and funk music, hip-hop dance rhythms, aspects of the jazz tradition, and Latin percussion. In some ways Tim Hagans' "Trumpet Sandwich" could be considered a brand of acid jazz. Bands known for this new hybrid style are Buckshot LeFonque (once associated with Branford Marsalis), Us3, Incognito, and Jamiroquai. Jazz artists

Contemporary smooth jazz artist Chris Botti performing in 2004 on his A Thousand Kisses Deep Tour.

such as trumpeter Russell Gunn and vocalist Cassandra Wilson, who are known for their work in more mainstream contexts, are also exploring this direction, which makes some sense since acid jazz relies heavily on important aspects of the jazz tradition—strong emotional content along with improvisation. This style of music provides an easy entry point for the uninitiated to become acquainted with jazz without wading in too deeply at first with bebop or classic jazz styles. These modern bands are providing an experience not dissimilar from that offered to 1920s music lovers who were drawn to jazz first through Paul Whiteman's music or the dance crowd who found jazz during the Swing Era, later to discover bebop and cool jazz. Acid jazz has become very popular in Japan, parts of Europe, and Latin America. It is a brand of jazz that is known by many names including "street soul," "electro jazz," "hip-bop," (check out Miles Davis' final recording *Doo-Bop*), and so forth, but the styles essentially bear the same salient features:

- Heavy bass lines that are often repetitive
- Lots of electronically processed sounds
- Danceable tempos and rhythms
- Strong drum beats (played by drummers or electronic drum machines) sometimes featuring back beat accents (emphasis on beats 2 and 4)
- Repetitive rhythms
- Melodies and harmonies informed by the blues

Whether it will survive and have a lasting influence remains to be seen. What is apparent is that jazz will continue to morph, bonding itself to any available music style, popular or not.

"Groove music," "jam jazz," or "bass 'n' drums" all essentially describe the same style, and something quite similar to acid jazz. This groove music often shows the following characteristics:

- Catchy rhythm grooves
- Rhythmically earthy and sometimes simplistic
- Reliance on strong repetitive bass lines
- Funky drum beats emphasizing numerous subdivisions of the basic beat
- Resemblance to the R&B tradition
- Simple harmonic form involving only a few chords

Artists who have participated in the style are often the same performers who are dedicated to many other styles of jazz and enjoy the challenge of diversity. Many of these groups feature organ and guitar much like the organ groups in the late 50s and 60s. Groups or artists that have pioneered this style are Medeski Martin and Wood and guitarist John Scofield. It is often difficult to separate hip-hop influenced jazz from acid jazz and this bass 'n drums jam style since they all share similar characteristics.

The Return of the Chanteuse and the Crooner

The 90s and the early years of this century have been kind to the jazz vocalist. There has not only been a rise in popularity of new vocalists singing music that is informed by the jazz tradition, but a rebirth of several older artists including Tony Bennett and Jon Hendricks. Hendricks sang an important role in Marsalis' *Blood on the Fields,* as did newcomer Cassandra Wilson. An eclectic vocalist who has been involved with projects that range from fringe to traditional, Wilson believes that "jazz has to be a current music for its survival. It has to be grounded in our lives as they are today."[10] Perhaps the biggest box office draw in recent years has been Canadian singer/pianist Diana Krall. Her romantic ballad style is in stark contrast to those female artists like Diane Schuur, who helped pave the way a decade earlier for renewed interest in jazz singers. Schuur, who continues to enjoy modest popularity, is a more robust singer in the Ella Fitzgerald tradition than Krall. Patricia Barber and Jane Monheit are newcomers along with Nora Jones, whose career was suddenly announced by her 2003 Grammy Award. Jones has created quite a stir as a new young singer, but despite her Blue Note label affiliation many question her classification as a jazz singer. Barber and Monheit, on the other hand, are more reverent, clearly showing their roots in the jazz vocal tradition. More seasoned artists like Dee Dee Bridgewater, Patti Austin, and Natalie Cole paid their dues for some time before enjoying greater exposure in recent years. Just as jazz labels sought out talented Young Lions in the image of Wynton Marsalis, they now are rushing to sign new young male and female vocalists in time to capitalize on the success of Krall and Jones. Who can blame these corporate efforts? They are no doubt made in an effort to energize record sales that have dropped 18 to 20 percent in recent years.

Diane Krall performs at Radio City Music Hall in New York City during the Look of Love Tour, March 29, 2002.

On the male side, Kurt Elling, Mark Murphy, Jamie Cullum, Kevin Mahogany, and, of course, Harry Connick, Jr., have all made contributions as relative newcomers to the contemporary jazz scene. Kurt Elling is best described as the kind of singer instrumentalists love, since he bases his impressive vocal technique on the best horn soloists, scatting and reinterpreting tunes like veteran jazz instrumentalists. Bobby McFerrin, the singer turned orchestral conductor, may have been responsible for the renewed and widespread interest in the jazz vocalist, though much of his repertoire in the 1990s was more about improvisation than it was specifically about jazz. He nevertheless is an amazing talent whose roots are unmistakably from the jazz and African traditions.

It is perhaps more difficult for vocalists than instrumentalists to bring anything significantly new to the tradition, and it seems many of the newcomers are enjoying popularity by recasting exceptional forgotten repertoire from the archives, or by introducing newly penned songs. It remains to be seen if any of these artists will have the same lasting influence as Billie Holiday, Sarah Vaughan, Ella Fitzgerald, Frank Sinatra, or Joe Williams. At the moment they are enjoying good press and have helped to rejuvenate sagging jazz label record sales.

World Music

While arch jazz purists are opposed to fusing jazz with ethnic influences from around the world, there seem to be a number of artists who have chosen this path, producing some very exciting new music. For many years, jazz artists have looked outside the Western world for inspiration, and it is certainly well known that improvisation plays a central role in the music of many other cultures, so the marriage is logical. Coltrane was one of the postmodern pioneers in this regard along with big band leader Don Ellis, but more recent trends toward drawing on world music styles may actually have been sparked by Paul Simon's successful Afro-pop Graceland recordings. It is only fitting that jazz and pop musicians are drawn to African music since the American styles are rooted in its music. Other world music styles that have been heavily mined by jazz artists during the 90s and early twenty-first century are various forms of Caribbean, Eastern and Western European including klezmer and Scottish, and, of course, Latin American. It is not surprising that many artists are turning to such influences to energize jazz, as no other country in the world can lay claim to such a culturally diverse population. Bob Moses, Roy Hargrove, Avashi Cohen, Peter Apfelbaum, Chucho Valdés, Bobby Sanabria, Poncho Sánchez, Michel Camillo, Dave Douglas, Danilo Pérez, and a host of other musicians have discovered the benefits of fusing jazz to certain aspects of non-American music, just as the boppers discovered in the 40s when they teamed with Cuban and Puerto Rican musicians to forge Cubop. Chapter 16 offers more detailed discussion about the marriage of jazz with Latin and Afro-Cuban styles.

A musician who has successfully exploited the merging of jazz with various world music styles is guitarist Pat Metheny, whose debut album *Bright Size Life* is

Guitarist Pat Metheny plays a concert in Tel-Aviv on April 12, 2000, with his trio including Larry Grenadier on bass and Bill Stewart on drums.

now legendary and helped to launch the ECM label. Jazz journalist Bob Blumenthal wrote that "Metheny . . . emerged in the 80s as the rare artistic/commercial success who could boldly rub shoulders with Ornette Coleman's circle after providing feel-good grooves for his larger audience."[11] Metheny brought a fresh, sophisticated approach to composition, conception, and production, and along with keyboard compadre Lyle Mays presented a new group sound concerned with improvisation, but draped in lush, contemporary electronic orchestral-like textures and Latin American–influenced grooves. His use of Latin American percussionists and indigenous instruments adds an element of authenticity to much of his music. Borrowing from Corea, Metheny also made use of vocalists, often imitating an instrument by using wordless syllables. Other world music styles such as Indian and Cambodian also serve to influence his music. Metheny and Mays first collaborated on *Water Colors* (1977) for the ECM label and, while personnel have changed and the addition of new electronic instruments, including the guitar synthesizer, have altered the band's sound over time, this first recording established the "graceful, lyrical and often tranquil" sound that became a recognizable Metheny trademark. As a composer, Metheny has also

Listening Guide

"Better Days Ahead" (Metheny) 3:03

Recorded 1989, Geffen 9 24245-2, *Letter from Home*

Pat Metheny: *guitars*

Lyle Mays: *piano, keyboards, Synclavier*

Steve Rodby: *bass*

Paul Wertico: *drums and percussion*

Pedro Aznar: *voice, acoustic guitar, marimba, vibes, additional percussion*

Armando Marçal: *percussion*

Pat Metheny Group

Form and Key: ABC in G major

0:00–0:08	*Introduction:* 4 bars of percussion	
0:08–0:40	*Initial Statement Song Melody,* 23 bars	
	0:08–0:19	*A section:* 8 bars
	0:19–0:30	*B section:* 8 bars
	0:30–0:40	*C section:* 7 bars that begins with 4-bar vamp with sustained melody, followed by 3-bar melodic tag that resolves momentarily before form repeats
0:40–1:11	*Second Statement Song Melody,* 23 bars	
	0:40–0:50	*A section:* 8 bars
	0:50–1:00	*B section:* 8 bars
	1:01–1:11	*C section:* 7 bars that begins with 4-bar vamp with sustained melody, followed by 3-bar melodic tag that resolves momentarily before form repeats
1:11–1:42	*First Chorus:* 23-bar improvised guitar solo	
1:42–2:14	*Second Chorus:* 23-bar improvised guitar solo; string-like countermelody begins as a background at 1:53	
2:14 to end	*Restatement of Song Melody,* 23 bars	
2:14–2:24	*A section:* 8 bars	
2:24–2:35	*B section:* 8 bars	
2:35 to end	*Extended C section with Coda:* begins with 8-bar vamp with sustained melody, followed by final 6–bar melodic tag ends on sustained chord with fermata	

enjoyed inventing music with complex rhythms, odd time signatures and less than predictable multithematic forms. As a guitarist, he is a master technician known to spin out clean, very long improvised phrases before pausing for a breath. Metheny is known for his approachable, listener friendly tunes, but is comfortable in many jazz styles, performing with musicians representing a wide range of preferences. He and his band continue to be a major force in the twenty-first century, contributing to film scores such as *Map of the World* and *The Falcon and the Snowman* as well as collaborations with choreographers and dance companies.

The Metheny performance included on the companion anthology epitomizes his successful crossover style in that, on the surface, the piece is very accessible with a strong, pleasant melody. Harmonically, however, it is complex, with chords that change frequently and present constant shifts from one key to another. It is also innovative in terms of the form since there is a deceptive ending 20 measures into the tune when the melody reaches a resting point at the repetitive vamp, but at this point it isn't over as an additional three measure melodic tag or coda completes the form. Twenty-three-measure tunes such as this are highly unusual. The irregular rhythmic phrasing of the melody set against a regular Brazilian-like rhythm background makes for a very cyclic feeling and a tune that seems to have no obvious beginning or ending. Metheny shows here that he is a wizard of modern jazz composition who can deliver listenable music that is simultaneously complex and challenging to the musicians who perform it.

Pianist Danilo Pérez is a young contemporary artist, who, because of his Panamanian heritage and American education, offers an excellent case study in which to more closely evaluate the potential for jazz drawing on numerous world music sources. The track from his CD *Motherland* included on the companion audio anthology was released at the dawn of this century and embraces a diverse worldview. He successfully molds elements of Caribbean, African, Andalucian, Moorish, and, of course, American jazz into something entirely new. The ethnicity of his group is as diverse as the music, featuring African-American, Brazilian, white-American, and other Latin-tinged musicians. Pérez, like many of his contemporaries, also has a penchant for exploring odd-time signatures, striving to make them sound as normal and comfortable as a 4/4 march or 3/4 waltz. Part 1 of his "Suite For The Americas" is reminiscent of Corea's earlier work in the 1970s in that it is multithematic and through composed in its organization and structure. **Through composed** is a compositional approach that resembles stream of consciousness writing in that typically there are no reoccurring themes, links from one to another or character development to provide a more traditional, discernable form or shape. One idea moves on to the next and is followed by yet another idea, and so on. In this case, Pérez does finally return briefly to the initial "A" theme and makes use of Arabic and Latin rhythms and bass ostinatos to help provide adhesive to help hold the various fragments together. This piece is a composition and not merely a tune that serves as the basis for improvised solos. In fact, there is very little improvisation in this entire piece. If you are trying to tap your toe and count along as you listen to this track, you will be challenged by the odd and changing meters, but the piece is primarily in 7/4 meter. Saxophonist Chris Potter, vocalist Luciana Souza, violinist Regina Carter, and, of course, pianist/composer Pérez are some of the most promising musicians of this young century.

Danilo Pérez

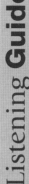

Listening Guide

"Suite For The Americas, Part 1" (Perez) 2:54

Recorded Feb-March 2000 New York City, *Motherland* Verve

3145439042

Danilo Pérez: *piano, Fender Rhodes*

Carlos Henriquez: *acoustic bass*

Antonio Sanchez: *drums*

Regina Carter: *violin*

Luciana Souza: *vocals*

Chris Potter: *soprano saxophone*

Luisito Quintero: *congas, small percussion, caja tambora, chimes, durban drums*

Ricuarte Villereal: *tambor repicador*

Form and Key: Sectional, through composed form using several different melodic elements, sometimes repeated; in several key centers including D-major/minor, B-modal-minor, and C#-minor; an overall Latin rhythmic feel in 7/4, 5/4 meters

0:00–0:17 *Introduction:* 8 bars of 7/4, *Latin groove in D-minor,* created by bass, drums, and piano

    2 bars: bass enters with 7/4 ostinato pattern

    2 bars: drums and percussion join bass

    4 bars: piano enters with chord, then sparse Latin comping

0:18–0:55 *"A" Theme section:* 17 bars of 7/4, *"A" Theme,* in D-minor played twice by piano, sax, and violin, with continuing rhythm section accompaniment

0:18–0:35 *Part 1:* 8 bars, *"A" Theme*

    4 bars: piano plays first phrase of "A" theme (2 + 2)

    2 bars: violin, sax, and piano play unison answering second phrase of "A" theme

    2 bars: piano plays ad-lib solo, with rhythm section accompaniment

0:35–0:55 *Part 2:* 9 bars, *"A" Theme* repeated 4 bars: violin, sax, and piano play unison 4 bars of "A" theme (2+2)

    2 bars: violin, sax and piano play unison answering 2 bars of "A" theme

    2 bars: piano and Fender Rhodes ad-lib solo with rhythm section accompaniment

    1 bar (7/4):   *Closing Idea* performed in unison by violin, sax, and piano, used as transition to "B" Theme section

0:55–1:19 *"B" Theme section:* 10 bars of 7/4, modulating *"B" Theme,* performed twice by voice, piano and saxophone, with continuing rhythm section accompaniment, "B" Theme repeat is varied

    0:55–1:06   *Part 1:* 5 bars: *"B" Theme* performed by voice, piano violin, and sax

    3 bars: first phrase of "B" Theme

    2 bars: second "answering" phrase of "B" Theme

1:07–1:19 *Part 2:* 5 bars: *"B" Theme* repeated by voice, piano, violin, and sax with variation at end

    3 bars: first phrase of "B" Theme

    2 bars: altered second phrase of "B" Theme, with dramatic held C# vocal note; violin, sax, and piano "break," and loud ensemble line that crescendos to climactic C# minor chord

1:19–1:42 *C section:* 10 bars of 7/4, *Long D-major Melodies*, performed by voice, violin, sax, and piano, with frequent rhythm section breaks

Listening Guide

1:43–2:02   *D section:* 8 bars of 7/4, *Modal "Arabic" B-minor Melodies*, performed by piano, voice, sax and violin

2 bars: piano, bass, drums, and percussion (tambourine) set up highly syncopated B Minor groove

2 bars: 1-bar vocal phrase answered by voice, sax, and violin

4 bars: voice elaborates 1-bar vocal phrase, with continued overlapping "answers" in sax and violin

2:03–2:24   *E section:* 9 bars of 7/4, *Vocal and Saxophone Solos*, with funky rhythm section led by electric piano, alternating between D-major and B-minor, with 1-bar closing acoustic piano break

2:25–2:34   *F section:* 4 bars in 7/4, *Ensemble "Shout" Theme*, in C#-minor, performed twice by voice, sax, violin, and piano, with rhythm section accompaniment

2:35–2:54   *"A" Theme section:* 8 bars in 5/4, *"A" Theme* paraphrased in C#-minor, performed twice by voice, sax, violin, and piano; first theme statement is unison, repeat is harmonized; with 1-bar (7/4) tag: *Closing Idea* in D, from end of "A" Theme section

Mature Artists Offer Seasoned Jazz

Some of the best jazz during the 90s seems to defy any clear categorization and was created by a group of musicians who, unlike the new wave of young musicians just beginning their careers, found themselves on the second or third leg of their journey. These artists reached a point in their careers where they transcended virtuosity for its own sake, and had surpassed their earlier phases of obsession with building technique and mastering the tradition. Their newfound freedom through complete instrumental control empowered them in the 90s to use what they had learned to create new work that was not bound or overly encumbered by tradition, but rather grew from it, while at the same time reflecting their contemporary society. In every case, these artists have found reward in exploring numerous styles throughout their careers, much like those many sidemen who had worked with Miles Davis years before. Bassist Dave Holland is an excellent example, since his small group and big band have frequently been in the news and polls throughout the opening years of the twenty-first century. Holland has been a visible figure since his first widespread exposure with Davis in the 70s, and to his new band of otherwise young musicians he brings the important elements of experience, wisdom, and sense of tradition. Recently, he has gained significant and long-overdue recognition for his work.

One of the final audio examples provides additional proof of the power that Davis exerted even after his death. John Scofield, who performed with Davis in the final stage of his career, has proven to be one of the most influential guitarists since John McLaughlin, and certainly one of the most important jazz artists in the new millennium. He is comfortable in quiet chamber ensembles, free form experiments, loud rock-influenced bands, progressive bop contexts, Latin grooves, soulful settings, and postmodern techno styles of jazz, and there is clear evidence of this diversity throughout his discography. Joe Lovano, his partner on the accompanying recording, exemplifies one of two new schools of tenor saxophone

Joe Lovano (right) sound checking with Tommy Smith (sax), John Scofield (guitar), and John Taylor (piano) at the Barbicon Centre, London on November 18, 2003, during the London Jazz Festival.

playing and, along with Michael Brecker, has become one of the most sought after and widely impersonated artists in today's jazz scene. Imitation in jazz is considered the highest form of flattery, and, while it discourages individuality, is a strong measure of an artist's impact on a future generation of performers. Lovano is somewhat steeped in what could be considered a modern day Lester Young school of playing, while Brecker is the contemporary equivalent of a Coleman Hawkins style player. "Some Nerve," included with the companion media, serves as an excellent example combining new and old aspects of the tradition. The drum groove is inspired by the funky, second-line, early New Orleans parade bands. The overall tenor of the piece is bluesy with both soloists reaching deeply into this rich tradition during their solos. Drummer Bill Stewart eventually moves to a modern straight-ahead, hard bop inspired approach during the tenor and guitar solos. Using the latest technology to modify his guitar sound, Scofield enables the instrument to sound like an organ while comping for Lovano. During the "head" and guitar solo, Scofield uses distortion devices to add a "grungy" element to the guitar sound.

Another musician who has undoubtedly reached the pinnacle of his career is saxophonist Michael Brecker. He has been on the scene for many years, pioneering fusion almost before anyone was ready to listen, performing as a sideman with Horace Silver along with his trumpet playing brother Randy, touring with Jaco Pastorius and drummer Billy Cobham, co-leading with his brother the successful Brecker Brothers fusion style band in the mid-1970s, and serving as founding member of the exceptional neo-bop Steps Ahead band. Much like other musicians from his generation, Brecker is at home in virtually any style of music. Consequently he

Saxophonist Michael Brecker performing on an electronic wind instrument (as heard on the companion CD audio anthology), July 3, 2004, in Barbicon Hall, London.

John Scofield and Joe Lovano

"Some Nerve"
(Scofield) 5:12

Recorded December
1990, John Scofield
Quartet *Meant To
Be,* Blue Note CDP 0777
7 95479-2

John Scofield: *guitar*

Joe Lovano: *tenor
saxophone*

Marc Johnson:
acoustic bass

Bill Stewart: *drums*

Listening Guide

Form and Key: Repeated 16-bar choruses (AB, 8+8) in C major in 2/4 (cut-time)
New Orleans-style "second-line" groove

0:00–0:07   *Introduction:* 8 bars, *Drum Solo* sets up New Orleans–style "second-line" groove

0:07–0:21   *First Chorus:* 16 bars, guitar and tenor sax play *Theme* in unison, with bass and drum "second-line" accompaniment

0:22–0:36   *Second Chorus:* 16 bars, guitar and tenor sax repeat *Theme* as in First Chorus

0:37–0:51   *Third Chorus:* 16 bars, *Guitar Solo* over song chord changes, with continuing bass and drum accompaniment

0:52–1:06   *Fourth Chorus:* 16 bars, guitar and tenor sax repeat *Theme* as in First Chorus

1:07–2:07   *Fifth to Eighth Choruses:* 16 bars each, *Tenor Sax Solo* over song chord changes, with continuing bass and drum "second-line" style accompaniment

2:07–2:53   *Ninth to Eleventh Choruses:* 16 bars each, *Sax Solo* continues, drums changing to swinging jazz feel, bass changing from "second-line" style to walking pattern

2:54–3:53   *Twelfth to Fifteenth Choruses:* 16 bars each, *Guitar Solo* over song chord changes, bass and drums return to "second-line" pattern accompaniment

3:53–4:38   *Sixteenth to Eighteenth Choruses:* 16 bars each, *Guitar Solo* continues, drums changing to swinging jazz feel, bass changing from "second-line" style to walking pattern

4:38–4:53   *Nineteenth Chorus:* 16 bars, guitar and tenor sax play *Theme* in unison, with bass and drum accompaniment, as in First Chorus

4:53–5:12   *Twentieth Chorus:* 16 bars, guitar and sax repeat *Theme* as in Second Chorus, with abrupt ending

has graced recordings by many jazz and pop musicians including James Taylor, John Lennon, Joni Mitchell, and Paul Simon. Brecker pioneered the use of the electronic wind instrument (EWI) that allows wind players to control synthesizers, applying their own technique and breath control to electronic tone generators, and, as volumes escalated, enabled saxophonists to compete with keyboard synthesizers, electric guitars, and other amplified instruments. Brecker has developed greater control of the saxophone than any who came before and many feel he is the next most important player to hit the scene since John Coltrane. His technical mastery of the instrument, including the ability to play far beyond the normal upper-range limit, and the use of harmonics in a musical fashion is as yet unequaled. His sound and very identifiable phrasing (like a distinct accent or speech pattern) on the tenor saxophone became the model for many young players in the last two decades of the twentieth century. He won *Down Beat* polls in the late 80s and was awarded a

Michael Brecker

"Suspone" (Mike Stern) 4:58

Recorded on ***Don't Try This at Home*** in 1988 on Impulse MCAD 42229

Michael Brecker: *tenor saxophone and Akai EWI*

Mike Stern: *guitar*

Joey Calderazzo: *piano*

Jeff Andrews: *bass*

Adam Nussbaum: *drums*

Listening Guide

Form and Key: Repeated 32-bar song form (AABA=chorus)

0:00–0:38   *First Chorus:* 32-bar AABA song form; Melody stated by EWI (electronic wind instrument), guitar, and piano; notice the two beat bass style with only occasional walking and drummer uses brushes; the melody displaces the usual strong downbeat since the melody of each A and B section begins not on beat 1 but on beat 4 from the previous measure.

     0:00–0:10   *A section:* 8 bars

     0:10–0:19   *A section:* first 8 bars are repeated

     0:19–0:29   *B section:* 8-bar bridge with same instrumentation

     0:29–0:38   *A section:* return of first 8-bar theme

0:38–1:15   *Second Chorus:* 32-bar AABA form continues with guitar improvisation; bass now walks but drummer continues to use brushes

1:15–1:52   *Third Chorus:* 32-bar AABA form continues with second guitar improvised chorus

1:52–2:29   *Fourth Chorus:* 32-bar AABA form continues now featuring improvised tenor sax solo; notice the lack of any comping by guitar or piano, but the drummer abruptly changes to sticks for contrast.

2:29–3:06   *Fifth Chorus:* 32-bar AABA form continues with second improvised tenor sax chorus; notice the light and sparse piano comping; also observe the double time phrases improvised at various points in the first two A sections

3:06–3:42   *Sixth Chorus:* 32-bar AABA form continues featuring improvised piano solo; bass implies single note (pedal point) during first two A sections and drum style changes from straight to swing feel; bass (and drums) play swing, walking style on bridge at 3:24.

3:42–4:18   *Seventh Chorus:* 32-bar AABA form continues with second improvised piano chorus; chorus begins with an allusion to "Lester Leaps In," a Swing Era "I've Got Rhythm" based tune

4:19–4:58   *Eighth Chorus:* 32-bar AABA form continues featuring an exact restatement of the entire theme with abrupt ending

Grammy for Best Jazz Performance for his work on *Don't Try This at Home*, the source of the final track in the companion collection. "Suspone" offers a glimpse at how contemporary jazz musicians continue to resurrect old traditions for it is a "rhythm changes" tune based on Gershwin's old model. Next to the blues, the rhythm changes scheme has had the most significant impact on shaping the jazz canon. Brecker and his band prove that this old form is still a worthy framework for improvisation and composition. He joins guitarist Mike Stern, another late Miles Davis alumnus, to state the initial tune on EWI before switching to tenor saxophone later for his improvised solo. The form and presentation is classic and reminiscent of the straightforward, meat and potatoes hard bop approach.

CONTEMPORARY JAZZ SCHOLARSHIP

Musicians were not the only ones working to take jazz to new heights at the close of the twentieth century. Scholarship in jazz had for years lagged behind research and writing about other forms of music, especially Western classical styles. James Lincoln Collier, Francis Davis, Gary Giddens, Burton Peretti, Lewis Porter, Paul Berliner, and Ted Gioia among others have raised the bar in terms of jazz scholarship. This new generation of jazz scholars looked more carefully at the music, those who created it, the times in which it had been created, and other factors that may have exercised influence on the musicians and their products. For the first time, jazz archives became important additions to existing nonjazz collections. Well-established institutions like the Rutgers Institute of Jazz Studies, the Smithsonian Institute, and the Library of Congress did much to acquire, cultivate, curate, and display their holdings, and scholars had access to treasure troves of material. Grants from various foundations to support historical research, video documentaries, aural history projects, and exhibits helped to raise Americans' awareness of jazz to heights not experienced since the Swing Era. While all of these accomplishments seem to indicate a promising future for the art form and its practitioners, the future isn't all rosy.

PROFILE OF THE TWENTY-FIRST-CENTURY JAZZ MUSICIAN

The strong economic climate during the 90s provided Americans with what became in retrospect an artificial sense of security and prosperity. The digital revolution continued to flourish through much of the decade with exploding markets and discoveries in desk top computing, personal digital assistants (PDA), wireless networks, cellular phones, DVD players and recorders, digital cameras, MP3 players, and global positioning devices all helping to serve what appears to be a common theme—communication of information and content sharing. But the shortage of jazz clubs in some cities made it more and more difficult for touring jazz artists to find regular work and those bands that did tour were primarily small groups. It has become almost impossible economically for big bands to maintain regular touring schedules, and for that matter, very few big bands exist on any regular basis aside from those sponsored by the armed services like the exceptional Airmen of Note and the Army Blues. Maynard Ferguson, the Mingus Big Band, Basie Band, and the Lincoln Center Jazz Orchestra are the only remaining big bands (aside from "ghost bands" or reunion bands like the Glenn Miller and Woody Herman bands, respectively) that continue regular touring schedules. Consequently, the steady flow of qualified, young jazz musicians groomed by an increasing number of university jazz programs have very few outlets for apprenticeships that were more readily available in earlier decades. In other words, there is a larger supply of musicians than ever but very little sustaining demand. Record sales plunged to new lows with jazz representing less than 2 percent of the market share, a low position it shares, ironically, with classical music. While it is difficult to understand, CBS dropped Pulitzer Prize winning Wynton Marsalis from their roster, along with other jazz artists, in a move not dissimilar from their jettisoning of Miles Davis in 1985 after a 29-year relationship. The younger artists struggling for record contracts with the smallest independent labels often see their recordings fall out of print before they have been given the opportunity for wider discovery. The Internet, CD recorders, and other forms that facilitate piracy have not helped the situation, and, coupled with a shrinking number of live venues for jazz, admission prices to concerts and clubs have soared. Consequently, many fans stay at home to listen to their CDs (quite possibly pirated from some illegal source) rather than pay what they feel to be too high an admission price. The younger generation, who in the past had supported jazz in many cases, now looks elsewhere for musical entertainment and questions the need to pay for it.

Deemed a national treasure by the U.S. Congress, "jazz is a unique American art form, and its musicians, the keepers and producers of this treasure, are recognized the world over as America's cultural ambassadors."[12] Yet, when viewed as an occupation, according to a recent study by Joan Jeffri, "making a living as a jazz musician can be very difficult."[13] It is even more difficult for emerging artists since "reissues of classic jazz recordings have [often] outsold all but the most popular contemporary jazz artists."[14] Jazz musicians are often loners, at least in terms of the freelance nature of their work. Like their music, they are independent, often working in many different groups as compared to the more regular ensemble existence of the symphony musician. There is a price to pay for this independence as about 66 percent of the working jazz musicians in the San Francisco area, a hub for experimental jazz, earned less than $7,000 in 2000, and more than half those musicians polled in a random survey reported that they had no retirement plans or health insurance. While private foundations have done their best to stimulate growth through grant funds, support from such organizations as The Lila Wallace–Reader's Digest Fund, the Doris Duke Charitable Trust, and the Pew Charitable Trust have largely gone to support presenters, organizations, and other such infrastructures aimed at promoting jazz. Their support typically goes to assisting well-established artists. While Congress may have designated jazz a "national treasure," since 1996 it has forbidden the National Endowment for the Arts to give grants to individuals aside from a select few senior artists awarded prestigious American Jazz Masters Fellowships. Consequently, emerging artists have very few avenues to turn to for assistance, as they had in earlier decades.

Despite these obstacles, women gained a much stronger foothold in the jazz scene by the close of the twentieth century. With champions like Joanne Brackeen, Jane Ira Bloom, Geri Allen, Regina Carter, Jamie Baum, Terri Lyne Carrington, Jane Bunnett, and big band leaders Toshiko Akiyoshi and Maria Schneider, a much more optimistic future seems to lie ahead. Diva and Maiden Voyage, while they don't work regularly, are both big band incubators for outstanding female jazz instrumentalists. Unfortunately though, surveys conducted in 2000 showed that an average of only 20 percent of the working jazz musicians were women compared to their 47 percent share of the overall U.S. workforce.

Odd as it may seem given the music's heritage, a disproportionate number of jazz musicians continue to be white as are their audiences. Despite their low pay, close to 50 percent of the working jazz musicians recently surveyed hold higher education degrees and at best only 55 percent make 100 percent of their living in the music business, and even less playing jazz. Most supplement their preference for playing jazz by a wide range of more commercial gigs. Considering the group's high level of educational achievement, and their contribution to the preservation and advancement of a "national treasure," they should be faring better economically. "This is the music that gives people hope when there is no hope,"[15] commented one of the survey respondents. Anywhere from 44 to 82 percent of those musicians surveyed indicated that their music was being broadcast via some medium—radio, TV, or Internet Web site. It is, therefore, safe to say that vast numbers of people are enjoying and profiting in some way from their work, but clearly we must do a better job of supporting these artists. A society without its art would certainly make for a drab and meaningless existence, and in many ways art helps to define a culture and its society; we are what we make and art is one of the most significant, lasting things left behind by a culture.

CLOSING THOUGHTS

On a more optimistic note, America has proven to be an amazingly resilient society, recovering from severe economic downturns, civil wars at home and world wars abroad, graft and corruption, divisive racial turmoil, terrorism, political controversy, social and moral revolutions, and every other imaginable trial. Just as American society has always recovered, jazz, too, has rebounded and musicians have more than once resuscitated it, often in unanticipated ways, and at times when it had been declared all but dead. But for jazz to remain ever present and a significant fiber in the American cultural fabric, it needs new audiences. These new listeners must embrace innovation, nurture preservation, encourage experimentation, and respect established technique. There is no need to debate the value of one style or trend over another, and, in fact, this form of divisiveness does more to harm the music than to help it. New audiences must be receptive to having their minds challenged, their values tested, and their tastes expanded. They must learn to welcome the unfamiliar. Learning to appreciate art can be compared to acquiring a taste for new foods—you often have to be willing to take the risk and try something new on the menu. New listeners will have to learn to appreciate, or at least give equal opportunity to what they don't understand and be curious enough to reconcile new experiences with old familiar ones. New audiences are needed to be proactive in supporting the most engaging artists, though they may be the most daring and obscure, operating against the grain in terms of what trends are dictated by popular culture. The power of the most unknown artist should not be underestimated, even though they often attract the least promotion for their work. Local clubs that feature the best area talent as well as nationally established performers should be patronized. Above all, don't accept at face value what someone else says is good. Individuals should form their own aesthetics and values based at least in part on sources such as *Experiencing Jazz*. The jazz art form needs to be experienced firsthand as much and as often as possible, for the enrichment accrued is well worth the effort.

Jazz in Perspective

The timeline that follows will put the developments of jazz discussed in this chapter into a larger historical context, providing you with a better sense of how landmark musical events may relate to others that match your personal areas of interest.

1990
- Russian leader Michael Gorbachev wins Nobel Peace Prize.
- Germany reunited under President Helmut Kohl.

- Civil liberties and political activist Nelson Mandela is freed from imprisonment.
- Kuwait is invaded by Iraq.

1991
- Gorbachev resigns as the last president of the USSR.
- Soviet Union is dissolved leaving 15 republics.
- President de Klerk of South Africa abolishes apartheid laws.
- United States' attack of Iraq to liberate Kuwait labeled Operation Desert Storm.

1992
- Bill Clinton elected U.S. president.
- Riots in LA over Rodney King verdict draw attention to racial profiling.
- South Africa bestows equal legal rights on blacks.
- Earth Summit held in an effort to protect habitat and environment.

1993
- Steven Speilberg's popular film *Schindler's List* draws new attention to Nazi Germany and persecution of Jews.
- Unified European market begins.
- Islamic terrorist bomb rocks World Trade Center in New York City.
- Waco, Texas, is site of 51-day standoff between U.S. officials and right-wing religious sect.
- Palestinian leader Arafat and Israeli Prime Minister Rabin sign peace agreement in United States.

1994
- LA experiences significant earthquake.
- 30,000-year-old paintings found in French cave.
- 16-million black voters elect Nelson Mandela president of South Africa.
- Sports legend OJ Simpson tried for murder.

1995
- Oklahoma federal building destroyed by car bomb.
- Peace agreement reached between leaders of Bosnia, Serbia, and Croatia.
- Israel's Prime Minister Rabin assassinated.
- OJ Simpson acquitted on murder charges.
- For the first time in 40 years, the Republican Party controls Congress.

1996
- Mad cow disease forces ban on beef by European Union.
- $10 million tobacco company settlement for treatment of smokers.
- Bill Clinton reelected U.S. president.
- Taliban take over Afghanistan.
- Church burnings in the United States fueled by racial hostilities.

1997
- Lamb is cloned by Scottish DNA researcher.
- Wynton Marsalis becomes first jazz artist to win Pulitzer Prize for *Blood on the Fields.*
- NASA space probe *Sojourner* sends back images of Mars.

1998
- Internet and e-mail see widespread use, revolutionizing commerce and exchange of information.
- Iraq bans UN weapons inspectors; the United States launches offensive.
- President Clinton impeached.
- Singer Frank Sinatra dies.
- Technology boom sparks Internet commerce and start-up industries.

1999
- Clinton acquitted by Senate of impeachment charges.

2000
- Stock market falters with decline of dot.com business and high-tech industries.
- International Space Station placed in orbit.
- G. W. Bush wins close, controversial election over Al Gore.
- Middle East tensions continue to rise.

2001
- Power crisis causes sporadic blackouts in California.
- Enron Corp. scandal shocks the United States.
- Al Qaeda terrorists use commercial airlines to destroy World Trade Center killing 3,000 Americans.
- President Bush vows revenge against terrorist attacks, invading Iraq.

CHAPTER SUMMARY

Jazz in the 1990s continued to include many diverse substyles. Other than the fact that women will continue to have more of an impact in jazz, one can only speculate about the lasting effects of the many new trends. It would seem, though, with the shrinking of the world via advances in communication, including the Internet, that jazz will continue to have an important world music aspect. The Pat Metheny Group and Panamanian pianist Danilo Pérez are just two of the many who have very successfully fused elements of world music with jazz.

Although not as popular as in the 1930s and 1940s, new big bands (and a few existing ones) came to the forefront, fueled by great soloists and outstanding composer/arrangers. 2005 Grammy Award winner Maria Schneider, one of the most original in this new group, leads an excellent band far different than 1940s swing bands. As is the case with so many other big bands, her group performs infrequently as the members work in many other musical settings. A notable aspect of Schneider's band is the fact that their recordings and arrangements are not available from the usual retail outlets, but only via her Web site. The Mingus Big Band and Lincoln Center Jazz Orchestra continue to keep big band music alive both through new compositions and the replication of classic arrangements.

A number of performers from previous jazz styles were "rediscovered" in the 1990s, giving their careers a second life. Tenor saxophonist Joe Henderson probably benefited from this trend the most, receiving multiple Grammy Awards in the 1990s. The popularity of the CD format encouraged companies to reissue long out of print LPs, a trend that probably helped the older players considerably. The downside of this, however, is that consumers use a large portion of their budgets purchasing reissues, leaving less to support new, emerging artists. Of the veteran jazz performers still active in the 1990s, a few stand out not only for their artistry, but also for their influence on young players. Guitarist John Scofield and tenor saxophonists Michael Brecker and Joe Lovano fit this category. Brecker and Lovano represent the two current schools of jazz tenor sax, much as Coleman Hawkins and Lester Young did years earlier. Scofield is probably the single most influential jazz guitarist since John McLaughlin.

Many other styles of jazz, including free/experimental jazz, jazz vocal styles, smooth jazz, and jam bands are also a part of the present-day jazz fabric. Experimental jazz performers, Ornette Coleman still among them, continue their journey. Many new artists have learned to include elements of rap or other popular styles into their music. At the other end of the spectrum, performers such as Kenny G perform a more easy listening, simplistic "smooth jazz" aimed at the mass market and frequently used as background or mood music in stores, restaurants, doctors' offices, and elevators. Jam bands like Medeski Martin and Wood have drawn sizable audiences with their repetitive, infectious grooves. While jazz vocal styles have changed less over the years than their instrumental counterparts, the popularity of Diana Krall and most recently Nora Jones have helped to boost sagging jazz record sales. It is anyone's guess what tomorrow will bring and only one thing can be certain—jazz will continue to be renewed, becoming even more surprising and different than it was yesterday.

KEY TERMS

Important terms, people, and bands.

TERMS
through composed

PEOPLE
Bob Brookmeyer
Jim McNeely
Maria Schneider
John Fedchock
Bob Mintzer
Kenny Wheeler
Andrew Hill
Vince Mendoza
Joe Henderson
Horace Silver
Geri Allen

Cassandra Wilson
Diana Krall
Diane Schuur
Patricia Barber
Jane Monheit
Nora Jones
Dee Dee Bridgewater
Patti Austin
Kurt Elling
Harry Connick, Jr.
Bobby McFerrin
Pat Metheny
Danilo Pérez
Joanne Brackeen
Jane Ira Bloom

Regina Carter
Jamie Baum
Terri Lyne Carrington
Jane Bunnett
Toshiko Akiyoshi

BANDS
Mingus Big Band
Lincoln Center Jazz
  Orchestra
Kronos Quartet
Turtle Island Quartet
World Saxophone
  Quartet

REVIEW QUESTIONS

1. Jazz was perhaps more fractured stylistically than ever before at the close of the twentieth century. Name the various styles and subcategories of jazz popular at this time.

2. Can you name the bandleader/composers who have sought to sustain the big band as a viable jazz medium over the past 20 years?

3. The advent of CDs has urged major record labels to reissue older artists' material. Can you name some of these living rediscovery figures that have profited from this new recording format?

4. Following Wynton Marsalis' lead, a number of young artists emerged capitalizing on the preservationist trend established in the 80s by Marsalis and other Young Lions. Name some of these new young artists.

5. European artists begin to emerge offering their own new view of jazz by the late twentieth and early twenty-first centuries. Name a few of these important artists.

6. How would you describe some of the new styles of jazz including acid, smooth, "bass 'n' drums," and jam jazz?

7. Record labels have capitalized on the increased popularity of the jazz vocal stylist. Name a few of these singers who have brought significant attention to their jazz-inspired music.

8. Music from around the world has always exerted influences on jazz, and in recent years this trend has intensified. Name some of the world influences that seem to have made the most impact on jazz in the late twentieth and early twenty-first centuries.

9. Why is Pat Metheny's music so popular?

10. Name two guitarists who have exerted significant influences on jazz in recent years.

11. Many contemporary artists like Michael Brecker, Pat Metheny, Dave Holland, Joe Lovano, Danilo Pérez, John Scofield, and others are very eclectic in their approach to jazz, displaying numerous interests and influences. When did this trend begin and with what artists that preceded those listed here?

12. Next to the blues, what form has exerted the most lasting influence on jazz, enduring for decades?

13. Women have finally established themselves in jazz, receiving significant attention for their contributions not just as singers, but as instrumentalists and composers. Name several in each category.

14. What seem to be the most significant problems facing jazz artists in the twenty-first century?

15. How has technology at the start of this century had an effect on jazz music and performers?

16. Who is the most significant saxophonist of the late twentieth and early twenty-first centuries, following John Coltrane?

> **Make sure that you also review material on the corresponding chapter of the CD-ROM.**

SUGGESTED SUPPLEMENTARY LISTENING

The abbreviation (iT) indicates that a particular recording cited in the text, or particularly demonstrative of the artist, is available from the Apple iTunes Web site. Other Web-based music distributors may also prove to be valuable resources. SCCJ indicates *Smithsonian Collection of Classic Jazz*.

LARGE ENSEMBLE MUSIC

Bob Brookmeyer
New Works Challenge

John Fedchock
No Nonsense Reservoir

Maria Schneider
Allegresse www.mariaschneider.com
Concert in the Garden www.mariaschneider.com

Jim McNeely
The Vanguard Jazz Orchestra: Music of Jim McNeely New World Records

Bob Mintzer
Bob Mintzer Big Band Live at Mcg Mcg Jazz

Kenny Wheeler
Music for Large and Small Ensembles ECM

Vince Mendoza

JAZZpana High Note

Wynton Marsalis

Blood on the Fields Sony (iT)
All Rise Sony
XXL Gordon Goodwin's Big Phat Band Silverline (iT)

REDISCOVERY FIGURES AND TRIBUTES

Mingus Band

Blues and Politics Dreyfus

Joe Henderson

Inner Urge Blue Note (iT)
In Pursuit of Blackness Milestone (iT)
So Near, So Far (Musings for Miles) Verve (iT)
Double Rainbow, The Music of Antonio Carlos Jobim Verve (iT)
Lush Life, The Music of Billy Strayhorn Verve (iT)

Marcus Roberts

Alone with Three Giants Windham Classics (iT)
In Honor of Duke Sony (iT)

Andrew Hill

Dance with Death Blue Note (iT)

ESTABLISHED ARTISTS

Dave Holland

Extended Play: Live at Birdland ECM
Prime Directive ECM

Charlie Haden

Liberation Music Orchestra Impulse! (iT)
Beyond The Missouri Sky (with Pat Metheny) Verve (iT)

Herbie Hancock

Gershwin's World Verve (iT)
New Standard Verve (iT)

Wayne Shorter

Footprints Live Verve
Alegria Verve

Wynton Marsalis

Magic Hour Blue Note

Joe Lovano

I'm All for You Blue Note
Gathering of the Spirits (with Brecker and Liebman) Telarc

Michael Brecker

Wide Angles Verve
Tales from the Hudson GRP

John Scofield

Quiet Polygram (Verve)
EnRoute Verve

Dave Douglas

Freakin RCA
Infinite RCA
Strange Liberation RCA

NEW YOUNG LIONS

Chris Potter

Unspoken Concord (iT)
Gratitude Verve (iT)

Joshua Redman

MoodSwing Warner Brothers
Wish Warner Brothers

Roy Hargrove

Family Polygram

Greg Osby

St. Louis Shoes Blue Note (iT)

Terence Blanchard

Let's Get Lost Sony
Jazz in Film Sony

Jason Moran

Modernistic Blue Note

Brad Mehldau

Live in Tokyo Nonesuch

James Carter

Live at Baker's Keyboard Lounge Warner Brothers

EXPERIMENTAL

David Murray

Gwotet Justin Time
Like a Kiss That Never Ends Justin Time
We Is Live at the Bop Shop Delmark

World Saxophone Quartet

Experience Justin Time

Don Byron

Bug Music Nonesuch (iT)
Ievy-Dievy Blue Note (iT)

The Kronos Quartet

Monk Suite: Kronos Quartet Plays Music of Thelonious Monk Savoy

Turtle Island String Quartet

Art of the Groove Koch International

Ornette Coleman

Ornette Coleman and Prime Time: Tone Dialing Harmolodic Record

Greg Osby

Public Blue Note (iT)

Art Ensemble of Chicago

The Meeting Pi Recordings (iT)

GROOVE MUSIC/ACID JAZZ/MODERN FUNK

John Scofield

Überjam Universal
Bump Polygram
Groove Elation Polygram
A Go Go Polygram
Medeski Martin and Wood
Combustication Blue Note

Roy Hargrove

Rh Factor Verve

Tim Hagans

Animation—Imagination Blue Note
Re-Animation: Live in Montreal Blue Note

Us3

Hand on the Torch Blue Note (iT)

Buckshot LeFonque

Buckshot LeFonque Sony (iT)

Incognito

Tribes, Vibes, and Scribes UMG Recordings, Inc. (iT)
No Time Like the Future UMG Recordings Inc. (iT)

Jamiroquai

The Return of the Space Cowboy Sony (iT)

WORLD MUSIC INFLUENCED

David Murray
Now Is Another Time Justin Time Records

Pat Metheny
Letter from Home Geffen
Imaginary Day Warner (iT)
Still Life Talking Geffen

Roy Hargrove
Habana Verve

Poncho Sanchez
Out of Sight Concord

Danilo Pérez
Motherland Verve

Avashi Cohen
Devotion Stretch Records

SMOOTH JAZZ

Kenny G
Breathless Arista (iT)

Rick Braun
Body and Soul Mesa Blue Moon (iT)

Larry Carlton
Alone/But Never Alone MCA Records (iT)

CONTEMPORARY WOMEN IN JAZZ

Geri Allen
The Gathering Verve (iT)

Jane Ira Bloom
The Red Quartets Arabesque
Art of Aviation Arabesque

Regina Carter
Rhythms of the Heart Polygram (Verve)

Terri Lyne Carrington
Jazz Is a Spirit The Act Company

Maria Schneider
Concert in the Garden www.mariaschneider.com

VOCALISTS

Patricia Barber

Live: A Fortnight in France Blue Note

Bobby McFerrin

The Voice Nonesuch
Beyond Words Blue Note

Jane Monheit

In Full Swing Sony
Taking a Chance on Love Sony

Diana Krall

Live in Paris Verve
When I Look in Your Eyes Verve

Cassandra Wilson

New Moon Daughter Blue Note
Glamoured Blue Note

Kurt Elling

Man in the Air Blue Note
Live in Chicago Blue Note

Harry Connick, Jr.

Only You Sony

Übersicht zu den Reisen des Kolumbus.

The Afro-Latin and Caribbean
Connection

"Today's American vernacular music would be impossible without a strongly symbiotic relationship between Caribbean nations and the North American."[1]

RENÉ LOPEZ AND DAVID CARP

The influence of Afro-Latin and Caribbean music on jazz is undeniable. From the very beginnings in New Orleans, music from the Caribbean and Latin America has had a profound effect on jazz as well as American popular and dance music. In a nearly predictable cycle since the outset of the twentieth century, new waves of Afro-Latin styles swept over the American music scene every decade or so, leaving a lasting impression on jazz and the ways it can be played. The close of the twentieth and early twenty-first centuries have witnessed a rekindling of interest in music that stems from the intersections of North and South American music. Collaborations between American jazz artists and Latin American and Afro-Cuban musicians continue to ignite exciting new possibilities. Some references have been made to these collaborative trends in earlier chapters, but without detailed discussion. Anything less than in-depth discussions about the influence this music has had on jazz would dilute the importance of Afro-Latin and Caribbean music to the ever-changing jazz landscape. Viewing these influences as a whole, as the material is chronologically presented in this chapter, underscores its importance so the reader will appreciate the full impact this music has had on jazz while understanding the broad, rich, deep, and lasting cultural relationships that exist between the American, Caribbean, and South American people.

Important supplements to this chapter are found on the CD-ROM. An introduction to the percussion instruments associated with Afro-Caribbean and Afro-Latin music is included in the corresponding chapter. All of the musical examples found in this chapter can be played from the CD-ROM and will help you to recognize these instruments and rhythmic concepts.

A great number of pioneers in the jazz field are black, and sought with their music to explore the roots of their African heritage. Previous discussions have more than alluded to the connections between jazz and African-derived rhythms. The link between American jazz musicians of color and Afro-Latin and Caribbean music is also close, since many black immigrants and African slaves landed in Latin America and the Caribbean islands. It is understandable that jazz musicians would be sympathetic and susceptible to the improvised nature of Afro-Latin and Caribbean music with its syncopation and rhythmic complexities. For example, jazz musicians who developed unique rhythms to identify different styles found a kinship with the varying drum rhythms that define a wide range of Afro-Carribean dance music. The quest for knowledge about the diverse origins of black music led jazz musicians to discover and assimilate aspects of Afro-Latin and Afro-Caribbean music styles ever since the beginnings of jazz in the Mississippi Delta region. For example, the rich tradition of improvisation found in Cuban music forms a common link with jazz. Much Afro-Latin and Caribbean music is a form of folklore, music of the people. This style of music is a language based on the spontaneous expression of emotions much like that found in African music. The emotional content of a song, which is frequently emphasized and brought about by rhythms, is of utmost importance to this music. Much jazz music demonstrates this same quality, since it is a rhythmically rich music that has been judged less on accuracy, unlike classical music standards, and more on spontaneity, individual creativity, and raw emotional content. Jazz, like much folk music including blues, is often assessed as much on emotional content as on sheer musicianship or virtuosity. In other words, you can be a terrific blues musician without having to be a fabulous guitarist or singer by traditional standards. Several common elements therefore exist between jazz and Afro-Latin music, serving as additional bonds. Such common bonds as spontaneity, rhythmic drive and complexity, improvisation, and individuality all contribute to an emotionally charged music. Different drum styles are central to and help define different styles of Afro-Caribbean music, just as they contribute to identifying numerous different jazz styles, exemplifying another common bond between jazz and Afro-Caribbean music.

In terms of European influences, it was Spanish culture that most influenced Caribbean music, largely because its political influence ranged over this entire area for decades. Spanish culture is not one-dimensional, but the result of the influence of many external cultures that at one time moved through this powerful European nation. These external influences included Arabic, Gypsy, Nordic, Indian, and Judaic. For example, the flamenco dance style is accompanied by music that is permeated with melodies derived from Middle Eastern and Indian scales featuring a singing style that sounds Arabic in nature. As the Spanish explorers conquered the New World, their hybrid music found yet a new sphere of influence in South America, Central America, and the Caribbean Islands. Latin American, Cuban, and other Caribbean music therefore is the result of influences from Spain and Africa, and much like early jazz styles, this music from the Caribbean and Latin America is derived largely from dance forms.

Since the 1500s, Cuban music demonstrated traits of European and African styles. Just as African slaves exerted their influences on American culture, they also brought music, religious ritual, and other African cultural practices to Cuba. African slaves came to Cuba from many of the same areas of the continent that supplied slave trade to the United States, namely, Nigeria, Congo, Dahomey, and the Sudan. Almost exclusively, African immigrants inhabited several regions in Cuba, so it is logical that a new music would emerge, identified as Afro-Cuban. African slaves had an impact on reshaping native Cuban music, particularly the rhythmic aspects.

Cuba became a safe haven not only for Africans but also Haitians in the 1700s and 1800s. Near the turn of the twentieth century (1900s) many Haitians, Cubans, and Puerto Ricans immigrated to New York City, settling in the eastern portion of the city's Harlem district. This area became known as "El Barrio," as it still is today. This term translated means "neighborhood," and became synonymous for Hispanic districts in cities throughout the United States. Evidence of this influx of musicians to New York is obvious when one examines the personnel in James Reese Europe's military and society bands from the early 1900s.

In the early 1800s, nearly 10,000 Haitian refugees immigrated to New Orleans commingling with the city's already culturally diverse population. Many Hispanic names and Creole (French-influenced) names appeared on the personnel rosters of bands active in New Orleans at the turn of the twentieth century. Louisiana was a melting pot of racial diversity, but in 1894 new legislation changed racial codes, forcing Creoles to lose the social status they had once enjoyed. Consequently, the Creoles who were a mix of French, Spanish, or black ethnicities, could no longer participate in the educational and cultural benefits afforded them in the past as residents of the more upscale "downtown" area of the "Crescent City." As author Gene Santoro points out, this forced Creoles to mingle with blacks, introducing yet another multicultural flavor to an already rich gumbo in New Orleans. Public celebrations including street dances and parades, particularly those associated with the Mardi Gras celebration in New Orleans' French Quarter district, often featured Cuban and Mexican derived music and dance, or European music influenced by these non-European styles.[2] It should be no surprise to hear the similarity between a second-line drum rhythm pattern associated with New Orleans street bands and a Latin American or Caribbean dance rhythm, since both often show a kinship with the habanera or clavé pattern. There are similar common threads that connect more contemporary salsa music with Haitian rhythms, both of which can be traced back further to African roots.

Audio files that further clarify the similarity between the early New Orleans style and African-influenced Latin and Caribbean rhythms can be found in the corresponding chapter on the CD-ROM.

EARLY FUSIONS

Louis Gottschalk was born in New Orleans in 1829 and was exposed to the Caribbean, French, and African-derived music that permeated the city at this time. Gottschalk was not only exposed to the vast variety of street music in New Orleans, but as a gifted young pianist also came into contact with serious French and other European classical music. His talent afforded him the opportunity to study piano and composition in Paris and his own compositions, flavored with the sounds of the New Orleans streets, won favor with European audiences. Over time, Gottschalk became heralded as one of the first important American composers. He traveled extensively to Cuba, Puerto Rico, and South America absorbing cultural traditions that he used liberally throughout his compositions. Many of his piano compositions were deeply inspired by his experiences with the folk music from these areas.

Lorenzo Tio, Jr., another important early Delta musician, was believed to be a Creole, but was actually of Mexican descent. Tio was an important musician around the turn of the century in the Crescent City and served as tutor to many early jazz musicians who emerged from this area.

The first wave of popular Latin music to hit the United States at a time when instrumental jazz was still in its infancy was the tango. The Christian establishment's reaction to the 1914 tango craze in the United States deserves some consideration. The tango was thought to be decadent and barbaric by members of the Christian establishment. Those who participated in this dance craze, and there were many, were accused of loose sexual morals and drug and alcohol abuse. This reaction was not terribly different from reactions to jazz musicians and their music during this same time (for that matter, rock and roll was initially received with similar mixed reviews by the more puritan community). A certain kinship existed then between Latin musicians and jazz performers, since both groups were victims of similar social and moral criticism. Jazz had been the brunt of similar allegations even in the black New Orleans press.

As early as 1914 W. C. Handy, remembered by many as the "father of the blues," incorporated a **tangana** (tango) rhythm in the first section and third sections of his "St. Louis Blues" and again in "Memphis Blues." Example 16.1 depicts the bass line from the "tango" section of Handy's "St. Louis Blues."

EXAMPLE 16.1

Bass line from W. C Handy's "St. Louis Blues" implies a tango rhythm.

 Example 16.1 can be heard on the corresponding CD-ROM chapter.

Early jazz pioneer Jelly Roll Morton referred to what he called the "Spanish tinge" evident in the rhythms of his music and the music of other jazz composers and performers of the 1920s. As jazz emerged from the cradle in these two important cities, New Orleans and New York, musicians of all nationalities had the opportunity to learn from one another and exchange musical traditions. For example, George Gershwin befriended a transplanted Cuban musician and borrowed one of his melodies that served as the basis of his "Cuban Overture."

Evidence of African, Afro-Cuban, Afro-Latin, and Afro-Caribbean music could be heard in numerous forms of popular American music in the early years of the 1900s in the United States. The dancing and improvisation, key components of Afro-Cuban folk music, merged well with early jazz, also driven by these same forces. For example, the fundamental Charleston dance rhythm, associated with the flappers of the 20s, is derived from the Cuban **habanera** and African rhythms of Ghana. Example 16.2 from the African Ghanain "Savou Dance" is clearly the antecedent to what became the Charleston rhythm and numerous ragtime rhythms.

EXAMPLE 16.2

For readers who do not understand music notation, the following graphic representation of Example 16.2 serves to illustrate one measure of the same rhythmic effect. The top line establishes the pulse or basic beat while the hand claps outline the specific rhythm notated above.

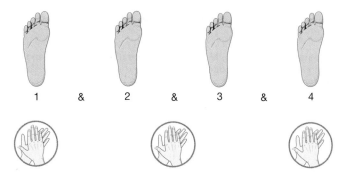

The rhythm that serves as the heart and soul of nearly all Latin or Afro-Cuban based jazz or dance music is the **clavé** rhythm, closely related to the habanera and to African bell patterns. While the clavé pattern can be played on any percussion instrument, the instrument named after this rhythm often plays it. The clavés are two round, highly polished hard wood sticks. Other different rhythms are layered on top of the basic clavé pattern that serves as a stabilizing anchor to the syncopated complex polyrhythmic mosaic that resembles similar concepts found in the rhythms of African music. The clavé pattern is presented as a two-measure phrase (in 4/4 meter) arranged in subgroupings of either 3-2 or 2-3. In other words, the first measure of the pattern implies one rhythmic grouping (3 or 2) and the second, the opposite grouping. The groupings that outline patterns of three provide an element of tension when played against a steady 4/4 pulse because of the upbeat syncopation following beat 2 and the implied meter subdivisions. Once the clavé pattern begins, it never stops or changes until the song ends and everything else throughout the song must always conform to the clavé, be constructed around it, and be played in relationship to it. The clavé pattern is closely related to the habanera and appears as a fundamental unifying rhythm to most Latin-jazz and folk styles. The clavé patterns are illustrated in Example 16.3. The first line shows the 3-2 grouping with the second line illustrating the implied rhythmic subdivisions. The third line illustrates the 2-3 clavé grouping and the bottom line shows the relationship of this rhythm to a rhythmic subdivision.

EXAMPLE 16.3
The clavé rhythm

Three note subdivisions on the 2nd and 4th lines do not represent triplets, but are shown to indicate rhythmic subdivisions that reinforce the 3-2 or 2-3 clavé accents. A single line music staff has been used, as it is frequently employed to notate nonpitched percussion instruments.

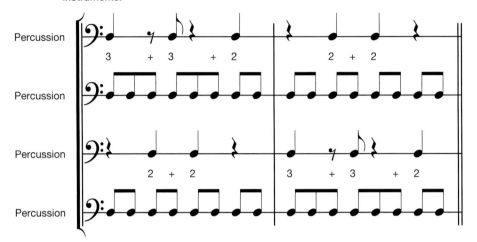

The following illustrations are graphic representations of the 3-2 clavé and 2-3 clavé patterns notated in the previous musical example. You should try executing them with your hands and feet.

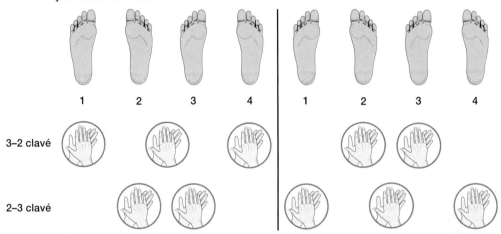

The CD-ROM includes demonstrations of the clavé rhythm as played by the instrument. The clavé as well as examples of numerous other indigenous Latin or Afro-Caribbean percussion instruments can also be found in the corresponding chapter on Latin and Afro-Caribbean music.

Early jazz artist Jelly Roll Morton spoke of the Spanish tinge in his music. A good example of what he meant by this is the habanera rhythm (displaced by one beat) found in the stop-time section of "Black Bottom Stomp" included in the CD audio anthology. This ensemble rhythm is found at 1:31 to 1:33 and again extensively from 1:49 to 2:08, where it is used as an accompaniment figure to the cornet solo.

There are many other similarities between dance rhythms that occur in Latin American and Caribbean folk music and rhythms found in jazz. The Haitian chant rhythm (Example 16.4), used to praise the demagogue Legba, is one such rhythm and shows a distinct similarity to rhythms of the early jazz period (ragtime and 20s style jazz). For that matter, the first measure of this two-bar phrase is closely related to the second half of the classic swing cymbal pattern that evolved in the 1930s.

EXAMPLE 16.4

This Haitian chant rhythm is closely related to the classic swing ride cymbal pattern.

Further clarification and audio examples of these rhythms are found in the special section about Afro-Cuban jazz found in the corresponding chapter on the CD-ROM.

MODERN JAZZ EMBRACES THE AFRO-CUBAN SPIRIT

America's infatuation with Latin dances came in waves, one after another, and each was popularized by Latin musicians who had taken up residence in the United States. Pérez (Prez) Prado, for instance, was a Cuban-born musician who helped popularize the mambo. The samba was also known among early jazz and popular musicians. Carmen Miranda, famous for her fruit cocktail headdresses, helped to further popularize this dance form in 1946 and it was reborn in the 1970s. The rumba entered the American scene in 1929, followed by the popular conga in 1937 through the promotion of noted Cuban bandleader Desi Arnez (Lucille Ball's husband). In 1950 the cha-cha craze spread through the United States. Many of these traditional dance rhythms underwent simplification or alteration to accommodate the demands of the dance-oriented American public. Xavier Cugat was largely responsible for some of this popular simplification. His great success enabled him to continually import Cuban musicians to replace those who left his employment to seek other opportunities with jazz bands.

The growing popularity of Latin music, combined with the increasing number of Latin musicians migrating to the United States, led jazz musicians to continue with experiments to integrate the two styles. Valve trombonist Juan Tizol performed with the Duke Ellington Orchestra in the 1930s. It was during this period that Ellington collaborated with Tizol to compose and record "Caravan," "Conga Brava," and "Bakiff," all possessing obvious Afro-Cuban rhythmic qualities.

Another Swing Era bandleader Cab Calloway recorded "Doin' the Rumba" in 1931. From time to time he employed Latin-American-born musicians such as trumpeter Mario Bauza. Bauza, who had played in the trumpet sections of big swing bands led by Chick Webb, Noble Sissle, Fletcher Henderson, and Don Redman, became an important catalyst in the formation of new Latin-jazz styles in the late 30s and throughout the 40s. His friendship with jazz trumpeter Dizzy Gillespie later becomes significant to the growth of Latin-jazz and Cubop in the late 1940s.

A smooth blending of jazz and Latin or Afro-Latin music was not accomplished overnight. Both sides were forced to overcome challenges encountered by the union of styles. Latin musicians were faced with jazz rhythms, similar to yet different from their native styles, and a more advanced harmonic and melodic vocabulary. Latin percussionists, using various hand drums such as congas and timbales, gradually learned how to coexist with jazz rhythm sections. Example 16.5 presents a variation of the Cuban son rhythm. This same rhythm is frequently played in jazz on the conga drum with only one small change—leaving out the initial downbeat of each measure, as shown in the second line of Example 16.5.

EXAMPLE 16.5

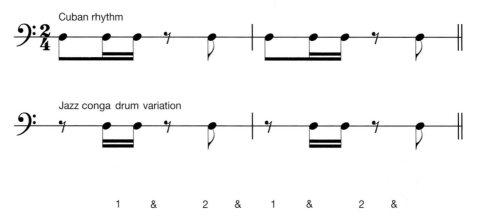

What follows is a graphic representation of the jazz conga drum variation. Tap your left foot in a steady tempo following the graphic while clapping the conga drum pattern.

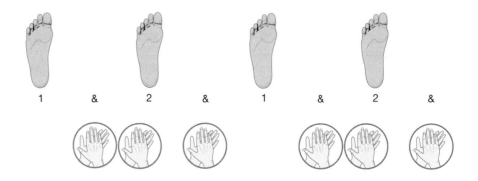

Modern American jazz artists, on the other hand, found it necessary because of the increasing popularity of Latin dance music to discover ways to incorporate the complex Latin rhythms into their own styles. Eventually, the exchange became mutual and Latin bands began exploring the more advanced harmonic and melodic possibilities that the jazz language presented. Machito's band of the 1940s was probably the most stable and successful in the integration of styles during this period. At any rate, jazz bands were hiring Latin musicians and vice versa, making for a healthy exchange of ideas. For example, Latin bandleader Rene Touzet hired jazz arranger Johnny Mandel, who had arranged for many artists including Frank Sinatra. Mandel then persuaded Touzet to employ ex–Stan Kenton jazz artists to complement his Latin band. Eventually the entire horn section of this band consisted of jazzmen and Mandel conducted extensive experiments superimposing Latin rhythms on jazz repertoire. The result was frequently referred to as "Cubop." "Barbados," recorded by Charlie Parker, is an excellent example of this style as is Bud Powell's "Un Poco Loco," which is also an early example confirming the similarities between much Cubop and modal jazz, a new approach in jazz that did not surface until 1958–1959 (Chapter 12). Parker also recorded the album *South of the Border* for the Mercury label featuring a bop approach to traditional Latin tunes.

Dizzy Gillespie was a prime force in the blending of jazz and Afro-Latin styles in the middle and late 1940s. Gillespie's early association with the Cab Calloway band served to introduce him to fellow trumpet section mate and arranger Mario Bauza. Gillespie and Bauza, who later became Machito's arranger, became friendly on and off the bandstand, attending after-hours sessions together at New York Latin music clubs. Gillespie's experiences sitting in with these Latin bands became a primary source in his training, inspiration, and lifelong obsession with Afro-Latin music. Gillespie hired master Cuban drummer Chano Pozo to be a member of his 1947 bebop big band and recorded the historically significant George Russell composition "Cubano Be, Cubano Bop" (according to Gillespie it was co-composed by Russell, himself, and Pozo). Other compositions associated with Gillespie that featured Afro-Latin rhythmic influences include his "A Night in Tunisia," "Manteca," "Con Alma," and "Gillespiana," the extensive multi-movement suite composed for the trumpeter by his Argentinean pianist Lalo Schifrin (composer of the "Mission Impossible" theme). Gillespie's own "A Night in Tunisia," has become a jazz classic and bears an amazing resemblance, though the rhythms have been displaced in the measure, to the Cuban bolero, as shown in Example 16.6.

EXAMPLE 16.6

You can hear this example found on the CD-ROM in the corresponding chapter.

Cuban bolero

Bass line from Dizzy Gillespie's "A Night in Tunisia"

One of the best examples of the outcome of blending bebop and Afro-Cuban influences is Gillespie's big band rendition of "Manteca" that features the legendary percussionist Chano Pozo. Gillespie's mid-1940s big band was a haven for some of the finest bebop musicians of the day, but, while it enjoyed some success, it became the victim of the economic downturn that affected all of the big bands by the close of the decade. The fact that the band avoided danceable repertoire also had a great deal to do with its short life span. However, the

Dizzy Gillespie and His Orchestra

"Manteca" (Gillespie, Fuller, Pozo) 3:06

Recorded 12/30/47, New York City, RCA Victor Vi20-3023

Reissued "The Complete RCA Victor Recordings" Bluebird 07863 66528-2

Dizzy Gillespie: *trumpet*

Dave Burns: *trumpet*

Elmon Wright: *trumpet*

Lamar Wright Jr.: *trumpet*

Benny Bailey: *trumpet*

William Shepard: *trombone*

Ted Kelly: *trombone*

John Brown: *alto saxophone*

Howard Johnson: *alto saxophone*

Joe Gayles: *tenor saxophone*

George "Big Nick" Nicholas: *tenor saxophone*

Cecil Payne: *baritone saxophone*

John Lewis: *piano*

Al McKibbon: *bass*

Kenny Clark: *drums*

Chano Pozo: *conga drums, bongos*

Listening Guide

Form and Key: Repeated 40-bar song form chorus (AABCA=chorus) in B♭ major, Latin Big Band arrangement

0:00–0:37   *Introduction:* 28 bars, *Afro-Cuban Latin Groove, Trumpet Solo:*

     0:00–0:18   *Section 1:* 14 bars, staggered entrances of conga drums, bass, drums, baritone sax, trumpets, and trombones set up Latin groove, with "Manteca" chanted vocals

     0:19–0:31   *Section 2:* 9 bars, improvised "Bebop" trumpet solo (Gillespie), over continuing Latin groove, concluded by 1-bar ensemble triplets with "fall"

     0:31–0:37   *Section 3:* 5 bars, conga, bass, and drum groove

0:38–1:47   *First Chorus:* 50-bar *Theme:*

     0:38–0:48   *A section:* 8 bars, repeated riff melody in saxes, answered by brass, followed by ensemble variation of brass riff, with conga fills

     0:49–0:59   *A section:* 8 bars, similar to A section

     1:00–1:10   *B section:* 8 bars, saxes play sustained bridge melody, with brass answer, swinging rhythm section accompaniment

     1:11–1:21   *C section:* 8 bars, trumpet (Gillespie) plays remainder of bridge melody, with sustained ensemble chords, Latin rhythm section accompaniment

     1:22–1:33   *A section:* 8 bars, similar to A section

     1:34–1:47   *Solo Send-off:* 10 bars, break down to rhythm section groove similar to Introduction (section 1), followed by 4-bar ensemble "shout" send-off to tenor solo

1:48–2:42   *Second Chorus:* 40-bar *Tenor Solo, Trumpet Solo, Theme*

     1:47–1:58   *A section:* 8 bars, improvised tenor solo (Nicholas); for full chorus with ensemble accents and riffs, swinging rhythm section accompaniment

     1:59–2:09   *A section:* 8 bars, tenor solo continues, ensemble tacit, with swinging rhythm section

     2:10–2:20   *B section:* 8 bars, ensemble "shout" variation of theme bridge melody, with swinging rhythm section

     2:21–2:32   *C section:* 8 bars, improvised trumpet solo (Gillespie), with sax sustained backgrounds, swinging rhythm section

     2:32–2:42   *A section:* 8 bars, ensemble theme similar to first chorus A sections, with "Manteca" vocals

2:43–3:06   *Coda:* 15 bars, ensemble Latin groove similar to introduction, with "Manteca" chants, staggered instrumental "exits," drum figure

Mario Bauza (bottom row, second from right) and Machito (bottom, far right) at the Club Brazil in 1946.

band was an exciting powerhouse ensemble that boasted a particularly muscular rhythm section to match Gillespie's own macho, bravado trumpet style. "Manteca" shows how Gillespie's band could move nearly seamlessly from Latin to swing-bop styles.

Chico O'Farrill, like many musicians who immigrated to the United States, was another product of Havana, Cuba. He arranged for Benny Goodman and Stan Kenton, but he is best known for his collaborations with Gillespie. O'Farrill's "Afro-Cuban Jazz Suite" is often referred to as the first successful landmark extended concert work, outside Russell's quirky "Cubano-Be, Cubano-Bop," which merged the two styles.

Parker and Gillespie weren't the only bebop musicians to explore the potential of merging bebop with Afro-Cuban music. Trumpeter Fats Navarro, who was part black, Chinese, and Cuban, formed an allegiance with Cuban percussionist Chano Pozo to create several memorable Cubop recordings in the late 40s. It is easy to speculate that the modal jazz concepts first emerging from Miles Davis' bands in 1958–1959 stemmed as a natural progression from the fusion of jazz improvisation with simple repetitive harmonies and bass lines central to much Afro-Cuban jazz of the 40s. Davis believed strongly in the significance of folk music and its importance to jazz, and much Afro-Caribbean music evolved first as folk music.

Stan Kenton and Johnny Richards, one-time Kenton arranger, were also pioneers in the mingling of jazz and Afro-Latin styles during this same period. Machito supplied the percussionists for Kenton's first band that enjoyed success with this new format. "Peanut Vendor" was Kenton's first recording success in this new vein and utilized a version of the Cuban bolero. The following quote from Stan Kenton accurately describes the atmosphere during this period of Afro-Latin influence:

Stan Kenton and his band, circa 1945.

Rhythmically, the Cubans play the most exciting stuff. We won't copy them exactly, but we will copy some of their devices and apply them to what we're trying to do. The guys in our rhythm section are doing just that. So are the guys in Woody's [Herman]. And while we keep moving toward the Cubans rhythmically, they're moving toward us melodically. We both have a lot to learn.[3]

Kenton's dynamic recording entitled the *Cuban Fire Suite* followed "Peanut Vendor." The suite of compositions on this recording are all composed by Johnny Richards (John Cascales) and are the product of his extensive study in Latin America, Mexico, Cuba, and the Latino sections of New York City. Each composition is based on a traditional Latin rhythm of predominantly Cuban origin. *Cuban Fire* represents a landmark Kenton recording in his lengthy discography and served to launch Richards' career as an arranger/composer. "La Suerte de los Tontos," the sixth movement from the suite, demonstrates the power and machismo that Kenton's band was known for. This project was followed by other Richards compositions with an Afro-Latin tinge including some produced for his own bands. Other big band leaders like Woody Herman followed the same path, recording the Rumba "Bijou" in 1945.[4]

Machito's own bands served as the training ground for many important Afro-Cuban musicians. Percussionists Tito Puente and Tito Rodriquez joined forces with Machito to form his Mambo Kings band before starting their own bands. To quote author Gene Santoro; "For Latin jazzers . . . the 50s were the glory days. [Tito] Puente and Tito Rodriguez both started bands in 1947 [no doubt motivated in part by the Cubop movement]. From then on, they shared with Bauza and Machito the creative shaping of New York Mambo."[5]

Stan Kenton

Form and Key: Song form (ABA') in D Major

Introduction

0:00–0:10	*Contrapuntal brass* playing variations to main theme
0:11–0:24	French horns enter, followed by saxes, trombones, tuba, and baritone sax stating initial motive
0:24–0:28	*Tuba solo*
0:28–0:33	*Percussion and brass* enter
0:34–0:38	*Percussion and rhythm section* establishes Latin tempo
0:39–1:13	*Contrapuntal layering*: bass (0:39), saxes (0:43), trombones (0:50), trumpets plus additional sax line (0:59); section crescendos as each new part enters

First Chorus

1:14–1:29	*Primary A theme*
1:30–1:45	*B section* featuring trumpets and French horns
1:46–1:57	A', variation on first A theme

Transition

1:58–2:04	Percussion interlude with French horns, trombones, and rhythm serves as transition to sax solo that follows

Second Chorus

2:05–2:44	Lennie Niehaus plays *alto sax solo* on ABA form with brass background figures added

Interlude

2:45–2:49	*Short interlude* links alto solo to trumpet solo that follows

Third Chorus

2:50–3:28	*Trumpet solo* on form with sax backgrounds

Interlude

3:29–3:33	Brief brass and percussion interlude

Fourth Chorus

3:34–3:41	A theme only partially restated
3:41–end	New material features exchanges between brass and percussion and represents the high point of the piece

Listening Guide

"La Suerte de los Tontos" (Fortune of Fools) composed/arranged by Johnny Richards, 4:17

Recorded 5/22-24/56, New York City, Capital Jazz (Blue Note) CDP77962602

Soloists: Lennie Niehaus, *alto sax;* Vinnie Tanno, *trumpet*

Ed Leddy, Sam Noto, Lee Katzman, Phil Gilbert, Al Mattaliano, Vince Tano: *trumpets*

Bob Fitzpatrick, Carl Fontana, Kent Larson, Don Kelly: *trombones*

Irving Rosenthal, Julius Watkins: *French horns*

Jay McAllister: *tuba*

Saxophones: Lennie Niehaus, *alto;* Bill Perkins, Lucky Thompson, *tenors;* Billy Root, *baritone*

Rhythm Section: Stan Kenton, *piano;* Ralph Blaze, *guitar;* Curtis Counce, *bass;* Mel Lewis, *drums*

Percussion: Saul Gubin or George Gaber, *tympani;* Willie Rodriguez, *bongo;* Tommy Lopez, *conga;* George Laguna, *timbale;* Roger Mozian, *clavés;* Mario Alvarez, *maracas*

Not all of the Afro-Cuban jazz experiments took place in the big band laboratory. Small group jazz musicians who explored the possibilities presented by the mixing of certain aspects of jazz and Afro-Cuban, Latin styles were English pianist George Shearing and hard bop tenor saxophonist Sonny Rollins. Shearing recorded *Latin Escapades* with a group of Afro-Cuban musicians. Rollins enjoyed popularity for his brand of calypso jazz first unveiled on his recording of "St. Thomas." It is no wonder that Rollins enjoyed a mild obsession with this brand of Caribbean music since his parents hailed from the West Indies.

POSTMODERN EXCHANGES

Miles Davis was a trendsetter since his early collaborations with Charlie Parker. His ventures in Spanish-influenced jazz include the Columbia release entitled *Sketches of Spain*, which featured arrangements by Gil Evans. Evans, like Johnny Richards, conducted extensive research in various Latin-Spanish forms prior to the creation of the music for *Sketches of Spain*. The entire recording reflects the predominant rhythmic, harmonic and melodic influences of Spanish Flamenco music. Other Davis ventures in Latin-Spanish and Afro-Latin jazz include "Flamenco Sketches" from the *Kind of Blue* recording, "Blues for Pablo" by Gil Evans from the *Miles Ahead* recording, and his later collaborations with Marcus Miller including the albums *Tutu* and *Amandla*.

Slavery of Africans in Brazil existed for over three centuries until it was abolished in the late 1800s. Once again, there is a clear link to Africa and certain African rhythmic practices from this country are evident in Brazilian music. While Brazilian music is rhythmically rich, it is also harmonically wealthy, which were no doubt the very characteristics that drew Stan Getz to this music. Tenor saxophonist Getz introduced the Brazilian bossa nova to American jazz audiences in the mid-1960s. The bossa nova sound track of the award winning film *Black Orpheus* also played a significant part in raising American audiences' awareness of this popular native Brazilian folk style. The bossa nova achieved a quick and fortuitous partnership with jazz and as a result Getz enjoyed several commercially successful recordings for the Verve label. His most popular recordings were "Desafinado," "Black Orpheus" (from the film), "The Girl from Ipanema," "Corcovado" (also known as "Quiet Nights"), "One Note Samba," and "How Insensitive." These recordings also included the Brazilian samba and a host of popular Brazilian song writers and performers. The basic bossa nova rhythm, which is highly syncopated, is shown in Example 16.7. Both the samba and bossa nova are dance styles associated with Brazil's four-day "Carnaval" celebration that features a countrywide celebration of street dances, parties, and parades culminating on Mardi Gras. The Mardi Gras tradition has spread to many parts of the United States, especially in our southernmost cities.

EXAMPLE 16.7

The pattern shown as follows represents a graphic interpretation of the musical notation that precedes it. Try tapping your foot and clapping the syncopated accents that capture the essence of the bossa nova rhythm.

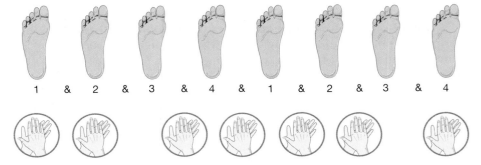

Listen to Getz's recording of "Só Danço Samba," included on the companion audio anthology. Try to follow the basic clavé rhythm as you listen. A special Latin and Afro-Cuban section can be found on the companion CD-ROM. Many of the examples in this section will be better understood by listening to these audio examples.

Horace Silver, jazz pianist and composer of Portuguese descent, produced the recordings *Cape Verdean Blues* and *Song for My Father* in which he included calypso-influenced tracks. Cuban-born drummer Mongo Santamaria was active as a sideman and leader during this same 1960s period. He attributes the Latin influence on jazz to the "African Negro heritage." Santamaria claimed that the popular wave of **salsa** music in the 1960s and 1970s was nothing more than a new look at the Afro-Cuban jazz and dance music of the 1930s and 1940s. Santamaria along with Ray Barretto and Willie Bobo were members of Puente's big band which is given much credit for creating the salsa style. According to Gene Santoro, salsa "was the tag for a fusion of Son vocals, jazz improvisation, and voicings [harmonic structures], Cuban rhythms, and, by the 1980s, rock chord sequences and electronics."[6] The term salsa is as broad and confusing as "jazz" or "rock," which now describe numerous species. Salsa, which means "sauce," is an Afro-Cuban musical "hot sauce" that reflects many different dance rhythms from Cuba, Mexico, Columbia, Venezuela, Puerto Rico, and Dominica. The one characteristic common to all varieties of salsa is the clavé pattern. **Son,** a national dance music of Cuba, is the direct predecessor of salsa and is closely related to African forms. It originated initially as percussion music played by the rural working classes to accompany song and dance in the early part of the twentieth century in the eastern regions of Cuba. Salsa also has roots in other Cuban dance forms such as the rumba and danzón.

While Cuba has been the primary source of influence on jazz, music from Argentina and Brazil have also impacted American music. The Argentinean **tango**, and its most popular composer Astor Piazzolla, provides a continued source of influence even today. Baritone saxophonist Gerry Mulligan collaborated with Piazzolla to create *Reunion Cumbre (Summit)* in 1974, and Argentinean tenor saxophonist Gato Barbieri gained fame and recognition in 1972 when his score for the film *Last Tango in Paris* won critical and popular acclaim.

It seems that with each new decade another wave of Afro-Latin or Afro-Cuban music has influenced jazz and become popular. In the 1970s artists such as Chick Corea, Airto Moreara and Flora Purim, as well as popular instrumental jazz artist Chuck Mangione popularized the Brazilian samba. There are many versions of the samba even in Brazil, where in the 1920s it became the predominant style for their "carnival" celebration. The traditional samba was of course altered somewhat from its original folk dance form as has been the case with all Afro-Latin rhythms adopted by jazz performers. Recordings such as Chick Corea's *Light as a Feather* were instrumental in rekindling interest in Latin-jazz during the 1970s. Mangione's recordings during this same period often alluded to Latin influences, though perhaps not as directly as Corea's. Listen to the bass (a **tumbao**-like bass rhythm) and drums in particular on Mangione's "Market Place" included on the companion audio anthology. The Corea track included on the audio anthology makes more direct use of Spanish influences than Latin American ones, particularly in the introduction. The success that Getz and Corea had in merging Brazilian styles with jazz paved the way for other jazz musicians in later years. Guitarist Pat Metheny (listen again to "Better Days Ahead" included on the audio anthology), percussionist Nana Vasconcelos and composer/pianist Egberto Gismonti emerged as important contributors to this trend during the 1980s.

Examples of the tumbao bass rhythm, **bossa nova,** jazz **samba, montuno** piano accompaniment figure, and other Afro-Cuban examples can be found in a special section about Latin and Afro-Caribbean jazz on the CD-ROM in the corresponding chapter.

THE BEAT GOES ON

Afro-Latin and Afro-Caribbean music will continue to bring rhythmic vitality to jazz, while the spontaneous nature of jazz and its harmonic complexity will interest Latin and Caribbean musicians. Contemporary jazz musicians like Paquito D'Rivera, Eddie Palmieri, Clare Fischer, Jerry Gonzalez, Claudio Roditi, Michel Camilo, Hilton Ruiz, Gonzalo Rubalcaba, Caribbean Jazz Project, Bobby Sanabria, Bobby Carcassés, Chucho Valdés, Luciana Souza, Rubén Blades, Danilo Pérez, and Arturo Sandoval continue to bring new focus to the Afro-Latin and Afro-Cuban jazz connection, each offering new exciting blends of these styles and featuring Latin musicians alongside American jazz artists. In some cases, Latino musicians play their own brand of Latin-influenced jazz. For example, the Cuban band Irakere nurtured several prominent Afro-Cuban jazz musicians including Valdes, Sandoval, and D'Rivera. One by one each of them sought exile in the United States, where they were free to travel and explore, through collaborations, the improvised music that to them represented freedom. D'Rivera was recently awarded the distinguished NEA Jazz Masters for his contributions to American music. Rubalcaba, like Valdés, is from Havana and both demonstrate a macho, fiery style of Afro-Cuban piano playing. The Dallas, Texas, born Young Lion Roy Hargrove took his trumpet to Cuba to learn firsthand about this invigorating music. Here he came into contact with Valdés and a number of other Cuban musicians. The result of their collaboration produced Hargrove's Crisol band and their recording *Habana* offers an electrifying mix of jazz and Cuban music. The mixes will no doubt continue as they have since the nineteenth century, when Latinos brought elements of their own native music to American jazz while American jazz musicians freely absorbed the rhythmic aspects of Latin American and Afro-Caribbean folk and popular music. Jazz has always been known for absorbing the cultural influences in its environment and spawning new hybrids. Hopefully, the Latin-jazz marriage will continue to offer spicy new outcomes.

CHAPTER SUMMARY

Although not immediately obvious in some styles, Afro-Latin and Caribbean music has had some kind of influence on most jazz styles. Like jazz, this music involves a mixing of elements from different cultures including Spanish music that developed somewhat separately from that of the rest of Europe. Trade that brought many black immigrants and slaves to the United States similarly affected Latin America and the Caribbean islands. The mixing of Afro-Latin and American jazz elements took place primarily in New Orleans and New York, since both cities had large numbers of Latin American immigrants.

One of the first jazz pieces to obviously fall under the influence of Latin music was W. C. Handy's "St. Louis Blues" (1914), which includes a tango section. The Argentinean tango was one of the numerous waves of dances that washed ashore from points south to excite dance-crazed Americans. The impact of Latin American dances can also be seen in the Charleston, a popular dance in the United States in the 1920s that shows rhythms similar to the Cuban habanera. Other Latin dances followed including the rumba, conga, mambo, and cha cha. These new dance rhythms found their way into big band repertoires exemplified by tunes such as "Caravan" (Duke Ellington) and "Doin' the Rumba" (Cab Calloway). In Cab Calloway's band, Cuban trumpeter/arranger Mario Bauza and future bebop great Dizzy Gillespie formed a bond that helped lead to the Afro-Cuban flavored approach to bebop known as Cubop. Gillespie compositions "A Night in Tunisia," "Con Alma," and "Manteca" are examples of this style and standards in the jazz repertoire.

Common to almost all Latin or Afro-Cuban dance music is the clavé rhythm. This is both an instrument and a simple 3-2 or 2-3 rhythmic grouping, over which other rhythms are layered. Even though each individual layer is typically simple by itself, the resulting interaction of the different layers forms complex polyrhythms.

In the 1950s, Stan Kenton's band recorded the Latin-influenced "Peanut Vendor," followed by a multimovement work entitled *Cuban Fire Suite*. So taken with the Latin influence, Kenton rewrote the band's theme, "Artistry in Rhythm," to reflect these Latin characteristics. Around the same time tenor saxophonist Sonny Rollins recorded his calypso jazz composition "St. Thomas," reflecting his West Indian heritage. During this same time, trumpeter Miles Davis collaborated with arranger/composer Gil Evans creating the landmark *Sketches of Spain* album.

Music from Latin America continued to impact jazz in the 1960s and 1970s. One of the more popular styles of jazz since the swing era was the bossa nova, popularized in the early 1960s by tenor saxophonist Stan Getz who merged the Brazilian style with jazz. Tunes like "Desafinado" and "The Girl From Ipanema" were his most popular recordings. Salsa, a dance that developed from the Cuban dance the Son, became popular in the United States in the 1960s and 1970s. Chick Corea's 1970s fusion band Return to Forever included many tunes in their repertoire based on the Brazilian samba and other Latin grooves. The band initially included Brazilians Airto Moreira (percussion) and Flora Purim (vocals). Flugelhornist/composer Chuck Mangione recorded many Latin influenced tunes including the 1977 pop hit "Feels So Good" and his Grammy winning *Children of Sanchez* film score.

Closer to the present, ChuCho Valdes, Paquito D'Rivera, and Arturo Sandoval, all former members of the Cuban band Irakere, defected to join the United States Latin jazz scene. Contemporary artists like Michel Camilo and Danilo Pérez continue to blend Latin styles with jazz while many American jazz artists such as Roy Hargrove and Pat Metheny incorporate Latin elements into their music.

KEY TERMS

Important terms, people.

TERMS	PEOPLE	
tangana	Louis Gottschalk	Charlie Parker
habanera	Lorenzo Tio	Stan Getz
clavé	W. C. Handy	Horace Silver
salsa	Jelly Roll Morton	Paquito D'Rivera
son	Desi Arnez	Gonzalo Rubalcaba
tango	Xavier Cugat	Luciana Souza
tumbao	Mario Bauza	Danilo Pérez
bossa nova	Dizzy Gillespie	Arturo Sandoval
samba	Machito	
montuno	Stan Kenton	

REVIEW QUESTIONS

1. What similarities exist between jazz and Afro-Caribbean music?

2. What is the connection between Caribbean islands, countries, and traditions to Africa?

3. What is the significance of Louis Gottschalk to a discussion of jazz and Afro-Caribbean music?

4. How can we confirm that there was a substantial Latin influence in New Orleans in the 1800s?

5. What W. C. Handy tune shows a Latin influence? What specifically is this influence?

6. What two American cities became the cradle and melting pot for Afro-Caribbean music and jazz?

7. What popular 1920s American dance is related rhythmically to the habanera?

8. The basic clavé rhythm can be organized in one of two rhythmic groupings. What are these groupings?

9. Which of the following styles has not been influential on jazz—tango, bossa nova, rumba, cha cha, samba, and conga?

10. What bebop pioneer was instrumental in creating the marriage of Cuban music to jazz? What was this style called?

11. Name other bebop artists who embraced this hybrid style in the late 1940s.

12. Name three big band leaders who embraced the Afro-Cuban style.

13. When was Cubop popular?

14. Who was Mario Bauza and what was his significance to jazz and Afro-Cuban jazz?

15. Who was Machito and what was his significance to jazz and Afro-Cuban jazz?

16. Why is Jelly Roll Morton mentioned in a discussion of the marriage of jazz and Afro-Caribbean music?

17. In the exchange, what has jazz borrowed from Afro-Caribbean music and what have the Afro-Caribbean musicians borrowed from jazz?

18. Name several Dizzy Gillespie compositions that show Afro-Cuban influences.

19. Miles Davis and Gil Evans borrowed more musically from what European country than they did from the Caribbean islands?

20. Who is the saxophonist that popularized Brazilian music and its fusion with jazz?

21. Can you name the pianist who worked with Stan Getz and also incorporated elements of Brazilian music into his brand of American jazz?

22. The fusion of jazz with Afro-Caribbean and Latin styles continues to flourish at the dawn of the twenty-first century. Name some of the contemporary artists who continue to pursue this exciting marriage.

> **Make sure that you also review material on the corresponding chapter of the CD-ROM.**

SUGGESTED SUPPLEMENTARY LISTENING

The abbreviation (iT) indicates that a particular recording cited in the text, or particularly demonstrative of the artist, is available from the Apple iTunes Web site. Other Web-based music distributors may also prove to be valuable resources. SCCJ indicates *Smithsonian Collection of Classic Jazz*.

James Reese Europe

"Memphis Blues" Memphis Archives
"St. Louis Blues" Memphis Archives

Dezi Arnez

Babalu Music! I Love Lucy's Greatest Hits Sony

Xavier Cugat

South America, Take it Away—24 Latin Hits Asv Living Era

Duke Ellington

Never No Lament: The Blanton-Webster Years RCA/BMG
Afro-Eurasian Eclipse Fantasy
"Caravan" (iT)
"Conga Brava" (iT)
"Bakiff" (iT)

Mario Bauza

The Tanga Suite Messidor

Dizzy Gillespie

Verve Jazz Master 10: Dizzy Gillespie Verve (iT)
Gillespiana Verve
Dizzy Gillespie/Chico O'Farril: Afro-Cuban Jazz Moods Original Jazz Classics
"Cubano Be, Cubano Bop" RCA (BMG) (iT)
"Manteca" RCA (BMG) (iT)
"A Night in Tunisia" RCA (BMG) (iT)
"Con Alma" RCA (BMG) (iT)

Stan Kenton

"Peanut Vendor" (iT)
Cuban Fire Suite Blue Note
Best of Stan Kenton Blue Note (Capitol) (iT)

Charlie Parker

South of the Border Verve (Polygram) (iT)

Machito

Mucho Macho: Machito and His Afro-Cuban Salseros Pablo
Kenya Cuban Jazz

Woody Herman

"Bijou" (iT)

Horace Silver

Song for My Father Blue Note (iT)
Cape Verdean Blues Blue Note (iT)

Mongo Santamaria

Afro-Roots Prestige

Gerry Mulligan

Summit—Reunion Cumbre (with Astor Piazzolla) Ans Records (iT)

Sonny Rollins

"St. Thomas" (iT)

Chick Corea

Light as a Feather Polygram (iT)
Return to Forever ECM (iT)
My Spanish Heart Polygram (iT)

Tito Peunte

King of Kings Buddha/BMG
Top Percussion RCA

Miles Davis

"Flamenco Sketches" (iT)
Sketches of Spain Sony (iT)
Tutu Warner Brothers
Amandla Warner Brothers

Stan Getz

Jazz Samba Verve
Getz/Gilberto Verve (iT)
Jazz Samba Encore Verve
Sweet Rain Verve
Getz a Go Go Verve (iT)

Clare Fischer

Lembrancas Concord

Paquito D'Rivera

Portraits of Cuba Chesky Records
Havana Café Chesky Records

Jerry Gonzalez

Rumba Para Monk Sunny Side
Moliendo Café Sunny Side (iT)

Michel Camilo

On Fire Sony
Rendezvous Sony (iT)

Gonzalo Rubalcaba

Paseo Blue Note (iT)
Super Nova Sony

Danilo Pérez

Motherland Verve (iT)

Arturo Sandoval

Hot House Encoded Music (iT)
Arturo Sandoval and the Latin Train GRP

Luciana Souza

Neruda Sunny Side (iT)
Brazilian Duos Sunny Side (iT)

Chucho Valdes

New Conceptions Blue Note
Briyumba Palo Congo Blue Note

Roy Hargrove

Habana Verve (iT)

Jane Bunnett

Spirits of Havana Universal Latino
Cuban Odyssey Blue Note

Pat Metheny

Letter from Home Geffen
Imaginary Day Warner (iT)
Still Life Talking Geffen

Irakere

The Best of Irakere Sony
Afro Cubanism Live! Bembe Records
Irakere Featuring Chucho Valdez: Yemayá Blue Note (iT)

Miscellaneous

The Original Mambo Kings: An Introduction to Afro-Cubop Verve
Mambo Mucho Mumbo: The Complete Columbia Masters Sony
Here and There with Cal Tjader and Poncho Sanchez Fantasy

Chapter 1

1. Pat Metheny, Keynote Address at 2001 International Association For Jazz Education Conference.
2. Bill Crow, *Jazz Anecdotes* (New York: Oxford University Press, 1990), p. 19.
3. Alan P. Merriam and Fradley H. Garner, "Jazz—The Word," in *The Jazz Cadence of American Culture* edited by Robert G. O'Meally (New York: Columbia University Press, 1998), pp. 7–31.
4. Ibid., p. 20.
5. Ibid., p. 20.
6. Ibid., p. 19.
7. Ibid., p. 20.
8. Ibid., pp. 7–31.
9. "New Word for Jazz Worth $1000" *Down Beat*, vol. 16, no. 10 (July 15, 1949); "Judges Named in 'Word' Contest—Prizes Pile Up," *Down Beat*, vol. 16, no. 1 (August 26, 1949); Don Read, "All That Crewcut," *Jazz Journal International*, vol. 50, no. 5 (May 1997), p. 10.

Chapter 2

1. Martin Williams, *The Jazz Tradition* (New York: Oxford University Press, 1970), p. 11.
2. Count Basie, CBS Television *60 Minutes*, Interview, 1981.
3. Robert Walser, editor, *Keeping Time: Readings in Jazz History* (New York: Oxford University Press, 1999), pp. 73–76.
4. Nat Hentoff, *Jazz Is* (New York: Limelight Editions, 1991), pp. 18–19.
5. Robert Walser, editor, *Keeping Time: Readings in Jazz History* (New York: Oxford University Press, 1999), p. 109.
6. André Hodeir, *Jazz, Its Evolution and Essence* (New York: Grove Press, 1956), p. 240.
7. Ibid., p. 195.
8. Leroy Ostransky, *Understanding Jazz* (Englewood Cliffs, NJ: Prentice Hall, 1977), p. 93.
9. Ibid., p. 80.
10. James Lincoln Collier, *Jazz: The American Theme Song* (New York: Oxford University Press, 1993), p. 25.
11. Michael Neal Jacobson, *A Comparison of the Improvisational Performance Practices of Jazz Saxophonists Charlie Parker, and Julian Adderley with the Embellishments Found in the Methodical Sonatas of Georg Philipp Teleman*, D.M.A. Treatise, The University of Texas, 1999.
12. "Improvisation," in *The New Grove Dictionary of Music and Musicians*, vol. 9, edited by Stanley Sadie (London: MacMillan Publishers Limited, 1980), p. 43.

13. Ibid., p. 49.
14. Nat Shapiro and Nat Hentoff, editors, *Hear Me Talkin' To Ya* (New York: Reinhart and Co., 1955), p. 19.
15. Joseph L. Levey, *The Jazz Experience* (Englewood Cliffs, NJ: Prentice Hall, 1983), p. 108 (cited from Jerry Coker, *Improvising Jazz*).
16. Pat Harris, "Pres Talks About Himself, Copycats," *Down Beat*, May 6, 1949, p. 15, reprinted from *Down Beat*, July 10, 1969, p. 25.
17. McCoy Tyner, from a presentation made at the University of the Arts, Philadelphia, PA, April 8, 2005.

Chapter 3

1. Paul Tanner, David Megill and Maurice Gerow, *Jazz* (New York: McGraw-Hill, 2005), p. 6.
2. Stanley Dance and Freddie Green, *The World of Swing* (New York: Da Capo Press, 1974), pp. 13–17.
3. Gene Ramey in an interview with Richard J. Lawn, Austin, Texas, 1982.
4. Leroy Ostransky, *The Anatomy of Jazz* (Seattle: University of Washington Press, 1960), p. 69.
5. Duke Ellington, *The Future of Jazz*, 1958.
6. Whitney Balliett, "Tom and Jeru," *The New Yorker*, March 15, 1990, pp. 93–95.
7. Dan Morganstern, "The Art of Playing," *Down Beat*, December 1994, pp. 46–47 (reprinted from *Down Beat*, October 22, 1964).
8. Ted Gioia, *The Imperfect Art, Reflections on Jazz and Modern Culture* (New York: Oxford University Press, 1988), pp. 50–69.
9. Scott DeVeaux, *The Birth of Bebop* (Los Angeles: University of California Press, 1997), p. 217.
10. Ibid., p. 208.
11. "Jazz Music in Motion: Dancers and Big Bands," in *The Jazz Cadence of American Culture*, edited by Robert G. O'Meally (New York: Columbia University Press, 1988), p. 282.

Chapter 4

1. John Miller Chernoff, *African Rhythm and African Sensibility: Aesthetics and Social Action in African Musical Idioms* (Chicago: University of Chicago Press, 1979), p. 30.
2. Gunther Schuller, *Early Jazz* (New York: Oxford University Press, 1968), p. 16.
3. Lewis Porter, *Jazz: A Century of Change* (New York: Schirmer Book, 1997), p. 127; James Reece Europe, "A Negro Explains Jazz," originally published in *Literary Digest*, 1919.
4. Lawrence W. Levine, "Jazz and American Culture," in *The Jazz Cadence of American Culture*, edited by

Robert G. O'Meally (New York: Columbia University Press, 1998), p. 435.

5. David A. Jansen and Gene Jones, *Spreadin' Rhythm Around: Black Popular Song Writers 1880–1930* (New York: Schirmer Books, 1998) p. 236.

6. Ibid., p. 237.

7. Ibid., p. 25.

Chapter 5

1. Frank Paterson, *Musical Courier* (May 11, 1922), p. 6, cited in James Lincoln Collier, *The Reception of Jazz in America: A New View* (New York: Institute for Studies in American Music, 1988), p. 14.

2. John Chilton, *Sidney Bechet: The Wizard of Jazz* (New York: Oxford University Press, 1987), p. 15.

3. H. O. Brunn, *The Story of the Original Dixieland Jazz Band* (London: Sidgwick and Jackson, 1963), pp. 108–109.

4. Ibid., p. 135.

5. Ibid., pp. 68–69.

6. Louis Armstrong, *The Complete Hot Five and Hot Seven Recordings*, Columbia/Legacy C4K 63527, New York, 2000.

7. William Howland Kenney, *Chicago Jazz: A Cultural History, 1904–1930* (New York: Oxford University Press, 1993), p. 46.

8. Martin Williams, *The Smithsonian Collection of Classic Jazz* (Washington: Smithsonian Institution, 1997), p. 36.

9. Scott E. Brown, liner notes on *Victory Stride: The Music of James P. Johnson* (Ocean: MusicMasters Classics, 1994), 01612-67140-2.

10. "Jazz and Jassism," *The Times-Picayune* (New Orleans), June 20, 1918, p. 4.

11. "Jazzing Away Prejudice," *Chicago Defender*, May 10, 1919, p. 20.

12. H. O. Brunn, *The Story of the Original Dixieland Jazz Band* (London: Sidgwick and Jackson, 1963), p. 107.

13. John R. McMahon, "Unspeakable Jazz Must Go," *The Ladies' Home Journal*, December 1921, pp. 34, 115–116.

14. "Does Jazz Put the Sin in Syncopation," *The Ladies' Home Journal*, August 1921, pp. 16, 34.

15. Ibid.

16. Ibid.

17. Robert Walser, *Keeping Time: Readings in Jazz History* (New York: Oxford University Press, 1999), p. 42.

18. Ibid., pp. 43–44.

19. Ibid., p. 50.

20. Ibid., p. 52.

21. James Lincoln Collier, *The Reception of Jazz in America: A New View* (New York: Institute for Studies in American Music, 1988), p. 11.

22. Ibid., p. 14.

23. Ibid.

24. H. O. Brunn, *The Story of the Original Dixieland Jazz Band* (London: Sidgwick and Jackson, 1963), pp. 73–74.

Chapter 6

1. Hoagy Carmichael, *Stardust Road* (New York: Reinhart, 1946), pp. 7–8.

2. William Howland Kenney, *Chicago Jazz: A Cultural History, 1904–1930* (New York: Oxford University Press, 1993), p. 14.

3. Ibid., p. 30.

4. Ibid., p. 24.

5. H. O. Brunn, *The Original Dixieland Jazz Band* (London: Sedgwick and Jackson, 1963), p. 173.

6. Neil Leonard, *Jazz and the White Americans* (Chicago: The University of Chicago Press, 1962), p. 37.

7. Ibid., p. 83.

8. James Lincoln Collier, *The Reception of Jazz in America: A New View* (New York: Institute for Studies in American Music, 1988) p. 18.

9. William Howland Kenney, *Chicago Jazz: A Cultural History, 1904–1930* (New York: Oxford University Press, 1993), p. 71.

10. Ibid., p. 45.

11. Ibid., p. 97.

12. James Lincoln Collier, *Jazz the American Theme Song* (New York: Oxford University Press, 1993), p. 201.

13. Wilder Hobson, *American Jazz Music* (New York: W.W. Norton, 1939), p. 126.

14. Richard M. Sudhalter, *Lost Chords: White Musicians and Their Contribution to Jazz* (New York: Oxford University Press, 1999), p. 450.

15. Ibid., p. 450.

16. Marshall Stearns, *The Story of Jazz* (New York: Oxford University Press, 1956), p. 165.

17. Henry Osgood, *So This Is Jazz* (Boston: Little Brown and Co., 1926), p. 136.

18. Robert Goffin, *Jazz, From the Congo to the Metropolitan* (Garden City, NY: Doubleday, 1946), p. 145.

19. James Lincoln Collier, *The Reception of Jazz in America: A New View* (New York: Institute for Studies in American Music, 1988), pp. 16–17.

20. William Howland Kenney, *Chicago Jazz: A Cultural History, 1904–1930* (New York: Oxford University Press, 1993), p. 30.

21. Ibid., p. 155.

22. Wilder Hobson, *American Jazz Music* (New York: W. W. Norton, 1939), p. 129.

23. Ibid., p. 127.

24. William Howland Kenney, *Chicago Jazz: A Cultural History, 1904–1930* (New York: Oxford University Press, 1993), p. 167–168.
25. Ibid., p. 168.
26. Ibid., p. 168.
27. Neil Leonard, *Jazz and the White Americans* (Chicago: The University of Chicago Press, 1962), p. 92.
28. James Lincoln Collier, *The Reception of Jazz in America: A New View* (New York: Institute for Studies in American Music Conservatory of Music, 1988), p. 18. (Reprinted from *Billboard*, February 14, 1925, p. 20.)
29. Neil Leonard, *Jazz and the White Americans* (Chicago: The University of Chicago Press, 1962), p. 74.
30. Paul Whiteman and Mary Margaret McBride, *Jazz* (New York: J. H. Sears and Co., 1926), p. 130.

Chapter 7

1. Duke Ellington, *Down Beat*, February, 1939, pp. 2, 16, 17.
2. Burton Peretti, *Jazz in American Culture* (Chicago: Ivan R. Dee, 1997), p. 67.
3. Cited from an interview with the author Richard Lawn, Fall 1982, Austin, Texas.
4. John Edward Hasse, editor, *Jazz: The First Century* (New York: Harper Collins, 1999), p. 73.
5. Burton Peretti, *Jazz in American Culture* (Chicago: Ivan R. Dee, 1997), pp. 61–75.
6. Cited from an interview with the author Richard Lawn, Fall 1982, Austin, Texas.
7. Scott DeVaux, *The Birth of Bebop: A Social and Musical History* (Berkley and Los Angeles: University of California Press, 1997), pp. 99–100.
8. John Edward Hasse, *Beyond Category: The Life and Genius of Duke Ellington* (New York: Simon and Schuster, 1993), pp. 14–19.
9. Robert Goffin, *Jazz, From the Congo to Swing* (London: Musicians Press, 1946), pp. 262–263.
10. Martin Williams, *The Smithsonian Collection of Classic Jazz* (Washington: Smithsonian Institution, 1997), p. 65.
11. Gunther Schuller, *The Swing Era: The Development of Jazz 1930–1945* (New York: Oxford University Press, 1989), pp. 11, 23, 44.
12. Cited from an interview with the author Richard Lawn, Fall 1982, Austin, Texas.
13. Ibid.
14. Gunther Schuller, *The Swing Era: The Development of Jazz 1930–1945* (New York: Oxford University Press, 1989), p. 567.
15. Gunther Schuller, *The Swing Era: The Development of Jazz 1930–1945* (New York: Oxford University Press, 1989), p. 702.

Chapter 8

1. Bernard Gendron, "Moldy Figs and Modernists: Jazz at War (1942–1946)," in *Jazz Among the Discourses* edited by Krin Garrard (Durham: Duke University Press, 1995), p. 17.
2. Ross Russell, *Jazz Style in Kansas City and the Southwest* (Berkley: University of California Press, 1971), p. 3.
3. Cited from an interview with the author Richard Lawn, Austin, Texas, Fall 1982.
4. Robert Walser, *Keeping Time: Readings in Jazz History* (New York: Oxford University Press, 1999), p. 112.
5. Ibid., pp. 111–120.
6. Cited from an interview with Art Vincent on the radio show "Art of Jazz," December 1, 1973.
7. Ross Russell, *Jazz Style in Kansas City and the Southwest* (Berkley: University of California Press, 1971), pp. 104–105.
8. Cited from an interview with the author Richard Lawn, Austin, Texas, Fall 1982.
9. George T. Simon, *The Big Bands* (New York: Macmillan, 1997), p. 4.
10. Robert S. Gold, *Jazz Talk* (Indianapolis: The Bobbs-Merrill Company, 1975), pp. 61, 47, 30, 128, 104.
11. Cited from an interview with the author Richard Lawn, Austin, Texas, Fall 1982.
12. Ibid.
13. John Edward Hasse, editor, *Jazz: The First Century* (New York: HarperCollins, 2000), p. 56.
14. Cited from an interview with the author Richard Lawn, Austin, Texas, Fall 1982.
15. "Billie Holiday: A Portrait in Testimony," compiled by Christopher Porter, *Jazz Times* (May 2005), p. 67.
16. Cited from an interview with the author Richard Lawn, Austin, Texas, Fall 1982.
17. John Edward Hasse, editor, *Jazz: The First Century* (New York: HarperCollins, 2000), p. 82.
18. Leonard Feather, "A Survey of Jazz Today," in *Esquire's 1945 Jazz Book* edited by Paul Eduard Miller (New York: A. S. Barnes & Company, 1945), pp. 15–27.
19. Wilder Hobson, *American Jazz Music* (New York: W. W. Norton, 1939), pp. 154–155.
20. Ibid., p. 156.

Chapter 9

1. Gunther Schuller, *The Swing Era: The Development of Jazz 1930–1945* (New York: Oxford University Press, 1989), p. 23.
2. Scott DeVaux, *The Birth of Bebop, A Social and Cultural History* (Berkley: University of California Press, 1997), pp. 243–244.

3. "The Petrillo Years," *International Musician*, 95, no. 4 (October 1996), p. 34.

4. Interview with the author Richard Lawn, Austin, Texas.

5. Scott DeVaux, *The Birth of Bebop: A Social and Cultural History* (Berkley: University of California Press, 1997), p. 156.

6. Roger Pryor Dodge, *Hot Jazz and Jazz Dance* (New York: Oxford University Press, 1995), p. 148.

7. Terry Gross interview of Stan Getz for NPR station WHYY, June 14, 1990.

8. Ira Gitler, *Jazz Masters of the '40s* (New York: Da Capo Press, 1966), p. 79 (quoted from Norman Granz, *Down Beat*, 1945).

9. Robert Walser, *Keeping Time* (New York: Oxford University Press, 1999), p. 153 (reprint of "Bop Will Kill Business Unless It Kills Itself First," *Down Beat* April 7, 1948, pp. 2–3).

10. Burton Peretti, *Jazz in American Culture* (Chicago: Ivan R. Dee, 1997), p. 103.

11. Ibid.

12. Marshall Stearns, *The Story of Jazz* (New York: Oxford University Press, 1956), p. 222.

13. John Birks Gillespie and Al Fraser, *To Be or Not to Bop, Memoirs of Dizzy Gillespie* (New York: Da Capo Press, 1979), p. 138.

14. *Down Beat*, 1955 (reprinted in *Down Beat*, 56., no.9, September 1989, p. 39).

15. Joe Goldberg, *Jazz Masters of the 50s* (New York: Da Capo Press, 1965), p. 44.

16. John Birks Gillespie and Al Fraser, *To Be or Not to Bop, Memoirs of Dizzy Gillespie* (New York: Da Capo Press, 1979), p. 193.

17. Ibid., p. 350.

Chapter 10

1. Ted Gioia, *West Coast Jazz, Modern Jazz in California 1945–1960* (Berkley: University of California Press, 1992), p. 187.

2. Joe Goldberg, *Jazz Masters of the 50s* (New York: Da Capo Press, 1965), p. 22.

3. Ibid., p. 12.

4. "Pipe and Slippers Jazz Is For Me: Gerry Mulligan," *Down Beat* (September 1989), p. 42.

5. Ted Gioia, *West Coast Jazz, Modern Jazz in California 1945–1960* (Berkley: University of California Press, 1992), p. 68.

6. Joe Goldberg, *Jazz Masters of the 50s* (New York: Da Capo Press, 1965), p. 154; http://vancouverjazz.com/forums/archive/index.php/t-98.html).

7. Ted Gioia, *West Coast Jazz, Modern Jazz in California 1945–1960* (Berkley: University of California Press, 1992), p. 77.

8. As told to the author Richard Lawn in an interview in Austin, Texas, September 2000.

9. Terry Gross interview of Stan Getz for WHYY and NPR, June 1, 1990.

10. Joe Goldberg, *Jazz Masters of the 50s* (New York: Da Capo Press, 1965), p. 117.

11. Lennie Tristano, "Why Don't They Leave Me Alone?" *Down Beat* (July 10, 1969) p. 28.

12. *The Birth of Third Stream*, liner notes by Gunther Schuller (p. 19–20), Columbia/Legacy, CK 64 929, 1996.

13. Ibid.

14. Robert Walser, editor, *Keeping Time: Readings in Jazz History* (New York: Oxford University Press, 1999), p. 247.

Chapter 11

1. David H. Rosenthal, *Hard Bop: Jazz and Black Music 1955–1965* (New York: Oxford University Press, 1992), p. 73.

2. Issac Newton, *Compton's Interactive Encyclopedia* (West Sussex: The Learning Company, 1998).

3. Burton W. Peretti, *Jazz In American Culture* (Chicago: Ivan R. Dee, 1997), p. 107.

4. David H. Rosenthal, *Hard Bop: Jazz and Black Music 1955–1965* (New York: Oxford University Press, 1992), p. 118, 163.

5. Ibid., p. 36.

6. Brian Priestly, *Jazz on Record* (New York: Billboard Books, 1991), p. 137.

7. David H. Rosenthal, *Hard Bop: Jazz and Black Music 1955–1965* (New York: Oxford University Press, 1992), pp. 62–73.

8. Ibid., pp. 117–129.

9. Ibid., p. 73.

10. Ibid., p. 129.

11. Don DeMicheal, "Cannonball Adderley: The Responsibilities of Success," *Down Beat* (June 21, 1962, reprint January 1996), pp. 34–35.

12. David H. Rosenthal, *Hard Bop: Jazz and Black Music 1955–1965* (New York: Oxford University Press, 1992), p. 111.

13. Mary Klages, "Postmodernism," www.colorado.edu/English/ENGL2012Klages/pomo.html.

14. A. B. Spellman, *Black Music: Four Lives* (New York: Schocken Books, 1971) p. 119.

15. Ibid.

16. Ibid.

17. John Litweiler, *Ornette Coleman, a Harmolodic Life* (New York: Da Capo, 1994), p. 46.

18. Peter Niklas Wilson, *Ornette Colemann, His Life and Music* (Berkley, CA: Berkley Hills Books, 1999), p. 35.

19. John Litweiler, *Ornette Coleman, a Harmolodic Life* (New York: Da Cappo Press, 1994), p. 73.
20. Ibid., p. 75.
21. Don Cherry, *Mind and Time*, liner notes, Contemporary 7569 Reissued on OJC OJCCD-342-2.
22. Pete Welding, review of *Free Jazz, Down Beat* (January, 1962) in *Keeping Time: Readings in Jazz History*, edited by Robert Walser (New York: Oxford; 1999), pp. 253–255.
23. Ibid.
24. John A. Tynan, "Double View of a Double Quartet," *Down Beat* (January 18, 1962), p. 28
25. Charles Mingus, *Beneath the Underdog* (New York: Alfred A. Knopf, 1971), in *Keeping Time: Readings in Jazz History*, edited by Robert Walser (New York: Oxford University Press, 1999), p. 225.
26. David H. Rosenthal, *Hard Bop: Jazz and Black Music 1955–1965*, (New York: Oxford University Press, 1992), p. 152.
27. Ted Gioia, *The History of Jazz* (New York: Oxford University Press, 1997), p. 330.
28. David H. Rosenthal, *Hard Bop: Jazz and Black Music 1955–1965* (New York: Oxford University Press, 1992), p. 83.
29. Ibid., p. 84.
30. Interview with Terry Gross for "Fresh Air," NPR station WHYY, June 1990, Philadelphia, PA.
31. Oscar Peterson, *A Jazz Odyssey* (New York: Continuum, 2002), p. 328.
32. David H. Rosenthal, *Hard Bop: Jazz and Black Music 1955–1965* (New York: Oxford University Press, 1992), p. 130.
33. James Lincoln Collier, *The Making of Jazz: A Comprehensive History* (Boston: Houghton Mifflin Co., 1978), p. 452.

Chapter 12
1. Miles Davis and Quincy Troupe, "Miles Davis Speaks His Mind," in *Keeping Time: Readings in Jazz History*, edited by Robert Walser (New York: Oxford University Press, 1999), p. 367.
2. Burton Peretti, *Jazz in American Culture* (Chicago: Ivan R. Dee, 1997), pp. 146–154.
3. Martin Williams, *The Jazz Tradition* (New York: Oxford University Press, 1970 reprint), p. 156.
4. Miles Davis and Quincy Troupe, *Miles: The Autobiography* (New York: Simon and Schuster, 1989), p. 119.
5. Miles Davis and Quincy Troupe, "Miles Davis Speaks His Mind," in *Keeping Time: Readings in Jazz History*, edited by Robert Walser (New York: Oxford University Press, 1999), p. 367.
6. Ibid., p. 366.
7. Miles Davis and Quincy Troupe, *Miles: The Autobiography* (New York: Simon and Schuster, 1989), p. 220.
8. Ibid., p. 104.
9. Ibid., p. 116.
10. Stephanie Stein Crease, *Gil Evans: Out of the Cool, His Life and Music* (Chicago: Cappella Books, 2002), p. 197.
11. Ibid., p. 199.
12. Todd Coolman, *The Quintet*, liner notes on *Miles Davis Quintet, 1965–1968*, Columbia/Legacy.
13. Ibid.
14. Ibid.
15. Miles Davis and Quincy Troupe, *Miles: The Autobiography* (New York: Simon and Schuster, 1989), p. 271.
16. Ibid., p. 272
17. Ibid., p. 297.
18. Ibid., p. 298.
19. Ibid.
20. Ibid., p. 299.
21. Ibid., p. 200.
22. Ibid., p. 352.
23. Ibid., p. 322.
24. Ibid., p. 205.
25. David H. Rosenthal, *Hard Bop Jazz and Black Music 1955–1965* (New York: Oxford University Press, 1992), p. 147.
26. Ted Gioia, *The History of Jazz* (New York: Oxford University Press, 1997) p. 245.
27. David H. Rosenthal, *Hard Bop Jazz and Black Music 1955–1965* (New York: Oxford University Press, 1992), p. 197.
28. Bill Shoemaker, "John Coltrane, Giant Steps," *Down Beat* (September 1989), p. 57.
29. Brian Priestley, *Jazz on Record* (New York: Billboard Books, 1991), p. 128.
30. Peter Watrous, "John Coltrane, A Life Supreme," *Musician* (July 12, 1987), p. 106.
31. Don DeMicheal, "John Coltrane and Eric Dolphy Answer the Critics," *Down Beat* (April 12, 1962, in reprint July 12, 1979), pp. 16, 52, 53.
32. Don De Michael, "John Coltrane and Eric Dolphy Answer the Jazz Critics," *Down Beat* (July 1994, reprint from November 23, 1961, by John Tynan), p. 72.
33. Ibid., p. 73.
34. Don DeMicheal, "John Coltrane and Eric Dolphy Answer the Critics," *Down Beat* (April 12, 1962, in reprint July 12, 1979), pp. 16, 52, 53.
35. Lewis Porter, *John Coltrane: His Life and Music* (Ann Arbor: The University of Michigan Press, 1999), p. 204.
36. Howard Mandel, *Down Beat* (July 12, 1979), p. 15.

37. "Still a Force in 1979, Musicians Talk About John Coltrane," *Down Beat* (July 12, 1979), p. 20.
38. *Down Beat* (December 1966).
39. Harvey Pekar, "Miles Davis: 1964–1969 Recordings," *in A Miles Davis Reader*, edited by Bill Kirchner (Washington: Smithsonian Institution Press, 1997), p. 166.
40. Miles Davis and Quincy Troupe, *Miles, The Autobiography* (New York: Simon and Schuster, 1989), p. 273.
41. Ibid., pp. 273–274.
42. Don Heckman and Wayne Shorter, liner notes, *Speak No Evil*, 1964, Blue Note CDP7 46509 2.

Chapter 13

1. Carlos Santana, "Remembering Miles and Bitches Brew," *Miles Davis the Complete Bitches Brew Sessions*, liner notes, 1989, p. 8, Columbia/Legacy.
2. Bill Milkowski, "Jazz Plugs In," *Down Beat* (July 1994), p. 58.
3. Ibid., p. 59.
4. Steve Bloom, "Second Generation of Fusion," *Down Beat* (August 9, 1979), pp. 22–25.
5. Stuart Nicholson, *Jazz-Rock: A History* (New York: Schirmer Books, 1998), pp. 166–181.
6. Larry Birnbaum, "Weather Report Answers Its Critics," *Down Beat* (July 1994), p. 60 (reprinted from February 8, 1979).
7. Stuart Nicholson, *Jazz-Rock: A History* (New York: Schirmer Books, 1998), p. 165.
8. Ibid., p. 166.
9. Josef Woodward, "Storm Surge, The Rise and Fall of Weather Report, The Best Jazz Band of the Past 30 Years," *Down Beat* (January 2001), p. 24.
10. Stuart Nicholson, *Jazz-Rock: A History* (New York: Schirmer Books, 1998), p. 176.
11. Elaine Guregian, "Weather Report," *Down Beat* (September 1989), p. 86.
12. Stuart Nicholson, *Jazz-Rock: A History* (New York: Schirmer Books, 1998), p.184.
13. Ibid., p. 186.
14. Ibid.
15. *Down Beat* (August 21, 1971), p. 15.
16. Herbie Hancock, *Head Hunters*, liner notes, Columbia/Legacy CK65123, 1996.
17. Scott Thompson, *Head Hunters*, liner notes, p. 9, Columbia/Legacy CK65123, 1996.
18. Stuart Nicholson, *Jazz-Rock: A History*, (New York: Schirmer Books, 1998), p. 136.
19. Ibid., p. 149.
20. Ibid., p. 200.
21. Ibid., p. 202
22. John Toner, "Chick Corea: Return to Forever," *Down Beat* (July 1994), p. 66 (reprinted from March 28, 1974).
23. Robin Tolleson, "David Sanborn: The Voice of Emotion," *Down Beat* (July 1994), p. 64 (reprint from March 1983).
24. Zan Stewart, "Chuck Mangione," *Music America Magazine*, vol. 1, no. 4 (January 1977), pp. 19–20.
25. John McDonough, "The Feeling's Back," review in *Down Beat* (June 1999), p. 56.

Chapter 14

1. Pat Metheny, *Down Beat* (September 1989), p. 78 (reprint from 1978).
2. Bob Suter, "How ECM Records Has Made Jazz Work For It," *Jazz*, vol. 4, no. 1 (Winter 1979), p. 65.
3. Ibid.
4. Ibid., p. 67.
5. Ibid., p. 68.
6. Robert Walser, *Keeping Time: Readings in Jazz History* (New York: Oxford University Press, 1999), p. 414.
7. Ibid., p. 412.
8. Ibid., p. 414.
9. Robert L. Doerschuk, "Keith Jarrett, Provocative Reflections on Creativity and the Crisis in Modern Music," *Keyboard* (March 1993), p. 83.
10. Chuck Berg, "Dexter Gordon Making His Great Leap Forward," *Down Beat* (September 1989), p. 83.
11. Jon Pareles, "Wynton Marsalis Takes a Long Look at Slavery," *The New York Times* (April 4, 1994), 13.
12. Lewis Porter, *Jazz, a Century of Change: Readings and New Essays* (New York: Schirmer Books, 1997), p. 269.
13. Bill Dobbins, "Cecil Taylor," in *The New Grove Dictionary of Jazz*, edited by Barry Kernfeld (New York: St. Martin's Press, 1995), p. 1190.
14. A. B. Spellman, *Black Music: Four Lives* (New York: Schocken Books, 1971), p. 29.
15. Bill Dobbins, "Cecil Taylor," in *The New Grove Dictionary of Jazz*, edited by Barry Kernfeld (New York: St. Martin's Press, 1995), p. 1190.
16. *Long Yellow Road, Toshiko Akiyoshi–Lew Tabackin Big Band*, liner notes by Leonard Feather, RCA 1976.
17. Ibid.
18. Art Lange, "The 80's," *Down Beat* (September 1989), p. 88.
19. Robert Walser, editor, *Keeping Time: Readings in Jazz History* (New York: Oxford University Press, 1999), p. 333.

Chapter 15

1. Rafi Zabor and Vic Garbaini, "Wynton vs. Herbie: The Purist and the Crossbreeder Duke It Out," *Musician* (March 1985) in *Keeping Time: Readings in Jazz History*, edited by Robert Walser (New York: Oxford University Press, 1999), p. 342.

2. Robert L. Doerschuk, "Keith Jarrett: Provocative Reflections on Creativity and the Crisis in Modern Music," *Keyboard* (March 1993), p. 89.

3. Lewis Porter, *Jazz a Century of Change: Readings and New Essays* (New York: Schirmer Books, 1997), p. 251.

4. Peter Watrous, "Jazz Moves Fast Forward Into the Past," *The New York Times* (September 18, 1988), in *Jazz, a Century of Change: Readings and New Essays*, edited by Lewis Porter, New York: Schirmer Books, 1997), p. 246.

5. Robert L. Doerschuk, "Keith Jarrett: Provocative Reflections on Creativity and the Crisis in Modern Music," *Keyboard* (March 1993), p. 88.

6. Lewis Porter, *Jazz, a Century of Change Readings and New Essays* (New York: Schirmer Books, 1997), p. 255.

7. Ibid., p. 256.

8. Tim Hagans (2004)—used by permission.

9. John McDonough, "Failed Experiment," in *Keeping Time: Readings in Jazz History,* edited by Robert Walser (New York: Oxford University Press, 1999), p. 398.

10. "Cassandra Wilson—Eclectic Vocalist," *The New Yorker* (December 2002).

11. Bob Blumenthal, "The Eighties," *Jazz Times* (September 2000), p. 47.

12. Joan Jeffri, *Changing the Beat: A Study of the Worklife of Jazz Musicians, Volume I Executive Summary* (Washington: National Endowment for the Arts, 2002), p. 4.

13. Ibid.

14. Ibid., p. 5.

15. Ibid., p. 12.

Chapter 16

1. René López and David Carp, "Cuba: Where the Music Is Hot" (New York: Jazz at Lincoln Center, 1997), www.jazzatlincolncenter.org/jazz/note/cuba.html.

2. Gene Santoro, "Latin Jazz," in *The Oxford Companion to Jazz,*" edited by Bill Kirchner (New York: Oxford University Press, 2000), pp. 522–533.

3. Marshall W. Stearns, *The Story of Jazz* (New York: Oxford University Press, 1956), p. 249.

4. Gene Santoro, "Latin Jazz," in *The Oxford Companion to Jazz*" edited by Bill Kirchner (New York: Oxford University Press, 2000), p. 529.

5. Ibid., p. 530.

6. Ibid., p. 531.

A

accelerando To gradually get faster.

accent Emphasis on a note or notes.

accompaniment The musical background for a solo performer or performers (e.g., a piano accompanying a trumpet solo).

acculturation The modification of a primitive culture by contact with an advanced culture.

ad lib To improvise or create on the spur of the moment. The term can relate to the work of musicians, comedians, actors, and visual artists, though all do not improvise.

aharmonic See **atonal.**

antiphonal A form of musical response, as of one singer, choir, or instrument answering another.

arco A manner of playing the double bass (or violin, viola, or cello) using a bow.

arpeggio Playing the notes of a chord consecutively one note at a time.

arrangement A reconstruction/adaptation of a musical composition for a specific ensemble of instruments. In a written arrangement, the arranger has written down the specific notes he wants each instrument to play. Also, a particular setting or interpretation of a precomposed piece of music.

arranger The individual who constructs new interpretations of precomposed works. Composers often serve as their own arrangers.

articulation A general term to describe the length of notes in performance, i.e., short or long or somewhere in between.

attack The manner of beginning a tone.

atonal Without a specific key or tonal center.

avant-garde A group (writers, musicians, artists, etc.) regarded as preeminent in the invention and application of new techniques.

B

backbeat rhythm A strong emphasis on beats two and four of a measure by the drummer.

ballad A slow to very slow song, often with romantic overtones, that uses the same melody for each verse.

bass line The lowest musical line; usually played by the tuba, string bass, or electric bass guitar.

black and tans Cabarets and saloons that catered to a mixed black and white clientele in the 1920s and 1930s.

blue notes The third, fifth, and seventh notes of a chord that are altered by lowering the pitch to create blues inflections. These alterations, which don't necessarily conform to precise semitones, are often

created through improvisatory interpretations rather than dictated by the printed, precomposed page.

boogie woogie Rhythmically charged, blues-inspired solo piano style that emerged in the mid-1920s. The style featured a repetitive left hand pattern.

bossa nova Brazilian dance style made popular in the United States in the 1960s.

brass section A section of an ensemble that includes trumpets, trombones, French horns, and tubas; in jazz ensembles, the brass section includes trumpets and trombones (bones).

break A point in an arrangement in which all instruments suddenly stop playing for two to four measures while the soloist/improviser continues to play.

bridge The middle section of a popular song also described formally as the "B" section. This second section is typically surrounded by the "A" section and often appears in a different key.

C

cadenza A solo by one instrument, often played without regard for strict tempo.

call and response An African-originated pattern used in jazz and in some religious music in which a call (by a solo vocalist or instrumentalist) is answered by another vocalist or instrumentalist, or by an ensemble of vocalists/instruments.

changes The entire sequence of chords used in a composition.

Chopin (1810–1849) A composer of Romantic music, particularly for the piano.

chart Musician's slang for arrangement.

chékere A percussion instrument of African origin made from a hollow gourd covered with a loose mesh of beads.

chords The simultaneous sounding of three or more notes. Also described as **harmony.**

chord progressions A series of successive chords. Also known as the **changes.**

chord voicing See **voicing.**

chorus The main body, refrain, or harmonic outline, as distinct from the verse (which comes first).

chromatic Half-step intervals of a scale or melody.

clavé An Afro-Caribbean rhythm pattern based on the organization of subgroupings 3 + 2 or 2 + 3 and derived from the Spanish habanera or Cuban rhythm. The clavé pattern serves as the foundation of many Afro-Caribbean music styles.

clavés A pair of round, polished, hard wood dowels that are struck together to create the clavé pattern.

cluster A group of notes very closely organized to form a dense chord. Clusters can be consonant or dissonant.

coda A passage at the end of a composition that may or may not contain material that was presented earlier in the composition.

collective improvisation A situation when all performers improvise simultaneously, as was the case in early jazz and in much free, avant-garde jazz.

comp(ing) A performance practice used to describe improvised harmonic accompaniment typically governed by those chords set forth in a prescribed chord progression. Any instrument capable of playing chords can "comp."

conga A Latin dance form. Also a Latin or Afro-Cuban drum.

conga drums Long round-bodied, single-headed Afro-Caribbean drums of varying sizes and pitches. The name is derived from an African line dance called the conga.

consonance and dissonance The very foundation of tonal music; consonance is created by the relationship of pitches that produce an agreeable effect, whereas dissonance is the result of disturbing musical relationships that create tension and often displeasure.

contrafact New melodies composed over chord progressions borrowed from other songs. This was a popular approach during the bebop period.

countermelody A secondary melody accompanying a primary voice or musical idea.

counterpoint Simultaneously occurring melodies.

contrapuntal Describes music that features counterpoint or simultaneously occurring melodies.

creole The result of intermarriage created by merging any combination of French, Spanish, and African-American descent. This race is associated with the New Orleans Delta area.

D

diatonic Notes within a given scale key and without alternation.

dissonance See **consonance**.

double-time Doubling a tempo, or implying such, so that the music becomes twice as fast in comparison to the initial tempo.

drone A sustained or repeated note, usually in the bass or lowest part, sounded while upper musical structures change.

dynamics The degree of volume of sound. The most common dynamic markings and definitions of relative volume are as follows:

pianissimo: pp — very soft
piano: p — soft
mezzo piano: mp — medium soft

mezzo forte: mf — medium loud
forte: f — loud
fortissimo: ff — very loud
crescendo < — gradually becoming louder
decrescendo or diminuendo: > — gradually becoming softer

E

extension tones Notes added to a four-note seventh chord and designed to enrich the harmony — usually the ninth, eleventh, and thirteenth.

F

fill Term used to describe a drummer or horn player's brief improvised passage.

flat To lower a pitch.

form Describes the architecture and overall organization of a piece of music and is defined by key melodic/harmonic components.

front line Refers to principle wind instruments associated with early New Orleans jazz and street bands which include cornet or trumpet, clarinet, and trombone. The percussion occupied the "second line," marching behind the wind instruments.

functional harmony Used to describe the tendency in much Western music harmony of one chord naturally leading to another chord — often moving away from and back to the tonic chord that defines the key or tonal center of a composition.

G

gig A musical engagement.

glissando To slide from note to note in a very smooth, legato fashion.

ground rhythm (ground pattern) A fundamental recurring pattern that serves as the foundation for other changing rhythms, melodies, and/or chords to be layered on top of.

guiro Afro-Caribbean percussion instrument fashioned from a long, cylindrical and serrated hollow gourd and played with a stick in a scraping motion.

H

habanera Spanish rhythm also associated with Cuba and serving as the heart of many Afro-Caribbean and Latin American folk styles and dance rhythms.

harmonic rhythm Describes the pace at which chords move from one to another.

harmonics Overtones (notes occurring above a fundamental tone or frequency) that result from the division of a vibrating string or air column.

harmony A collection of two or more notes played simultaneously. See **chords** and **chord progression.**

head The main theme (composed melody) as stated in jazz performance. The head is usually played first before improvised solos.

head charts (arrangements) Impromptu arrangements that were improvised by members of a band and often performed from memory rather than from notated scores.

high hat (hi hat) A synonym for the sock cymbal, which is an integral part of the drum set. This pair of inverted cymbals is caused to clap together by a foot pedal.

homophonic Describes music that consists of only one predominant melodic line accompanied by chords defining harmony.

I

interval The distance separating two different pitches.

intonation The degree of accuracy, based on a particular agreement concerning the matching of two pitches, in a performance of music.

K

key Defines the tonality and tonal center of a piece of music, and serves to further describe the key signature.

key center Central pitch that defines the tonal center of a composition.

key signature Refers to sharps and flats that regulate the tonality and tonal center of a piece of music. The key signature instructs the performer to alter certain notes by raising or lowering them one half step, i.e., one flat in the key signature implies either F major or D minor and requires the performer to flat (lower by one half-step) the note B.

kit An abbreviation for a drum set or a drum kit.

L

lay back A style of performing where musicians play slightly behind a consistent beat or tempo creating a slight tension.

lay out An abbreviation designating the performer to rest or not play; also **tacet** or **tacit.**

lead player The principal or first player in a group. In a big band this often refers to the first trumpet player who sets the standard for interpretation for all the other wind players to follow.

legato Very smooth and connected playing without noticeable tonguing and often without emphasis on any particular note.

lick A melodic phrase that has become an accepted part of the jazz language, often, but not always, associated with a specific musician who first created it.

locked hand Refers to a piano style in which chords are voiced closely in both left and right hands, and all voices move in parallel motion. A style of solo piano playing using chords rather than single-note lines accompanied by chords.

M

measure/bar The space between vertical lines (bar lines) in written music; a means of division of music that groups beats together in specific, consistent numbers (see **time signature**).

melody A succession of single tones varying in pitch and rhythm, and having a recognizable shape.

meringue A fast, Latin or Afro-Cuban two-beat dance rhythm originating from the Dominican Republic.

meter A division of beats or pulses into unaccented and accented groupings of two beats, three beats, etc.

modality The use of harmonic and melodic formations based on the church modes, as opposed to those based on the minor scales. Also refers to a particular **tonality.**

mode Used synonymously with the term **scale**, since the seven Greek labeled "church modes" are contrived by rearranging the occurrence of notes found within the fundamental or parent major scale.

modulate To change key or tone center.

Moldy Figs Term used to describe fans who supported traditional jazz (New Orleans Dixieland and Chicago jazz) during the more modern swing and bebop movements.

monophonic Describes a single melodic line without accompaniment.

monorhythm One rhythm.

montuno Refers to a recurring, vamp-like piano accompaniment that often serves at the heart of much Afro-Cuban music.

motif A short melodic fragment of a few notes that recurs through a composition or a section as a unifying element. It is distinguished from a theme or subject by being shorter. It is often derived from themes (analogues to riffs).

motive Smallest recognizeable musical idea; see **motif.**

multiphonic Two or more notes sounded simultaneously by a wind instrument.

mute A device for softening, muffling, and altering the sound of a musical instrument, particularly brass instruments.

N

neoclassicism A movement of twentieth-century music characterized by the inclusion of seventeenth- and eighteenth-century musical features into contemporary style music.

O

obligato An accompanying but important melody that is less prominent and plays a secondary role to the main melody of a composition. These melodies are often improvised.

oral tradition All spoken or sung testimonies about the past and the process by which traditions are passed on through generations.

orchestration The ways in which instruments are assigned to play certain roles in a musical arrangement. To orchestrate is the act of orchestration, or assigning instruments to certain notes and musical lines in a score.

ostinato A persistently repeated rhythmic and/or melodic phrase, and sometimes an accompaniment phrase, that is repeated over and over again in a composition.

outside playing Refers to a performance practice in which musicians elect to purposely draw attention to dissonant relationships by playing musical ideas that run contrary to traditional notions of consonance in music. A term often associated with free and postmodern jazz styles.

overtones See **harmonics.**

P

pedal point See **drone.**

pentatonic Implies five notes, as in "pentatonic scale."

percussive To play in a strongly emphasized manner; to strike.

phrase A small unit or subdivision of a melody. It can also refer to a particular manner in which a musician interprets a melody as compared to how an individual enunciates a sentence.

pizzicato A manner of playing the double bass (or other string instrument) using only the fingers to pluck the strings.

polymeters Simultaneous use or implication of several meters.

polyphony Music that combines several simultaneous melodies.

polyrhythms Simultaneous use of several rhythms.

Prohibition Act A United Sates law, also known as the Volstead Act, passed on January 16, 1920, declaring the importation, exportation, transportation, sale, and manufacturing of alcoholic beverages as illegal activities punishable by law.

Q

quartet Ensemble of four musicians.

quintet Ensemble of five musicians.

R

race records Records marketed in the 1920s for black listeners featuring largely black, female blues singers who were often accompanied by jazz instrumentalists.

ragtime Originally a solo piano style popular in the United States from 1895 to 1915, this European-derived form followed a rondo scheme also featured in marches along with 2/4 meter, simple right-hand syncopations with very regular, oom-pah-like left-hand chord accompanishment. Ragtime was initially a composed, not improvised style. It is considered the first style of American music to enjoy widespread popularity, and demonstrates that a music highly influenced by black performers and composers could be the basis of commercial success.

range The distance between the lowest and highest notes capable of being played on an instrument or sung. Can also refer to the highest and lowest pitches in a song.

reed A thin, elongated piece of cane wood or other material that is fixed at one end but free to vibrate at the other end. In clarinets and saxophones, a column of air passes rapidly between the reed and mouthpiece causing the reed to vibrate, creating a sound.

reed (or woodwind) section A group of saxophones, clarinets, flutes, and, occasionally, oboes that performs together in a jazz ensemble.

rhythm The whole feeling of forward movement in music as defined by the speed at which the melody moves and the different durations of those notes comprising a melody.

rhythm and blues (R&B) A popular music style that uses African-American musical elements such as the 12-bar blues progression, blue notes, repetitious chords over heavily emphasized rhythms, heavy, gutsy vocals, and lyrics that often communicate a sense of melancholy, disappointment, or other such emotion.

rhythm section Refers to standard instrumentation including piano, bass, drums, and sometimes guitar.

ride A synonym often used in early jazz styles to indicate improvise, i.e., "take a ride." Ride means to improvise a solo.

ride cymbal Generally the larger cymbal in a drum kit on which a steady, somewhat repetitive pattern is played usually by the right hand, helping to establish the tempo.

riff A short repeated musical phrase played by a soloist or a group.

ritardondo (ritard) To gradually slow down the tempo or pace of music.

rondo A classical form in origin, where one section of a musical composition (A) recurs with contrasting sections (B,C,D) that are juxtaposed (such as ABACADA, etc.)

rubato Flexible, free, inconsistent tempo permitting interpretation by the performer.

S

samba Brazilian folk music style closely associated with dance and the Carnival celebration.

salsa A broad term that evolved in the 1960s to describe music of Afro-Cuban descent. Now the term can imply elements of son, rock and roll, jazz, and other Afro-Caribbean influences.

scale A precise progression of notes upward or downward in stepwise motion.

scat An improvised jazz solo by a singer using meaningless syllables.

sequence An architecturally or geometrically equal musical restatement of a series of pitches but without repeating the same notes; a reoccurring shape or gesture but with different notes at a different pitch level — either higher or lower.

seventh chord A chord consisting of four different pitches and arranged with a major or minor third between each. Seventh chords serve as the foundation of jazz and popular music harmony.

sharp To raise a pitch.

sheets of sound Term used to describe John Coltrane's practice of playing rapidly ascending, harp-like gestures of notes that together represent the sound of an entire harmony.

shout chorus A chorus or section of an arrangement (usually big band) that involves the entire ensemble, features new material, and serves to bring the piece to a climax. The shout chorus usually appears near the end of the composition.

shuffle A medium tempo style using the boogie-woogie rhythm as the basis.

sideman A musician who is not the leader of a band.

soli When a group of instruments (often from the same family) perform in a featured, soloistic fashion.

solo break A point in a piece of music lasting usually two to four measures when everyone in the ensemble stops playing except the soloist.

son A popular dance style of Spanish and African origins that served as the foundation for later styles including salsa.

song form Term used to define the architecture of the classic American popular song following a symmetrical ABA or AABA structure.

staccato Played short and crisply.

stock or **stock arrangement** A standard rendition or arrangement usually referring to a popular dance band arrangement from the Swing Era.

stomp A style of music in which the band plays certain heavily accented rhythmic patterns over and over again in riff fashion, providing momentum and excitement through syncopation and repetition.

stop time A series of short notes played by the band in tempo and on certain major beats (often 1, 2, and 3) that usually serves as accompaniment to solo improvisations.

stride A type of piano playing derived from ragtime. It often has no prescribed form, is frequently improvised, can be blues influenced, and is faster and more intense than rags.

style The characteristic manner in which something is performed.

swing Rhythmic phenomenon associated with jazz performance practice and referring to the rhythmic buoyancy created by the uneven, skipping rhythms that anticipate primary beats and are sometimes a consequence of syncopated rhythms.

syncopation A music rhythm that emphasizes a weak or normally unaccented beat or portion of a beat.

T

tacet (tacit) Be silent—an indication in printed music designating the performer to not play a particular passage.

tag A short addition to the end of a musical composition often based on the repetition of ingredients of the main melody.

tailgate Refers to a New Orleans–style of trombone playing in which the musician smears notes together using the instrument's slide to perform glissandos. This technique was forced by limited space on flatbed, horse-drawn wagons that forced trombonists to sit on the "tailgate" as the band paraded through the streets.

tangana Argentinean folk dance form that served as the predecessor of the tango.

tango Argentinean dance form.

tempo The rate of speed of a musical composition; the speed at which the melody is performed.

territory bands Bands that had limited tours to specific geographic regions and were well known in these areas. Some territory bands eventually made a national impact through recordings and touring.

texture The character of the musical fabric of a composition determined by the arrangement of musical elements. The density, selection, organization, and range of instruments all contribute to the "texture."

theme A melody forming the basis for variations or improvisation in composition.

32-bar structure A musical form that takes 32 bars to complete. It can be used as a popular song form.

through composed A compositional approach that resembles stream of consciousness writing in that typically there are no recurring themes that provide a more traditional, discernable form or shape. Musical ideas seem to evolve organically, each moving freely from one to the next.

timbales Afro-Caribbean percussion drums made of a resonant metal shell and a single, tightly stretched head (plastic or calf-skin membrane) hit with sticks.

timbre The quality of a sound that distinguishes it from other sounds and dictated by the number of overtones (harmonics) present in the sound. By comparison, a pure sine wave has no overtones. Each instrument has its own unique set of overtones and timbre.

time signature The numbers at the beginning of a composition indicating the groupings of beats for each measure (for example, in 3/4 time, the "3" indicates the number of beats to each measure, while the "4" indicates the note value that receives one beat).

tonality Tonal character as determined by the relationship of the tones to the keynote or key center. Tonality is defined by a series of chords dictated by **functional harmony** or modality.

tonic The fundamental pitch or keynote (first note of a scale) that defines the **key center** of a piece of music.

trading fours Two solo instrumentalists or instrument groups alternately playing four measures each. A typical jazz solo practice where instrumentalists exchange solos with a drummer.

trap set A synonym for a drum set usually consisting of a bass drum, snare drum, sock cymbal, ride cymbal, and one or more tom toms.

tremolo A rapid alteration between two notes.

triad A three-note chord or sonority described as either major, minor, diminished, or augmented in quality.

trill a rapid alternation of two immediately adjacent tones (whole or half step apart).

trio Three performers playing as a group.

12-tone technique Relating to, consisting of, or based on an atonal arrangement of the 12 chromatic tones.

tumbao A recurring bass pattern associated with Afro-Cuban music that creates a sense of syncopation and tension since it rarely emphasizes the first beat of the measure.

V

vamp A repeated chord or rhythmic progression of indefinite length used as filler until the soloist is ready to start, or as accompaniment to a solo, or as a filler to delay the next section of a piece. This repetition can also occur at the beginning or end of a composition.

variation A melody that has been altered.

vibraharp/vibraphone/vibes A musical instrument that has metal bars and rotating disks in the resonators to produce a **vibrato.**

vibrato The regulated fluctuation of a tone. Used to add warmth and expression to a tone created by a singer or instrumentalist except piano.

voicing The manner of organizing, doubling, omitting, or adding to the notes of a chord, and the assignment of notes to each particular instrument in the case of an arrangement for an ensemble.

W

walking bass A bass line that moves like a scale, four notes per bar in 4/4 meter.

whole step A musical interval comprising two half steps — for example, from C to D is a whole step, from C to C# is a half step.
Chromatic Scale Starting on C:
whole   step
C   (C#)   D
    half step

woodshed or **shed** Jazz slang term to mean diligent, self-disciplined practice on an instrument in an effort to improve one's performance abilities

woodwind doubler A musician who is a proficient performer on more than one woodwind instrument; i.e., saxophone, clarinet, and flute.

work song Spontaneous, often improvised music associated with menial labor. Often sung by prison work forces, chain gangs, and slaves performing field labor.

WPA President Franklin D. Roosevelt's Works Progress Administration as a federal relief program and an aspect of his "New Deal" that was designed to create employment and improve unemployment following the Depression.

Chapter 1

Dom Cerulli, Burt Korall, and Mort Nasatir, editors, *The Jazz Word* (New York: Da Capo Press, 1960).

Bill Crow, *Jazz Anecdotes* (New York: Oxford University Press, 1990), pp. 19–22.

James Reese Europe, "A Negro Explains Jazz," *Literary Digest*, April 26, 1919, pp. 28–29.

Sidney Finkelstein, *Jazz: A People's Music* (New York: The Citadel Press, 1948).

Ted Gioia, *The Imperfect Art* (New York: Oxford University Press, 1988).

Robert Goffin, *Jazz: From the Congo to the Metropolitan* (New York: Doubleday and Co., 1946), pp. 1–22.

Wilder Hobson, *American Jazz Music* (New York: W. W. Norton and Co. Inc., 1939).

Barry Kernfeld, *The New Grove Dictionary of Jazz* (New York: St. Martins Press, 1995).

Henry O. Osgood, *So This Is Jazz* (Boston: Little Brown and Co., 1926).

Leroy Ostransky, *The Anatomy of Jazz* (Seattle: University of Washington Press, 1960), pp. 14–21.

Winthrop Sargeant, *Jazz: Hot and Hybrid* (London: Jazz Book Club, 1946).

Tony Sherman, "What Is Jazz: An Interview With Wynton Marsalis," *American Heritage*, October 1995, pp. 67–85.

Smithsonian Collection of Classic Jazz, Notes by Martin Williams and Ira Gitler (Washington: The Smithsonian Collection of Recordings, Smithsonian Institution, 1997).

Marshall W. Stearns, *The Story of Jazz* (New York: Oxford University Press, 1956), pp. 275–282.

Paul Whiteman and Mary Margaret McBride, *Jazz* (New York: J. H. Sears, 1926).

Chapter 2

James Lincoln Collier, *Jazz the American Theme Song* (New York: Oxford University Press, 1993), pp. 25–70.

Sidney Finkelstein, *Jazz: A People's Music* (New York: The Citadel Press, 1948).

Samuel A. Floyd, Jr., "African Roots of Jazz," in *The Oxford Companion to Jazz,* edited by Bill Kirchner (New York: Oxford University Press, 2000), pp. 7–16.

Wilder Hobson, *American Jazz Music* (New York: W. W. Norton, 1939), pp. 40–73.

André Hodeir: *Jazz: Its Evolution and Essence* (New York: Grove Press, 1956), pp. 195–241.

Roger Kamien, *Music and Appreciation* (New York: McGraw-Hill, 1988), pp. 1–88.

Barry Kernfeld, *The New Grove Dictionary of Jazz* (New York: St. Martin's Press, 1995).

Henry O. Osgood, *So This Is Jazz* (Boston: Little Brown and Co., 1926).

Leroy Ostransky, *Understanding Jazz* (Englewood Cliffs, NJ: Prentice Hall, 1977), pp. 47–93.

Winthrop Sargeant, *Jazz: Hot and Hybrid* (London: Jazz Book Club, 1946).

Smithsonian Collection of Classic Jazz, Notes by Martin Williams and Ira Gitler (Washington: The Smithsonian Collection of Recordings, Smithsonian Institution, 1997).

Marshall W. Stearns, *The Story of Jazz* (New York: Oxford University Press, 1956), pp. 275–282.

Jeff Taylor, "The Early Origins of Jazz," in *The Oxford Companion to Jazz,* edited by Bill Kirchner (New York: Oxford University Press, 2000), pp. 39–52.

William H. Youngren, "European Roots of Jazz," in *The Oxford Companion to Jazz,* edited by Bill Kirchner (New York: Oxford University Press, 2000), pp. 17–28.

Chapter 3

Scott DeVeaux, *The Birth of Bebop* (Los Angeles: University of California Press, 1997), pp. 202–235.

Leroy Ostransky, *Understanding Jazz* (Englewood Cliffs, NJ: Prentice Hall, 1977), pp. 73–115.

Lewis Porter and Michael Ullman, *Jazz: From Its Origins to the Present* (Englewood Cliffs, NJ: Prentice Hall, 1993), pp. 449–459.

Paul Tanner, David Megill, and Maurice Gerow, *Jazz* (New York: McGraw-Hill, 2005), pp. 1–13.

Chapter 4

Edward A. Berlin, *Ragtime: A Musical and Cultural History* (Berkley: University of California Press, 1980), pp. 5–20.

Ken Burns, *The Story of America's Music,* Columbia/Legacy CSK 61432.

Clifton Daniels, editor, *Chronicle of America* (Mount Kisco, NY: Chronicle Publications, 1990).

James Reese Europe's 369th U.S. Infantry "Hell Fighter" Band, Memphis Archives, 1996, MA7020.

Ted Gioia, *The History of Jazz* (New York: Oxford University Press, 1997), pp. 3–28.

W. C. Handy Memphis Blues Band, Memphis Archives, 1994, MA7006.

André Hodeir, *Jazz: Its Evolution and Essence* (New York: Grove Press, 1956).

Anne Lemon, "Robert Johnson Biography," from the *The Robert Johnson Notebooks,* edited by Courtney Danforth and Adriana Rissetto, 1997, http://xroads.virginia.edu/~music/rjhome.html (July 7, 1997).

Richard Marshall, editor, *Great Events of the 20th Century* (Pleasantville, NY: The Reader's Digest Association, Inc., 1977).

William J. Schafer, with assistance from Richard B. Allen, *Brass Bands and New Orleans Jazz* (Baton Rouge, LA: Louisiana State University Press, 1977).

Gunther Schuller, *Early Jazz* (New York: Oxford University Press, 1968), pp. 3–88.

The Smithsonian Collection of Classic Jazz, notes by Martin Williams and Ira Gitler (Washington, Smithsonian Institute, 1997).

Marshall Stearns, *The Story of Jazz* (New York: Oxford University Press, 1956), pp. 3–150.

Jim Steinblatt, "The Handy Man Can," ASCAP, *Playback,* Summer 1996.

www.deltahaze.com/johnson/bio.html

Chapter 5

Louis Armstrong: The Complete Hot Five and Hot Seven Recordings, liner notes by Phil Schaap and Robert G. O'Meally (Columbia/Legacy C4K 63527).

H. O. Brunn, *The Story of the Original Dixieland Jazz Band* (London: Sidgwick and Jackson, 1963).

James Lincoln Collier, *Jazz the American Theme Song* (New York: Oxford University Press, 1993).

James Lincoln Collier, *The Reception of Jazz in America: A New View* (New York: Institute for Studies in American Music, 1988).

James Lincoln Collier, "Sidney Bechet," in *The New Grove Dictionary of Jazz,* Barry Kernfeld, editor (New York: St. Martin's Press, 1995), pp. 88–90.

Clifton Daniel, editor, *Chronicle of America* (Mount Kisco, NY: Chronicle Publications, 1990).

Ted Gioia, *The History of Jazz* (New York: Oxford University Press, 1997), pp. 29–54.

Lawrence Gushee, "Joe 'King' Oliver," in *The New Grove Dictionary of Jazz,* Barry Kernfeld, editor (New York: St. Martin's Press, 1995), pp. 935–936.

Wilder Hobson, *American Jazz Music* (New York: W.W. Norton, 1939).

André Hodeir, *Jazz: Its Evolution and Essence* (New York: Grove Press, 1956).

José Hosiasson, "Kid Ory," in *The New Grove Dictionary of Jazz,* Barry Kernfeld, editor (New York: St. Martin's Press, 1995), p. 945.

Richard Marshall, editor, *Great Events of the 20th Century* (Pleasantville, NY: The Reader's Digest Association, Inc., 1977).

John McDonough, "Jass Record #1, Original Dixieland Jazz Band," *Down Beat,* February 1992.

Burton Perretti, *Jazz in American Culture* (Chicago: Ivan R. Dee, 1997), pp. 10–60.

Lewis Porter, *Jazz a Century of Change: Readings and New Essays* (New York: Schirmer Books, 1997), pp. 121–158.

Lewis Porter and Michael Ullman, *Jazz From Its Origins to the Present* (Englewood Cliffs, NJ: Prentice Hall, 1992), pp. 7–73.

Willa Rouder, "James P. Johnson," in *The New Grove Dictionary of Jazz,* Barry Kernfeld, editor (New York: St. Martin's Press, 1995), pp. 619–621.

Gunther Schuller, *Early Jazz* (New York: Oxford University Press, 1968), pp. 89–241.

Gunther Schuller, "Jelly Roll Morton," in *The New Grove Dictionary of Jazz,* Barry Kernfeld, editor (New York: St. Martin's Press, 1995), pp. 804–806.

The Complete Original Dixieland Jazz Band, 1917–1936, Jazz Tribune No. 70, RCA/BMG, 1992.

Chapter 6

Clifton Daniel, editor, *Chronicle of America* (Mount Kisco, NY: Chronicle Publications, 1990).

Ted Gioia, *The History of Jazz* (New York: Oxford University Press, 1997), pp. 70–91.

William Howland Kenney, *Chicago Jazz: A Cultural History, 1904–1930* (New York: Oxford University Press, 1993).

William Howland Kenney, "Historical Context and the Definition of Jazz: Putting More of the History in 'Jazz in History'," in *Jazz Among the Discourses,* edited by Krin Gabbard (Durham, NC: Duke University Press, 1995), pp. 100–116.

Neil Leonard, *Jazz and the White Americans* (Chicago: The University of Chicago Press, 1962), p. 29–107.

Richard Marshall, editor, *Great Events of the 20th Century* (Pleasantville, NY: The Reader's Digest Association, Inc., 1977).

Ronald L. Morris, *Wait Until Dark: Jazz and the Underworld, 1880–1940* (Bowling Green, KY: Bowling Green University Popular Press, 1980).

Burton Peretti, *Jazz in American Culture* (Chicago: Ivan R. Dee, 1997), pp. 31–60.

Burton Peretti, *The Creation of Jazz: Music, Race and Culture in Urban America* (Urbana, IL: University of Illinois Press, 1992).

Lewis Porter, *Jazz, A Century of Change: Readings and New Essays* (New York: Schirmer Books, 1997), pp. 121–158.

Marshall Stearns, *The Story of Jazz* (New York: Oxford University Press, 1956), pp. 151–194.

Richard M. Sudhalter, *Lost Chords: White Musicians and Their Contribution to Jazz* (New York: Oxford University Press, 1999).

Chapter 7

James Lincoln Collier, *Duke Ellington* (New York: Oxford University Press, 1987).

James Lincoln Collier, "Fletcher Henderson," in *The New Grove Dictionary of Jazz,* edited by Barry Kernfeld (New York: St. Martin's Press, 1995), pp. 514–516.

Clifton Daniel, editor, *Chronicle of America* (Mount Kisco, NY: Chronicle Publications, 1989).

Scott DeVaux, *The Birth of Bebop; A Social and Musical History* (Berkley and London: University of California Press, 1997), pp. 1–31, 35–269.

Fletcher Henderson, A Study in Frustration, Notes by Frank Driggs and John Hammond, Columbia/Legacy 557596.

Ted Gioia, *The History of Jazz* (New York: Oxford University Press, 1997), pp. 93–197.

Richard Marshall, editor, *Great Events of the 20th Century* (Pleasantville, NY: The Reader's Digest Association, Inc., 1977).

Dave McAleer, compiler, *The Book of Hit Singles* (San Francisco: Miller Freeman Books, 1999), pp. 10–85.

Burton Peretti, *Jazz in American Culture* (Chicago: Ivan R. Dee, 1997), pp. 61–84.

Lewis Porter, "Coleman Hawkins," in *The New Grove Dictionary of Jazz*, edited by Barry Kernfeld (New York: St. Martin's Press, 1995), pp. 505–507.

Brian Priestley, *Jazz on Record* (New York: Billboard Books, 1991), pp. 43–87

Ken Rattenbury, *Duke Ellington, Jazz Composer* (New Haven: Yale University Press, 1990).

Gunther Schuller, *Early Jazz* (New York: Oxford University Press, 1968), pp. 242–357.

Gunther Schuller, *The Swing Era* (New York: Oxford University Press, 1989), pp. 3–157, 323–325, 426–449.

George T. Simon, *The Big Bands* (New York: Macmillan Publishing Co., 1974), pp. 33–39.

Mark Tucker, *Ellington the Early Years* (Urbana, IL: University of Illinois Press, 1991), pp. 3–118.

Robert Walser, *Keeping Time: Readings in Jazz History* (New York: Oxford University Press, 1999), pp. 71–150.

Chapter 8

James Lincoln Collier, "Billie Holiday," in *The New Grove Dictionary of Jazz*, edited by Barry Kernfeld (New York: St. Martin's Press, 1995), pp. 533–534.

Clifton Daniel, editor, *Chronicle of America* (Mount Kisco, NY: Chronicle Publications, 1989).

Bernard Gendron, "Moldy Figs and Modernists: Jazz at War (1942–1946)," in *Jazz Among the Discourses*, edited by Krin Gabbard (Durham: Duke University Press, 1995), pp. 31–51.

John Edward Hasse, *Jazz, the First Century* (New York: HarperCollins, 1999), pp. 53–85.

Felicity Howlett and J. Bradford Robinson, "Art Tatum," in *The New Grove Dictionary of Jazz*, edited by Barry Kernfeld (New York: St. Martin's Press, 1995), pp. 1187–1188.

Richard Marshall, editor, *Great Events of the 20th Century* (Pleasantville, NY: The Reader's Digest Association, Inc., 1977).

Lewis Porter, "Lester Young," in *The New Grove Dictionary of Jazz*, edited by Barry Kernfeld (New York: St. Martin's Press, 1995), pp. 1317–1319.

Fredric Ramsey, Jr. and Charles Edward Smith, editors, *Jazzmen* (New York: Harcourt Brace Jovanovich, 1939).

J. Bradford Robinson, "Ella Fitzgerald," in *The New Grove Dictionary of Jazz*, edited by Barry Kernfeld (New York: St. Martin's Press, 1995), pp. 388–389.

J. Bradford Robinson, "Mary Lou Williams," in *The New Grove Dictionary of Jazz*, edited by Barry Kernfeld (New York: St. Martin's Press, 1995), pp. 1294–1295.

Ross Russell, *Jazz Style in Kansas City and the Southwest*, (Berkley: University of California Press, 1971).

Gunther Schuller, *The Swing Era* (New York: Oxford University Press, 1989), pp. 222–262.

Gunther Schuller and Martin Williams, liner notes from *Big Band Jazz: From the Beginnings to the Fifties* (Washington: Smithsonian Collection of Recordings).

George T. Simon, *The Big Bands* (New York: Macmillan, 1967), pp. 3–72.

Chapter 9

Clifton Daniel, editor, *Chronicle of America* (Mount Kisco, NY: Chronicle Publications, 1989).

Scott DeVaux, *The Birth of Bebop: A Social and Musical History* (Berkley: University of California Press, 1997), pp. 1–31, 202–317.

Scott DeVaux, "The Advent of Bebop," in *The Oxford Companion to Jazz*, edited by Bill Kirchner (New York: Oxford University Press, 2000), pp. 292–304.

Ira Gitler, *Jazz Masters of the 40s* (New York: Da Capo Press, 1966).

Max Harrison, "Tadd Dameron," in *The New Grove Dictionary of Jazz*, edited by Barry Kernfeld (New York: St. Martin's Press, 1995), p. 264.

Barry Kernfeld, "Sonny Rollins," in *The New Grove Dictionary of Jazz*, edited by Barry Kernfeld (New York: St. Martin's Press, 1995), pp. 1058–1060.

Barry Kernfeld, "Sarah Vaughan," in *The New Grove Dictionary of Jazz*, edited by Barry Kernfeld (New York: St. Martin's Press, 1995), pp. 1241–1242.

Richard Marshall, editor, *Great Events of the 20th Century* (Pleasantville, NY: The Reader's Digest Association, Inc., 1977).

Thomas Owens, "Fats Navarro," in *The New Grove Dictionary of Jazz*, edited by Barry Kernfeld (New York: St. Martin's Press, 1995), pp. 830–831.

Burton W. Peretti, *Jazz in American Culture* (Chicago: Ivan R. Dee, 1997), pp. 83–108.

Lewis Porter, "Dexter Gordon," in *The New Grove Dictionary of Jazz*, edited by Barry Kernfeld (New York: St. Martin's Press, 1995), p. 442.

Lewis Porter, "J. J. Johnson," in *The New Grove Dictionary of Jazz*, edited by Barry Kernfeld (New York: St. Martin's Press, 1995), pp. 621–622.

Brian Priestly, *Jazz on Record* (New York: Billboard Books, 1991), pp 86–106.

J. Bradford Robinson, "Oscar Pettiford," in *The New Grove Dictionary of Jazz*, edited by Barry Kernfeld (New York: St. Martin's Press, 1995), pp. 974–975.

J. Bradford Robinson, "Bud Powell," in *The New Grove Dictionary of Jazz*, edited by Barry Kernfeld (New York: St. Martin's Press, 1995), pp. 995–996.

Geoffrey C. Ward, "Bird on a Wire," *Vanity Fair* (November 2000).

Ollie Wilson and J. Bradford Robinson, "Kenny Clarke," in *The New Grove Dictionary of Jazz*, edited by Barry Kernfeld (New York: St. Martin's Press, 1995), pp. 218–219.

Ollie Wilson and J. Bradford Robinson, "Max Roach," in *The New Grove Dictionary of Jazz*, edited by Barry Kernfeld (New York: St. Martin's Press, 1995), pp. 1045–1050.

Martin Williams, *The Jazz Tradition* (New York: Oxford University Press, 1970), pp. 103–130.

Chapter 10

Larry Blumenfeld, "The Good Reverend Caine," *Jazziz* (January 2001), pp. 38–42.

Bob Blumenthal, "When Worlds Collide," *Jazz Times* (January/February 2001), pp. 51–53.

Wayne Delacoma, "Stravinsky Dug Jazz," *Jazziz* (January 2001), pp. 43–45.

Clifton Daniel, editor, *Chronicle of America* (Mount Kisco, NY: Chronicle Publications, 1989).

Scott DeVaux, "Harmonic Convergence," *Jazziz* (January 2001), p. 36.

Joe Goldberg, *Jazz Masters of the 50s* (New York: Da Capo Press, 1965), pp. 9–23, 113–131, 154–167.

Ted Gioia, "Cool Jazz and West Coast Jazz," in *The Oxford Companion to Jazz*, edited by Bill Kirchner (New York: Oxford University Press, 2000), pp. 332–342.

Ted Gioia, *The History of Jazz* (New York: Oxford University Press, 1997), pp. 277–313.

Ted Gioia, *West Coast Jazz, Modern Jazz in California 1945–1960* (Berkley: University of California Press, 1992), pp. 60–99, 167–199.

Ira Gitler, *Jazz Masters of the 40s* (New York: Da Capo Press, 1966), pp. 226–26l.

Charlotte Greig, *100 Best Selling Albums of the 50s* (New York: Barnes and Noble Books, 2004).

Richard Marshall, editor, *Great Events of the 20th Century* (Pleasantville, NY: The Reader's Digest Association, Inc., 1977).

Brad Mehldau, "Brahms, Interpretation and Improvisation," *Jazz Times* (January/February 2001), pp. 55–56, 180–181.

Burton Peretti, *Jazz in American Culture* (Chicago: Ivan R. Dee, 1997), pp. 109–133.

Brian Priestley, *Jazz on Record* (New York: Billboard Books, 1991), pp. 94–121.

J. Bradford Robinson, "Lennie Tristano," in *The New Grove Dictionary of Jazz*, edited by Barry Kernfeld (New York: St. Martin's Press, 1995), pp. 1218–1219.

Bill Shoemaker, "Third Stream From the Source: Gunther Schuller," *Jazz Times* (January/February 2001), p. 54.

Lucy Tauss, "When Worlds Collide," *Jazziz* (January 2001), pp. 48–49.

Terry Teachout, "Jazz and Classical Music: The Third Stream and Beyond," in *The Oxford Companion to Jazz*, edited by Bill Kirchner (New York: Oxford University Press, 2000), pp. 343–356.

Robert Walser, editor, *Keeping Time: Readings in Jazz History* (New York: Oxford University Press, 1999), pp. 195–249.

Martin Williams, *Jazz Masters in Transition* (New York: Da Capo Press, 1970), pp. 112–119.

Chapter 11

Julian Cannonball Adderley, "Cannonball Looks at Ornette Coleman,"*Down Beat* (May 26, 1960), pp. 20–21.

John Chilton, "Jimmy Smith," in *The New Grove Dictionary of Jazz*, edited by Barry Kernfeld (New York: St. Martin's Press, 1955), pp. 1138–1139.

Clifton Daniel, editor, *Chronicle of America* (Mount Kisco, NY: Chronicle Publications, 1989).

Ted Gioia, *West Coast Jazz, Modern Jazz in California 1945–1960* (Berkley, CA: University of California Press, 1922), pp. 331–359.

Don Heckman, "Inside Ornette Coleman Pt. I," *Down Beat* (September 9, 1965), pp. 13–15.

Don Heckman, "Inside Ornette Coleman Pt. II," *Down Beat* (December 16, 1965), pp. 20–21.

Richard Marshall, editor, *Great Events of the 20th Century* (Pleasantville, NY: The Reader's Digest Association, Inc., 1977).

Charles Mingus, "Mingus on Ornette Coleman," *Down Beat* (May 26, 1960), p. 21.

John Litweiler, *Ornette Coleman, A Harmolodic Life* (New York: Da Capo Press, 1944).

John Litweiler, *The Freedom Principle: Jazz After 1958* (New York: William Morrow and Co., 1984), pp. 31–58.

Burton Peretti, *Jazz in American Culture* (Chicago: Ivan R. Dee, 1997), pp. 109–133.

Lewis Porter, "Wes Montgomery,"in *The New Grove Dictionary of Jazz*, edited by Barry Kernfeld (New York: St. Martin's Press, 1955), pp. 792–793.

Brian Priestley, *Jazz on Record* (New York: Billboard Books, 1991), 122–145.

David H. Rosenthal, *Hard Bop: Jazz and Black Music 1955–1965* (New York: Oxford University Press, 1922).

Gene Seymour, "Hard Bop," in *The Oxford Companion to Jazz*, edited by Bill Kirchner (New York: Oxford University Press, 2000), pp. 373–388.

A.B. Spellman, *Black Music, Four Lives* (New York: Schocken Books, 1971), pp. 71–150.

Robert Walser, editor, *Keeping Time: Readings in Jazz History* (New York: Oxford University Press, 1999), pp. 253–293.

Martin Williams, *The Jazz Tradition* (New York: Oxford University Press, 1970), pp. 177–182.

Martin Williams, "Ornette Coleman 10 Years After," *Down Beat* (December 1969), pp. 24–25.

Ollie Wllson, "Clifford Brown," in *The New Grove Dictionary of Jazz* edited by Barry Kernfeld (New York: St Martin's Press, 1955), pp. 156–157.

Peter Niklas Wilson, *Ornette Coleman: His Life and Music* (Berkley, CA: Hills Books, 1999).

Chapter 12

Bob Belden, "Miles Davis," in *The Oxford Companion to Jazz*, edited by Bill Kirchner (New York: Oxford University Press, 2000) pp. 389–402.

Bob Belden and John Ephland, "Miles Davis, What Was That Note," *Down Beat* (December 1995), pp. 16–22.

Joachim Berendt, *The Jazz Book: From New Orleans to Rock and Free Jazz* (New York: Lawrence Hill and Co., 1973), pp. 92–117.

Bitches Brew, liner notes by Carlos Santana, Michael Cuscuna, Ralph J. Gleason, Quincy Troupe, and Bob Belden, Columbia/Legacy, 1998.

Marc Crawford, "Miles Davis and Gil Evans, Portrait of a Friendship," *Down Beat* (February 1994, reprint from February 12, 1961), pp. 28–29.

Clifton Daniel, editor, *Chronicle of America* (Mount Kisco: Chronicle Publications, 1989).

Down Beat (September 1989), pp. 74–92.

Down Beat, "Louder Than Words" (June 1998), pp. 20–27.

Leonard Feather, "Miles Davis: Miles and the Fifties," *Down Beat* (March 1995, reprint from July 2, 1964), pp. 36–39.

Pat Harris, "Nothing But Bop? 'Stupid,' Says Miles," *Down Beat* (July 1994, reprint from January 27, 1950).

Bill Kirchner, editor, *A Miles Davis Reader* (Washington: Smithsonian Institution Press, 1997).

John Litweiler, *The Freedom Principle: Jazz After 1958* (New York: William Morrow and Co., Inc., 1984), pp. 59–128.

Richard Marshall, editor, *Great Events of the 20th Century* (Pleasantville, NY: The Reader's Digest Association, Inc., 1977).

Dan Ouellette, "Bitches Brew: The Making of the Most Revolutionary Jazz Album in History," *Down Beat* (December 1999), pp. 32–37.

Dan Ouellette, "Dark Prince in Twilight, Band Members and Associates Discuss the Last Years of Miles Davis' Life," *Down Beat* (May 2001), pp. 25–29.

Burton Peretti, *Jazz in American Culture* (Chicago: Ivan R. Dee, 1997), pp. 134–176.

Gene Santoro, "Miles Davis, the Enabler Pt. II," *Down Beat* (November 1988), pp. 16–19.

Greg Tate, "The Electric Miles Pt. I," *Down Beat* (July 1983), pp. 16–18.

Peter Watrous, "John Coltrane: A Life Supreme," *Musician* (July 1987), pp. 103–112, 136–138.

Chapter 13

Christopher Collins, "Joe Zawinul," *Jazz Education Journal* (May/June 2002), pp. 45–50.

Clifton Daniel, editor, *Chronicle of America* (Mount Kisco, NY: Chronicle Publications, 1989).

Ted Gioia, *The History of Jazz* (New York: Oxford University Press, 1997), pp. 64–374.

Richard Marshall, editor, *Great Events of the 20th Century* (Pleasantville, NY: The Reader's Digest Association, Inc., 1977).

Barry Kernfeld, "Grover Washington, Jr.," in *The New Grove Dictionary of Jazz*, edited by Barry Kernfeld (New York: St. Martin's Press, 1995), p. 1265.

Stuart Nicholson, *Jazz-Rock: A History* (New York: Schirmer Books, 1998).

Burton Peretti, *Jazz in American Culture* (Chicago: Ivan R. Dee, 1997), pp. 155–176.

Brian Priestley, *Jazz on Record* (New York: Billboard Books, 1991), p. 158.

Zan Stewart, "Chuck Mangione," *Music America Magazine*, vol. 1, no. IV (January 1977), pp. 16–20.

Patrick T. Will, "Steps Ahead," in *The New Grove Dictionary of Jazz*, edited by Barry Kernfeld (New York: St. Martin's Press, 1995), p. 1159.

Chapter 14

The Complete Solid State Recordings of the Thad Jones/Mel Lewis Orchestra, liner notes by Bill Kirchner, Mosaic Records.

Clifton Daniel, editor, *Chronicle of America* (Mount Kisco: Chronicle Publications, 1989).

Ted Gioia, *The History of Jazz* (New York: Oxford University Press, 1997), pp. 377–395.

Nat Hentoff, *Jazz Is* (New York: Limelight Editions, 1991), pp. 225–233.

Peter Keepnews, "Jazz Since 1968," in *The Oxford Companion to Jazz*, edited by Bill Kirchner (New York: Oxford University Press, 2000), pp. 488–501.

John Litweiler, *The Freedom Principle: Jazz After 1958* (New York: William Morrow and Co., Inc., 1984), pp. 200–221.

Richard Marshall, editor, *Great Events of the 20th Century* (Pleasantville, NY: The Reader's Digest Association, Inc., 1977).

Tom Moon, "Keith Jarrett," *Jazz Times* (May 1999), pp. 38–46.

Lewis Porter, *Jazz a Century of Change: Readings and New Essays* (New York: Schirmer Books, 1997), pp. 219–273.

Brian Priestley, *Jazz On Record* (New York: Billboard Books, 1991), pp. 150–151, 167, 172–194.

Chapter 15

Whitney Balliett, "Young Guns," *The New Yorker* (June 5, 1955, vol. 71), pp. 97–99.

Bob Blumenthal, "Survival of the Biggest," *Jazz Times* (September 1998), pp. 28–31, 35, 50.

Clifton Daniel, editor, *Chronicle of America* (Mount Kisco, NY: Chronicle Publications, 1989).

Francis Davis, "Like Young," *Atlantic Monthly* (July 1996), pp. 92–98.

Martin Johnson, "Where the Past & Future Collide, Acid Jazz," *Down Beat* (April 1997), pp. 16–21.

Wynton Marsalis, www.jazzatLincolnCenter.org/jazz/arti/lcjo/marsalis.html.

Richard Marshall, editor, *Great Events of the 20th Century* (Pleasantville, NY: The Reader's Digest Association, Inc., 1977).

Bill Milkowski, "Wynton Marsalis and John Zorn," *Jazz Times* (March 2000), pp. 28–39, 118–121.

Robert Walser, *Keeping Time: Readings in Jazz History* (New York: Oxford University Press, 1999), pp. 389–424.

Peter Watrous, "The Nineties," *Jazz Times* (September 2000), pp. 51–55.

Andrew Soloman, "The Jazz Martyr," *The New York Times Magazine* (February 9, 1997), pp. 32–35.

Chapter 16

Stephanie L. Stein Crease, "Jazz and Brazilian Music," in *The Oxford Companion to Jazz,*" edited by Bill Kirchner (New York: Oxford University Press, 2000), pp. 548–558.

Down Beat, April, 1974, pp. 35–36.

Down Beat, November 1974, p. 10.

G. Duran, *Latin Music, Recordings of Latin American Songs and Dances: An Annotated Selected List of Popular and Folk Music* (Washington: Pan American Union).

H. Gurlander, *The Drum and the Hoe* (Berkley: University of California Press, 1960).

Stan Kenton, *Cuban Fire Suite*, Capital/EMI, T731.

D. Lewiston, *Black Music of South America*, Nonesuch Records, H-72036.

Fred B. Lindstrom and Naomi Lindstrom, "Adorno Encounters Cu-Bop, Experimental Music as a Task for Critics and Their Audiences," *Sociological Perspectives*, vol. 1, no. 2. (April 1986), pp. 284–304.

René López and David Carp, "Cuba: Where the Music Is Hot" (New York: Jazz at Lincoln Center, 1997), www.jazzatlincolncenter.org/jazz/note/cuba.html.

D. Owen, *Panorama of American Popular Music* (Englewood Cliffs, NJ: Prentice Hall, 1957).

Brian Priestley, *Jazz on Record* (New York: Billboard Books, 1991), pp. 88–89, 99.

Winthrop Sargeant, *Jazz: Hot and Hybrid* (New York: E. P. Dutton and Co., Inc., 1946).

Gunther Schuller, *Early Jazz* (New York: Oxford University Press, 1968), pp. 3–62.

Nicolas Slonimsky, *Music of Latin America* (New York: Da Capo Press, 1972).

Marshall W. Stearns, *The Story of Jazz* (New York: Oxford University Press, 1956), pp. 243–256.

For those readers who have become real aficionados and want to not only hear but also see their favorite performers, there is a plethora of readily available resources. The home video explosion that began in the late 1970s with videotape and moved to DVD in recent years has attributed to an entirely new industry supporting fans, educators, and students of jazz. Instructional, documentary, and full-length films featuring musical scores by jazz artists or starring jazz performers are now plentiful. The following list is a brief selection of recommended videos, many of which have been aired by Arts and Entertainment, Bravo!, and PBS television stations. Sources for acquiring these jazz videos, aside from libraries and local rental establishments, can be easily found on the Internet. A "must have" resource for jazz film and video collectors is David Meeker's *Jazz in the Movies*, published in 1981 by Da Capo Press. Meeker's book is a filmography, supplying detailed information about when films were produced, who produced them, and a listing of jazz artists associated with each film. Another such reference source is *Jazz on Film* by Scott Yanow, published in 2004 by Back Beat Books.

Biographical

The Billie Holiday Story

But Then She's Betty Carter

Women in Jazz: The Instrumentalists

A Duke Named Ellington

Reminiscing in Tempo (Ellington)

Biography: Legendary Entertainers Series—*Ella Fitzgerald*

The Miles Davis Story

Thelonious Monk—American Composer

Thelonious Monk—Straight, No Chaser

Jazz Masters Series: *Charlie Parker*

Celebrating the Bird (Charlie Parker)

American Masters: *Charlie Parker*

American Masters: *John Hammond*

American Masters: *Sarah Vaughan: The Devine One*

American Masters: *Dizzy Gillespie*

American Masters: *Ella Fitzgerald: Something to Live For*

American Masters: *Duke Ellington*

American Masters: *Benny Goodman*

American Masters: *Billie Holiday*

Lady Day, The Many Faces of Billie Holiday

Time Is All You've Got (Artie Shaw)

The Coltrane Legacy

The World According to John Coltrane

Satchmo: Louis Armstrong

Toshiko Akiyoshi: Jazz Is My Native Language

Oscar Peterson, Life of a Legend

40 Years of the Modern Jazz Quartet

Charlie Christian: Solo Flight

Charles Mingus: Mingus in Greenwich Village

Charles Mingus—Triumph of the Underdog

Let's Get Lost (Chet Baker)

Historical Documentaries

Duke Ellington's Washington

The Story of Jazz

Trumpet Kings (history of jazz trumpet players)

Reed Royalty (history of jazz saxophonists)

On the Road With Duke Ellington

Minnie the Moocher and Many, Many More (features Cab Calloway with Louis Armstrong, Count Basie, Nat "King" Cole, Fats Waller, Duke Ellington, and Lena Horne)

Jazz (10-part, 19-hour series by Ken Burns)

Adventures in the Kingdom of Swing (Benny Goodman)

Swingin' The Blues (Count Basie)

Legends of Jazz Drumming Parts I & II

Piano Legends (hosted by Chick Corea)

The Last of the Blues Devils: The Kansas City Jazz Story

Phil Woods—A Life in E Flat

Performance/Instructional

The Universal Mind (Bill Evans)

Women in Jazz, The Vocalists: Scatting—Carmen McRae host

Jivin' In Bebop (1947 Dizzy Gillespie Big Band)

The Sound of Jazz (1957 CBS TV broadcast featuring Count Basie Band, Gerry Mulligan, Billie Holiday, Lester Young, Coleman Hawkins, and Thelonious Monk)

Blue Note: A Story of Modern Jazz

Born to Swing (Count Basie)

Jazz Life Volume 2—Mike Mainieri Group and Art Blakey & The Jazz Messengers (with Marsalis brothers)

Jazz at the Smithsonian: Art Blakey and the Jazz Messengers (with Wynton Marsalis)

Jazz Casual—Cannonball Adderley

Charles Mingus Sextet

Ornette Coleman Trio

Wes Montgomery—Belgium, 1965

Eric Dolphy—Last Date

Chick Corea—A Very Special Concert

Herbie Hancock and the Rocket Band

Brecker Brothers: Return of the Brecker Brothers

Steps Ahead—Copenhagen Live

Grover Washington, Jr. In Concert

Keith Jarrett: Standards

Keith Jarrett: Last Solo

Keith Jarrett/Gary Peacock/ Jack DeJohnette: Tokyo 1996

Dexter Gordon: More Than You Know

Sonny Rollins and Dexter Gordon

Dexter Gordon: Live at the Maintenance Shop

Wynton Marsalis: Blues and Swing

Branford Marsalis: The Music Tells You

Jazz Casual—Thad Jones/Mel Lewis and Woody Herman

Cecil Taylor: Burning Poles

Sun Ra: Space is the Place

Sun Ra—Make a Joyful Noise

Branford Marsalis: The Music Tells You

Jam Miami—A Celebration of Latin Jazz

Antonio Carlos Jobim: An All-Star Tribute

Important Feature Films

St. Louis Blues (1929, Bessie Smith, James P. Johnson, W. C. Handy Choir)

King of Jazz (1930, Paul Whiteman film)

Minnie the Moocher (1932, Betty Boop cartoon with music by Cab Calloway)

I Heard (1933 Betty Boop cartoon featuring music by Don Redman)

Stormy Weather (1943, Cab Calloway, Fats Waller, Lena Horne, and others)

The Fabulous Dorseys (1947, Tommy and Jimmy Dorsey feature with Art Tatum, Paul Whiteman, Charlie Barnet, Helen O'Connell, Ziggy Elman)

I Want to Live (1958, music by Mundell Lowe, Gerry Mulligan, Art Farmer, etc.)

Asphalt Jungle (1959, Duke Ellington score)

Anatomy of a Murder (1959, Duke Ellington score)

Paris Blues (1961, Duke Ellington score)

Mickey One (1965, music by Stan Getz)

Alfie (1966, with music by Sonny Rollins, Oliver Nelson, Kenny Burrell, etc.)

Round Midnight (1986, featuring Herbie Hancock, Dexter Gordon, etc)

The Color of Money (1986, with music by Gil Evans)

Bird (1988, film by Clint Eastwood about Charlie Parker)

Chapter 1
2 (both) The Granger Collection, New York; 4 (top): © Frank Driggs Collection/Getty Images; 4 (bottom): The Granger Collection, New York; 6: © ArenaPal/Topham/The Image Works; 7: © R. Andrew Lepley

Chapter 2
10: © Jeff Christensen/AP Photo; 10 (inset): The Granger Collection, New York; 13: © Photodisc Collection/Getty Images; 14: © Guy LeQuerrec/Magnum Photos; 19: © Frank Driggs Collection/Getty Images; 26: © BBC/CORBIS

Chapter 3
30 (top): © Nubar Alexanian/CORBIS; 30 (bottom, left): © Digital Vision/Getty Images; 30 (bottom, 2nd and 3rd from left): © Brand X Pictures/PunchStock; 30 (bottom, 3rd from right): © Photodisc Collection/Getty Images; 30 (bottom, 2nd from right): © C Squared Studios/Getty Images; 30 (bottom, right): © Royalty-Free/CORBIS; 33: © Photodisc Collection/Getty Images; 44: © Frank Driggs Collection

Chapter 4
48 (both): The Granger Collection, New York ; 57: © Bettmann/CORBIS; 58: The Granger Collection, New York; 60: U.S. Stamp; 62: © Roger-Viollet/Topham/The Image Works; 64: © John Springer Collection/CORBIS; 67, 68: The Granger Collection, New York; 71: © Frank Driggs Collection

Chapter 5
76 (top): © Hulton Archive/Getty Images; 76 (bottom): © Bettmann/CORBIS; 79: Library of Congress #b0916-1; 80: © Topham/The Image Works; 81: © Frank Driggs Collection; 83: © The Art Archive/Culver Pictures/The Picture Desk; 85: © Topham/The Image Works; 88, 89: © Frank Driggs Collection/Getty Images;

91: © CORBIS; 94: © Bettmann/CORBIS; 96: © Charles Peterson/Getty Images; 97: © Bettmann/CORBIS; 100: *Does Jazz Put the Sin in Syncopation* by Anne Shaw Faulkner. Copyright August 1921, Reprinted with permission of LADIES' HOME JOURNAL, Meredith Corporation

Chapter 6
106: © Frank Driggs Collection/Getty Images; 106 (inset): © Mary Evans Picture Library/The Image Works; 108: © Frank Driggs Collection; 111: Photographer: J. W. Taylor. Source: Chicago Historical Society (ICHi-01436); 112, 114: © Frank Driggs Collection; 115: © Frank Driggs Collection/Getty Images; 117: © Michael Ochs Archives.com; 119: © Universal/THE KOBAL COLLECTION; 122: © Bettmann/CORBIS; 124: © Frank Driggs Collection/Getty Images; 126: © Bettmann/CORBIS

Chapter 7
134: © Paramount/THE KOBAL COLLECTION; 134 (inset): © George Kleiman/CORBIS; 139: © Underwood & Underwood/CORBIS; 141 (top): The Granger Collection, New York; 141 (bottom): © Mosaic Images/CORBIS; 144: © Frank Driggs Collection/Getty Images; 146: © Bettmann/CORBIS; 148: © Frank Driggs Collection/Getty Images; 154: © Bettmann/CORBIS; 158: © Frank Driggs Collection; 159: © Frank Driggs Collection/Getty Images; 162: © Bettmann/CORBIS

Chapter 8
170: © Topham/The Image Works; 170 (inset) : © Bettmann/CORBIS; 174: © Frank Driggs Collection/Getty Images; 175: Image Courtesy of Kansas City Public Library; 176: © Bettmann/CORBIS; 177, 179: © Metronome/Getty Images; 182: © 2005 VNU Business Media, Inc. Used with permission; 185: © Charles Hewitt/Getty Images; 187: © ArenaPal/Topham/The Image Works; 189: © Charles Peterson/

Getty Images; 191: US Armed Services

Chapter 9
200: © Metronome/Getty Images; 200 (inset): © Bettmann/CORBIS; 206: Library of Congress #LC-GLB23-0626; 207: © George Karger/Pix Inc./Time Life Pictures/Getty; 212: Library of Congress #LC-GLB23-0315; 215: © Thierry Orban/CORBIS SYGMA; 217: © Bob Parent/Getty Images; 218: © Frank Driggs Collection/Getty Images; 219, 220, 221, 222, 224: © Mosaic Images/CORBIS; 226: © Herman Leonard/Hulton Archive/Getty Images; 227: © Metronome/Getty Images

Chapter 10
240 (both): © Bettmann/CORBIS; 243 (both): Courtesy of EMI; 245: © Lebrecht Music & Arts; 247: © Herman Leonard Photography/Redferns Music Picture Library; 250: © Michael Ochs Archives.com; 254: © JazzSign/Lebrecht/The Image Works; 258: © BMI/Michael Ochs Archives.com; 260: © Herman Leonard/Hulton Archive/Getty Images; 263: © Metronome/Getty Images

Chapter 11
272 (top): © Mosaic Images/CORBIS; 272 (bottom): © Flip Schulke/CORBIS; 276: © Mosaic Images/CORBIS; 280 (top): © Shepard Sherbell/CORBIS; 280 (bottom): © Ted Williams/CORBIS; 281, 282, 286: © Mosaic Images/CORBIS; 288: Image: © Francis G. Mayer/CORBIS. Artwork: © Pollock-Krasner Foundation / Artists Rights Society (ARS), New York; 291: © JazzSign/Lebrecht/The Image Works

Chapter 12
302: © Tad Hershorn/Hulton Archive/Getty Images; 302 (inset): © Digital Vision/Getty Images; 309: © Frank Driggs Collection/Getty Images; 313: © Bill Spilka/

Getty Images; **315:** © David Redfern/
Redferns Music Picture Library;
320: Courtesy of Sony Music
Entertainment, Inc.; **322:** © Lynn
Goldsmith/CORBIS; **328:** © ArenaPal/
Topham/The Image Works; **329:**
© Mosaic Images/CORBIS

Chapter 13

342: © Derick A. Thomas; Dat's
Jazz/CORBIS; **342 (inset):** © Howard
Ruffner/Time & Life Pictures/Getty
Images; **345:** © BBC Photo Library/
Redferns Music Picture Library;
349: © Roger Ressmeyer/CORBIS;
352: © CORBIS; **354:** © Richard
Melloul/Sygma/CORBIS; **358:** © Laura
Friedman; **359:** © Neal Preston/
CORBIS; **360:** © Julian Wasser//Time
Life Pictures/Getty Images

Chapter 14

370: © ArenaPal/Topham/The Image
Works; **370 (inset):** © Bettmann/
CORBIS; **372:** ECM Records;
374: © Deborah Feingold/CORBIS;
380: © Ted Thai//Time Life
Pictures/Getty Images; **382:** Courtesy
of RCA; **387:** © Lee Tanner; **389:** Frank
Driggs Collection

Chapter 15

400: © Adam Rountree/Getty Images;
400 (inset): © Peter Turnley/CORBIS;
403: © Carlo Allegri/Getty Images;
405: © Tim Krautkraemer; **407:** © Tim
Mosenfelder/Getty Images;
409: © Frank Micelotta/ImageDirect/
Getty Images; **410:** © Uzi Keren/
Newsmakers/Getty Images; **415 (top):**
© Retna Pictures Ltd.; **415 (bottom) :**
© Allan Titmuss/ArenaPal/Topham/
The Image Works

Chapter 16

430: Frank Driggs Collection;
430 (inset): © Hulton Archive/Getty
Images; **441:** Frank Driggs Collection;
442: © Metronome/Getty Images

A

AABA song form model
  chord progression and, 65
  explanation of, 22
  modal tunes and, 309
  repetition and, 26
  rhythm changes model and, 316
AACM (Association for the Advancement
  of Creative Music), 289
Abrams, Muhal Richard, 289
Accents, 36
Acid jazz, 346, 407–409
Acoustic Alchemy, 407
Acoustic jazz
  Corea and, 357
  Davis and, 319
  ECM sound, 371–376
  electronic instruments and, 346
  Hancock and, 352
  rebirth of, 376–385
Adderley, Cannonball, 228, 275,
  279–280, 306–307, 309, 312,
  320, 345, 347, 360–361, 371
Adderley, Nat, 280
Aeolian mode, 308
Affirmative action, 389
African music
  blues and, 58–66
  early vocal music, 56–58
  influence of, 14–15, 49–56
"Afro Blue," 326–327
Afro-Cuban music, 437–444
Afro-Latin music
  early fusions, 434–437
  influence of, 431–434
  postmodernism and, 444–446
Ailey, Alvin, 379
Airmen of Note, 418
Akiyoshi, Toshiko, 344, 386, 388–389,
  391, 419
Akoustic (band), 358
Alcohol use, 206
Aleatoric classical music, 286
All-American Rhythm Section, 177
Allen, Geri, 405, 419
Almeida, Laurindo, 263
Altissimo notes, 37
Altschul, Barry, 355
American Dance Theater, 379
American Federation of Musicians,
  202–203
American Jazz Masters Fellowship, 419
American label, 362
Ammons, Albert, 121
Ammons, Gene, 211
Amplification, 139
Amplivox, 127
Anderson, Cat, 153
Antoine, Marc, 407

Apflebaum, Peter, 410
Apollo Theater, 125, 183, 187, 227
Apple, 390
Arista Records, 359
Armstrong, Louis, 16, 25, 27, 36, 38, 40,
  54, 64, 81–82, 87–89, 92–95,
  108, 112, 114–116, 122, 127, 137,
  140, 143–144, 146, 148, 158,
  185–186, 206–207, 222, 256,
  265, 291, 323, 371
Armstrong, Neil, 303
Army Blues, 418
Arnez, Desi, 437
Arpeggio, 82, 146, 179
Arrangement
  defined, 35–36
  Morton and, 90–91
  swing and, 137, 141–142
Arshawsky, Arthur, 138, 161–165
Art Ensemble of Chicago, 289, 344,
  381–382
Articulation, 36, 146
Astro Intergalactic Infinity Arkestra, 381
Atlantic label, 284, 287–288
Atonal music, 17
Audobon Ballroom, 183
Auricle (band), 347
Austin High Gang, 111, 156, 162
Austin, Patti, 409
Avant-garde jazz style
  Braxton and, 226
  Chicago and, 381
  Coleman and, 274, 285
  experimentalists, 405–407
  Hubbard and, 279
  Monk and, 223
  Shepp and, 226
  Taylor and, 224, 226, 384–385
Average White Band, 359
Ayler, Albert, 288, 371

B

Babbitt, Milton, 261–262
Baby boomer generation, 265
Bach, J. S., 24, 242
Bailey, Buster, 144
Bailey, Pearl, 313
Baker, Chet, 244, 247–249, 260, 391
Baker, David, 404
Ball, Lucille, 437
Banjo, 32, 82
Banks, Carl, 175
Banks, Julius, 175
Bar (measure), 12, 177
Baraka, Amiri, 287
Barber, Patricia, 409
Barbieri, Gato, 445
Baritone sax, 154

Barnet, Charlie, 121, 158–159, 162,
  218, 225
Baroque period, 24
Barretto, Ray, 445
Basie, William "Count," 16, 121, 138,
  141–142, 152, 173, 175–180,
  182–185, 193, 210, 228, 280,
  344, 386, 391, 418
Bass
  bebop and, 209
  cool jazz and, 252
  hard bop and, 274
  as jazz instrument, 32, 82
Bass drum
  bebop and, 225
  cymbals and, 83
  depicted, 33
  Jones and, 177
  swing and, 209
Bass 'n' drums, 409
Bassoon, 32
Bauer, Billy, 260
Baum, Jamie, 419
Bauza, Mario, 211, 438–439, 441–442
Beasley, Walter, 407
Beatles, 181, 279, 304
Bebop style
  Afro-Cuban influence and, 439
  cool jazz and, 244
  development of, 27
  Ellington and, 153
  first recordings, 207–211
  Hawkins and, 147
  horn players, 211–221
  Johnson, James P. and, 97
  Kenton and, 386
  musical characteristics, 205–208
  musicians, 211–228
  Parker and, 38
  rhythm section players, 211–227
  swing compared to, 210
  timeline for, 8
  Trumbauer and, 117
Bechet, Sidney, 32, 70, 80–81, 95–96,
  127, 192
Bee, Easy Moe, 323
Beethoven, Ludwig van, 24
Beiderbecke, Bix, 112, 115–119, 123, 128,
  142, 178, 250, 256
Belafonte, Harry, 265, 294
Belden, Bob, 405–406
Bellson, Louis, 153
Bend special effect, 37
Bennett, Tony, 256, 409
Benoit, David, 407
Benson, George, 319, 361
Berg, Bob, 277, 306
Berigan, Bunny, 157, 183
Berlin, Irving, 79, 99–100, 141–142
Berliner, Paul, 418

Rudd, Roswell, 380
Ruiz, Hilton, 446
Rumba, 437, 445
Rushing, Jimmy, 175, 184
Russell, George, 241, 247, 252, 261, 264, 439
Russell, Ross, 171, 176, 215
Rutgers Institute of Jazz Studies, 418
Rypdal, Terje, 372

S

Safranski, Eddie, 260
Salsa, 433, 445
Samba, 258, 355–356, 437
San Francisco
    cool jazz and, 244
    hard bop and, 275
    "love-ins," 304
    musician pay scale, 419
Sanabria, Bobby, 410, 446
Sanborn, David, 358–359, 361
Sánchez, Poncho, 410
Sanders, Pharoah, 288, 329, 380
Sandoval, Arturo, 446
Santamaria, Mongo, 445
Santana, Carlos, 343, 354
Santoro, Gene, 433, 442, 445
Saturday Night Fever, 346
Saturday Night Live, 359
Sauter, Eddie, 256
Savoy Ballroom
    Gale and, 183
    Harlem renaissance and, 125
    radio broadcasts and, 127
    Swing Era and, 142
Saxophone
    baritone, 154
    bebop and, 208
    C-melody, 116
    cool jazz and, 245
    funky jazz and, 281
    Gordon and, 220
    as jazz instrument, 31–32, 112
    Shorter and, 330–331
    soli and, 40
    special effects, 37
    Swing Era jazz bands, 138
    Trumbauer and, 117
Scale
    defined, 18
    improvisation and, 37
    modality and, 307–308
Scat
    Armstrong and, 93
    defined, 40
    Fitzgerald and, 187
    Vaughan and, 227
Schaeffer, Paul, 359

Schifrin, Lalo, 439
Schneider, Maria, 391, 402–403, 419
Schoebel, Elmer, 113–114
School segregation, 265, 328, 389
Schottisches, 70
Schuller, Gunther, 52, 54, 123, 156, 160–161, 220–221, 259, 261–262, 286–287, 291, 372, 404
Schuur, Diane, 409
Scofield, John, 281, 306, 323, 409, 414–415
Scoop special effect, 37
Scott, James, 52, 66
Scott, Shirley, 281
Seawind (band), 347
Sebesky, Don, 402
Serverinsen, Doc, 249, 388
Seventh chord, 20
Shadowfax, 407
Shake special effect, 37
Shakti, 354
Shank, Bud, 263
Shavers, Charlie, 211
Shaw, Artie, 138, 161–162, 181–182, 185
Shaw, Woody, 376, 391
Shearing, George, 443
Sheets of sound, 325
Shell toms, 33
Shepp, Archie, 226, 288, 380
Shields, Larry, 85–86
Shorter, Wayne, 276, 279, 306, 315, 317–318, 320, 328, 330–332, 347–348, 350, 352, 378, 403
Shout chorus, 39–40
Showboating, 83
Silver, Horace, 275–279, 307, 330, 384, 403, 415, 445
Simeon, Omer, 91–92
Simon and Garfunkel, 403
Simon, Paul, 410, 416
Sims, Zoot, 386
Sinatra, Frank, 119, 163, 203, 263, 294, 410
"Singin' the Blues," 117–118
Sissie, Noble, 438
Slang expressions, 182–183, 279
Small's Paradise Club, 126
Smith, Bessie, 62–64, 88, 97, 143, 228
Smith, Buster, 175
Smith, Jimmy, 279, 281–282
Smith, Joe, 62
Smith, Mamie, 64
Smith, Pine Top, 121
Smith, Tommy, 415
Smith, Willie "The Lion," 96
Smithsonian Institute, 418
Smithsonian Masterworks Jazz Orchestra, 404
Smoker, Paul, 405
Smooth jazz, 346, 360–361, 407

Snare, 33
Snyder, Frank, 114
"So Danço Samba," 259
Sock cymbal; *see* Hi-hat cymbal
Soli, 40, 143
Solo break
    defined, 86
    double time, 93
    Morton and, 91
Soloff, Lew, 345
"Some Nerve," 415–416
Son rhythm, 438, 445
Song form, 22, 26
"Sophisticated Lady," 151–153
Soul-jazz, 276, 279–280, 358–363
Sound recordings, 25, 203
Sousa, John Phillip, 67, 100
Southern Syncopated Orchestra, 96
Souza, Luciana, 412, 446
"Spanish Key," 321
Sparbarrow, Tony, 85
Special effects, 37
Speed, 354
Spirituals, 56–57, 279
Spitalny, Phil, 173
Spyro Gyra, 344, 347
Sri Chinmoy, 353
St. Cyr, Johnny, 80, 91–92, 94, 111
"St. Louis Blues," 64–66, 97
Stacy, Jess, 157
Stafford, Jo, 163
Standards Trio, 374
Star, Kay, 163
State Department, 265
Stearns, Marshall, 118, 264
Steinbeck, John, 137
Steinem, Gloria, 304
Stein's Dixie Jass Band, 84
Stenson, Bobo, 372
Steps Ahead, 362–363, 415
Stern, Mike, 306, 323, 417
Stewart, Bill, 415
Stewart, Rex, 148
Stewart, Slam, 189–190, 209, 225
Sting, 377
Stitt, Sonny, 211, 213, 324
Stokowski, Leopold, 100
Stone, Sly, 319–320, 322, 351
Storyville district (New Orleans), 79–81
Stravinsky, Igor, 158, 354, 380, 384
Strayhorn, Billy, 154, 312
Street soul, 408
Stride, 8, 69, 97
String instrument family, 32
Stringham, Edwin J., 109
"Strollin'," 278
Strong, Jimmy, 95
Students for a Democratic Society (SDS), 304
Studio Rivbea, 381